Scott Foresman - Addison Wesley
MIDDLE SCHOOL MATH
Course 2

Randall I. Charles   John A. Dossey   Steven J. Leinwand
Cathy L. Seeley   Charles B. Vonder Embse

L. Carey Bolster • Janet H. Caldwell • Dwight A. Cooley • Warren D. Crown
Linda Proudfit • Alma B. Ramírez • Jeanne F. Ramos • Freddie Lee Renfro
David Robitaille • Jane Swafford

Prentice
Hall

Needham, Massachusetts
Upper Saddle River, New Jersey
Glenview, Illinois

Cover artist: Robert Silvers, 28, started taking photographs and playing with computers at the same time, over 20 years ago. He always thought of computer programming as a way to express himself much as he does with photography. Silvers has melded his interests to produce the image on this cover.

Prentice Hall

ISBN 0-13-054110-9

3 4 5 6 7 8 9 10   04 03 02

FROM THE AUTHORS

Dear Student,

We have designed a unique mathematics program that answers the question students your age have been asking for years about their math lessons: "When am I ever going to use this?"

In *Scott Foresman - Addison Wesley Middle School Math,* you'll learn about math in your own world and develop problem-solving techniques that will work for you in everyday life. The chapters have two or three sections, each with a useful math topic and an interesting theme. For example, you'll relate decimals to space probes, proportions to whales, and algebra to amusement parks.

Each section begins with an opportunity to explore new topics and make your own conjectures. Lessons are presented clearly with examples and chances to try the math yourself. Then, real kids like you and your friends say what they think about each concept and show how they understand it. And every section contains links to the World Wide Web, making your math book a dynamic link to an ever-expanding universe of knowledge.

You will soon realize how mathematics is not only useful, but also connected to you and your life as you continue to experience the real world. We trust that each of you will gain the knowledge necessary to be successful and to be everything you want to be.

Randall I. Charles   *John A. Dossey*   *Steven J. Leinwand*

Cathy L. Seeley   *Charles B. Vonder Embse*

L. Carey Bolster	*Janet H. Caldwell*	*Dwight A. Cooley*	*Warren D. Crown*	*Linda Proudfit*
Alma B. Ramirez	*Jeanne F. Ramos*	*Freddie Lee Renfro*	*David Robitaille*	*Jane Swafford*

Authors

L. Carey Bolster
Public Broadcasting System
Alexandria, Virginia

Randall I. Charles
San Jose State University
San Jose, California

Warren D. Crown
Rutgers, the State University of New Jersey
New Brunswick, New Jersey

Steven J. Leinwand
Connecticut Department of Education
Hartford, Connecticut

Alma B. Ramírez
Oakland Charter Academy
Oakland, California

Freddie Lee Renfro
Fort Bend Independent School District
Sugarland, Texas

Cathy L. Seeley
Texas SSI in Math and Science
Austin, Texas

Charles B. Vonder Embse
Central Michigan University
Mount Pleasant, Michigan

Janet H. Caldwell
Rowan College of New Jersey
Glassboro, New Jersey

Dwight A. Cooley
M. L. Phillips Elementary School
Fort Worth, Texas

John A. Dossey
Illinois State University
Normal, Illinois

Linda Proudfit
Governors State University
University Park, Illinois

Jeanne F. Ramos
Nobel Middle School
Los Angeles, California

David Robitaille
University of British Columbia
Vancouver, British Columbia, Canada

Jane Swafford
Illinois State University
Normal, Illinois

Problem Solving in Chapter 1

Using real-world data, you'll solve problems about geography and sports.

TECHNOLOGY

• Graphing Utility
• Data Analysis Package
• World Wide Web
• Interactive CD-ROM

 Algebra

You'll graph data to make scatter-plots and use your scatterplots to look for trends.

CHAPTER

1	2	3	4	5	6	7	8	9	10	11	12

MAKING SENSE OF THE WORLD OF DATA...2

SECTION 1A
Communicating with Data

SECTION 1B
Trends and Relationships in Data

Problem Solving in Chapter 2

By using algebra, you'll solve problems about cars and other machines.

TECHNOLOGY

- Spreadsheet
- Scientific Calculator
- World Wide Web
- Interactive CD-ROM

Algebra

You'll investigate ways to solve equations involving variables.

CHAPTER

| 1 | **2** | 3 | 4 | 5 | 6 | 7 | 8 | 9 | 10 | 11 | 12 |

THE LANGUAGE OF ALGEBRA: FORMULAS, EXPRESSIONS, AND EQUATIONS...52

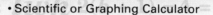

Problem Solving in Chapter 3

Decimals and fractions help you investigate astronomical distances and musical passages.

TECHNOLOGY

- Scientific or Graphing Calculator
- Spreadsheet
- World Wide Web
- Interactive CD-ROM

✗ Algebra

You'll use your equation-solving skills to solve problems involving decimals.

CHAPTER

| 1 | 2 | **3** | 4 | 5 | 6 | 7 | 8 | 9 | 10 | 11 | 12 |

NUMBER SENSE: DECIMALS AND FRACTIONS...102

Problem Solving
in Chapter 4

TECHNOLOGY

 Algebra

Using fractions, you'll solve problems about the stock market and about construction projects.

- Spreadsheet
- Fraction Calculator
- World Wide Web
- Interactive CD-ROM

You'll see how to solve equations involving fractions and mixed numbers.

CHAPTER

| 1 | 2 | 3 | **4** | 5 | 6 | 7 | 8 | 9 | 10 | 11 | 12 |

OPERATIONS WITH FRACTIONS...164

Problem Solving in Chapter 5

Geometric formulas will help you solve problems involving unusual buildings, game boards, and sports fields.

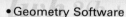
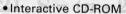
TECHNOLOGY

• Geometry Software
• World Wide Web
• Interactive CD-ROM

X Algebra

You'll use formulas to find perimeters and areas of geometric shapes.

CHAPTER

| 1 | 2 | 3 | 4 | **5** | 6 | 7 | 8 | 9 | 10 | 11 | 12 |

GEOMETRY AND MEASUREMENT...208

Ratios, rates, and proportions help you investigate the human body and explore different species of whales.

- Scientific Calculator
- World Wide Web
- Interactive CD-ROM

You'll use proportions to solve for unknown values such as the time it takes a dolphin to swim a given distance.

CHAPTER

| 1 | 2 | 3 | 4 | 5 | **6** | 7 | 8 | 9 | 10 | 11 | 12 |

RATIOS, RATES, AND PROPORTIONS...270

SECTION 6A

Ratios and Rates

SECTION 6B

Proportional Quantities

Problem Solving in Chapter 7

Maps and models of movie monsters show why scales are useful and important. Rates help you solve problems related to conservation.

TECHNOLOGY

- Geometry Software
- World Wide Web
- Interactive CD-ROM

x Algebra

You'll use proportions to solve for unknown lengths in geometric figures, on maps, and on scale models.

CHAPTER

| 1 | 2 | 3 | 4 | 5 | 6 | **7** | 8 | 9 | 10 | 11 | 12 |

PROPORTION, SCALE, AND SIMILARITY...320

Problem Solving
in Chapter 8

TECHNOLOGY

 **Algebra**

Percents help you solve a variety of problems, from finding the number of vampire bat species to calculating prices at a discount mall.

• Spreadsheet
• World Wide Web
• Interactive CD-ROM

You'll use your equation-solving skills to find unknown percents.

CHAPTER

| 1 | 2 | 3 | 4 | 5 | 6 | 7 | **8** | 9 | 10 | 11 | 12 |

PERCENTS...382

SECTION 8A

Understanding and Estimating Percents

SECTION 8B

Problem Solving with Percents

Positive and negative numbers help you describe and analyze the earth's structure and rides at an amusement park.

- Spreadsheet
- World Wide Web
- Interactive CD-ROM

Understanding operations with integers will allow you to solve equations that include negative numbers.

CHAPTER

| 1 | 2 | 3 | 4 | 5 | 6 | 7 | 8 | **9** | 10 | 11 | 12 |

INTEGERS...428

SECTION 9A

Using Integers

SECTION 9B

Operations with Integers

Equation-solving skills can be used to explore facts about insects, the weather, and situations involving young entrepreneurs.

- Graphing Utility
- World Wide Web
- Interactive CD-ROM

You'll solve equations involving integers by using tables, graphing, and using inverse operations.

CHAPTER

| 1 | 2 | 3 | 4 | 5 | 6 | 7 | 8 | 9 | **10** | 11 | 12 |

THE PATTERNS OF ALGEBRA: EQUATIONS AND GRAPHS...478

Problem Solving in Chapter 11

Surface areas and volumes help you measure sculptures and children's toys. Kaleidoscope patterns provide practice with transformations.

TECHNOLOGY

• Spreadsheet
• Geometry Software
• World Wide Web
• Interactive CD-ROM

 Algebra

You'll use formulas to find surface areas and volumes of three-dimensional figures.

| 1 | 2 | 3 | 4 | 5 | 6 | 7 | 8 | 9 | 10 | **CHAPTER 11** | 12 |

GEOMETRY: SOLIDS, CIRCLES, AND TRANSFORMATIONS...550

Problem Solving
in Chapter 12

Examples from detective work and board games will illustrate how you can use probability to analyze a situation.

TECHNOLOGY

- Graphing Calculator
- World Wide Web
- Interactive CD-ROM

x **Algebra**

You'll use formulas to help find geometric probabilities.

CHAPTER

1	2	3	4	5	6	7	8	9	10	11	**12**

COUNTING AND PROBABILITY...622

Internet Connections

The world of math is connected to the world around you in so many interesting ways. We'd like to invite you to explore these connections on the World Wide Web.

To begin your journey, you will need a web browser. Use your browser to visit the home page for *Mathsurf* by typing in *http://www.mathsurf.com.*

You'll find more web addresses at the top of each chapter opener and section opener that send you directly to pages that relate to your chapter or section.

Problem Solving and Applications

Math is all around you. Having good math skills can help you solve problems every day. What kinds of problems can you solve using mathematics?

Problem Solving
Understand
Plan
Solve
Look Back

Problem Solving STRATEGIES

Problem Solving TIP

WHAT DO YOU THINK?

Sports

90 ft **90 ft** **90 ft** **90 ft**

page 247

How far do you have to throw a baseball to catch a runner stealing second?

Whales

Species	Rate
Gray	36 ft/4 sec
Fin	36 ft/3 sec
Right	29 ft/4 sec

page 298

How can you compare the speeds of different whale species?

Geology

Mt. Everest, Nepal, 29,028 ft — 30,000 ft
Mt. McKinley, AK, 20,320 ft — 20,000 ft
Mt. Whitney, CA, 14,494 ft
Guadalupe Peak, TX, 8,749 ft — 10,000 ft
— 0 ft—Sea level
Dead Sea, 1,312 ft
— 10,000 ft
Deepest point,
Gulf of Mexico, 14,370 ft
Plaquemines Borehole, — 20,000 ft
22,570 ft

page 432

How far is it from the top of a mountain to the bottom of the ocean?

Insects

European Bee Honey Production

Honey (kg): 500, 400, 300, 200, 100, 0
Hives: 1, 2, 3

page 500

Which type of bee produces the most honey?

Toys

8 cm   9 cm   5.4 cm   6.5 cm

page 597

If you stretched out a Slinky® all the way, how long would it be?

Kaleidoscopes

page 605

How can you use mathematics to describe a kaleidoscope pattern?

Math is also connected to the other subjects you are studying.
Look on these pages to find some examples of how math is connected to:

Science

p. 9	p. 20	p. 58	p. 69
p. 114	p. 123	p. 177	p. 190
p. 216	p. 226	p. 277	p. 280
p. 347	p. 392	p. 397	p. 401
p. 435	p. 440	p. 493	p. 503

History

p. 15	p. 89	p. 107	p. 181
p. 189	p. 195	p. 236	p. 251
p. 311	p. 335	p. 342	p. 351
p. 422	p. 456	p. 560	p. 576
p. 581	p. 591	p. 598	p. 657

Geography

p. 9	p. 28	p. 76	p. 172
p. 220	p. 235	p. 257	p. 324
p. 327	p. 331	p. 332	p. 336
p. 339	p. 342	p. 398	p. 436
p. 458	p. 577	p. 604	p. 609

PROBLEM SOLVING HAND BOOK

We live in an Information Age. Today, by using the Internet and other tools, you can find more information more quickly than ever before. But knowing how to *find* information and knowing how to *use* it are two very different skills!

The key to success in almost any career is the ability to solve problems. If you don't have good problem-solving skills, you won't be able to use even the most accurate, up-to-date information.

Your teacher and textbook will help guide you, but to become a better problem solver, you must do the real exploring yourself. As you investigate challenging problems, you'll need to think logically, use technology appropriately, and work with others cooperatively.

Along the way, you'll find yourself asking and answering the question, "What do you think?" By asking this question, you'll learn about creative strategies used by your classmates. By answering it, you'll learn how to present your ideas to others with clarity and confidence.

The students shown here will be sharing their thinking with you throughout this book. But the key question will always be

"What do you think?"

1. Why is it important to hear about creative strategies used by your classmates?

2. How can sharing your ideas with other students help you become a better problem solver?

Solving Problems

You've solved many problems in your previous math classes. Now you'll look more closely at some methods that can help you solve problems. ◄

Problem Solving Getting Started

You solve problems every day. Some, like the problem of how much change you should get back when you pay for something, are straightforward. You can usually apply your knowledge of mathematics to find a quick solution to a problem such as this.

Others, such as the problem of which school activities to join, are harder to solve. There are many choices, and the result of each choice is not clear. Still others, such as the problem of which occupation to choose, may not even have exact or permanent solutions. You solve them the best way you can. But you should be ready to take another look at your solution if the situation changes.

No matter what problem you're tackling, you need a plan or a strategy for solving it. A plan or strategy will help you to understand the problem, to work out a creative solution, and to check that the solution makes sense.

Problem Solving

Understand
Plan
Solve
Look Back

PROBLEM-SOLVING GUIDELINES

❶ UNDERSTAND the Problem

- What do you know?
- What do you need to find out?

❷ Develop a PLAN

- Have you ever solved a similar problem?
- What strategies can you use?
- Estimate an answer.

❸ SOLVE the Problem

- Do you need to try another strategy?
- What is the solution?

❹ LOOK BACK

- Did you answer the right question?
- Does your answer make sense?

Example

Mrs. Cutler wants to install pine paneling on one wall of her den. The wall is 8 ft tall and 12 ft wide. An 8 ft panel that is 9 in. wide costs $9.95. Find the cost of the panels.

① UNDERSTAND the Problem

You *know* the size of the wall and the size and cost of a panel. You *need to find* the cost of all the panels needed to cover the wall.

② Develop a PLAN

You've *solved similar problems* involving the cost of a number of items that have the same price. To find the total cost, multiply the number of items by the unit price.

You can *estimate the answer*. Each panel is about 1 ft wide, so about 12 panels are needed. The total cost should be about 12 · $10, or $120.

One possible *strategy* is to draw a diagram to find the number of panels.

③ SOLVE the Problem

As you begin to sketch the wall, you might decide to use division to find out how many panels to draw.

But once you know the number of panels, you don't need a sketch! So *try another strategy*. Use division to find the number of panels.

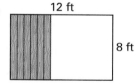

Number of panels = 144 ÷ 9 = 16   12 ft = 144 in.

Total cost = 16 · $9.95, or $159.20

The *solution* is that the panels will cost $159.20.

④ LOOK BACK

You *answered the right question*. Because your answer is close to your estimate of $120, *your answer makes sense*.

Check | Your Understanding

1. What other strategies could you have used to solve the problem?

2. Why is it important to have a plan before you begin a solution?

Problem Solving
STRATEGIES

- Look for a Pattern
- Make an Organized List
- Make a Table
- Guess and Check
- Work Backward
- Use Logical Reasoning
- Draw a Diagram
- Solve a Simpler Problem

Look for a Pattern

Sometimes the numbers in a problem form a pattern. To solve the problem, you can find the rule that creates the pattern and use the rule to find the answer. ◄

Example

Debra made a list of her direct ancestors. She called herself Generation 1, her parents Generation 2, her grandparents Generation 3, and so on. How many people were there in Generation 6?

List the information you know:

Generation 1: 1 person

Generation 2: 2 parents

Generation 3: 4 grandparents

Each generation has twice as many people as the previous one. Use this rule to continue the pattern:

Generation 4: $4 \times 2 = 8$ great-grandparents

Generation 5: $8 \times 2 = 16$ great-great grandparents

Generation 6: $16 \times 2 = 32$ great-great-great grandparents

There were 32 people in Generation 6.

Try It

a. Lincoln School students use a phone tree to convey important information. The chairperson makes 3 calls to start the phone tree. On the second round, 9 calls are made. On the third round, 27 calls are made. How many calls are made on the fifth round?

b. In one week, a tomato plant grew from 0.78 meters tall to 0.87 meters tall. If the plant continues to grow at the same rate, how tall will it be three weeks later?

Make an Organized List

Problem Solving STRATEGIES

• Look for a Pattern
• Make an Organized List
• Make a Table
• Guess and Check
• Work Backward
• Use Logical Reasoning
• Draw a Diagram
• Solve a Simpler Problem

Sometimes a problem asks you to find the number of ways in which something can be done. To solve the problem, you can list and count all the possibilities. The key to a correct solution is to organize your list carefully so you don't overlook any possibilities. ◄

Example

Fruit juice costs 40¢ in a vending machine. How many different combinations of quarters, dimes, and nickels must the machine be programmed to accept?

Since 2 quarters make 50¢, there can be no more than 1 quarter in any combination. Start by listing combinations with 1 quarter.

Then list combinations with 0 quarters. First list 4-dime combinations, then 3-dime combinations, and so on.

Finally, list combinations with 0 quarters and 0 dimes, only nickels.

The machine must be programmed to accept 7 different combinations of quarters, dimes, and nickels.

Quarters	Dimes	Nickels
1	1	1
1	0	3
0	4	0
0	3	2
0	2	4
0	1	6
0	0	8

Try It

a. All telephone area codes in one region of the country consist of the digits 2, 3, and 7. If no digit can be repeated, how many area codes containing only 2, 3, and 7 are possible?

b. Wise Owl book bags come in square or teardrop shapes. Each shape is available in red, blue, green, or yellow, and in small, medium, or large sizes. How many shape-color-size choices are available?

Problem Solving

STRATEGIES

- Look for a Pattern
- Make an Organized List
- **Make a Table** ──
- Guess and Check
- Work Backward
- Use Logical Reasoning
- Draw a Diagram
- Solve a Simpler Problem

Make a Table

A problem involving a relationship between two sets of numbers can often be solved by making a table. A table helps you organize data so you can spot the numerical relationship and find the answer. ◄

Example

In January, Hershel started a job that paid $2500 per month. In February, Keithia started a job that paid $3000 per month. In what month were the total amounts that the two had earned the same?

Make a table to organize data about each person's total earnings.

Month	January	February	March	April	May	June
Hershel's Total	2,500	5,000	7,500	10,000	12,500	15,000
Keithia's Total		3,000	6,000	9,000	12,000	15,000

The table shows that the amount by which Hershel's total exceeded Keithia's total decreased each month from February through June.

In June, both total amounts were the same.

Try It

a. In April, canned peaches sold for 79¢ and canned pears sold for 91¢. If the price of peaches increases 3¢ each month and the price of pears increases 1¢ each month, how much will both types of fruit sell for when their prices are the same?

b. At a traffic checkpoint, environmental safety officers checked every 18th car for excess carbon monoxide and every 15th car for a damaged exhaust system. If the first car at the checkpoint is car 1, what will be the number of the first car to be checked for both problems?

Roz Chast ©1995 from the New Yorker Magazine, Inc.

Guess and Check

Problem Solving

STRATEGIES

- Look for a Pattern
- Make an Organized List
- Make a Table
- Guess and Check
- Work Backward
- Use Logical Reasoning
- Draw a Diagram
- Solve a Simpler Problem

If you're not sure how to solve a problem, make an educated guess at the answer. Then check your guess. If it's wrong, revise your guess up or down. Repeat the pattern of *guess-check-revise* until you find the answer, or until you have an estimate that is close enough. ◄

Example

A rectangle has an area of 60 in². The length exceeds the width by 7 inches. Find the dimensions of the rectangle.

Guess: For a first guess, choose a length and width that multiply to 60.

Try $l = 10$ and $w = 6$. $10 \times 6 = 60$

Check: The length should be 7 greater than the width. $10 - 6 = 4$

Think: The difference isn't great enough. I need to increase the length.

Revise: Try $l = 15$ and $w = 4$. $15 \times 4 = 60$

Check: $15 - 4 = 11$

Think: Now the difference is *too* great. I need a length *between* my two guesses.

Revise: Try $l = 12$ and $w = 5$. $12 \times 5 = 60$

Check: $12 - 5 = 7$ ✔

The length of the rectangle is 12 in. and the width is 5 in.

Try It

a. Leon made long distance calls to two friends. One call lasted 8 minutes longer than the other. According to his phone bill, the two calls lasted a total of 42 minutes. How long was each call?

b. Two trains are 225 miles apart and traveling in opposite directions on parallel and adjacent tracks. If the eastbound train averages 50 miles per hour and the westbound train averages 40 miles per hour, how long will it take before they pass each other?

Problem Solving

STRATEGIES

• Look for a Pattern
• Make an Organized List
• Make a Table
• Guess and Check
• Work Backward
• Use Logical Reasoning
• Draw a Diagram
• Solve a Simpler Problem

Work Backward

A problem may give you the result of a series of steps and ask you to find the initial value. To solve the problem, you can work your way backward, step by step, to the beginning. ◄

Example

The Astro calculator was introduced in 1993. In 1994, the price was raised $8. In 1995, the price was lowered $14 because of lower demand. In 1996, the price was halved to $18 because of competition from a new calculator. Find the original price.

The problem describes three steps occurring in order (price raised, price lowered, price halved). It also tells you the end result (the final price was $18). To solve the problem, work backward to the beginning.

Step	What Happened	Conclusion
3	The price was halved to $18.	Before this step, the price was *twice* $18, or $36.
2	The price was lowered $14 to $36.	Before this step, the price was $14 *greater than* $36, or $50.
1	The price was raised $8 to $50.	Before this step, the price was $8 *less than* $50, or $42.

The original price of the calculator was $42.

Try It

a. At a sale, T-shirts were marked down $4. Pei bought 3 T-shirts. A sales tax of $2 was added to her bill, bringing the total cost to $26. Find the price of T-shirts before the sale.

b. Mount Whitney, Harney Peak, Mount Davis, and Woodall Mountain are the highest points in California, South Dakota, Pennsylvania, and Mississippi, respectively. Mount Whitney is about twice as tall as Harney Peak. Mount Davis is about 4020 feet less tall than Harney Peak and 4 times as tall as 806 ft Woodall Mountain. About how tall is Mount Whitney?

Use Logical Reasoning

Problem Solving

STRATEGIES

• Look for a Pattern
• Make an Organized List
• Make a Table
• Guess and Check
• Work Backward
• Use Logical Reasoning
• Draw a Diagram
• Solve a Simpler Problem

To solve a problem using logical reasoning, decide how the facts of the problem are related to each other. Then work your way, step by step, from the given facts to a solution. As you work, be careful not to make false assumptions or to draw conclusions that are not based on facts. ◄

Example

Freda, Miguel, and Ann are a teacher, a miner, and a writer, though not necessarily in that order. Ann is the sister of the teacher. Miguel has never met the teacher or the miner. Match the people with their jobs.

Take clues one at a time. Use a grid to keep track of your conclusions.

1. Ann is the sister of the teacher, so she is not the teacher.

	Teacher	Miner	Writer
Freda			
Miguel			
Ann	no		

2. Miguel has never met the teacher or the miner.

   Miguel must be the writer.

   Freda must be the teacher.

   That means Ann is the miner.

	Teacher	Miner	Writer
Freda			
Miguel	no	no	yes
Ann	no		

Try It

a. Xiao, Gina, and Dena like math, history, and art best. Dena dislikes art. Gina knows the students who like art and math best. Match the students with their favorite subjects.

	Teacher	Miner	Writer
Freda	yes	no	no
Miguel	no	no	yes
Ann	no	yes	no

b. Antoine, Bill, and Carlos live in Dallas, Seattle, and Miami. Bill is the brother of the man who lives in Seattle. Either Antoine or Carlos lives in Dallas. Antoine is an only child. Match the people with their cities.

Problem Solving

STRATEGIES

• Look for a Pattern
• Make an Organized List
• Make a Table
• Guess and Check
• Work Backward
• Use Logical Reasoning
• Draw a Diagram
• Solve a Simpler Problem

Draw a Diagram

A problem may involve objects, places, or positions. To solve such a problem, it may help to draw a diagram and look for relationships among the given data. Then use the relationships to find the answer. ◄

Example

Alicia, Brenda, Cal, and Damont are in line in the cafeteria. Damont is somewhere behind Brenda. Alicia is somewhere behind Cal. Brenda is somewhere behind Alicia. Find the order of the four students.

Draw a diagram to straighten out the relationships among the students. Use letters to represent their positions.

Begin with the first item of information: Damont is behind Brenda.

Front B   D

The second item gives no information about Damont or Brenda, so skip to the third: Brenda is behind Alicia. Add Alicia to the diagram.

Front A   B   D

Now use the second item: Alicia is behind Cal.

Front C   A   B   D

The order of the students is Cal, Alicia, Brenda, and Damont.

Try It

a. Clint is older than Laleh but younger than Bonnie. Adam is older than Laleh but younger than Clint. Bonnie is younger than Dylan. Order the 5 students from oldest to youngest.

b. A birthday cake measures 12 in. by 9 in. There are candles at the 4 corners and at 1-inch intervals around the border. How many candles are there on the cake?

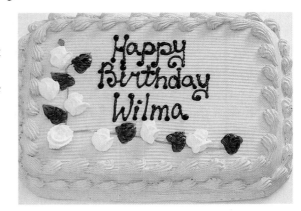

Solve a Simpler Problem

Problem Solving

STRATEGIES

• Look for a Pattern
• Make an Organized List
• Make a Table
• Guess and Check
• Work Backward
• Use Logical Reasoning
• Draw a Diagram
• Solve a Simpler Problem

A problem may contain large numbers or appear to require many steps. Instead of solving the given problem, solve a similar but simpler problem. Look for shortcuts, patterns, and relationships. Then use what you've learned to solve the original problem. ◄

Example

There are 64 teams in the state soccer tournament. A team is eliminated if it loses a game. How many games must be played to determine the state soccer champion?

You could draw a diagram listing 64 teams and count the number of games that must be played. But that would be very complicated. Instead, look at some simpler tournaments.

Number of Teams	Games Needed	
2	1	Team 1 plays Team 2 — **Champion!**
3	2	Team 2 plays Team 3 — Team 1 plays Team 2 or 3 — **Champion!**
4	3	Team 1 plays Team 2 — Team 1 or 2 — Team 3 plays Team 4 — Team 3 or 4 — plays — **Champion!**

The number of games needed is always 1 less than the number of teams. So a 64-team tournament requires $64 - 1 = 63$ games.

Try It

a. How many cuts must you make in a long rope to create 47 jump ropes?

b. How many paths are there from *A* to *B?* You may move only in the directions of the arrows.

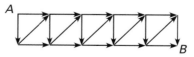

1 Making Sense of the World of Data

Cultural Link
www.mathsurf.com/7/ch1/people

Entertainment Link
www.mathsurf.com/7/ch1/ent

People of the World

A line graph of the population of Asia would be a steep curve. In 1750, it was 476,000,000. In 1950, it was 1,368,000,000. A line graph of the population of Antarctica would have a flat line.

Arts & Literature

The Oxford English Dictionary lists at least 1000 words for nearly every letter of the alphabet. With only 152 words, the letter x is an outlier.

Entertainment

The Hart Memorial Trophy is awarded to the most valuable hockey player in the National Hockey League. The hockey player who has received this award most often is Wayne Gretzky.

Science

A scatterplot can demonstrate a strong trend between the amount of snow in the winter and the chances of a flood the following spring.

Social Studies

Quillayute, Washington is considered the wettest area in the continental United States. It receives an average rainfall of 105 inches each year.

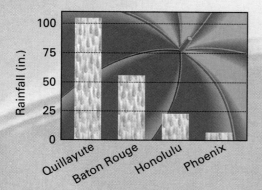

Annual Rainfall

KEY MATH IDEAS

Displaying information in bar graphs, line graphs, line plots, and stem-and-leaf diagrams can help you interpret the data.

A bar graph with a broken or inconsistent scale can be misleading.

The average, middle, and most common values in a data set are its mean, median, and mode.

A scatterplot is a graph that shows relationships between two types of data.

Drawing a trend line for points on a scatterplot can help you make predictions about the data.

CHAPTER PROJECT

Problem Solving

Understand
Plan
Solve
Look Back

In this project, you will plan and conduct your own Olympics with many different games. Your events might include math, trivia, or other intellectual contests as well as athletic ones. Begin the project by listing the games you decide on. The competitions can be held and scored at different times.

Problem Solving Focus

Problem Solving

Understand
Plan
Solve
Look Back

Reading the Problem

As you read a problem, you may be overwhelmed by information. Breaking the information into small parts can help you understand what the problem is saying. Ask yourself questions to be sure you understand each part.

Read each problem, and answer the questions about the problem.

1 The Oben triplets made a memory quilt by sewing together squares of material cut from their baby blankets. Jo cut 12 squares. Tyra cut 4 less than Jo. Tasha cut twice as many as Tyra. How many squares did they cut all together?

a. What is the problem about?

b. What is the problem asking for?

c. How many squares did Jo cut?

d. How many squares did Tyra cut?

e. Write and answer a question of your own.

2 At the Amish Quilting Shop, Mike sees a Lone Star quilt for $550 and a Country Love quilt for twice as much. The dealer offers Mike both quilts in exchange for Mike's Wedding Wreath quilt, which is worth $800, and his Sampler quilt, which is worth $900. Should Mike make this trade?

a. What is the problem about?

b. What is the problem asking for?

c. How much is Mike's Sampler quilt worth?

d. How much is the Country Love quilt worth?

e. Write and answer a question of your own.

Communicating with Data

A World of Geography

With its high mountains and deep valleys, lush rain forests and arid deserts, this Earth is an amazing place. The study of the earth's physical features is called *geography*. Geographers study the world's size, shape, and features.

Geographers use mathematics to help make sense of the world. Think about the world's population. You probably know that it is growing rapidly, but this is not enough to help you understand the details of population growth. Mathematics can be used to describe data in many ways:

• At its present rate of growth, the world's population is doubling every 40 years.

• About 180 million babies are born each year, 500,000 each day, 21,000 each hour, 350 each minute.

• Nearly 90% of the world's population is crowded onto 20% of the land.

In the lessons that follow, you will learn how to use mathematics to organize, display, and interpret data.

1 Give an example showing how geographic data helps people make sense of the world.

2 Describe a way you could visually display one of the facts given about population.

5

Interpreting Graphs

▶ **Lesson Link** In the past, you've seen many different types of graphs used to display information. In this lesson, you'll read and interpret two of the most common types of graphs. ◀

You'll Learn ...

■ to read and interpret bar graphs

■ to read and interpret circle graphs

... How It's Used

Meteorologists use bar and circle graphs to show weather-related data. For instance, a bar graph can be used to compare this year's rainfall to the average.

Vocabulary

circle graph

sector

bar graph

vertical axis

horizontal axis

Explore | Graphs

Population Pictures

Use these graphs of population in Southeast Asia to answer each question.

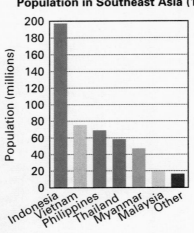

Population in Southeast Asia (1995)

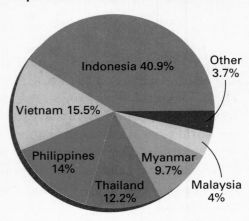

Population in Southeast Asia (1995)

Indonesia 40.9%
Other 3.7%
Vietnam 15.5%
Philippines 14%
Thailand 12.2%
Myanmar 9.7%
Malaysia 4%

1. Which country has a population of about 60 million? Which graph did you use? Why?

2. Which country has nearly half the population of Southeast Asia? Which graph did you use? Why?

3. Which graph best shows the actual population of each country? Explain.

4. Which graph best shows the portion of the population of Southeast Asia that is in each country? Explain.

5. What can you learn from each type of graph that the other type doesn't tell you?

A **circle graph** is divided into wedge-shaped **sectors**. The sectors show how portions of a set of data compare with the whole set.

The size of the sector can be compared to the entire circle. The data values can also be compared to each other by looking at the sizes of sectors.

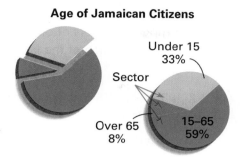

Age of Jamaican Citizens

Under 15
33%

Sector

Over 65
8%

15–65
59%

Remember

100% = the whole of any quantity. **[Previous course]**

Examples

The circle graph displays information about the labor force in Australia.

1 What type of job is most common?

Finance. It has the largest sector, 34%.

2 What two job types together make up half of the total labor force?

16% + 34% = 50%, so finance and industry make up half of the total labor force.

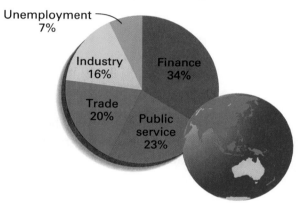

Australian Labor Force

Unemployment
7%

Industry
16%

Finance
34%

Trade
20%

Public
service
23%

Try It

What two job types together make up 43% of the total labor force in Australia?

A **bar graph** uses bars to display numerical data. The length of the bar tells you the value of the data. In the bar graph, the size of each data value can be found by looking at the **vertical axis**. The **horizontal axis** has a label for each bar. Bar graphs can be used to describe data values and to compare data values.

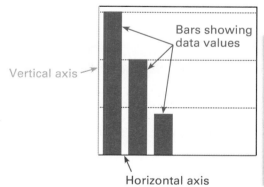

Bars showing
data values

Vertical axis

Horizontal axis

▶ **Language Link**

It is easy to remember which axis is horizontal—picture the sun going down over the horizon, where the land meets the sky!

Examples

Decide whether a bar graph or a circle graph best displays the information.

3 The number of barrels of oil exported by Saudi Arabia in each of the last 4 years.

A bar graph. The number of barrels can be read from the vertical axis.

4 The comparison between the money spent on pumping a barrel of oil and the total cost of producing a barrel of oil.

A circle graph. The sector that represents the pumping costs can be compared to the entire circle.

Try It

Which type of graph would be the best to display the cost of a barrel of oil in each of the past 3 years?

An axis in a bar graph can be "broken" to make the graph easier to read. Breaking an axis, however, can mislead the reader. In a voter preference poll, Smith (32%) and Jones (30%) were almost tied.

But on the graph with the broken vertical axis, it looks as though Smith is far ahead of Jones. This is an example of a misleading graph.

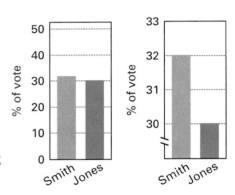

Check | Your Understanding

1. When is it best to use a bar graph to display data? A circle graph?

2. Explain why the sum of the percents in a circle graph is always 100.

3. How can a bar graph with a broken vertical axis give a misleading impression?

Practice and Apply

Getting Started Use the bar graph for Exercise 1, and the circle graph for Exercise 2.

1. a. Which volcano is the highest? The lowest?

   b. Which two volcanoes are closest in height?

   c. What does the vertical axis show?

2. a. Number Sense List the oceans in order of size, from the largest to smallest.

   b. Estimation About what percent of the earth's surface that is covered by water is the Pacific Ocean?

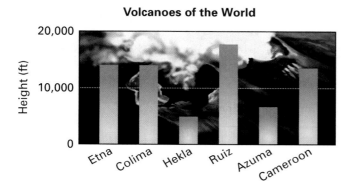

Volcanoes of the World

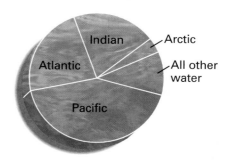

Ocean Sizes

3. Geography Decide whether a bar graph or a circle graph would best display:

   a. The heights of the six tallest mountains in the Andes.

   b. The percent of the world's annual coal supply produced by several nations.

   c. The amount of time you spend each day in different activities.

Use the graph showing the amount of water stored behind the world's 10 largest dams for Exercises 4 and 5.

4. Science The Waditharthar Dam stores enough water to take about 1 billion showers. Use the graph to estimate the number of showers you could take with Owens Falls water.

5. **Test Prep** Which dams store more water than the Aswan High Dam?

   Ⓐ Waditharthar and Zeya

   Ⓑ Kariba and Akosombo

   Ⓒ Owens Falls and Bratsk

   Ⓓ Bratsk and Kariba

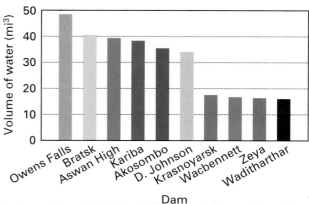

Volume of Water Behind World's Greatest Dams

6. Social Studies The bar graph below is misleading. About how many times greater than the population of Seoul are the populations of Tokyo and Bombay?

Predicted 2015 Populations of Some Asian Cities

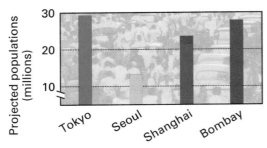

7. Chance The graph shows how your best friend spends her Saturday afternoons. What are you most likely to find her doing if you stop by unexpectedly?

Saturday Afternoon Activities

Relaxing
Homework
Gardening
Shopping
Housework

Problem Solving and Reasoning

These two graphs show the same information. Use them for Exercises 8 and 9.

Composition of Earth's Crust

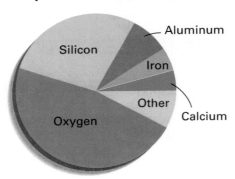

Aluminum
Silicon
Iron
Other
Oxygen
Calcium

Composition of Earth's Crust

8. Critical Thinking Why do the graphs show "other"?

10. Critical Thinking Give an example of two sets of data that would best be represented by: **a.** A circle graph and **b.** A bar graph.

9. Communicate Use one of the graphs to compare the amounts of silicon and aluminum in the earth's crust. Which graph did you use? Explain.

11. Journal Circle graphs are often called "pie charts." Explain why you think this name is used.

Mixed Review

Write each as a number. *[Previous course]*

12. three thousand two hundred one

13. sixteen thousand two

14. 15 million

Add. *[Previous course]*

15. 34 + 99

16. 28 + 176

17. 543 + 395

18. 196 + 952

19. 25 + 27 + 56

20. 379 + 32 + 8

Making Bar Graphs

▶ **Lesson Link** You've read and interpreted data that is displayed in a bar graph. Now you will create bar graphs from tables of data. ◀

Explore Bar Graphs

Bars and Stripes

Materials: Graphing utility

The table shows the heights of the eight highest waterfalls.

Waterfall	Height (ft)
Angel Falls, Venezuela	3212
Tugela, South Africa	2014
Utigord, Norway	2625
Mongefossen, Norway	2540
Yosemite Falls, United States	2425
Ostre Mardola Foss, Norway	2154
Tyssestrengane, Norway	2120
Kukenaom, Venezuela	2000

1. Enter the data on a graphing utility. Make the minimum value on the vertical axis 0 and the maximum value on the vertical axis 4000. Then create a bar graph.

2. In what ways does the graph display the data effectively? In what ways is the display not effective?

3. Change either the maximum or the minimum on the vertical axis so that the data can be compared more easily. Describe the change and how you decided on it. Is the new display misleading?

You'll Learn ...

■ to create a bar graph from a table of data

■ to create a double-bar graph

... How It's Used

Newspapers and magazines need to show information in a format that is easily understood. Bar graphs do this.

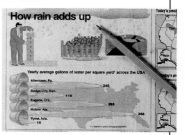

Vocabulary

scale

interval

double-bar graph

Learn Making Bar Graphs

The **scale** of a bar graph is the "ruler" that measures the heights of the bars. The **interval** is the amount of space between the values on the scale. Before you create a bar graph, you need to choose the scale and the interval.

You also have to decide if you will use vertical or horizontal bars. Your decision may be based on what you want the graph to communicate.

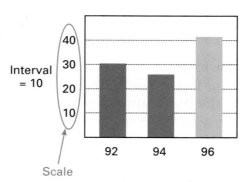

Example 1

Create a bar graph using data on the world's longest mountain ranges.

Step 1 Decide whether you will use vertical or horizontal bars. Since mountain ranges run horizontally, a horizontal graph seems better for displaying this data.

World's Five Longest Mountain Ranges		
Mountain Range	**Continent**	**Length (mi)**
Andes	South America	4500
Rocky Mountains	North America	3750
Himalayas-Karakoram	Asia	2400
Great Dividing Range	Oceania	2250
Transantarctic	Antarctica	2200

Step 2 Determine the scale and interval. The greatest value on the scale should be slightly greater than the greatest data value. It should also be easy to divide into equal intervals.

A number ending in one or more zeros is often a good choice. Use 5000 for the greatest scale value, and an interval of 1000.

Step 3 Draw a bar for each data value, using the scale to determine its length.

Step 4 Label and color the bars and give the graph a title.

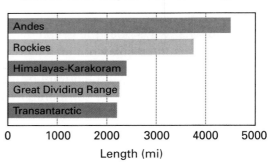

World's Five Longest Mountain Ranges

Because of the way data is arranged, you may decide to break a scale, or to start it at a number other than zero. In either case, be aware that readers may be misled.

Double-bar graphs allow you to compare two related data sets. Each double bar compares data for a given year. Changes from one year to the next are also easy to see.

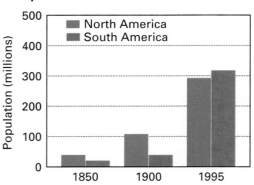

Populations of North and South America

Example 1

Example 2

The table compares the populations of New York City and Mexico City metropolitan areas. Create a double-bar graph of the data.

Populations of New York City and Mexico City (millions)		
Year	Mexico City	New York City
1950	3.1	12.3
1970	9.4	16.2
1990	20.2	16.2

Mexico City

In creating a double-bar graph, you must consider both sets of data. Otherwise, the steps are the same as for a single-bar graph.

Step 1 Use a vertical bar graph.

Step 2 Determine the scale and the interval. The greatest value should be slightly greater than the greatest value in *both* columns of the table. Use 24 for the greatest scale value and an interval of 6.

Step 3 Draw pairs of bars to represent the data values for each year and assign a color to the data in each column. Indicate the color assigned to each bar.

Step 4 Label the axes and give the graph a title.

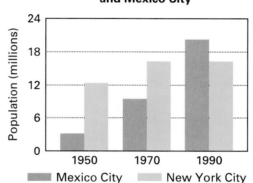

Populations of New York City and Mexico City

New York City

Try It

Make a double-bar graph of the irrigation data.

Irrigated Land (millions of acres)		
Year	India	United States
1960	27.1	28.7
1970	20.9	29.6
1980	18.1	26.1
1990	16.7	22.4

Study TIP

In a double-bar graph, you need to indicate which color bar belongs to which set of data.

Check Your Understanding

1. How can you decide what scale and interval to use on a bar graph?

2. Can any data be displayed in a bar graph? Explain.

3. How can a vertical bar graph be changed to a horizontal bar graph?

PRACTICE 1-2

Practice and Apply

1. **Getting Started** Use the population graph to answer each question.

   a. What is the greatest value shown on the vertical axis?

   b. What is the interval?

2. **Geography** Follow the steps below to make a bar graph of the lengths of some of Europe's rivers.

   a. Which type of bar graph would best show this data—horizontal or vertical?

   b. Rank the rivers in order, from shortest to longest.

   c. What should you choose as the greatest value on your axis? As the interval?

   d. Make a bar graph of the data.

Populations (1991)

River	Length (mi)
Danube	1780
Ebro	570
Volga	2200
Elbe	720
Rhine	820
Loire	630

3. **Test Prep** In which month was there the greatest difference in rainfall between Nashville and Seattle?

   Ⓐ April   Ⓑ July

   Ⓒ November Ⓓ December

Monthly Rainfall

Choose a convenient scale and interval to use for graphing each set of data.

   4. 70, 35, 55, 10, 43, 25, 80

   5. 4700, 2000, 3400, 1650, 2800

   6. 5, 8, 12, 11, 3, 6, 2, 9, 14

   7. 190, 234, 179, 140, 322, 356

8. **History** In the year 1910, many people immigrated to the United States—460,935 from northern and western Europe, 465,356 from eastern and southern Europe, 89,534 from the Americas, 23,533 from Asia, and 1,072 from Africa. Make a bar graph to show this data.

9. **Social Studies** The data shows the heights, in meters, of the world's 10 tallest buildings. Make a bar graph with a broken axis. 415, 421, 452, 348, 374, 443, 417, 452, 369, 381

10. Make a double-bar graph of the data from South America's three most populated cities.

Population—1994 and estimated 2015 (thousands)		
City	1994	2015
São Paolo, Brazil	16,110	20,800
Buenos Aires, Argentina	10,914	12,400
Rio de Janeiro, Brazil	9,817	11,600

Problem Solving and Reasoning

11. **Critical Thinking** Look at the table showing Armando's salary for the years 1996–2000.

    a. Would this data best be shown on a bar graph or a circle graph?

    b. Make a graph of the data.

    c. What do you notice about Armando's salary in the years 1996–1999?

    d. What do you think happened to Armando in the year 2000?

Year	Salary ($)
1996	20,000
1997	23,000
1998	26,000
1999	29,000
2000	35,000

12. **Journal** Sometimes a graph has a "broken" axis. Explain what this means and why you sometimes need to use one.

Mixed Review

Write each number in words. *[Previous course]*

13. 428   14. 2,489   15. 43,185   16. 130,396   17. 3,734,790

Subtract. *[Previous course]*

18. 94 − 23   19. 45 − 29   20. 147 − 32   21. 235 − 49   22. 527 − 76

Project Progress

Design the events for your games by making rules for the athletic events and deciding on questions and scoring methods for the thinking ones. Over the next few days, conduct your games. As each event takes place, record the results for each competitor on the chart.

Problem Solving

Understand
Plan
Solve
Look Back

1-3

Line Plots and Stem-and-Leaf Diagrams

You'll Learn ...

■ to make a line plot

■ to make a stem-and-leaf diagram

... How It's Used

Basketball coaches need to keep track of each player's progress. A line plot gives a clear view of how well a player is performing.

Vocabulary

line plot

outlier

stem-and-leaf diagram

▶ Lesson Link You know how to use a bar graph to display information. In this lesson, you will learn two ways to show how frequently values occur and how they are distributed. ◀

Explore | Line Plots

Double Time

Doubling time is the length of time it takes a population to double. The faster a population grows, the shorter its doubling time. The table shows the doubling times of the 44 African countries south of the Sahara Desert.

Population Doubling Times (yr)						
25	23	23	21	21	22	21
27	28	20	24	26	25	28
27	22	28	35	19	19	24
22	22	20	23	25	48	26
22	22	23	38	20	28	25
27	26	22	20	19	19	22
18	22					

1. Draw and label a number line to include every doubling time in the table. Put in an × for each doubling time. Stack ×'s one above the other. The ×'s for 23, 24, and 25 are shown.

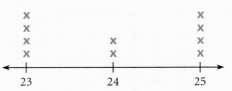

2. What does your completed plot show you?

3. How is the plot like a bar graph? How is it different?

4. In 1994, the nation of Namibia had a population of 1.5 million and a doubling time of 22 years. If its doubling time does not change, in what year is Namibia's population expected to be 3 million? Explain.

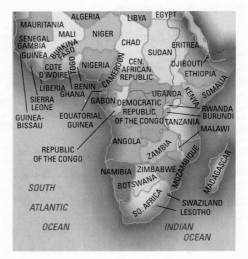

A **line plot** shows how many times each data value occurs. A number line and ×'s are used to organize the data. Line plots make it easy to see data values that are separated from the rest. Such data values are called **outliers**.

Line plot

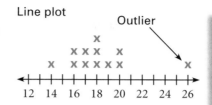

DID YOU KNOW?

Lacrosse is a very old game that was first played by Native Americans. A lacrosse stick has a net at the end, in which players catch the ball.

Example 1

Make a line plot of the data and describe the resulting plot.

Number of Players on a Team					
Baseball	9	Handball, team	7	Rugby, league	13
Basketball	5	Hockey	6	Rugby, union	15
Cricket	11	Lacrosse, men's	10	Soccer	11
Field hockey	11	Lacrosse, women's	12	Softball, fast-pitch	9
Football, American	11	Netball	7	Speedball	11
Football, Canadian	12	Polo	4	Volleyball	6
Football, Gaelic	15	Roller hockey	15	Water polo	7

Step 1 Decide on a scale. Because the smallest data value is 4 and the largest data value is 15, choose a scale from 4 to 16. Use an interval of 2.

Step 2 Mark an × for each data value.

The line plot shows that the most common team size is 11. More than half of the data values fall in the interval from 9 to 13. Teams of 7 and 15 are also common.

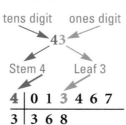

Number of players on a team

Problem Solving TIP

It is easy to miss a value, so be sure the number of ×'s you make matches the number of data values in the table.

Like a line plot, a **stem-and-leaf diagram** shows how often data values occur and how they are distributed. A stem-and-leaf diagram displays data horizontally.

Each data value is split into a *stem* and a *leaf*. For a two-digit value, the tens digit is the stem and the ones digit is the leaf. Single-digit values have stems of 0. For a three-digit value, the first two digits make up the stem.

123 is written as 12 | 3.

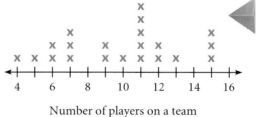

Example 2

▶ **Social Studies Link**

Auckland is the largest city in New Zealand, but Wellington is the capital. New Zealand was the first nation to allow women to vote.

The table gives the high temperature in Auckland, New Zealand, on each day during the month of April. Make a stem-and-leaf diagram of the data.

Daily High Temperatures in Auckland, New Zealand (°F)					
75	67	83	90	79	74
70	71	72	78	76	67
66	80	77	77	84	74
64	76	79	82	76	85
71	81	69	83	75	84

Step 1 Order the data values from smallest to largest.

64, 66, 67, 67, 69, 70, 71, 71, 72, 74, 74, 75, 75, 76, 76, 76, 77, 77, 78, 79, 79, 80, 81, 82, 83, 83, 84, 84, 85, 90

Step 2 Separate each item into a stem and a leaf. Use the tens digit for the stem and the ones digit for the leaf.

Step 3 List the stems in a column from largest to smallest. List the leaves in order beside their stems.

Stem	Leaf
9	0
8	0 1 2 3 3 4 4 5
7	0 1 1 2 4 4 5 5 6 6 6 7 7 8 9 9
6	4 6 7 7 9

The diagram shows that most of the data values are in the 70s. The plot also clearly shows the highest temperature, 90°F, and the lowest temperature, 64°F.

Problem Solving TIP

Make an organized list.

Try It

a. Make a line plot of the data.

b. Make a stem-and-leaf diagram of the data.

c. Compare the two graphs.

Ages of Employees Surveyed					
21	27	30	33	17	20
15	23	21	30	42	24
30	17	21	16	22	23
16	21	30	17	23	28

Check Your Understanding

1. How would you put 589 on a stem-and-leaf diagram? What about 6?

2. How do you think the stem-and-leaf diagram got its name?

3. Explain how you could use a line plot to decide if there were any outliers in a data set.

Practice and Apply

1. **Getting Started** Follow the steps below to make a line plot of the number of raisins in each of 24 boxes.

32	35	29	31	30	33	31	32	34	32	36	33
32	34	33	30	35	31	33	33	32	32	34	32

a. Find the smallest number of raisins shown.

b. Find the largest number of raisins shown.

c. Draw a section of the number line to include these two values.

d. Choose an interval.

e. Mark an × for each value in the chart.

f. Are there any outliers?

2. **Sports** Baseball Hall-of-Famer Rod Carew had 3053 hits in his major-league career. His home-run total for each of the 19 seasons he played from 1967 through 1985 is given in the table.

8	1	8	4	2	0	6	3	14	9
14	5	3	3	2	3	2	3	2	

a. Make a line plot of the number of home runs hit by Rod Carew.

b. What does the line plot tell you about Rod Carew's home runs?

3. The stem-and-leaf diagram shows the number of phone calls made by 20 of Joan's classmates over a two-week period. What was the greatest number of phone calls made? The least?

Phone Calls Made

Stem	Leaf
4	7
3	5 9
2	0 1 2 6
1	1 2 2 4 5 6 6 7
0	0 3 5 8 8

4. Show the data from Question 3 on a line plot. What does it show more clearly than the stem-and-leaf diagram?

5. **Test Prep** A data value with a stem of 52 and a leaf of 4 is displayed in a stem-and-leaf diagram. The number represented is:

Ⓐ 4   Ⓑ 52.4   Ⓒ 452   Ⓓ 524

Make a line plot for each set of data and name any outliers.

6. 2, 3, 1, 2, 1, 4, 2, 2, 4, 2

7. 11, 13, 14, 17, 11, 12, 12, 14, 17, 12

Make a stem-and-leaf diagram for each set of data.

8. **Science** Days of incubation for birds of various species: 27, 19, 35, 28, 25, 16, 40, 39, 32, 29, 31

9. Number of students in various school clubs: 12, 38, 5, 23, 8, 25, 14, 19, 25, 16, 23, 28, 17, 20

Problem Solving and Reasoning

10. **Critical Thinking** The back-to-back stem-and-leaf diagram shows the average daily April temperatures for Boston, MA, and Portland, OR. Use the plot to compare the pattern of April temperatures in the two cities.

Boston, MA		Portland, OR
	7	1
2 2	6	0 0 0 1 1 1 1 2 3 4 5
9 8 7 7 7 5 3 3 1 1 1 0	5	2 5 5 5 6 6 6 7 8 9 9
8 8 8 7 4 4 2 2 0 0	4	2 2 3 4 4 5
6 6 4 3 3 0	3	

11. **Critical Thinking** The table shows the ages of the first 20 American presidents when they took office.

   a. Make a stem-and-leaf diagram to show this data.

   b. What conclusions can you draw from your diagram?

   c. Would a line plot be a sensible way to show this data? Explain.

12. **Journal** How are line plots and stem-and-leaf diagrams alike? How are they different?

President	Age	President	Age
George Washington	57	James Polk	49
John Adams	61	Zachary Taylor	64
Thomas Jefferson	57	Millard Fillmore	50
James Madison	57	Franklin Pierce	48
James Monroe	58	James Buchanan	65
John Quincy Adams	57	Abraham Lincoln	52
Andrew Jackson	61	Andrew Johnson	56
Martin Van Buren	54	Ulysses Grant	46
William Harrison	68	Rutherford Hayes	54
John Tyler	51	James Garfield	49

Mixed Review

Multiply. *[Previous course]*

13. 82×5

14. 6×68

15. 89×40

16. 17×44

17. 130×62

18. 42×556

19. 850×417

20. 526×421

21. 23×907

Round to the nearest thousand. *[Previous course]*

22. 9,489

23. 100,687

24. 543

25. 23,500

26. 187,555

27. 4,499

28. 1,475,327

29. 499

30. 1,750

31. 9,631

Mean, Median, Mode, and Range

▶ **Lesson Link** You have used different types of graphs to display all the values in a data set. Now you will learn to use a single number to describe a collection of data. ◀

Explore   Mean

Food for Thought

Materials: Graph paper, Scissors, Tape

As populations increase, more food is needed to feed the world's people. *Arable land* is land fit for raising crops.

1. Use graph paper to make a horizontal bar graph of the data. Make the graph big enough so that you can easily cut out the bars.

2. Cut out each bar and tape the narrow sides together to form one large bar. Be sure the bars do not overlap. Fold the large bar in half, then in half again, then in half one more time.

3. Unfold the large bar and count the number of sections. What does the number of sections represent? What does the length of the large bar represent?

4. Measure the length of a section. How is the length of a section related to the length of the large bar?

5. Explain how the length of a section summarizes the table.

| Central American Arable Land (%) ||
Country	Amount
Belize	2
Costa Rica	6
El Salvador	27
Guatemala	12
Honduras	14
Mexico	12
Nicaragua	9
Panama	6

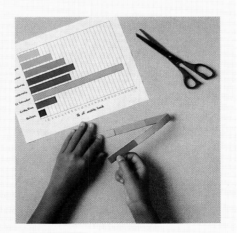

You'll Learn ...

■ to find the mean, median, mode, and range for a set of data

■ to decide if the mean, median, or mode best summarizes a set of data

... How It's Used

When making decisions about planting crops, farmers need to consider the average temperature, rainfall, and yield.

Vocabulary

mean

median

mode

range

Four numbers are commonly used to summarize a collection of data. Each has its own purpose.

The **mean** is the *average* of a set of data. We find the mean by dividing the sum of the data values by the number of data values.

The **median** is the *middle* data value when the values are arranged in order. If there is no single middle value, the median is the mean of the two middle values.

The **mode** is the *most common* data value. If no value occurs more than once, there is no mode. If two or more values occur more than once and equally, there are two or more modes.

The **range** is the difference between the highest and lowest data values.

Example 1

Find the mean, median, and range of the data values.

36, 8, 3, 13, 75

Mean

$$\frac{36 + 8 + 3 + 13 + 75}{5} = 27$$ Divide the sum by the number of values.

The mean is 27.

Median

3, 8, $\boxed{13}$, 36, 75   Put the values in order.

↑

The middle data value is 13.

The median is 13.

Range

$75 - 3 = 72$ Subtract the lowest data value from the highest.

The range is 72.

Try It

Find the mean, median, and range of the data values.

a. 28, 14, 59, 41, 50   **b.** 54, 45, 28, 36, 90, 23

The mean is the number used most often to summarize data. But when there are outliers, the median often gives a better summary than the mean. The mode can be used to summarize a few data values when most are the same.

Example 2

Find the mean, median, and mode of the data on life expectancies in the six Caribbean countries and decide which gives the best summary of the data.

Life Expectancy in Caribbean Countries					
Country	Cuba	Puerto Rico	Jamaica	Trinidad and Tobago	Dominican Republic	Haiti
Life Expectancy (yr)	77	75	75	70	69	45

Mean

$$\frac{77 + 75 + 75 + 70 + 69 + 45}{6}$$ Add the data values.

$$= \frac{411}{6} = 68.5$$ Divide by the number of data values.

The mean is 68.5 years.

Median The median is the mean of 70 and 75.

$$\frac{70 + 75}{2}$$ Add the two middle values.

45 69 **70**   **75** 75 77

$$= \frac{145}{2} = 72.5$$ Divide by the number of middle values.

The median is 72.5 years.

Mode A life expectancy of 75 years appears twice. The mode is 75 years.

The *mean* (68.5) was influenced by Haiti (an outlier), so it is smaller than five of the six data values. The *mode* (75) is near the high end of the data. The best summary of the data is the *median* (72.5).

Test Prep

Sometimes a list of data that are all whole numbers has a mean and/or a median that are fractions or decimals.

Check Your Understanding

1. Why would you want to know the mean, median, or mode of a data set?

2. How does an outlier affect the mean, median, and mode?

Practice and Apply

1. **Getting Started** Order each data set from the lowest to highest. Then find the median for each set.

   a. 5, 17, 6, 23, 34, 26, 19

   b. 48, 39, 27, 52, 45, 47, 49, 38

2. Look at this set of data: 2, 5, 8, 4, 3, 7, 5, 4, 6, 4, 8. How often does each value appear? Find the mode(s) for the data set.

3. The table shows the heights of the students in Ms. McPherson's class.

Height (in.)	57	58	59	60	61	62	63	64
Number of Students	2	5	8	7	4	2	0	2

   a. Find the mean, median, range, and mode.

   b. Which of these measures best summarizes the class?

4. Mei Li scored 85, 78, 65, 77, 91, 88, 80, 93, and 90 points on her math tests.

   a. How many tests did she take?

   b. How many points did she score all together?

   c. What was her average (mean) score?

5. **Sports** In the 1994 season, American Football Conference football teams allowed 234, 204, 352, 327, 298, 306, 406, 356, 312, 327, 320, 320, 323, and 396 points to be scored against their teams. What was the mean number of points allowed? The median? The mode(s)? The range?

6. **Number Sense** Decide if the mean, median, or mode is the best summary of the data set 10, 4, 11, 33, 6, 12, 9, 4, 7. Explain.

7. **Social Studies** To answer the questions, use the table showing the 1993 populations of the 13 states that formed the original colonies.

   a. Find the mean population of these 13 states.

   b. Would the mean be a good number to summarize these populations? Explain.

State	NH	MA	RI	CT	NY	NJ	PA	DE	MD	VA	NC	SC	GA
Population (100,000s)	11	60	10	33	181	78	120	7	49	63	67	36	66

8. **Number Sense** Use the line plot. Estimate the mean.

9. Find the mean, median, and mode of the data.

10. What is the median score represented by the stem-and-leaf diagram?

11. **Test Prep** Look at this set of data: 16, 24, 17, 18, 16, 22, 23, 18, 18. The number 18 is:

Ⓐ the mean only.

Ⓑ the mean and median only.

Ⓒ the median and mode only.

Ⓓ the mean, median, and mode.

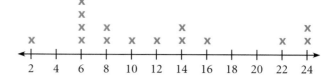

Stem	Leaf
4	4 5 7 8 9 9
3	0 2 5 5 8
2	3 7 7 7

Problem Solving and Reasoning

12. **Choose a Strategy** Six piglets in a litter had an average or mean weight of 8 lb. Find two possibilities for the weight of each pig.

13. **Communicate** You can always find the mean and median for a set of data, but sometimes you may not be able to find the mode. Why?

14. **Critical Thinking** Carlotta was being interviewed for a job. She was told that the median salary at the company was $43,000. Should Carlotta expect to receive that salary? Explain.

15. **Critical Thinking** The average population density of Alaska is 0.99 people per square mile. Explain this statement.

Problem Solving

STRATEGIES

- Look for a Pattern
- Make an Organized List
- Make a Table
- Guess and Check
- Work Backward
- Use Logical Reasoning
- Draw a Diagram
- Solve a Simpler Problem

Population

Mixed Review

Divide. [*Previous course*]

16. 56 ÷ 8

17. 47 ÷ 5

18. 567 ÷ 9

19. 682 ÷ 7

20. 588 ÷ 34

Order from least to greatest. [*Previous course*]

21. 7,286 6,999 8,003

22. 13,145 13,201 12,895

23. 288 8,822 8,282 28 8,882 82 2,228

TECHNOLOGY

Using a Data Analysis Package • Box-and-Whisker Plots

Problem: During the first seven days of the school year, a store sold 8, 12, 23, 5, 8, 15, and 3 calculators and 8, 8, 7, 10, 15, 9, and 2 computers. Construct a box-and-whisker plot for each data set. Which set is more "spread out"? Which points seem to be outliers?

You can use a data analysis package to help answer these questions. Data analysis packages are part of statistics programs and are featured on graphing calculators.

① Enter each data set. If you use a graphing calculator, enter each set as a list. With a data analysis package, enter each data set in a column.

② On your graphing calculator, select your statistics plotting menu. For your first plot, graph L1 as a box plot; for your second, graph L2 as a box plot. If you are using a data analysis package, select the box plot icon.

③ Interpret your box plots. The line in the middle of the box shows the median of the data. The ends of the box are *quartiles*—the medians of the lower and upper half of the data. The ends of the whiskers show the least and greatest values in the data set.

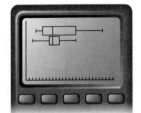

Solution: In step 3, the top box plot (calculators) appears to be more spread out. In the top plot, 23 seems to be an outlier. In the bottom plot, both 2 and 15 computers seem to be outliers.

TRY IT

Construct a box-and-whisker plot and answer the questions in the problem for the following data sets:

a. 33, 38, 43, 30, 29, 40, 51, 27, 42, 23, 31

b. 11, 14, 18, 5, 16, 8, 19, 10, 17, 20, 34

ON YOUR OWN

▶ How does a graphing calculator or data analysis package make it easier to interpret data?

▶ What would a box with extremely long whiskers tell you about a data set?

▶ Suppose two data sets have the same median and equally long whiskers. If the box of one box plot is longer, what can you say about the two data sets?

You saw at the beginning of this section that geography is used to help people make better sense of the world. Now you will have a chance to make decisions about displaying and summarizing geographic data.

A World of Geography

Materials: Art supplies for creating a display

1. Study the table. What relationships among data values do you see? When you have discovered something in the data that might help others make better sense of the world, write a sentence or two describing your discovery.

Country	People (per mi²)	Annual Population Increase (%)	Life Expectancy at Birth (yr)	Annual Income per Inhabitant ($)	Percent Living in Cities
Belgium	854	0.2	76	15,440	95
Brazil	48	1.9	65	2,680	74
Egypt	151	2.4	60	600	45
Guinea	86	2.5	42	480	22
Haiti	636	2.9	45	370	29
Nepal	383	2.5	50	170	8
Poland	320	0.4	71	1,700	61
Singapore	14,206	1.4	75	12,310	100
S. Africa	93	2.6	64	2,520	56
S. Korea	1,190	1.1	71	5,400	74

2. Create two different types of graphs or plots that help communicate relationships that you have noticed among data values.

3. Calculate the mean, median, and mode for each of your two data collections. Decide which summaries of the data will help others better understand what you are showing. Explain.

REVIEW 1A

Use the graphs for Exercises 1 and 2.

1. About what percent of the labor force in Canada is not employed in services?

2. Which graph best shows the fraction of people in manufacturing?

Canadian Labor Force (1996)

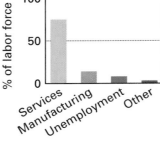

Canadian Labor Force (1996)

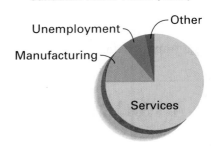

The line plot shows temperatures in several U.S. cities. Use it for Exercises 3–5.

3. Are any outliers shown?

4. Find the median and mode for the temperatures shown.

5. Make a stem-and-leaf diagram of this data.

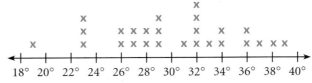

Average December Temperatures in Some U.S. Cities

Geography Use the table for Exercises 6–9.

6. Make a horizontal bar graph to show the data.

7. Which country has the longest canal system?

8. Find the mean length of the canals in the table.

9. **Journal** If France's 15,000-km canal system is included, how will it affect the answer to Exercise 8?

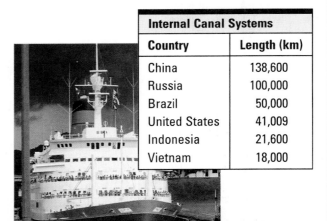

Internal Canal Systems	
Country	**Length (km)**
China	138,600
Russia	100,000
Brazil	50,000
United States	41,009
Indonesia	21,600
Vietnam	18,000

Test Prep

On a multiple-choice test, if you are given the mean for a number of unlisted data values, and asked to find the total of the data values, multiply the mean by the number of items.

10. A set of five data values has a mean of 26. What is the total of the data values?

Ⓐ 26   Ⓑ 31   Ⓒ 130   Ⓓ 265

Trends and Relationships in Data

▶ **Health Link** ▶ **Career Link** ▶ **www.mathsurf.com/7/ch1/sports**

Sports Around the World

"GOOOOAAAL!" The home soccer team scores again and the crowd cheers. Competition is fierce at every level, whether the game is a backyard contest or the World Cup final. All around the world, sports cross the barriers of language and distance. Whether it's soccer or basketball, swimming or tennis, you will find fans everywhere, studying their team's progress and prospects for the future.

Coaches keep track of many different types of statistics—both their own team's and their opponents'. All these statistics help show how good a team is now and help to predict its future performance.

Lists of facts and numbers take time to study, but a graph can show such information more clearly. Now you will learn how to analyze and display data.

1 Describe a trend you have seen in everyday life.

2 What are some statistics that a coach might want to keep track of? How can those statistics be measured?

3 How would you identify the most popular sport?

1-5 Line Graphs

You'll Learn ...

■ to read and interpret line graphs

■ to recognize trends

... How It's Used

Physical therapists can quickly see how a patient's performance is improving by checking a line graph of his or her statistics.

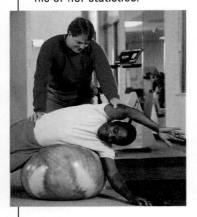

Vocabulary

line graph

trend

double-line graph

▶ **Lesson Link** In the last section, you learned to create displays of data. Now you will see how to display data that changes over time, and to use your displays to predict the future behavior of data. ◀

Explore | Line Graphs

Materials: Graphing utility

A Trendy Tournament

1. Enter the first column of data on a graphing utility. Decide on a scale. Then create a line graph of the first column of data. Enter the second column of data.

2. Describe both lines. How are they alike? How are they different?

3. One of the lines shows a trend. Which is it? How can you use this line to make a prediction about future values of the data?

4. Predict the expected total attendance at the 1998 World Cup in France. Explain how you made your prediction.

Men's World Cup Soccer Tournament		
Year	Attendance (millions)	Goals (per game)
1962	0.8	2.8
1966	1.6	2.8
1970	1.7	3.0
1974	1.8	2.6
1978	1.6	2.7
1982	1.8	2.8
1986	2.4	2.5
1990	2.5	2.2
1994	3.7	2.7

Learn | Line Graphs

The bar graph shows the winning height for the women's high jump at the Olympics from 1968 through 1996. If the tops of the bars are connected by a line and the bars are erased, a **line graph** is created.

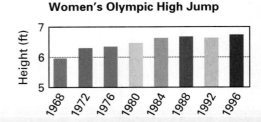

Women's Olympic High Jump

A line graph shows how data changes over time. A **trend** is a clear direction in a graph that suggests how the data will behave in the future. The line graph shows that the winning heights have an increasing trend.

If you extend a line graph, the direction of the data can be used to predict the future behavior of the data.

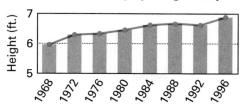
Women's Olympic High Jump

Examples

1 Make a line graph of the following data.

Number of Teams in the NBA							
Year	Teams	Year	Teams	Year	Teams	Year	Teams
1960	8	1970	14	1980	22	1990	27
1965	9	1975	18	1985	23	1995	29

Step 1 Draw and label the axes. Time lines are usually horizontal, so put units of time on the horizontal axis. Decide on the scale for the vertical axis.

Have the scale run from zero to a number that ends in zero, if possible. Divide the scale into intervals that are easy to read and understand.

Step 2 Plot a point for each data value. Then connect the points.

Step 3 Give the graph a title.

NBA Teams

2 Use the graph to predict the number of NBA teams in the year 2010.

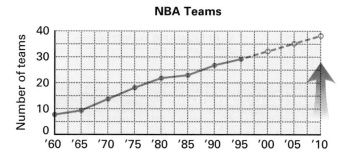
NBA Teams

To predict the number of teams in 2010, extend the graph in a reasonable way. The extension shown gives a prediction of about 38 teams. Keep in mind that the prediction will be true only if the trend continues.

Problem Solving TIP

Be sure that the greatest value shown on your axis is greater than the greatest data value you need to show.

► **History Link**

In 1891, a physical education teacher named James Naismith nailed two peach baskets to the gym balcony and asked his students to try tossing a ball into them. Basketball was born!

A line graph can be misleading if the scale is broken or begins at a number other than zero. The scale of this graph extends from 8% to 11%. As a result, it shows a sharp increase that one with a scale from 0% to 11% would not.

Be alert for misleading line graphs in newspapers and magazines. Be sure that any changes you make in your own line graphs are clearly marked.

You can graph two sets of related data on a **double-line graph** .

Example 3

Make a double-line graph and describe the graph.

U.S. Athletic Shoe Sales								
	1987	1988	1989	1990	1991	1992	1993	1994
Basketball Shoes ($ millions)	169	226	293	428	449	456	407	407
Aerobic Shoes ($ millions)	401	327	425	389	381	376	318	305

Remember

You need to color-code the lines to avoid confusion.

One line is drawn to represent each set of data and the lines are labeled. The graph shows that as the sales of basketball shoes increased, the sales of aerobic shoes decreased.

U.S. Athletic Shoe Sales

Try It

Make a double-line graph of the data and describe the graph.

Features of New Homes			
	1970	1980	1990
Central Air-Conditioning (%)	34	63	76
At Least One Fireplace (%)	35	56	66

Check Your Understanding

1. Why is a line graph a good way to display data that changes with time? How do line graphs show trends?

2. Give an example of a data set for which a bar graph could be used, but a line graph couldn't be used.

Practice and Apply

Countries Competing in the Olympics

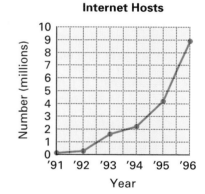

Getting Started The graph shows the number of countries taking part in the summer Olympic games from 1948 through 1972.

1. What trend do you notice in the graph?

2. What is the interval on the horizontal axis? The vertical?

3. **Sports** The table shows Josie's total score after each frame of bowling. Make a line graph to show this information.

Frame	1	2	3	4	5	6	7	8	9	10
Score	8	24	40	48	67	76	104	123	132	150

Technology Use the graph of Internet hosts (computer sites where Web pages are stored) for Exercises 4 and 5.

4. Predict the number of hosts in 1998.

5. What other kind of graph could be used to show this data?

Social Studies Use the table of the mean number of people per household in the United States from 1850 through 1980 for Exercises 6 and 7.

Year	1850	1860	1870	1880	1890	1900	1910	1920	1930	1940	1950	1960	1970	1980
Mean	5.50	5.28	5.09	5.04	4.93	4.76	4.54	4.34	4.11	3.67	3.37	3.33	3.14	2.75

6. Make a line graph to show this data.

7. Describe any trend you see in the graph.

8. Use the data in the table to make a double-line graph. Describe the graph.

Transportation Used by Commuters				
	1960	1970	1980	1990
Private Vehicles (%)	69	81	86	88
Public Transportation (%)	13	8	6	5

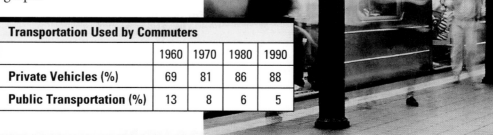

9. **Test Prep** The world record time for the 4 × 400 meter relay has been decreasing over the years. Which of these graphs could represent this?

Ⓐ 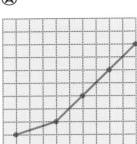 Ⓑ 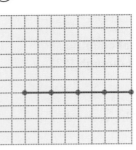 Ⓒ 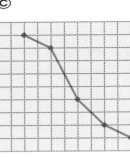 Ⓓ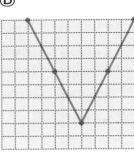

Problem Solving and Reasoning

Critical Thinking The Carolina Panthers joined the NFL in 1995. The double-line graph shows the number of points scored and allowed by the Panthers in the first nine games of their first season. Use the graph for Exercises 10 and 11.

10. Estimate the most points scored by the Panthers in a game. Estimate the fewest points allowed in a game.

11. In how many games did the Panthers score more points than their opponents? How can you tell? How could you tell if there was a tie game?

12. **Communicate** A line graph is useful in predicting future data values. Will your prediction necessarily be accurate? Explain.

Carolina Panthers (1995)

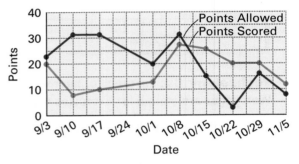

Mixed Review

Add or subtract. *[Previous course]*

13. 4,512 + 9,439

14. 6,302 − 2,154

15. 34,293 + 67,262

16. 89,684 − 56,158

17. 452,972 + 318,964

18. 579,532 − 417,359

Choose a convenient scale and interval to use for making a bar graph of the data. *[Lesson 1-2]*

19. 270, 100, 430, 650, 280

20. 1300, 2400, 3400, 400

21. 20, 110, 90, 130

22. 1000, 1500, 750, 250

23. 21, 12, 35, 47

24. 1138, 1257, 1049, 1317

Scatterplots and Relationships

▶ **Lesson Link** You have drawn double-bar graphs and double-line graphs to compare related data values. Now you will see a type of graph that can be used to explore those relationships. ◀

Explore   Scatterplots

Plots of Lots of Shots

The U.S. women's fast-pitch softball team won the 1994 World Championship. The graph shows data for some players in this tournament.

1. Who had the most hits? How many did she have?

2. Which players had the same number of hits? How many did they have?

3. Which players had the same number of times at bat? How many did they have?

4. What would a point on the vertical axis represent? Explain.

5. Imagine a line from the point representing 0 hits and 0 times at bat to 10 hits and 10 times at bat. Why are there no points below the line?

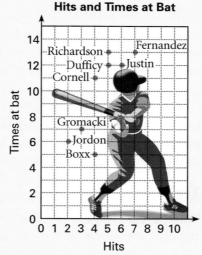

Hits and Times at Bat

Learn   Scatterplots and Relationships

You can investigate the relationship between two sets of data by drawing a **scatterplot** . Each set of data is represented by an axis with its own scale. Each pair of values is represented by a point.

To plot a point, find the value of the data on each axis. Extend a horizontal line from one axis and a vertical line from the other axis. Put a point where the lines meet.

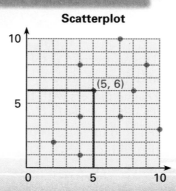

Scatterplot

(5, 6)

Example 1

Make a scatterplot of the data. Describe the scatterplot.

City	Altitude (ft)	Highest Temperature (°F)
Denver, CO	5283	99
Helena, MT	4157	98
Phoenix, AZ	1092	113
Reno, NV	4500	102
Spokane, WA	1898	101
Syracuse, NY	408	88

Step 1 Choose the axes and scale. The horizontal axis has been chosen to represent altitudes. The altitude scale runs from 0 to 6000 feet. There are no temperatures below 88°F, so the temperature scale begins at 85°F.

Step 2 Plot each point. Point *H* represents Helena's 98°F temperature and 3828 ft altitude.

Step 3 Label the scatterplot.

Most of the temperatures are clustered around 100°F. Altitudes are distributed fairly evenly from 0 ft to 6000 ft.

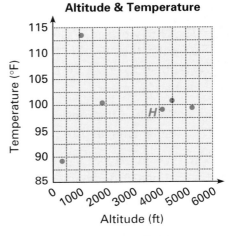

Altitude & Temperature

Try It

Make a scatterplot of the data and describe the result.

Famous U.S. Bridges		
Bridge	Length (ft)	Width (no. of lanes)
Brooklyn	1595	6
George Washington	3500	14
Golden Gate	4200	6
Verrazano Narrows	4260	12

This scatterplot displays data on goals and games played by the National Hockey League players with the most career goals. The plot shows that a player's goal total tends to increase as the number of games played increases.

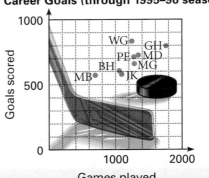

Career Goals (through 1995–96 season)

When two sets of data increase at the same time, the sets show a **positive relationship** . A scatterplot of a positive relationship slants upward to the right.

When one set of data increases as the other decreases, the sets show a **negative relationship** . A scatterplot of a negative relationship slants downward to the right.

When two sets of data neither increase nor decrease together, they show **no relationship** .

Positive Relationship

Negative Relationship

No Relationship

Examples

Decide whether each set of data would show a positive, a negative, or no relationship.

2 The number of students doing a job and the length of time it takes.

The *greater* the number working, the *less* time the job takes: *negative.*

3

Student's Age	11	18	7	13	15	10	9
Student's Area Code	205	302	408	508	914	610	818

The scatterplot shows a random arrangement of points. There is *no relationship* between the sets.

Try It

Decide whether the sets would show a positive, a negative, or no relationship.

a. The number of hours you've been awake and the number of hours until you go to bed.

b. The number of magazines you buy and the total price you pay.

Age and Area Code

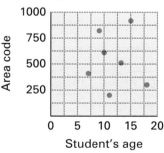

Study TIP

It is better to get a full night's sleep before an important test than to stay up late studying.

Check Your Understanding

1. How are scatterplots and line plots alike? How are they different?

2. Why is it sometimes better to choose a scale that does not begin at zero?

PRACTICE 1-6

Practice and Apply

1. **Getting Started** Follow the steps to draw a scatterplot.

   a. Choose a scale for both axes.

   b. Mark the interval on each axis.

   c. Label both axes.

   d. Plot the points.

   e. What kind of a relationship does the scatterplot show?

Points Scored in Super Bowl, 1990–95						
Winning Team	55	20	37	52	30	49
Losing Team	10	19	24	17	13	26

Science Use the scatterplot showing the life expectancies and sizes of some African animals for Exercises 2 and 3.

2. Which animal has the longest life expectancy? The shortest?

3. What is the life expectancy of a gorilla? A rhinoceros?

4. **Sports** Make a scatterplot to show the data. Determine if there is any relationship between the two sets of data.

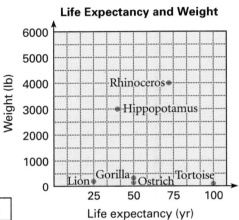

Life Expectancy and Weight

Games Played	4	7	9	14	15	18	20	23
Total Service Aces	13	20	28	44	47	56	59	70

5. The table shows the heights in inches of some students and of their mothers. Make a scatterplot to show this information.

	A	B	C	D	E	F	G	H	I	J
Mother	54	52	60	56	60	66	60	66	64	62
Student	54	58	58	60	62	62	66	66	68	60

Decide whether the sets would show a positive, a negative, or no relationship.

6. The time it takes a parachutist to land and the altitude of the plane when the parachutist jumps.

7. The time it takes to run 400 meters and the speed of the runner.

8. The time spent waiting in line and the length of the movie.

9. **Test Prep** Which point on the scatterplot represents a perfect score on a test?

Ⓐ P   Ⓑ Q   Ⓒ R   Ⓓ S

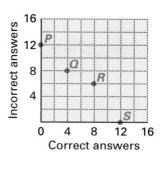
Correct answers

10. **Sports** Which of these scatterplots might show the length of stride against the number of strides taken in a 100-meter sprint?

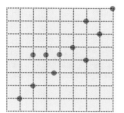   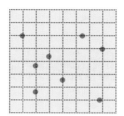   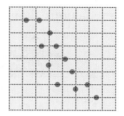

11. **Communicate** Describe a set of paired data that has a negative relationship.

Problem Solving and Reasoning

12. **Critical Thinking** The scatterplot shows total goals scored in a series of soccer matches plotted against the total number of attempts. Is there anything surprising about the plot? Explain your thinking.

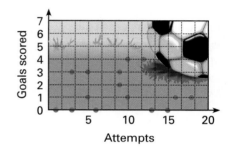

13. **Critical Thinking** The scatterplot shows the number of cars crossing a toll bridge on the different days in May. Describe any patterns you see.

Cars on Toll Bridge

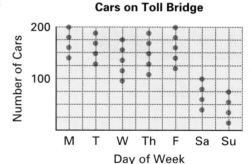

Mixed Review

Multiply or divide. *[Previous course]*

14. 345 × 531   **15.** 842 ÷ 22   **16.** 6,241 × 390

17. 5,924 ÷ 50   **18.** 7,238 × 942   **19.** 6,319 × 2,733

Make a stem-and-leaf diagram for each set of data. *[Lesson 1-3]*

20. 23, 32, 24, 34, 32, 31, 25, 36, 28, 27, 21, 41, 29   **21.** 7, 4, 8, 12, 14, 9, 21, 23, 17, 21, 10, 11, 16, 19, 12

Project Progress

After all of your events have been completed, look at the data you collected for each event. Decide which type of graph would best show the event's results, and make the graph. Find the winner of each event. You may wish to have a closing ceremony in which all the winners are announced.

Problem Solving

Understand
Plan
Solve
Look Back

Trend Lines

You'll Learn ...

■ to construct trend lines

■ to use trend lines to make predictions

... How It's Used

Coaches need to see whether the training schedules they are using are having the desired results. One way to see this is to make a scatterplot and check the trend.

Vocabulary

trend line

▶ **Lesson Link**   You know how to construct a scatterplot to display the relationship between two sets of data. Now you will see how to use that relationship to make predictions about the data. ◀

Explore | Trend Lines

Trends and Relations

Use the box score from the 1996 NCAA Women's Basketball Championship game to answer each question.

University of Tennessee Boxscore				
Player	**Height (ft-in)**	**Minutes**	**Assists**	**Points**
Holdsclaw	6-2	34	3	16
Conklin	6-3	23	3	14
Johnson	6-4	28	1	16
Marciniak	5-9	37	5	10
Davis	5-6	32	8	8
Jolly	5-10	10	1	2
Laxton	6-0	12	0	4
Thompson	6-1	21	0	12

1. Make a scatterplot using "Minutes Played" and "Points" data. Make a second scatterplot using "Assists" and "Height" data.

2. Describe the difference between the shapes of the scatterplots. Is there anything special about the data that might account for this?

3. Do players who are tall tend to have a lot of assists? Do players who play for many minutes tend to score a lot of points?

4. Suppose a player played for 40 minutes. What would be a good prediction for the number of points she scored? Explain.

5. Suppose a player had 10 assists. What would be a good prediction for her height? Explain.

6. Describe the method you used to make your predictions. What are some factors that determine if the prediction is likely to come true?

Learn | Trend Lines

When sets of data show a positive or negative relation-ship, you can draw a **trend line** to approximate the data. A trend line should have about the same number of data points above and below it. By extending the trend line, you can make predictions about the data.

Trend Line

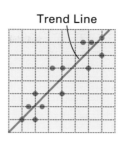

Examples

1 Draw a scatterplot and a trend line for the number of wins and years of coaching for the eight college football coaches with the most total wins.

Years	30	44	27	30	38	33	57	23
Wins	259	319	234	278	323	238	314	231

The scatterplot shows a positive relation-ship between wins and years of coaching.

To draw a trend line, take a clear plastic ruler and position it until an equal number of points lie above and below the trend line. Then, draw the line.

2 Use the trend line to predict the num-ber of wins for a coach who coached for 35 years.

Wins and Years Coached

The point on the trend line directly above 35 (years) is approximately 270 (wins). So, the trend line suggests that a coach would win 270 games in 35 years.

Try It

a. Draw a scatterplot and a trend line for this data:

Hours Watching TV (average per day)	2.4	5.1	1.8	3.3	3.9	4.7
Books Read (average per year)	11	3	12	6	6	2

b. Use the trend line to predict the number of daily hours watching TV for someone who reads 14 books per year.

Test Prep

It is better to use a clear ruler than a wooden straightedge so that you can see where all the data points are.

▶ **History Link**

Television was invented in 1923. The first TV broadcast that could be seen all over the United States was on September 4, 1951, when President Truman spoke in San Francisco.

WHAT DO YOU THINK?

Taro and Melissa wanted to estimate a fair price for a 10-year-old snowmobile. Here is the data they found in the classified ads.

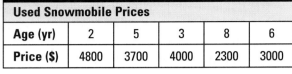

Used Snowmobile Prices					
Age (yr)	2	5	3	8	6
Price ($)	4800	3700	4000	2300	3000

Taro thinks ...

I'll make a line graph of the data and extend the line.

From the trend of the graph, I estimate a price of $1,500.

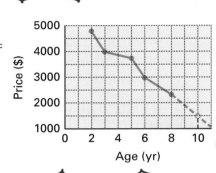

Melissa thinks ...

I'll make a scatterplot of the data and draw a trend line.

From the trend line, I estimate a price of $1,500.

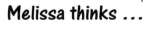

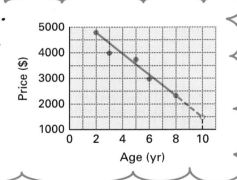

What do you think?

1. What might cause either estimate to be far off the mark?

2. Which method is more certain? Which involves more of a guess?

Check Your Understanding

1. How do you decide where to draw a trend line?

2. For a given scatterplot, is more than one trend line possible? Explain.

Practice and Apply

1. **Getting Started** The Sybox Open Golf Tournament increased ticket prices each of the last 4 years. Use the table to make a scatterplot for the average daily attendance for each ticket price.

   a. Choose a scale for both axes.

   b. Mark the intervals on your axes.

   c. Label both axes and plot the points.

   d. Place your ruler so that about an equal number of data points are above and below its edge.

   e. Draw the trend line.

Sybox Open Golf Tournament Average Daily Attendance	
Ticket Price ($)	**Average Attendance**
14	5261
15	4706
16	3968
17	3350

2. The scatterplot shows the number of fish caught and the time spent fishing. Copy the graph and draw a trend line. Predict the number of fish you might catch in 6 hours.

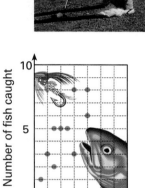

3. **Consumer** Make a scatterplot of the data shown in the table. Draw the trend line.

Price of CD ($)	13.99	12.99	11.99	17.99	19.99	21.99	22.99
Number of Songs	15	23	18	14	25	16	22

4. **Test Prep** The graph shows attempted shots at goal and goals scored by the players on a hockey team. If the trend continues, which of these numbers is a good prediction of how many goals might be scored by a player making 15 attempts?

   Ⓐ 0   Ⓑ 2   Ⓒ 5   Ⓓ 8

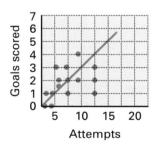

5. **Nutrition** The table shows the grams of fat and number of calories in one 8-ounce serving of milk.

   a. Make a scatterplot and draw a trend line.

   b. Use your trend line to predict how many calories there are in milk with 6.0 grams of fat.

Fat and Calories in Milk		
Type of milk	**Fat (g)**	**Calories**
Whole	8.5	150
2% Low-Fat	4.7	120
1% Low-Fat	2.5	100
Skim	0.4	85

6. **Communicate** The scatterplot shows areas of some states and their 1996 populations.

   a. Describe the plot.

   b. Could you use the plot to make any predictions?

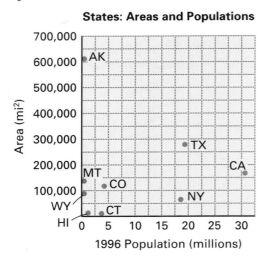

States: Areas and Populations

7. **Sports** The table shows the number of medals won by six countries at the 1996 Olympics.

   a. Make a scatterplot and draw a trend line.

   b. Use your trend line to predict how many gold medals could be expected for a country that won a total of 200 medals.

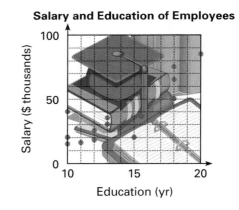

1996 Olympic Medals		
Country	**Gold**	**Total**
United States	44	101
Germany	20	65
Russia	26	63
China	16	50
Australia	9	41
France	15	37

Problem Solving and Reasoning

8. **Critical Thinking** The scatterplot shows the years of education completed and average income for the employees in a company.

   a. Is there an overall trend?

   b. Which points appear to go against the overall trend?

9. **Critical Thinking** Would you expect a scatterplot showing the number of basketball games played to the total number of points scored by a player to show a positive or a negative trend? Why?

10. **Journal** Describe how scatterplots and trend lines are used to make predictions about future values of data.

Salary and Education of Employees

Mixed Review

Add, subtract, multiply, or divide. *[Previous course]*

11. $349 + 468 + 2713$

12. $47,362 \times 25$

13. $60,042 - 5,476$

14. $23\overline{)4839}$

15. 3748×406

16. $9,365 - 8,715$

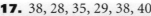

Find the mean, median, and mode(s) for each data set. *[Lesson 1–4]*

17. 38, 28, 35, 29, 38, 40   **18.** 11, 37, 28, 37, 37, 18   **19.** 109, 98, 92, 94, 112

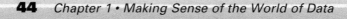

Section 1B Connect

In this section, you have seen that sets of data are sometimes related, and you have learned ways to discover and analyze those relationships. Now you will use what you have learned to look for relationships in baseball statistics.

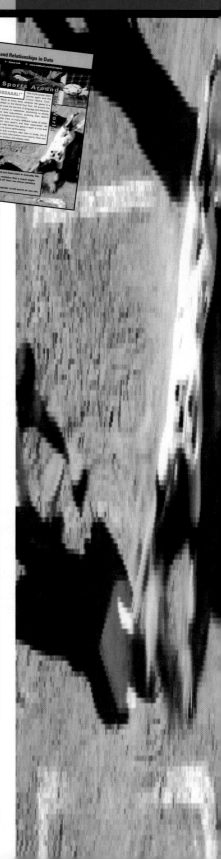

Sports Around the World

The Florida Marlins baseball team has players that have the power to hit home runs and the speed to steal bases. *Home runs* (HR) are usually balls hit over the outfield fence. *Runs batted in* (RBI) are runs that happen as a result of the batter's actions. *Stolen bases* (SB) happen when a base runner runs to the next base as the ball is pitched. The 1995 season totals for the Florida starting lineup are given.

1. Make a scatterplot with home runs on the horizontal axis and runs batted in on the vertical axis.

2. Determine if there is a positive, a negative, or no relationship between home runs and runs batted in. If there is a relationship, draw a trend line.

Player	HR	RBI	SB
Gary Sheffield	16	46	19
Jeff Conine	25	105	2
Terry Pendleton	14	78	1
Greg Colbrunn	23	89	11
Quilvio Veras	5	32	56
Andre Dawson	8	37	0
Kurt Abbott	17	60	4
Charles Johnson	11	39	0
Chuck Carr	2	20	25

3. Make a scatterplot with home runs on the horizontal axis and stolen bases on the vertical axis.

4. Determine if there is a relationship between home runs and stolen bases. If there is, draw a trend line.

5. Predict the number of runs batted in for a Marlins player who hits 30 home runs. Explain how you made your prediction.

6. Predict the number of stolen bases for a Marlins player who hits 30 home runs. Explain.

1. Sketch an example of a scatterplot showing:

   a. a positive relationship.   **b.** a negative relationship.

   c. no relationship.

2. The table gives the total braking distance for a car at various speeds. Make a line graph of the data. Use your line graph to predict the braking distance for a car traveling 70 mi/hr.

3. **Communicate** If the braking distance for 50 mi/hr changed to 200 ft, how would your prediction change? Explain.

4. **Journal** Describe the difference between a line graph and a scatterplot.

Braking Distance	
Speed (mi/hr)	Braking Distance (ft)
50	188
20	45
30	78
10	20
40	125

Use the table for Exercises 5–7.

5. Make a scatterplot of the data.

6. Draw a trend line on your scatterplot.

7. Use your trend line to predict the expected average attendance for a team with 110 wins.

American League West Attendance, 1995		
Team	Wins	Average Attendance
Minnesota	56	14,690
Cleveland	100	40,038
Milwaukee	65	15,318
Kansas City	70	17,614
Chicago	68	22,673

Test Prep

You are often asked to match data sets to graphs. It is a good idea to make a quick sketch of just enough data points to recognize a match. It also helps to check for any easily identified features, such as repeated data values.

8. Which of these could be the graph for this set of data?

Year	1990	1991	1992	1993	1994	1995	1996
Wins	19	22	25	18	20	24	23

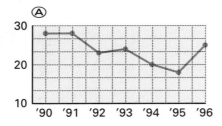

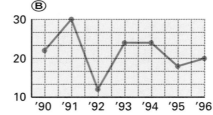

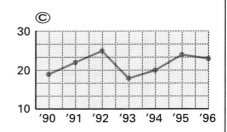

Histograms

You've displayed data in several different ways. A histogram is another commonly used way to illustrate numerical data.

A radio station surveyed 100 people in each of five different age groups to find out how many enjoyed rap music. The frequency table shows the results of the survey. The frequency column shows how many from each age group said they enjoy rap music.

Age Group	Frequency
50–59	5
40–49	9
30–39	18
20–29	40
10–19	28

You can display this data in a bar graph called a histogram. In a histogram, there is no space between the bars.

The age groups are shown at the bottom of the histogram. The height of each bar indicates the number of people in each group.

Notice that the number of years in each age group is the same. When you display data in a histogram, all of the groups must be the same size.

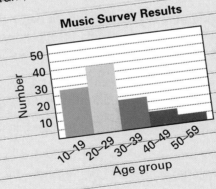

Music Survey Results

Try It

Work in groups to make a histogram showing the following information.

Median U.S. Weekly Earnings, 1993				
Age Group	25–34	35–44	45–54	55–64
Earnings ($)	439	519	543	492

Graphic Organizer

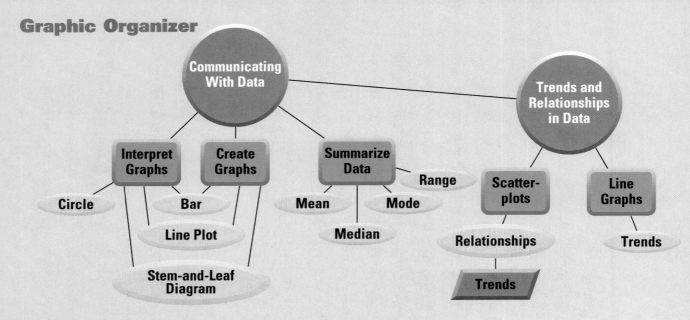

Section 1A Communicating with Data

Summary

■ A **circle graph** uses **sectors** of a circle to represent data.

■ Data is represented in a **bar graph** by the length of each bar. Bars may be **horizontal** or **vertical**. A **scale** and an **interval** must be chosen to make a bar graph. **Double-bar graphs** show two sets of data on the same graph.

■ In a **line plot**, columns of ×'s show how frequently data values occur. It is easy to see which items appear most often and which are **outliers**.

■ Use a **stem-and-leaf diagram** to show how data values are distributed.

■ The **mean** of a data set is the sum of the data values divided by the number of data values. The **mode** is the number(s) that appears most often. The **median** is the middle value in an ordered set of data. The **range** is the difference between the highest and lowest data values.

Review

1. Make a bar graph to show the data.
45, 23, 10, 62, 73, 50, 35

2. Find the mean, median, mode(s), and range.
14, 23, 7, 25, 23, 19, 7, 51, 11, 23

3. Make a stem-and-leaf diagram to show:
32, 22, 45, 23, 33, 37, 41, 28, 34, 42

4. What type of graph best displays the varieties of music among a student's CDs?

5. Which two continents cover about half the land in the world between them?

Areas of Continents

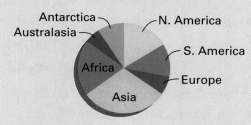

6. Make a bar graph with a broken vertical axis to display the world's four busiest airports in 1994. Explain why your graph could be misleading.

Airport	Passengers (millions)
Chicago O'Hare	66
Atlanta Hartsfield	54
Dallas/Ft. Worth	53
London Heathrow	52

7. Make a line plot to show the times of finishers in a race.

Minutes	30	50	60	70	80	90	120
Finishers	5	4	8	7	6	3	2

Section 1B Trends and Relationships in Data

Summary

- A **line graph** shows data plotted as points and then connected with a line. Two sets of related data can be displayed using a **double-line graph**. The **trend** of the data can be seen from a line graph.

- **Scatterplots** show if paired data has a **positive relationship**, a **negative relationship**, or **no relationship**. A **trend line** can be drawn on a scatterplot and used to make predictions about data values.

Review

8. Which scatterplot shows a positive relationship?

a.

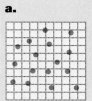

b.

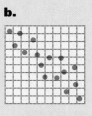

c.

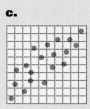

9. The table gives the singles ranking of professional tennis player Conchita Martinez at the end of each year. Make a line graph to display the data.

Year	1991	1992	1993	1994	1995
Ranking	9	8	4	3	2

10. Make a scatterplot of the data for players on a volleyball team. Draw a trend line and use it to predict the expected number of service errors for a player with 20 aces.

Service Aces	4	5	8	10	15
Service Errors	7	12	16	21	33

Social Studies Use the circle graph showing the 1990 U.S. population by age for Questions 1 and 2.

U.S. Population 1990

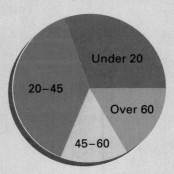

1. Which age group forms the largest part of the 1990 U.S. population?

2. Which two age groups together are about the same size as the Under 20 age group?

3. Explain why these two graphs of the average monthly temperatures in Dallas–Fort Worth look so different.

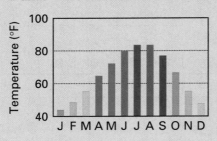

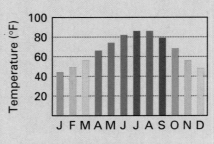

Use the table for Questions 4–6.

4. How many children are there in the largest family? How many children are there all together?

Children in Family	1	2	3	4	5	6	7
Number of Families	5	8	7	3	2	0	1

5. Make a line plot of the data. Use it to name any outliers.

6. Find the mean, median, mode(s), and range for the data. Which best summarizes the information about the families—mean, median, or mode?

7. Make a scatterplot of the data in the table. Draw the trend line and use it to predict the height of a 25-year-old man. Does this prediction make sense?

Age (yr)	Birth	2	4	8	12	16	18
Height (in.)	20	34	40	51	59	68	69

Performance Task

Oceania is the name given to Australia, Melanesia, New Zealand, and Papua New Guinea. Make two types of displays of the data in the table and describe how each helps you understand the data.

	Australia	Melanesia	New Zealand	Papua New Guinea
1995 Population	18,100,000	5,800,000	3,600,000	4,300,000
2025 Population (estimate)	24,700,000	10,100,000	4,400,000	7,500,000

Performance Assessment

Choose a problem.

POPULAR PETS

Pets are often important parts of our lives. Whether they swim in a bowl or curl up on the rug, they require care and attention. Make a survey to find out which types of pets are most popular in your class. Find out the average cost of keeping each type and the amount of time spent in caring for them. Make a poster to show your results. Be sure to display your data in some of the ways you have learned in this chapter.

Capital Capers

Our nation is made up of 50 states, each of which has a capital. Make a list of the capitals. Count the letters each state capital has in its name. Show your results in a line plot. Does it seem as if there are any outliers? Do they appear to cluster about any particular number of letters? Choose a typical capital to represent the states. Find out how it got its name and how long it has been the state capital. Is it older or younger than the capital of your state?

Roll a Score!

Roll a set of four number cubes 100 times and record the total shown each time. Make a stem-and-leaf diagram to show your results. Describe any patterns you see. Choose another way to show your data and compare the two graphs. Explain what your second display shows that the stem-and-leaf diagram does not.

WHAT DO THEY WATCH?

A television network wants to sell advertising time for four of its programs. The network conducted a poll to determine the number of viewers. Numbers represent millions of viewers.

Program	Women	Men	Teens	Children
A	6.1	3.9	9.0	8.5
B	8.0	3.7	4.6	3.4
C	5.0	7.4	1.8	0.5
D	4.4	4.0	5.8	4.2

Make a double-bar graph to use when selling advertising in TV programs that would appeal to adults. Make a second to use when selling advertising in programs for teens and children. As a manufacturer of a new skateboard, use the graphs to decide in which programs you would probably buy advertising time. Explain your choices.

Entertainment

An Olympic diver's score equals the scores from the judges multiplied by the degree of difficulty of the dive.

Arts & Literature

When writing *David Copperfield*, Charles Dickens was paid according to a formula based on the number of words he wrote. *David Copperfield* was one of his longest works.

People of the World

In 1700 B.C. Ahmes, an Egyptian priest, was the first person to use a symbol for equality.

Expressions, and Equations

Social Studies Link
www.mathsurf.com/7/ch2/social

Science

You can use the chirps of the snowy tree cricket to determine the temperature.

KEY MATH IDEAS

A **variable** is a symbol that represents one or more numerical values.

A **formula** shows how several variables are related. Formulas describe real-world relationships.

The **order of operations** tells what to do first, second, and so on when you find the value of an expression.

When you **solve** an equation or inequality, you find the value(s) of the variable that makes the equation or inequality true.

An **inverse operation** undoes an operation. When you solve an equation or inequality, you use inverse operations to isolate the variable.

Social Studies

The abacus from ancient China was one of the first calculators. Electronic calculators that performed the order of operations automatically didn't come until the 1900s.

Problem Solving
Understand
Plan
Solve
Look Back

CHAPTER PROJECT

In this project, you will make a plan for running a business. Begin the project by thinking about the type of business you would like to run. You might consider mowing lawns, baby-sitting, pet care, or other services.

Problem Solving Focus

Finding Unnecessary Information

Sometimes a problem contains more information than you need. To better understand the problem, you need to sort through all of the information and decide which of the facts are necessary to solve the problem.

For each problem, identify the unnecessary numerical information. Some problems may not have unnecessary information. (You do not need to solve the problem.)

❶ The pied woodpecker can peck at a tree 14 times in one second. There are 209 different species of woodpeckers. How many times would a pied woodpecker drum on a tree in 15 seconds of continuous pecking?

❷ An adult roadrunner is about 600 centimeters long. Over short distances, a roadrunner can run at a speed of 20 kilometers per hour. If a roadrunner ran for 2 hours, how far would it run?

❸ Emperor penguins produce only one egg per breeding pair every year. Suppose there are 180 breeding emperor penguins in a colony. In one year, how many eggs would you expect these penguins to lay?

❹ The most expensive domesticated bird is the hyacinth macaw. These birds can cost up to $12,000, and live an average of 50 years in captivity. A hyacinth macaw in an exotic-bird park is 7 years old. It cost the park $7,000. How much longer would you expect this macaw to live?

America Loves Cars... From Olds to New

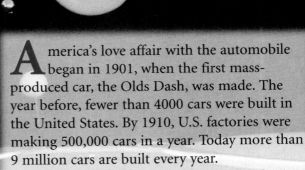

America's love affair with the automobile began in 1901, when the first mass-produced car, the Olds Dash, was made. The year before, fewer than 4000 cars were built in the United States. By 1910, U.S. factories were making 500,000 cars in a year. Today more than 9 million cars are built every year.

Many people of all ages dream about driving a brand-new car. Sometimes they have to give up the dream after they calculate the costs of buying and taking care of the car.

You need to use mathematics to calculate the total cost of owning and driving a car to decide if you can afford it. Mathematical relationships and symbols let you calculate the cost of your "dream machine."

1 Why is it important to consider other costs besides the actual price of a car?

2 What kinds of costs are part of owning and driving a car?

3 Other than while thinking about cars, when do people use mathematics to find out total costs?

Formulas and Variables

You'll Learn ...

■ to use formulas to show relationships among quantities

■ to use variables to represent quantities

■ to substitute values for variables

... How It's Used

Environmental analysts use formulas to determine the amount of acid found in rain.

▶ **Lesson Link**　In the last chapter, you used line graphs and scatterplots to display relationships among quantities. Now you will learn how to show relationships by using symbols. ◀

Explore | Formulas

Start Your Engines!

1. The 24 Hours of Daytona is an automobile race held each year in Daytona Beach, Florida. Teams of 3 to 5 drivers drive their cars as many miles as possible in 24 hours. The table shows the average speeds, in mi/hr, of several cars that finished the 1996 race. You can calculate the number of miles that a car is driven in the race if you multiply the car's average speed by 24. Copy and complete the table.

Average Speed	103	96	95	93	90	88	82
Miles							

2. Use symbols to give a relationship among the average speeds of cars, the distance, and the time it takes to complete the race.

3. Explain how you could use the relationship alone to find the number of miles driven by a car with an average speed of 110 mi/hr.

4. The first Daytona race, in 1962, was only 3 hours long. Dan Gurney drove a Lotus Ford at an average speed of 104 mi/hr to win. Change your relationship to find the number of miles traveled by Gurney's Lotus Ford. Explain the change in the relationship.

Learn | Formulas and Variables

A **formula** is a rule showing relationships among quantities. A **variable** is used to represent a quantity whose values may change or vary. Formulas usually contain variables.

Letters are often used to represent variables. Choose letters that remind you of what they represent.

To find the relationship between the perimeter of (distance around) a square and the length of a side, let the variable s represent the length of a side of a square and the variable p represent the perimeter of the square. The relationship is the formula $p = 4 \cdot s$. Notice that $4 \times s$ is written as $4 \cdot s$. It can also be written as just $4s$.

Formula

$p = 4 \cdot s$

Variables

Sometimes you know the values of some of the variables in a formula. You can replace these variables with the values you know. Replacing variables with values is called **substituting**.

Examples

1 The formula for the cost (C) of a tank of gas is $C = p \cdot g$. Find the cost of a tank of gas if the price per gallon (p) is \$1.70 and the number of gallons (g) is 12.

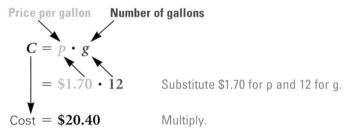

Price per gallon   Number of gallons

$C = p \cdot g$

$\quad = \$1.70 \cdot 12$ Substitute \$1.70 for p and 12 for g.

Cost $= \$20.40$ Multiply.

The cost of the tank of gas is \$20.40.

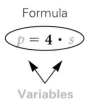
2 Jeremy is a cook at the Home Cooking Restaurant. He uses the formula $c = \frac{f}{8}$ to change fluid ounces (f) into cups (c). Find out how many cups are equal to 32 fluid ounces.

$c = \dfrac{f}{8} = \dfrac{32}{8}$ Substitute 32 for f.

$\quad = 4$ Divide.

Four cups are equal to 32 fluid ounces.

Try It

a. The formula for the average (A) of two numbers (a and b) is $A = \dfrac{a + b}{2}$. Use the formula to find the average of 10 and 18.

b. The cost of a tune-up (C), the hourly charge (h), and the number of hours worked (n) are related by the formula $C = h \times n$. If the hourly charge is \$40, find the cost of a tune-up that takes 4 hours.

▶ **Science Link**

The metric system of measurement is used by scientists around the world. A liter is about the same as 34 fluid ounces, or a little more than a quart.

1. Give an example of a variable and explain what it represents.

2. Give an example of a formula you use in everyday life.

2-1 Exercises and Applications

Practice and Apply

1. **Getting Started** The formula $p = 2 \cdot l + 2 \cdot w$ can be used to find the perimeter of a rectangle.

   a. Name the variables in this formula.

   b. Use the formula to find the perimeter of a rectangle with length (l) 6 cm and width (w) 4 cm.

Geometry You can use the formula $A = l \cdot w$ to find the area of a rectangle. Substitute the given values into the formula. Then use the formula to find A.

2. $l = 15$ cm, $w = 5$ cm

3. $l = 10$ m, $w = 23$ m

4. $l = 8$ in., $w = 14$ in.

5. $l = 12$ ft, $w = 20$ ft

Science The formula $r = \dfrac{d}{t}$ is used to find rate or average speed when you know d (distance) and t (time). Substitute the values for d and t into the formula. Then use the formula to find r.

6. $d = 150$ mi, $t = 3$ hr

7. $d = 10$ km, $t = 23$ hr

8. $d = 800$ mi, $t = 1$ hr

9. $d = 12$ km, $t = 20$ hr

Science Use the table for Exercises 10 and 11.

Animal	Cheetah	Lion	Zebra	Giraffe	Elephant	Chicken
Maximum Speed (mi/hr)	70	50	40	32	25	9

10. At these speeds, how far would a cheetah travel in 30 min? An elephant?

11. How much farther than a giraffe could a lion travel in 30 min?

12. **Health** The formula $C = 13m$ relates calories "burned" (C) and minutes of running (m). Find the number of calories "burned" in 30 minutes of running.

13. $\boxed{\text{Test Prep}}$ Use the formula $g = \frac{c}{16}$ to convert cups (c) to gallons (g). How many gallons are equal to 64 cups?

    Ⓐ $\frac{1}{4}$ gal   Ⓑ 4 gal   Ⓒ 48 gal   Ⓓ 1024 gal

Problem Solving and Reasoning

14. You have to get your car stereo fixed. The repair shop charges $10 per hour, plus $30 for the visit. Use the formula $C = 10h + 30$, where C is cost and h is hours.

  a. How much will it cost if the repairs take 3 hours?

  b. Choose a Strategy Is this the same amount you would pay if you brought the stereo in once for 1 hour and once for 2 hours? Explain your reasoning.

15. Communicate Think of a formula that you have used before. Write a real-world problem for which you would use this formula.

16. Critical Thinking Some formulas that were used in the past have become obsolete. Units called palms (p), digits (d), and spans (s) were once used to measure lengths.

  a. For $p = d \div 4$ and $s = p \div 3$, how many spans long is an object that measured 24 digits?

  b. Where do you think the words *digits, palms,* and *spans* (and feet) came from?

> **Problem Solving**
> ## STRATEGIES
> • Look for a Pattern
> • Make an Organized List
> • Make a Table
> • Guess and Check
> • Work Backward
> • Use Logical Reasoning
> • Draw a Diagram
> • Solve a Simpler Problem

Mixed Review

Round each number as indicated. *[Previous course]*

17. 23,685; nearest 1,000   **18.** 45,684; nearest 10   **19.** 7,466; nearest 100

20. 754,391; nearest 1,000   **21.** 295,972; nearest 100   **22.** 1,864; nearest 10

23. 74,614; nearest 100   **24.** 8,397; nearest 10   **25.** 146,199; nearest 1,000

26. 187,243; nearest 10,000   **27.** 3,824,341; nearest 10,000   **28.** 4,179,486; nearest 10,000

Make a line graph to show each set of data. *[Lesson 1-5]*

29.

Year	'90	'91	'92	'93
Height (in.)	42	46	47	49

30.

Year	'80	'85	'90	'95
Profit ($1000)	328	625	763	947

You'll Learn ...

■ to use the order of operations to find the values of expressions

■ to use the associative, commutative, and distributive properties

... How It's Used

Astronomers use the associative, commutative, and distributive properties to solve and simplify complicated equations describing the motions of stars and planets.

Vocabulary

expression

Commutative Property

Associative Property

Distributive Property

▶ **Lesson Link** You've used formulas to show relationships among quantities. Now you'll see how to use formulas that involve several operations. ◄

Explore | Order of Operations

May I Take Your Order?

Materials: Scientific calculator

1. Enter 12 [+] 9 [÷] 3. What answer do you get? Which of the operations—addition or division—does your calculator do first?

2. Some calculators give an answer of 7 to Step 1. How might these calculators do the problem?

3. Enter (12 [+] 9) [÷] 3. What answer do you get? How did your calculator find the answer?

4. Use your calculator to find the value of each expression. Tell which operation it performed first.

   a. $4 + 3 \times 2$ **b.** $(4 + 3) \times 2$ **c.** $16 - 4 \div 2$ **d.** $(16 - 4) \div 2$

5. Suppose you are using a scientific calculator and a formula with three operations. One of the operations is addition or subtraction. One is multiplication or division. One is done inside parentheses. Which operation will your calculator do first? Second? Third?

Learn | Order of Operations

An **expression** is a mathematical phrase that can be made up of variables and/or numbers and operations. $4 + 3 \cdot 2$ and $b + 4$ are both expressions.

The value of an expression can depend on the order in which you do operations. Here are two ways that could be used to find the value of $7 + 3 \times 2$:

Add 7 + 3 first.	Multiply 3 × 2 first.
↓	↓
$7 + 3 \times 2 = 10 \times 2 = \mathbf{20}$	$7 + 3 \times 2 = 7 + 6 = \mathbf{13}$

The result of evaluating a formula such as $D = a + b \cdot c$ also depends on the order in which you do the operations.

To indicate which order to use, sometimes we need to use grouping symbols. Parentheses and division bars are two kinds of grouping symbols.

ORDER OF OPERATIONS	$2 + 3^2 \times (4 + 3)$
1. Simplify inside parentheses or above or below the division bar.	$2 + 3^2 \times (7)$
2. Simplify exponents.	$2 + 9 \times 7$
3. Multiply and divide from left to right.	$2 + 63$
4. Add and subtract from left to right.	65

There are many ways to show multiplication.

3 times n can be written $3 \times n$, $3 \cdot n$, $3(n)$, or $3n$, and $a \cdot b$ is also written ab.

On a spreadsheet, an asterisk (*) is used to show multiplication: $3 * n$.

Examples

1 Find the value of $2(6 + 4) - 3 \cdot 5$.

$$2(6 + 4) - 3 \cdot 5 = 2(10) - 3 \cdot 5 \qquad \text{Do operations within grouping symbols first.}$$
$$= 20 - 15 \qquad \text{Multiply 2(10) and } 3 \cdot 5.$$
$$= 5 \qquad \text{Subtract.}$$

2 An auto mechanic ordered eight car spark plugs and four truck spark plugs. Car spark plugs cost $0.75, and truck spark plugs cost $3.00. Find the value of $8 \cdot 0.75 + 4 \cdot 3$, the total cost of these parts.

$$8 \cdot 0.75 + 4 \cdot 3 = 6 + 12 \qquad \text{Multiply } 8 \cdot 0.75 \text{ and } 4 \cdot 3.$$
$$= 18 \qquad \text{Add.}$$

The cost of the parts is $18.

Try It

Find the value of each expression.

a. $3 + 8 \div 2$

b. $\dfrac{6 + 3}{3} - 1$

c. $(2 \times 5) - 1 + 5^2 \div 5$

d. $14 \div 7 + 8(3)$

Along with order-of-operation rules, the **commutative** , **associative** , and **distributive** properties will help you find values of expressions.

PROPERTY	EXAMPLE (numbers)	EXAMPLE (variables)
Commutative Property of Addition	$2 + 7 = 7 + 2$	$a + b = b + a$
Commutative Property of Multiplication	$4 \cdot 9 = 9 \cdot 4$	$ab = ba$
Associative Property of Addition	$3 + (5 + 1) = (3 + 5) + 1$	$a + (b + c) = (a + b) + c$
Associative Property of Multiplication	$8 \cdot (2 \cdot 9) = (8 \cdot 2) \cdot 9$	$a(bc) = (ab)c$
Distributive Property	$5(7 + 2) = 5 \cdot 7 + 5 \cdot 2$	$a(b + c) = ab + ac$

- The commutative properties state that *order* doesn't matter when you add or multiply.
- The associative properties state that *grouping* doesn't matter when you add or multiply.
- The Distributive Property states that multiplying a sum of two numbers by a third number is the same as multiplying each number in the sum by the third number, then adding.

Example 3

MENTAL MATH

When multiplying a large number by a small one, split the large number into two numbers that are easier to multiply and use the distributive property to multiply in your head.

Only 104 Dual-Ghia automobiles were ever built. The formula $T = 4D$ relates the number of tires (T) to the number of Dual-Ghias (D). How many tires were needed for all the Dual-Ghias?

$T = 4(104)$	Substitute.
$= 4(100 + 4)$	Rewrite 104 as 100 + 4.
$= 4 \cdot 100 + 4 \cdot 4$	Use the distributive property.
$= 400 + 16$	Multiply.
$= 416$	Add.

416 tires were needed.

Try It

Evaluate.   **a.** $6(405)$ **b.** $307 \cdot 8$ **c.** $12 \cdot 205$

Check | Your Understanding

1. Are parentheses necessary in the expression $7 + (10 \div 2)$? Explain.

2. Is there a commutative property for subtraction? For division? Explain.

Practice and Apply

Getting Started Name the operation that should be done first.

1. $12 - 6 \times 2$ **2.** $18(24 + 36)$ **3.** $64 \div 2 \cdot 3$ **4.** $\dfrac{16 + 4}{5}$

Does the expression contain grouping symbols? What are they?

5. $24 \div (6 - 5)$ **6.** $24 \div 12 + 2$ **7.** $\dfrac{14 + 4}{9}$ **8.** $20 \cdot 3 \div 2$

Find the value of each expression.

9. $16 - 12 \div 4$ **10.** $3^2 \cdot 2 - (8 - 2) \div 3$ **11.** $83 + 2(4 - 1)$

12. $11(3 + 1) \div 2^2 + 3$ **13.** $72 - 30 \div (2 + 3)$ **14.** $7^2 - \dfrac{5^2 + 1}{2} \cdot 3$

15. **Test Prep** Find the value of $a + 2 \cdot b$ if b is 4 and a is 3.

Ⓐ 10   Ⓑ 11   Ⓒ 18   Ⓓ 20

Operation Sense Copy each statement below. Insert parentheses to make each sentence true.

16. $18 + 12 \div 3 + 1 = 11$ **17.** $18 + 12 \div 3 + 1 = 21$

18. $7 \times 2 + 3 \times 6 = 102$ **19.** $7 \times 2 + 3 \times 6 = 140$

Which property is being shown?

20. $12 + 48 = 48 + 12$ **21.** $12 \cdot (14 \cdot 16) = (12 \cdot 14) \cdot 16$

22. $28 + (30 + 34) = (28 + 30) + 34$ **23.** $47 \cdot 39 = 39 \cdot 47$

24. $5(3 + 4) = 5 \cdot 3 + 5 \cdot 4$ **25.** $(6 + 2) \cdot (5 + 7) = (5 + 7) \cdot (6 + 2)$

26. You are organizing a pet show. Forty dogs will be shown the first morning. You need to allow 4 minutes for each dog to be shown and 1 minute for cleanup after each dog. How long will the morning session be? What property could you use to find the answer?

27. **Consumer** The formula $C = p + ip$ gives the total cost (C) of an item where p is the cost of the item before tax and i is the tax rate.

    a. What is the total cost of a $62 car battery if the tax rate is 5% (0.05)?

    b. The formula $C = p(1 + i)$ will also give you the total cost. Use this formula to find the total cost of a $62.00 battery at the same tax rate.

    c. How are the two formulas related?

Problem Solving and Reasoning

28. **Critical Thinking** Use exactly four 4's and a combination of $+$, $-$, $\times$, $\div$, and parentheses to write three different expressions that equal 1.

29. **Journal** Jose uses the formula $p = 2l + 2w$ to find the perimeter (p) of a rectangle with length (l) and width (w). Phan uses the formula $p = 2(l + w)$. Will both find the correct perimeter? Explain.

30. **Critical Thinking** Wanda invites four friends to lunch. Each one orders a salad and a drink. There are two ways to compute the bill. What are they? Which property is illustrated by the fact that both methods give the same result?

TRUCK STOP CAFE

Menu

Salad	$1.49
Soup	$1.29
Burger	$1.89
Drinks	$0.79

Mixed Review

Estimate each sum. *[Previous course]*

31. 48 + 27

32. 275 + 305

33. 89 + 38 + 61

34. 7,846 + 4,874

35. 32 + 61 + 78

36. 3,275 + 2,305

37. 97 + 78 + 35

38. 15,321 + 26,453

Make a scatterplot to show the data. Describe the relationship. *[Lesson 1-6]*

39.

Child's age	2	6	3	4	8	5	7	3	8	2
Cousins	7	3	6	3	4	4	8	3	7	8

40.

Games	5	2	7	8	4	1	6	10	3
Hits	9	3	10	14	4	3	8	13	5

Project Progress

Think about the costs of starting and running your business. Make a chart that lists the things you would need for your business and how much it would cost to serve the number of customers you expect.

Problem Solving

Understand

Plan

Solve

Look Back

PROBLEM SOLVING 2-2

TECHNOLOGY

Using a Spreadsheet • Formulas and Operations

Problem: Your basketball team has scored 85, 90, 73, 100, 76, 92, 87, and 75 points in its last eight games. How many points did your team score in all? What is your team's average score?

You can use your spreadsheet's built-in formulas to answer these questions.

1 Enter the scores into the spreadsheet as shown:

	A	B	C	D	E	F	G	H	I
1	Points Scored	85	90	73	100	76	92	87	75
2	Total =								
3	Average =								

	A	B	C	D	E	F	G	H	I
1	Points Scored	85	90	73	100	76	92	87	75
2	Total =	678							
3	Average =								

2 In cell B2, enter your spreadsheet's built-in summing formula. This may have an icon that looks like Σ.

3 In cell B3, enter your spreadsheet's built-in averaging formula.

	A	B	C	D	E	F	G	H	I
1	Points Scored	85	90	73	100	76	92	87	75
2	Total =	678							
3	Average =	84.75							

Solution: The total is 678 points. The average is 84.75 points.

TRY IT

a. Find the sum and average of 721, 789, 765, 345, 234, 143, 908, and 709.

b. Find the sum and average of 23, 34, 67, 88, 54, 27, 28, 21, 41, and 55.

ON YOUR OWN

▶ Why do you think spreadsheets have built-in formulas?

▶ What are the advantages and disadvantages of using a spreadsheet to find an average? Explain.

▶ Enter the customized formula "=(B1+C1+D1+E1+F1+G1+H1+I1)/8" in cell B4. Compare the answer with the average in cell B3. Explain what you see.

Formulas and Tables

▶ **Lesson Link** You know how to substitute values when you are given a formula. Now you will create tables from formulas and find formulas from tables. ◀

Explore | Formulas and Tables

Auto Biographies

Materials: Spreadsheet software

On a spreadsheet, if you want to multiply the number in cell A2 by 5 and store the result in C2, type "=A2*5" into C2 and press Enter.

The spreadsheet gives data on the Motorette, a car sold from 1946 to 1948.

1. What pattern do you see relating the values in columns A and B? What formula would you use for cell B5?

2. Enter the Motorette information on a spreadsheet. Complete the next 4 rows.

	A	B
1	Number of Cars	Number of Wheels
2	1	3
3	2	6
4	3	9
5	4	

This data is for a 1983 car, the Thrust 2.

3. What pattern do you see relating the values in columns A and B? What formula would you use for cell B5?

4. Enter the Thrust 2 information on a spreadsheet. Complete the next 7 rows.

	A	B
1	Distance (mi)	Time (hr)
2	633	1
3	1266	2
4	1899	3
5	2532	

5. Make a spreadsheet for the 1955 Eshelman roadster. Complete the next 2 rows.

	A	B	C	D
1	Number of Cars	Weight (lb)	Distance (mi)	Gas (gal)
2	1	250	70	1
3	2	500	140	2

6. What was unusual about the Motorette, the Thrust 2, and the Eshelman?

Learn Formulas and Tables

You can use a formula to make a table of values. The rows and columns of a table need to be labeled. The values come from substituting into the formula.

Example 1

The sales tax formula in Nebraska is $t = 0.05 \times c$, where c is the cost of goods or services and t is the sales tax. Use the formula to make a sales tax table for services offered by Sparkling Car Wash.

Multiply the cost of each service by 0.05.

Services	Basic	Special	Deluxe	Super	Custom
Cost (c)	$4.00	$5.00	$8.00	$11.00	$16.00
Sales Tax (t)	$0.20	$0.25	$0.40	$0.55	$0.80

Try It

The area of a square can be found using the formula $A = s \cdot s$, where A is the area and s is the length of a side. Use the formula to make a table for the areas of squares with sides of length 2, 3, 5, 8, 10, and 12 in.

If you *begin* with a table of values, you can use your number sense to find the formula that was used to make the table.

Example 2

Find a formula relating t and d.

Time (t)	1	2	3	4	5	6
Distance Driven (d)	50	100	150	200	250	300

Study the table. Notice that in each column, the distance driven is equal to the time multiplied by 50.

The formula is $d = 50t$.

Try It

Find a formula relating the variables.

a.

x	1	2	3	4
y	8	16	24	32

b.

m	6	7	8	9
n	2	3	4	5

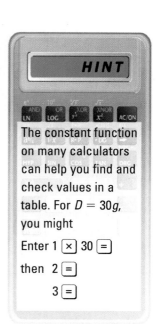

HINT

The constant function on many calculators can help you find and check values in a table. For $D = 30g$, you might

Enter 1 ⊠ 30 ⊟

then 2 ⊟

3 ⊟

WHAT DO YOU THINK?

The table gives data on the number of representatives (*r*) a state might have in the House of Representatives, and the total number of members of Congress (*t*) the state would have. Find a formula relating *r* and *t*.

Representatives (*r*)	1	2	3	4	5	6
Total Members (*t*)	3	4	5	6	7	8

Kimberly thinks ...

In each column, the value of *t* is 2 more than the value of *r*.

The formula is $t = r + 2$.

Jacob thinks ...

In each column the value of *r* is 2 less than the value of *t*.

The formula is $r = t - 2$.

What do you think?

1. Will both methods allow you to find *r* if you know *t*? Which one is easier to use if you know *t*?

2. Will both methods allow you to find *t* if you know *r*? Which one is easier to use if you know *r*?

Check | Your Understanding

1. Suppose the rows and columns of a table are switched. Does the new table show different information? Explain.

2. Do you think there is a formula relating *any* two sets of numbers? Explain.

Practice and Apply

1. | **Getting Started** | The formula $H = 24 \cdot D$ relates the number of hours (H) to the number of days (D).

  a. Substitute 3 for D to find the number of hours in 3 days.

  b. Substitute 4 for D to find the number of hours in 4 days.

  c. Use your answers to **a** and **b** to begin filling in the table. Fill in the rest of the table.

Days	3	4	5	6	7	8
Hours						

2. **Consumer** In 1973, the average price for regular gasoline in the United States was $0.39 per gallon. The formula $C = 0.39G$ relates cost (C) to the number of gallons bought (G). Make a table that shows the cost of 2, 5, 7, 9, and 12 gallons of gasoline in 1973.

3. **Science** The Kelvin temperature scale is sometimes used in science. The formula $K = 273 + C$ relates degrees Kelvin (K) to degrees Celsius (C). Make a table that shows the Kelvin temperatures for the Celsius temperatures of 0°, 20°, 40°, 60°, 80°, and 100°.

Find a formula relating the variables.

4.

u	1	2	3	4
v	5	6	7	8

5.

x	3	4	5	6
y	15	20	25	30

6.

p	7	8	9	10
q	2	3	4	5

7.

m	2	3	4	5
n	12	18	24	30

8.

x	5	6	7	8
y	50	60	70	80

9.

w	11	12	13	14
v	1.1	1.2	1.3	1.4

10. `Test Prep` Which formula gives the relationship of the variables in the table?

k	4	6	8	12
j	2	3	4	6

   Ⓐ $j = 2k$ Ⓑ $j = 2 + k$ Ⓒ $k = 2j$ Ⓓ $k = 2 + j$

11. Health To decide how much adult medicine to give a child, some doctors use the formula $C = \frac{Y}{Y + 12} \cdot A$, where C is the amount of medicine to give the child, Y is the child's age in years, and A is the amount of medicine normally given to an adult. Make a table for a 4-year-old child to show the amount of medicine to give the child when the adult dose is 4 g, 8 g, 12 g, and 16 g.

Problem Solving and Reasoning

12. Communicate Sound travels at about 1480 meters per second in 20°C water. The formula $D = 1480s$ relates distance (D) and seconds (s).

   a. Make a table of values to see how far sound travels in 0 to 10 seconds.

   b. In 10°C water, sound travels 1450 meters per second. How does this change the values in the table? The formula?

13. Critical Thinking The intensity of sound decreases quickly as you move away from the source of the sound. The formula $I = \frac{100}{d \cdot d}$ gives the intensity (I) of a sound that has 100 watts of power at a given distance (d) from the source of the sound. How many times more intense is this sound at 1 foot away than at 10 feet away?

Mixed Review

Estimate each difference. *[Previous course]*

14. $52 - 24$ **15.** $81 - 32$ **16.** $625 - 238$ **17.** $499 - 328$

18. $81 - 47$ **19.** $572 - 297$ **20.** $8324 - 7632$ **21.** $7811 - 3236$

Make a scatterplot to show the data. Draw a trend line and predict the value of y when $x = 9$. *[Lesson 1-7]*

22.

x	2	5	3	7	3	8	2	5	1	6	4
y	4	6	5	7	4	6	3	5	3	5	4

23.

x	10	8	3	4	7	1	4	6
y	2	1	7	7	3	9	4	4

In this section you've seen how variables and formulas can help you understand relationships among real-world quantities. Now you'll have a chance to apply what you have learned to a situation that could occur: You have just turned 16 and someone has given you a new car. The question is, can you afford to operate it?

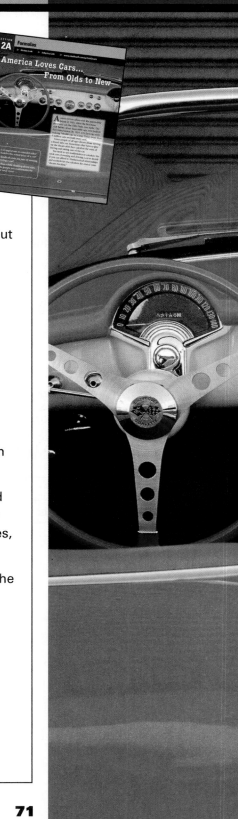

America Loves Cars ... From Olds to New

You've just been given a new four-cylinder Freebie. The car was free, but the day-to-day expenses are your responsibility. There are brakes to maintain, gas to buy, and an engine to keep up. The American Automobile Association estimates that for a four-cylinder car, costs average about $0.08 per mile.

1. Complete the table for a four-cylinder car.

Miles Driven (m)	10	20	50	100	500	1000	2000
Cost (c)							

2. Write a formula relating the two variables in the table.

3. Estimate the average distance you would drive each day. How much would it cost you to operate your car for one day? For one year?

The table shows that the day-to-day costs of operating your car depend on how far you drive. But there are other *fixed costs* that you must pay whether you drive or not—insurance, license and registration fees, taxes, and so on. These can amount to thousands of dollars a year.

4. Suppose the fixed costs for your car are $3000 per year. Complete the table to show the total annual cost, including the $3000.

Annual Mileage (m)	6,000	9,000	12,000	18,000	24,000
Annual Cost (a)					

5. Write a formula relating the annual mileage (m) and the annual cost (a).

6. Using your estimate from Step 3, find how much it will cost you to operate your car for one year.

Evaluate each expression.

1. $9 + 12 \div 3 - 3$

2. $\dfrac{3^2 + 3}{3 \cdot 2^2}$

3. $14 \div 7 \cdot 4 - 1$

4. $42 \cdot 2 - 2.1$

5. $\dfrac{2 + 6}{2} + 3 \cdot 4$

6. $6^2 \div 4 + 5 \cdot 3 + 1$

Place parentheses to make each statement true.

7. $9 \times 9 - 9 \div 9 = 0$

8. $9 \times 9 - 9 \div 9 = 8$

9. $9 \times 9 - 9 \div 9 = 80$

Evaluate each formula for the given values.

10. $t = \dfrac{D}{r}$, $D = 1000$, $r = 50$

11. $C = ph$, $p = 12$, $h = 10$

Find a formula relating the variables.

12.

u	1	2	3	4
v	10	11	12	13

13.

x	2	4	5	6
y	6	12	15	18

14. The formula $t = \dfrac{d}{s}$ measures a storm's travel time in hours. A major storm is located 160 miles from Miami. Complete the table to estimate the number of hours it will take to reach Miami for the different speeds.

Speed (s) in mi/hr	5	8	10	20
Travel Time (t) in hr				

15. Journal Describe the steps you use to substitute values into a formula.

Test Prep

When you are asked to find the value of an expression that has several operations in it, it is a good idea to write the expression on a separate sheet of paper and carefully use the order of operations in a step-by-step manner.

16. Find the value of $12 + 3 \cdot 4^2(7 - 5) + \dfrac{4 + 2}{3}$.

Ⓐ 62   Ⓑ 110   Ⓒ 146   Ⓓ 482

REVIEW 2A

An Efficient Machine?

👉 Is it a compliment to call an invention a "Rube Goldberg" machine? Cartoonist Rube Goldberg (1881–1970) enjoyed poking fun at America's love of machines. He "invented" many complicated but useless machines. Here, a cartoon shows an invention used to avoid oversleeping.

👉 His "inventions" became so widely known that *Webster's New World Dictionary* added "Rube Goldberg" to its listing. *Webster's* defines it as "any very complicated invention…contrived to perform a seemingly simple operation." Goldberg's machines involve a series of actions done in a certain order.

👉 Mathematical operations, too, can often be described in terms of a series of actions. In this section you'll learn about some of these operations. You'll see how both doing and "undoing" operations can help you solve problems much more easily than Rube Goldberg's machine can wake a person up!

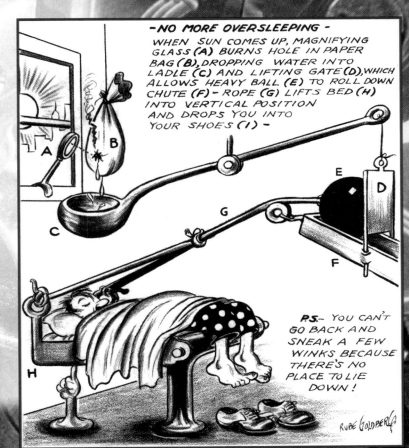

-NO MORE OVERSLEEPING -
WHEN SUN COMES UP, MAGNIFYING GLASS (A) BURNS HOLE IN PAPER BAG (B), DROPPING WATER INTO LADLE (C) AND LIFTING GATE (D), WHICH ALLOWS HEAVY BALL (E) TO ROLL DOWN CHUTE (F) - ROPE (G) LIFTS BED (H) INTO VERTICAL POSITION AND DROPS YOU INTO YOUR SHOES (I) -

P.S.- YOU CAN'T GO BACK AND SNEAK A FEW WINKS BECAUSE THERE'S NO PLACE TO LIE DOWN!

RUBE GOLDBERG

1 How do you write "triple five, then add two" mathematically?

2 Describe a mathematical formula that involves several steps.

You'll Learn ...

■ to use inverse operations

... How It's Used

A computer game designer often has to work backward and undo the steps of a game to fix errors and make improvements.

Vocabulary

inverse operations

▶ **Lesson Link**   You have used formulas, variables, and the order of operations to express relationships and find the values of expressions. Now you will *reverse* the order of operations to solve problems. ◀

Explore   Working Backward

Friday, Thursday, Wednesday ...

An inventor has created a machine that makes swim goggles for dogs. The following clues describe the "doggle" (dog-ull) machine's first week of operation.

A. Monday went well except for telephone interruptions from pet store owners wanting to find out when they could order doggles.

B. Tuesday was a success. The machine produced twice as many doggles as it did on Monday.

C. On Wednesday a bottle of glue fell into the machine, gumming it up for 2 hours. The day's output was 4 fewer than the previous day.

D. On Thursday, two workers called in sick. The day's output was only half Wednesday's.

E. On Friday, 23 pairs of doggles were produced, 5 more than on Thursday.

1. Begin with the last clue and work backward to find how many pairs of doggles were produced on Monday.

2. Explain how you solved the problem.

Problem Solving TIP

Make a table to keep track of the doggles made on each day.

Learn   Inverse Operations

Suppose you ride your bike north for 4 miles and decide that you need to return to where you started. You need to ride your bike south for 4 miles. Riding north and riding south are inverse actions because they "undo" each other.

Suppose you add 5 to a number and want to return to the number you started with. You would subtract 5. Addition and subtraction are called **inverse operations** . So are multiplication and division. The inverse of the action of multiplying by 4 is dividing by 4. Inverse operations "undo" each other.

$$2 \boxed{+5} = 7 \qquad 7 \boxed{-5} = 2$$

$$2 \boxed{\cdot 4} = 8 \qquad 8 \boxed{\div 4} = 2$$

Sometimes more than one action needs to be undone. The order in which the actions are done affects the order in which they are undone. You may have put on a sock, then a shoe, in the morning before school. To undo those actions, you need to take off the shoe first, then take off the sock. Inverse operations work the same way.

Examples

1 The machine below is an inverse operation machine. If 9 is entered, what will be the result?

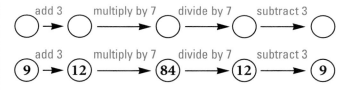

The result is 9.

2 A number is multiplied by 4, then 5 is subtracted from the result. What operations are needed to return to the original number?

Five needs to be added to undo the subtraction, then the sum needs to be divided by 4 to undo the multiplication.

Try It

a. If 12 is entered in the machine in Example 1, what will be the result?

b. A number is divided by 2, then 3 is added to the quotient. What operations are needed to return to the original number?

Check Your Understanding

1. How can you use inverse operations to check a sum? A product?

2. How does an inverse operation "undo" an operation?

Practice and Apply

Getting Started Name the inverse action of each.

1. Drive 5 mi east

2. Turn on a heater

3. Run up three flights of stairs

4. Subtract 643

5. Add $4.50

6. Divide by 65

The machine below is an inverse operation machine. What will be the result when each is entered into the machine? Record each step.

7. 25

8. 12

9. 44

10. *m*

11. Operation Sense What labels does the machine below need so that the output will be the same as the input?

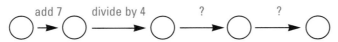

12. **Test Prep** A number is multiplied by 5, then 7 is added to the result. What operations are needed to return to the original number?

Ⓐ Subtraction and division

Ⓑ Addition and multiplication

Ⓒ Division and addition

Ⓓ None of these

13. Geography When Les flew from Ohio to Oregon, he set his watch back 3 hours. What should he do to his watch when he flies back to Ohio?

14. Geography Pilot Denny Zimmerman flies all over the United States delivering overnight mail. On one trip, he traveled from Baltimore northwest to Pittsburgh, then southwest to Dallas. The following night, he flew from Dallas northwest to San Francisco and then north to Seattle. What route would Captain Zimmerman need to follow if he wants to return to Baltimore by going through the same cities?

15. Science A wolf had 10 pups in her third litter. The number of pups was twice as many as in her second litter, and her second litter had 3 more pups than her first. Find the number of pups in her first litter.

Problem Solving and Reasoning

16. 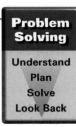 **Journal** Suppose you lost your wallet or purse. How can inverse operations or actions help you find it? Give an example.

17. Communicate Write a set of actions and then describe the steps you would do to undo these actions.

18. Critical Thinking Copy and complete the table. Explain how you found the missing numbers.

n	Add 8	Subtract 8
4	12	4
12	20	?
18	?	18
?	10	?
?	?	10
n	?	?

Mixed Review

Estimate each product. [Previous course]

19. 31×8
20. 14×58
21. 28×52
22. 715×16

23. 129×419
24. 318×104
25. 4792×617
26. 4122×108

Multiply. [Previous course]

27. $10 \times 10 \times 10$
28. $4 \times 4 \times 4 \times 4$
29. $5 \times 5 \times 5$

30. $7 \times 7 \times 7 \times 7$
31. $10 \times 10 \times 10 \times 10$
32. $2 \times 2 \times 2 \times 2 \times 2$

33. $10 \times 10 \times 10 \times 10 \times 10$
34. $3 \times 3 \times 3 \times 3 \times 3 \times 3$
35. $8 \times 8 \times 8 \times 8 \times 8$

Project Progress

Look at the costs you listed earlier. As you learn more about equations, write and solve an equation to find how much to charge each customer to meet your costs. Then decide how much you will charge for your service. Prepare a report describing your business and explaining how you decided on the price you will charge.

Problem Solving

Understand
Plan
Solve
Look Back

2-5 Translating Words to Expressions

▶ Lesson Link You have learned to find the value of a given expression. Now you will write expressions by translating words into mathematical symbols. ◀

You'll Learn ...
- to translate words and phrases into algebraic expressions
- to translate algebraic expressions into words and phrases

... How It's Used
Inventors must be able to explain their inventions clearly. They often use mathematical symbols rather than written descriptions.

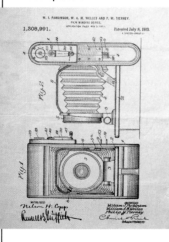

Vocabulary
algebraic expression

Explore | Number Tricks

Next Time, I'll Make a Rabbit Disappear

1. [Pick a number. Write it down.] → [Double the number.] → [Subtract 5.] → [Add 5.] → [Halve the number. Write the result.]

2. Repeat Step 1 three times using a different starting number each time.

3. What do you notice about your results? Why do you think this happens?

4. Use variables, operations, and numbers, to translate this "number trick" into symbols.

5. Make up a number trick like this one. Use at least four words that describe number operations. (The trick above uses *double*, *subtract*, *add*, and *halve*.) Try out your trick on another student.

Learn | Translating Words to Expressions

An **algebraic expression** is an expression that contains a variable, like x, $b - 4$, and $5(n + 3)$. When solving a real-world problem, you may have to translate words or phrases into algebraic expressions. The chart shows the operations that may be suggested by words or phrases.

Addition	Subtraction	Multiplication	Division
plus	minus	times	divided by
sum	difference	product	quotient
more than	less than	double	half of
increased by	decreased by	by	separate equally
gain of	less	of	per

Examples

Write an algebraic expression for each phrase.

1 Five less than a number c

$c - 5$

2 Four times the sum of a number n and 3

$4(n + 3)$

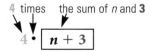

4 times   the sum of n and **3**

$4 \cdot \boxed{n + 3}$

Study TIP

Be careful when you translate subtraction phrases. Sometimes you will need to switch the word order: *5 less than 7* means $7 - 5$, not $5 - 7$.

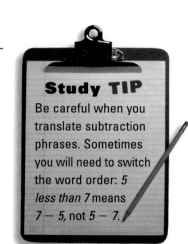

Try It

Write an algebraic expression for each phrase.

a. Half of a number h

b. d dollars more than a price of $25

c. The product of a number d and the difference of a number v and 5

You can also translate algebraic expressions into phrases.

Examples

Write a phrase for each algebraic expression.

3 $x + 7$

One answer is "a number x increased by 7." Others are possible.

4 $4n - 5$

One answer is "five less than four times a number n." Others are possible.

Remember

An expression is a mathematical phrase made up of variables and/or numbers and operations. **[Page 60]**

Try It

Write a phrase for each algebraic expression.

a. $12 - g$ **b.** $3a + 4b$ **c.** $11(5 - r)$

Check Your Understanding

1. Are the expressions $a + 2$ and $2 + a$ equal? Explain.

2. Are the expressions $x - 4$ and $4 - x$ equal? Explain.

3. Give a phrase in which "of" suggests multiplication.

4. Give a phrase in which "quotient" suggests division.

Practice and Apply

Getting Started Tell what operation the action suggests.

1. Loses 18 yards

2. Deposits $25

3. Gains 25 lb

Write an algebraic expression for each phrase.

4. 6 more than a number x

5. Double a number k

6. Half of a number y

7. 4 less than a number u

8. The product of a number w and 4

9. 8 more than twice a number c

10. A number p decreased by 6

11. Four times the difference of a number n and 6

12. 6 times a number m

13. 3 times the sum of a number x and 15

Write a phrase for each algebraic expression.

14. $2m$

15. $6 - x$

16. $2(b - 5)$

17. $2r + 3$

18. $n - 4$

19. $\dfrac{f}{2}$

20. $4a + 2b$

21. $3(d + 3)$

22. $\dfrac{w - 4}{u + 3}$

23. $\dfrac{3}{c + 2} + 4$

24. **Test Prep** Choose the correct algebraic expression for the phrase "three times the sum of a number and 6."

Ⓐ $3(n + 6)$　　Ⓑ $3 + 6n$　　Ⓒ $3n + 6$　　Ⓓ $6 + 3n$

25. **Industry** A machine can produce 267 bolts in one hour. Write an expression to describe:

a. The number of bolts produced in n hours.

b. The number of usable bolts produced in n hours if 25 had to be thrown away because they were defective.

26. **Career** A dentist earns twice as much as she did in her last job, 3 years before. If her salary 3 years ago was p, write an algebraic expression for her current salary.

27. **Science** A 5-ft pine tree was planted and grew 2 ft each year. Write an algebraic expression for the height after y years.

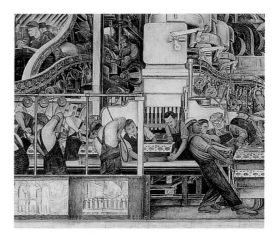

Detroit Industry (detail), 1932–1933, mural by Diego Rivera.

28. Fine Art This sculpture is made of cars and concrete. Each row contains four cars. Write an algebraic expression for the number of cars in x rows of the sculpture.

Problem Solving and Reasoning

29. Critical Thinking Geometric figures can be used to model algebraic expressions. The figure below is a model for $x + 3$.

a. Write an algebraic expression for the figure below.

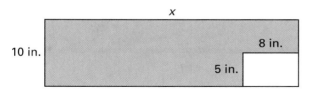

b. Write another algebraic expression for the figure.

c. Can the expressions in **a** and **b** be shown to be equal without the model? Explain.

30. Choose a Strategy The area of a rectangle is equal to its length times its width. Write an algebraic expression to describe the area of the shaded portion of the large rectangle. Explain your reasoning.

x

10 in.

8 in.

5 in.

31. Write an algebraic expression using each of these three words or phrases: product, sum, and less than. Explain what each word or phrase means.

Long Term Parking, 1975–1983, sculpture by Arman.

Problem Solving

STRATEGIES

- Look for a Pattern
- Make an Organized List
- Make a Table
- Guess and Check
- Work Backward
- Use Logical Reasoning
- Draw a Diagram
- Solve a Simpler Problem

PROBLEM SOLVING 2-5

Mixed Review

Estimate each quotient. *[Previous course]*

32. $65 \div 8$ **33.** $83 \div 5$ **34.** $49 \div 11$ **35.** $66 \div 16$

36. $144 \div 11$ **37.** $784 \div 39$ **38.** $4843 \div 528$ **39.** $6324 \div 157$

You can use the formula $P = 2l + 2w$ to find the perimeter of a rectangle. Substitute the given values into the formula. Then use the formula $A = lw$ to find the area. *[Lesson 2-1]*

40. $l = 11$ in., $w = 7$ in.   **41.** $l = 31$ ft, $w = 20$ ft

42. $l = 18$ cm, $w = 12$ cm   **43.** $l = 62$ m, $w = 40$ m

2-6

Solving Addition and Subtraction Equations

You'll Learn ...

■ to write and solve addition and subtraction equations

... How It's Used

Chemists use addition and subtraction equations when they plan and experiment with chemical reactions.

Vocabulary

equation

solve

solution

▶ **Lesson Link** You've learned that addition and subtraction are inverse operations. Now you'll use that fact to solve equations involving addition and subtraction. ◀

Explore | Addition and Subtraction Equations

More or Less

You can use a balanced scale to represent an equation.

1. The balanced scale represents the equation $x + 3 = 7$.

2. What would you do to get x by itself on one side of the scale and still keep the scale in balance? What is the value of x?

3. Sketch a balanced scale that shows $x + 7 = 9$. What is the value of x?

4. What inverse operation did you use to get x by itself on one side of the equation $x + 7 = 9$? Why did it make sense to use this operation?

Learn | Solving Addition and Subtraction Equations

An **equation** is a statement that two expressions are equal.

To **solve** an equation containing a variable means to find the value(s) of the variable that make(s) the equation true.

$x = 4$ is a **solution** to the equation $x + 6 = 10$ because $\boxed{4} + 6 = 10$ is true.

$x = 11$ is *not* a solution because $\boxed{11} + 6$ is not equal to 10.

Expressions		⟶ Equation
$3 + 5$	8	$3 + 5 = 8$
$x + 6$	10	$x + 6 = 10$

$x + 6 \stackrel{?}{=} 10$

$\boxed{4} + 6 \stackrel{?}{=} 10$

$10 = 10$

$x + 6 \stackrel{?}{=} 10$

$\boxed{11} + 6 \stackrel{?}{=} 10$

17 is not equal to **10.**

Using inverse operations, you solve an addition equation using subtraction and a subtraction equation using addition. When you change one side of an equation, you must change the other side in the same way to keep it "in balance."

$$x + 3 = 8$$

$$x + 3 \boxed{-3} = 8 \boxed{-3}$$

The equation $x + 3 = 8$ can represent many situations. Here are two. If 3 more cars were sold, for a total of 8 cars, how many were there originally? Or, what quantity added to 3 equals 8?

Examples

1 Solve $x - 5 = 12$.

$x - 5 + 5 = 12 + 5$ To undo subtracting 5, add 5 to *both* sides.

$x = 17$ Add.

Check: $\boxed{17} - 5 \overset{?}{=} 12$

$12 = 12 \checkmark$ The solution checks.

2 In 1940, a farmer using modern machinery could produce food for 13 people. This was 9 more people than a farmer in 1860 could feed. How many people could a farmer feed in 1860?

Let n = the number a farmer could feed in 1860.   Choose a variable.

$13 = n + 9$ Translate the phrases into an equation.

$13 - 9 = n + 9 - 9$ To undo adding 9, subtract 9 from both sides.

$4 = n$ Subtract.

A farmer could feed 4 people in 1860.

Try It

a. Solve $148 = x - 33$.

b. The price of a product includes the materials and labor cost plus the markup. A breadmaker, marked up $67, sold for $122. Write and solve an equation to find the materials and labor cost.

Check Your Understanding

1. How are the equations $7 = y + 3$ and $7 - 3 = y + 3 - 3$ related?

2. Write a problem for $x - 8 = 17$ and describe how to solve it.

3. Can $x + 4$ take on the value of 100? Explain.

Practice and Apply

Getting Started Write the first step in solving each equation.

1. $d - 80 = 70$ **2.** $s + 89 = 154$ **3.** $f + 16 = 32$ **4.** $a - 80 = 320$

Tell if the given number is a solution to the equation.

5. $x - 19 = 84$; 103   **6.** $y + 26 = 78$; 56   **7.** $25 + r = 129$; 156   **8.** $u - 47 = 29$; 18

Solve each equation. Check your answer.

9. $d + 83 = 92$ **10.** $r - 77 = 99$ **11.** $45 = 36 + f$ **12.** $102 = v - 66$

13. $x - 22 = 66$ **14.** $987 = 16 + m$ **15.** $1.5 = p + 1.5$ **16.** $w - 56 = 560$

17. $55 = h - 13$ **18.** $48 = d + 23$ **19.** $937 = f - 63$ **20.** $0 = y - 87.4$

21. $138 + g = 150$ **22.** $2098 = k - 536$ **23.** $651 + c = 800$ **24.** $71 = s - 583$

25. **Test Prep** Which is the first step in solving $x - 3 = 3$?
Ⓐ Add 3 to the left side.   Ⓑ Subtract 3 from both sides.
Ⓒ Subtract 3 from the left side.   Ⓓ Add 3 to both sides.

Write an equation for each statement.

26. The number of hours (h) increased by 12 equals 54.

27. The amount of profit (p) decreased by $25 is $180.

28. **Science** The chemical element aluminum was discovered in 1825 by Hans Christian Oersted. This was 18 years after Sir Humphry Davy discovered the element sodium. Write and solve an equation to find the year (y) that sodium was discovered.

29. **Literature** In Douglas Adams's five-book trilogy, *The Hitchhiker's Guide to the Galaxy,* the answer to Life, the Universe, and Everything is a number. This number (n) is 17 less than 59. Write and solve an equation to find n.

30. Write a word problem that would be solved by the equation $z - 16 = 28$.

Sodium

Aluminum

31. Industry Arty's Auto is suffering a slump. Last month Arty's salespeople sold a record 250 cars. The number of cars sold this month is 127 less than last month's number. Write and solve an equation to find the number of cars sold this month (n).

Estimation Estimate a solution to each equation.

32. $673 = x + 104$ **33.** $1{,}789 - t = 391$ **34.** $c - 9{,}422 = 3{,}207$ **35.** $12{,}949 + s = 19{,}323$

Problem Solving and Reasoning

Communicate Explain what was done to the first equation to get the second.

36. $x + 21 = 27 \rightarrow x = 6$ **37.** $16 = q - 13 \rightarrow q = 29$

38. **Journal** You have learned to write algebraic expressions and equations. Explain the difference between the two.

39. Critical Thinking Igor Sikorsky built and flew the first practical helicopter in 1939, making it possible for vertical landing and takeoff in remote places. A helicopter was flying at 1300 feet, landed to pick up a load, and then took off. If the loaded helicopter flew at a height 115 feet lower than before, write and solve an equation to find the new height (h).

40. Choose a Strategy You have been told that there is buried treasure somewhere due north of your house. You also know that it is exactly 3 miles from a large oak tree that is 12 miles due north of your house. How could you use equations to decide where to dig?

Problem Solving
STRATEGIES
- Look for a Pattern
- Make an Organized List
- Make a Table
- Guess and Check
- Work Backward
- Use Logical Reasoning
- Draw a Diagram
- Solve a Simpler Problem

Mixed Review

Name the inverse action of each. *[Lesson 2-4]*

41. Subtract 17   **42.** Divide by 4

43. Multiply by 20   **44.** Add 32

Find the value of each expression. *[Lesson 2-2]*

45. $6 \div (12 - 9) + 5$ **46.** $4 + 3 \times 7 - 5$ **47.** $1 + 2 \times 3 - 4$ **48.** $2 \times 32 - 8 \div 4$

49. $9 + 8 - 7 + 6$ **50.** $23 - 48 \div 6$ **51.** $12 \div 2 \times 3$ **52.** $12 - (2 + 6) \div 4$

2-7 Solving Multiplication and Division Equations

You'll Learn ...

■ to write and solve multiplication and division equations

... How It's Used

Scientists use multiplication and division equations to help analyze the growth of equations.

▶ **Lesson Link** | In the last lesson, you used inverse operations to solve addition and subtraction equations. Now you will see how inverse operations can help you solve multiplication and division equations. ◀

Explore | Multiplication and Division Equations

Matching Equals

1. The balanced scale represents the equation $3x = 12$.

2. What would you do to get just one x by itself on one side of the scale and still keep the scale in balance? What is the value of x?

3. Sketch a balanced scale that shows $2x = 6$. What is the value of x?

4. How did you use an inverse operation to get x by itself on one side of the equation $2x = 6$?

5. Sketch a balanced scale that shows $\frac{1}{2}x = 7$ or $x \div 2 = 7$. What is the value of x?

Learn | Solving Multiplication and Division Equations

Because multiplication and division are inverse operations, you can solve a multiplication equation using division. To solve division equations, use multiplication. When you change one side of an equation by multiplication or division, you must change the other side the same way to keep the "balance."

$$x \cdot 3 = 12$$

$$x \cdot 3 \boxed{\div 3} = 12 \boxed{\div 3}$$

Examples

1 Solve: $\frac{x}{4} = 5$

$\quad\quad \frac{x}{4} \times 4 = 5 \times 4$ To undo dividing by 4, multiply both sides by 4.

$\quad\quad\quad\quad x = 20$ Multiply.

Check: $\boxed{20} \div 4 \stackrel{?}{=} 5$

$\quad\quad\quad\quad\quad 5 = 5$ ✓ The solution checks.

Study TIP

Always remember to check your solution.

2 In 1793, Eli Whitney invented a cotton gin for separating cotton fiber from its seed. A person using a gin could work 50 times faster than a person working by hand. Suppose a person with a gin can clean 400 lb of cotton. In the same amount of time, how much could a person clean by hand?

Let c = the amount a person could clean by hand.   Choose a variable.

Using a gin cleans 50 times as much as cleaning by hand.   Describe the situation.

$\quad 400 \quad = \quad 50 \quad \cdot \quad\quad c$ Write an equation.

$\quad\quad \frac{400}{50} = \frac{50c}{50}$ To undo multiplying by 50, divide **both** sides by 50.

$\quad\quad\quad 8 = c$ Divide.

A person working by hand could clean 8 pounds of cotton.

3 In 1993, 7 times as many cars were manufactured in the United States as were manufactured in Mexico. If there were about 5,950,000 cars made in the United States that year, how many were made in Mexico?

Let m = number of cars made in Mexico.   Choose a variable.

Number of U.S. cars was 7 times cars made in Mexico.   Describe the situation.

$\quad 5,950,000 \quad\quad = 7 \quad \cdot \quad\quad m$ Write an equation.

$\quad\quad \frac{5,950,000}{7} \quad\quad = \frac{7m}{7}$ To undo multiplying by 7, divide by 7.

$\quad\quad\quad 850,000 = m$ Divide.

About 850,000 cars were made in Mexico.

Try It

a. Solve: $x \div 35 = 7$ **b.** Solve: $4s = 888$

c. The cost of running an appliance equals the number of kilowatts of power used times the cost per kilowatt. The cost is $0.15 per kilowatt. How many kilowatts did Stacey use if the cost of running her air conditioner was $18?

► **History Link**

In about 1764, James Hargreaves, an Englishman, invented the Spinning Jenny. Samuel Slater brought the new methods to the United States and, together with Americans Francis Lowell and Eli Whitney, revolutionized the cotton industry.

WHAT DO YOU THINK?

In 1986, cyclist Fred Markham set the world speed record for bicycles, 65 mi/hr. Wendy and Luis want to know how long it would take for a rider to travel the 260 miles from Cincinnati to Detroit if he could sustain that rate.

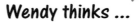

Wendy thinks ...

I'll make a table of values.

Time (hr)	1	2	3	4
Distance (mi)	65	130	195	260

It would take 4 hours.

Luis thinks ...

I'll write and solve an equation. I'll let t = the time it will take.

The equation is $65t = 260$ because rate times time equals distance.

To undo multiplying by 65, I'll divide both sides by 65: $\dfrac{65t}{65} = \dfrac{260}{65}$

Then I'll get: $t = 4$

It would take 4 hours.

What do you think?

1. When does it make sense to use Wendy's method? When doesn't it make sense?

2. Why did Luis divide 260 by 65 rather than multiply by 65?

Check | Your Understanding

1. How are the equations $k \div 4 = 9$ and $k \div 4 \times 4 = 9 \times 4$ related?

2. How are solving a multiplication equation and an addition equation alike?

Practice and Apply

Getting Started What is the first step in solving each equation?

1. $15d = 1200$

2. $m \div 43 = 2$

3. $\frac{f}{16} = 32$

4. $80k = 4.80$

Is the given number a solution to the equation?

5. $k \div 19 = 76; 4$

6. $j \cdot 25 = 75; 3$

7. $25m = 125; 3125$

8. **Test Prep** Which equation shows the next step in solving $3g = 33$?

Ⓐ $3g - 3 = 33 - 3$　　Ⓑ $3g + 3 = 33 + 3$　　Ⓒ $3g \div 3 = 33 \div 3$　　Ⓓ None of these

Solve each equation. Check your answer.

9. $m \cdot 45 = 90$

10. $\frac{s}{77} = 11$

11. $36 = 36p$

12. $100 = \frac{w}{66}$

13. $60 \div 4 = d$

14. $216 = n \div 2$

15. $1.5 = y \cdot 1.5$

16. $33j = 198$

17. $7r = 147$

18. $\frac{t}{17} = 16$

19. $268 = \frac{h}{13}$

20. $352 = 8z$

21. **Test Prep** Which of these numbers is the solution to $72x = 936$?

Ⓐ 13　　Ⓑ 864　　Ⓒ 1008　　Ⓓ 67,392

22. Science A winch raises a weight 6 feet for each turn of the handle. Write an equation that shows how many turns it would take to raise a weight 20 feet.

23. Geometry Two rectangles each have an area of 12 square centimeters. What is the height of each rectangle if the base of one is 4 cm and the base of the other is 6 cm?

24. History A league was an early measure of distance. A league is about 3 miles long. A horse was traveling at 9 leagues per hour. Write an equation to show how many leagues the horse could travel in 2 hours.

25. Geography The average area of each state in the United States is about 75,500 square miles. What is the area of the United States?

26. James bakes some cookies and gives 8 to each of his 9 friends. Write and solve an equation to find the number of cookies (c) that James baked.

Estimation Estimate a reasonable solution to each equation.

27. $9320 = 321k$ **28.** $\frac{t}{487} = 3$ **29.** $\frac{t}{5} = 3979$ **30.** $7{,}943p = 15{,}887$

Problem Solving and Reasoning

31. Choose a Strategy Fingernails grow about 1.5 inches per year. The world record for the longest fingernails is 37 inches. Which equation shows how long it might take to grow nails 37 inches long?

Ⓐ $1.5 + y = 37$ Ⓑ $\frac{y}{1.5} = 37$

Ⓒ $1.5y = 37$ Ⓓ $y = 1.5 \cdot 37$

32. Communicate Write an equation that can be solved using multiplication and another that can be solved using division. Explain how to solve the equations.

33. Critical Thinking What is the solution to the equation $0 \cdot j = 0$? Explain.

34. Communicate In September 1996, one U.S. dollar was worth 110 Japanese yen, and one yen was worth 811 Turkish lira. If you had a million Turkish lira, would you be able to buy a house, a car, a pizza, or a newspaper? Explain how you decided.

35. Critical Thinking Each roll of Hua's film allows her to take 36 photographs. Write an equation to calculate how many rolls (n) of film she needs to take a picture of each member of a school with 1235 students. Use your equation to find out how many rolls of film she must buy.

> **Problem Solving**
> ## STRATEGIES
> • Look for a Pattern
> • Make an Organized List
> • Make a Table
> • Guess and Check
> • Work Backward
> • Use Logical Reasoning
> • Draw a Diagram
> • Solve a Simpler Problem

Mixed Review

Use mental math to estimate each measurement. *[Previous course]*

36. The height of a house

37. The length of a city block

38. The height of a soda can

39. The height of an elephant

Write an algebraic expression for each phrase. *[Lesson 2-5]*

40. Seven more than a number x

41. Three less than twice a number c

42. A number n increased by 5

43. A number r decreased by 10

44. Triple the sum of 2 and a number d

Problem Solving with Two-Step Equations

▶ **Lesson Link**   You've solved equations by using inverse operations. Now you'll use inverse operations to solve equations with more than one operation. ◀

Explore   Two-Step Equations

Watch Your Balance

1. The balanced scale represents the equation $2x + 3 = 13$.

2. What steps would you take to get one x alone on one side of the scale and still keep the scale in balance? What is the value of x?

3. Sketch a balanced scale that shows $3x + 1 = 7$. What is the value of x?

4. How did you use inverse operations to get x by itself on one side of $3x + 1 = 7$?

5. When you solve an equation like $3x + 1 = 7$, would you first try to find out what $3x$ without the 1 equals, or first find out what x equals? Explain.

You'll Learn ...

■ to use more than one inverse operation to solve an equation

... How It's Used

Contractors need to understand equations that have more than one operation because they have to work with fixed costs and variable costs.

Learn   Problem Solving with Two-Step Equations

If an equation involves two operations, you need to use inverse operations one at a time. The order of operations says to do multiplication and division before addition and subtraction. So you need to undo any addition or subtraction first. Then undo any multiplication or division.

$$2w \boxed{+ 3} = 9 \qquad \text{Undo addition first.}$$

$$2w + 3 \boxed{- 3} = 9 \boxed{- 3} \qquad \text{Undo by subtracting 3.}$$

$$\frac{2w}{2} = \frac{6}{2} \qquad \text{Undo multiplication by dividing.}$$

$$w = 3$$

DID YOU KNOW?

The Wrights' 1903 plane traveled just 120 ft through the air. If it had taken off inside a Boeing 747 at the nose end, it would have touched down 111 ft from the tail—still inside the plane!

Examples

1 Solve: $3p - 10 = 8$

$3p - 10 + 10 = 8 + 10$ To undo subtracting 10, add 10 to **both** sides.

$3p = 18$ Add.

$\dfrac{3p}{3} = \dfrac{18}{3}$ To undo multiplying by 3, divide **both** sides by 3.

$p = 6$ Divide.

Check: $3(6) - 10 \overset{?}{=} 8$

$18 - 10 = 8$ ✓ The solution checks.

2 Orville and Wilbur Wright began experimenting with a glider in 1900. The 40-foot wings of their 1903 airplane were 8 feet longer than twice the length of the wings of the glider. How long were the glider's wings?

Let $w = $ the length of the glider's wings.   Choose a variable.

$40 = 8 + 2 \cdot w$ Write an equation.

$40 - 8 = 8 + 2w - 8$ To undo adding 8, subtract 8 from **both** sides.

$32 = 2w$ Subtract.

$\dfrac{32}{2} = \dfrac{2w}{2}$ To undo multiplying by 2, divide **both** sides by 2.

$16 = w$ Divide.

The glider's wings were 16 feet long.

Try It

a. Solve: $\dfrac{x}{3} - 12 = 5$

b. Chris earns $5 per hour as a waiter. One evening, he took home his regular earnings plus $48 in tips, for a total of $73. How many hours did he work?

Check | Your Understanding

1. When you use inverse operations, how is their order related to the order of operations?

2. Describe how you would solve $897 = 34x + 412$ using a calculator.

3. Can $3x + 5$ ever take on the value of 17? Explain.

Practice and Apply

Getting Started For each equation, tell which operation you would undo first.

1. $2x + 3 = 10$

2. $6x - 3 = 33$

3. $\dfrac{x}{4} - 6 = 10$

4. **Test Prep** Which of the following have a solution of $m = 16$?

Ⓐ $m + 8 = 8$ Ⓑ $\dfrac{m}{16} = 256$ Ⓒ $2m - 10 = 22$ Ⓓ $4m + 4 = 68$

Solve each equation. Check your answer.

5. $45n + 45 = 90$

6. $\dfrac{k}{7} + 11 = 11$

7. $36 = 6u + 30$

8. $10 = \dfrac{t}{66} + 9$

9. $60 \div 4 = 2m$

10. $216 = \dfrac{r}{2} + 214$

11. $10 = 15s - 5$

12. $4h - 8 = 8$

13. $5u - 7 = 13$

14. $14 = 6t + 2$

15. $12s - 10 = 50$

16. $23 = 8g + 7$

17. $7x + 2 = 51$

18. $9k - 3 = 78$

19. $15 = \dfrac{s}{4} + 11$

20. $14 = 5 + 3b$

21. Marco is making a mobile like the one in the photograph. Write an equation to show the mobile is balanced. What should each of the small boxes weigh?

22. 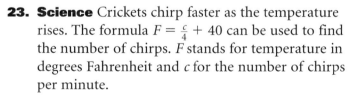 When you solve an equation, you must do the same operation to both sides. Explain why this is true.

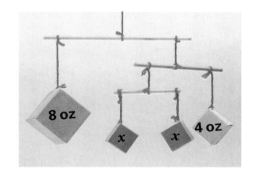

23. **Science** Crickets chirp faster as the temperature rises. The formula $F = \dfrac{c}{4} + 40$ can be used to find the number of chirps. F stands for temperature in degrees Fahrenheit and c for the number of chirps per minute.

a. How many times will crickets chirp if the temperature is 84°F?

b. How many times will crickets chirp if the temperature is 44°F?

Acheta domestica

24. Sara helps sell strawberries at her family's fruit stand. The family pays $10 a day to rent the stand, and they earn $0.80 for each basket of strawberries they sell. How much does the family make on a day when they sell 90 baskets of strawberries?

Problem Solving and Reasoning

25. Critical Thinking A man's shoe size (s) is determined by the formula $s = 3x - 25$, where x is the length of the foot in inches. The formula for a woman is $s = 3x - 22$. Is there any value for x that would give the same size for a man and a woman? Explain.

26. Communicate Kim solved this equation for y: $6y + 5 = 29$. She got the answer 5.67, which was incorrect. What should the answer have been and what mistake do you think Kim made?

27. Critical Thinking New skis have been invented to help skiers turn more easily. They are called parabolic, or hourglass, skis. Renting these skis costs $22 per day plus a flat fee of $10 for insurance. If Hawke's rental bill was $98, for how many days did he rent the skis?

Communicate Explain what was done to the first equation to get the second.

28. $2x + 1 = 5 \rightarrow x = 2$

29. $\frac{x}{4} + 6 = 10 \rightarrow x = 16$

Mixed Review

Solve each equation. *[Lesson 2-6]*

30. $3 + x = 7$
31. $x - 11 = 15$
32. $6 + x = 13$
33. $123 - x = 47$
34. $32 - x = 27$
35. $x + 34 = 97$
36. $234 = x + 107$
37. $106 = 963 - x$

Find a formula relating the variables. *[Lesson 2-3]*

38.

f	3	4	5	6
g	9	12	15	18

39.

d	11	12	13	14
e	15	16	17	18

40.

p	7	8	9	10
q	1	2	3	4

41.

x	2	3	4	5
y	18	27	36	45

Section 2B Connect

You have learned to solve a variety of equations. Now you will solve a problem using an equation and a Rube Goldberg–type machine.

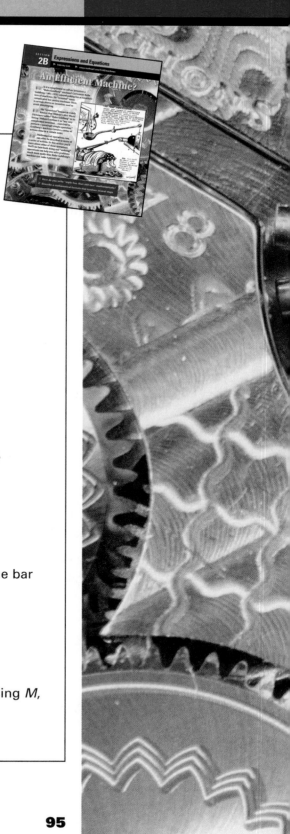

Check It Out!

The last digit in a 12-digit bar code "checks" the accuracy of the first 11 digits. Here's how it works:

M = sum of digits in odd positions

N = sum of digits in even positions (except for the check digit)

In the bar code shown:

4 51702 00836 6

$M = 4 + 1 + 0 + 0 + 8 + 6$ $M = 19$

$N = 5 + 7 + 2 + 0 + 3$ $N = 17$

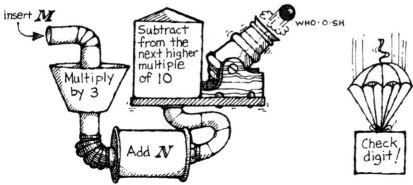

insert M

Multiply by 3

Subtract from the next higher multiple of 10

Add N

WHO·O·SH

Check digit!

1. Check that the machine sends out the correct check digit for the bar code above.

2. Find the check digit for these bar codes.
   a. 3 21635 00481 ?   **b.** 5 90335 26648 ?

3. One digit is missing from this bar code: 1 32832 69?25 6
   a. Find N for the bar code.
   b. The sum of $3M$ and N is 84. Write and solve an equation using M, the number 84, and the value of N you found above.
   c. Explain how you found the missing digit.

1. A driver opens the car door, gets in, sits down, closes the door, and fastens her seatbelt before driving home. Describe the inverse operations she would use after arriving home and turning the engine off.

Write an algebraic expression for each phrase.

2. Seven less than a number p

3. y dollars more than a price of $32

4. The product of a number h and the sum of a number j and 9

Write a phrase for each algebraic expression.

5. $28 - f$

6. $4c + 3d$

7. $6(g - 8)$

8. $(s - 3) \div (8 - t)$

Find the value of each expression.

9. $15 - 4 \times 3 - 2$

10. $\dfrac{11 - 3}{2} + 4 \cdot 5$

11. $5 \cdot 4 + 3 - 2$

12. $12 - \dfrac{8}{4}$

13. Journal Write an algebraic expression using each of these three phrases: "increased by," "difference," and "half of."

Solve each equation.

14. $g - 8 = 12$

15. $k + 6 = 14$

16. $16 + 5y = 51$

17. $27 = z - 11$

18. $6t + 18 = 18$

19. $3x - 5 = 1$

20. $21 = 3q$

21. $7 = \dfrac{k}{7}$

22. Ken went rowing. The rental was $6.00 for the first hour and $4.50 for each hour after that. If Ken's rental was $24.00, how long did he row?

23. Science Physicists use the formula $F = ma$ to relate force (F), mass (m), and acceleration (a). Substitute 20 for F and 5 for a, then solve to find the mass.

Test Prep

When you are asked to find the correct solution to an equation, it may be quickest to substitute each of the given values into the equation and see which one works.

24. Which of these numbers is the solution to $8w - 9 = 15$?

ⓐ 24 ⓑ 1 ⓒ 3 ⓓ 0.75

Functions

A function is a relationship between numbers. You can think of the function as taking a number and transforming it into another number.

Function machines can be a useful way to think about functions. This machine seems to be using the rule "double it" to decide which number it puts out.

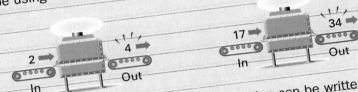

The equation that represents the "double it" function can be written as $y = 2x$. The input number is x and the output number is y.

When you know the equation for the function, you can substitute an input (x) value to find the output (y) value that goes with it.

If $y = 3x + 5$, what's the y-value for an x-value of 2?

$y = 3(2) + 5$	Substitute 2 for x.
$y = 6 + 5$	Multiply.
$y = 11$	Add.

Try It

Evaluate each function for the given values.

1. $y = 5x$ for $x = 1$, 2, and 3
2. $y = x + 2$ for $x = 6$, 8, and 10
3. $y = 2x - 1$ for $x = 5$, 7, and 9
4. $y = 4x + 2$ for $x = 2$, 3, and 4

Think of each table as a function machine. Copy and complete each one. Then write an equation for the table.

5.

x	1	2	3	4	5
y	5	10	15		

6.

x	1	2	3	4	5
y	3	5	7		

Chapter 2 Summary and Review

Graphic Organizer

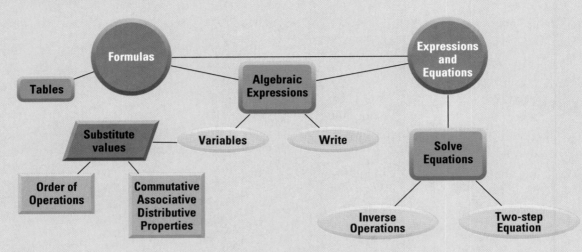

Section 2A   Formulas

Summary

■ A **formula** is a rule showing relationships among quantities. A **variable** represents a quantity whose values may change. Formulas usually contain variables.

■ An **expression** can be made up of variables and/or numbers and operations.

■ You must do operations in the correct order. First do operations in parentheses, or above or below a division bar, then multiplication and division, from left to right, and finally addition and subtraction from left to right.

■ Along with order-of-operation rules, the **commutative, associative,** and **distributive properties** will help you find the values of expressions.

■ You can use a formula to make a table of values.

Review

1. The formula $A = \frac{1}{2}bh$ gives the area of a triangle. Find the area of a triangle with base (b) 8 ft and height (h) 5 ft.

2. A taxi ride costs $2 plus $3 for each mile. Let $C = 3m + 2$, where C is the cost and m is the number of miles. How much will it cost to travel 6 miles?

3. Find the value of $3 + 4 \times 5$.

4. Find the value of $5 \times (6 - 2) \div 2$.

5. Tell which operation you would do first to evaluate $\frac{(5 + 4) \times 6}{18}$.

6. Which property is suggested by the formulas $P = 2l + 2w$ and $P = 2(l + w)$?

7. Find a formula relating the variables.

x	1	2	3	4	5	6	7
y	4	8	12	16	20	24	28

8. Use the formula $d = rt$ to make a table of values showing the distance (d) traveled in 0, 1, 2, 3, 4, and 5 hours (t) at a rate (r) of 40 mi/hr.

Section 2B Expressions and Equations

Summary

■ Addition and subtraction and, likewise, multiplication and division are called **inverse operations** because they undo each other.

■ An **algebraic expression** is an expression that contains a variable.

■ An **equation** is a statement that two expressions are equal.

■ To **solve** an equation containing a variable means to find the value of the variable that makes the equation true.

■ You can use inverse operations to solve addition, subtraction, multiplication, and division equations.

■ Some equations contain more than one operation, so you will need to use two or more inverse operations to solve them.

Review

9. Name the inverse of flying 260 miles north.

10. Tell if 35 is a solution to $p \div 5 = 7$.

11. Write and solve an equation for the statement: The number of dogs (d) increased by 7 is 23.

12. A number is divided by 11. What operation is needed to return to the original number?

13. Tell if 18 is a solution to $x + 6 = 26$.

14. Solve $25x = 325$. Check your solution.

15. Solve $a + 15 = 32$. Check your solution.

16. Solve $8 = \frac{n}{12}$. Check your solution.

17. Solve $108 = x - 27$. Check your solution.

18. Solve $\frac{x}{5} - 3 = 21$. Check your solution.

19. Eighteen is added to a number. The result is multiplied by 3. What operations are needed to return to the original number?

20. Write algebraic expressions for
   a. 21 more than a number (k).
   b. The product of 10 and a number (u).

21. Solve $3x - 5 = 16$. Check your solution.

22. Write a phrase for
   a. $5z$ **b.** $12(j - 4)$ **c.** $\frac{d + 5}{14}$

1. You can use the formula $V = lwh$ to find the volume of a box. Find the volume (V) of a box with length (l) 12 in., width (w) 8 in., and height (h) 5 in.

2. Shelly is riding a bicycle at a rate (r) of 15 km/hr. Use the formula $d = rt$ to make a table of values showing the distance (d) traveled in 0, 1, 2, 3, and 4 hours (t).

3. Find the value of $8 \times 7 - 20 \div 5$.

4. Write a phrase for $\dfrac{x + 12}{8}$.

5. If 18 is entered into this inverse operation machine, what will be the result?

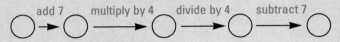

add 7   multiply by 4   divide by 4   subtract 7

6. Find a formula relating the variables.

x	10	11	12	13	14	15
y	4	5	6	7	8	9

7. Write algebraic expressions for

   a. Thirty-two less than a number k.

   b. Three times the difference between a number g and five.

8. Can you find one value for the variable w that will make both equations true?

$$3w + 11 = 20 \qquad 3w - 7 = 20$$

Explain your thinking.

9. Solve and check your solution.

   a. $65 = x + 27$ **b.** $x \div 3 = 28$

10. Solve and check your solution.

   a. $4a - 15 = 37$ **b.** $23 = \dfrac{k}{12} - 7$

11. Which operation would you do first?

$$\dfrac{100}{18 \times 2} - 26$$

12. Twenty-three is subtracted from a number. The result is divided by 12. What operations are needed to return to the original number?

13. A mail-order company sells compact discs for $14 each, with a $4 shipping charge for the entire order. Let $C = 14d + 4$, where C is the cost and d is the number of discs. Athena placed an order for 7 discs. How much will she have to pay?

14. Raul drove 2100 miles in 3 days. He drove the same number of miles each day. Write and solve an equation to find the number of miles he drove each day.

Copy each statement. Insert parentheses to make each sentence true.

15. $10 + 14 \div 2 + 5 = 12$

16. $10 + 14 \div 2 + 5 = 17$

17. $36 \div 6 + 6 \div 2 = 6$

18. $36 \div 6 + 6 \div 2 = 4$

Performance Task

Consider the expression $3 + 5 \times 4 - 1 \times 2$. Find all possible ways to insert a single pair of parentheses and evaluate the expression. For example, $3 + (5 \times 4 - 7) \times 2 = 29$. How many different ways of evaluating the expression can you find?

Multiple Choice

Choose the best answer.

1. Which type of graph is the best choice for displaying a corporation's profits over the last five years? *[Lessons 1-1, 1-3, 1-5]*

Ⓐ Circle graph   Ⓑ Line graph

Ⓒ Line plot   Ⓓ Stem-and-leaf plot

2. Consider the data 2, 5, 3, 7, 5, 4, 3, 6, 3, 7. Which of the following is 4.5? *[Lesson 1-4]*

Ⓐ Mean   Ⓑ Mean and median

Ⓒ Mode and mean   Ⓓ Median

3. The scatterplot shows the daily high and low temperatures in Junction City over a 2-week period. The low temperature the next day was 43°. Use the scatterplot to give the best estimate of the high temperature on that day. *[Lesson 1-7]*

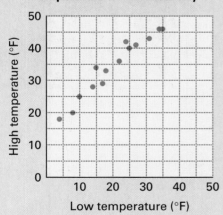

Temperature in Junction City

Ⓐ 30°   Ⓑ 45°   Ⓒ 55°   Ⓓ 70°

4. Use the formula $h = \frac{m}{60}$ to relate minutes (*m*) and hours (*h*). How many hours are equal to 240 minutes? *[Lesson 2-1]*

Ⓐ 4 hr   Ⓑ 180 hr

Ⓒ 300 hr   Ⓓ 14,400 hr

5. What property is suggested by the equation $(3 + 4) + 5 = 3 + (4 + 5)$? *[Lesson 2-2]*

Ⓐ Distributive property

Ⓑ Associative property of addition

Ⓒ Order of operations

Ⓓ Commutative property of addition

6. Which formula was used to create the table? *[Lesson 2-3]*

x	3	4	5	6	7
y	9	12	15	18	21

Ⓐ $x = 3y$ Ⓑ $y = x + 6$

Ⓒ $y = \frac{x}{3}$ Ⓓ $y = 3x$

7. Thirty-five is added to a number. What operation is needed to return to the original number? *[Lesson 2-4]*

Ⓐ Divide by 35   Ⓑ Multiply by 35

Ⓒ Subtract 35   Ⓓ Subtract from 35

8. Which expression shows 5 less than twice a number (*n*)? *[Lesson 2-5]*

Ⓐ $2n - 5$ Ⓑ $2 \times (n - 5)$

Ⓒ $5 - 2n$ Ⓓ $n - 2 \times 5$

9. Solve $x + 15 = 53$. *[Lesson 2-6]*

Ⓐ 705   Ⓑ 62

Ⓒ 38   Ⓓ 32

10. Solve $2y - 3 = 17$. *[Lesson 2-7]*

Ⓐ $y = 10$ Ⓑ $y = 7$

Ⓒ $y = 40$ Ⓓ $y = 25.5$

Entertainment

The highest scoring 7-letter word in Scrabble® is quartzy. It is worth 126 points on the first move.

People of the World

After the United States, the people of Germany make the most international telephone calls in the world. They make about 1.0116×10^9 calls per year.

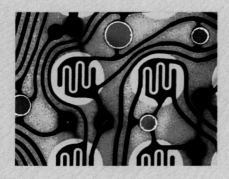

Science

The hexadecimal number system is used by electrical engineers. It has sixteen digits. The letters A through F represent the digits ten through fifteen.

Arts & Literature

Michael Crichton's best-selling novel, *Jurassic Park*, has sold over 10^6 copies.

KEY MATH IDEAS

When multiplying or dividing decimal numbers, you must be careful to locate the decimal point in the answer correctly.

Scientific notation uses decimal numbers and powers to express very large or very small numbers conveniently.

One number is a factor of another if it divides that number with no remainder. A prime number has only two factors, one and itself.

To compare two fractions, first write them with a common denominator. The fraction with the larger numerator is greater.

Social Studies

The world's largest university is the University of Calcutta, India. It has 300,000 students.

CHAPTER PROJECT

Problem Solving

Understand
Plan
Solve
Look Back

In this project, you will make a display that shows the number of animals of a certain type (species) that might exist after several generations. Begin the project by thinking of an animal species you would like to research.

Problem Solving Focus

Reading the Problem

Before you can solve a problem, you need to understand it. Some problems look harder than they are because they have unexpected twists. Going back over a problem a second time may help you understand what the problem is really asking.

Read each problem, and answer the questions about the problem.

❶ The children's clinic held a walkathon. Each sponsor paid walkers $2.00 a mile. June got 8 sponsors and walked 4 miles. Greg walked twice as far as June did, but had half as many sponsors. Lou had 3 times as many sponsors as Greg and walked as far as June did. Who earned the most money?

a. What is the problem about?

b. What is the problem asking for?

c. How much did each sponsor pay for a mile walked?

d. Which two walkers earned the same amount of money?

e. Write and answer a question of your own that can be solved using the information in this problem.

❷ Three radio stations, including WEFG, volunteered free radio airtime to publicize the walkathon. WEBC donated 20 minutes each day for 3 days. WAFT donated the same amount of time per day, but for 3 extra days. The walkathon had 6 hours of free airtime. How much time did WEFG donate?

a. What is the problem about?

b. What is the problem asking for?

c. How many minutes of airtime did WEBC donate each day?

d. How many total minutes did WAFT donate?

e. Write and answer a question of your own that can be solved using the information in this problem.

The Lonely Planets

When astronauts Neil Armstrong and Buzz Aldrin landed on the moon in 1969, they were the first people ever to visit another celestial body. Over the next three years, 10 more astronauts walked on the moon. At that time, many people believed that traveling to the moon and even to other planets would be common by the year 2000.

However, in the 25 years since then, no one has been back to the moon and no one has visited another planet. Many scientists believe that no one ever will. The reason is that our solar system is so huge. Armstrong and Aldrin took four days to get to the moon. At the speed they traveled, it would take nearly two *years* to reach Mars, the nearest planet with conditions that humans could stand. The planet Jupiter is 20 years farther than that, and Pluto, the most distant planet, 100 years farther yet.

Working with huge numbers is something astronomers and space explorers do every day. They carefully measure time and distance as they try to make the dream of understanding and visiting other worlds come true. Keeping these records and making calculations with large numbers is made simpler by using decimal notation.

1 How many times as far away from Earth is Pluto than the moon? Explain.

2 Give examples of things you can find on Earth that need very large or very small numbers to express.

3 The moon is about 240,000 miles from Earth. Estimate Armstrong and Aldrin's average speed in mi/hr. How does their speed compare with typical speeds on Earth?

3-1

Place Value: Comparing and Ordering Decimals

You'll Learn ...

■ to compare and order decimals

... How It's Used

Environmental scientists need to compare the decimal values of pollutants that they find in the air or in water.

▶ **Lesson Link** You have worked with whole numbers. Now you'll begin to study decimals by deciding which of two decimals is greater. ◀

Explore | Comparing and Ordering Decimals

Model Behavior

Materials: Graph paper, Colored pencils

Modeling Decimals

The graph paper shows a model of the number 1.47. To model a decimal:

1.47

* Color a complete 10-by-10 grid for each whole in the decimal.

* Draw another 10-by-10 grid next to the last complete grid.

* In this grid, color one 10-by-1 strip for each tenth in the decimal. Color a small square for each hundredth.

1. Draw a grid model for each decimal.

    a. 1.3   **b.** 1.29   **c.** 0.8   **d.** 1.30   **e.** 0.51   **f.** 0.99

2. What do you notice about the models for 1.3 and 1.30? What does this tell you about these numbers? Explain.

3. Rank the decimals from smallest to largest. Explain your reasoning.

4. The number 51 is greater than 8. Why is 0.8 greater than 0.51?

5. Could you use this method to model 1.354? Explain.

Learn | Comparing and Ordering Decimals

The place value of each digit of a whole number is one-tenth of the value of the place to its left. Moving to the right of a decimal point, you can create the place values *tenths, hundredths, thousandths,* and so on.

Place	thousands	hundreds	tens	ones	•	tenths	hundredths	thousandths
Place Value	1000	100	10	1		$\frac{1}{10}$ or 0.1	$\frac{1}{100}$ or 0.01	$\frac{1}{1000}$ or 0.001

As with whole numbers, the value of each digit in a decimal is the product of the digit and its place value.

Examples

1 Read 8052.468.

The number is read "eight thousand fifty-two *and* four hundred sixty-eight thousandths."

2 Give the value of each 8 in 8052.468.

The first 8 is in the thousands place. Its value is $8 \times 1000 = 8000$.

The second 8 is in the thousandths place. Its value is $8 \times \frac{1}{1000} = \frac{8}{1000}$ or 0.008.

Remember

The symbol $<$ means *less than*. The symbol $>$ means *greater than*.
[Previous course]

To compare and order decimals, write the numbers with their decimal points lined up. Then compare the digits in each place, moving left to right. Sometimes one number has more decimal places than another. *Annex* zeros to the right of the decimal part of each number so that each number has the same number of digits after the decimal point.

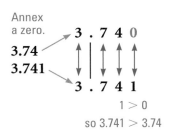

Annex a zero.

3 . 7 4 **0**

3.74

3.741

3 . 7 4 **1**

$1 > 0$

so 3.741 > 3.74

Example 3

America's first two manned space flights that orbited Earth took place in 1962. Compare the time in orbit of the two astronauts.

4 . 9 2 3 **0** Annex a zero.

4 . 9 3 4 **7** Compare digits in each place.

$2 < 3$

Astronaut	Time in Orbit
John Glenn	4.923 hr
Scott Carpenter	4.9347 hr

Glenn's time of 4.923 hr was less than Carpenter's time of 4.9347 hr.

Try It

Compare using $<$, $>$, or $=$.

a. 58.7351 ☐ 58.73   **b.** 3.24 ☐ 3.240

▶ **History Link**

The first woman in space was Valentina Tereshkova, of the U.S.S.R. Between June 16 and 19, 1963, she made 48 orbits of Earth in 70.83 hours.

Check | Your Understanding

1. Explain the relationship between place values in a decimal and a grid model.

2. You know that 3 is less than 27. Is 0.3 less than 0.27? Explain.

3-1 Exercises and Applications

Practice and Apply

Getting Started **Write each decimal in words.**

1. 36.5   **2.** 124.84   **3.** 4792.639   **4.** 306.306

Give the value of each 6.

5. 125.067   **6.** 16.136   **7.** 42.68   **8.** 634.16   **9.** 46,600.66

10. **Test Prep** Which of these numbers has the same value as the 5 in this number: 247.358?

ⓐ 50   ⓑ 5.0   ⓒ 0.5   ⓓ 0.05

Compare using $<$, $>$, or $=$.

11. 0.034 ☐ 0.340   **12.** 1.01 ☐ 1.013   **13.** 487.835 ☐ 487.838

14. 16.2 ☐ 16.201   **15.** 5.831 ☐ 6.813   **16.** 196.789 ☐ 196.987

17. **Science** The table shows levels of ozone-depleting chemicals in the air. Which year had the greatest level? The least?

Year	1991	1992	1993	1994	1995
Level (parts per billion)	2.981	3.133	3.148	3.138	3.124

18. **Test Prep** Which of these numbers is the smallest?

ⓐ 36.397   ⓑ 36.400

ⓒ 36.399   ⓓ 3.700

19. **Consumer** You are deciding which of two brands of yogurt to buy. Both brands cost $1.69 per container.

     a. Which is the better deal? Explain.

     b. Which brand is lower in fat? Explain.

PRACTICE 3-1

Problem Solving and Reasoning

20. Critical Thinking Here is a decimal with some missing digits:
☐ 3. ☐ 8 ☐. If no two digits of this number are alike, what is the
largest possible number this can be? The smallest? Fill in the missing
digits to make the closest possible number to $53\frac{1}{2}$.

21. Communicate Write three decimals that are greater than 3.71 but less
than 3.72. Order them from the least to the greatest. Could you write
more than three of these numbers? Is there a limit to how close you can
get to 3.72 without actually reaching it? Explain your answers.

22. Journal Explain how you would put the three numbers 1.01, 1.029, and
1.103 in order from least to greatest.

23. Critical Thinking Number lines can be used to display and order decimals. Compare 3.2, 3.4, and 4.3 by plotting each on a number line. How
can you tell the order of the three decimals?

24. Critical Thinking The books in a library are arranged according to *call
number;* the lower call numbers are on the left side of the shelf and the
higher numbers are on the right. The call numbers for six books on
planetary astronomy are lettered a–f. Give the order in which they
should appear on the shelf.

a. 523.1   **b.** 523.70   **c.** 523.43   **d.** 523.45   **e.** 523.4   **f.** 523.449

Mixed Review

Order each data set from least to greatest. Then find the median for each set.
[Lesson 1-4]

25. 34, 65, 23, 78, 46, 45, 89, 43, 29

26. 164, 215, 432, 653, 671, 564

27. 3, 6, 8, 5, 3, 4, 6, 8, 5, 3, 2, 7, 9, 6

28. 65, 67, 73, 83, 53, 65, 75, 49, 71

Write a phrase for each algebraic expression. *[Lesson 2-5]*

29. $x - 7$

30. $63c$

31. $8(n - 4)$

32. $42k + 17$

33. $\dfrac{d + 3}{4}$

34. $4 - 3y$

35. $5 - n$

36. $12c + 16w$

Estimating by Rounding

You'll Learn ...

■ to round to the nearest decimal place

■ to estimate by rounding to whole numbers

■ to use front-end estimation and compatible numbers to estimate

... How It's Used

Contractors need to estimate costs in order to make a realistic bid for a job. They often have to round quantities and expenses to give a customer a quote.

▶ **Lesson Link** You have rounded whole numbers when you didn't need exact answers or when you wanted to estimate. Now you'll see how to round decimal numbers. ◀

| Explore | Estimating by Rounding |

How Far Is Mars?

Gail was writing a report on space probes. In 1971, NASA engineers placed the *Mariner 9* space probe in orbit around the planet Mars. Gail needed to find the distance from Earth to Mars. Three sources of information gave three different distances:

40 million miles   **36,862,000 miles**   **36.9 million miles**

1. A NASA report said, "At the moment it went into Martian orbit, *Mariner 9* was _____ from Earth." Which of the three distances was probably in the report? Why do you think so?

2. A World Wide Web page said, "Mars is about _____ from Earth." Which of the three distances probably was given? Why?

3. In 1978, the *Pioneer 12* probe was placed in orbit around the planet Venus. A newspaper report said, "*Pioneer 12* is 7.3 million miles closer to Earth than *Mariner 9*'s _____ when it went into Martian orbit in 1971." Which distance did the newspaper probably give? Why?

4. Give another distance from Earth to Mars Gail might have found and where she might have found it. Why would the source give that distance?

| Learn | Estimating by Rounding |

Sometimes decimals are more exact than you really need to give a useful answer. Or you may want to estimate an answer by using numbers simple enough for mental math. In both cases, you can simplify your work by *rounding*.

5.3485 to nearest tenth   **34.287 to nearest hundredth**

5. 3 485	Find the place value.
5. 3 485	Look at the digit to the right.
5. 3 485 ↑ no change	If the digit is 5 or greater, add 1 to the place value digit. If it is less than 5, do not change the place value digit.
5.3	Delete all digits to the right.

34.2 8 7   Find the place value.

34.2 8 7   Look at the digit to the right.

34.2 8 7
↑
add 1

34.29

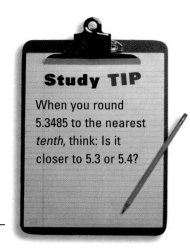
Example 1

The planet Saturn is 9.5549 times as far from the sun as Earth is. Round 9.5549 to the nearest tenth, hundredth, and thousandth.

tenths place

9. 5 549
↑
5 or more. Add 1 to the previous digit

hundredths place

9.5 5 49
↑
4 or less. Don't change the previous digit.

thousandths place

9.55 4 9
↑
5 or more. Add 1 to the previous digit.

To the nearest tenth, 9.5549 rounds to 9.6.

To the nearest hundredth, 9.5549 rounds to 9.55.

To the nearest thousandth, 9.5549 rounds to 9.555.

Try It

Round 7.865 to the nearest tenth, hundredth, and thousandth.

There are several ways to use rounding to estimate answers to problems that contain decimals.

One way to estimate is to round each number to the highest place value. Then add, subtract, multiply, or divide.

$$456.39 - 213.94 = \boxed{4}56.39 - \boxed{2}13.94 = 500 - 200 = 300$$

Hundreds is the highest place value.   Round to the nearest hundred place.   Estimate.

To estimate using *compatible numbers,* replace the numbers with the nearest numbers that are easy to use.

$356.4 \div 84.7$

Round 356.4 to 360. If you replace 84.7 with 80, it is not compatible with 360. Instead, replace 84.7 with 90. $360 \div 90 = 4$.

Examples

Estimate.

2 14.779 + 20.24

14.779 rounds to 15. 20.24 rounds to 20. Estimate: 15 + 20 = 35

3 23.12 × 37.627

Round to the nearest ten. 23.12 rounds to 20.
37.627 rounds to 40. Estimate: 20 × 40 = 800

4 319.24 ÷ 68.93

Use compatible numbers. 319.24 rounds to 320.
Replace 68.93 with 80 instead of 70. Estimate: 320 ÷ 80 = 4

Try It

Estimate. **a.** 67.54 − 32.45   **b.** 12.5 × 58.44   **c.** 428.9 ÷ 88.3

▶ **Technology Link**

When you use your calculator, it is important to estimate your answer first. Then you will know if you have pressed the wrong keys.

In some situations, rounding to the nearest place does not make sense. Suppose you have $6 in your pocket and want to buy as many comic books as possible. The cost of each comic book is $2.39 with tax. If you round $2.39 to $2 (the nearest whole number) you will estimate that you could buy three comic books (6 ÷ 2 = 3). But three comic books will cost more money than you have. It is better to replace $2.39 with $3 and estimate two comic books (6 ÷ 3 = 2).

Example 5

Your astronomy club plans to wash cars to raise money for a new telescope. With tax, the telescope costs $317.19. Estimate how many cars will have to be washed if you charge $5.00 per car.

Replace 317.19 with a compatible number to make dividing by 5 easier. The nearest compatible number is 300. To be sure the club makes enough money to buy a telescope, however, it is better to replace 317.19 with 350. Estimate: 350 ÷ 5 = 70.

About 70 cars should be washed.

Study TIP

When you choose compatible numbers, keep the math as simple as possible: 320 and 350 can both be divided by 5; it is easier to divide 350 by 5.

Check | Your Understanding

1. Why is it a good idea to estimate before solving a problem?

2. Give an example of a situation when you might decide not to round a decimal to the nearest whole number to make an estimate.

Practice and Apply

Getting Started Round each number to the nearest tenth by looking at the digit to the *right* of the tenths digit.

1. 3.084   **2.** 22.247   **3.** 17.458   **4.** 138.985

Round each number to the nearest whole number.

5. 15.2   **6.** 2.43   **7.** 10.39   **8.** 158.942

Round each number to the nearest whole number and multiply.

9. 14.92×0.98 **10.** 21.94×1.34 **11.** 1.68×9.4 **12.** 72.8×19.68

Estimate.

13. 163.2×5.4 **14.** $37.19 + 100.94$ **15.** $\dfrac{45.4}{4.75}$ **16.** $47.49 - 16.85$

17. $39.23 + 246.49$ **18.** 6343.2×2.57 **19.** $376.82 - 139.28$ **20.** $37.19 \div 8.18$

21. 42.3×239.23 **22.** $731.37 - 36.48$ **23.** $\dfrac{289.29}{42.52}$ **24.** $5893.4 + 2169.3$

25. $\dfrac{5314.3}{2128.2}$ **26.** 942.94×3.184 **27.** $842.4 - 294.31$ **28.** 739.12×423.9

Round each number to the nearest: (a) hundredth (b) tenth (c) thousandth

29. 23.3825   **30.** 312.5504   **31.** 19.0096   **32.** 99.9999

33. 0.0464   **34.** 81.8181   **35.** 43.4343   **36.** 67.6767

37. Your astronomy club wants to buy five different eyepieces for a new telescope. The 6-, 12-, and 20-millimeter lenses cost $42.95 each, and the 32- and 40-millimeter lenses cost $58.95 each. Estimate the total cost of the lenses.

38. Social Studies A social service agency finds that, on the average, 2.87 of every 100 families need help from the agency. About how many families can they expect to help in a town of 966 families?

PRACTICE 3-2

39. **Test Prep** Which would give the best estimate for 483.64×29.78?

   Ⓐ 483×29 Ⓑ 484×30 Ⓒ 400×30 Ⓓ 500×25

40. **Career** A tailor needs three pieces of fabric, 1.67 yards long, 1.5 yards long, and 1.25 yards long. Estimate how many yards of material he should buy.

41. **Science** *Voyager 2* travels at an average speed of about 466.73 million km per year. About how many years would it take to get to each planet in the table?

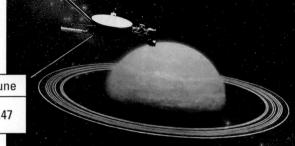

Planet	Mars	Jupiter	Saturn	Neptune
Distance from Earth (million km)	78.34	628.73	1277.38	4346.47

Problem Solving and Reasoning

42. **Choose a Strategy** Measured on a map with a scale of 150 miles per inch, the distance from Chicago to New York is 4.75 inches. How could you use estimation to find out about how many miles it is from Chicago to New York?

43. **Critical Thinking** An Internet service provider charges $2 per hour of use. A customer called to say that she used the Internet for 1 hour and 1 minute and was charged $4. Her friend, who uses the same Internet service provider, used the Internet for 1 hour and 50 minutes and was also charged $4. How do you think the charge was calculated? Give a more fair way to charge each user.

44. **Journal** Describe a situation where estimation could be used by a group of friends in a restaurant.

Problem Solving
STRATEGIES

- Look for a Pattern
- Make an Organized List
- Make a Table
- Guess and Check
- Work Backward
- Use Logical Reasoning
- Draw a Diagram
- Solve a Simpler Problem

Mixed Review

Make a line graph for each set of data. *[Lesson 1-5]*

45.

Year	1987	1988	1989	1990	1991
Profit ($)	3248	4165	4421	4230	4684

46.

Year	1975	1980	1985	1990	1995
Number	230	325	460	435	390

Solve each equation. *[Lesson 2-6]*

47. $x - 7 = 15$ **48.** $u + 19 = 34$ **49.** $125 = m - 72$ **50.** $365 = h + 148$

51. $y + 12 = 15$ **52.** $16 + u = 23$ **53.** $45 = n - 10$ **54.** $145 = p + 76$

Problem Solving: Sums and Differences of Decimals

▶ **Lesson Link** | You have solved addition and subtraction equations with whole numbers. Now you'll see how to solve addition and subtraction equations that contain decimals. ◄

Explore | Sums and Differences of Decimals

A Different Walk

Astronaut Mark Lee took part in an "extra-vehicular activity" (EVA) during a 1994 mission of the space shuttle *Discovery*. He wore a propulsion module to "walk" in space 200 miles above the earth.

The propulsion module is stored in an airlock unit aboard the shuttle.

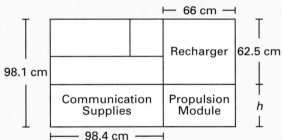

EVA Storage Unit
Total Weight Not to Exceed 177.43 kg

66 cm

Recharger 62.5 cm

98.1 cm

Communication Supplies | Propulsion Module

h

98.4 cm

1. Find the length of the EVA propulsion module in storage. How did you get your answer?

2. Let *h* equal the height of the module. Write an addition equation that you can use to find *h*.

3. Find the height of the module. How did you get your answer?

4. The combined weight of the stored items other than the propulsion module is 139.83 kg. Let *w* equal the maximum weight of the propulsion module. Write a subtraction equation that you can use to find *w*.

5. Find the maximum weight of the propulsion module. How did you get your answer?

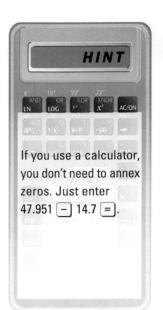

Learn | Sums and Differences of Decimals

To solve addition and subtraction equations that contain decimals, you need to add and subtract decimals.

ADDING AND SUBTRACTING DECIMALS

- Write the numbers with their decimal points lined up.
- Annex zeros as needed.
- Add or subtract the digits.
- Place the decimal point in the answer.

$$4.2 + 3.76$$

$$\begin{array}{r} 4.20 \\ + 3.76 \\ \hline 7.96 \end{array}$$

Place decimal point.

Solving decimal equations is very similar to solving whole-number equations. Remember to estimate before finding the exact solution and to check to see if your solution is reasonable.

Example 1

When Halley's comet is at its maximum distance from the sun, it is 25.72 AU (astronomical units) farther from the sun than Saturn is. Saturn's distance from the sun is 9.55 AU. Find the maximum distance of Halley's comet from the sun.

Let x = Halley's Comet's maximum distance.

Choose a variable.

Saturn's distance plus 25.72 AU equals maximum distance.

Describe the situation.

$$9.55 + 25.72 = x$$

Write an equation.

$$\begin{array}{r} \overset{1}{1}9.55 \\ +25.72 \\ \hline 35.27 \end{array}$$

Estimate: $10 + 26 = 36$

Add the digits and place the decimal point.

$$35.27 = x$$

The estimate was 36, so the solution is reasonable.

Halley's comet's maximum distance from the sun is 35.27 AU.

Try It

Solve. **a.** $x - 4.5 = 8.6$ **b.** $x + 16.05 = 37.4$

Shawon and Nedra are buying a birthday present for their mother that costs $42.95 . Nedra has $18.75 with her. How much money does Shawon have to come up with to get the present?

Shawon thinks ...

I'll let a = the amount I need.

My amount plus Nedra's amount equals the total cost.

$$a + 18.75 = 42.95$$

$$a + 18.75 - 18.75 = 42.95 - 18.75$$

$$
\begin{array}{r}
42.95 \\
- 18.75 \\
\hline
24.20
\end{array}
$$

$$a = 24.20$$

I need to add $24.20 to Nedra's amount to buy the present.

Nedra thinks ...

The amount Shawon has to come up with is the difference between the cost of the birthday present and the amount that I have with me. I'll represent the difference between 42.95 and 18.75 with the expression $42.95 - 18.75$.

Shawon needs to add $24.20 to my amount to buy the present.

$$
\begin{array}{r}
42.95 \\
- 18.75 \\
\hline
24.20
\end{array}
$$

Study TIP

When you add or subtract decimals, check your answer for reasonableness by using rounding to estimate the answer.

What do you think?

1. How are the two ways of finding the solution alike?

2. Would it have been helpful for Shawon and Nedra to estimate first?

Check | Your Understanding

1. Why do you line up decimal points when you add or subtract decimals?

2. How is solving a decimal equation like solving a whole-number equation?

Practice and Apply

1. **Getting Started** Follow the steps to find the difference between 42.4 and 42.268.

   a. Decide which of the two numbers is greater, and put it on top.

   b. Align the decimal points.

   c. Annex zeros.

   d. Subtract to find the difference.

Estimate each sum or difference.

2. $12.3 + 32.1$ **3.** $119.07 + 53.3$ **4.** $148 + 147.99$ **5.** $0.066 + 0.183 + 0.10$

6. $16.9 - 16.09$ **7.** $1.333 - 0.667$ **8.** $0.00882 - 0.00679$ **9.** $0.00726 + 0.00251$

10. $68.28 + 931.2$ **11.** $0.0386 - 0.003$ **12.** $634.2 - 428.34$ **13.** $0.049 + 0.134 + 0.082$

Solve each equation.

14. $121.4 + x = 437.734$ **15.** $x - 53.204 = 31.1$ **16.** $34.02 = x + 9.881$

17. $4.095 = x - 12.3$ **18.** $x + 0.047 = 0.176$ **19.** $0.0073 = x - 0.008367$

20. Science The formula that relates degrees Kelvin (K) to degrees Celsius (C) is $K = 273 + C$. Write and solve an equation to find the degrees Celsius for 384.9 K. Write and solve an equation to find the degrees Kelvin for 37.2°C.

21. **Test Prep** Which is the solution to the equation $13.5 = d + 5.027$?

    Ⓐ 8.473   Ⓑ 8.527   Ⓒ 13.5   Ⓓ 18.527

22. **Journal** Find the sum $0.2 + 0.07 + 0.08 + 0.1 + 0.01 + 0.3 + 0.2$ mentally. Explain the strategy you used to find your answer.

23. Sports In the 1995 National Football League regular-season games, the Dallas Cowboys averaged 27.1875 points, and the Miami Dolphins averaged 24.875 points. How many more points did the Cowboys average?

24. The top ten money-earning films of 1994 included *The Lion King*, at $298.88 million; *Forrest Gump*, at $298.10 million; and *The Santa Clause*, at $134.56 million. How much did these three films earn all together?

Forrest Gump

PRACTICE 3-3

Problem Solving and Reasoning

25. Critical Thinking Planetary probes have small engines that technicians on Earth can use to correct the path of a probe while it is traveling between planets. A probe to Jupiter started with 55.7 kg of fuel for its engine. The engine has been used three times. Use the table to calculate how much fuel has been used and how much is remaining.

Engine Firing	1	2	3
Fuel Used (kg)	12.87	9.3	11.22

26. Critical Thinking At a fruit stand, Green Valley apples are $0.75 each, Del-Ray apples are $0.85 each, and pears are $0.65 each. Kim buys one of each and pays with a $20 bill. The cash register has just broken. Write and solve an equation to help the clerk determine how much change he owes Kim.

27. Communicate In some cases it's wise to round a very small decimal value to 0, and in some cases it's not. For each of the following, tell whether you would round 0.001 to 0 and explain why or why not.

  a. $0.009 - 0.001 + 0.0007$

  b. $131.10085 + 143.9784 + 0.001 + 5.3534$

28. **Test Prep** Jennifer is following directions to Suki's house. The directions say, "At the corner of Route 9 and Bancroft, turn right and go exactly 4.8 miles on Bancroft. The driveway will be on your left." At the corner, Jennifer's odometer reads 47,253.8. What odometer reading should she watch for in order to find Suki's driveway?

  Ⓐ 8.6   Ⓑ 47,259.0   Ⓒ 47,244.8   Ⓓ 47,258.6

Mixed Review

Draw a scatterplot and trend line for each set of data. *[Lesson 1-6]*

29.

x	1	5	7	2	5	8	3	6
y	2	4	5	3	3	6	4	4

30.

x	6.4	3.2	7.1	9.1	4.3	8.1	2.9	8.3
y	4.2	7.1	3.9	1.8	5.5	2.7	7.0	2.6

Solve each equation. Check your solution. *[Lesson 2-7]*

31. $6v = 72$ **32.** $195 = x \cdot 16$ **33.** $7 = c \div 20$ **34.** $j \div 42 = 6$

35. $\frac{w}{5} = 12$ **36.** $211 = y \cdot 12$ **37.** $9 = \frac{d}{8}$ **38.** $23e = 368$

Problem Solving: Products and Quotients of Decimals

You'll Learn ...

■ to multiply and divide decimal numbers

■ to solve multiplication and division equations containing decimals

... How It's Used

Caterers must purchase food in large quantities. Because recipes and packages do not always use measures that are whole numbers, a caterer must be able to multiply and divide decimals.

▶ **Lesson Link** ☐ You've solved addition and subtraction equations containing decimals. Now you'll solve multiplication and division equations containing decimals. ◄

Explore | Products and Quotients of Decimals

Lighten Up!

Materials: Spreadsheet software

Objects on Venus weigh 0.9 times what they weigh on Earth. A space probe that weighs 9.4 pounds on Earth has landed on Venus.

	A	B
1		Venus
2	Pull of gravity	0.9
3	Probe weight on Earth	9.4
4	Probe weight on planet	

1. Set up your spreadsheet as shown. To find the weight of the probe on Venus, enter the formula "=B2*B3" into cell B4. How much does the probe weigh on Venus?

2. The table compares the force of gravity on other planets with that on Earth. Enter the planet names in row 1 and their gravity factors in row 2 of your spreadsheet. Then use the spreadsheet to calculate the weight on each planet of a probe that weighs 9.4 lb on Earth.

Body	Mars	Jupiter	Saturn	Neptune
Pull of Gravity	0.38	2.58	1.11	1.4

3. Without finding the answer, how can you tell whether a probe's weight on a planet will be greater or less than its Earth weight?

Learn | Products and Quotients of Decimals

You can use models to multiply decimals. The large square represents 1. Each row and column represents one-tenth of the large square, or 0.1. Each small square represents 0.01.

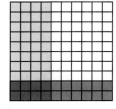

Each factor in 0.4×0.2 has 1 decimal place, but the product 0.08 has 2 places.

Example 1

A *year* is the time it takes a planet to orbit the sun. An Earth year lasts 365.3 days. A year on Mars is 1.88 times as long. Find the length of a year on Mars.

Let x = the length of a Martian year.   Choose a variable.

A Martian year is 1.88 times an Earth year.   Describe the situation.

$x = 1.88 \times 365.3$ Write an equation.

$$\begin{array}{r} 365.3 \\ \times\ 1.88 \\ \hline 29224 \\ 29224 \\ 3653 \\ \hline 686.764 \end{array}$$

365.3 1 decimal place
× 1.88 2 decimal places

Estimate: 2 × 400 = 800

686.764 . 3 decimal places

$x = 686.764$

The estimate was 800, so the solution is reasonable.

A Martian year is 686.764 Earth days.

Try It

Solve.   **a.** $x = 0.3 \times 5.391$ **b.** $x = 23.41 \times 6.5$

You can also use models to divide decimals. The model shows $0.3 \div 6$. Notice that if the decimal point is moved one place to the right in both the dividend (0.3) and the divisor (6), you get the same quotient ($3 \div 60 = 0.05$).

$$46.58 \div 7.2 \to 7.2\,\overline{)46.58}$$

$$72\,\overline{)465.8}$$

> **Problem Solving TIP**
>
> Because the problem asks you to find the length of a year on Mars, you should make the variable (x) equal to the length of a year on Mars. When you solve the equation, you will have the solution to the problem.

> **DID YOU KNOW?**
>
> The planet with the longest year is Pluto. You would have to wait 248.5 Earth years between birthdays if you lived on Pluto!

Examples

ESTIMATION

An estimate can help you with the placement of the decimal point.

2 Divide: $11.68 \div 0.8$

$$0.8\overline{)11.68}$$ | Estimate: $12 \div 1 = 12$ |

$$
\begin{array}{r}
14.6 \\
8\overline{)116.8} \\
\underline{8} \\
36 \\
\underline{32} \\
48 \\
\underline{48}
\end{array}
$$

The quotient is 14.6.

3 Divide: $16.51 \div 2.54$

$$2.54\overline{)16.51}$$ | Estimate: $18 \div 3 = 6$ |

$$
\begin{array}{r}
6.5 \\
254\overline{)1651} \\
\underline{1524} \\
1270 \\
\underline{1270}
\end{array}
$$

The quotient is 6.5.

Try It

Divide. **a.** $13.8 \div 0.4$ **b.** $9.966 \div 15.1$

Sometimes you need to multiply or divide by decimals to solve equations.

Example 4

DID YOU KNOW?

On August 20, 1960, two dogs named Strelka and Belka orbited Earth in a Russian satellite. One of their puppies was given to President Kennedy.

Use the formula $d = rt$ to find the time (t) it took a space probe that traveled at an average rate (r) of 2,342.36 mi/hr to go a distance (d) of 43,143.8 miles.

$43,143.8 = 2,342.36t$ Substitute the values for r and d.

$$\frac{43,143.8}{2,342.36} = \frac{2,342.36t}{2,342.36}$$ Undo multiplication by 2,342.36 by dividing by 2,342.36.

| Estimate: $40,000 \div 2000 = 20$ | 43143.8 $\boxed{\div}$ 2342.36 $\boxed{=}$ 18.418945

$18.418945 = t$

The estimate was 20, so the solution is reasonable.

The space probe took about 18.42 hours.

Try It

Solve. **a.** $3.4x = 32.21$ **b.** $\dfrac{n}{4.1} = 48.28$

Check   Your Understanding

1. Two decimals are both less than 1. How does their product compare with the numbers themselves? Explain.

2. How is dividing decimals like dividing whole numbers? How is it different?

Practice and Apply

1. **Getting Started** Follow these steps to solve $\frac{x}{9.1} = 4.2$.

   a. Round and estimate.

   b. Undo division by 9.1 by multiplying.

   c. Compare the answer to your estimate. Is it reasonable?

Estimate each product or quotient.

2. 2.3×32

3. 11.7×3.3

4. 2.47×3.5

5. 4.98×2.46

6. 37.2×2.6

7. $\frac{4.6}{2.3}$

8. $\frac{2.3}{4.6}$

9. $\frac{0.046}{0.0023}$

10. $\frac{0.0046}{0.023}$

11. $\frac{0.0023}{0.0046}$

12. 3.6×1.2

13. 3.6×0.12

14. 0.36×0.012

15. 0.036×0.12

16. 4.3×5.07

17. $\frac{8.47}{0.35}$

18. $\frac{0.36}{7.2}$

19. $\frac{2.42}{0.108}$

20. $\frac{36.18}{0.048}$

21. $\frac{0.0038}{0.0689}$

Solve each equation.

22. $0.12x = 0.432$

23. $5.06 = \frac{u}{0.092}$

24. $\frac{c}{1.23} = 14.568$

25. $4.785 = 1.7x$

26. $3.278s = 2.34$

27. $0.28 = \frac{a}{3.56}$

28. $45.3 = 4.7x$

29. $\frac{k}{12.67} = 0.04$

30. **Measurement** The formula $c = 2.54i$ relates the number of inches (i) and the number of centimeters (c). Find how many inches are in 15 centimeters.

31. **Test Prep** Juice boxes cost $3.89 for a six-pack. Which is the best estimate for the price of one juice box?

    Ⓐ $23.34   Ⓑ $0.65   Ⓒ $0.80   Ⓓ $1.54

32. **Science** The number of times a telescope magnifies an image is equal to its length divided by the focal length of the eyepiece. If a 0.996-m-long telescope has a 0.0125-m eyepiece, what is the telescope's magnification? How many decimal places are there in your answer? Do you think you need to describe the magnification to this number of decimal places? Explain.

Problem Solving and Reasoning

33. Communicate Ilse's mother commutes 41.7 miles every day. If her car averages 27.3 miles per gallon and gasoline costs $1.399 per gallon, how much are her gasoline costs for one 5-day work week? Explain how you found your answer.

34. Critical Thinking As part of her research in astronomy, Nava has been calculating the speed of travel of the moons in the solar system. Here is some of the data she has collected for some of the moons of Jupiter:

Copy and complete the table.

Moon	Io	Ganymede	Callisto
Orbital Radius (km × 1,000,000)	0.42		
Period (days)	1.77	7.15	16.69
Orbital Distance (radius × 6.28)		6.7196	11.8064
Speed ($\frac{distance}{period}$)		0.94	

Io, a moon of Jupiter

35. Critical Thinking Use inverse operations to solve $4.3w - 3.7 = 9.5$. Give a reason for each step.

Mixed Review

Find the value of each expression. *[Lesson 2-2]*

36. $43 + 15 \div 5$

37. $7 \times (84 - 32)$

38. $\dfrac{96 - 18 \times 3}{12 - (3 + 2)}$

39. $\dfrac{45 \div (8 - 3)}{2 \times 4 + 1}$

Solve each equation. Check your answer. *[Lesson 2-8]*

40. $3y + 7 = 28$

41. $12g - 13 = 71$

42. $8x - 17 = 63$

43. $339 = 23x + 17$

44. $\dfrac{k}{12} + 24 = 73$

45. $100 = \dfrac{w}{7} - 18$

46. $\dfrac{x}{4} - 3 = 32$

47. $\dfrac{c}{17} + 39 = 57$

Project Progress

Draw a picture or diagram of one set of animal parents (the *first* generation). Do library research to find out how many babies this pair might have at one time (the *second* generation). Indicate the number of babies on your picture.

Problem Solving

Understand
Plan
Solve
Look Back

PROBLEM SOLVING 3-4

Powers of 10 and Scientific Notation

▶ **Lesson Link** You've seen that some numbers are too large to be written down easily. Now you'll use a method created by scientists that makes it easier to write and work with very large numbers. ◀

You'll Learn …

■ to use exponents to write powers of 10

■ to write large numbers in scientific notation

… How It's Used

Scientific notation helps scientists write and calculate with huge numbers that are involved in distances and speeds related to space.

Explore Expressing Numbers as Powers of 10

Table for 10

Materials: Scientific or graphing calculator

1. Copy and complete the table.

Multiply	10	10 · 10	10 · 10 · 10	10 · 10 · 10 · 10	10 · 10 · 10 · 10 · 10
Result	10	100			
No. of 0s	1	2			

Study the patterns in the table. Then answer the following questions.

2. How is the number of zeros related to the number of 10s multiplied?

3. How many times must you multiply 10 by itself to get 100,000,000,000,000,000,000,000?

Now use the patterns in the first two columns to complete this table.

2 × 100	7.2 × 10,000	3.5 × 1000		36.8 × 1,000,000,000
200	72,000		4,800,000	

4. How does your calculator display the result in the last column?

Vocabulary

exponent

base

power

standard form

scientific notation

Learn Powers of 10 and Scientific Notation

A number like 1000 can be written as $10 \times 10 \times 10$. When factors are repeated, you can use an **exponent** and a **base**. You can write $10 \times 10 \times 10$ as 10^3 because there are three 10s multiplied together. The product (1000) is called a **power** of 10. 10, 100, and 10,000 are also powers of 10.

3 factors

$10 \times 10 \times 10$

$= 10^3$ Exponent

Base

Example 1

Evaluate 3^5.

$3^5 = 3 \cdot 3 \cdot 3 \cdot 3 \cdot 3$ Use the meaning of an exponent.

$\quad = 243$ Multiply.

You can multiply a decimal or a whole number by a power of 10 simply by moving the decimal point. A calculator or pencil-and-paper calculation will show that $3.2 \times 10,000 = 32,000$.

If you annex zeros, you can see that the decimal point in 32,000.0 is four places to the right of the decimal point in 3.20000.

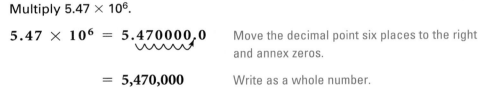

If 10,000 is written as 10^4, you can see that the exponent (4) tells you the number of places to the right to move the decimal point.

Example 2

Multiply 5.47×10^6.

$5.47 \times 10^6 = 5.470000{,}0$ Move the decimal point six places to the right and annex zeros.

$\quad = 5,470,000$ Write as a whole number.

Scientists use an understanding of powers of 10 to help them write very large numbers.

The numbers you have used so far have been written in **standard form**. The number 88,000 is written in standard form.

88,000 can be expressed many ways using powers of 10.

$8,800 \times 10$ $\qquad\qquad$ 880×100, or 880×10^2

88×1000, or 88×10^3 $\qquad$ $8.8 \times 10,000$, or 8.8×10^4

The last notation, 8.8×10^4, is called **scientific notation**. Scientific notation is a way of writing large numbers. A number written in scientific notation has three parts:

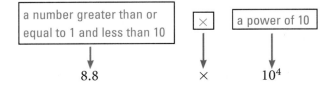

To write a number in scientific notation, count how many places you must move the decimal point to get a number greater than or equal to 1 and less than 10. The number of places you move the decimal point is the power of 10.

$$24,000.0 = 24,000.0$$

4 places, 2.4 is between 1 and 10.

$$2.4000.0 \times 10^4$$

Examples

3 The average distance of Jupiter's moon Callisto from Jupiter is 1,880,000 km. Write the distance in scientific notation.

$$1,880,000.0 \longrightarrow 1.88 \times 10^6 \longleftarrow \text{number of places decimal point moved}$$

Check: $1.88 \times 10^6 = 1.88 \times 1,000,000 = 1,880,000$

The distance in scientific notation is 1.88×10^6 km.

4 The total number of cars, trucks, and buses in the world in 1992 was about 6.13×10^8. Write the number in standard form.

Reverse the procedure you use to write a number in scientific notation.

$6.13 \times 10^8 \longleftarrow$ number of places *to move* the decimal point to the right

$$6.13000000.0 \Big\} \longrightarrow 613,000,000$$
8 places right

The number of vehicles was about 613,000,000, or 613 million.

> ► **Science Link**
>
> Astronomers have so far discovered 16 moons of Jupiter, ranging in size from the tiny Leda, with a diameter of 16 km, to the giant Ganymede, which is 5,260 km across. Four of Jupiter's moons are larger than the planet Pluto.

Galileo's observations of Jupiter's moons.

Try It

Write in scientific notation.   **a.** 31,700,000,000   **b.** 9,600.5

Write in standard form.   **c.** 4.1×10^5 **d.** 2.894×10^{12}

Check Your Understanding

1. What advantages does scientific notation have over standard notation?

2. Is 52.6×10^4 written in scientific notation? Is 1×10? Explain both answers.

Practice and Apply

1. [Getting Started] Follow these steps to write 16,120,000 in scientific notation.

    a. Move the decimal point to the left until it is between the first two digits.

    b. Count how many spaces the decimal point moved.

    c. Use that number as the exponent of 10. $16{,}120{,}000 = \underline{\hspace{1cm}} \times 10\text{---}$

Evaluate.

2. 2^3 **3.** 3^2 **4.** 5^3 **5.** 10^4 **6.** 2^6

Write each number in scientific notation.

7. 9,370,000,000   **8.** 8,500   **9.** 175   **10.** 93,000

11. 1,010,000,000   **12.** 10,100,000   **13.** 36,540,000   **14.** 384,200

15. 990,000,000,000,000,000   **16.** 96,500   **17.** 243,000,000   **18.** 439,300,000

19. [Test Prep] In scientific notation, 40,240,000,000 is written:

    Ⓐ 40.240×10^6 Ⓑ 40.240×10^9 Ⓒ 4.024×10^{10} Ⓓ 4.024×10^{11}

Write each number in standard form.

20. 8×10^6 **21.** 6×10^8 **22.** 5.2×10^8 **23.** 1.2×10^{12}

24. 1.35×10^2 **25.** 4.98×10^5 **26.** 2.368×10^{10} **27.** 5.69×10^6

28. Science The illustration shows the masses of the nine planets in the solar system in kilograms. List their masses in order from least to greatest.

Mars 6.42×10^{23}

Venus 4.87×10^{24}

Neptune 1.02×10^{26}

Mercury 3.30×10^{23}

Earth 5.98×10^{24}

Jupiter 1.90×10^{27}

Saturn 5.69×10^{26}

Uranus 8.69×10^{25}

Pluto 1.32×10^{22}

PRACTICE 3-5

29. Social Studies In 1994, the U.S. national debt (the amount of money owed by the U.S. government) was 4.721 trillion dollars. There were 260 million people in the country. Use your calculator to determine how much money each person in the U.S. would have had to contribute that year to pay off the national debt.

30. Patterns How many zeros are there in a billion? In 10^{10}? In 10^{20}? In 10^{100}?

Problem Solving and Reasoning

31. Literature In 1994, about 2,274,400,000 books were sold in the United States. Express this number in scientific notation.

32. Critical Thinking Use your calculator to divide 2.50×10^{14} by 1.25×10^{14}. Explain why the result is not in scientific notation.

33. Social Studies During the 1994–1995 school year, there were about 43.9 million students in United States public schools. States spent a total of 239.1 billion dollars on these schools. What was the average spent per pupil? Round your answer to the nearest dollar.

34. Communicate Large corporations and countries keep track of budgets that total billions or even trillions of dollars, but they never use scientific notation to express these numbers. Explain when and why scientific notation is not useful to express some very large numbers.

35. Choose a Strategy In a laboratory experiment, two colonies of bacteria are being observed. One is growing at the rate of 1.5×10^5 bacteria per half-hour. The other is growing at the rate of 3.2×10^5 bacteria per hour. Which is growing faster? How do you know?

36. Critical Thinking Describe how you can add two numbers that are in scientific notation. Consider the case where the exponents are the same and the case where the exponents are different.

Problem Solving
STRATEGIES

- Look for a Pattern
- Make an Organized List
- Make a Table
- Guess and Check
- Work Backward
- Use Logical Reasoning
- Draw a Diagram
- Solve a Simpler Problem

Mixed Review

Give the inverse of each action. [Lesson 2-4]

37. Add 5

38. Multiply by 7

39. Stand up

40. Go up 4 steps

Estimate, then find the exact sum. [Lesson 3-3]

41. 4.23 + 7.821

42. 8.471 + 3.196

43. 3.645 + 2.946

44. 3.4 + 0.34 + 0.034

45. 14.7 + 93.74

46. 5.23 + 4.2 + 0.039

47. 3.856 + 84.28

48. 4.8943 + 3.541

TECHNOLOGY

Using a Scientific Calculator • Scientific Notation

Problem: What is the product of 106,000,000,000,000 and 22,220,000,000,000,000?

You can use your scientific calculator's built-in exponential notation key to help simplify this problem.

1 **Express each number in scientific notation as shown:**
$106{,}000{,}000{,}000{,}000 = 1.06 \cdot 10^{14}$
$22{,}220{,}000{,}000{,}000{,}000 = 2.222 \cdot 10^{16}$

2 **Enter the first number into your scientific calculator as** [1] [.] [0] [6] [EE] [1] [4]. **Press the** [×] **key, then enter the second number as** [2] [.] [2] [2] [2] [EE] [1] [6]. **(Note: Your calculator may use** [E] **instead of** [EE].**)**

3 **Press the** [=] **key to find the product.**

Solution: The product of 106,000,000,000,000 and 22,220,000,000,000,000 is 2.35532×10^{30}, which equals 2,355,320,000,000,000,000,000,000,000,000.

TRY IT

a. What is the sum of 345,901,120,000 and 111,111,234,000,000?

b. What is the quotient of 145,124,000,000,000,000 and 4,000,000,000,000?

ON YOUR OWN

▶ When you enter a large number into your calculator, why is it sometimes necessary to express the number in scientific notation?

▶ If your calculator gives an answer that uses an exponent, how can you change it to standard notation?

▶ Are there some very large numbers that you could not enter into a scientific calculator? If so, explain why and give an example. If not, explain why not.

Section 3A Connect

You've seen how decimals can be used to better understand the solar system. Now you'll use decimals to describe a planet.

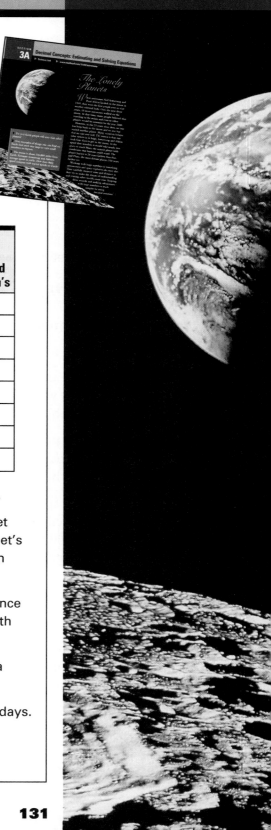

The Lonely Planets

1. Column 2 shows how the mass of each planet compares with Earth's. Order the masses from least to greatest.

Planet	Mass Compared with Earth's	Distance from Sun (mi)	Distance from Sun Compared with Earth's	Day (hr)	Length of Year Compared with Earth's
Mercury	0.0553	3.59×10^7	0.39	1407.6	0.24
Venus	0.8150	6.72×10^7	0.72	5832.2	0.62
Mars	0.1074	1.42×10^8	1.53	24.6	1.88
Jupiter	317.89	4.84×10^8	5.21	9.9	11.86
Saturn	95.18	8.87×10^8	9.55	10.7	29.46
Uranus	14.54	1.78×10^9	19.20	17.2	84.01
Neptune	17.15	2.79×10^9	30.10	16.1	164.76
Pluto	0.002	3.67×10^9	39.46	153.3	247.65

Choose a planet. Use data on your planet to answer these questions.

2. Write your planet's distance from the sun in standard notation. Let d = Earth's average distance from the sun. Use data on your planet's distance from the sun (columns 3–4) to write an equation you can solve to find Earth's distance from the sun.

3. Solve the equation you wrote in Question 2. What is Earth's distance from the sun to the nearest million miles? Write the answer in both standard and scientific notation.

4. Earth's *rotation* period is 23.9 hr. How much longer or shorter is a "day" on your planet than it is on Earth?

5. Earth's *revolution* period—the length of one Earth year—is 365.3 days. How long is your planet's year in Earth days?

6. Write a paragraph that compares your planet with Earth.

Section 3A Review

Compare using <, >, or =.

1. a. $9.501 \, \square \, 9.5$ **b.** $0.067 \, \square \, 0.670$ **c.** $756.38 \, \square \, 756.380$

2. Round to the underlined place value.   **a.** 10.6$\underline{7}$4   **b.** 5.$\underline{8}$19   **c.** 56.09$\underline{8}$6

Estimate.

3. 23×3.2 **4.** $153.3 - 9.07$ **5.** $13.34 + 32.01 + 36.8$ **6.** 652.3×7.57

7. $\dfrac{5.6}{2.8}$ **8.** 5.52×4.91 **9.** $\dfrac{0.0038}{0.019}$ **10.** $37.48 - 29.93$

Solve each equation. Estimate the solution first.

11. $\dfrac{x}{3.2} = 2.8$ **12.** $x - 23.5 = 17.3$ **13.** $3.24x = 15.86$ **14.** $15.76 + x = 23.89$

15. Write in scientific notation.   **a.** $12{,}100$ **b.** $5{,}206{,}000$ **c.** $4{,}860{,}000{,}000$

16. Write in standard form.   **a.** 5×10^3 **b.** 7×10^5 **c.** 7.2×10^7 **d.** 1.6×10^{14}

17. **Journal** Describe the way you can use rounding and estimation of decimals when shopping for groceries to decide which items have the best value.

18. Science A space probe can carry 50 lb of scientific instruments on its journey. Can 72 identical instruments, each weighing 6.75 oz, be carried? Explain. (Hint: 1 lb = 16 oz.)

19. Consumer After spending the morning shopping, Joe has $14.37 left. He needs $2.65 bus fare to get home, and he needs to keep $5.00 to pay back a debt. About how much can he afford to spend on lunch?

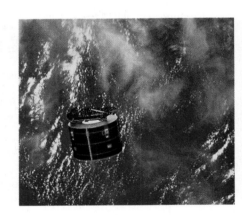

Test Prep

On a multiple choice test, when you are asked to find the answer to a decimal calculation or the solution to a decimal equation, a reasonable estimate can often help you eliminate some choices right away.

20. Find the sum of 3.89, 72.076, and 2.6.
- (A) 0.78566
- (B) 7.8566
- (C) 78.566
- (D) 785.66

21. Find the difference of 97.24 and 1.308.
- (A) 9.5932
- (B) 84.16
- (C) 95.932
- (D) 971.092

REVIEW 3A

One,
Two,
Three ...
Play!

Music and mathematics are closely related. For example, music travels as sound "waves" in the air. The pitch of a musical note depends on the number of waves per second.

Music also involves fractions. Fractions determine the notes of a musical scale, a fact discovered some 2500 years ago by the Greek mathematician Pythagoras. Fractions help musicians keep time, too. Knowing how long a "whole" note should last, the players can determine the length of a "half" note, a "quarter" note, and so on. This allows them to play together as a group.

Some modern music is based almost entirely on mathematics. The Austrian composer Arnold Schönberg (1874–1951) wrote complete pieces using sets of 12-note musical phrases that changed continually according to strict mathematical rules.

Today, computers can replace musicians altogether, using electronically produced digital sounds.

1 How many "eighth" notes would it take to equal a "half" note? Explain how you decided.

2 Give examples of the importance of mathematics to other arts such as theater, writing, dance, or painting.

Divisibility and Prime Factorization

▶ **Lesson Link**   You've divided with whole numbers. Now you'll see how to tell whether there is a remainder when one whole number is divided by another. ◀

Explore   Factoring and Prime Numbers

Materials: 36 small objects

Row, Row, Row Your Band

Mrs. Buchanan is planning marching routines for the school band. The band might have 30 to 36 members. Band members can march in any number of rows as long as each row has the same number of members.

1. Use the objects to figure out how many arrangements there are for each number of members from 30 to 36. Show your results in a table like the one started here.

Number of Members	30	30
Members per Row	1	2
Number of Rows	30	15

2. What number of members gives the most possible arrangements? The fewest? What do you notice about numbers that give many arrangements? Few arrangements?

3. Describe patterns that will help you predict whether arrangements of 2, 3, and 6 members per row are possible for other sizes of bands.

Learn   Divisibility and Prime Factorization

A music store window displayed 12 trumpets in groups of 4. We say that 12 is **divisible** by 4 because 12 can be divided into groups of 4 with no remainder. 12 is also divisible by 6. We say that 4 and 6 are **factors** of 12 because 12 is divisible by 4 and 6.

$$12 \div 4 = 3 \qquad 12 \div 6 = 2$$

Five is not a factor of 12 because $12 \div 5$ equals 2 with a remainder of 2.

Example 1

Give the ways 8 students can be divided into groups of the same size.

Divide 8 by each number from 1 to 8. Look for quotients with remainders of zero.

$8 \div 1 = 8$, remainder 0 $8 \div 5 = 1$, remainder 3

$8 \div 2 = 4$, remainder 0 $8 \div 6 = 1$, remainder 2

$8 \div 3 = 2$, remainder 2 $8 \div 7 = 1$, remainder 1

$8 \div 4 = 2$, remainder 0 $8 \div 8 = 1$, remainder 0

Eight students can be divided into groups of 1, 2, 4, and 8.

You can use divisibility rules to help you find the factors of a number.

DIVISIBILITY RULES

A number is divisible by
- 2 if the ones digit is 0, 2, 4, 6, or 8.
- 3 if the sum of the digits is divisible by 3.
- 4 if the number formed by the last two digits is divisible by 4.
- 5 if the ones digit is 0 or 5.
- 6 if the number is divisible by both 2 and 3.
- 8 if the number formed by the last three digits is divisible by 8.
- 9 if the sum of the digits is divisible by 9.
- 10 if the ones digit is 0.

DID YOU KNOW?

You can use the divisibility rule for 4 to check which years are leap years.

Example 2

Test the number 4320 for divisibility by 2, 3, 4, 5, 6, 8, 9, and 10.

2?   Yes   The last digit is 0.

3?   Yes $4 + 3 + 2 + 0 = 9$, which is divisible by 3.

4?   Yes   The number formed by the last two digits (20) is divisible by 4.

5?   Yes   4320 ends in 0.

6?   Yes   4320 is divisible by both 2 and 3.

8?   Yes   The number formed by the last three digits (320) is divisible by 8.

9?   Yes $4 + 3 + 2 + 0 = 9$, which is divisible by 9.

10?   Yes   The ones digit is 0.

4320 is divisible by 2, 3, 4, 5, 6, 8, 9, and 10.

Try It

Check each number for divisibility by 2, 3, 4, 5, 6, 8, 9, and 10.

a. 84   **b.** 845   **c.** 128   **d.** 162

A **prime number** is a whole number greater than 1 that has exactly two factors, 1 and itself. Seven is a prime number because its only factors are 1 and 7.

A **composite number** is a whole number greater than 1 that has more than two factors. Fifteen is a composite number.

Composite

$12 = 1 \cdot 12$
$2 \cdot 6$
$3 \cdot 4$
6 factors

Prime

$11 = 1 \cdot 11$
2 factors

When you write a composite number as a product of prime numbers, the product is called the **prime factorization** of the composite number. The prime factorization of 18 is $2 \times 3 \times 3$. You should use exponents to write repeated factors, so $2 \times 3 \times 3$ is written 2×3^2.

Example 3

Write the prime factorization of 84.

You can use a **factor tree** to find a prime factorization. At each "branch," find factors using divisibility rules. You'll get the same prime factorization no matter which factor you begin with.

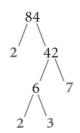

84 is divisible by 2, 3, 4, and 6. Choose one to start.

84 is divisible by 2: $84 \div 2 = 42$.

42 is divisible by 6: $42 \div 6 = 7$.

6 is divisible by 3: $6 \div 3 = 2$.

The "leaves" at the ends of the branches give the prime factorization $2 \times 2 \times 3 \times 7$. Use exponents to write this as $2^2 \times 3 \times 7$.

The prime factorization of 84 is $2^2 \times 3 \times 7$.

Try It

Find the prime factorization of each number.

a. 124   **b.** 63   **c.** 308   **d.** 102

Check | Your Understanding

1. What is the prime factorization of a prime number?

2. Give the difference between a prime number and a composite number.

3. How can you find a number if you know its prime factorization?

Practice and Apply

Getting Started Is the first number divisible by the second number?

1. 571; 2   **2.** 3560; 5   **3.** 8394; 3   **4.** 6737; 4

5. 675; 9   **6.** 558; 6   **7.** 82240; 8   **8.** 5605; 10

Test each number for divisibility by 2, 3, 4, 5, 6, 8, 9, and 10.

9. 291   **10.** 582   **11.** 585   **12.** 592

13. 5920   **14.** 5921   **15.** 5922   **16.** 5925

Determine whether each of these numbers is composite or prime.

17. 63   **18.** 89   **19.** 116   **20.** 201

21. 152   **22.** 167   **23.** 323   **24.** 153

Use factor trees to find the prime factorizations of the following numbers. Use exponents to write repeated factors.

25. 18   **26.** 180   **27.** 185   **28.** 285

29. 360   **30.** 864   **31.** 1125   **32.** 1512

33. **Test Prep** Which of these numbers is *not* a prime factor of 168?

     Ⓐ 2   Ⓑ 3   Ⓒ 4   Ⓓ 7

34. The longest pipe in many pipe organs is 32 feet long. Find the prime factorization of 32. Use exponents to write repeated factors.

35. **Science** Eva is analyzing a radio wave. She finds that the waveform repeats every 378 seconds. What other, shorter periods of waveforms divide evenly into 378 seconds?

36. **Number Sense** Find the prime numbers that are less than 30.

37. Find a number between 60 and 90 that has exactly two prime factors.

38. **Test Prep** Satu is evaluating bottle racks for use in a packing plant. The number of bottles in the rack must be divisible by both 6 and 4. Which of the following rack capacities can she use?

     Ⓐ 120   Ⓑ 126   Ⓒ 148   Ⓓ 164

PRACTICE 3-6

Problem Solving and Reasoning

39. Critical Thinking Raoul is building a fish tank. He wants it to hold 12 liters (12,000 mL) of water. The formula $V = lwh$ tells the volume (V) in milliliters of a tank with length (l), width (w), and height (h) in centimeters. He wants the length, width, and height to be whole numbers.

a. List three sets of dimensions that will result in a 12,000 mL tank.

b. Which shape do you think requires the most glass?

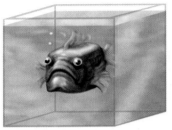

40. Choose a Strategy Suggest one way a computer program that tests whether or not large numbers are prime might work.

41.  Describe how you can find more than one factor tree for some composite numbers. Will the prime factorization be the same? Give an example.

42. Critical Thinking There are 248 different cards in a fantasy card game. Laura stores her cards in 9-card plastic sheets. Will the last sheet be completely full? Explain how you found the answer.

43. Critical Thinking The number 1,758,289,141 is not divisible by 4. What is the smallest number larger than 1,758,289,141 that *is* divisible by 4? How did you find this number?

> **Problem Solving**
> ### STRATEGIES
> • Look for a Pattern
> • Make an Organized List
> • Make a Table
> • Guess and Check
> • Work Backward
> • Use Logical Reasoning
> • Draw a Diagram
> • Solve a Simpler Problem

Mixed Review

Make a stem-and-leaf diagram for each set of data. *[Lesson 1-3]*

44. 32, 43, 51, 32, 41, 53, 61, 39, 47

45. 17, 23, 31, 43, 15, 29, 41, 38, 26

46. 83, 79, 71, 74, 83, 74, 91, 73, 89

47. 95, 103, 87, 94, 99, 105, 117, 86

Compare using $<$, $>$, **or** $=$. *[Lesson 3-1]*

48. 1.9999 ☐ 1.999   **49.** 0.307 ☐ 0.0307   **50.** 12.345 ☐ 123.4   **51.** 2.709 ☐ 2.71

52. 2.08 ☐ 2.123   **53.** 195.5 ☐ 19.55   **54.** 4.55 ☐ 4.555   **55.** 0.064 ☐ 0.0064

GCF and LCM

▶ **Lesson Link**   You've looked at the factors of whole numbers. Now you'll find which of several factors common to two or more numbers is the greatest. You'll also find which of the multiples common to several numbers is the least. ◀

Explore   Greatest Common Factor

Marching in Prime Time

Materials: 42 small objects

The 12-member Phoenix Middle School marching band is marching in the Thanksgiving Day parade behind the 30-member Jacksonville Middle School marching band. The rows in both bands have to be the same width.

1. Use the objects to find the widest row that can be used by both bands.

2. Find the prime factorizations of 12 and 30 and list them one above the other. Line up equal factors (for example, 2 above 2, 3 above 3, and so on).

3. Using only the factors that are common to both numbers, suggest a rule you could use to find the row width you found in Step 1.

4. Test your rule using bands of 28 and 42 students.

Learn   GCF and LCM

Numbers often have *common factors*.

Factors of 42 = ☐1☐, ☐2☐, ☐3☐, ☐6☐, 7, 14, 21, 42

Factors of 12 = ☐1☐, ☐2☐, ☐3☐, 4, ☐6☐, 12

The common factors of 42 and 12 are **1, 2, 3**, and **6**. The **greatest common factor** (GCF) is **6.**

One way to find the GCF of two or more numbers is to list their common factors. The greatest of these is the GCF.

You'll Learn ...

■ to find the greatest common factor of a pair of numbers

■ to find the least common multiple of a pair of numbers

... How It's Used

Warehouse management involves using space efficiently. Using GCFs and LCMs can help the workers organize the stacks.

Vocabulary

greatest common factor (GCF)

common multiple

least common multiple (LCM)

Example 1

Find the GCF of 24 and 40.

Use divisibility rules to find factors of 24. Begin with 1 and 24. Divide each factor you find into 24 to get another factor.

Factor: 2   Think: $24 \div 2 = 12$, so 12 is also a factor.

Factor: 3   Think: $24 \div 3 = 8$, so 8 is also a factor.

Factor: 4   Think: $24 \div 4 = 6$, so 6 is also a factor.

Factors of 24: ☐1☐, ☐2☐, 3, ☐4☐, 6, ☐8☐, 12, 24

Factors of 40: ☐1☐, ☐2☐, ☐4☐, 5, ☐8☐, 10, 20, 40

The common factors are 1, 2, 4, and 8.

The *greatest* common factor (GCF) of 24 and 40 is 8.

▶ **Music Link**

The tuba plays very low notes, but it is not the lowest member of the orchestra. That honor falls to the piano, which also plays the highest notes.

When a musical instrument produces a note, you actually hear many notes at once. The note you hear most clearly is the *fundamental*. But you also hear notes called the *first overtone*, the *second overtone*, and so on. Each note is caused by a vibration, or sound wave.

Here are the prime factorizations of the second overtones of two tuba notes:

$212 = 2^2 \times 53$ $244 = 2^2 \times 61$

You can use prime factorizations to find the GCF. The GCF is the product of the common prime factors. The common prime factors are 2^2, so the GCF is $2^2 = 4$.

Example 2

Two wooden planks measuring 63 in. and 84 in. are to be cut into the longest possible shelves of equal length. How long will the shelves be?

Each plank can be cut into lengths that are factors of the total length. The greatest common factor is the longest common shelf length.

$63 = 3 \times \boxed{3} \times \boxed{7}$ Write the prime factorizations. Box the common
$84 = 2 \times 2 \times \boxed{3} \times \boxed{7}$ **prime factors.**

The GCF is $3 \times 7 = 21$. The shelves will be 21 in. long.

Try It

Find the GCF.   **a.** 18, 36   **b.** 144, 168   **c.** 78, 91   **d.** 20, 26

A *multiple* of a number is the product of the number and a whole number. The first five non-zero multiples of 5 are 5, 10, 15, 20, and 25.

$5 = 5 \cdot 1$ $10 = 5 \cdot 2$ $15 = 5 \cdot 3$ $20 = 5 \cdot 4$ $25 = 5 \cdot 5$

You've seen that numbers can have common factors. They also have **common multiples** . Listed below are some multiples of 4 and 6.

Multiples of 4: 4 (1 · 4), 8 (2 · 4), 12 (3 · 4), 16 (4 · 4), 20 (5 · 4), 24 (6 · 4)

Multiples of 6: 6 (1 · 6), 12 (2 · 6), 18 (3 · 6), 24 (4 · 6)

Common multiples of 4 and 6 include 12 and 24. The **least common multiple** (LCM) of 4 and 6 is 12.

One way to find the LCM of two or more numbers is to list their common multiples. The least of these is the LCM.

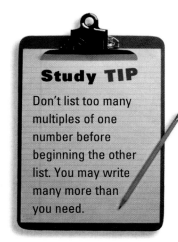
Examples

3 Find the LCM of 8 and 10.

	1 • 8	2 • 8	3 • 8	4 • 8	5 • 8	6 • 8	7 • 8
Multiples of 8:	8	16	24	32	40	48	56

	1 • 10	2 • 10	3 • 10	4 • 10	5 • 10
Multiples of 10:	10	20	30	40	50

The LCM is 40.

4 In one part of a musical composition, the triangle player in an orchestra plays once every 12 beats. The tympani player plays once every 9 beats. How often do they play together?

You need to find the LCM of 12 and 9.

	1 • 12	2 • 12	3 • 12
Multiples of 12:	12	24	36

	1 • 9	2 • 9	3 • 9	4 • 9
Multiples of 9:	9	18	27	36

The LCM of 12 and 9 is 36.

The triangle and tympani play together once every 36 beats.

▶ **Science Link**

We have a pair of *tympani* in our heads! Tympanic membrane is the name for an *eardrum.*

Try It

Find the LCM. **a.** 5, 15   **b.** 12, 16   **c.** 10, 12   **d.** 7, 9

1. Can the greatest common factor of two numbers be equal to one of the numbers? Explain.

2. What is the GCF of two different prime numbers? What is the LCM?

3-7 Exercises and Applications

Practice and Apply

1. **Getting Started** Follow these steps to find the GCF of 42 and 63.
   a. Find all of the factors of 42.
   b. Find all of the factors of 63.
   c. List the factors that 42 and 63 have in common.
   d. Find the greatest factor common to both numbers.

Find the GCF by listing all the factors of each number.

2. 54, 90   3. 84, 96   4. 125, 175   5. 323, 391

Find the GCF by writing the prime factorization of each number.

6. 54, 81   7. 432, 378   8. 24, 117   9. 405, 486

10. **Test Prep** The GCF of 198 and 220 is:
    Ⓐ 22   Ⓑ 11   Ⓒ 26   Ⓓ 4

Find the LCM of each pair of numbers.

11. 9, 15   12. 12, 20   13. 15, 20   14. 16, 24

15. 8, 14   16. 15, 24   17. 8, 30   18. 14, 24

19. **Pattern** A local restaurant is offering a free meal to every 25th customer and a free hat to every 12th customer. Which customer will be the first to get both a free meal and a free hat?

20. **Career** Bennie is catering a wedding and is putting finger food on plates. He has 72 cheese puffs and 48 carrot sticks. He wants both kinds of food on each plate. He wants to distribute the food evenly, and he doesn't want any left over. What is the largest number of plates he can use, and how many of each type of food should he put on each plate?

21. Music Aaron is composing music for a pair of synthesizers. One instrument's part contains 595 bars of music; the other contains 680 bars of music. What is the greatest number of bars of music that divides evenly into both instruments' parts?

22. ▮Test Prep▮ Find the LCM and the GCF of 18 and 27.

Ⓐ LCM: 108; GCF: 3   Ⓑ LCM: 54; GCF: 3

Ⓒ LCM: 108; GCF: 9   Ⓓ LCM: 54; GCF: 9

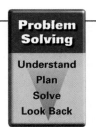

Problem Solving and Reasoning

23. Critical Thinking Give a method for finding the LCM of two numbers by using prime factorizations.

Critical Thinking For each number, find three pairs of numbers for which the given number is the GCF.

24. 9 **25.** 14 **26.** 7 **27.** 25

28. Communicate A and B are two different whole numbers. Their GCF is A. Their LCM is B. Which one is greater? Explain.

Mixed Review

Make a bar graph for each set of data. *[Lesson 1-2]*

29.

Color	Red	Blue	Green
Number	13	21	9

30.

Student	Ralph	Joan	Liz
Height (in.)	48	39	45

Estimate each product or quotient. *[Lesson 3-4]*

31. 23.4×7.81 **32.** $20.01 \div 8.7$ **33.** $6.73 \cdot 0.037$ **34.** $1.68 \div 0.35$

35. $\dfrac{639.9}{161.5}$ **36.** 281.19×29.42 **37.** $214.34 \div 2.45$ **38.** $0.048 \cdot 4.59$

▮ **Project Progress**

Use exponents to show how many animals can result from your original pair in the third through the eighth generation. (Assume each baby survives to find a mate, and that there are always equal numbers of males and females.) Make a poster that shows the growth in the population. Express large numbers in scientific notation.

Problem Solving

Understand
Plan
Solve
Look Back

Equivalent Fractions and Lowest Terms

▶ **Lesson Link**
You've learned to find the greatest common factor of two numbers. Now you'll use the GCF to write fractions that are equivalent. ◀

You'll Learn ...

■ to write equivalent fractions

■ to rewrite fractions in lowest terms

... How It's Used

Brokers sometimes use equivalent fractions to compare prices of stocks and bonds.

Vocabulary

fraction

numerator

denominator

equivalent

lowest terms

Explore Equivalent Fractions

Materials: Calculator

The Key to Fractions

When you strike a piano key, a string vibrates. The vibration produces the sound that you hear. Here are the names of 12 piano keys and their *frequencies*—the number of times their strings vibrate each second.

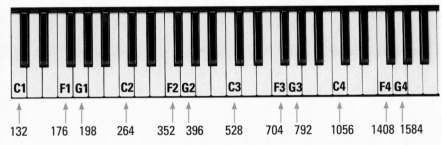

C1	F1	G1	C2	F2	G2	C3	F3	G3	C4	F4	G4
132	176	198	264	352	396	528	704	792	1056	1408	1584

1. Compare the frequency of C1 with C2, C2 with C3, and C3 with C4. What pattern do you find? How is each C-note related to the next one?

2. Repeat Question 1, comparing the F-notes. Repeat again, comparing the G-notes.

3. Compare C1 with F1, C2 with F2, and so on. What do you find?

4. Compare C1 with G1, C2 with G2, and so on. What do you find?

5. Make conjectures about the frequencies of C5, F5, and G5. Explain.

Learn Equivalent Fractions and Lowest Terms

$\frac{a}{b}$ where a and b are whole numbers and $b \neq 0$ is a **fraction** . $\frac{a}{b}$ means $a \div b$. The top number is the **numerator** . The bottom number is the **denominator** .

$$1 \div 4 = \frac{1}{4} \begin{array}{l} \leftarrow \text{numerator} \\ \leftarrow \text{denominator} \end{array}$$

If two fractions represent the same quantity, they are **equivalent** : $\frac{1}{4}$ and $\frac{2}{8}$ are equivalent.

$\frac{1}{4}$ $\frac{2}{8}$

You can use a calculator to decide if two fractions are equivalent.

$1 \; \boxed{\div} \; 4 \; \boxed{=} \; 0.25$

$2 \; \boxed{\div} \; 8 \; \boxed{=} \; 0.25$

$\frac{1}{4}$ and $\frac{2}{8}$ both equal 0.25, so they are equivalent.

You can create an equivalent fraction by multiplying or dividing the numerator and denominator of a fraction by the same number.

Example 1

Find two fractions equivalent to $\frac{12}{16}$.

Multiply or divide by any convenient numbers.

$\frac{12 \times 2}{16 \times 2} = \frac{24}{32}$ Multiply by 2. $\frac{12 \div 4}{16 \div 4} = \frac{3}{4}$ Divide by 4.

$\frac{24}{32}$ and $\frac{3}{4}$ are equivalent to $\frac{12}{16}$.

Try It

Find two equivalent fractions for each fraction. **a.** $\frac{6}{9}$ **b.** $\frac{25}{30}$ **c.** $\frac{10}{12}$ **d.** $\frac{15}{21}$

Test Prep

You may sometimes be asked to give a fraction in *simplest form*. Don't be confused! *Simplest form* means the same thing as *lowest terms*.

When 1 is the only common factor of the numerator and the denominator of a fraction, the fraction is in **lowest terms** . The fraction $\frac{10}{15}$ is not in lowest terms because 5 is a common factor of the numerator and the denominator.

$\frac{10}{15} = \frac{10 \div 5}{15 \div 5} = \frac{2}{3}$ 1 is the only common factor of 2 and 3.

You can rewrite a fraction in lowest terms by dividing the numerator and denominator by a common factor several times or by dividing the numerator and denominator by the GCF of both numbers to reach lowest terms in one step.

Example 2

Show that $\frac{8}{10}$ and $\frac{20}{25}$ are equivalent.

Two fractions that are the same in lowest terms are equivalent.

$\frac{8}{10} = \frac{8 \div 2}{10 \div 2} = \frac{4}{5}$ $\frac{20}{25} = \frac{20 \div 5}{25 \div 5} = \frac{4}{5}$

$\frac{8}{10}$ and $\frac{20}{25}$ both equal $\frac{4}{5}$ in lowest terms, so they are equivalent.

Try It

Decide whether the fractions are equivalent.

a. $\frac{3}{4}$ and $\frac{12}{15}$ **b.** $\frac{9}{10}$ and $\frac{19}{20}$ **c.** $\frac{10}{30}$ and $\frac{6}{18}$ **d.** $\frac{4}{14}$ and $\frac{6}{21}$

▶ **Language Link**

Look at the word *equivalent*. It tells you what it means: *equi-* always means "equal" and *valent* is related to the word *value*. So *equivalent* means "having equal value."

Of the 84 students in the school band, 24 play brass instruments. For an article for the school paper, Brett and Lorena want to know the fraction of band members who play brass instruments.

Brett thinks ...

I need to write $\frac{24}{84}$ in lowest terms.

$\frac{24 \div 2}{84 \div 2} = \frac{12}{42}$ Divide by 2.

$\frac{12 \div 2}{42 \div 2} = \frac{6}{21}$ Divide by 2 again.

$\frac{6 \div 3}{21 \div 3} = \frac{2}{7}$ Divide by 3.

The fraction is $\frac{2}{7}$.

Lorena thinks ...

I need to write $\frac{24}{84}$ in lowest terms. $24 = 2^3 \times 3$

$84 = 2^2 \times 3 \times 7$

The GCF of 24 and 84 is $2^2 \times 3 = 12$.

I'll divide by the GCF: $\frac{24 \div 12}{84 \div 12} = \frac{2}{7}$

The fraction is $\frac{2}{7}$.

What do you think?

1. When does Brett's method work well? When does Lorena's work well?

2. If you're using mental math, whose method is easier?

Check | Your Understanding

1. Is there any limit to the number of equivalent fractions one fraction can have? Explain.

2. The numerator of a fraction in lowest terms has 2 as a factor. Is 2 a factor of the denominator? Explain.

Practice and Apply

1. **Getting Started** Follow these steps to use the GCF to express $\frac{16}{24}$ in lowest terms.

   a. Find all of the factors of 16.

   b. Find all of the factors of 24.

   c. What is the GCF of 16 and 24?

   d. Divide the numerator and denominator by the GCF.

Find an equivalent fraction with (a) a smaller and (b) a larger denominator.

2. $\frac{20}{24}$ 3. $\frac{15}{27}$ 4. $\frac{6}{21}$ 5. $\frac{16}{22}$ 6. $\frac{8}{52}$

Express each fraction in lowest terms.

7. $\frac{54}{81}$ 8. $\frac{36}{68}$ 9. $\frac{28}{36}$ 10. $\frac{18}{76}$ 11. $\frac{32}{40}$ 12. $\frac{34}{52}$

13. $\frac{42}{63}$ 14. $\frac{21}{69}$ 15. $\frac{24}{32}$ 16. $\frac{36}{54}$ 17. $\frac{36}{48}$ 18. $\frac{25}{35}$

19. $\frac{60}{90}$ 20. $\frac{90}{108}$ 21. $\frac{14}{98}$ 22. $\frac{64}{144}$ 23. $\frac{117}{243}$ 24. $\frac{42}{77}$

25. $\frac{36}{50}$ 26. $\frac{60}{72}$ 27. $\frac{25}{110}$ 28. $\frac{128}{288}$ 29. $\frac{96}{212}$ 30. $\frac{144}{216}$

31. **Test Prep** Which one of the following fractions is not equivalent to the others?

   Ⓐ $\frac{24}{96}$ Ⓑ $\frac{8}{32}$ Ⓒ $\frac{25}{97}$ Ⓓ $\frac{23}{92}$

32. **Industry** A saxophone manufacturer made 800 saxophones last year. Of these, 720 passed final quality checks. What fraction of the saxophones passed final quality checks? An order for 20 saxophones came from a music store. How many of the next 20 saxophones made are likely to be "good"?

33. **Data** In 1864, 2,218,388 of the 4,031,887 votes in the U.S. presidential election went to Abraham Lincoln. About what fraction of the votes did Lincoln receive?

PRACTICE 3-8

34. Science Over her lifetime, a female green turtle lays an average of 1800 eggs. Of these, about 1395 do not hatch, about 374 young turtles quickly die, and only about 3 live long enough to breed. About what fraction of a green turtle's eggs survive to breed? Write your answer in lowest terms.

Problem Solving and Reasoning

Critical Thinking Fill in the missing number to make the fractions equivalent.

35. $\dfrac{14}{18} = \dfrac{x}{27}$ **36.** $\dfrac{72}{84} = \dfrac{x}{77}$ **37.** $\dfrac{51}{85} = \dfrac{45}{x}$ **38.** $\dfrac{48}{216} = \dfrac{26}{x}$

39. Choose a Strategy How would you rewrite $\dfrac{4352}{4608}$ in lowest terms if you did not have a calculator? What method would you use if you did have a calculator? Explain your answers. Try both methods and see how well they work.

40. Critical Thinking A batting average in softball or baseball is the number of hits divided by the number of times at bat. A batting average of .285 means that the batter would be expected to get a hit 285 times in 1000 at-bats. The fraction $\dfrac{285}{1000}$ can be used to represent a batting average of .285. Use equivalent fractions to help you complete the following table. Use a calculator to check your answers.

> **Problem Solving**
> ### STRATEGIES
> - Look for a Pattern
> - Make an Organized List
> - Make a Table
> - Guess and Check
> - Work Backward
> - Use Logical Reasoning
> - Draw a Diagram
> - Solve a Simpler Problem

	Maria	Sophie	Ja	Mia
Hits			24	18
Times at Bat	80	90		
Batting Average	.250	.300	.400	.200

Mixed Review

Solve each equation. Check your solutions. *[Lesson 2-7]*

41. $3t = 27$ **42.** $8j = 864$ **43.** $26 = 13x$ **44.** $162 = z \cdot 27$

45. $n \div 17 = 12$ **46.** $31 = \dfrac{s}{8}$ **47.** $y \div 51 = 8$ **48.** $\dfrac{b}{50} = 374$

Use rounding to whole numbers to estimate. *[Lesson 3-2]*

49. $23.7 + 6.872$ **50.** $64.3 - 2.41$ **51.** 46.62×9.63 **52.** $\dfrac{55.86318}{7.236751}$

53. $14.45 + 72.5$ **54.** $179.734 - 22.176$ **55.** $7.13 \cdot 8.449$

Comparing and Ordering Fractions

▶ **Lesson Link** | You have learned how to decide whether two fractions are equivalent. Now you'll learn how to order a set of fractions that are not equivalent. ◀

Explore | Comparing Fractions

As Time Goes By

Materials: Graph paper

| Whole note | Half note | Quarter note | Eighth note | Sixteenth note | Thirty-second note |

A written musical note tells you the length of time the note should be played. If a "whole" note lasts 4 beats, then a "half" note lasts 2 beats, a "quarter" note lasts 1 beat, and so on.

1. Write each of the following notes or sets of notes as a fraction.

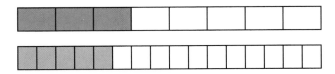

2. Using graph paper, model each of the fractions in Step 1. Let an 8 × 8 square (64 squares) represent a whole note.

3. Order the fractions from least to greatest. Explain your method.

You'll Learn ...

■ to compare the values of fractions

■ to order fractions

... How It's Used

Mechanics need large collections of socket wrenches. It is much easier to find the right wrench for a job if they are organized by size.

Vocabulary

common denominator

Learn | Comparing and Ordering Fractions

There are many ways to compare fractions. One way is to use a model.

The first model represents $\frac{3}{8}$. The second represents $\frac{5}{16}$. By visually comparing lengths, we can see that $\frac{5}{16}$ is less than $\frac{3}{8}$.

Example 1

Martin is building a recorder. He needs to choose the smaller of two drill bits measuring $\frac{3}{4}$ in. and $\frac{5}{8}$ in. Which bit should he choose?

You can use a model to compare fourths and eighths. Since $\frac{5}{8} < \frac{3}{4}$, Martin should choose the $\frac{5}{8}$ in. bit.

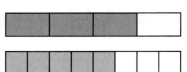

If two fractions have the same denominator, the one with the larger numerator is greater.

$$\frac{8}{11} > \frac{7}{11}$$

Fractions with the same denominator are said to have a **common denominator**. If the denominators are different, you can still compare the fractions by making equivalent fractions that have a common denominator.

Examples

2 Compare $\frac{2}{3}$ and $\frac{11}{18}$.

Look at the denominators. You know that 18 is a multiple of 3. Since $3 \cdot 6 = 18$, change $\frac{2}{3}$ to an equivalent fraction with a denominator of 18.

$$\frac{2}{3} = \frac{2 \times 6}{3 \times 6} = \frac{12}{18}$$ Multiply the numerator and the denominator by 6.

$$\frac{12}{18} > \frac{11}{18}, \text{ so } \frac{2}{3} > \frac{11}{18}.$$

3 Compare $\frac{5}{6}$ and $\frac{3}{4}$.

You can get equivalent fractions with a common denominator by multiplying the numerator and denominator of each fraction by the denominator of the other.

$$\frac{5}{6} = \frac{5 \times 4}{6 \times 4} = \frac{20}{24}$$ Multiply by 4, the denominator of $\frac{3}{4}$.

$$\frac{3}{4} = \frac{3 \times 6}{4 \times 6} = \frac{18}{24}$$ Multiply by 6, the denominator of $\frac{5}{6}$.

Using a common denominator of 24, you can see that $\frac{20}{24} > \frac{18}{24}$, so $\frac{5}{6} > \frac{3}{4}$.

Try It

Compare using $<$, $>$, or $=$.

a. $\frac{3}{4} \square \frac{7}{12}$ **b.** $\frac{3}{5} \square \frac{4}{7}$ **c.** $\frac{7}{10} \square \frac{8}{11}$

> **Problem Solving TIP**
>
> Notice that 12 is the LCM for 6 and 4. You could change the denominators to 12 in your head.

1. How can you tell which of two fractions on a ruler is greater?

2. Describe a method for comparing a decimal and a fraction.

3-9 Exercises and Applications

Practice and Apply

1. **Getting Started** Follow the steps to compare $\frac{6}{7}$ and $\frac{7}{8}$.

   a. Multiply the numerator and denominator of $\frac{6}{7}$ by the denominator of $\frac{7}{8}$.

   b. Multiply the numerator and denominator of $\frac{7}{8}$ by the denominator of $\frac{6}{7}$.

   c. Compare the numerators found in **a** and **b**. Which fraction is larger?

Compare using $<$, $>$, or $=$.

2. $\frac{20}{24}$ ☐ $\frac{28}{36}$ **3.** $\frac{15}{27}$ ☐ $\frac{5}{9}$ **4.** $\frac{6}{7}$ ☐ $\frac{18}{22}$ **5.** $\frac{16}{22}$ ☐ $\frac{25}{33}$

6. $\frac{8}{9}$ ☐ $\frac{9}{10}$ **7.** $\frac{22}{30}$ ☐ $\frac{7}{10}$ **8.** $\frac{19}{24}$ ☐ $\frac{24}{30}$ **9.** $\frac{33}{48}$ ☐ $\frac{8}{12}$

10. $\frac{21}{25}$ ☐ $\frac{20}{26}$ **11.** $\frac{5}{9}$ ☐ $\frac{10}{18}$ **12.** $\frac{12}{14}$ ☐ $\frac{24}{28}$ **13.** $\frac{16}{24}$ ☐ $\frac{8}{12}$

14. $\frac{23}{27}$ ☐ $\frac{24}{26}$ **15.** $\frac{11}{15}$ ☐ $\frac{33}{45}$ **16.** $\frac{22}{55}$ ☐ $\frac{3}{10}$ **17.** $\frac{13}{52}$ ☐ $\frac{16}{64}$

18. **Science** Hummingbirds are among the smallest birds in the world. Order the weights of the hummingbirds in the table from least to greatest.

actual size = 2 in.

Name	Bee Hummingbird	Giant Hummingbird	Costa's Hummingbird	Calliope Hummingbird
Weight	$\frac{1}{14}$ oz	$\frac{2}{3}$ oz	$\frac{1}{9}$ oz	$\frac{1}{11}$ oz

19. **Music** Theresa is building a guitar for her daughter. The guitar must be between $\frac{1}{2}$ and $\frac{3}{4}$ of the size of a full-sized guitar. Find and list in order, from least to greatest, four fractions in that range. Express the fractions in lowest terms.

PRACTICE 3-9

20. **Test Prep** Louise has to sort bolts from smallest to largest. In what order should she sort the following bolts: $\frac{3}{4}$ in., $\frac{11}{16}$ in., $\frac{5}{8}$ in., $\frac{23}{32}$ in.?

Ⓐ $\frac{3}{4}, \frac{23}{32}, \frac{11}{16}, \frac{5}{8}$

Ⓑ $\frac{5}{8}, \frac{11}{16}, \frac{3}{4}, \frac{23}{32}$

Ⓒ $\frac{5}{8}, \frac{11}{16}, \frac{23}{32}, \frac{3}{4}$

Ⓓ $\frac{5}{8}, \frac{23}{32}, \frac{11}{16}, \frac{3}{4}$

Problem Solving and Reasoning

21. Communicate Carly sees the same item advertised in two different stores. One store is advertising $0.20 off per dollar and the other is advertising $\frac{1}{4}$ off. Which store has the better deal? Explain.

22. Critical Thinking Name a fraction between 0 and $\frac{1}{10}$ whose numerator is not 1. Name a fraction between $\frac{1}{3}$ and $\frac{1}{2}$ whose denominator is 10. Express the fraction in lowest terms.

23. Communicate Describe a method you could use to quickly compare two fractions with the same numerator and different denominators.

24. Write an explanation of how you can compare and order mixed numbers such as $2\frac{3}{4}$ and $2\frac{4}{5}$.

Mixed Review

Make a scatterplot for each set of data. *[Lesson 1-6]*

25.

x	2	3	4	5	6	7	8	9
y	8	6	7	5	4	6	4	3

26.

x	2.3	4.6	3.6	6.3	8.2	9.1	5.3	7.1
y	3.7	4.2	5.3	6.1	8.0	8.7	5.8	6.3

Write each number in scientific notation. *[Lesson 3-5]*

27. 475,600

28. 580,000

29. 93,000,000

30. 3,210,000

31. 830

32. 904,000,000

33. 50

34. 6,535,000,000,000

Write each number in standard form. *[Lesson 3-5]*

35. 4.6×10^4

36. 8.36×10^2

37. 6.2×10^8

38. 9.9×10^{10}

39. 3.47×10^5

40. 2.589×10^7

41. 7.49×10^{14}

42. 5×10^{18}

43. In 1996, the Colorado Symphony Orchestra had 1.02×10^2 members. Of these, 5.0×10^1 played stringed instruments. What fraction of the orchestra members played stringed instruments? Write your answer in lowest terms.

Converting Between Fractions and Decimals

▶ **Lesson Link**   You've worked with both fractions and decimals. Now you'll learn to convert from one to the other. ◀

Explore   Converting Fractions to Decimals

Repeat After Me

Materials: Calculator

1. Write $\frac{1}{9}$, $\frac{4}{9}$, and $\frac{7}{9}$ as decimals by dividing the numerator by the denominator. Describe the pattern in your results.

2. Predict the decimal for $\frac{5}{9}$. Check your prediction on your calculator.

3. Write $\frac{13}{99}$, $\frac{41}{99}$, and $\frac{67}{99}$ as decimals. What patterns do you find?

4. Predict the decimal for $\frac{83}{99}$.

5. Write $\frac{157}{999}$ and $\frac{632}{999}$ as decimals.

6. Predict a fraction that has 0.418418418... for its decimal. Then check your prediction.

... How It's Used

Counter clerks in the deli department need to be able to read $\frac{1}{4}$ lb on a scale that has a decimal readout.

Vocabulary

terminating decimal

repeating decimal

Learn   Converting Between Fractions and Decimals

Fractions and decimals are different ways of writing the same quantity. Sometimes one way is better than the other, so you should know how to convert from one to the other.

To convert from a decimal to a fraction, think of the fractional equivalents of place values. You may even want to *read* the decimal.

To write 0.7 as a decimal, think: seven *tenths*.

$$0.7 = \frac{7}{10} \begin{matrix} \leftarrow \text{ seven} \\ \leftarrow \text{ tenths} \end{matrix}$$

one tenth $= \dfrac{1}{10}$

one hundredth $= \dfrac{1}{100}$

one thousandth $= \dfrac{1}{1000}$

After converting a decimal to a fraction, you may need to rewrite the fraction in lowest terms.

Example 1

A sound meter recorded the *piano* (soft) section of a symphony at 0.24 times the loudness of the *forte* (loud) section. Write 0.24 as a fraction in lowest terms.

$$0.24 = \frac{24}{100} = \frac{24 \div 4}{100 \div 4} = \frac{6}{25}$$

The orchestra played $\frac{6}{25}$ as loud during the *piano* section.

Try It

Convert to a fraction in lowest terms.   **a.** 0.3   **b.** 0.75   **c.** 0.368

To convert from a fraction to a decimal, divide the numerator by the denominator. The decimal you obtain will terminate or repeat.

A **terminating decimal** ends.

$$8 \overline{)3.000} \rightarrow \frac{3}{8} = 0.375$$

A **repeating decimal** repeats a pattern of digits.

$29 \div 111 = 0.261261261\ldots \rightarrow \frac{29}{111} = 0.\overline{261}$ ← Use a bar to indicate the repeating pattern.

Examples

Convert to a decimal. Tell whether the decimal terminates or repeats.

2 $\frac{5}{33}$

$5 \div 33 = 0.151515\ldots$

$0.\overline{15}$; the decimal repeats

3 $\frac{13}{16}$

$13 \div 16 = 0.8125$

0.8125; the decimal terminates

Try It

Convert to a decimal. Tell if the decimal terminates or repeats.

a. $\frac{17}{20}$

b. $\frac{2}{3}$

c. $\frac{9}{32}$

Test Prep

You may see *terminating* and *repeating decimals* referred to as *rational numbers*.

Check Your Understanding

1. When might 0.5 be preferred over $\frac{1}{2}$? When might $\frac{1}{2}$ be preferred?

2. Can 0.23 and 0.230 be expressed as the same fraction? Explain.

Practice and Apply

1. **Getting Started** Convert 0.025 to a fraction and rewrite it in lowest terms.

   a. Write 0.025 as a fraction with a power of 10 as the denominator.

   b. Rewrite the resulting fraction in lowest terms.

Convert to a fraction in lowest terms.

2. 0.75   3. 0.12   4. 0.325   5. 0.040

6. 0.179   7. 0.108   8. 0.555   9. 0.812

Convert to a decimal. Tell if the decimal terminates or repeats.

10. $\frac{4}{9}$ 11. $\frac{4}{7}$ 12. $\frac{11}{16}$ 13. $\frac{14}{21}$

14. $\frac{12}{15}$ 15. $\frac{16}{20}$ 16. $\frac{10}{18}$ 17. $\frac{26}{50}$

18. **Science** The masses of the moon and planets differ from Earth's mass. Each planet's pull of gravity also differs from Earth's. The following decimals represent the pull of gravity on the moon and planets compared to the pull of gravity on Earth. Convert to fractions and rewrite in lowest terms.

    a. Moon: 0.16   **b.** Mercury: 0.37

    c. Mars: 0.38   **d.** Venus: 0.88

Surface of Venus

19. **Test Prep** Which fraction forms a terminating decimal?

    Ⓐ $\frac{8}{9}$ Ⓑ $\frac{5}{6}$ Ⓒ $\frac{7}{8}$ Ⓓ $\frac{10}{11}$

20. **Music** To use a computer to write music, you need to write notes as decimals. What decimals are entered for a half note, quarter note, eighth note, and sixteenth note?

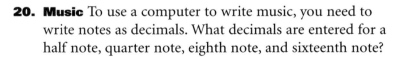

Number Sense Use a calculator to convert each repeating decimal to a fraction.

21. $0.\overline{83}$ 22. $0.\overline{1}$ 23. $0.\overline{18}$ 24. $0.\overline{5}$

PRACTICE 3-10

Problem Solving and Reasoning

25. Critical Thinking For each problem, is it better to use a fraction or a decimal to solve the problem? Explain.

a. Sam, Dean, and Matt agree to evenly split the cost of dinner, which totals $100.00. How much does each owe?

b. Miriam has a recipe that serves 12 and she wants to serve 4. The recipe calls for 2 cups of sugar. How much sugar should she use?

c. Every third seat in a music hall has a pair of rental binoculars attached to the seat back. There are 1000 seats in the music hall. How many pairs of binoculars are there?

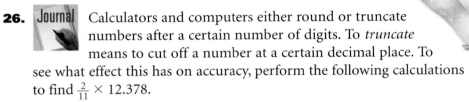

26. **Journal** Calculators and computers either round or truncate numbers after a certain number of digits. To *truncate* means to cut off a number at a certain decimal place. To see what effect this has on accuracy, perform the following calculations to find $\frac{2}{11} \times 12.378$.

a. First, find the decimal equivalent of $\frac{2}{11}$. Truncate the decimal to the thousandths place. Then multiply the answer by 12.378 and write the result. Truncate the result to the thousandths place.

b. Solve the problem as in **a**, but round the decimals to the thousandths place rather than truncating.

c. Multiply 12.378 by 2 first, and then divide the answer by 11. Truncate the result to the thousandths place.

d. Solve the problem as in **c**, but round the decimals to the thousandths place rather than truncating them.

e. Which result is the most accurate? Describe the results in your journal.

Mixed Review

Find the mean of each set of data. *[Lesson 1-4]*

27. 34, 64, 55, 72, 61, 73, 84, 63

28. 86, 97, 103, 136, 70, 157, 324

29. 11, 20, 25, 61, 62, 84, 93, 97

30. 3, 4, 7, 10, 12, 14, 15, 17

31. Julie's car gets 36 miles per gallon. Use the formula $m = 36g$ to make a table showing how many miles (m) Julie can travel on 1, 2, 3, 4, and 5 gallons (g) of gas. *[Lesson 2-3]*

32. WidgetWorx makes 532 widgets per hour. Use the formula $w = 532t$ to make a table showing how many widgets (w) are made in 1, 2, 3, 4, and 5 hours (t). *[Lesson 2-3]*

You've learned about some of the connections between music and fractions. Now you'll use what you've learned to identify notes in one of America's most beloved songs.

One, Two, Three ... Play!

A violin string is 360 mm long. To produce a musical note, a violinist draws the bow across the string while touching the string d mm from the nut. You can use the fraction $\frac{d}{360}$ to find the note produced.

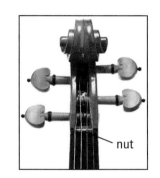

nut

1. There are seven different notes in the first line of the song "Home on the Range." The music below names the seven notes and gives the distance (d) that will produce each note.

Note:	A	A	D	E	F#	D	C#	B	G	G	G
Distance: (mm)	120	120	180	200	216	180	168	144	225	225	225

Oh, give me a home where the buf - fa - lo roam,

Complete the table, writing $\frac{d}{360}$ in lowest terms.

	A	B	C#	D	E	F#	G
d	120	144					
$\frac{d}{360}$							

2. Write each fraction as a decimal rounded to the nearest thousandth. State whether the decimal terminates or repeats.

3. The violinist hit a sour note given by the fraction $\frac{5}{12}$. How far from the nut did the violinist touch the string? Between what two notes was the sour note?

Section 3B Review

Compare using <, >, or =.

1. $0.059 \,\square\, 0.590$ **2.** $2.67 \,\square\, 2.671$ **3.** $412.437 \,\square\, 412.347$ **4.** $4.5 \,\square\, 4.50$

5. $\dfrac{19}{23} \,\square\, \dfrac{27}{35}$ **6.** $\dfrac{12}{27} \,\square\, \dfrac{4}{9}$ **7.** $\dfrac{13}{15} \,\square\, \dfrac{25}{29}$ **8.** $\dfrac{11}{18} \,\square\, \dfrac{14}{23}$

Solve.

9. $0.17w = 1.445$ **10.** $\dfrac{x}{28.5} = 16$ **11.** $c - 3.25 = 23.47$ **12.** $81.212 = 3.16n$

Find the prime factorization of each number.

13. 54   **14.** 275   **15.** 175   **16.** 288   **17.** 144

Find the GCF and the LCM.

18. 24, 40   **19.** 81, 90   **20.** 60, 100   **21.** 135, 162

22. **Journal** Many industries are concerned with fitting many objects or containers inside a larger object or container. Describe how factors and factorization can be used to solve these problems.

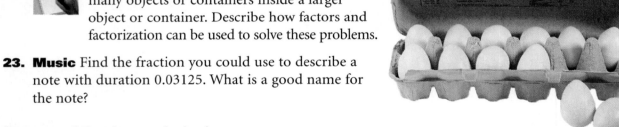

23. **Music** Find the fraction you could use to describe a note with duration 0.03125. What is a good name for the note?

Convert each fraction to a decimal.

24. $\dfrac{7}{9}$ **25.** $\dfrac{3}{7}$ **26.** $\dfrac{13}{16}$ **27.** $\dfrac{12}{18}$

Test Prep

On a multiple-choice test, you may need to rewrite fractions in lowest terms. Recognizing that there is an even number in the numerator and the denominator, so they are both divisible by 2, can help you work more quickly.

28. In which of the following fractions are both the numerator and the denominator divisible by 2?

Ⓐ $\dfrac{9}{16}$ Ⓑ $\dfrac{8}{15}$ Ⓒ $\dfrac{16}{22}$ Ⓓ $\dfrac{15}{26}$

Binary and Hexadecimal Numbers

Most of the numbers you see in everyday life are decimal, or base 10, numbers. The "10" in base 10 means that, as you move to the left, each place value is worth 10 times as much. You need 10 digits (0–9) to be able to express any base 10 number.

Decimal (base 10) number

1000s place	100s place	Tens place	Ones place
2,	0	7	4

$\times 10 \quad \times 10 \quad \times 10$

Computers use numbers in other bases. Binary (base 2) numbers have only two digits, 0 and 1. For each step to the left of the ones place, the place value doubles.

Binary (base 2) number

Eights place	Fours place	Twos place	Ones place
1	0	1	1

$\times 2 \quad \times 2 \quad \times 2$

To write the binary number 11011 in decimal form, use place value. The number in decimal form is $16 + 8 + 0 + 2 + 1 = 27$.

Number	1	1	0	1	1
Place Value	16	8	4	2	1
Product	$1 \times 16 = 16$	$1 \times 8 = 8$	$0 \times 4 = 0$	$1 \times 2 = 2$	$1 \times 1 = 1$

Computers also use hexadecimal (base 16) numbers. The letters A–F are used to represent digits 10 through 15. For each step to the left of the ones place, the place value of the digits is multiplied by 16.

Hexadecimal (base 16) number

4096s place	256s place	16s place	Ones place
1	C	2	A

$\times 16 \quad \times 16 \quad \times 16$

Here is how you can convert the hexadecimal number 2BCF to decimal form. The number in decimal form is $8,192 + 2,816 + 192 + 15 = 11,215$.

Number	2	B	C	F
Place Value	4096	256	16	1
Product	$2 \times 4096 = 8192$	$11 \times 256 = 2816$	$12 \times 16 = 192$	$15 \times 1 = 15$

Try It

Write each binary number in decimal form.

1. 101   **2.** 1100   **3.** 1011   **4.** 11001   **5.** 11111

Write each hexadecimal number in decimal form.

6. 16   **7.** A7   **8.** C9   **9.** 1OF   **10.** ABC

159

Graphic Organizer

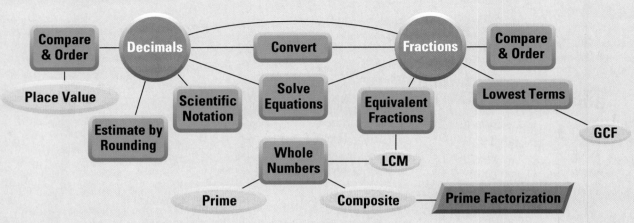

Section 3A Decimal Concepts: Estimating and Solving Equations

Summary

■ Decimals can be compared by writing the numbers with their decimal points lined up and comparing digits in each place, from left to right.

■ To add or subtract decimals, write the numbers with their decimal points lined up, then add or subtract the digits as usual.

■ When you multiply decimals, the decimal in the product has the same number of decimal places as the sum of the decimal places in the factors.

■ To divide decimals, move the decimal point the same number of places to the right in both the divisor and dividend until the divisor is a whole number. Then divide the same way as you divide by a whole number.

■ **Scientific notation** can be used to express large numbers.

Review

1. Give the value of each 4 in 3428.6341.

2. Compare 8.041 and 8.04.

3. Round 18.6359 to the nearest hundredth.

4. Estimate: $602.34 + 239.28$

5. Estimate: $\dfrac{319.28}{54.71}$

6. Find the sum: $326.78 + 16.835$

7. Solve: $12.34 + y = 56.123$

8. Find the product: 12.85×2.3

9. Solve: $\dfrac{e}{4.56} = 12.9$

10. Solve: $3.2p = 144.96$

11. Write 7.234×10^5 in standard form.

12. Write 1,739,000 in scientific notation.

Summary

- One number is **divisible** by another if the first can be divided by the second with no remainder. In this case, the second number is a **factor** of the first. Divisibility tests can be used to tell if one number is a factor of another.

- A whole number greater than 1 is a **prime number** if it has exactly two factors, 1 and itself. If it has more than two factors, it is a **composite number**.

- When you write a composite number as a product of prime numbers, the product is the **prime factorization** of the composite number. You can use a **factor tree** to find a prime factorization.

- The **greatest common factor** (GCF) of two whole numbers is the greatest whole number that is a factor of both numbers.

- The **least common multiple** (LCM) of two whole numbers is the smallest whole number (other than 0) that is a multiple of both numbers.

- A fraction is a number written in the form $\frac{a}{b}$, which means $a \div b$. The top number is the **numerator**. The bottom number is the **denominator**. Fractions are **equivalent** if they represent the same quantity.

- A fraction is in **lowest terms** if 1 is the only common factor of the numerator and the denominator. You can rewrite a fraction in lowest terms by dividing the numerator and denominator by common factors.

- To convert from a decimal to a fraction, think of the fractional equivalents of place values. To convert from a fraction to a decimal, divide the numerator by the denominator.

- A **terminating decimal** ends. A **repeating decimal** repeats a pattern of digits.

Review

13. Test the number 330 for divisibility by 2, 3, 4, 5, 6, 8, 9, and 10.

14. Use a factor tree to find the prime factorization of 276.

15. Find the GCF of 45 and 65.

16. Find the LCM of 12 and 15.

17. Give two fractions that are equivalent to $\frac{15}{18}$.

18. Rewrite $\frac{28}{112}$ in lowest terms.

19. Rewrite $\frac{75}{165}$ in lowest terms.

20. Compare $\frac{24}{31}$ and $\frac{23}{31}$.

21. Compare $\frac{9}{16}$ and $\frac{5}{9}$.

22. Convert 0.24 to a fraction in lowest terms.

23. Convert 0.528 to a fraction in lowest terms.

24. Convert $\frac{9}{11}$ to a decimal. Tell if the decimal terminates or repeats.

Chapter 3 Assessment

1. Give the value of each 7 in 71,267.073.

2. Compare 5.6999 and 5.07.

3. Round 63.849 to the nearest tenth.

4. Estimate: $1512.7 \div 301.6$

5. Find the difference: $37.65 - 4.238$

6. Solve: $k - 82.37 = 731.2$

7. Solve: $297.57 = 6.5x$

8. An Earth year is 365.3 days. A year on Jupiter is 11.86 times as long as a year on Earth. Find the length of a year on Jupiter (in Earth days).

9. Write 8.37×10^7 in standard form.

10. Write 87,560,000,000 in scientific notation.

11. Test the number 672 for divisibility by 2, 3, 4, 5, 6, 8, 9, and 10.

12. Use a factor tree to find the prime factorization of 600.

13. Find the GCF of 84 and 108.

14. Find the LCM of 10 and 25.

15. Give two fractions that are equivalent to $\frac{42}{64}$.

16. Of the 78 students in Mr. Takagi's classes, 18 earned a grade of A last semester. What fraction of the students earned A's? Express your answer in lowest terms.

17. Compare $\frac{19}{35}$ and $\frac{8}{15}$.

18. Convert 0.35 to a fraction in lowest terms.

19. Convert $\frac{13}{16}$ to a decimal. Tell if the decimal terminates or repeats.

Performance Task

Suppose a Martian calendar used 8-day weeks and 30-day months. If the first day of a month fell on a Monday, how many more days would it take before another first day fell on a Monday? How does your answer relate to the numbers 8 and 30? Explain why this relationship makes sense.

Performance Assessment

Choose one problem.

Going by the Book

Choose a page in each of two different kinds of books. Count how many one-syllable, two-syllable, three-syllable (and so on) words are on each page. Make two line plots, one for each book, to display your results. Do you notice any patterns in the line plots? Which book seems to be intended for more advanced readers? Explain how you reached your conclusion.

Monkeys and Strawberries

Write four different problems that can be solved using the equation $6x + 5 = 47$. You must include at least one of these words or phrases in each problem: more than, product, pickles, dollars, increased by, strawberries, less than, sum, monkeys, times. Pick one of the problems and show how to solve it. Explain each step.

Keeping Gizmos in Stock

Gizmos are packed in crates of 12. You manage a store that normally sells 35 Gizmos per day. In addition, Mr. Garcia comes in every two weeks to purchase 17 Gizmos. Your employer has asked you to determine how many crates of Gizmos need to be ordered from the manufacturer every month. Write a report to your employer, explaining how you solved an equation to answer his question.

Drawing the Solar System

The table shows how far each planet is from the sun, in astronomical units. Make a poster which shows the orbits of all the planets as accurately as possible. (Hint: Start with Pluto so that you'll be sure that you have enough space!)

Planet	Distance from Sun (AU)
Mercury	0.39
Venus	0.72
Earth	1.00
Mars	1.53
Jupiter	5.21
Saturn	9.55
Uranus	19.20
Neptune	30.10
Pluto	39.46

Science Link
www.mathsurf.com/7/ch4/science

Arts & Literature Link
www.mathsurf.com/7/ch4/arts

Science

The Department of Agriculture recommends that no more than $\frac{3}{10}$ of the calories in a person's diet come from fat. About $\frac{45}{88}$ of the calories in a breakfast of 8 oz of orange juice, two fried eggs, buttered toast, and two strips of bacon come from fat.

Arts & Literature

In music, the sum of the time value of the notes in a measure must equal the time signature. If the time signature is $\frac{3}{4}$, the measure could contain 2 quarter notes and 2 eighth notes:
$$\frac{1}{4} + \frac{1}{4} + \frac{1}{8} + \frac{1}{8} = \frac{3}{4}.$$

People of the World

The ancient Babylonians used fractions whose denominators were powers of 60. In this system, they would have written $\frac{1}{8}$ as $\frac{7}{60} + \frac{30}{60^2}$.

Entertainment

According to Motion Picture Association of America estimates, about $\frac{1}{7}$ of the people attending movies are younger than age 16.

Social Studies

People living in Aswan, Egypt, get about $\frac{1}{50}$ of an inch of rain each year. Yuma, Arizona, the driest city in the United States, gets $2\frac{13}{20}$ inches of rain, which is $132\frac{1}{2}$ times more rain than Aswan.

KEY MATH IDEAS

Before adding or subtracting fractions, write them with a common denominator. Then find the sum or difference of the numerators.

You can express a fractional number greater than one as an improper fraction or a mixed number.

Two numbers are reciprocals if their product is 1. To divide by a fraction, multiply by its reciprocal.

Most lengths are not whole numbers. You often need to multiply and divide fractions when you solve area problems.

CHAPTER PROJECT

Problem Solving

Understand
Plan
Solve
Look Back

In this project, you will use fractions to describe and graph the populations of the world's nations. To begin this project, find current population figures for the world and the five most populous countries.

Problem Solving Focus

Finding Unnecessary Information

It is important to analyze the information in a problem carefully. You need to understand which information will help you solve the problem, and which information is unnecessary and can be ignored.

For each problem, identify the unnecessary numerical information. Some problems may not have unnecessary information. (You do *not* need to solve the problem.)

1 The Strand Movie Theater charges $7.50 per ticket. Senior citizen prices are $2.00 less. For his thirteenth birthday, Damien takes 4 of his school friends to the movies. How much money does he need for the tickets?

2 At the theater, Damien buys popcorn and trail mix for himself and his friends. He gives the cashier a ten dollar bill and gets $1.20 in change. What is the average amount of money Damien spent on each friend?

3 Damien asked for $\frac{3}{4}$ of a pound of trail mix. The scale read 0.80 and the trail mix cost $4.60. Did Damien receive the correct amount of trail mix?

4 The movie was about a young woman who tried to sail around the world. Her planned route was 28,000 miles long. Unfortunately, her boat capsized, and she barely made it to shore in Australia, 7,500 miles from her starting point. Fortunately, she became a famous pop music star there, selling 2,500,000 CDs in 7 months. What fraction of her planned route did she complete?

Sums and Differences of Fractions

Taking $tock in the Market

Frantic people race from place to place, each yelling to be heard above the others. Bells ring. Facts speed across a computer screen. Is there an emergency? No, this is just the way it is every day at the New York Stock Exchange.

What are they yelling about? They are buying and selling stocks in companies. Owning a *share* of stock means owning part of a company. Companies raise money by selling stock. If the company does well, more people buy shares and the price paid for each share of the stock goes up.

Buyers want to "buy low" so they need to keep track of changes in the price of stock. Sometimes prices rise, sometimes they fall, but price changes are always measured in fractional amounts. An increase of $1\frac{3}{8}$ (about $1.38 per share) may not sound like much, but it means that someone who owns thousands of shares will make a lot of money.

1 Which is greater, an increase of $1\frac{3}{8}$ dollars or an increase of $1\frac{1}{2}$ dollars?

2 Explain why $1\frac{3}{8}$ dollars is about the same as $1.38.

3 You own a stock whose price increased $1\frac{3}{8}$, then decreased $\frac{5}{8}$, then increased $\frac{7}{8}$. Is your stock worth more or less than it was at first?

Estimating: Fractions and Mixed Numbers

You'll Learn ...

■ to estimate solutions to problems involving fractions

... How It's Used

Investment managers must be able to check the progress of stocks and bonds as prices rise and fall by fractional amounts.

Vocabulary

mixed number

▶ **Lesson Link**   You have estimated solutions to decimal problems. Now you'll see how you can estimate solutions to problems involving fractions. ◀

Explore   **Estimating with Fractions**

Super Stocks

Mary, an investor on the American Stock Exchange, found that eight of her stocks rose in price yesterday. She decided to sell the stocks that were up by an amount close to 0, to hold on to the stocks that were up by close to $\frac{1}{2}$, and to buy more of the stocks that were up by an amount close to 1. Here are the stocks and the amounts the stocks rose.

| Wesco | $+\frac{7}{16}$ | PLM | $+\frac{7}{8}$ | IGI | $+\frac{11}{16}$ | Azco | $+\frac{1}{8}$ | HK |
| IRIS | $+\frac{51}{64}$ | Norex | $+\frac{5}{8}$ | Espey | $+\frac{15}{16}$ | Sportsclb | $+\frac{3}{32}$ | Yp |

MARKET PROFILES   MOST ACTIVE

1. Into which category should Mary put each of the eight stocks? Explain your reasoning.

2. Mary has another stock that was up $\frac{1}{4}$. What category should it go into? Is there only one answer? Explain.

3. Suppose a stock is up by an amount with a denominator of 16. How can you use the numerator to tell what category it is in?

Learn   **Estimating: Fractions and Mixed Numbers**

One way to estimate sums and differences of fractions is to round the fractions to either 0, $\frac{1}{2}$, or 1 and add or subtract mentally. You can use a number line to help decide if a fraction is closer to 0, $\frac{1}{2}$, or 1.

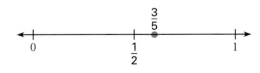

Example 1

A recording company whose stock trades on the New York Stock Exchange was up $\frac{3}{8}$ on Monday and up $\frac{15}{16}$ on Tuesday. Estimate the total amount the stock was up at the end of the two days.

Use a number line to round each fraction to 0, $\frac{1}{2}$, or 1.

Since $\frac{3}{8}$ is close to $\frac{1}{2}$, it rounds to $\frac{1}{2}$. Since $\frac{15}{16}$ is close to 1, it rounds to 1.

$\frac{3}{8} + \frac{15}{16}$ is about $\frac{1}{2} + 1 = 1\frac{1}{2}$.

The stock was up about $1\frac{1}{2}$.

Try It

Estimate.

a. $\frac{4}{9} + \frac{2}{11}$ **b.** $\frac{8}{10} - \frac{3}{14}$ **c.** $\frac{7}{9} + \frac{12}{15}$

ESTIMATION

When the numerator and denominator are close in value, the fraction is close to 1. When the numerator is about half the denominator, the fraction is close to $\frac{1}{2}$. When the numerator is much smaller than the denominator, the fraction is close to 0.

Recall that a **mixed number** is made up of a nonzero whole number and a fraction. $4\frac{1}{2}$ and $2\frac{2}{7}$ are mixed numbers. You can estimate sums, differences, and products of mixed numbers by rounding to the nearest whole number.

Example 2

Estimate: $4\frac{3}{16} + 7\frac{6}{10}$

$4\frac{3}{16}$ rounds to 4. $7\frac{6}{10}$ rounds to 8.

$4\frac{3}{16} + 7\frac{6}{10} \approx 4 + 8 = 12$

Try It

Estimate.

a. $3\frac{5}{12} + 5\frac{9}{11}$ **b.** $9\frac{2}{15} - 4\frac{7}{11}$ **c.** $7\frac{3}{21} \cdot 2\frac{9}{14}$

You can use compatible numbers to estimate quotients of mixed numbers. Round the divisor first, then replace the dividend with the nearest compatible number. You can also use compatible numbers to estimate products of fractions and whole numbers.

Examples

3 Estimate: $43\frac{2}{3} \div 8\frac{2}{15}$

First round $8\frac{2}{15}$ to 8.

Both 40 and 48 are compatible with 8, so replace $43\frac{2}{3}$ with 40, which is closer.

$$43\frac{2}{3} \div 8\frac{2}{15} \approx 40 \div 8 = 5$$

4 Precious metals like gold, silver, and platinum sell on the options market. If gold sells for $392.50 an ounce, estimate the value of $\frac{1}{4}$ ounce of gold. Determine if the estimate is too high or too low.

$$\$392.50 \times \frac{1}{4} \approx \$400 \times \frac{1}{4} = \$100$$

The value of the gold is about $100. The estimate is high because $392.50 was rounded to $400, a greater number.

Gold ingot

Try It

Estimate.

a. $23\frac{4}{9} \div 5\frac{3}{13}$ **b.** $32\frac{4}{5} \div 6\frac{3}{4}$ **c.** $21\frac{7}{8} \times 8\frac{1}{6}$

Check | Your Understanding

1. Explain how you would use rounding to estimate $3\frac{7}{9} - 1\frac{3}{4}$.

2. $20 \div 1\frac{3}{4}$ is about $20 \div 2 = 10$. Is the estimate of 10 for the quotient high or low? Explain.

3. How can you use a number line to help round a fraction?

4. To what number would you round $\frac{3}{8}$ if you were adding $\frac{13}{14}$ and $\frac{3}{8}$? To what number would you round $\frac{3}{8}$ if you were adding $4\frac{13}{14}$ and $9\frac{3}{8}$? If your answers to these questions are different, explain why.

Practice and Apply

Getting Started Round each fraction to 0, $\frac{1}{2}$, or 1.

1. $\frac{3}{8}$ **2.** $\frac{7}{8}$ **3.** $\frac{1}{5}$ **4.** $\frac{3}{5}$ **5.** $\frac{1}{8}$

Estimate each sum or difference.

6. $\frac{1}{8} + \frac{2}{5}$ **7.** $\frac{6}{7} - \frac{3}{8}$ **8.** $\frac{2}{3} + \frac{1}{9}$ **9.** $\frac{9}{10} - \frac{7}{8}$ **10.** $\frac{3}{16} - \frac{1}{8}$

11. $\frac{3}{8} + \frac{3}{7}$ **12.** $\frac{7}{8} + \frac{12}{13}$ **13.** $\frac{3}{4} - \frac{3}{8}$ **14.** $\frac{5}{6} + \frac{1}{4}$ **15.** $\frac{4}{5} - \frac{1}{8}$

Round each mixed number to the nearest whole number, then estimate each sum or difference.

16. $3\frac{3}{4} + 2\frac{1}{9}$ **17.** $5\frac{4}{10} + 6\frac{5}{7}$ **18.** $12\frac{4}{5} - 7\frac{2}{3}$ **19.** $11\frac{2}{5} - 9\frac{9}{10}$

20. $6\frac{1}{4} + 1\frac{5}{9}$ **21.** $10\frac{3}{4} + 3\frac{1}{6}$ **22.** $5\frac{3}{5} - 4\frac{1}{3}$ **23.** $15\frac{4}{5} - 11\frac{7}{8}$

Use compatible numbers to estimate each product or quotient.

24. $17 \times \frac{1}{3}$ **25.** $18\frac{7}{8} \div 5\frac{1}{6}$ **26.** $\frac{1}{5} \times 31$ **27.** $52\frac{4}{11} \div 6\frac{1}{2}$

28. $23 \times \frac{1}{2}$ **29.** $13\frac{3}{4} \div 2\frac{1}{3}$ **30.** $\frac{1}{3} \times 11$ **31.** $61\frac{4}{5} \div 7\frac{1}{5}$

32. The length of a chicken egg can be $1\frac{15}{16}$ in. The length of an ostrich egg can be $6\frac{3}{8}$ in. Use rounding to estimate the difference between the lengths of these eggs.

33. An ostrich can weigh up to 280 lb. If a chicken weighs $8\frac{1}{2}$ lb, use rounding to estimate how many times heavier the ostrich is than the chicken.

34. **Test Prep** Use compatible numbers to find the best estimate for the following product, then tell whether the estimate is high or low: $\frac{1}{7} \times 40$.

   Ⓐ 5; low   Ⓑ 5; high   Ⓒ 6; low   Ⓓ 6; high

35. **Measurement** About how many $6\frac{3}{4}$-inch pieces can be cut from a board measuring $37\frac{1}{5}$ inches? Estimate to find your answer.

Problem Solving and Reasoning

36. **Communicate** $45 \div 9\frac{1}{3}$ is about $45 \div 9 = 5$. Is the estimate of 5 for the quotient high or low? Explain.

37. **Critical Thinking** A share of Stock A is selling for $5\frac{1}{8}$. A share of Stock B is selling for $4\frac{3}{4}$. Suppose you have $100. Can you buy 10 shares of Stock A and 10 shares of Stock B? Estimate to find your answer. Explain how you know your answer is correct.

38. [Journal] Write about a situation in which an estimated sum or an estimated difference might be more useful than an exact calculation.

Prices on Tokyo Stock Exchange

Mixed Review

Use the bar graph to answer each question. *[Lesson 1-1]*

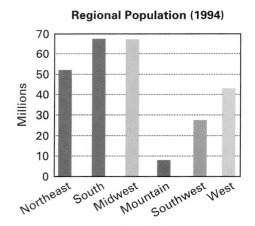

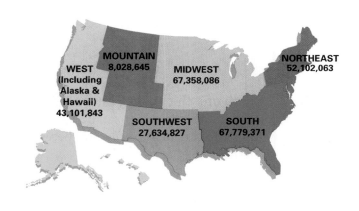

39. Which region has the highest population? The lowest?

40. Which two regions are closest in population?

Use < or > to compare the numbers. *[Lesson 3-1]*

41. 8.30 ☐ 8.299   **42.** 15.40 ☐ 16.39   **43.** 6.825 ☐ 6.725

44. 8.638 ☐ 8.647   **45.** 0.078 ☐ 0.780   **46.** 18.05 ☐ 18.051

Adding and Subtracting Fractions

► **Lesson Link** You've estimated sums and differences of fractions. Now you'll find exact sums and differences of fractions and solve equations that contain fractions. ◄

Explore Adding Fractions

Fraction Action

Materials: Graph paper
Colored pencils

Adding Two Fractions

- Draw three rectangles on graph paper. Use the denominators to determine the length and width of the rectangles.

- In the first rectangle, color the number of squares equal to the first fraction.

- In the second rectangle, color the number of squares equal to the second fraction.

- In the third rectangle, color one square for each colored square in the first two rectangles. Describe the result.

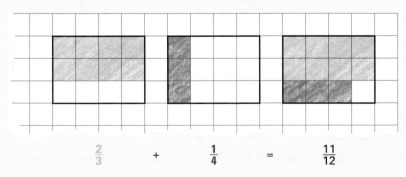

$$\frac{2}{3} \quad + \quad \frac{1}{4} \quad = \quad \frac{11}{12}$$

1. Model each sum.

　a. $\frac{1}{2} + \frac{2}{5}$ 　　**b.** $\frac{2}{5} + \frac{1}{3}$ 　　**c.** $\frac{1}{4} + \frac{3}{5}$ 　　**d.** $\frac{1}{2} + \frac{1}{3}$

2. How are the denominators of the fractions that are added related to the denominators of your answers?

3. Does $\frac{1}{4} + \frac{1}{5}$ have the same answer as $\frac{1}{5} + \frac{1}{4}$? Explain.

4. How is adding two fractions similar to adding two decimals?

You'll Learn ...

- to find sums and differences of fractions

- to solve equations involving fractions

... How It's Used

Fragrance manufacturers have to add fractional amounts of different flower essences when developing new perfumes.

Vocabulary

least common denominator (LCD)

4-2 • Adding and Subtracting Fractions **173**

To add or subtract fractions, think of each fraction as a portion of a whole.

In the model, each fraction gives the portion of a whole circle that is shaded. Each denominator gives the number of equal parts into which the circle is divided.

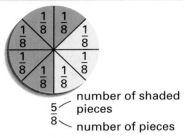

number of shaded pieces
$\frac{5}{8}$
number of pieces

Each numerator gives the number of equal parts that are shaded.

ADDING OR SUBTRACTING FRACTIONS WITH THE SAME DENOMINATOR

- Add or subtract their numerators.
- Write the sum or difference over the denominator.
- Rewrite in lowest terms.

Remember

You can find the LCM by listing both sets of multiples until you find the first match.

[Page 141]

If the denominators are different, the fractions need to be rewritten so that they have a common denominator. The **least common denominator (LCD)** is the least common multiple (LCM) of the denominators.

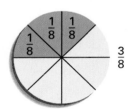 $\frac{3}{8}$

 $\frac{1}{4} = \frac{2}{8}$

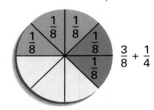 $\frac{3}{8} + \frac{1}{4} = \frac{5}{8}$

ADDING OR SUBTRACTING FRACTIONS WITH DIFFERENT DENOMINATORS

- Rewrite the fractions using the LCD.
- Add or subtract.
- Rewrite in lowest terms.

Example 1

Add. Rewrite in lowest terms. $\frac{1}{10} + \frac{3}{10}$

$\frac{1}{10} + \frac{3}{10} = \frac{1 + 3}{10}$ The denominators are the same, so add the numerators.

$= \frac{4 \div 2}{10 \div 2} = \frac{2}{5}$ Rewrite in lowest terms by dividing the numerator and denominator by 2.

Example 2

Subtract. $\frac{1}{4} - \frac{1}{6}$

$$\frac{1}{4} - \frac{1}{6} = \frac{1 \cdot 3}{4 \cdot 3} - \frac{1 \cdot 2}{6 \cdot 2}$$

Find the LCD. Multiples of 4 are 4, 8, 12, 16, …
Multiples of 6 are 6, 12, 18, … Use 12 as the LCD.

$$= \frac{3}{12} - \frac{2}{12}$$

Rewrite the fractions using the common denominator.

$$= \frac{1}{12}$$

Subtract.

You can solve equations that contain fractions the same way as you solve equations that contain whole numbers and decimals.

Example 3

Lucia bought the stock *MorganF* on the American Stock Exchange yesterday. Today the stock closed at a price of $\frac{5}{8}$, which was down $\frac{1}{16}$. Down $\frac{1}{16}$ represents the loss of $\frac{1}{16}$ of a dollar. At what price did Lucia buy the stock?

Let $b =$ the buying price.

Choose a variable.

$$b - \frac{1}{16} = \frac{5}{8}$$

Write an equation.

$$b - \frac{1}{16} + \frac{1}{16} = \frac{5}{8} + \frac{1}{16}$$

To undo subtracting $\frac{1}{16}$, add $\frac{1}{16}$ to both sides.

$$b = \frac{5 \cdot 2}{8 \cdot 2} + \frac{1}{16}$$

Find the LCD. Multiples of 8: 8, 16, 24, …
Multiples of 16: 16, 32, 48, … Use 16 as the LCD.

$$= \frac{10}{16} + \frac{1}{16}$$

Rewrite with the LCD.

$$= \frac{11}{16}$$

Add.

Lucia bought the stock for a price of $\frac{11}{16}$.

► **History Link**

The American Stock Exchange was founded in 1921, 129 years later than the New York Stock Exchange, which was founded in 1792. The Philadelphia Stock Exchange is even older; it was founded in 1790.

Study TIP

You can always find a common denominator by multiplying the numerator and denominator of each fraction by the denominator of the other.

Try It

Solve. **a.** $d + \frac{1}{4} = \frac{5}{6}$ **b.** $w - \frac{3}{5} = \frac{1}{3}$ **c.** $h + \frac{1}{2} = \frac{5}{6}$

Check | Your Understanding

1. Why do you need common denominators to add or subtract fractions?

2. Is the least common denominator always the only possible denominator to use when you add or subtract fractions? Explain.

4-2 Exercises and Applications

Practice and Apply

Getting Started Can each pair of fractions be added or subtracted as written or does it need to be rewritten with a common denominator?

1. $\dfrac{3}{4}, \dfrac{1}{4}$ **2.** $\dfrac{1}{3}, \dfrac{1}{4}$ **3.** $\dfrac{2}{3}, \dfrac{3}{8}$ **4.** $\dfrac{2}{5}, \dfrac{2}{7}$ **5.** $\dfrac{7}{8}, \dfrac{3}{8}$ **6.** $\dfrac{3}{4}, \dfrac{3}{5}$

Find the least common denominator for each pair of fractions.

7. $\dfrac{2}{3}, \dfrac{1}{4}$ **8.** $\dfrac{3}{8}, \dfrac{3}{4}$ **9.** $\dfrac{7}{8}, \dfrac{1}{6}$ **10.** $\dfrac{1}{3}, \dfrac{2}{5}$ **11.** $\dfrac{3}{5}, \dfrac{1}{4}$ **12.** $\dfrac{1}{3}, \dfrac{1}{4}$

Find each sum or difference. Rewrite in lowest terms.

13. $\dfrac{3}{10} + \dfrac{5}{10}$ **14.** $\dfrac{11}{12} - \dfrac{7}{12}$ **15.** $\dfrac{3}{16} + \dfrac{11}{16}$ **16.** $\dfrac{13}{24} - \dfrac{5}{24}$ **17.** $\dfrac{3}{4} - \dfrac{1}{3}$

18. $\dfrac{4}{5} - \dfrac{1}{3}$ **19.** $\dfrac{1}{6} + \dfrac{5}{9}$ **20.** $\dfrac{5}{8} - \dfrac{1}{6}$ **21.** $\dfrac{2}{5} + \dfrac{1}{10}$ **22.** $\dfrac{4}{21} + \dfrac{5}{7}$

Solve each equation.

23. $y + \dfrac{2}{3} = \dfrac{8}{9}$ **24.** $t - \dfrac{2}{5} = \dfrac{1}{3}$ **25.** $\dfrac{3}{7} + n = \dfrac{3}{4}$ **26.** $r - \dfrac{3}{8} = \dfrac{1}{6}$

27. Consumer The price of Mary's stock went up $\dfrac{5}{8}$ the day she bought it. The next day the price went up $\dfrac{1}{4}$. What was the total increase over the 2 days?

28. Algebra What do you know about n if the sum $\dfrac{1}{2} + n$ is:

  a. Equal to 1?   **b.** Greater than 1?

29. **Test Prep** Which fraction, when added to $\dfrac{1}{6}$, results in a sum of $\dfrac{2}{3}$?

  Ⓐ $\dfrac{1}{2}$ Ⓑ $\dfrac{1}{3}$ Ⓒ $\dfrac{1}{4}$ Ⓓ $\dfrac{1}{5}$

Madrid Stock Exchange

30. Science The circle graph shows the different ways electrical energy is produced in the United States.

a. How much of the total energy is produced by gas and hydroelectric generators?

b. How much more of the total energy is produced by coal than by oil?

c. How much more of the total energy is produced by nuclear generators than hydroelectric generators?

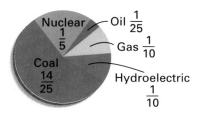
Sources of Electric Power

Problem Solving and Reasoning

31. Choose a Strategy Andrea watched the prices of two stocks for a week. Which stock had the greatest gain?

	Monday	Tuesday	Wednesday	Thursday	Friday
Stock A	$+\frac{1}{4}$	$+\frac{1}{8}$	$-\frac{5}{8}$	$+\frac{1}{2}$	$-\frac{1}{8}$
Stock B	$+\frac{1}{8}$	$-\frac{7}{8}$	$+\frac{1}{8}$	$+\frac{1}{4}$	$+\frac{3}{8}$

Problem Solving

STRATEGIES

• Look for a Pattern
• Make an Organized List
• Make a Table
• Guess and Check
• Work Backward
• Use Logical Reasoning
• Draw a Diagram
• Solve a Simpler Problem

32. Critical Thinking Using each number only once, use the numbers 2, 4, 6, and 8 to write an expression with two proper fractions that have:

a. The largest possible sum
b. The largest possible difference
c. The smallest possible sum
d. The smallest possible difference

Mixed Review

Solve each equation. Check your answer. *[Lesson 2-8]*

33. $5p + 2 = 37$

34. $21k - 18 = 273$

35. $11u - 31 = 47$

36. $97 = 9d + 7$

37. $\frac{a}{12} + 31 = 114$

38. $67 = \frac{w}{3} - 36$

39. $\frac{x}{31} - 3 = 93$

40. $\frac{c}{17} + 52 = 209$

Estimate. *[Lesson 3-2]*

41. $86.342 - 37.5$

42. $\frac{361.2}{118.7}$

43. 62.7×20.19

44. $32.78 + 117.32$

45. $72.01 + 39.25$

46. $269.03 - 41.7$

47. 31.2×48.7

48. $248.6 \div 51.03$

49. $92.1 - 36.7$

50. $\frac{108.5}{53.1}$

51. 47.2×9.87

52. $31.42 + 31.98$

53. $213.9 - 84.7$

54. $\frac{5,280}{10.2}$

55. 104.16×51.97

56. $247.54 + 598.217$

Adding and Subtracting Mixed Numbers

You'll Learn ...

■ to find sums and differences of mixed numbers

■ to solve equations involving mixed numbers

... How It's Used

Plumbers have to deal with fractional lengths when they work with water pipes.

Vocabulary

improper fraction

▶ **Lesson Link** You've seen how to add and subtract fractions. Now you'll add and subtract mixed numbers. ◀

Explore   Adding Mixed Numbers

Mixed Results

Materials: Graph paper
Colored pencils

Adding Two Mixed Numbers

• Model each mixed number using squares. Make the side lengths of the squares equal to the denominators of the fractions.

• To find the sum, first copy the filled squares. Then combine the fractionally-filled squares. When you combine these fractions, make as many complete squares as you can.

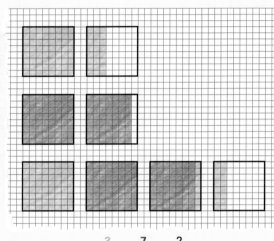

$$1\frac{3}{8} + 1\frac{7}{8} = 3\frac{2}{8}$$

1. Model each sum.

a. $1\frac{3}{5} + 2\frac{1}{5}$ **b.** $1\frac{3}{4} + 2\frac{1}{4}$ **c.** $1\frac{2}{5} + 1\frac{4}{5}$

2. When adding mixed numbers, how do you find the two parts of the sum?

3. How is adding two mixed numbers like adding two fractions?

DID YOU KNOW?

Mixed numbers are called *mixed* because they are written in two kinds of math notation.

Learn   Adding and Subtracting Mixed Numbers

When you add mixed numbers, you add the whole numbers and fractions separately. Sometimes you get a fraction such as $\frac{9}{4}$. A fraction that is greater than or equal to 1, such as $\frac{9}{4}$, is called an **improper fraction** . You can use division to rewrite an improper fraction as a mixed number.

To rename $\frac{9}{4}$ as a mixed number, think: $9 \div 4 = 2$ with remainder 1, so $\frac{9}{4} = 2\frac{1}{4}$.

To write a mixed number such as $3\frac{4}{5}$ as an improper fraction:

$$3\frac{4}{5} = \frac{15}{5} + \frac{4}{5}$$ Rewrite the whole number. Use the same denominator as the fraction.

$$= \frac{19}{5}$$ Add.

Examples

1 Last year, Margot bought stock in a medical equipment company at $6\frac{7}{8}$. Since then, the price has gone up $4\frac{3}{8}$. Find the current price.

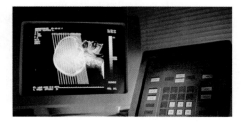

Estimate: $7 + 4 = 11$

$$6\frac{7}{8} + 4\frac{3}{8} = 10 + \frac{10}{8}$$ Add the whole numbers and add the fractions.

$$= 10 + 1\frac{2}{8}$$ Rewrite the improper fraction as a mixed number.

$$= 11\frac{2}{8} = 11\frac{1}{4}$$ Add and rewrite in lowest terms.

The current price of the stock is $11\frac{1}{4}$.

2 Solve. $w + 3\frac{3}{4} = 5\frac{1}{5}$

$$w + 3\frac{3}{4} - 3\frac{3}{4} = 5\frac{1}{5} - 3\frac{3}{4}$$ To undo adding $3\frac{3}{4}$, subtract $3\frac{3}{4}$ from both sides.

$$w = 5\frac{4}{20} - 3\frac{15}{20}$$ Rewrite fractions using the LCD.

$$w = 4 + \frac{20}{20} + \frac{4}{20} - 3\frac{15}{20}$$ Rewrite 5 as $4 + \frac{20}{20}$.

$$w = 4\frac{24}{20} - 3\frac{15}{20}$$ Combine the whole numbers and fractions.

$$w = 1\frac{9}{20}$$ Subtract whole numbers and fractions.

Try It

Add or subtract.

a. $4\frac{1}{2} + 3\frac{5}{8}$ **b.** $3 - 1\frac{1}{3}$ **c.** $6\frac{2}{5} - 2\frac{1}{2}$

Ramon and Melissa own stock in the MATHtoys Company. One week the price went from $2\frac{5}{8}$ to $5\frac{1}{8}$ per share. They want to know the price increase.

Ramon thinks ...

I'll subtract the whole number parts and the fraction parts.

$$5\frac{1}{8} - 2\frac{5}{8} = 4\frac{9}{8} - 2\frac{5}{8} = 2\frac{4}{8} = 2\frac{1}{2}$$

The price went up $2.50 per share.

Melissa thinks ...

I'll write as improper fractions and then subtract.

$$5\frac{1}{8} - 2\frac{5}{8} = \frac{41}{8} - \frac{21}{8} = \frac{20}{8} = 2\frac{4}{8} = 2\frac{1}{2}$$

The price went up $2.50 per share.

What do you think?

1. How did Ramon's method differ from Melissa's?

2. How did Melissa know that $5\frac{1}{8}$ is equal to $\frac{41}{8}$?

Check | Your Understanding

1. Explain how to write $\frac{11}{3}$ as a mixed number.

2. When you subtract mixed numbers, when do you need to rewrite a whole number as a whole number plus a fraction?

Practice and Apply

Getting Started Rewrite each improper fraction as a mixed number.

1. $\frac{24}{7}$ **2.** $\frac{16}{3}$ **3.** $\frac{34}{9}$ **4.** $\frac{61}{5}$ **5.** $\frac{39}{8}$ **6.** $\frac{49}{4}$

Rewrite each mixed number as an improper fraction.

7. $3\frac{1}{8}$ **8.** $5\frac{4}{5}$ **9.** $7\frac{3}{4}$ **10.** $4\frac{7}{9}$ **11.** $6\frac{7}{8}$ **12.** $8\frac{5}{11}$

Find each sum or difference.

13. $7\frac{7}{8} - 3\frac{5}{8}$ **14.** $5\frac{2}{9} + 2\frac{4}{9}$ **15.** $4\frac{1}{7} - 1\frac{6}{7}$ **16.** $6\frac{8}{9} + 8\frac{4}{9}$

17. $9 - 2\frac{1}{5}$ **18.** $10\frac{1}{2} + 5\frac{2}{3}$ **19.** $6\frac{3}{8} - 3\frac{1}{2}$ **20.** $25\frac{7}{9} + 18\frac{2}{3}$

Solve each equation.

21. $n + 3\frac{3}{7} = 6\frac{2}{3}$ **22.** $11\frac{7}{9} + x = 26\frac{1}{10}$ **23.** $y - 4\frac{2}{5} = 2\frac{1}{4}$ **24.** $z - 8\frac{5}{6} = 9\frac{7}{8}$

25. Geometry Find the perimeter of each figure.

a.

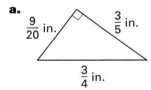

$\frac{9}{20}$ in. $\frac{3}{5}$ in.

$\frac{3}{4}$ in.

b.

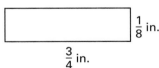

$\frac{1}{8}$ in.

$\frac{3}{4}$ in.

26. History On October 29, 1929, known as Black Tuesday, the stock market crashed. The Dow Jones average, which measures stock prices, started that day at $298\frac{97}{100}$, and finished $38\frac{33}{100}$ points lower. What was the Dow Jones average at the end of the day?

27. Science One *Astronomical Unit* (AU) is the average distance from Earth to the sun. If, when they are lined up, Mars is about $1\frac{1}{2}$ AU from the sun and Jupiter is about $3\frac{7}{10}$ AU from Mars, how far is Jupiter from the sun?

28. **Test Prep** Find the sum expressed in lowest terms: $3\frac{5}{6} + 7\frac{3}{4} = 10\frac{38}{24}$

Ⓐ $5\frac{19}{12}$ Ⓑ $10\frac{19}{12}$ Ⓒ $11\frac{14}{24}$ Ⓓ $11\frac{7}{12}$

29. **Social Studies** Many newspapers publish daily stock market reports. The reports usually include the high and the low price for that day as well as the last, or closing, price for the day.

a. What was the difference in cost between the high and the low for a share of Dig Video?

b. For Dig Video, how much higher than the low was the last price of the day?

STOCK	HIGH	LOW	LAST
DigiLink	$17\frac{1}{2}$	$16\frac{3}{16}$	$16\frac{3}{16}$
Dig Mic	$17\frac{3}{4}$	$15\frac{5}{8}$	$17\frac{1}{2}$
Dig Video	$9\frac{1}{2}$	$9\frac{3}{8}$	$9\frac{7}{16}$
Dionex	35	$32\frac{1}{4}$	35

Problem Solving and Reasoning

30. **Choose a Strategy** Find three mixed numbers with different denominators that have a sum of $10\frac{3}{4}$.

31. **Communicate** Write an explanation of the method you would use to subtract $2\frac{4}{5}$ from $4\frac{3}{5}$.

32. **Critical Thinking** Kara's bedroom is $15\frac{1}{4}$ feet long and $10\frac{1}{6}$ feet wide. She is getting a new carpet that is sold in rolls that are 12 feet wide. How much excess width will there be when the carpet is installed?

Problem Solving

STRATEGIES

- Look for a Pattern
- Make an Organized List
- Make a Table
- Guess and Check
- Work Backward
- Use Logical Reasoning
- Draw a Diagram
- Solve a Simpler Problem

Mixed Review

Science You can use the formula $d = r \cdot t$ to find the distance (d) traveled when you know the rate (r) and the amount of time (t). Substitute the given values into the formula. Then use the formula to find d. *[Lesson 2-1]*

33. $r = 25$ mi/hr, $t = 2$ hr
34. $r = 16$ ft/sec, $t = 42$ sec
35. $r = 75$ km/hr, $t = 5$ hr

36. $r = 82$ m/sec, $t = 40$ sec
37. $r = 55$ mi/hr, $t = 4$ hr
38. $r = 120$ ft/sec, $t = 90$ sec

Solve each equation. *[Lesson 3-3]*

39. $132.63 + x = 201.49$
40. $x - 62.75 = 31.87$
41. $69.31 = x + 23.75$

42. $6.234 = y - 15.7$
43. $p + 0.093 = 0.142$
44. $g - 0.072 = 6.39$

Project Progress

Using the population data you have collected, find the fraction of the world's population that lives in each of the 5 most populous countries. Round numbers to the nearest ten million when you make your fractions, and write them in lowest terms. Make a bar graph showing the populations of these countries.

Problem Solving

Understand
Plan
Solve
Look Back

You saw at the beginning of this section that investors need to understand fractions well if they are to succeed in the stock market. Now you will have an opportunity to follow the fortunes of one young investor.

Taking Stock in the Market

Felipe saved $55 from his paper route. He decided to buy one share of stock in the newspaper he delivered.

1. Felipe bought his share of stock on Monday, July 1. The price was $52\frac{3}{4}$. How much money did he have left?

2. During July, the stock reached a high of $56\frac{7}{16}$, then fell $1\frac{1}{8}$. Find the price at the end of the month.

3. On August 1, the stock rose $5\frac{3}{4}$. On August 2, it rose another $2\frac{7}{8}$. Find how much it rose during the first 2 days of August.

4. On August 3, the stock fell $3\frac{1}{2}$. Find the price at the close of trading on August 3.

5. By August 31, the stock had gained $2\frac{5}{8}$ from its August 3 price. How does the price compare with the price on August 1?

6. Felipe sold his stock on August 31. Find how much money he gained or lost. Write a paragraph that describes the performance of Felipe's stock.

Round each addend to 0, $\frac{1}{2}$, or 1, then estimate each sum or difference.

1. $\frac{4}{5} - \frac{1}{6}$ **2.** $\frac{2}{7} + \frac{7}{8}$ **3.** $\frac{1}{3} + \frac{8}{9}$ **4.** $\frac{6}{7} + \frac{1}{8}$ **5.** $\frac{7}{8} - \frac{2}{3}$

Round each mixed number to the nearest whole number, then estimate each sum or difference.

6. $8\frac{3}{4} - 6\frac{1}{3}$ **7.** $4\frac{5}{7} + 3\frac{2}{9}$ **8.** $11\frac{5}{6} - 7\frac{7}{9}$ **9.** $14\frac{1}{2} + 5\frac{9}{10}$

Find each sum or difference.

10. $\frac{4}{5} - \frac{1}{2}$ **11.** $\frac{2}{3} + \frac{1}{8}$ **12.** $\frac{6}{7} - \frac{1}{4}$ **13.** $\frac{5}{9} + \frac{2}{5}$ **14.** $\frac{2}{9} + \frac{5}{8}$

15. $4\frac{2}{5} + 3\frac{4}{5}$ **16.** $8\frac{1}{2} - 4\frac{3}{8}$ **17.** $10\frac{1}{2} - 5\frac{7}{10}$ **18.** $9\frac{2}{7} + 6\frac{3}{4}$ **19.** $2\frac{7}{8} + 3\frac{3}{4}$

20. **Journal** Describe several ways you might express 4 as an improper fraction.

Solve each equation.

21. $z + 2\frac{2}{5} = 5\frac{3}{4}$ **22.** $m - 6\frac{2}{3} = 3\frac{2}{7}$ **23.** $x - 4\frac{3}{8} = 5\frac{1}{2}$ **24.** $a + 1\frac{3}{4} = 8\frac{7}{8}$

25. Science Every year, the World Frog Jump Championships are held in Angels Camp, California. One year, the frog Free Willy won the contest by jumping 19 feet, $\frac{1}{2}$ inch, in 3 hops. The world record is 21 feet, $5\frac{3}{4}$ inches, held by Rosie the Ribeter. How much farther than Free Willy did Rosie the Ribeter jump?

Test Prep

On a multiple choice test, recognizing that the best answer choice is usually in lowest terms can help you work more quickly.

26. Find the sum: $3\frac{5}{8} + 5\frac{7}{40}$

Ⓐ $8\frac{32}{40}$ Ⓑ $8\frac{16}{20}$ Ⓒ $8\frac{8}{10}$ Ⓓ $8\frac{4}{5}$

27. Find the difference: $9\frac{1}{3} - 1\frac{5}{6}$

Ⓐ $6\frac{3}{6}$ Ⓑ $6\frac{1}{2}$ Ⓒ $7\frac{3}{6}$ Ⓓ $7\frac{1}{2}$

Building It Piece by Piece

"You won again?" says Mom. "Congratulations! I really think we need to build some shelves to hold your trophies." So off you go to measure the alcove in your room. It seems as though it should be an easy task to build a few shelves—a couple of pieces of wood, some brackets, and some nails. No problem.

When you start to measure, you find that none of the numbers are nice and simple. Is that width 3 feet $3\frac{1}{4}$ inches or 3 feet $3\frac{5}{8}$ inches? It certainly isn't exactly 3 feet 3 inches. You plan to build three shelves with brackets at even intervals. How will you figure out how much shelving to buy and how many brackets? How long should the nails be?

To make decisions like these, do-it-yourselfers and construction workers, carpenters and carpet layers, tile setters and plumbers all need to understand how to multiply and divide with fractions.

1 Why do you think a tile setter would need to work with fractions?

2 Why would it matter whether you knew how much shelving you needed?

3 If the three shelves were each 3 feet $3\frac{1}{4}$ inches long, would 10 feet of shelving be sufficient? Explain.

185

4-4

Multiplying Fractions

You'll Learn ...

■ to multiply fractions

... How It's Used

Costume designers often have to make several identical outfits for a show. They will need to multiply fractions to order the right amounts of fabric.

▶ **Lesson Link** You've added and subtracted fractions and solved equations involving addition and subtraction of fractions. Now you'll multiply fractions. ◄

Explore | Multiplying Fractions

A Model for Our Times

Materials: Graph paper
Colored pencils

Multiplying a Fraction by a Fraction

$\frac{2}{3} \times \frac{3}{4} = \frac{6}{12}$

- Draw a rectangle on graph paper. Use the denominators of the fractions you are multiplying to determine the length and width of the rectangle.

- Color a rectangle to represent the first fraction.

- Color a rectangle to represent the second fraction. Describe the section in the model where the two fractions overlap.

1. Model each product.   **a.** $\frac{1}{2} \cdot \frac{2}{3}$ **b.** $\frac{1}{4} \cdot \frac{4}{5}$ **c.** $\frac{2}{5} \cdot \frac{3}{7}$ **d.** $\frac{3}{4} \cdot \frac{5}{6}$

2. How do the denominators of the fractions that are multiplied relate to the denominators of your answers? How are the numerators related?

3. Does $\frac{1}{2} \cdot \frac{1}{3}$ have the same answer as $\frac{1}{3} \cdot \frac{1}{2}$? Explain.

4. When you multiply two fractions that are between 0 and 1, is the product less than or greater than the original fractions?

Learn | Multiplying Fractions

You can use a rectangle to model the product of two fractions. Recall that the formula for the area (A) of a rectangle with length l and width w is $A = lw$.

The first rectangle shows that $2 \cdot 3 = 6$.

The second rectangle shows that $\frac{1}{2} \cdot \frac{1}{3} = \frac{1}{6}$.

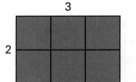

$\frac{1}{2} \times \frac{1}{3} = \frac{1}{6}$

MULTIPLYING FRACTIONS

- Multiply the numerators and multiply the denominators.
- Simplify the product if possible.

Examples

1 Most nails are round. A *spike*, the longest and strongest type of nail, has a square cross section. The greater the area of the cross section, the harder a spike is to remove. A $\frac{3}{8}$ in. square spike requires 6000 lb of force to remove it from a piece of locust wood. Find the cross-sectional area of the spike.

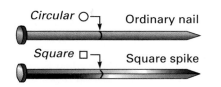

Remember

The formula for the area of a rectangle is $A = lw$. **[Page 58]**

$A = lw = \frac{3}{8} \cdot \frac{3}{8}$ Substitute $\frac{3}{8}$ for both *l* and *w*.

$= \frac{3 \cdot 3}{8 \cdot 8}$ Multiply the numerators and denominators.

$= \frac{9}{64}$ Simplify.

The cross-sectional area is $\frac{9}{64}$ square inches.

Cross section

$\frac{3}{8}$ in. $\frac{3}{8}$ in.

▶ **History Link**

The most famous *spike* is probably the Golden Spike, which completed the Central Pacific Railroad tracks at Promontory Point, Utah, in 1869.

2 Multiply. Rewrite in lowest terms. $\frac{2}{5} \cdot \frac{7}{8}$

$\frac{2}{5} \cdot \frac{7}{8} = \frac{2 \cdot 7}{5 \cdot 8}$ Multiply the numerators and the denominators.

$= \frac{14}{40}$ Simplify.

$= \frac{14 \div 2}{40 \div 2}$ Divide the numerator and denominator by 2 to rewrite in lowest terms.

$= \frac{7}{20}$ Simplify.

Try It

Multiply. Rewrite in lowest terms.

a. $\frac{3}{7} \cdot \frac{5}{8}$ **b.** $\frac{8}{9} \cdot \frac{3}{4}$ **c.** $\frac{3}{10} \cdot \frac{5}{6}$ **d.** $\frac{2}{3} \cdot \frac{1}{4}$ **e.** $\frac{3}{5} \cdot \frac{1}{6}$

Remember

The GCF is the largest factor that divides evenly into two numbers.

[Page 139]

You can save yourself work by dividing the numerator and the denominator by common factors *before* you multiply.

$$\overset{1}{\cancel{4}}\cdot\frac{15}{\cancel{8}} \qquad$$ Divide 4 and 8 by 4, a common factor.
$$\frac{\cancel{4}}{10}\cdot\frac{15}{\cancel{8}}$$
$$_{}\,_{2}$$

$$=\frac{\overset{1}{\cancel{4}}}{\underset{2}{\cancel{10}}}\cdot\frac{\overset{3}{\cancel{15}}}{\underset{2}{\cancel{8}}} \qquad$$ Divide 15 and 10 by 5, a common factor.

$$=\frac{3}{4} \qquad$$ Multiply the factors that remain.

Examples

3 Multiply. Rewrite in lowest terms. $\dfrac{5}{8}\cdot\dfrac{4}{7}$

$$\frac{5}{8}\cdot\frac{4}{7}=\frac{5}{\underset{2}{\cancel{8}}}\cdot\frac{\overset{1}{\cancel{4}}}{7} \qquad$$ Divide 8 and 4 by 4, a common factor.

$$=\frac{5}{14} \qquad$$ Multiply the fractions that remain.

4 Multiply. Rewrite in lowest terms. $\dfrac{49}{50}\cdot\dfrac{25}{28}$

$$\frac{49}{50}\cdot\frac{25}{28}=\frac{49}{\underset{2}{\cancel{50}}}\cdot\frac{\overset{1}{\cancel{25}}}{28} \qquad$$ Divide 25 and 50 by 25, a common factor.

$$=\frac{\overset{7}{\cancel{49}}}{\underset{2}{\cancel{50}}}\cdot\frac{\overset{1}{\cancel{25}}}{\underset{4}{\cancel{28}}} \qquad$$ Divide 49 and 28 by 7, a common factor.

$$=\frac{7}{8} \qquad$$ Multiply the fractions that remain.

Try It

Multiply. Rewrite in lowest terms.

a. $\dfrac{14}{15}\cdot\dfrac{20}{21}$ **b.** $\dfrac{12}{27}\cdot\dfrac{18}{24}$ **c.** $\dfrac{18}{35}\cdot\dfrac{21}{50}$ **d.** $\dfrac{3}{5}\cdot\dfrac{5}{6}$ **e.** $\dfrac{16}{34}\cdot\dfrac{17}{32}$

HINT

If your calculator has a fraction key, you can use it to multiply fractions. To multiply $\frac{7}{12}\cdot\frac{5}{9}$, enter 7 ▢/▢ 12 ▢×▢ 5 ▢/▢ 9 ▢=▢. The product is $\frac{35}{108}$.

Check Your Understanding

1. How can the greatest common factor be used to help multiply fractions?

2. Two fractions are each less than 1. Is their product less than 1? Explain.

3. Erica said, "When I multiply $\frac{1}{4}$ times a number, I'm really finding $\frac{1}{4}$ of the number." Is she correct? Explain.

Practice and Apply

Getting Started | Multiply the numerators and the denominators to find each product.

1. $\frac{1}{2} \cdot \frac{2}{3}$ **2.** $\frac{2}{5} \cdot \frac{3}{7}$ **3.** $\frac{4}{5} \cdot \frac{2}{9}$ **4.** $\frac{1}{10} \cdot \frac{1}{3}$ **5.** $\frac{1}{4} \cdot \frac{3}{5}$

Find each product. Rewrite in lowest terms.

6. $\frac{1}{2} \cdot \frac{2}{9}$ **7.** $\frac{3}{5} \cdot \frac{2}{3}$ **8.** $\frac{3}{4} \cdot \frac{6}{7}$ **9.** $\frac{4}{9} \cdot \frac{3}{4}$ **10.** $\frac{1}{3} \cdot \frac{3}{8}$

11. $\frac{4}{5} \cdot \frac{3}{8}$ **12.** $\frac{3}{4} \cdot \frac{5}{9}$ **13.** $\frac{5}{7} \cdot \frac{1}{5}$ **14.** $\frac{6}{11} \cdot \frac{5}{6}$ **15.** $\frac{2}{9} \cdot \frac{3}{4}$

Divide the numerator and the denominator of the following fractions by common factors *before* you multiply. Then multiply the fractions that remain.

16. $\frac{8}{15} \cdot \frac{5}{16}$ **17.** $\frac{9}{14} \cdot \frac{7}{18}$ **18.** $\frac{15}{27} \cdot \frac{18}{25}$ **19.** $\frac{8}{21} \cdot \frac{15}{16}$ **20.** $\frac{4}{35} \cdot \frac{7}{24}$

21. $\frac{18}{35} \cdot \frac{14}{45}$ **22.** $\frac{24}{49} \cdot \frac{35}{48}$ **23.** $\frac{20}{49} \cdot \frac{21}{40}$ **24.** $\frac{27}{56} \cdot \frac{35}{36}$ **25.** $\frac{14}{36} \cdot \frac{18}{35}$

26. Measurement Find the area of each rectangle.

a.
$\frac{7}{8}$ in.

$\frac{7}{16}$ in.

b.
$\frac{3}{4}$ in.

$\frac{3}{8}$ in.

27. **Test Prep**   What will the denominator be when the product $\frac{27}{48} \cdot \frac{24}{45}$ is expressed in lowest terms?

   Ⓐ 3   Ⓑ 10   Ⓒ 45   Ⓓ 2160

28. Career A tile setter is tiling a floor with tiles that measure $\frac{3}{4}$ ft on each side. If he uses 17 tiles along a wall, how long is the wall?

29. History From 1892 until 1954, New York's Ellis Island was the entry point to the United States for most immigrants coming over the Atlantic Ocean. In 1911, 650,000 people arrived at Ellis Island. About $\frac{1}{50}$ of those were turned away for economic or health reasons. How many people were turned away?

30. **Science** Gravitational attraction on the moon isn't as strong as gravity on Earth because of the moon's smaller mass. The weight of an object on the moon is about $\frac{1}{6}$ of what it would weigh on Earth. What would be the weight of each animal if it were on the moon?

   a. Otter: 13 lb

   b. Raccoon: 21 lb

   c. Coyote: 75 lb

   d. Alligator: 150 lb

Problem Solving and Reasoning

31. **Critical Thinking** A square yard measures 3 ft by 3 ft. How many square yards of floor space are in a 2 ft by 6 ft closet?

32. **Choose a Strategy** Find three different common factors you could use to divide the numerator and denominator of each fraction in the following problem: $\frac{12}{30} \cdot \frac{24}{60}$.

33. **Communicate** Explain why the answer is larger than the number you start with when you multiply a whole number by a whole number and smaller when you multiply a whole number by a proper fraction.

34. **Journal** You have a recipe that makes enough punch for twelve people. Explain how multiplication of fractions can help you adjust the recipe for nine people.

Problem Solving

STRATEGIES

- Look for a Pattern
- Make an Organized List
- Make a Table
- Guess and Check
- Work Backward
- Use Logical Reasoning
- Draw a Diagram
- Solve a Simpler Problem

Mixed Review

Make a bar graph for each set of data. *[Lesson 1-2]*

35.

Grade	6	7	8
No. of Students	421	635	507

36.

Dog	Lucky	Rex	Spot
Weight (lb)	35	51	23

Solve each equation. *[Lesson 3-4]*

37. $8.26p = 9.499$

38. $0.64 = \dfrac{s}{5.23}$

39. $39.52 = 10.4u$

40. $\dfrac{z}{1.873} = 5.01$

41. $0.73x = 1.9345$

42. $\dfrac{g}{38.42} = 21.75$

43. $76.858 = 8.3y$

44. $3.72 = \dfrac{k}{0.057}$

Multiplying Mixed Numbers

▶ **Lesson Link** You have found products of fractions. Now you'll find products of mixed numbers. ◀

Explore | Multiplying Mixed Numbers

The Math Writing on the Wall

Your kitchen has a length of 18 ft and a width of 9 ft. You've hired a contractor to knock down a wall and build an addition that will increase the width by 7 ft.

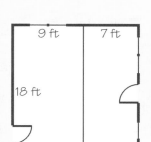

1. Find the area of the "old" kitchen, the addition, and the "new" kitchen.

2. Explain how your results show that
$18(9 + 7) = (18 \cdot 9) + (18 \cdot 7)$.

3. Draw a sketch that models each equation.

   a. $24(11 + 7) = (24 \cdot 11) + (24 \cdot 7)$ **b.** $6\left(2 + \frac{1}{3}\right) = (6 \cdot 2) + \left(6 \cdot \frac{1}{3}\right)$

4. Describe two ways you can find the product $4 \cdot 8\frac{1}{2}$.

You'll Learn ...

■ to multiply mixed numbers

... How It's Used

Gardeners need to multiply mixed numbers when they mix fertilizers.

Learn | Multiplying Mixed Numbers

Jenny wanted to find the area of the large rectangle. She knew that she could use the formula $A = lw$. She decided that she would add the areas of the two smaller rectangles.

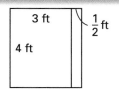

area of large rectangle = area of left rectangle + area of right rectangle

$l \cdot w$		$l \cdot w$		$l \cdot w$
$4 \cdot 3\frac{1}{2}$	$=$	$(4 \cdot 3)$	$+$	$\left(4 \cdot \frac{1}{2}\right)$
	$=$	12	$+$	2
	$=$	14 ft^2		

Remember

The Distributive Property states that $a(b + c) = ab + ac$.
[Page 62]

Jenny's method shows that the distributive property can be used to multiply a whole number by a mixed number. Using the distributive property, you may be able to find the product mentally.

You can also multiply mixed numbers by rewriting them as improper fractions. Then multiply the numerators and multiply the denominators.

Examples

1 Multiply: $12 \times 4\frac{2}{3}$

$$= \frac{\overset{4}{\cancel{12}}}{1} \times \frac{14}{\underset{1}{\cancel{3}}}$$ Divide 12 and 3 by 3, a common factor.

$$= \frac{4 \times 14}{1 \times 1}$$ Multiply numerators and denominators.

$$= 56$$ Multiply.

2 The measure of a piece of lumber in *board feet* equals $l \cdot w \cdot t$. Length (*l*) and width (*w*) are measured in feet and thickness (*t*) is measured in inches. Find the number of board feet in the plank.

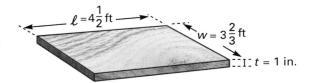

$l = 4\frac{1}{2}$ ft $w = 3\frac{2}{3}$ ft $t = 1$ in.

$$4\frac{1}{2} \cdot 3\frac{2}{3} \cdot 1 = \frac{9}{2} \cdot \frac{11}{3} \cdot \frac{1}{1}$$ Write mixed numbers as improper fractions.

$$= \frac{9 \cdot 11 \cdot 1}{2 \cdot 3 \cdot 1}$$ Multiply numerators and denominators.

$$= \frac{\overset{3}{\cancel{9}} \cdot 11 \cdot 1}{2 \cdot \underset{1}{\cancel{3}} \cdot 1}$$ Divide 9 and 3 by 3, a common factor.

$$= \frac{33}{2}$$ Multiply.

$$= 16\frac{1}{2}$$ Change to a mixed number.

The plank measures $16\frac{1}{2}$ board feet.

Try It

Multiply. Rewrite in lowest terms.

a. $8 \cdot 2\frac{1}{4}$ **b.** $4\frac{2}{7} \cdot 1\frac{2}{5}$ **c.** $2\frac{1}{10} \cdot 2\frac{1}{7}$ **d.** $3\frac{3}{10} \cdot 5$ **e.** $6\frac{1}{2} \cdot 2\frac{2}{3}$

Study TIP

Although it is quicker to divide by the GCF, any common factor will do. Sometimes it is easier to divide by a smaller factor several times.

Andy and Paula are helping their parents build a storage shed. They need to know the area of the 6 ft by $5\frac{1}{3}$ ft space where the shed will go.

Andy thinks ...

I'll use the distributive property to multiply.

$6 \cdot 5\frac{1}{3} = 6(5 + \frac{1}{3})$ Rewrite $5\frac{1}{3}$ as a sum.

$= (6 \cdot 5) + (6 \cdot \frac{1}{3})$ Use the distributive property.

$= 30 + 2$ Multiply.

$= 32$ Add.

The area is 32 square feet.

Paula thinks ...

I'll rewrite the mixed number as an improper fraction and then multiply.

$6 \cdot 5\frac{1}{3} = 6 \cdot \frac{16}{3}$ Rewrite $5\frac{1}{3}$ as an improper fraction.

$= \frac{\cancel{6}^{2}}{1} \cdot \frac{16}{\cancel{3}_{1}}$ Divide 6 and 3 by 3, a common factor.

$= 32$ Multiply.

The area is 32 square feet.

What do you think?

1. Whose method would you use to multiply $90 \times 100\frac{1}{3}$?

2. Can both methods be used for the product $4\frac{2}{3} \times 2$?

Remember

An improper fraction is always greater than or equal to 1, so the numerator is always greater than or equal to the denominator.
[Page 178]

Check   Your Understanding

1. How can you find $3\frac{1}{2} \cdot 4$ using addition? Using the distributive property?

2. How can you find the product of a mixed number and a fraction less than 1?

Practice and Apply

Getting Started Rewrite each mixed number as an improper fraction.

1. $3\frac{3}{8}$ **2.** $5\frac{4}{5}$ **3.** $8\frac{7}{8}$ **4.** $6\frac{5}{7}$ **5.** $2\frac{1}{6}$

Use the distributive property to find each product mentally.

6. $5 \cdot 1\frac{1}{3}$ **7.** $4 \cdot 3\frac{1}{2}$ **8.** $7 \cdot 2\frac{1}{5}$ **9.** $5\frac{1}{3} \cdot 3$ **10.** $1\frac{3}{4} \cdot 12$

Find each product.

11. $5\frac{3}{5} \cdot 2\frac{6}{7}$ **12.** $7\frac{1}{5} \cdot 3\frac{8}{9}$ **13.** $6\frac{2}{3} \cdot 8\frac{2}{5}$ **14.** $10\frac{4}{5} \cdot 4\frac{4}{9}$ **15.** $3\frac{1}{3} \cdot 2\frac{7}{10}$

16. $2\frac{4}{5} \cdot 3\frac{1}{3}$ **17.** $4\frac{1}{6} \cdot 1\frac{3}{5}$ **18.** $5\frac{1}{3} \cdot 2\frac{3}{5}$ **19.** $9\frac{3}{4} \cdot 7\frac{1}{2}$ **20.** $6\frac{2}{5} \cdot 4\frac{3}{4}$

21. $1\frac{4}{9} \cdot 2\frac{2}{3}$ **22.** $6\frac{1}{3} \cdot 3\frac{1}{6}$ **23.** $7\frac{1}{2} \cdot 5\frac{4}{5}$ **24.** $2\frac{3}{8} \cdot 6\frac{1}{4}$ **25.** $7\frac{3}{7} \cdot 1\frac{1}{4}$

26. Science As a roller-coaster car reaches the bottom of a slope and begins to go up the next slope, its acceleration, combined with the downward pull of gravity, can make you feel $3\frac{1}{2}$ times your weight—a sensation called supergravity, or *super-g's*. Calculate how heavy a 120 lb person would feel in a speeding roller coaster experiencing super-g's.

27. Number Sense Is the product of two mixed numbers less than or greater than each factor? Explain your answer.

28. Social Studies The area of the Pacific Ocean is about $12\frac{1}{2}$ times greater than the area of the Arctic Ocean. If the area of the Arctic Ocean is about 5,105,000 mi², about what is the area of the Pacific Ocean?

29. Problem Solving In a dog show, breeds are divided into *groups*. The terrier group, which includes the Airedale, has $1\frac{3}{10}$ times as many breeds as the working group, which includes the Great Dane. If there are 20 breeds in the working group, how many are there in the terrier group?

30. [Test Prep] Choose the best estimate for the product of the expression $4\frac{6}{7} \cdot 5\frac{1}{8}$.

Ⓐ 20 Ⓑ 25 Ⓒ 30 Ⓓ 35

31. History Susan B. Anthony was a leader in the women's suffrage movement. A special $1.00 coin was minted in 1979 to honor her. The coin is $\frac{3}{4}$ copper and $\frac{1}{4}$ nickel. It weighs $8\frac{1}{2}$ grams. How many grams of copper are in the coin?

Problem Solving and Reasoning

32. Choose a Strategy Find the areas of the rooms diagrammed. How much larger than the dining room is the area of the family room?

Family Room
16 1/2 ft by 17 1/6 ft

Dining Room
10 7/12 ft by 14 ft

Problem Solving

STRATEGIES

• Look for a Pattern
• Make an Organized List
• Make a Table
• Guess and Check
• Work Backward
• Use Logical Reasoning
• Draw a Diagram
• Solve a Simpler Problem

33. Communicate Write a step-by-step description of the method you would use to multiply 8 and $4\frac{3}{4}$.

34. [Journal] Draw a diagram to illustrate the product $2\frac{1}{2} \cdot 1\frac{3}{4}$.

Mixed Review

Make a line plot for each set of data and name any outliers. *[Lesson 1-3]*

35. 23, 25, 22, 26, 35, 24, 23, 23, 26

36. 3, 5, 8, 4, 7, 3, 7, 6, 4, 3, 7, 2, 4, 1

37. 7, 9, 12, 13, 8, 9, 13, 10, 6, 9, 9, 7

38. 42, 44, 43, 45, 33, 44, 46, 41, 43

Write each number in scientific notation. *[Lesson 3-5]*

39. 18

40. 625,000

41. 42,100,000

42. 867,530,900

43. 127,000,000

44. 2,600

45. 19,330

46. 2,700,000,000,000

47. 270

48. 186,000

49. 93,000,000

50. 5,555,230,000,000

TECHNOLOGY

Using a Spreadsheet • Writing Formulas

Problem: You are the statistician for the school's basketball team. So far this season, Kobi has scored 7 3-point baskets, 37 2-point baskets, and 15 1-point free throws. How many points did she score?

You can use the capabilities of a spreadsheet to answer this question quickly.

1 Enter Kobi's data into the spreadsheet.

	A	B
1	3-point baskets	7
2	2-point baskets	37
3	1-point free throws	15

	A	B
1	3-point baskets	7
2	2-point baskets	37
3	1-point free throws	15
4	Total points	=(3*B1)+(2*B2)+B3

2 To calculate Kobi's total number of points, multiply the number in B1 by 3, add this to 2 times the number in B2, and add the number in B3. As a spreadsheet formula, this is:
=(3*B1)+(2*B2)+B3

	A	B
1	3-point baskets	7
2	2-point baskets	37
3	1-point free throws	15
4	Total points	110

3 If you type this formula into cell B4 and press enter, the spreadsheet calculates Kobi's point total.

Solution: Kobi has scored 110 points so far this season.

Notice that, in spreadsheet formulas, multiplication is usually shown by *. In spreadsheets, division is usually shown by /.

TRY IT

a. So far this season, Audrey has scored four 3-point baskets, sixteen 2-point baskets, and nine 1-point free throws. Use a spreadsheet to find how many points she has scored.

b. A family of four is charged $7.00 each for movie tickets, and they have a $10 gift certificate. Use a spreadsheet to find how much they pay.

ON YOUR OWN

▶ Why might you want to use a spreadsheet to find Kobi's point total instead of calculating it yourself? (*Hint:* The season isn't over yet.)

▶ Explain how you would set up a spreadsheet to find the point totals for every player on a 10-player team.

Dividing Fractions and Mixed Numbers

▶ Lesson Link You've seen how to add, subtract, and multiply fractions and mixed numbers. Now you'll divide fractions and mixed numbers. ◀

Explore | Dividing Fractions

You Can Rule the World!

A building inspector carries a 6-ft measuring tape. To measure a 12-ft room, the inspector used 2 lengths of the tape. That's because $12 \div 6 = 2$.

1. Suppose the inspector forgot the tape and had only a $\frac{1}{2}$-ft ruler. How many lengths of the ruler would be needed to measure a 12-ft room? What is $12 \div \frac{1}{2}$? Explain.

2. Copy and complete the table for measuring rooms with rulers of the given lengths.

Length of Room	Length of Ruler	Number of Lengths of Ruler
12 ft	$\frac{1}{2}$ ft	24
12 ft	$\frac{1}{4}$ ft	
18 ft	$\frac{1}{2}$ ft	
18 ft	$\frac{1}{4}$ ft	

3. How could you find $18 \div \frac{1}{2}$ by multiplying instead of dividing? How could you find $12 \div \frac{1}{3}$ by multiplying instead of dividing?

Learn | Dividing Fractions and Mixed Numbers

When you divide, you find out how many times the divisor is contained in a number.

$14 \div 2$ means "How many 2's are there in 14?"

$3 \div \frac{1}{4}$ means "How many $\frac{1}{4}$'s are in 3?"

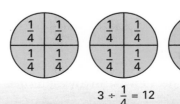

$$3 \div \frac{1}{4} = 12$$

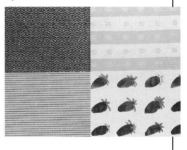

You can use **reciprocals** when you divide by a fraction or a mixed number. Two numbers are reciprocals if their product is 1.

The reciprocal of $\frac{4}{11}$ is $\frac{11}{4}$ because $\frac{4}{11} \cdot \frac{11}{4} = \frac{44}{44} = 1$.

To divide by a fraction, multiply by the reciprocal of the fraction. Simplify if possible.

Example 1

MENTAL MATH

To find the reciprocal of a fraction, simply interchange the numerator and denominator. The reciprocal of a whole number greater than zero is 1 over that number.

Divide. Rewrite in lowest terms. $\frac{5}{6} \div \frac{2}{3}$

$\frac{5}{6} \div \frac{2}{3} = \frac{5}{6} \cdot \frac{3}{2}$ Multiply by the reciprocal of $\frac{2}{3}$.

$= \frac{5 \cdot \overset{1}{\cancel{3}}}{\underset{2}{\cancel{6}} \cdot 2}$ Divide 3 and 6 by 3, a common factor.

$= \frac{5}{4} = 1\frac{1}{4}$ Multiply.

To divide with mixed numbers, rewrite the mixed numbers as improper fractions. Then multiply by the reciprocal of the divisor.

Example 2

▶ **Science Link**

A knot in a piece of wood is a lump where a branch grows out. When cut across, knots provide attractive designs in the grain of wood.

Mary needs to cover her $112\frac{1}{2}$-in.-long wall with $9\frac{3}{8}$-in.-wide knotty pine paneling. How many panels does she need?

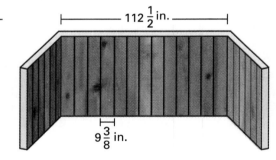

$112\frac{1}{2}$ in.

$9\frac{3}{8}$ in.

$112\frac{1}{2} \div 9\frac{3}{8} = \frac{225}{2} \div \frac{75}{8}$ Rewrite the mixed numbers as improper fractions.

$= \frac{225}{2} \cdot \frac{8}{75}$ Multiply by the reciprocal of $\frac{75}{8}$.

$= \frac{\overset{3}{\cancel{225}} \cdot \overset{4}{\cancel{8}}}{\underset{1}{\cancel{2}} \cdot \underset{1}{\cancel{75}}}$ Divide 225 and 75 by 75. Divide 8 and 2 by 2.

$= 12$ Multiply.

Twelve panels are needed.

Try It

Divide. Rewrite in lowest terms.   **a.** $5 \div \frac{1}{7}$ **b.** $\frac{3}{7} \div \frac{12}{21}$ **c.** $3\frac{7}{9} \div 2\frac{5}{6}$

1. Make a model to show that $3\frac{3}{8} \div 1\frac{1}{8} = 3$.

2. How can you use the rule for multiplying by the reciprocal to find $20 \div 5$?

4-6 Exercises and Applications

Practice and Apply

Getting Started | Find the reciprocal of each fraction.

1. $\frac{1}{2}$　　　　**2.** $\frac{3}{8}$　　　　**3.** $\frac{3}{10}$　　　　**4.** $\frac{2}{5}$　　　　**5.** $\frac{1}{4}$

Change each mixed number to an improper fraction and write its reciprocal.

6. $1\frac{1}{8}$　　　**7.** $3\frac{1}{2}$　　　**8.** $2\frac{3}{5}$　　　**9.** $4\frac{3}{4}$　　　**10.** $3\frac{2}{3}$

Rewrite each division expression as a multiplication expression to find the quotient.

11. $\frac{3}{8} \div \frac{1}{4}$　　　**12.** $\frac{1}{2} \div \frac{2}{7}$　　　**13.** $\frac{3}{5} \div \frac{1}{3}$　　　**14.** $\frac{3}{4} \div \frac{2}{3}$

15. $\frac{5}{8} \div 3\frac{1}{2}$　　　**16.** $1\frac{1}{2} \div 2\frac{2}{3}$　　　**17.** $2\frac{2}{5} \div \frac{5}{6}$　　　**18.** $4\frac{5}{8} \div 3\frac{1}{3}$

Find each quotient. Rewrite in lowest terms.

19. $\frac{3}{7} \div \frac{3}{5}$　　　**20.** $\frac{7}{8} \div \frac{1}{6}$　　　**21.** $\frac{5}{8} \div \frac{1}{4}$　　　**22.** $\frac{2}{3} \div \frac{1}{4}$

23. $5\frac{3}{4} \div 3\frac{2}{3}$　　　**24.** $2 \div \frac{2}{3}$　　　**25.** $7\frac{3}{4} \div 1\frac{2}{3}$　　　**26.** $4\frac{3}{4} \div 2\frac{2}{3}$

27. **Test Prep** Choose the correct operation to complete the sentence. The reciprocal of a number is the number that when _____ the original number results in the answer 1.

Ⓐ added to　　　Ⓑ subtracted from　　　Ⓒ multiplied by　　　Ⓓ divided by

28. **Measurement** A nail weighs about $\frac{1}{10}$ oz. How many nails are in a 5-lb box?

29. Ranchers in the American West often wear what is called a ten-gallon hat. However, a ten-gallon hat actually holds only $\frac{3}{4}$ of a gallon. How many ten-gallon hats would be needed to hold ten gallons?

30. **Measurement** A developer plans to subdivide 12 acres of land into $\frac{3}{4}$-acre building sites. How many building sites will there be?

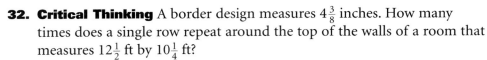

Problem Solving and Reasoning

31. **Journal** Explain why, when you divide a whole number other than zero by a proper fraction, the quotient is always greater than the whole number.

32. **Critical Thinking** A border design measures $4\frac{3}{8}$ inches. How many times does a single row repeat around the top of the walls of a room that measures $12\frac{1}{2}$ ft by $10\frac{1}{4}$ ft?

33. **Critical Thinking** Write an equation to solve for x. Then solve the equation.

a.

$2\frac{1}{4}$ in.

| Area = $3\frac{1}{2}$ in² | x in. |

b.

x in.

| Area = $5\frac{1}{5}$ in² | $\frac{5}{8}$ in. |

Mixed Review

Make a line graph for each set of data. [Lesson 1-5]

34.

Month	Jan.	Feb.	Mar.	Apr.	May
Profit ($)	2460	3820	1760	2340	2900

35.

Game	1	2	3	4	5
Score	18	25	12	31	28

Test each number for divisibility by 2, 3, 4, 5, 6, 8, 9, and 10. [Lesson 3-6]

36. 385   37. 642   38. 94   39. 6230   40. 1028

Project Progress

Draw or trace a world map, and show the 5 most populous countries. Find the *total* fraction of the world's population that lives in these countries, and find the fraction of the population that does not live in these countries.

Problem Solving

Understand
Plan
Solve
Look Back

You've learned about the importance of fractions in architecture and building. Now you will have an opportunity to apply what you've learned to the remodeling of a home. This home is in the Greek revival style. To be historically accurate, it has no closets or kitchen.

Building It Piece by Piece

Below is a blueprint for the first floor of a Greek revival–style home.

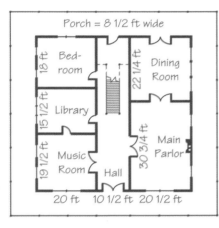

1. Find the length and width of the house, not including the porch.

2. Estimate the area of each room and the hall.

3. The dining room carpet comes on 12-foot-wide rolls. How many feet of carpet must be ordered?

4. The porch must be painted with a special paint that costs $17.85 per gallon. If a gallon covers 200 square feet, how many gallons must be purchased for the porch floors? What will the cost be?

5. Wood for the library floor costs $6 per square foot. How much will the floor cost?

6. Sections of crown molding, each $2\frac{9}{16}$ ft in length, will circle the main parlor at the tops of the walls. How many sections will be needed?

7. The kitchen is to be built as a separate rectangular building. It is to be bigger than the library but smaller than the dining room. Neither the length nor the width will have whole-number measurements. Draw a possible floor plan. Show the measurements on your diagram.

Find each sum or difference.

1. $\dfrac{4}{7} - \dfrac{1}{3}$
2. $\dfrac{4}{9} + \dfrac{1}{2}$
3. $9\dfrac{1}{4} - 5\dfrac{3}{8}$
4. $7\dfrac{3}{5} + \dfrac{5}{6}$

Find each product. Rewrite in lowest terms.

5. $\dfrac{1}{3} \cdot \dfrac{3}{8}$
6. $\dfrac{2}{7} \cdot \dfrac{3}{4}$
7. $\dfrac{3}{5} \cdot 2\dfrac{5}{6}$
8. $\dfrac{3}{8} \cdot \dfrac{5}{9}$
9. $\dfrac{7}{8} \cdot \dfrac{2}{3}$

10. $3\dfrac{4}{7} \cdot \dfrac{7}{8}$
11. $\dfrac{2}{5} \cdot 2\dfrac{7}{10}$
12. $5 \cdot \dfrac{3}{8}$
13. $\dfrac{7}{9} \cdot 7$
14. $2\dfrac{1}{4} \cdot \dfrac{3}{4}$

Find each quotient. Rewrite in lowest terms.

15. $\dfrac{1}{2} \div \dfrac{1}{4}$
16. $\dfrac{5}{7} \div \dfrac{1}{4}$
17. $\dfrac{3}{4} \div 6$
18. $\dfrac{1}{4} \div \dfrac{1}{2}$
19. $\dfrac{2}{5} \div 1\dfrac{1}{4}$

20. $\dfrac{4}{5} \div 3\dfrac{1}{3}$
21. $5\dfrac{4}{5} \div 9\dfrac{2}{7}$
22. $10\dfrac{3}{4} \div 4$
23. $8\dfrac{1}{8} \div 12$
24. $3\dfrac{1}{4} \div 5\dfrac{1}{12}$

25. Science The length of a kangaroo's leap can be up to $6\dfrac{1}{2}$ times its height. If a kangaroo is $6\dfrac{3}{4}$ feet tall, about how far can it jump?

26. DeWayne is building a 72-ft-long dock. If each plank is $\dfrac{3}{4}$ of a foot wide, how many planks does he need?

Test Prep

On a multiple choice test in which you are asked to multiply fractions, recognizing that common factors can be used to divide the numerators and denominators of fractions before multiplying will help you work more quickly.

27. Multiply. $\dfrac{27}{56} \cdot \dfrac{42}{81}$

  Ⓐ $\dfrac{1}{4}$ Ⓑ $\dfrac{1}{3}$ Ⓒ $\dfrac{2}{3}$ Ⓓ $\dfrac{3}{4}$

28. Multiply. $\dfrac{10}{33} \cdot \dfrac{11}{20}$

  Ⓐ $\dfrac{1}{12}$ Ⓑ $\dfrac{1}{6}$ Ⓒ $\dfrac{5}{12}$ Ⓓ $\dfrac{3}{4}$

Measurement Tools

Every profession has its own set of measuring tools. Carpenters use tape measures to measure length, and pharmacists use balance scales to measure weight. The purpose of the measurement helps you decide which tool and measurement unit to choose.

The accuracy of a measurement depends on the unit you use. The smaller the unit, the more precise the measurement. But no matter how small a unit you use, there is some uncertainty, or *error*, to the measurement.

The greatest possible error in a measurement is half the smallest unit used. If your doctor says your height is 5 feet 2 inches, you know you are at least 5 feet $1\frac{1}{2}$ inches tall, but less than 5 feet $2\frac{1}{2}$ inches tall. The greatest possible error is plus or minus $\frac{1}{2}$ inches, written $\pm\frac{1}{2}$ inches (or ±0.5 inches).

What is the possible error in the baby's weight measurement?

The smallest unit being used is an ounce. So the possible error is $\pm\frac{1}{2}$ ounce.

A ruler has divisions every $\frac{1}{8}$ of an inch. What is the possible error of a measurement taken with this ruler?

The smallest unit is $\frac{1}{8}$ of an inch. Half of $\frac{1}{8}$ is $\frac{1}{16}$, so the possible error is $\pm\frac{1}{16}$ inch.

IT'S A GIRL!

Crystal Ann Jones
6 pounds, 7 ounces
Born 9:52 A.M.
December 1, 1997

When a measurement is expressed as a whole number or decimal, its *significant digits* are all of the digits that are known exactly and the last digit, which is estimated. You'll learn more about significant digits in science courses.

Try It

Name a tool and unit of measure that can be used to measure:

1. Length
2. Weight
3. Distance
4. Time

Give the greatest possible error for each measurement.

5. 6 meters
6. 7 feet 2 inches
7. 12.3 kilograms
8. Any measurement on a scale with divisions every $\frac{1}{4}$ ounce.

203

Graphic Organizer

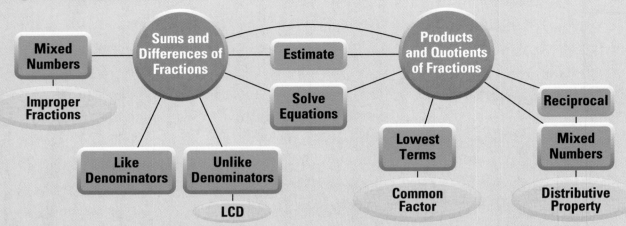

Section 4A Sums and Differences of Fractions

Summary

- To estimate sums and differences of fractions, round the fractions to 0, $\frac{1}{2}$, or 1, then add or subtract mentally.

- A **mixed number** is made up of a whole number and a fraction.

- To estimate sums, differences, and products of mixed numbers, round to the nearest whole.

- Use compatible numbers to estimate quotients of mixed numbers and products of fractions and whole numbers.

- To add or subtract fractions with the same denominator, add or subtract the numerators. Write the result over the denominator and rewrite in lowest terms.

- The **least common denominator (LCD)** of two fractions is the LCM of the denominators. To add or subtract fractions with different denominators, rewrite the fractions using the LCD.

- Equations containing fractions can be solved using inverse operations.

- An **improper fraction** is a fraction that is greater than or equal to one.

- Add mixed numbers by adding the whole numbers and the fractions separately. You may have to change the resulting fraction to a mixed number and add it to the whole number.

- Subtract mixed numbers by subtracting the whole numbers and subtracting the fractions. Sometimes you need to rewrite the whole-number part of the first number to subtract the fractions.

- Another way to add and subtract mixed numbers is to rewrite both numbers as improper fractions, then add or subtract.

Review

1. Estimate the sum $\frac{5}{8} + \frac{15}{16}$.

2. Estimate the difference $\frac{10}{11} - \frac{8}{9}$.

3. Use compatible numbers to estimate the quotient $24\frac{3}{4} \div 5\frac{1}{3}$.

4. Paul bought a stock at $32\frac{11}{16}$. Estimate the price after it went down $3\frac{3}{4}$.

5. Find the sum $\frac{13}{15} + \frac{7}{10}$.

6. Solve the equation $x + \frac{1}{6} = \frac{8}{9}$.

7. Find the difference $\frac{11}{12} - \frac{3}{5}$.

8. Write $3\frac{7}{8}$ as an improper fraction.

9. Find the sum $2\frac{3}{4} + 6\frac{5}{8}$.

10. Find the difference $13\frac{2}{3} - 7\frac{4}{5}$.

Section 4B   Products and Quotients of Fractions

Summary

- To multiply fractions, multiply the numerators and multiply the denominators. Simplify the product if possible.

- You can multiply mixed numbers by using the distributive property or by rewriting them as improper fractions.

- Two numbers are **reciprocals** if their product is 1.

- To divide by a fraction, multiply by its reciprocal.

- To divide mixed numbers, first rewrite them as improper fractions.

Review

11. Find the product $\frac{2}{3} \cdot \frac{9}{11}$.

12. Find the product $\frac{16}{21} \cdot \frac{15}{8}$.

13. Find the area of a rectangular piece of wood with dimensions $\frac{3}{8}$ ft by $\frac{5}{6}$ ft.

14. Susan is $2\frac{1}{4}$ times as old as Hal. Hal is 16. How old is Susan?

15. Find the product $3\frac{1}{7} \cdot 5\frac{8}{11}$.

16. Find the product $8\frac{3}{8} \cdot 7\frac{2}{5}$.

17. Find the quotient $\frac{7}{8} \div \frac{14}{9}$.

18. Find the quotient $2\frac{4}{15} \div 1\frac{5}{6}$.

19. A floppy disk holds $1\frac{11}{25}$ megabytes. How many disks are needed for 60 megabytes?

20. A cupcake weighs $3\frac{1}{2}$ ounces. How many cupcakes are there in a 28-ounce package?

Chapter 4 Assessment

Estimate each sum, difference, or quotient.

1. $\frac{1}{15} + \frac{5}{11}$

2. $\frac{7}{13} - \frac{11}{23}$

3. $20\frac{5}{8} \div 7\frac{1}{3}$

4. Karen bought a stock at $41\frac{3}{8}$. Her stock went up $6\frac{3}{4}$ points. Estimate the new price.

Find each sum or difference.

5. $\frac{7}{16} + \frac{3}{10}$

6. $\frac{9}{14} - \frac{2}{7}$

7. $\frac{13}{16} + \frac{7}{12}$

8. $32\frac{6}{7} - 14\frac{1}{4}$

9. $6\frac{8}{15} + 17\frac{7}{20}$

10. $63\frac{1}{5} - 39\frac{2}{3}$

11. Solve the equation $y - \frac{3}{8} = \frac{1}{6}$.

12. Write $\frac{53}{11}$ as a mixed number.

13. In a 3-day hike, Ka-fei walked $7\frac{3}{4}$ miles the first day, $12\frac{4}{5}$ miles the second day, and $9\frac{5}{8}$ miles the third day. How far did he walk altogether?

Find each product or quotient.

14. $\frac{4}{5} \cdot \frac{3}{10}$

15. $\frac{7}{30} \cdot \frac{50}{21}$

16. $5\frac{3}{8} \cdot 12\frac{2}{3}$

17. $\frac{1}{4} \cdot 10\frac{7}{8}$

18. $\frac{6}{19} \div \frac{12}{13}$

19. $8\frac{2}{5} \div 3\frac{5}{9}$

20. Rodney has $4200 in his bank account. If Esmeralda's account balance is $2\frac{5}{7}$ times Rodney's balance, how much money does she have in her account?

21. A plank is $6\frac{3}{4}$ in. wide. How many planks need to be laid side by side to form a walkway that is 54 in. wide?

Performance Task

Two-thirds of the people working at Happy Homes Realty are sales agents and the rest are clerical employees. If five-eighths of the agents are women and four-sevenths of the clerical employees are men, find the fraction of the people in the office who are male agents, female agents, male clerical employees, and female clerical employees.

a. Make a chart to show your results.

b. If there are 21 male sales agents, find how many people are employed all together and how many people are in each category.

Multiple Choice

Choose the best answer.

1. Find the mean of 41, 31, 36, 31, 27, 38, 41, 31, 47, and 29. *[Lesson 1-4]*

   Ⓐ 31   Ⓑ 33.5   Ⓒ 35.2   Ⓓ 41

2. Which formula was used to create the table below? *[Lesson 2-3]*

x	2	3	4	5	6
y	7	10	13	16	19

   Ⓐ $y = 2x + 3$ Ⓑ $y = 4x - 5$

   Ⓒ $y = 3x + 1$ Ⓓ $y = 4x - 1$

3. A music club advertises, "Buy a CD for $15, then take as many as you want for $8 each." Fran ordered five CDs from the club. How much will she pay? *[Lesson 2-8]*

   Ⓐ $40   Ⓑ $47   Ⓒ $55   Ⓓ $75

4. Estimate the product 12.8×19.7. *[Lesson 3-4]*

   Ⓐ 200   Ⓑ 230   Ⓒ 260   Ⓓ 300

5. Express the number 64,000,000 in scientific notation. *[Lesson 3-5]*

   Ⓐ 6.4×10^6 Ⓑ 6.4×10^7

   Ⓒ 64×10^6 Ⓓ 0.64×10^8

6. Find the GCF of 96 and 72. *[Lesson 3-7]*

   Ⓐ 12   Ⓑ 16   Ⓒ 24   Ⓓ 288

7. Which is the solution to the equation $6.523 = u - 3.45$? *[Lesson 3-3]*

   Ⓐ 3.073   Ⓑ 9.973

   Ⓒ 9.568   Ⓓ 22.50435

8. Which one of the following fractions is not equivalent to the others? *[Lesson 3-8]*

   Ⓐ $\frac{12}{15}$ Ⓑ $\frac{20}{25}$ Ⓒ $\frac{25}{30}$ Ⓓ $\frac{28}{35}$

9. Which fraction forms a repeating decimal? *[Lesson 3-10]*

   Ⓐ $\frac{11}{50}$ Ⓑ $\frac{32}{125}$ Ⓒ $\frac{10}{13}$ Ⓓ $\frac{39}{256}$

10. Estimate the sum $\frac{1}{11} + \frac{5}{12}$. *[Lesson 4-1]*

    Ⓐ 0   Ⓑ $\frac{1}{2}$ Ⓒ 1   Ⓓ $\frac{3}{2}$

11. Which is the solution to the equation $y + \frac{3}{20} = \frac{5}{8}$? *[Lesson 4-2]*

    Ⓐ $\frac{19}{40}$ Ⓑ $\frac{1}{8}$ Ⓒ $\frac{31}{40}$ Ⓓ $\frac{2}{7}$

12. Find the sum $8\frac{21}{22} + 12\frac{25}{33}$. *[Lesson 4-3]*

    Ⓐ $20\frac{113}{66}$ Ⓑ $20\frac{46}{55}$

    Ⓒ $114\frac{173}{726}$ Ⓓ $21\frac{47}{66}$

13. Find the product $\frac{9}{22} \cdot \frac{55}{12}$. Reduce to lowest terms. *[Lesson 4-4]*

    Ⓐ $\frac{54}{605}$ Ⓑ $\frac{45}{24}$ Ⓒ $\frac{15}{8}$ Ⓓ $\frac{659}{132}$

14. A record on a turntable rotates every $1\frac{4}{5}$ seconds. How many times does it rotate in 45 seconds? *[Lesson 4-6]*

    Ⓐ 15 times   Ⓑ 20 times

    Ⓒ 25 times   Ⓓ 30 times

5 Geometry and Measurement

Cultural Link
www.mathsurf.com/7/ch2/people

Entertainment Link
www.mathsurf.com/7/ch5/ent

People of the World

The area of a bedroom in Japan is measured in units called *tatamis.* The tatami is about the size of a small single bed.

Entertainment

A spiral track on a compact disc is more than 3.5 miles long!

Arts & Literature

A sonnet written in iambic pentameter is a poem that has a length of 14 lines, where each line has 10 syllables and every even numbered syllable is stressed.

Shall **I** Com**pare** thee **to** a **sum**mer's **day**?
Thou **art** more **love**ly **and** more **temp**erate:
Rough **winds** do **shake** the **dar**ling **buds** of **May**,
And **sum**mer's **lease** hath **all** too **short** a **date**:

Science

A crystal's shape can help classify it. A cross section of an emerald is a hexagon. The cross section of a salt crystal is a square.

Social Studies

The Nile is the world's longest river. It flows through four countries (Egypt, Sudan, Tanzania, and Uganda) and measures 6670 km.

KEY MATH IDEAS

A straight line extends forever in two directions. Rays and segments are parts of lines.

Angles are made of rays. They are measured in degrees.

A polygon is a figure whose sides are straight. The number of sides of a polygon tells you the sum of its angle measures.

The distance around a figure is its perimeter. The space it encloses is its area. You can use formulas to calculate the areas of many types of polygons.

You can use the Pythagorean Theorem to find the length of a side in a right triangle. Solving for the side length involves squaring numbers and finding their square roots.

Problem Solving

Understand
Plan
Solve
Look Back

CHAPTER PROJECT

In this project, you will calculate the area of your school's ground floor. Begin the project by sketching the floor plan of your school building or buildings.

**Problem
Solving**

Understand
Plan
Solve
Look Back

Identifying Missing Information

As you plan how you are going to solve a problem, you need to be sure you have all the necessary information. Sometimes you will encounter a problem that is missing important information.

Problem Solving Focus

Identify any additional information needed to solve each problem. If a problem is not missing any information, give its solution.

❶ A *mat* is an open cardboard rectangle that fits between a photograph and its frame. Lou has several photographs to mat and frame. Each mat costs $15.00. A frame costs $5.00 more than a mat. How many pictures can Lou afford to mat and frame?

❷ Lou's favorite photograph is $3\frac{1}{2}$ inches by 5 inches. She wants to center it in an 8 inch by $9\frac{1}{2}$ inch mat with equal space on all sides. How many inches of mat will there be on each side of the photograph?

❸ For the next photograph, Lou wants 2 inches of mat on all sides. How large should the mat be?

❹ One of Lou's photos is 4 inches by 6 inches. What size frame should Lou buy for this photo?

FROM THE DOME

to Your Home ...

What's more than two football fields wide, can withstand 200-mile-per-hour winds, protects 75,000 people from the weather, and looks like a hemisphere but isn't?

Answer: *The dome on the Louisiana Superdome, the world's largest indoor stadium. Covering almost 10 acres, the dome is the crown on one of the world's most unusual buildings.*

The dome isn't really a hemisphere. Instead, it's constructed of lines and angles that form simple geometric figures. Other unusual buildings, such as the Transamerica Pyramid in San Francisco, are also based on geometric figures.

From the pyramids of ancient Egypt to today's most modern buildings, architectural design has used the simple figures of geometry. Now you'll also learn to spot geometric figures in the buildings around you—in your school, your home or apartment, and in the office buildings in your town.

1 What does it mean to say that the dome "isn't really a hemisphere"?

2 Describe some of the shapes you see in the dome. Name any figures you recognize.

3 Name an unusual building that you're familiar with. How is geometry used in the design of the building?

211

Angles

You'll Learn ...

■ to name angles

■ to measure angles

... How It's Used

Airplane navigators must measure angles very accurately to keep their planes on course.

Vocabulary

ray

angle

vertex

acute angle

right angle

obtuse angle

straight angle

complementary

supplementary

congruent

bisect

angle bisector

▶ **Lesson Link**   You've seen angles in circle graphs. Now you'll look more closely at angles to see how they are named, drawn, and measured. ◀

Explore   Angles

What's Your Angle?

Materials: Protractor, Transparent paper

The 1815-foot-tall CN Tower in Toronto, Ontario, Canada, is the world's tallest unsupported building. It contains the 7-story Skypod, the tower's revolving restaurant and office complex.

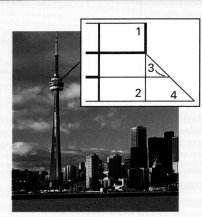

1. Copy the four labeled angles shown on the Skypod.

2. The measure of the angle labeled with a 4 is 45 degrees. Use your protractor to determine how the measurement is made. Extend the sides of the angle if necessary.

3. Find the measures of angles 1, 2, and 3.

4. Explain how to measure an angle with a protractor. Be sure to include different types of angles in your explanation.

Learn   Angles

Recall that a *line* extends without end in both directions. You can think of a **ray** as part of a line. A ray has one endpoint and extends without end in *one* direction.

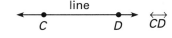

A ray is named by its endpoint and one other point on the ray. The figure shows ray $\overrightarrow{AB}$, written $\overrightarrow{AB}$. Notice that the arrow points from the endpoint through another point on the ray.

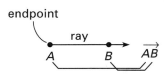

Two rays with a common endpoint form an **angle** . The two rays are the sides of the angle. The common endpoint is the **vertex** .

You can use the angle symbol (∠), the vertex, and a point on each side to name an angle. You can use the vertex alone, or a number, to name the angle if there is no chance of confusion.

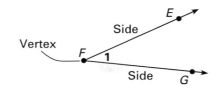

Vertex Side E

F 1

Side G

∠*EFG* or ∠*GFE* or ∠*F* or ∠1
Always write the vertex letter
in the middle.

Angles are measured in degrees (°). They can be classified according to their measures.

  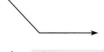

An **acute angle** has a measure less than 90°.

A **right angle** has a measure of exactly 90°.

An **obtuse angle** has a measure greater than 90° and less than 180°.

A **straight angle** has a measure of exactly 180°.

▶ **Language Link**

When the word *right* refers to an angle, it has nothing to do with left and right or wrong and right. This usage is like *upright,* meaning "standing up straight."

You can use a protractor to find the measure of an angle.

Example 1

Name the angle and find its measure.

The angle is ∠*LTK*, ∠*KTL*, or ∠*T*.

To find the measure, place a protractor on the angle so that the center mark is on the vertex and the 0° lines match one side of the angle.

L

T

K

Study TIP

You can lengthen the sides of angle *T* by tracing over it and drawing the rays so that they extend to the edge of your protractor.

Find the point where the other side of the angle meets the degree scale on the protractor. Read the measure: 76°. Use the letter *m* to write the measure: $m\angle T = 76°$.

Two angles are **complementary** if the sum of their measures is 90°. Two angles are **supplementary** if the sum of their measures is 180°.

50° + 40° = 90°

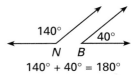

140° + 40° = 180°

Examples

2 Find the measures of a complement and a supplement of ∠N.

The sum of the measures of ∠N and an angle complementary to it is 90°.

A complement of ∠N measures 90° − 54° = 36°.

The sum of the measures of ∠N and an angle supplementary to it is 180°.

A supplement of ∠N measures 180° − 54° = 126°.

54°

N

3 Identify a pair of supplementary angles in the supports of the bridge. If the measure of the acute angle is 60°, what is the measure of the other angle?

Since a straight angle measures 180°, any pair of angles that share a side and lie along a line is supplementary. If the acute angle measures 60°, the other angle measures 180° − 60° = 120°.

60°

Try It

Find the measures of a complement and a supplement of a 43° angle.

If two angles have the same measure, they are **congruent**. The symbol ≅ means "is congruent to." A ray that divides an angle into two congruent angles **bisects** the angle. The ray is the **angle bisector**. In this figure, $\overrightarrow{GM}$ bisects ∠FGH, so ∠FGM ≅ ∠MGH.

H

M

G   F

Check   Your Understanding

1. Tell whether you agree or disagree with this statement: The complement of an acute angle must be an acute angle. Explain.

2. What are the measures of the angles formed by the bisector of a right angle? A straight angle?

Study TIP

Notice that **C** comes before **S**, and 90° is less than 180°, so **Complementary** refers to 90° and **Supplementary** to 180°.

Practice and Apply

1. **Getting Started** Follow these steps to measure an angle using a protractor.

a. Draw two intersecting rays that form an angle.

b. Place the protractor on the angle so that the center mark is on the vertex and the 0° line matches one side of the angle.

c. Find the point where the other side of the angle meets the degree scale on the protractor. Read the measure.

Name each angle and give its measure.

2.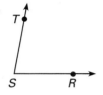

3.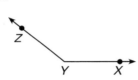

4.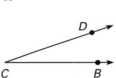

5.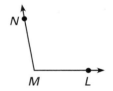

Find the measures of a complement and a supplement of ∠N.

6. 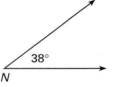 38°

7. 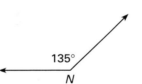 135°

8. 88°

9. 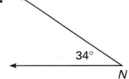 34°

Measure each angle using a protractor.

10.

11.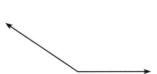

12.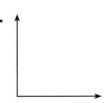

13.

Classify each angle.

14.

15.

16.

17.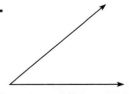

18. **Science** When a beam of light strikes a flat mirror, the light reflects at the same angle at which it hit the mirror's surface.

a. If light strikes a mirror at a 50° angle, at what angle will the light reflect?

b. What is the measure of the angle *between* the angle at which light strikes the mirror (50°), and the angle at which the light reflects?

19. **Test Prep** Which of the following is not correct?

Ⓐ Obtuse angle: 37°　　Ⓑ Acute angle: 79°　　Ⓒ Right angle: 90°　　Ⓓ Straight angle: 180°

Problem Solving and Reasoning

20. **Critical Thinking** Tell what type of angles are formed when each angle is bisected. Make a sketch to help show your answers.

a. An obtuse angle　　　　　　　　**b.** A right angle

c. A straight angle　　　　　　　　**d.** An acute angle

21. **Journal** Draw an angle. Use the method shown below to bisect the angle with a compass and straightedge.

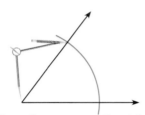

1. Place the compass tip at the vertex of the angle. Make an arc that intersects both sides of the angle.

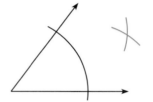

2. Place the compass tip at a point where the arc intersects the angle. Make an arc. Make another arc with the tip at the other intersection point.

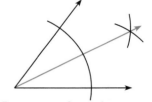

3. Draw a ray from the vertex of the angle through the point where the arcs you made in Step 2 cross. This ray bisects the angle.

Mixed Review

Use > or < to compare each pair of numbers. *[Lesson 3-1]*

22. 8.40 ☐ 7.41　　**23.** 6.423 ☐ 64.23　　**24.** 2.875 ☐ 2.758　　**25.** 5.246 ☐ 5.245

26. 3.899 ☐ 3.9　　**27.** 23.74 ☐ 23.477　　**28.** 9.127 ☐ 9.217　　**29.** 0.8 ☐ 0.0999

Find the GCF and the LCM of each pair of numbers. *[Lesson 3-7]*

30. 34, 42　　**31.** 165, 85　　**32.** 42, 63　　**33.** 84, 96

34. 525, 630　　**35.** 198, 363　　**36.** 1001, 1275　　**37.** 36, 56

Parallel and Perpendicular Lines

▶ **Lesson Link**   You have seen that rays are related to lines. Now you'll look more closely at lines, especially those that never meet and those that meet to form right angles. ◀

Explore | Parallel and Perpendicular Lines

The Game Is on the Line!

Materials: Lined paper, Straightedge, Protractor

Select two lines on your paper that are more than one space apart.

1. Describe the lines on your paper. What's special about them?

2. Draw a slanted line through these lines and label the angles as shown. Measure angles 1–8 and record your measurements.

3. Did you find any congruent angles? If so, name them.

4. Did you find any supplementary angles? If so, name them.

5. Redraw the figure. Now draw a vertical line through the two lines you selected. What is the measure of each angle now?

Learn | Parallel and Perpendicular Lines

A **plane** is an infinite, flat surface. Lines in a plane that never meet are called **parallel** lines. The figure shows parallel ribs (red) near the base of Paris's famous Eiffel Tower. To strengthen the tower, designer Gustave Eiffel constructed slanted struts (blue) across the parallel ribs. Lines that intersect two or more parallel lines in this way are called **transversals** .

You'll Learn ...

■ to recognize parallel lines and their properties

■ to recognize perpendicular lines and their properties

... How It's Used

Railroad construction engineers need to build tracks that are exactly parallel. The ties that hold the track in place must be perpendicular to the tracks.

Vocabulary

plane

parallel

transversal

alternate interior angles

corresponding angles

vertical angles

midpoint

congruent segments

segment bisector

perpendicular

perpendicular bisector

When a transversal intersects two parallel lines, pairs of congruent angles are formed. Here are some of the congruent angles:

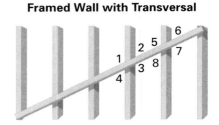

Alternate Interior Angles	$\angle 3 \cong \angle 5, \angle 4 \cong \angle 6$
Corresponding Angles	$\angle 1 \cong \angle 5, \angle 2 \cong \angle 6, \angle 3 \cong \angle 7, \angle 4 \cong \angle 8$
Vertical Angles	$\angle 1 \cong \angle 3, \angle 2 \cong \angle 4, \angle 5 \cong \angle 7, \angle 6 \cong \angle 8$

Example 1

A carpenter has framed a wall with six parallel studs crossed by a transversal brace. If $m\angle 2 = 62°$, what are $m\angle 3$, $m\angle 8$, $m\angle 6$, and $m\angle 4$?

Framed Wall with Transversal

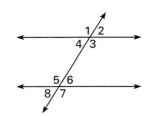

Vertical angles $\angle 2$ and $\angle 4$ are congruent, so $m\angle 4 = 62°$.

Alternate interior angles $\angle 2$ and $\angle 8$ are congruent, so $m\angle 8 = 62°$.

Corresponding angles $\angle 2$ and $\angle 6$ are congruent, so $m\angle 6 = 62°$.

$\angle 2$ and $\angle 3$ form a straight angle, so they are supplementary.

$$m\angle 3 + m\angle 2 = 180° \qquad \text{∠2 and ∠3 are supplementary.}$$
$$m\angle 3 + 62° = 180° \qquad \text{Substitute 62° for } m\angle 2.$$
$$m\angle 3 + 62° - 62° = 180° - 62° \qquad \text{To undo adding 62°, subtract 62° from both sides.}$$
$$m\angle 3 = 118° \qquad \text{Subtract.}$$

Try It

Name each angle pair.

a. $\angle 2, \angle 6$ **b.** $\angle 5, \angle 7$ **c.** $\angle 4, \angle 6$

$m\angle 3 = 121°$. Find the measure of each angle.

d. $\angle 4$ **e.** $\angle 5$ **f.** $\angle 7$ **g.** $\angle 2$

A line segment is formed by two endpoints and all the points between them. Line $\overleftrightarrow{EF}$ intersects line segment $\overline{KL}$ at its **midpoint** M, the point that divides it into two **congruent segments**. Congruent segments have equal lengths.

$\overleftrightarrow{EF}$ is the **segment bisector** of $\overline{KL}$ because it passes through the midpoint M. The two marks on $\overline{KL}$ show the equal parts.

Line segment

Now imagine that $m\angle EMK$ is increased to 90°. **Perpendicular** lines, rays, and line segments form right angles. The symbol $\perp$ means "is perpendicular to." $\overleftrightarrow{EF} \perp \overleftrightarrow{KL}$, so $\overleftrightarrow{EF}$ is the **perpendicular bisector** of $\overline{KL}$.

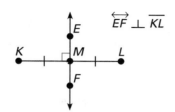

$$\overleftrightarrow{EF} \perp \overline{KL}$$

Example 2

An archer places an arrow 16 in. from each end of the bowstring. The arrow makes a 90° angle to the string. Why is the arrow the perpendicular bisector of the bowstring?

The arrow forms a right angle with the bowstring, so the arrow is perpendicular to the string.

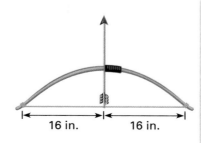

16 in.   16 in.

The arrow also intersects the string at its midpoint, 16 in. from each end.

Since the arrow is perpendicular to the segment at its midpoint, the arrow is the perpendicular bisector of the segment.

► **History Link**

From the 1300s to the 1500s, the Perpendicular Style of Gothic architecture developed in England. Westminster Abbey is an example of this style of building.

Try It

a. Identify any midpoint on the kite and tell why it is a midpoint.

b. Identify any perpendicular bisector on the kite and tell why it is a perpendicular bisector.

$$\overline{CE} \cong \overline{ED}$$

Check   Your Understanding

1. Point out a pair of parallel lines and a pair of perpendicular lines in your classroom.

2. Explain how you could determine if two lines are parallel; if two lines are perpendicular.

3. Suppose a transversal intersects two parallel lines. If it is perpendicular to one of the parallel lines, is it perpendicular to the other? Explain.

4. Is it possible for two nonintersecting lines *not* to be parallel? If so, describe or give an example of such lines. If not, explain why not.

Practice and Apply

Getting Started Determine if each pair of lines is parallel, perpendicular, or neither.

1. **2.** **3.** **4.**

Write the word that describes the lines or line segments.

5. Two rails of a railroad track

6. Adjacent edges of a square floor tile

7. Top and side of a door

8. Opposite sides of a basketball court

9. Telephone pole and the street

10. Shelves of a bookcase

Use the figure to name each set of angles or lines.

11. A pair of parallel lines

12. A pair of perpendicular lines

13. A pair of supplementary angles

14. Two pairs of congruent angles

15. **Measurement** Draw a line segment, then measure it and identify its midpoint. Use the midpoint and your protractor to draw a perpendicular bisector.

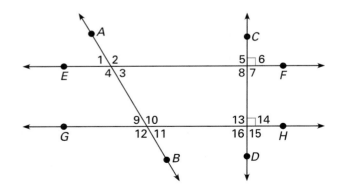

Geography Use the street map of downtown Washington, DC, for Exercises 16–18.

16. Name two streets that are parallel.

17. Name two streets that are transversals of the parallel streets you identified.

18. Name two streets that are perpendicular.

19. **Test Prep** If a perpendicular bisector divides a 7 cm segment into two congruent segments, how long will each one be?

Ⓐ 3.5 cm   Ⓑ 5 cm   Ⓒ 9 cm   Ⓓ 14 cm

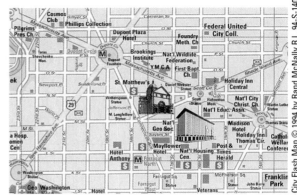

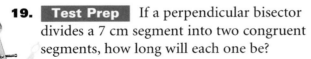

Problem Solving and Reasoning

Critical Thinking Identify parallel and perpendicular lines on the buildings in the photos.

20.

21.

Neue Staatsgalerie Museum, Munich, Germany

22. Communicate Two lines that do not intersect and are not parallel are *skew*. Describe to a friend two pairs of skew lines that you observe in your classroom.

23. Draw a line segment. Use the method shown below to construct its perpendicular bisector with a compass and straightedge.

  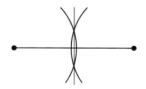

1. Open your compass to more than half of the segment's length. Place the point of your compass on one endpoint and make an arc.

2. Using the same compass setting, make an arc from the other endpoint. It should intersect your first arc in two places.

3. Draw the line joining these points. This line is the perpendicular bisector of the segment.

Mixed Review

Estimate. *[Lesson 3-2]*

24. $12.95 + 26.34$

25. $184.3 - 98.6$

26. 7.86×9.23

27. $373.28 \div 24.78$

28. $63.21 - 19.42$

29. $\dfrac{842.7}{23.75}$

30. 39.67×17.3

31. $931.5 + 68.3$

Express each fraction in lowest terms. *[Lesson 3-8]*

32. $\dfrac{24}{36}$

33. $\dfrac{18}{54}$

34. $\dfrac{44}{121}$

35. $\dfrac{42}{91}$

36. $\dfrac{38}{95}$

37. $\dfrac{72}{105}$

38. $\dfrac{81}{192}$

39. $\dfrac{45}{80}$

Triangles and Quadrilaterals

You'll Learn ...

■ to name and classify triangles

■ to name and classify quadrilaterals

■ to find the measures of angles in these figures

... How It's Used

Interior designers use triangles and quadrilaterals to help create patterns.

Vocabulary

equilateral triangle

isosceles triangle

scalene triangle

acute triangle

right triangle

obtuse triangle

quadrilateral

parallelogram

rhombus

trapezoid

▶ **Lesson Link** You've looked at some important angle properties. Now you'll investigate commonly seen figures that have three or four angles. ◀

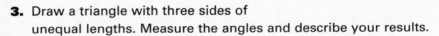

Explore | **Triangles**

Sides and Angles

Materials: Ruler, Protractor

1. Draw a triangle with three congruent sides. Measure the angles and describe your results.

2. Draw a triangle with two congruent sides; make the third side a different length. Measure the angles and describe your results.

3. Draw a triangle with three sides of unequal lengths. Measure the angles and describe your results.

4. Repeat Steps 1–3, changing the lengths of the sides you use.

5. Describe the relationship between the number of congruent sides and the number of congruent angles that a triangle has.

Learn | **Triangles and Quadrilaterals**

Architects use triangles in their buildings for strength as well as for their visual appeal. You can classify triangles by the number of congruent sides they have.

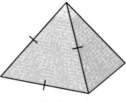

Equilateral

Isosceles

Scalene

You can also classify triangles by their angle measures.

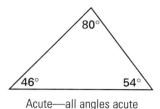

Acute—all angles acute   Right—one right angle   Obtuse—one obtuse angle

▶ **Science Link**

Classification, or grouping things by their properties, is a very important part of scientific study.

A **quadrilateral** is a four-sided figure. You have already learned to identify rectangles and squares. The chart gives three new types of quadrilaterals, **parallelograms**, **rhombuses**, and **trapezoids**, and relates all the types of quadrilaterals according to their properties.

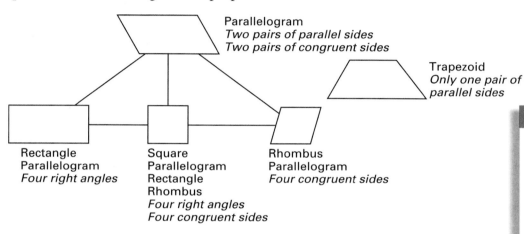

Parallelogram
Two pairs of parallel sides
Two pairs of congruent sides

Trapezoid
Only one pair of parallel sides

Rectangle
Parallelogram
Four right angles

Square
Parallelogram
Rectangle
Rhombus
Four right angles
Four congruent sides

Rhombus
Parallelogram
Four congruent sides

▶ **Language Link**

Quadri- means "four." It comes from the Latin word *quattuor*. *Quattuor* is also the root word for "quarter," which means "one fourth."

Examples

Classify each figure in as many ways as you can.

1

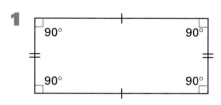

The figure is a quadrilateral, a parallelogram, and a rectangle.

2

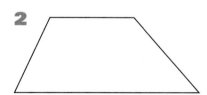

The figure is a quadrilateral and a trapezoid.

The figure illustrates a special property of triangles. The three angles of any triangle can be rearranged to form a straight angle. Recall that the measure of a straight angle is 180°. This means that the sum of the measures of the angles of any triangle is 180°.

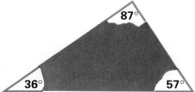

Notice that any quadrilateral can be divided into two triangles. The sum of the measures of the angles of any quadrilateral is 180° + 180°, or 360°.

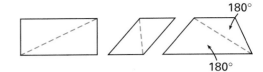

Examples

3 An ancient building in Tulum, Mexico, had the quadrilateral foundation shown. If its angle measures are 98°, 82°, 98°, and $x°$, find the measure of the unknown angle.

$x + 98 + 82 + 98 = 360$ The sum of the angles of a quadrilateral is 360°.

$x + 278 = 360$ Add 98, 82, and 98.

$x + 278 - 278 = 360 - 278$ To undo adding 278, subtract 278 from both sides.

$x = 82°$ Simplify.

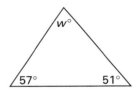

4 Find the measure of the unknown angle.

$w + 57 + 51 = 180$ The sum of the angles of a triangle is 180°.

$w + 108 = 180$ Add 57 and 51.

$w + 108 - 108 = 180 - 108$ To undo adding 108, subtract 108 from both sides.

$w = 72°$ Simplify.

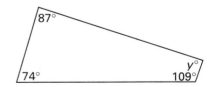

Try It

a. Find the measure of the unknown angle.

Check Your Understanding

1. Can a quadrilateral be both a rhombus and a rectangle? Explain.

2. Can a triangle be both equilateral and right? Isosceles and obtuse? Explain.

Practice and Apply

1. **Getting Started** Follow these steps to find the measure of an unknown angle in a quadrilateral.

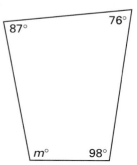

    a. Identify the known and unknown angle measures.

    b. Write an equation using the known and unknown angle measures and 360.

    c. Add the known angle measures together. Subtract the sum from each side of the equation.

    d. Write the difference.

Classify each triangle by its sides and by its angles.

2. 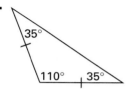   **3.**   **4.** 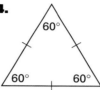   **5.**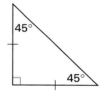

Classify each quadrilateral in as many ways as you can.

6.   **7.** 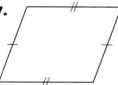   **8.**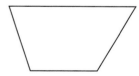

9. 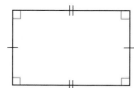   **10.**   **11.**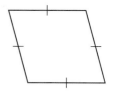

Find the measure of each unknown angle.

12. In triangle ABC, $m\angle A = 50°$, $m\angle B = 22°$, $m\angle C = x$.

13. In triangle XYZ, $m\angle X = 104°$, $m\angle Y = 38°$, $m\angle Z = t$.

14. In quadrilateral $DEFG$, $m\angle D = 88°$, $m\angle E = 93°$, $m\angle F = 74°$, $m\angle G = x$.

15. In quadrilateral $MNOP$, $m\angle M = 107°$, $m\angle N = 44°$, $m\angle O = 32°$, $m\angle P = x$.

16. Science A molecule of boron fluoride forms a molecular arrangement, as shown. An atom of boron is bonded to three atoms of fluorine. The angle between each bond measures 120°. Find the total measure of all the angles formed between the bonds.

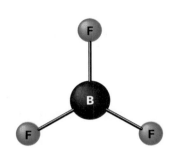

Problem Solving and Reasoning

17. **Journal** Place a piece of paper over the bottom of a gym shoe and make a crayon rubbing of the tread print. Identify different geometric shapes in the tread rubbing.

Critical Thinking Identify the types of triangles or quadrilaterals in the buildings.

18.

The Legal Center, Newark, NJ

19.

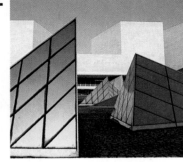

National Gallery, Washington, DC

20.

Los Angeles Museum of Contemporary Art

Mixed Review

Solve each equation. *[Lesson 3-3]*

21. $23.64 = y - 8.31$

22. $u + 0.643 = 1.86$

23. $x - 12.73 = 0.05$

24. $364.21 + c = 584.17$

25. $k - 38.2 = 68.375$

26. $129.6 = d + 18.31$

Use >, <, or = to compare each pair of numbers. *[Lesson 3-9]*

27. $\frac{6}{7} \square \frac{5}{6}$

28. $\frac{16}{20} \square \frac{19}{25}$

29. $\frac{22}{42} \square \frac{17}{32}$

30. $\frac{45}{63} \square \frac{40}{56}$

31. $\frac{3}{14} \square \frac{6}{27}$

32. $\frac{18}{25} \square \frac{23}{30}$

33. $\frac{3}{11} \square \frac{5}{13}$

34. $\frac{19}{49} \square \frac{24}{63}$

Project Progress

Measure the dimensions of the building(s) in the floor plan you sketched for your school. You may need to estimate some lengths that you cannot measure directly.

Problem Solving

Understand
Plan
Solve
Look Back

Polygons

▶ Lesson Link In the last lesson, you learned about geometric figures with three or four sides. Now you'll investigate figures that have more than four sides. ◀

Explore Many-Sided Figures

Getting in Shape

Materials: Pattern blocks

1. Name the pattern block shapes.

2. Use combinations of pattern blocks to create as many different five-sided figures as you can. Trace each figure on your paper.

3. Use combinations of pattern blocks to create as many different six-sided figures as you can. Trace each figure on your paper.

4. Look at the figures you traced. Find a way to classify the figures into different groups, other than by the number of sides.

Learn Polygons

Many of the shapes that you see in the design of buildings are **polygons** . A polygon is a geometric figure with at least three sides.

In the last lesson, you worked with two types of polygons—triangles and quadrilaterals. The sides meet at vertices, with exactly two at each vertex.

A polygon is classified by the number of sides it has.

You'll Learn ...
- to classify polygons
- to find the angle sum of polygons

... How It's Used
Structural engineers use many different shapes in the design of bridges and railroad trestles.

Vocabulary
polygon

pentagon

hexagon

octagon

regular polygon

3 sides
triangle

4 sides
quadrilateral

5 sides
pentagon

6 sides
hexagon

8 sides
octagon

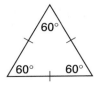

In a **regular polygon**, all of the sides and all of the angles are congruent. An equilateral triangle and a square are examples of regular polygons.

Examples

Classify each polygon and determine if it is regular.

1
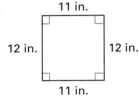

It has four sides. The angles are congruent. The sides are not congruent.

Nonregular quadrilateral.

2
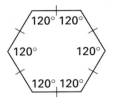

It has six sides. The angles are congruent. The marks show that the sides are congruent.

Regular hexagon.

In the last lesson, you saw that a quadrilateral could be divided into two triangles to find the sum of the measures of the angles. You can divide any polygon into triangles to find the sum of the measures of the angles.

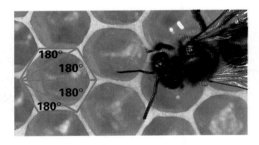

$180° + 180° + 180° + 180° = 720°$

Example 3

Find the sum of the measures of the angles of a hexagon.

- Sketch a hexagon.
- Choose one vertex and draw segments to as many other vertices as possible.
- There are four triangles, so $4 \cdot 180° = 720°$.

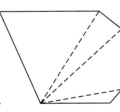

The sum of the measures of the angles of a hexagon is 720°.

Try It

a. Find the sum of the measures of the angles of an octagon.

b. Find the sum of the measures of the angles of a 12-sided polygon.

The number of triangles you can divide a polygon into is 2 less than the number of sides it has. You can find the sum of the angle measures by subtracting 2 from the number of sides, then multiplying by 180°.

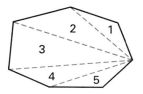

7 sides, 5 triangles

You can use the formula $S = (n - 2)180°$ to find the sum (S) of the measures of the angles of a polygon with n sides.

Find the sum of the measures of the angles of a stop sign.

WHAT DO YOU THINK?

Winona thinks ...

I'll use the formula.

$S = (n - 2)180°$ Use the formula for the sum of the measures of the angles.

$= (8 - 2)180°$ Substitute 8 for n.

$= 1080°$ Simplify.

The sum is 1080°.

Ramon thinks ...

I'll sketch a stop sign and draw triangles from a vertex. There are six triangles. I'll multiply 6 by 180°.

The sum is 1080°.

What do you think?

1. Explain Ramon's method. Could he draw the triangles another way?

2. Give another way to find the answer.

Check Your Understanding

1. Is a rectangle a regular polygon? Is a rhombus? Explain.

2. Name a regular polygon with three sides; with four sides.

Practice and Apply

Getting Started | Classify each polygon and determine if it is regular.

1.

Each angle measures 120°.

2.

3.

4.

Each angle measures 60°.

Tell why each polygon is not a regular polygon.

5. **6.** **7.** **8.**

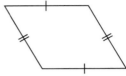
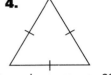

Use the picture of each building to identify as many polygons as you can.

9.

10.

Find the sum of the measures of the angles of each polygon.

11. 7-sided polygon   **12.** 15-sided polygon   **13.** 20-sided polygon

14. Science Mica is a type of mineral that can be split into flexible sheets that are thinner than paper. These sheets are often hexagon-shaped. If a piece of mica can be split into 142 hexagon-shaped sheets, what is the total number of sides of all the hexagons that are formed?

15. Draw a nonregular example of each of the following polygons, then describe what makes the polygon nonregular.

    a. Pentagon   **b.** Hexagon   **c.** Octagon

PRACTICE 5-4

16. Regular polygons are both equilateral, which means having congruent sides, and equiangular, which means having congruent angles. Non-regular polygons sometimes have one of these characteristics but not the other.

   a. Sketch an equilateral polygon that is not equiangular.

   b. Sketch an equiangular polygon that is not equilateral.

17. **Test Prep** How many triangles will be formed if you sketch an octagon, choose one vertex, and draw diagonals to as many other vertices as possible?

Ⓐ 8   Ⓑ 7   Ⓒ 6   Ⓓ 5

Problem Solving and Reasoning

Choose a Strategy The sum of the measures of the angles of a polygon is given. How many sides does each polygon have?

18. 1620°   **19.** 1980°   **20.** 2520°

Critical Thinking Find the measure of each angle in the polygon.

21. Regular pentagon   **22.** Regular hexagon

23. Regular octagon   **24.** Regular decagon

25. **Journal** A friend was out ill during this lesson. Write a paragraph to him or her explaining what a polygon and a regular polygon are. Use your own words.

26. **Communicate** The polygons you have worked with in this section are called *convex* polygons. Two examples of *concave* polygons are shown at the right. Describe the difference between the two types of polygons.

> **Problem Solving**
> **STRATEGIES**
> • Look for a Pattern
> • Make an Organized List
> • Make a Table
> • Guess and Check
> • Work Backward
> • Use Logical Reasoning
> • Draw a Diagram
> • Solve a Simpler Problem

Convex   Concave

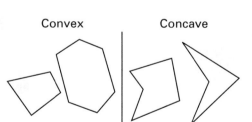

Mixed Review

Solve each equation. *[Lesson 3-4]*

27. $1.82m = 6.552$ **28.** $\dfrac{s}{81.45} = 7.89$ **29.** $8.468 = 5.8y$ **30.** $3.72 = \dfrac{k}{0.057}$

31. $3.75x = 36.9$ **32.** $130.5 = \dfrac{a}{7.43}$ **33.** $79.744 = 6.23b$ **34.** $\dfrac{x}{4.7531} = 4.6$

Convert to a decimal. Tell if the decimal terminates or repeats. *[Lesson 3-10]*

35. $\dfrac{7}{16}$ **36.** $\dfrac{8}{15}$ **37.** $\dfrac{3}{7}$ **38.** $\dfrac{5}{6}$

39. $\dfrac{21}{160}$ **40.** $\dfrac{16}{21}$ **41.** $\dfrac{7}{8}$ **42.** $\dfrac{11}{18}$

T E C H N O L O G Y

Using Dynamic Geometry Software • Investigating Polygons

Problem: What happens to the sum of the angle measures of a triangle when its shape and size are changed?

You can use dynamic geometry software to explore this problem.

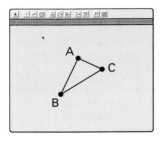

1 Use your software to make a triangle. Label its vertices *A*, *B*, and *C*.

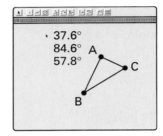

37.6°
84.6° A
57.8°
C
B

2 Use the angle measurement tool to find *m∠BAC*. (You will probably need to click on points *B, A,* and *C* in that order.) Then, find *m∠ABC* and *m∠BCA*. Drag the measures to the upper left corner of your screen.

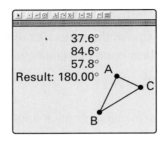

37.6°
84.6°
57.8° A
Result: 180.00° C
B

3 Use the software's calculator to find the sum of the three angle measures.

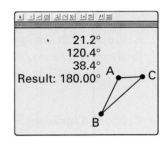

21.2°
120.4°
38.4° A C
Result: 180.00°
B

4 Click on a vertex and hold down the mouse button. Drag the vertex around the screen.

Solution: The measures of the individual angles change, but the sum of the angle measures stays the same at 180°.

TRY IT

a. What happens to the sum of the angle measures of a convex quadrilateral when you change its shape and size?

b. What happens to the sum of the angle measures of a convex pentagon when you change its shape and size?

ON YOUR OWN

▶ What are some advantages and disadvantages of using geometry software to measure an angle instead of using a protractor?

▶ Why do you think you have to select three vertices in the proper order when you measure an angle with geometry software?

Perimeter and Area

▶ **Lesson Link**   You've seen formulas for the areas and perimeters of squares and rectangles. Now you'll look more closely at the relationships between the areas and perimeters of those quadrilaterals. ◀

Explore   Perimeter and Area

Cut and Compare

Materials: Graph paper, Scissors

1. Draw a 4 by 6 rectangle on graph paper. Find its area and perimeter.

2. Cut out the rectangle. Then cut it in half. Find the perimeters of the two pieces and add them. Is the sum of the perimeters the same as the perimeter of the original rectangle?

3. Find the areas of the two pieces and add them. Is the sum of the areas the same as the area of the original rectangle?

4. Rearrange the pieces to form a different rectangle. How do its perimeter and area compare with those of the rectangle you drew in Step 1?

You'll Learn ...

■ to examine the relationship between perimeter and area

... How It's Used

City planners use the relationship between perimeter and area to make sure they use land in the most efficient way.

Learn   Perimeter and Area

The area of a geometric figure is the number of square units needed to cover the figure. Recall that the formula $A = lw$ gives the area (A) of a rectangle with length l and width w.

Area = 6 ft²

The words *base* and *height* are often used instead of *length* and *width*. The formula $A = bh$ can be used to find the area (A) of a rectangle with base b and height h. The perimeter, or distance around, any polygon can be found by adding the lengths of the sides.

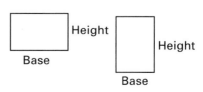

Perimeter is a distance, so it is measured in units of length.

Examples

The Palace Museum, in Beijing, China, is the world's largest palace. It contains more than 75 buildings and over 9000 rooms. The palace grounds are rectangular, with a length of 3150 ft and a width of 2460 ft.

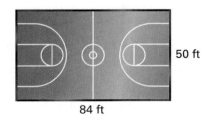

1 A moat surrounds the palace grounds. Find the length of the moat.

The length of the moat is the perimeter of the palace grounds.

$p = 3150 + 2460 + 3150 + 2460$ Add the length of each side.

$= 11{,}220$ Add.

The moat is 11,220 ft ($2\frac{1}{8}$ miles!) long.

2 Find the area of the palace grounds.

$A = bh$ Use the formula for the area of a rectangle.

$= 3{,}150 \cdot 2{,}460$ Substitute 3,150 for b and 2,460 for h.

$= 7{,}749{,}000$ Multiply.

The area is about 7.75 million ft^2. Note that ft^2 means "square feet."

Try It

The maintenance supervisor of Logan Middle School is planning to refinish the basketball court.

a. What is the perimeter of the court?

b. Find the area to be refinished.

50 ft

84 ft

Check | Your Understanding

1. Explain the difference between measurements made in ft and in ft^2.

2. How can you use the rectangle formulas to find the perimeter and area of a square? Why does it make sense to do so?

3. Two rectangles have the same area. Do they have the same perimeter? Use an example to explain.

Practice and Apply

1. **Getting Started** | Follow these steps to determine the perimeter and the area of a rectangle with a base of 14 ft and a height of 10 ft.

    a. Add the lengths of the sides to find the perimeter.

    b. Use the formula $A = bh$ to find the area of the rectangle. Substitute 14 for b and 10 for h.

    c. Simplify the equation.

Find the perimeter and area of each rectangular playing area.

	Game	Base (length)	Height (width)	Perimeter	Area
2.	Table tennis	9 ft	5 ft		
3.	Basketball	26 m	14 m		
4.	Soccer	100 m	73 m		
5.	Football	120 yd	53 yd		

Find the perimeter and area of the base of each rectangular building.

6. Largest multilevel industrial building: Kwai Chung container port, Hong Kong, China—906 ft by 958 ft

7. Largest ground area, commercial building: flower auction building, Aalsmeer, Netherlands—2546 ft by 2070 ft

8. Geography The state of Colorado is shaped like a rectangle, with a base measuring about 385 miles and a height of about 275 miles. Find the approximate perimeter and area of Colorado.

Science The National Air and Space Museum in Washington, DC, held a contest in which students attempted to land their paper and balsa wood airplanes inside a rectangle 35 feet away.

9. The rectangle inside which students must land their planes measures 12 ft by 9 ft. Find the perimeter and the area of the rectangle.

10. In the final portion of the contest, students must land their planes on a tiny "runway" measuring 1 ft by 5 ft. Find the perimeter and the area of the runway.

11. History The Woolworth Building in New York City was once the tallest in the world. It is 241 m tall. Its base is nearly rectangular, with a length of about 60 m and a width of about 46 m. Find the approximate area of the base of the Woolworth Building.

12. <u>Test Prep</u> If the length of the side of a square is given in centimeters, the perimeter would be given in which units?

Ⓐ cm   Ⓑ cm²   Ⓒ m   Ⓓ m²

Problem Solving and Reasoning

13. Choose a Strategy Is it possible for one rectangle to have a greater area than another but a smaller perimeter? If so, give an example. If not, explain why not.

14. Communicate Use addition to find the perimeter of a rectangle that measures 14 m by 9 m. Then find the perimeter using the following formula: $P = 2b + 2h$. Substitute 14 for b and 9 for h. Explain which method you prefer for finding perimeter.

15. **Journal** Make a list of times when you would need to know the perimeter of something. Do the same for area. Are there any times when you would need to know both?

Problem Solving
STRATEGIES

- Look for a Pattern
- Make an Organized List
- Make a Table
- Guess and Check
- Work Backward
- Use Logical Reasoning
- Draw a Diagram
- Solve a Simpler Problem

Mixed Review

Use the circle graph for Exercises 16–18. *[Lesson 1-1]*

16. Which age group has the largest number of workers?

17. About what percent of workers are 55 or older?

18. Which age group has about $\frac{1}{4}$ of the workers?

U.S. Workers by Age, 1993

45–54
15.28%

55+
10.09%

16–24
22.63%

35–44
24.25%

25–34
27.75%

Round each mixed number to the nearest whole number, then estimate each sum or difference. *[Lesson 4-1]*

19. $3\frac{2}{3} + 7\frac{5}{8}$ **20.** $12\frac{2}{7} - 2\frac{3}{8}$ **21.** $9\frac{3}{4} + 6\frac{1}{3}$

22. $4\frac{13}{16} - 1\frac{1}{8}$ **23.** $18\frac{4}{5} - 7\frac{3}{16}$ **24.** $6\frac{8}{9} + 7\frac{2}{5}$

25. $67\frac{2}{11} - 32\frac{6}{7}$ **26.** $45\frac{4}{9} + 52\frac{7}{10}$ **27.** $18\frac{3}{10} + 16\frac{5}{8}$

Section 5A Connect

You've learned about some of the world's most unusual buildings. You've seen how architects use angles, parallel and perpendicular lines, and polygons in the design of their buildings. Now you'll have a chance to design a building of your own.

From the Dome to Your Home ...

Materials: Inch or metric ruler, Protractor, Drawing paper

You've been chosen to design the headquarters of a company that produces a familiar product.

1. Decide on the product the company produces. It could be a well-known food product, a brand of clothing, an entertainment device, an item of sporting equipment, or any other product that you enjoy. Choose a product with features that you can somehow show in your building design.

Gas station, Zillah, WA

2. Draw the floor plan and one outside view of company headquarters. Use one sheet of paper for each. Include as many of the following as possible in your design:

   a. Different types of angles.

   b. Parallel lines and perpendicular lines.

   c. Different types of triangles and quadrilaterals.

   d. Different types of polygons with more than 4 sides.

   e. Creative ideas that reflect some of the characteristics of the product you chose in Step 1.

3. Explain how you used the items listed in Step 2 in your design.

Find the missing angle in each quadrilateral.

1.

2.
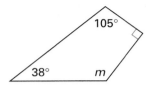

3.
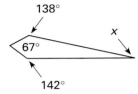

Classify each figure in as many ways as you can.

4.

5.

6.

Find the sum of the measures of the angles of each polygon.

7. Nine-sided polygon   **8.** Eleven-sided polygon   **9.** Sixteen-sided polygon

10. **Journal** Draw any angle and label the vertex A. Use a protractor to draw its bisector. Draw any segment $\overline{AB}$. Use a protractor to draw its perpendicular bisector. Explain the methods you have used.

11. **Social Studies** The National Portrait Gallery in Washington, DC, houses portraits of all the presidents of the United States, as well as portraits of other famous Americans. What are the perimeter and the area of the courtyard of the gallery?

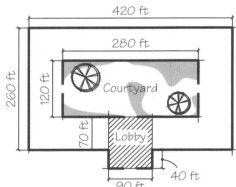

Test Prep

On a multiple choice test where you are asked to find an unknown angle measure in a triangle that has two of its angles given, you can add each possible angle to the two that are given. When you get a sum of 180°, you have the correct answer.

12. Find the measure of the unknown angle.

Ⓐ 10°   Ⓑ 31°   Ⓒ 35°   Ⓓ 45°

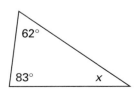

Shaping Up

Long before you heard of geometry, you understood shapes. You probably enjoyed putting shapes into toy mail slots, putting jigsaw puzzles together, or drawing a hopscotch game on the sidewalk. For all of those, you needed to know about shapes.

When you got older, you began to play board games such as Chutes and Ladders® and checkers—both the American and Chinese kinds! Then you moved on to bigger and better things—basketball, football, baseball, tennis, or soccer.

All these games involve shapes. Imagine trying to play basketball on a round court. Or volleyball on a baseball diamond! Every game has its own particular playing area, whether it's an enormous football field or a simple chessboard. The shape and size of that playing area are part of what gives the game its identity. Geometry is all about shapes—how they fit together, how big they are, how to draw them, and how to measure them.

1 How many differently shaped playing areas—boards or fields—can you think of?

2 Which do you think is larger, a soccer field or a football field? How could you find out?

239

5-6 Squares and Square Roots

You'll Learn ...

■ to find the side of a square when you know its area

■ to find a square root

... How It's Used

Surveyors use square roots to calculate distances they can't directly measure.

Vocabulary

perfect square

square root

radical sign

▶ **Lesson Link** You've learned to use the length of a side of a square to find the area. Now you'll use the area to find the length of a side. ◀

Explore   Squares and Square Roots

I'm Board with Squares

Materials: Geoboard, Rubber bands

The square shown on the geoboard has sides 1 unit long. Its area is 1 square unit.

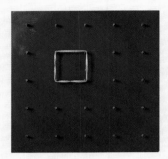

1. Make squares with areas of 4, 9, and 16 square units on your geoboard. What is the length of a side of each square?

2. Make a square with an area of 2 square units. How do you know that the area of your square is 2 square units?

3. How do you know that the figure you made is a square?

4. Estimate the length of a side of your square. How did you decide on your estimate?

5. Make a square with an area of 8 square units. Estimate the length of a side. Compare your estimate to your estimate for Step 4.

Learn   Squares and Square Roots

Recall that you can use an exponent to show that a number has been multiplied by itself one or more times. You can write 7×7 as 7^2, or 7 *squared*.

A **perfect square** is the square of a whole number. The number 16 is a perfect square because $16 = 4^2$. The number 29 is not a perfect square because there is no whole number that can be squared to get 29.

You know that 36 is the square of 6 because $6^2 = 36$.

You can also say that 6 is the **square root** of 36. The square root of a number is the length of the side of a square with an area equal to the number.

Use a **radical sign**, $\sqrt{}$, to write a square root.

Example 1

A square chessboard has an area of 144 square inches. How long is each side of the board?

Look for a number that equals 144 when it is squared.

$12^2 = 144$. So $\sqrt{144} = 12$.

Each side of the chessboard is 12 inches long.

Try It

Find each square root.

a. $\sqrt{81}$ **b.** $\sqrt{121}$ **c.** $\sqrt{225}$ **d.** $\sqrt{10,000}$ **e.** $\sqrt{64}$

You can use a calculator to find square roots.

Examples

2 Find $\sqrt{1024}$.

Enter 1024 $\boxed{\sqrt{x}}$

$\sqrt{1024} = 32$

3 Find $\sqrt{33}$.

Enter 33 $\boxed{\sqrt{x}}$

$\sqrt{33} \approx 5.7445626$

$\sqrt{33} \approx 5.74$ Round to 2 decimal places.

Try It

Find each square root. Round to 2 decimal places.

a. $\sqrt{85}$ **b.** $\sqrt{41}$ **c.** $\sqrt{73}$ **d.** $\sqrt{90}$ **e.** $\sqrt{300}$

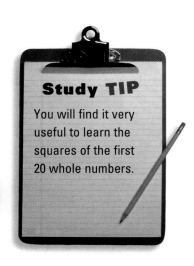

Study TIP

You will find it very useful to learn the squares of the first 20 whole numbers.

Check | Your Understanding

1. If you know the area of a square, how can you find the length of a side?

2. Give two consecutive whole numbers that have $\sqrt{29}$ between them. Explain how you chose the numbers.

Practice and Apply

Getting Started Give the value of each expression.

1. 4^2 **2.** 11^2 **3.** 25^2 **4.** 30^2 **5.** 9^2

6. $(0.9)^2$ **7.** $(0.11)^2$ **8.** $\left(\dfrac{1}{2}\right)^2$ **9.** $\left(\dfrac{3}{8}\right)^2$ **10.** $\left(\dfrac{2}{3}\right)^2$

Determine if each number is a perfect square.

11. 4   **12.** 12   **13.** 16   **14.** 49   **15.** 164

Find each square root.

16. $\sqrt{289}$ **17.** $\sqrt{100}$ **18.** $\sqrt{169}$ **19.** $\sqrt{81}$ **20.** $\sqrt{900}$

21. $\sqrt{225}$ **22.** $\sqrt{121}$ **23.** $\sqrt{10{,}000}$ **24.** $\sqrt{144}$ **25.** $\sqrt{625}$

Use a calculator to find each square root. Round the answer to two decimal places.

26. $\sqrt{175}$ **27.** $\sqrt{544}$ **28.** $\sqrt{1264}$ **29.** $\sqrt{731}$ **30.** $\sqrt{125}$

31. $\sqrt{98}$ **32.** $\sqrt{105}$ **33.** $\sqrt{57}$ **34.** $\sqrt{1572}$ **35.** $\sqrt{12}$

36. Measurement A softball diamond has an area of 3600 ft². How long is each side of the diamond?

37. Number Sense What counting number is the same as its square root?

38. Measurement The area of the four-square court is 100 ft². What is the length of a side of the court?

39. Architecture Architect I. M. Pei designed a pyramid-shaped addition for the Louvre museum in Paris. The square base of the structure covers about 13,225 ft². What is the approximate length of each side?

40. Schoolchildren in Ghana play the game of Achi on a board like the one shown. If the perimeter of an Achi board is 192 cm, what is its area?

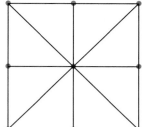

41. **Test Prep** Between which consecutive whole numbers does $\sqrt{267}$ lie?

 Ⓐ 6 and 7   Ⓑ 16 and 17

 Ⓒ 133 and 134   Ⓓ 265 and 266

Problem Solving and Reasoning

42. **Communicate** The scatterplot shows the relationship between the whole numbers from 0 to 100 and their square roots.

 a. Use the scatterplot to find the square root of 49. Explain how you did this.

 b. Use the scatterplot to estimate the square root of 10. Explain how you did this.

 c. Use the scatterplot to estimate the square root of 56. Explain how you did this.

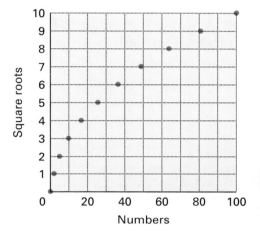

43. **Critical Thinking** Find two perfect squares that have a sum of 100.

Mixed Review

Make a scatterplot for each set of data. *[Lesson 1-6]*

44.

x	2	3	4	5	6	7	8	9
y	3	5	4	6	7	5	8	4

45.

x	3.2	4.3	5.1	6.4	7.2	7.8	8.3	9.7
y	7.6	8.2	6.3	4.2	3.1	3.5	4.4	6.6

Find each sum or difference. Rewrite in lowest terms. *[Lesson 4-2]*

46. $\dfrac{2}{3} + \dfrac{5}{6}$ **47.** $\dfrac{11}{12} - \dfrac{3}{4}$ **48.** $\dfrac{3}{5} + \dfrac{4}{7}$ **49.** $\dfrac{21}{25} - \dfrac{4}{15}$

50. $\dfrac{5}{12} - \dfrac{1}{8}$ **51.** $\dfrac{7}{16} + \dfrac{23}{40}$ **52.** $\dfrac{30}{49} - \dfrac{11}{28}$ **53.** $\dfrac{4}{7} + \dfrac{5}{13}$

54. $\dfrac{3}{4} + \dfrac{1}{12}$ **55.** $\dfrac{9}{20} - \dfrac{4}{15}$ **56.** $\dfrac{21}{50} + \dfrac{11}{18}$ **57.** $\dfrac{99}{100} - \dfrac{9}{11}$

The Pythagorean Theorem

You'll Learn ...

■ to use the special relationship among the sides of a right triangle

■ the Pythagorean Theorem

... How It's Used

Construction workers from the ancient Egyptians to the workers of today have used the Pythagorean Theorem to make the corners of their buildings square.

Vocabulary

hypotenuse

leg

▶ **Lesson Link** You've seen several types of triangles. Now you will see an important relationship among the lengths of the sides of a right triangle. ◀

Explore | Side Lengths in Right Triangles

The Rights of Triangles

Materials: Metric ruler, Graph paper, Calculator

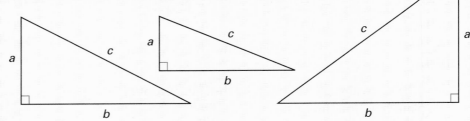

1. Begin a table like the one shown. Measure each triangle in millimeters and fill in the table. The first triangle is started for you.

a	b	c	$a^2 + b^2$	c^2
24	45	51	2601	

2. Describe any patterns you see in your table.

3. On your graph paper, draw a right triangle by using two perpendicular line segments of any length. Then connect the endpoints to form a triangle. Label the sides *a, b,* and *c,* using *c* for the longest side. Measure the sides and add the results to your table. Do your results match the pattern you saw in Step 2?

4. Now draw a triangle that is *not* a right triangle. Add its measurements to your table. Do the results match the pattern you saw in Step 2?

Learn | The Pythagorean Theorem

The **hypotenuse** of a right triangle is the side opposite the right angle and is the longest side. The other two sides are called **legs**.

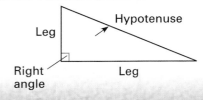

The triangle shown has legs that are 3 units and 4 units long and a hypotenuse 5 units long. Notice that $3^2 + 4^2 = 5^2$.

THE PYTHAGOREAN THEOREM

In a right triangle, the sum of the squares of the lengths of the legs is equal to the square of the length of the hypotenuse.

$a^2 + b^2 = c^2$

It is also true that if a triangle's side lengths satisfy $a^2 + b^2 = c^2$, then the triangle must be a right triangle.

Examples

1 Find the crosscourt distance on a tennis court.

$a^2 + b^2 = c^2$	Use the Pythagorean Theorem.
$36^2 + 78^2 = c^2$	Substitute 36 for a and 78 for b.
$1296 + 6084 = c^2$	Square 36 and 78.
$7380 = c^2$	Add.
$\sqrt{7380} = c \approx 86$	Find $\sqrt{7380}$ and round to the nearest whole number.

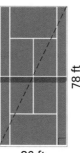

78 ft

36 ft

The crosscourt distance is about 86 ft.

2 Find the length of the shorter leg.

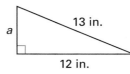

13 in.

12 in.

$a^2 + b^2 = c^2$	Use the Pythagorean Theorem.
$a^2 + 12^2 = 13^2$	Substitute 12 for b and 13 for c.
$a^2 + 144 = 169$	Square 12 and 13.
$a^2 + 144 - 144 = 169 - 144$	To undo adding 144, subtract 144 from both sides.
$a^2 = 25$	Subtract.
$a = \sqrt{25} = 5$ in.	Find $\sqrt{25}$.

Try It

Find the missing length in each right triangle.

a.

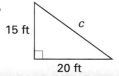

15 ft c

20 ft

b.

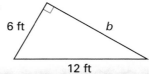

6 ft b

12 ft

1. How can you use the side lengths of a triangle to decide if it is a right triangle?

2. Can a leg of a right triangle ever be longer than the hypotenuse? Explain.

5-7 Exercises and Applications

Practice and Apply

Getting Started Name the hypotenuse and legs of each triangle.

1.
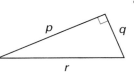

2.
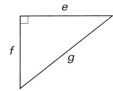

3.
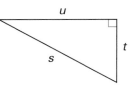

4.
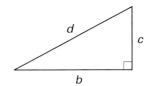

Use the Pythagorean Theorem to write an equation expressing the relationship between the legs and the hypotenuse for each triangle.

5.
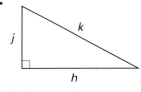

6.
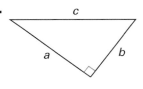

7.
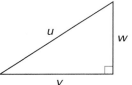

8.
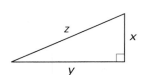

Determine if each triangle is a right triangle.

9.
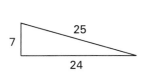

10.
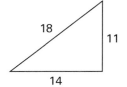

11.
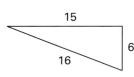

12.
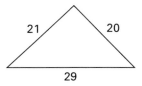

Find the missing length in each right triangle.

13.
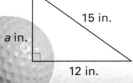

14.
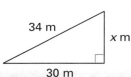

15.
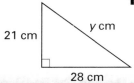

16.
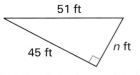

17. Measurement The runner is trying to steal second base. The catcher makes a perfect throw from home plate to second base. The runner is out! How far was the throw from home plate to second base?

18. Science Engineers who build bridges often use truss construction. The basic unit of a truss is a triangle. A king post is often used to strengthen a truss. What is the length of the king post shown in the diagram?

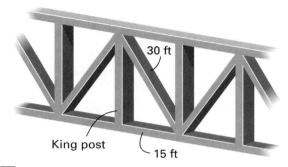

19. **Test Prep** In triangle ABC, $\overline{AB}$ measures 5 cm, $\overline{BC}$ measures 5 cm, and $\overline{CA}$ measures about 7.07 cm. Which of these best describes triangle ABC?

  Ⓐ Right triangle   Ⓑ Scalene triangle

  Ⓒ Isosceles right triangle   Ⓓ Scalene right triangle

Problem Solving and Reasoning

20. Choose a Strategy An 8 ft ladder leans against a building with the base of the ladder 3 ft from the building. How high is the point where the ladder touches the building?

21. Communicate Would you expect to get another right triangle by adding 1 to the length of each side of a right triangle? By doubling each side? Explain.

22. Critical Thinking A square diving pool has sides 30 ft long. Would a 45 ft length of rope be long enough to reach diagonally across the pool?

Problem Solving

STRATEGIES

- Look for a Pattern
- Make an Organized List
- Make a Table
- Guess and Check
- Work Backward
- Use Logical Reasoning
- Draw a Diagram
- Solve a Simpler Problem

Mixed Review

Draw a scatterplot and a trend line for each set of data. *[Lesson 1-7]*

23.

x	8	6	3	8	5	4	3	7
y	3	4	6	4	5	6	5	3

24.

x	7.2	4.7	7.6	3.2	9.3	6.4	2.3	5.8
y	6.5	5.7	5.2	6.3	5.4	6.1	5.7	6.0

Find each sum or difference. *[Lesson 4-3]*

25. $12\frac{7}{12} + 7\frac{9}{16}$ **26.** $7\frac{3}{8} - 3\frac{1}{5}$ **27.** $8\frac{5}{7} + 13\frac{4}{5}$ **28.** $4\frac{7}{18} - 1\frac{41}{66}$

29. $7\frac{3}{10} - 3\frac{4}{7}$ **30.** $18\frac{1}{2} + 31\frac{7}{8}$ **31.** $53\frac{5}{7} - 17\frac{2}{3}$ **32.** $63\frac{1}{6} + 54\frac{2}{3}$

Areas of Triangles

You'll Learn ...

■ to find the area of a triangle

... How It's Used

Installers of siding need to be able to calculate triangular areas to make a reasonable estimate for a job.

▶ **Lesson Link** You know the formula for the area of a rectangle. Now you'll relate that formula to the formula for the area of a triangle. ◀

Explore Triangles

Wreck a Rectangle

Materials: Graph paper, Scissors

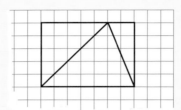

1. Draw a rectangle with any length and width on graph paper. Inside, draw a triangle as shown.

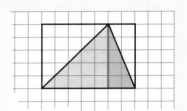

2. Draw a second rectangle and triangle exactly like the first. Draw a perpendicular line from a vertex of the triangle to the opposite base.

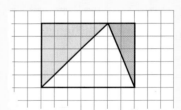

3. Cut out the second triangle. Then cut it into two pieces along the perpendicular line.

4. Return to the first rectangle. Fit the two new triangles onto the parts of the rectangle that are *not* contained in the first triangle.

5. How does the area of the triangle you drew in Step 1 compare with the area of the rectangle? Explain.

6. Draw a different rectangle and repeat Steps 1–5. Describe your results.

The *height* (*h*) of a triangle is the line segment drawn perpendicular to the *base* (*b*) from the vertex opposite the base. The length of that segment is also called the height.

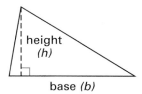 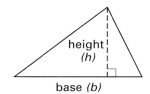 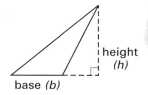

Remember

An obtuse angle is between 90° and 180°.
[Page 213]

Notice that a height of an obtuse triangle may be outside the triangle.

AREA OF A TRIANGLE

The area of a triangle is half the product of the lengths of the base and the height.

$$A = \frac{1}{2}bh$$

MENTAL MATH

When you calculate the area of a triangle, see if the base or height is an even number. If so, you can save time by first dividing the even number by 2.

Examples

1 Find the area of the shaded portion of the "Sixteen Soldiers" game board shown at right. The base of the shaded triangle is 12 cm and the height is 9 cm.

$A = \frac{1}{2}bh$ Use the formula for area of **a triangle.**

$= \frac{1}{2} \cdot 12 \cdot 9$ Substitute 12 for **b** and 9 for **h**.

$= 54$ Multiply.

The area of the shaded portion is 54 cm².

2 Find the area of the triangle.

$A = \frac{1}{2}bh$

$= \frac{1}{2} \cdot 8 \cdot 3$

$= 12$

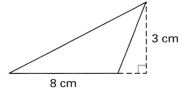

3 cm

8 cm

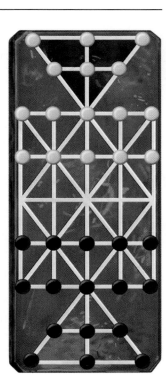

The area is 12 cm².

Every triangle has three bases, and a height can be drawn for each base.

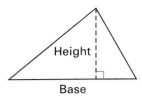

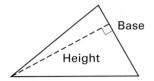

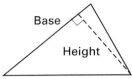

In the game of Tangoes™, players rearrange seven geometric figures into shapes of people, animals, and other figures. Often the pieces are arranged so the bases are not horizontal.

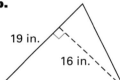

Example 3

Find the area of the outlined triangle.

$A = \frac{1}{2}bh$ Use the formula for area of a triangle.

$= \frac{1}{2} \cdot 4 \cdot 2$ Substitute 4 for b and 2 for h.

$= 4$ Multiply.

The area is 4 in².

Try It

Find the area of each triangle.

a.

6 in.

14 in.

b.

19 in.

16 in.

c.

24 ft

5 ft

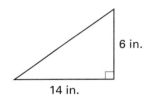

Check | **Your Understanding**

1. Compare the areas of the triangles with the area of the rectangle.

2. Two triangles with different shapes both have bases of 6 cm and heights of 4 cm. Do they have the same areas? Explain.

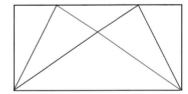

Practice and Apply

1. **Getting Started** Follow these steps to find the area of the triangle shown.

   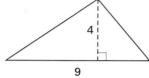

   a. What is the base?

   b. What is the height?

   c. Multiply the base by the height.

   d. Multiply the product by $\frac{1}{2}$ to determine the area of the triangle.

Find the area of each triangle.

2. $b = 12$ m

   $h = 20$ m

3. $b = 25$ ft

   $h = 5$ ft

4. $b = 3.5$ cm

   $h = 1.4$ cm

5. $b = 20$ in.

   $h = \frac{2}{3}$ in.

6.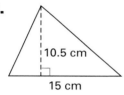

7.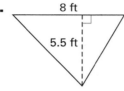

8.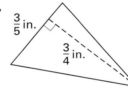

9.

Find the missing measurement of each triangle.

10. $b = 20$ m

    $h = ?$

    $A = 150$ m^2

11. $b = 18$ ft

    $h = ?$

    $A = 162$ ft^2

12. $b = ?$

    $h = 44$ cm

    $A = 792$ cm^2

13. $b = ?$

    $h = 72$ in.

    $A = 3240$ in^2

14. $b = 100$ mm

    $h = 0.2$ mm

    $A = ?$

15. $b = ?$

    $h = 25$ yd

    $A = 225$ yd^2

16. $b = 54$ cm

    $h = ?$

    $A = 4536$ cm^2

17. $b = ?$

    $h = 95$ in.

    $A = 1235$ in^2

18. **History** The ancient Egyptians built great pyramids to serve as tombs for their kings. Each face of the largest pyramid has a base about 230 meters long. The height of each face is about 92 meters. What is the area of a face?

19. Social Studies The game of Chinese checkers is thought to have originated in China and migrated to Europe in the early 1800s. The game is played on a star-shaped board. If the base of the triangle is 4 in. and its height is 3.5 in., what is the area of the triangle-shaped part of the star?

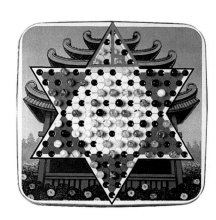

20. **Test Prep** Which triangle has the smallest area?

   Ⓐ $b = \frac{1}{2}$, $h = 12$ Ⓑ $b = 3$, $h = 4$

   Ⓒ $b = \frac{2}{3}$, $h = 15$ Ⓓ $b = \frac{3}{4}$, $h = 16$

Problem Solving and Reasoning

21. Communicate True or false: All triangles with equal bases and heights have equal areas. Explain your answer.

22. Choose a Strategy Draw and label the following triangles. Include labels for both base and height.

   a. Two different triangles, each with an area of 6 square units

   b. Two different triangles, each with an area of 15 square units

   c. Two different triangles, each with an area of 24 square units

23. **Journal** Draw a triangle on graph paper. Count the number of squares inside the triangle to estimate its area. Then measure the base and height of the triangle to calculate its area. Tell how close your estimate was to your calculation of the triangle's area.

> **Problem Solving**
> ### STRATEGIES
> • Look for a Pattern
> • Make an Organized List
> • Make a Table
> • Guess and Check
> • Work Backward
> • Use Logical Reasoning
> • Draw a Diagram
> • Solve a Simpler Problem

Mixed Review

Test each number for divisibility by 2, 3, 4, 5, 6, 8, 9, and 10. *[Lesson 3-6]*

24. 562   **25.** 843   **26.** 78   **27.** 3125

28. 6578   **29.** 48,628   **30.** 78,376   **31.** 364,859

Find each product. Rewrite in lowest terms. *[Lesson 4-4]*

32. $\frac{5}{7} \cdot \frac{7}{9}$ **33.** $\frac{13}{16} \cdot \frac{28}{39}$ **34.** $\frac{5}{12} \cdot \frac{6}{35}$ **35.** $\frac{5}{9} \cdot \frac{21}{25}$

36. $\frac{7}{15} \cdot \frac{3}{8}$ **37.** $\frac{5}{11} \cdot \frac{22}{45}$ **38.** $\frac{3}{5} \cdot \frac{7}{13}$ **39.** $\frac{8}{9} \cdot \frac{7}{25}$

40. $\frac{3}{10} \cdot \frac{2}{15}$ **41.** $\frac{5}{8} \cdot \frac{11}{12}$ **42.** $\frac{7}{24} \cdot \frac{12}{14}$ **43.** $\frac{6}{19} \cdot \frac{19}{6}$

Areas of Parallelograms and Trapezoids

▶ **Lesson Link** You've found the areas of rectangles, squares, and triangles. Now you'll find the areas of parallelograms and trapezoids. ◀

You'll Learn ...

■ to find the area of a parallelogram

■ to find the area of a trapezoid

... How It's Used

Quilters sometimes use parallelogram-shaped pieces of cloth in their designs.

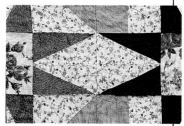

Explore Areas of Parallelograms

Tangling with Rectangles

Materials: Graph paper, Scissors, Straightedge

1. Draw a parallelogram on graph paper. Draw a perpendicular line from a vertex to the opposite base.

2. Cut out the parallelogram, then cut it into two pieces along the perpendicular line. Arrange the two pieces to form a rectangle. What are the base and the height of the rectangle?

3. Repeat Steps 1–2 with a different parallelogram.

4. Describe a method for finding the area of a parallelogram.

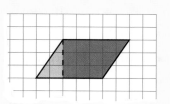

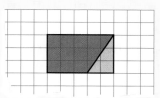

Learn Areas of Parallelograms and Trapezoids

The *height* of a parallelogram or trapezoid is the length of a segment that connects two parallel bases. It is perpendicular to both bases.

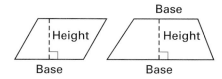

You can use the base and the height of a parallelogram to find its area.

AREA OF A PARALLELOGRAM

The area of a parallelogram is the product of its height and the length of its base.

$A = bh$

Example 1

This window in Jerusalem, designed by Marc Chagall, is made of small pieces of stained glass. Find the area of the parallelogram-shaped piece of glass.

$A = bh$ Use the formula for area of a parallelogram.

$= 6 \cdot 2$ Substitute 6 for b and 2 for h.

$= 12$ Multiply.

The area is 12 cm^2.

Try It

Find the area of each parallelogram.

a.

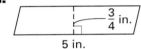

$\frac{3}{4}$ in.

5 in.

b.

11 m

23 m

c.

2.4 km

1.2 km

To find the area of a trapezoid, you must know the length of each base and the height. The bases are usually given the labels b_1 and b_2.

AREA OF A TRAPEZOID

The area of a trapezoid is half its height multiplied by the sum of the lengths of its two bases.

$A = \frac{1}{2}h(b_1 + b_2)$

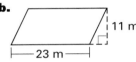

b_1

h

b_2

Example 2

Find the area of the trapezoid shown in the diagram at the right.

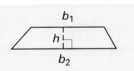

9 ft

4 ft

6 ft

$A = \frac{1}{2}h(b_1 + b_2)$ Use the formula for the area of a trapezoid.

$= \frac{1}{2} \cdot 4(6 + 9)$ Substitute 4 for h, 6 for b_1, and 9 for b_2.

$= \frac{1}{2} \cdot 4(15)$ Add.

$= 30$ ft^2 Multiply.

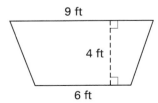

Example 3

In international basketball, the free-throw lane is different from the one used in the United States. How much greater is the area of the international lane?

The international free-throw lane is shaped like a trapezoid.

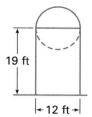

International free-throw lane

United States free-throw lane

$A = \frac{1}{2}h(b_1 + b_2)$ Use the formula for the area of a trapezoid.

$= \frac{1}{2} \cdot 19(12 + 19.7)$ Substitute 19 for h, 12 for b_1, and 19.7 for b_2.

$= \frac{1}{2} \cdot 19(31.7)$ Add.

$= 301.15 \text{ ft}^2$ Multiply.

The U.S. free-throw lane is shaped like a rectangle.

$A = bh$ Use the formula for the area of a rectangle.

$= 12 \cdot 19$ Substitute 12 for b and 19 for h.

$= 228 \text{ ft}^2$ Multiply.

$301.15 - 228 = 73.15 \text{ ft}^2$

The area of the international free-throw lane is 73.15 ft² greater.

Try It

Find the area of each trapezoid.

a.
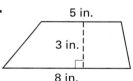
5 in.
3 in.
8 in.

b.

1.2 cm
5 cm
4.1 cm

c.

$2\frac{3}{8}$ in.
3 in.
$3\frac{1}{4}$ in.

Check Your Understanding

1. A rectangle and a parallelogram have the same base and height. How are their areas related?

2. How can you use the Distributive Property to write the formula for the area of a trapezoid in a different form?

Practice and Apply

Getting Started Name the height and base(s) for each figure.

1.
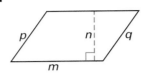

2.
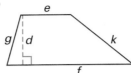

3.
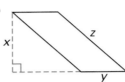

4.
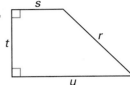

Which formula would you use to find the area of each figure, $A = bh$ or $A = \frac{1}{2}h(b_1 + b_2)$?

5.

6.

7.

8.

Find the area of each parallelogram.

9.
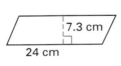

7.3 cm

24 cm

10.
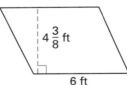

$4\frac{3}{8}$ ft

6 ft

11.
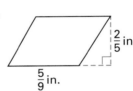

$\frac{2}{5}$ in.

$\frac{5}{9}$ in.

12.
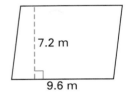

7.2 m

9.6 m

Find the area of each trapezoid.

13.
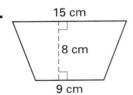

15 cm

8 cm

9 cm

14.
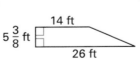

14 ft

$5\frac{3}{8}$ ft

26 ft

15.
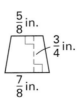

$\frac{5}{8}$ in.

$\frac{3}{4}$ in.

$\frac{7}{8}$ in.

16.
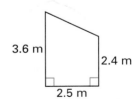

3.6 m

2.4 m

2.5 m

17. Measurement The game of tiddlywinks is thought to have originated in England. Although it is often thought of as a children's game, it is popular on university campuses. How much larger is the area of the 2-point portion of the board than the area of the 10-point portion?

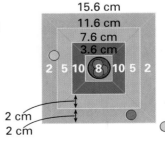

15.6 cm

11.6 cm

7.6 cm

3.6 cm

2 5 10 8 10 5 2

2 cm
2 cm

18. Geography The state of Nevada is shaped like a trapezoid. Calculate the approximate area of Nevada using the formula for area of a trapezoid.

19. [Test Prep] Which trapezoid has the greatest area?

Ⓐ $b_1 = 10$, $b_2 = 6$, $h = 3.1$

Ⓑ $b_1 = 8$, $b_2 = 7$, $h = 3.2$

Ⓒ $b_1 = 10$, $b_2 = 4$, $h = 3.4$

Ⓓ $b_1 = 9$, $b_2 = 4$, $h = 3.5$

20. History "Morris" games, where you need to get three pieces in a row, have been popular around the world for centuries. Versions of these games have been found in a 4400-year-old Egyptian temple and a 2900-year-old Viking ship. A game board for Twelve Men's Morris is shown. Find the areas of the highlighted trapezoids.

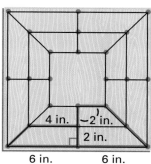

4 in.   ~2 in.
2 in.
6 in.   6 in.

Problem Solving and Reasoning

21. Communicate Explain how the area of a parallelogram is related to the area of a triangle with the same base and height.

22. Communicate One problem at sporting events is the availability of parking. A standard slant parking spot is 9 ft by 24 ft. What is the area of one parking space?

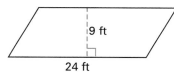

9 ft

24 ft

23. [Journal] Using the two small triangles and the square from a set of Tangoes™, make a rectangle, a trapezoid, and a parallelogram. Make drawings of the figures you form or trace around the figures. If the area of a small triangle is 1 square unit, what are the areas of your figures?

Mixed Review

Find the GCF and the LCM of each pair of numbers. *[Lesson 3-7]*

24. 336, 210   **25.** 54, 88   **26.** 81, 126   **27.** 210, 168

28. 165, 195   **29.** 780, 510   **30.** 385, 390   **31.** 420, 270

Find each product. *[Lesson 4-5]*

32. $4\frac{3}{5} \cdot 7\frac{2}{3}$ **33.** $4\frac{8}{9} \cdot 3\frac{6}{7}$ **34.** $9\frac{4}{5} \cdot 5\frac{2}{3}$ **35.** $6\frac{1}{2} \cdot 8\frac{1}{2}$

36. $3\frac{2}{3} \cdot 1\frac{1}{3}$ **37.** $2\frac{1}{6} \cdot 7\frac{2}{3}$ **38.** $8\frac{1}{4} \cdot 10\frac{7}{10}$ **39.** $4\frac{3}{8} \cdot 3\frac{1}{3}$

PROBLEM SOLVING 5-9

5-10

Problem Solving: Areas of Irregular Figures

You'll Learn ...

■ to find the areas of irregular shapes

... How It's Used

Developers work with areas of irregular figures when planning new housing tracts.

▶ **Lesson Link** You've found the areas of several common geometric figures. Now you'll see how you can find areas of *composite*, or *irregular*, figures. ◀

Explore | Irregular Figures

Par for the Course

The seventh hole at Marty's Miniature Golf is shown. Marty needs to order new carpet to cover the entire hole.

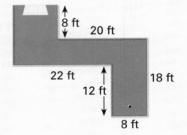

1. Determine the lengths of each of the two missing sides. Explain.

2. Draw horizontal or vertical segments to divide the hole into three rectangles. Is there more than one way to divide the hole into three rectangles? Explain.

3. Find the area of each rectangle. Add them to find the total area.

4. Divide the hole into three rectangles another way and find the total area. Is the area the same?

5. Suppose this hole has a windmill whose triangular base is cut out of the middle of the carpet. How would you find the area of the carpeted part of the hole?

Learn | Problem Solving: Areas of Irregular Figures

You can find the area of an irregular figure by dividing it into familiar figures, then adding the area of each part. There are often several different ways to divide an irregular figure.

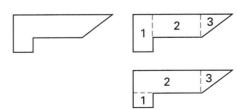

Example 1

Find the area of the figure.

Divide the figure into a rectangle and a triangle.

$A = lw = 6 \cdot 10$ Find the area of the rectangle.

$\quad = 60$ Multiply.

$\frac{1}{2}bh = \frac{1}{2} \cdot 8 \cdot 5$ Find the area of the triangle.

$\quad = 20$ Multiply.

Total area = area of rectangle + area of triangle

$\quad\quad = \quad\quad 60 \quad\quad + \quad\quad 20$

$\quad\quad = 80$

The area is 80 ft².

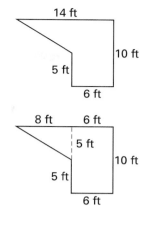

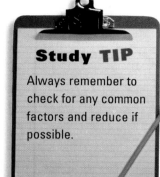

Study TIP

Always remember to check for any common factors and reduce if possible.

Try It

Find the area of the figure.

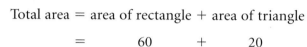

Sometimes you need to subtract to find the area of a geometric figure. You can find the area of a figure with a hole or opening in it by finding the total area of the figure and subtracting the area of the hole or opening.

Example 2

Find the area of the carpeted portion of the miniature golf hole shown. Find the total area, then subtract the area of the square.

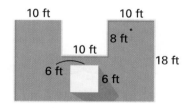

Rectangle 1	**Rectangle 2**	**Rectangle 3**
$lw = 10 \cdot 8$	$lw = 30 \cdot 10$	$lw = 10 \cdot 8$
$= 80$	$= 300$	$= 80$

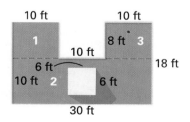

Area of rectangles = 80 + 300 + 80 = 460

Area of square = $s^2 = 6^2 = 36$

Total area = area of rectangles − area of square

$\quad\quad = 460 - 36 = 424$

The area of the carpeted portion of the hole is 424 ft².

Jyotsna and Taro are helping their friends install a deck. What is the area of the deck?

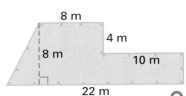

Jyotsna thinks ...

I'll add the areas of a trapezoid and a rectangle.

Trapezoid $= \frac{1}{2}h(b_1 + b_2) = \frac{1}{2} \cdot 8 \cdot (8 + 12) = 80$

Rectangle $= lw = 4 \cdot 10 = 40$

Total area $= 80 + 40 = 120$ m^2

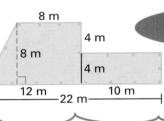

Taro thinks ...

I'll add the areas of a triangle and two rectangles.

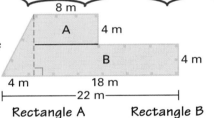

	Triangle	Rectangle A	Rectangle B
	$\frac{1}{2}bh = \frac{1}{2} \cdot 4 \cdot 8$	$lw = 8 \cdot 4$	$lw = 18 \cdot 4$
	$= 16$	$= 32$	$= 72$

Total area $= 16 + 32 + 72 = 120$ m^2

What do you think?

1. What other way could you find the area?

2. How can you decide which is the best way to divide a figure?

Check | Your Understanding

1. Why is it helpful to divide an irregular figure into rectangles and triangles to find the area?

2. Name some other familiar figures you can divide irregular figures into.

Practice and Apply

1. **Getting Started** Follow these steps to find the area of the irregular figure shown.

   a. Divide the figure into two rectangles.

   b. Find the area of each rectangle.

   c. Add the areas of the rectangles to determine the area of the irregular figure.

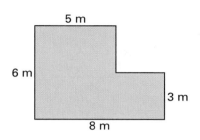

Find the area of each shaded region.

2.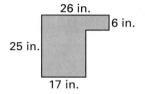

3.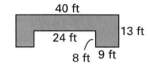

4.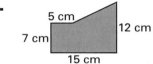

5.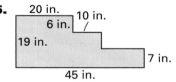

6.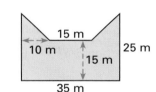

7.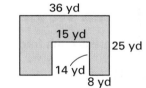

8.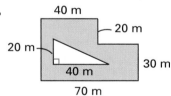

9.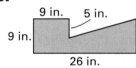

10.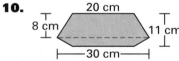

11. **Social Studies** The Great Ball Court at Chichen Itza, in Mexico, was the site of ceremonial Mayan ball games. Use the diagram to find the area of the Great Ball Court.

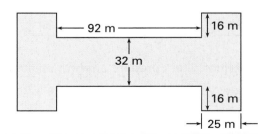

12. **Test Prep** Which of these areas could be divided into a square and a trapezoid?

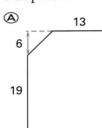

Ⓐ 13
6
19
19

Ⓑ ├─13─┤
4
16
19

Ⓒ 12
6
2
11

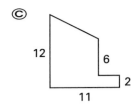

Ⓓ 15
3
15
3

Problem Solving and Reasoning

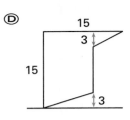

13. Critical Thinking A rectangular table measures 48 in. by 30 in. A square chessboard 24 in. on a side is set on the table. What amount of the table's area is *not* covered by the chessboard?

14. Communicate This 8 cm by 8 cm square has been divided into four triangles of equal size. What is the area of one of the triangles? Explain how you found your answer.

8 cm

Mixed Review

Express each fraction in lowest terms. *[Lesson 3-8]*

15. $\frac{25}{35}$ **16.** $\frac{16}{42}$ **17.** $\frac{12}{54}$ **18.** $\frac{49}{84}$

19. $\frac{63}{96}$ **20.** $\frac{38}{95}$ **21.** $\frac{52}{100}$ **22.** $\frac{75}{375}$

Find each quotient. Rewrite in lowest terms. *[Lesson 4-6]*

23. $\frac{3}{7} \div \frac{8}{9}$ **24.** $\frac{5}{6} \div \frac{2}{3}$ **25.** $\frac{6}{7} \div \frac{3}{14}$ **26.** $\frac{1}{3} \div \frac{3}{4}$

27. $2\frac{3}{4} \div 5\frac{2}{5}$ **28.** $3\frac{2}{7} \div 2\frac{4}{9}$ **29.** $1\frac{7}{8} \div 4\frac{1}{2}$ **30.** $9\frac{3}{4} \div 3\frac{1}{4}$

Project Progress

Calculate the area of your school's ground floor. Then prepare a report explaining how you made your measurements and how you calculated the area. Be sure to include the floor plan you drew in your report.

Problem Solving

Understand
Plan
Solve
Look Back

You've used formulas to find the areas and sides of some geometric figures. You've used estimation to find others. Now you'll apply what you've learned to the design of a multi-game play area.

Shaping Up

Materials: Graph paper

You've been hired to create the ground plan for a game park containing five play areas.

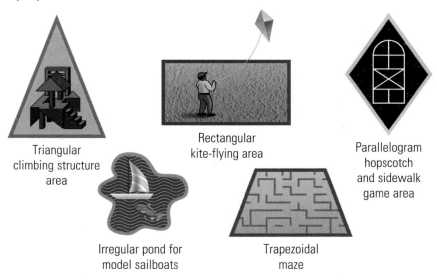

Triangular climbing structure area

Rectangular kite-flying area

Parallelogram hopscotch and sidewalk game area

Irregular pond for model sailboats

Trapezoidal maze

1. Geometric Park is a square with an area of 1024 yd². Draw the boundaries of the park on graph paper. Let each square represent an area of 1 square yard.

2. Decide where you will put each of the five play areas and how big each will be. Then draw the outline of each area within the park boundaries. Most of the park should be occupied by the five areas, with only a few small walkways and resting areas separating them.

3. Describe each play area as fully as possible in terms of topics you have studied in this section. Some of the things you might want to describe, calculate, or estimate are lengths, widths, bases, heights, perimeters, areas, and side lengths.

Find the perimeter and area for each rectangle.

1. $l = 25$ m; $w = 12$ m

2. $l = 3.9$ cm; $w = 2.4$ cm

3. $l = 4\frac{3}{8}$ in.; $w = 3\frac{1}{4}$ in.

Find the value of each expression.

4. 12^2

5. $\sqrt{121}$

6. $(0.27)^2$

7. $\left(\frac{9}{10}\right)^2$

8. $\sqrt{169}$

Find the missing length in each right triangle.

9.
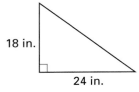
18 in.
24 in.

10.
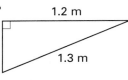
1.2 m
1.3 m

11.
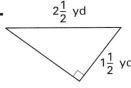
$2\frac{1}{2}$ yd
$1\frac{1}{2}$ yd

12.
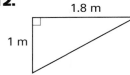
1.8 m
1 m

Find the area of each figure.

13.
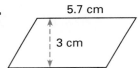
5.7 cm
3 cm

14.
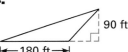
90 ft
180 ft

15.

0.8 mi
0.6 mi
2.2 mi

16.
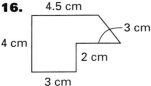
4.5 cm
3 cm
4 cm
2 cm
3 cm

17. **Journal** Write about the difference between the formula for the area of a triangle and the formula for the area of a trapezoid.

18. **Measurement** A swimming pool measures 50 m by 21 m. A typical water polo playing area measures 30 m by 20 m. How much greater than the water polo playing area is the area of the pool?

Test Prep

On a multiple choice test on which you are asked to find the area of a figure, recognizing that certain figures can be divided into smaller areas will help you work more quickly.

19. This rectangle is divided into two triangles of equal size. If you are given the area of the rectangle, how do you determine the area of one of the triangles?

Ⓐ Divide the given area by 2.　　　Ⓑ Multiply the given area by 2.

Ⓒ Square the given area.　　　Ⓓ The answer is not given here.

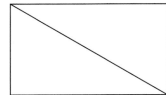

REVIEW 5B

Inductive and Deductive Reasoning

Most people do not believe everything they hear. Inductive and deductive reasoning are different ways to convince people that a statement is true.

When you test an idea many times and look for a pattern in the results, you use *inductive* reasoning. When you use logic to show that an idea is true, you use *deductive* reasoning. Mathematicians use deductive reasoning to prove that theorems, like the Pythagorean Theorem, must be true.

Here's how you might use the two types of reasoning to show that *the acute angles of a right triangle are complementary.*

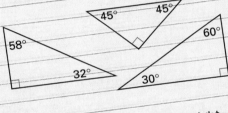

Inductive reasoning:
I've drawn lots of right triangles and measured their angles. The measures of the acute angles always add up to 90°. So, the acute angles of a right triangle are complementary.

Deductive reasoning:
I know that the angle measures in a triangle always add up to 180°. The right angle in the right triangle measures 90°. So there must be 180° − 90° = 90° left for the two acute angles. Since their measures must add up to 90°, the acute angles of a right triangle are complementary.

An example that shows that an idea is *not* true is called a *counterexample.* One counterexample is enough to show that a statement is false. If you drew just one right triangle whose acute angle measures did not add up to 90°, you would disprove the statement *the acute angles of a right triangle are complementary.*

Try It

Tell whether each situation is an example of inductive or deductive reasoning.

1. It's rained every day this month. I'd better take my umbrella today.

2. If a triangle has two congruent sides, then it is isosceles. This triangle has two congruent sides, so it is isosceles.

Give a counterexample for each statement.

3. All birds can fly.

4. If a quadrilateral has four congruent sides, then it is a square.

Chapter 5 Summary and Review

Graphic Organizer

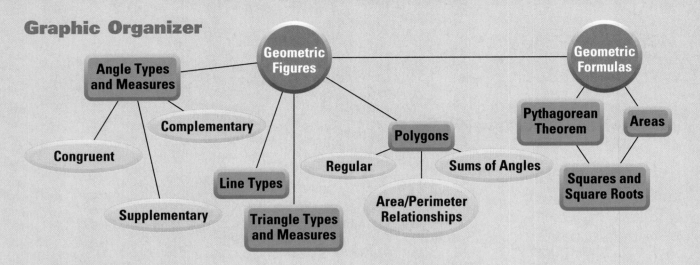

Section 5A Geometric Figures

Summary

- Two **rays** with a common endpoint form an **angle**.

- An **acute** angle measures less than 90°, a **right** angle measures 90°, and an **obtuse** angle measures between 90° and 180°. A **straight** angle measures 180°. **Complementary** angles add up to 90°; **supplementary** ones add up to 180°. **Congruent** angles have the same measure.

- Lines in a plane that never meet are **parallel. Perpendicular** lines, rays, and segments form right angles.

- A triangle may be classified by its sides, as **equilateral, isosceles,** or **scalene,** or by its angles, as **acute, right,** or **obtuse.**

- A **rhombus** is a **quadrilateral** with all sides congruent. A **trapezoid** is a quadrilateral with just one pair of parallel sides. The angles of a triangle total 180° and the angles of a quadrilateral total 360°. In **regular polygons,** all sides and angles are congruent.

- The area of a rectangle is the base (length) times the height (width): $A = bh$. The perimeter of a figure is the distance around its edge.

Review

1. Draw a line $\overleftrightarrow{AB}$ and a ray $\overrightarrow{CD}$ intersecting to form $\angle AED$.

2. What is the sum of the measures of the angles of a 10-sided polygon?

3. If $\angle RST$ measures 48°:

  a. What is the measure of an angle supplementary to $\angle RST$?

  b. What is the measure of an angle complementary to $\angle RST$?

4. Lines $\overleftrightarrow{AB}$ and $\overleftrightarrow{CD}$ are parallel. Name an angle congruent to $\angle AEF$ and explain why it is congruent to $\angle AEF$.

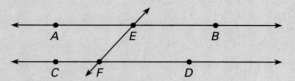

5. Find the perimeter and area of the rectangular floor of a storage shed 4 ft wide and 6 ft long.

6. Fill in the blanks with *acute, right,* or *obtuse:* All angles of a square are _____ angles. All angles of an equilateral triangle are _____ angles. The angles of any other regular polygon are _____ angles.

Section 5B Geometric Formulas

Summary

■ A **perfect square** is the square of a whole number. The **square root** of a number is the length of the side of a square whose area is that number.

■ The **hypotenuse** of a right triangle is the side opposite the right angle. The other sides are called **legs**. The **Pythagorean Theorem** says that the sum of the squares of the lengths of the legs of a right triangle is equal to the square of the length of the hypotenuse.

■ A triangle's area is half the product of its base length and height: $A = \frac{1}{2}bh$. The area of a parallelogram is the product of the length of its base and its height: $A = bh$. The area of a trapezoid is half its height multiplied by the sum of the lengths of its bases: $A = \frac{1}{2}h(b_1 + b_2)$.

Review

7. Find a perfect square between 45 and 55.

8. Find $\sqrt{17}$ to three decimal places.

9. Find the length of the hypotenuse of a triangle whose legs measure 6 ft and 8 ft.

10. Find the area of a trapezoid whose height is 4 cm and whose bases are 3 and 11 cm long.

11. Find the area of the obtuse triangle.

12. Find the area of the side of the building.

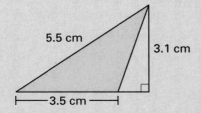

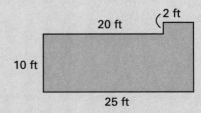

The floor plans for two triangular buildings with a passageway between them is shown. Use them to answer Questions 1–6.

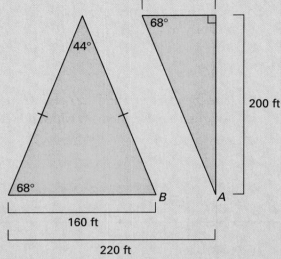

1. What is the measure of the angle at corner *A*?

2. Classify each of the two triangles as equilateral, isosceles, or scalene and as acute, right, or obtuse.

3. What is the measure of ∠*B*? What is true about angles *A* and *B*?

4. Find the length, to two decimal places, of one side of the passage between the two parts of the building.

5. Find the floor area of the passage.

6. What two methods would give you the total area of both buildings? Use either method to find that area.

7. If ∠*ABC* measures 81°:
   a. What is the measure of an angle complementary to ∠*ABC*?
   b. What is the measure of an angle supplementary to ∠*ABC*?

8. Find the sum of the angles of a regular heptagon (seven-sided polygon).

9. List all of the perfect squares between 60 and 130.

10. Find $\sqrt{225}$.

11. Find the area of an isosceles right triangle with legs measuring 15 cm.

12. Find the area of a trapezoid whose bases are 4 cm and 12 cm and whose height is 6 cm.

13. Draw an obtuse triangle with a ray bisecting the obtuse angle.

14. Draw a 3 in. line segment with a 5 in. perpendicular bisector.

Performance Task

This is a three-dimensional shape called an *octahedron*. What shape does each of its eight outside surfaces have? (Be as specific as you can.) What is the sum of the angle measures on one of these surfaces? What is the sum of the angle measures on all of these surfaces?

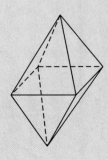

Performance Assessment

Choose one problem.

Saying **More** with **Less**

Draw the outline of a floor plan for a building that uses three different regular polygons. Using the smallest number of lengths possible, describe the dimensions of the building completely. Explain how you can use those measurements to find the others and calculate the area of the plan.

You Can Run, and Hide

According to legend, Queen Dido fled to Africa after her husband was killed. There, she begged a king for land. He granted her only as much as she could enclose with an oxhide.

Queen Dido sliced the oxhide into strips, then used the strips to surround a large area. According to the story, this land became the city of Carthage.

Suppose you have a 24-foot-long strip of hide. If you made an equilateral triangle out of the strip, how much area would it enclose? What area would you get if you made a square? A regular hexagon? If you were Queen Dido, which of these shapes would you choose for your city and why?

THE MYSTERY OF METER MOUNTAIN

Meter Mountain is 10 km across, but no one knows how tall it is. It's an easy 8 km hike to the top of the mountain on its west side. No one has ever climbed the steeper east side. Find:

e, the length of the hike up the east side.

h, the height of Meter Mountain.

Explain how you found your answers.

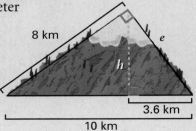

8 km

e

h

3.6 km

10 km

Cold Facts

If two buildings are identical except for the shapes of their bases, the one with the greater perimeter loses more heat. On graph paper, draw a square with an area of 64 square units, then experiment with a compass to draw a circle with about the same area. Compare their perimeters. If you lived in a cold climate, which shape would you prefer for a home? Why?

Ratios, Rates, and Proportions

➤ **Entertainment Link**
www.mathsurf.com/7/ch6/ent

➤ **Arts & Literature Link**
www.mathsurf.com/7/ch6/arts

People of the World

In 1992, the literacy rate for people over the age of 15 in Japan and the United Kingdom was reported to be 100%. This would mean that *everyone* in the population over 15 years of age could read.

Arts & Literature

The average amount of music written in a year by the Russian composer Tchaikovsky would take about 2.65 hours to perform.

Entertainment

In modern movies, the film advances at a rate of 24 frames per second. This is equivalent to 1440 frames per minute. A 2-hour feature length film contains 172,800 frames.

Science

When sitting quietly, the average 150-pound adult burns about 50 calories an hour.

Social Studies

Between 1980 and 1990 the population of Los Angeles, California, grew at a rate of 17.41% per decade, while the population of Houston grew at a rate of 2.22%.

KEY MATH IDEAS

Ratios can be used to compare any two numbers.

Rates compare numbers whose units are different. Different rates related to the human body help doctors test a patient's health.

A unit rate compares a number to 1. Unit rates are convenient to work with when solving problems.

A proportion is an equation with equal ratios. By using proportions, you can use a small number of tests to make predictions about a larger population.

There are several ways to solve a proportion. You can use tables, unit rates, or cross multiplication.

CHAPTER PROJECT

Problem Solving

Understand
Plan
Solve
Look Back

In this project, you will conduct a price survey of different stores in your neighborhood and decide which one has the best prices. Begin the project by identifying the six to ten grocery items that your family buys most often.

Interpreting Mathematical Phrases

When you make a problem solving plan, you may need to translate words into mathematical symbols. For example, the phrase "more than" may mean "+", and "is" or "was" may mean "=".

Problem Solving Focus

For each problem below, write the answer and the arithmetic you used to find the answer. (For example, if you added 5 to 7 to get 12, write "5 + 7 = 12.")

1 A tropical storm is classified as a hurricane when its maximum wind speed reaches at least 75 mi/hr. In 1960, Hurricane Donna's winds were 105 mi/hr more than the minimum. How fast were Hurricane Donna's winds?

2 The maximum winds of 1996's Hurricane Edouard were 40 mi/hr less than those of Hurricane Donna. How fast were Hurricane Edouard's winds?

3 Wind speeds inside a tornado may be 20 mi/hr more than twice as fast as Hurricane Edouard's winds. What is the wind speed in a tornado?

4 A wind whose speed is $\frac{1}{2}$ of a tornado's is powerful enough to uproot trees. Find the speed of this wind.

Ratios and Rates

Human Comparisons

A patient has just come into the Emergency Room, complaining of chest pains. A doctor exclaims, "I need pulse, BP, and EKG, stat!" Immediately, a nurse wraps a blood pressure cuff around the patient's arm and checks his pulse. Another connects an electronic device to the patient's chest and a large display screen comes alive with numbers and graphs. The doctors and nurses quickly read and write down the results, trying to understand what they mean. What are the doctors and nurses measuring?

What is a normal human body like? How do you know if a heart is working properly? To make quick life-and-death decisions, doctors need to read and understand computer displays that show many pieces of information.

Instead of measurements based on a single number, doctors often work with comparisons, such as *beats per minute* and *pounds per square inch*. Now, you'll investigate the mathematics behind these types of comparisons.

1 Why might a doctor find "80 beats per minute" more useful than "80 beats?"

2 Do you think a reading of 60 beats per minute and a reading of 240 beats in 4 minutes are the same? Explain.

Exploring and Estimating Ratios

► **Lesson Link**
You've learned how to compare whole numbers, decimals, and fractions. Now you'll use ratios to compare quantities of all kinds. ◄

You'll Learn ...

■ what a ratio is

■ to compare quantities using division

... How It's Used

Transportation planners need to compare the number of drivers to the number of cars.

Vocabulary

ratio

| Explore | Comparing Quantities |

Materials: Metric ruler

Do Your Chin-Ups!

1. For each figure, find and record measurements for the height from the chin up, the height from the chin down, and the total height. Round to the nearest millimeter.

2. Choose one figure. Write as many fractions as you can to compare the measurements you made.

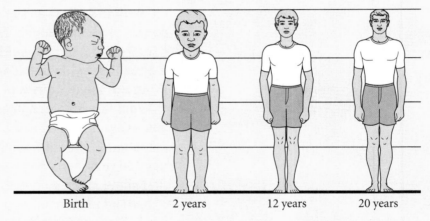

Birth   2 years   12 years   20 years

3. Use your fractions to describe the way people change as they age.

► **Science Link**

The 8 cranial bones enclose the brain.

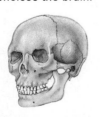

| Learn | Exploring and Estimating Ratios |

A **ratio** compares two quantities. There are three ways to write a ratio comparing the number of cranial bones to the number of facial bones in a human skull:

$\frac{8}{14}$ 8:14   8 to 14   All of these ratios are read "8 to 14."

Example 1

In a group of 7th graders, 34 were right-handed and 5 were left-handed. Find the ratio of right-handers to left-handers.

$$\frac{\text{right-handers}}{\text{left-handers}} = \frac{34}{5}$$ Write the ratio in words, then substitute numbers.

The ratio of right-handers to left-handers is $\frac{34}{5}$.

Ratios are left as improper fractions and not rewritten as mixed numbers.

In Example 1, the ratio compared two quantities. In Example 2, you'll see how a ratio can compare a part to a whole.

Examples

▶ **History Link**

The game of checkers is over 3,000 years old. It was first played by aristocrats in ancient Egypt.

2 Write a ratio comparing the number of squares with checkers on them to the total number of squares.

$$\frac{9 \text{ squares with pieces}}{64 \text{ squares}} = \frac{9}{64}$$ Write the ratio using words, then use only numbers.

The ratio of squares with checkers to the total number of squares is $\frac{9}{64}$.

3 The painting is the *Mona Lisa* by the Italian artist Leonardo da Vinci (1452–1519). Estimate the ratio of the length of Mona Lisa's nose to the length of her face.

Imagine Mona Lisa's face divided into three equal sections. The length of the nose is approximately equal to the length of the middle section. The ratio of the length of the nose to the length of the face is about 1:3.

▶ **Art Link**

The *Mona Lisa* is also known as *La Gioconda,* which means "the Smiling Lady." The portrait hangs in the Louvre in Paris, France.

Try It

The photo shows the Capitol in Washington, DC. Estimate the ratio of the height of the dome to the height of the entire building.

1. How is a ratio like a fraction? How is it different?

2. Why do you think ratios are not written as mixed numbers?

6-1 Exercises and Applications

Practice and Apply

1. **Getting Started** Follow these steps to write the ratio of the number of shaded squares to the total number of squares.

   a. Find the number of shaded squares in the pattern.

   b. Find the total number of squares in the pattern.

   c. Write a ratio comparing the number of shaded squares to the total number of squares. Rewrite the ratio in lowest terms.

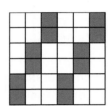

Number Sense Write each ratio three ways. Write in lowest terms if possible.

2. 8 months out of 12 months

3. 14 dogs to 16 cats

4. 3 computers out of 8 computers

5. 36 shoes to 27 socks

6. 9 runs in 4 innings

7. 88¢ for 2 oranges

Science The table gives the number of bones found in the human *axial skeleton,* which is made up of the head, neck, and trunk. Write each of the following ratios in lowest terms.

Head		Neck and Trunk	
Skull	22	Vertebral column	33
Middle ear	6	Thoracic cage	37
Hyoid	1		

8. Middle ear to vertebral column

9. Thoracic cage to hyoid

10. Skull to head

11. Skull to neck and trunk

12. Head to neck and trunk

13. Head to total axial skeleton

14. **Estimation** The Taj Mahal, in Agra, India, is considered by many people to be the world's most beautiful building. Estimate the ratio of the height of the main dome to the height of the entire building.

15. Estimation The horse pictured stands 16 *hands* tall at the shoulders. Estimate the ratio of the horse's height from the shoulders up to its height from the shoulders down. Use hands as the unit of measurement.

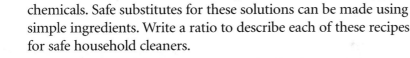

16. Science Many household cleaning solutions contain hazardous chemicals. Safe substitutes for these solutions can be made using simple ingredients. Write a ratio to describe each of these recipes for safe household cleaners.

    a. Vinyl cleaner: 1 ounce vinegar, 32 ounces water

    b. Window cleaner: $\frac{1}{4}$ cup vinegar, 1 cup water

17. **Test Prep** Write the ratio 400 to 150 in lowest terms.

    Ⓐ 40 to 15   Ⓑ 8 to 3   Ⓒ 4 to 1   Ⓓ 4 to 15

Problem Solving and Reasoning

18. Choose a Strategy Last year, the Brown Middle School basketball team won 8 games and lost 4. This year, the team won 10 games and lost 2.

    a. Write a ratio comparing the number of wins to the number of games played in each season. Remember to rewrite each ratio in lowest terms.

    b. Did the team improve from last year to this year? Explain.

19. Communicate Leonardo da Vinci, Michelangelo and other artists made careful studies of the mathematical relationships of the human body. One of the ratios they used was $\dfrac{\text{height of head}}{\text{height of entire body}} = \dfrac{2}{15}$. Find several magazine or newspaper photos and measure the people to find the ratio. Is it always $\dfrac{2}{15}$?

> **Problem Solving**
> **STRATEGIES**
> - Look for a Pattern
> - Make an Organized List
> - Make a Table
> - Guess and Check
> - Work Backward
> - Use Logical Reasoning
> - Draw a Diagram
> - Solve a Simpler Problem

Mixed Review

Science The formula $t = \frac{d}{r}$ gives the time (*t*) it takes to travel a distance (*d*) at a given rate (*r*). Substitute the given values into the formula. Then use the formula to find *t*. *[Lesson 2-1]*

20. $d = 140$ mi, $r = 40$ mi/hr   **21.** $d = 2000$ ft, $r = 50$ ft/sec

Classify each angle and give its measure. *[Lesson 5-1]*

22.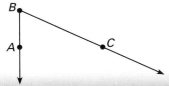

23.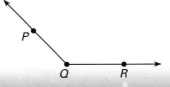

24.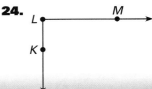

6-2

You'll Learn ...

■ to compare two quantities with different units of measure

■ to make comparisons to one unit

... How It's Used

Police officers watch for cars whose rate of speed is above the legal limit.

Vocabulary

rate

unit rate

unit price

▶ Lesson Link You've learned that a ratio is a comparison of two quantities. Now you'll see how to compare two quantities with different units of measure. ◀

Explore | Estimating Rates

How Fast Does Your Hair Grow?

1. Answer each question by making a reasonable estimate. Give estimates in terms that are easy to understand. For example, an estimate such as "1 mile in 6 hours" is easier to understand than "five-millionths of a mile in one-tenth of a second."

2. Explain how you made each estimate.

3. Compare your estimates with the ones your classmates made. Are they about the same? Why or why not?

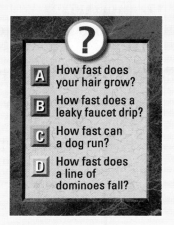

A How fast does your hair grow?

B How fast does a leaky faucet drip?

C How fast can a dog run?

D How fast does a line of dominoes fall?

Learn | Exploring and Estimating Rates

A ratio is called a **rate** when the units of measure of the quantities are different. A rate shows how quantities with different units are related to each other.

$$\frac{6 \text{ miles}}{5 \text{ miles}}$$ Both measured in miles
→ Not a rate

$$\frac{6 \text{ miles}}{5 \text{ hours}}$$ One measured in miles, one measured in hours
→ Rate

You can read the rate as "6 miles *per* 5 hours." It means "6 miles in 5 hours."

If the measure of the second quantity in a rate is one unit, the rate is called a **unit rate**. Unit rates allow you to compare rates easily.

Rate	Unit Rate
$\frac{40 \text{ points}}{5 \text{ games}}$	$\frac{8 \text{ points}}{1 \text{ game}}$
40 points per 5 games	8 points per game, or 8 points/game

To convert a rate to a unit rate, divide both its numerator and denominator by the number in the denominator.

Example 1

Your respiration rate measures the number of breaths you take per minute. Reggie counted 48 breaths in 3 minutes and Toan counted 34 breaths in 2 minutes. Who has the higher respiration rate?

Reggie: $\dfrac{48 \text{ breaths}}{3 \text{ minutes}} = \dfrac{16 \text{ breaths}}{1 \text{ minute}}$ Divide numerator and denominator by 3.

Toan: $\dfrac{34 \text{ breaths}}{2 \text{ minutes}} = \dfrac{17 \text{ breaths}}{1 \text{ minute}}$ Divide numerator and denominator by 2.

Reggie's respiration rate is 16 breaths per minute. Toan's respiration rate is 17 breaths per minute. Toan's respiration rate is higher.

A unit rate that gives the cost of one item is called a **unit price** . You can use unit prices when you want to compare prices of different quantities of an item.

Example 2

Super Sports sells 5 table tennis balls for $1.95. Sports City sells 6 table tennis balls for $2.28. Which is the better price?

$\dfrac{\$1.95}{5 \text{ balls}} = \dfrac{\$0.39}{1 \text{ ball}}$ Divide numerator and denominator by 5.

$\dfrac{\$2.28}{6 \text{ balls}} = \dfrac{\$0.38}{1 \text{ ball}}$ Divide numerator and denominator by 6.

$0.38 < $0.39, so $2.28 for 6 table tennis balls is the better price.

Try It

a. Four inches of rain fell in 16 hours. Find the amount of rainfall per hour.

b. Which is the better price: $5.12 for 3 videotapes or $8.42 for 5 videotapes?

Check Your Understanding

1. Is a rate a ratio? Is a ratio a rate? Explain.

2. How do you use division when you're working with rates?

3. Is an item with a lower unit price always the better buy? Explain why or why not.

▶ **Science Link**

Medical professionals often count a patient's breaths for 10 to 15 seconds, then multiply to calculate the respiration rate.

DID YOU KNOW?

In China, table tennis players are among the best-known athletes.

Practice and Apply

1. **Getting Started** Follow these steps to find the unit rate for a car that traveled 480 miles in 8 hours.

   a. Write the ratio of the two quantities.

   b. Rewrite the ratio so the denominator is 1 hour.

   c. Write the unit rate, using the numerator and the word *per*.

Write each expression as a rate. Remember to include units in your rates.

2. 96 students in 3 classrooms   3. 260 miles using 8 gallons   4. 44 breaths in 2 minutes

Express each rate as a unit rate.

5. $12.00 for 3 notebooks   6. 48 chairs for 6 tables

7. 54 cookies for 18 students   8. 50 jumping jacks in 50 seconds

9. $22.00 paid for 4 hours work   10. 56 points in 4 quarters

Consumer Use unit prices to find the better buy.

11. Strawberries: $1.48 for 2 baskets or $2.07 for 3 baskets

12. Potatoes: $1.60 for 5 pounds or $0.90 for 3 pounds

13. Cheese: $1.80 for 12 slices or $3.36 for 24 slices

14. Soda: 6 bottles for $2.16 or 8 bottles for $2.96

Determine whether each ratio is also a rate. Write *yes* or *no*.

15. $\dfrac{70 \text{ eighth-graders}}{80 \text{ seventh-graders}}$ 16. $\dfrac{30 \text{ miles traveled}}{\text{gallon of fuel}}$ 17. $\dfrac{40 \text{ sit-ups}}{30 \text{ seconds}}$

18. $\dfrac{16 \text{ cats}}{14 \text{ dogs}}$ 19. $\dfrac{3 \text{ cans red paint}}{2 \text{ cans yellow paint}}$ 20. $\dfrac{125}{500}$

21. **Science** Births of two or more babies at one time are called *multiple births*. In the United States, about 1% of all births are multiple births. Suppose one hospital has 12 sets of twins out of 1000 births. Write this information as a rate.

22. **Industry** Vermont leads the United States in maple syrup production. Sap from maple trees is boiled to make the syrup. As the sap boils, water evaporates until pure maple syrup remains. If it takes 120 gallons of sap to make 3 gallons of maple syrup, find the unit ratio.

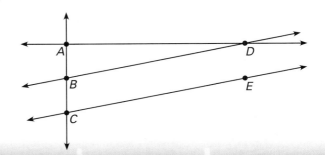

23. **Science** The planet Mercury travels about 756,000 miles in its orbit in the 7 hours that make up a typical school day. Find the unit rate.

24. **Sports** Basketball players often use unit rates to compare statistics. Which represents the higher unit rate, 210 points in 8 games or 153 points in 6 games?

25. **Test Prep** Find the best unit price for apples.

Ⓐ $0.79 per pound Ⓑ $\dfrac{\$2.40}{3\text{-pound bag}}$ Ⓒ $\dfrac{\$4.10}{5\text{-pound bag}}$ Ⓓ $\dfrac{\$8.00}{10\text{-pound bag}}$

Problem Solving and Reasoning

26. **Critical Thinking** Some jobs pay hourly wages; other jobs pay a salary for a week's work. One job pays $7.00 for each hour's work. A second job pays $320.00 for 40 hours of work each week. Which job has a higher unit rate? Explain.

27. **Communicate** A friend was absent from school, so he wants you to explain the difference between a rate and a ratio. Explain to your friend how a rate is a special kind of ratio.

Mixed Review

Find the value of each expression. *[Lesson 2-2]*

28. $41 + 27 \div 3$

29. $3 \times (62 - 14)$

30. $2 \times 5 + 6 \times 7$

31. $(24 + 28) \div 4$

32. $\dfrac{14 + 7}{3} - \dfrac{30}{10}$

33. $17 - 56 \div 7$

34. $\dfrac{56 - 4 \times 5}{2 \times 4 + 4}$

35. $\dfrac{64 \div (8 - 6)}{10 - 2 \times 3}$

Use the figure to name each pair of lines. *[Lesson 5-2]*

36. A pair of parallel lines

37. A pair of perpendicular lines

38. A pair of lines that are neither parallel nor perpendicular

Equivalent Ratios and Rates

You'll Learn ...

■ to find equivalent ratios and rates

... How It's Used

Physicians' assistants use equivalent rates when they take a patient's pulse.

Vocabulary

equivalent ratios

equivalent rates

▶ **Lesson Link** You've seen that two fractions or decimals can be equivalent. In this lesson, you'll find equivalent ratios and equivalent rates. ◀

Explore | Equivalent Rates

Knock on Wood

Materials: Watch with a second hand

1. Determine your "tapping rate" by counting the number of times you can tap your finger rapidly on your desk in 5 seconds. Have a partner time you.

2. Use your tapping rate to estimate the number of times you can tap your finger in 1 second. Explain how you found the number.

3. Estimate how long it would take you to tap 200 times. Explain how you found your answer. Are you making any assumptions?

4. Can you tap your finger 1000 times in 3 minutes? Explain.

Learn | Equivalent Ratios and Rates

Recall that equivalent fractions name the same number. **Equivalent ratios** and **equivalent rates** also name the same number. The ratio $\frac{3 \text{ bones}}{1 \text{ ear}}$ is equivalent to $\frac{6 \text{ bones}}{2 \text{ ears}}$.

You can find equivalent ratios and equivalent rates the same way as you find equivalent fractions—by multiplying or dividing both parts of the ratio or rate by the same number.

The middle ear has 3 bones.

anter 6 • Ratios, Rates, and Proportions

Examples

1 Find two ratios equivalent to $\frac{9}{15}$.

Multiply or divide the numerator and denominator by the same number.

Multiply   Divide

$\frac{9 \times 2}{15 \times 2} = \frac{18}{30}$ $\frac{9 \div 3}{15 \div 3} = \frac{3}{5}$

The ratios $\frac{18}{30}$ and $\frac{3}{5}$ are equivalent to $\frac{9}{15}$.

2 As José jogged at a steady rate on a treadmill, his heart beat 420 times in 4 minutes. Find the number of times his heart would beat in triple that amount of time. (Assume that the rate stays the same.)

$\text{rate} = \frac{420 \text{ beats}}{4 \text{ minutes}}$

To find an equivalent rate over *3 times* the time, multiply both parts of the rate by 3.

$\frac{420 \text{ beats} \times 3}{4 \text{ minutes} \times 3} = \frac{1260 \text{ beats}}{12 \text{ minutes}}$

José's heart would beat 1260 times in 12 minutes.

3 A 6-pack of boxed orange juice sells for $2.45. Predict the price of a 24-pack by creating equal rates.

The price is $\frac{\$2.45}{6 \text{ boxes}}$. Notice that 24 is 4 × 6. So to predict the price of 24 boxes, multiply both parts of the rate by 4.

$\frac{\$2.45 \times 4}{6 \text{ boxes} \times 4} = \frac{\$9.80}{24 \text{ boxes}}$

A 24-pack of juice should cost $9.80.

Science Link

A heart rate that is too rapid can put extra stress on the heart. Regular exercise can help lower your resting heart rate.

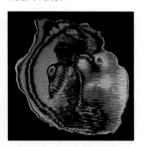

Remember

Multiplying or dividing the numerator and the denominator of a fraction by the same number does not change the value of the fraction. **[Page 145]**

Try It

a. Use multiplication and division to find two ratios equivalent to $\frac{6}{14}$.

b. The last time Jason made buttermilk biscuits, he used 8 cups of flour to make 60 biscuits. Today he plans to make one-fourth as many biscuits. If the flour-to-biscuit rate remains the same, how much flour should he use?

Check Your Understanding

1. How can you tell if two ratios or two rates are equivalent?

2. Give an example showing how you can use equivalent ratios or rates in everyday life.

Practice and Apply

1. **Getting Started** Follow these steps to find two ratios equivalent to $\frac{8}{20}$.

   a. Choose a number. Multiply the numerator and the denominator by the number you chose.

   b. Write the equivalent ratio.

   c. Try to find a number that both the numerator and denominator are divisible by.

   d. Divide the numerator and the denominator by the number, then write the equivalent ratio.

Multiply and divide to find two ratios equivalent to each ratio.

2. $\frac{6}{9}$ 3. $\frac{10}{14}$ 4. $\frac{15}{20}$ 5. $\frac{22}{24}$ 6. $\frac{25}{35}$

7. $\frac{27}{45}$ 8. $\frac{36}{54}$ 9. $\frac{40}{75}$ 10. $\frac{64}{80}$ 11. $\frac{100}{175}$

12. **Health** The human body gets energy from food. This energy is measured in calories. If a person burns 2.9 calories per minute while walking, how many calories would that person burn during a 20-minute walk?

13. Suppose one U.S. dollar can be exchanged for 125 Spanish pesetas. At this rate of exchange, how many pesetas would you receive for eight U.S. dollars?

14. **Chance** Use equivalent rates to explain which game you would have a better chance of winning.

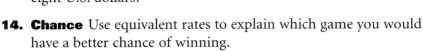

PLAY RING THE BELL!

One in four players wins a PRIZE!!

Try Race The Rocket!

One-third of our players win a PRIZE!!

PRACTICE 6-3

15. Science It takes 10 seconds for sound to travel 9 miles underwater. How long does it take sound to travel 6 times that distance?

16. **Test Prep** The number of breaths per minute for a person at rest is about 16. About how many breaths are taken in 30 minutes by a person at rest?

Ⓐ 8   Ⓑ 14   Ⓒ 46   Ⓓ 480

Problem Solving and Reasoning

17. Critical Thinking Some animated films, such as the film *A Close Shave*, by Nick Park, are made by using clay models. At the beginning of a scene, the models are placed in position and a picture is taken. The models are then moved slightly— a finger curls, an eye opens wider—and the next picture is taken. Each picture, or *frame*, is seen for only $\frac{1}{24}$ of a second on the movie screen. How many frames are needed to make 30 seconds of animated film using this method? Write an equivalent ratio to show this quantity.

©Aardman Animations/ Wallace and Gromit Ltd.1995

18. Critical Thinking It is estimated that 13 out of every 100 pounds of garbage in the United States is recycled. An average person in the United States throws away about 4 pounds of garbage per day. About how many pounds of garbage does an average person recycle in 50 days? 100 days?

19.  Identify a ratio that describes something in your classroom, such as the number of legs per desk. Write the unit ratio for the item. Then count the total number of items and write the equivalent ratio based on the number you count. (Remember to include units!)

Mixed Review

Compare using <, >, or =. *[Lesson 3-9]*

20. $\frac{6}{13} \square \frac{7}{26}$ **21.** $\frac{10}{13} \square \frac{11}{14}$ **22.** $\frac{16}{24} \square \frac{22}{33}$ **23.** $\frac{16}{21} \square \frac{33}{40}$

24. $\frac{20}{32} \square \frac{9}{15}$ **25.** $\frac{32}{50} \square \frac{40}{64}$ **26.** $\frac{5}{17} \square \frac{4}{15}$ **27.** $\frac{18}{42} \square \frac{35}{80}$

Classify each triangle by its sides and by its angles. *[Lesson 5-3]*

28.   **29.**    **30.**

Using Tables to Explore Ratios and Rates

You'll Learn ...

■ to use a table to find equivalent ratios and rates

... How It's Used

Manufacturers use tables to make sure parts are distributed correctly throughout the manufacturing process.

▶ **Lesson Link** You know how to find a ratio or a rate that is equivalent to a given ratio or rate. Now you'll see how to use a table to find as many equivalent ratios or rates as you want. ◀

Explore | **Rate Tables**

Grizzlies, Mice, and You

Biologists have discovered that nearly all mammals, regardless of size, breathe about once for every 4 heartbeats.

1. Complete a table like the one below for breaths numbering from 1 to 8. Describe any patterns you see.

No. of Breaths	1	2	3	4	5	6	7	8
No. of Heartbeats	4							

2. A grizzly bear breathes about 10 times per minute. Find the grizzly's heart rate. How did you find the answer?

3. A mouse's heart beats about 700 times in 1 minute. How many times does a mouse breathe in 1 minute? How did you find the answer?

4. Give a method for finding a mammal's heart rate if you know how many times it breathes in a minute. Can you use this method to find the number of breaths per minute if you know the heart rate? Explain.

Learn | **Using Tables to Explore Ratios and Rates**

To create a table of equivalent ratios or rates, use the same method you use to create equivalent fractions. Multiply or divide the numerator and the denominator of a known ratio or rate by the same number. The table shows that $\frac{3}{4}$ is equal to $\frac{6}{8}$.

$3 \cdot 2$

3	6	
4	8	

$4 \cdot 2$

Example 1

Complete the table to create five ratios equivalent to $\frac{4}{9}$.

4	8	12	16	20	24
9					

A row in a table is a horizontal line of entries. A vertical line of entries is called a column. To remember this, think of the up-and-down *columns* in famous buildings.

To find the first equivalent ratio, notice that the second number in the top row, 8, is 4 × 2. To find the second number in the bottom row, multiply 9 by 2: **9** × 2 = 18.

	4×2	4×3	4×4	4×5	4×6
4	8	12	16	20	24
9	18	27	36	45	54
	9 × 2	**9** × 3	**9** × 4	**9** × 5	**9** × 6

The five ratios are $\frac{8}{18}$, $\frac{12}{27}$, $\frac{16}{36}$, $\frac{20}{45}$, and $\frac{24}{54}$.

Try It

Use the table to create five ratios equivalent to $\frac{2}{5}$.

2				
5				

You can also use tables to estimate and make predictions about ratios and rates. First find the number you know (or numbers close to it) in one row of the table. Then find the corresponding number(s) in the other row.

Example 2

The table gives the number of sit-ups Laurie did during three workouts last week. Estimate how long it will take her to complete 35 sit-ups.

Sit-Ups	20	30	40
Time (sec)	24	36	48

To estimate the time it takes Laurie to do 35 sit-ups, think:

The number of sit-ups is in the top row of the table. Although 35 is not in the top row, 35 is halfway between 30 and 40. So the time is the number halfway between 36 and 48 in the bottom row. 42 is halfway between 36 and 48.

A good estimate for the time to complete 35 sit-ups is 42 seconds.

WHAT DO YOU THINK?

Ramon and Paula are lab partners in science class. They find that a volume of 5 cubic centimeters (cm³) of sulfur has a mass of 11 grams (g). They need to find the volume of 55 g of sulfur.

Ramon thinks ...

I'll make a table.

Volume (cm³)	5	10	15	20	25
Weight (g)	11	22	33	44	55

From the $\frac{25}{55}$ column of my table, I can tell that 55 g of sulfur has a volume of 25 cm³.

Paula thinks ...

The ratio of the volume to the weight is $\frac{5 \text{ cm}^3}{11 \text{ g}}$. I know that 55 is 11 × 5. So I can multiply both parts of the ratio by 5.

$$\frac{5 \text{ cm}^3 \times 5}{11 \text{ g} \times 5} = \frac{25 \text{ cm}^3}{55 \text{ g}}$$

So 55 g of sulfur has a volume of 25 cm³.

What do you think?

1. Suppose Ramon and Paula needed to find the volume of 46 g of sulfur. Whose method would be more helpful? Explain why you think so.

2. Describe a method you could use to *estimate* the volume of 100 g of sulfur. What is your estimate?

Check | Your Understanding

1. Suppose you know one out of two numbers in a ratio. With a table of ratios equivalent to that ratio, how can you use the table to find the missing number?

2. How can you find two rates that are equivalent to 1.2 miles in 15 minutes?

Practice and Apply

1. **Getting Started** Follow these steps to make a table of five ratios equivalent to $\frac{4}{7}$.

 a. Make a table containing 6 columns and 2 rows.

 b. In the column at the far left of the table, write 4 in the top row and 7 in the bottom row.

 c. Multiply both the numerator and the denominator by 2 and enter the result in the second column of your table.

 d. Multiply the 4 and the 7 by 3, 4, 5, and 6 to complete your table.

2. Using multiplication, complete the table to find five ratios equivalent to $\frac{5}{8}$.

5	10	15	20	25	30
8					

3. Using division, complete the table to find five ratios equivalent to $\frac{48}{72}$.

48	24	16	12	8	6
72					

Fill in each table to find four ratios equivalent to the ratio in the first column.

4.

3			21
5	15		

5.

32		4	
64			128

Use the table to make an estimate.

6. **Estimation** In 1984, Paul Forthomme of Belgium set the record for the greatest distance walked in a day. Forthomme averaged about 29 miles every 5 hours. Estimate how long it took him to walk 100 miles.

Distance Walked (mi)	29	58	87	116	145
Time (hr)	5	10	15	20	25

7. **Consumer** Used video games are on sale at 2 for $17. Estimate how many you could buy for $100.

Video Games	2	4	6	8	10
Cost ($)	17	34	51	68	85

PRACTICE 6-4

Use a table to find two rates equivalent to each rate.

8. 3 home runs in 7 games

9. 25 words typed per minute

10. 15 miles in 3 hours

11. 21 points in 24 minutes played

Science Make a table for each animal to find five rates equivalent to its unit rate.

12. Three-toed sloth: 7 feet per minute

13. Tortoise: 15 feet per minute

14. Snail: $2\frac{1}{2}$ feet per minute

15. **Test Prep** A ratio is equivalent to $\frac{3}{8}$. The numerator is 24. Which of these numbers is the denominator?

    Ⓐ 9   Ⓑ 64   Ⓒ 72   Ⓓ 192

Problem Solving and Reasoning

16. **Critical Thinking** Estelle has built two towers of blocks. There are 12 blocks in Tower A and 18 blocks in Tower B. If she takes one block from each tower, will the ratio of blocks remain the same? Is there any number she could remove from each tower to keep the ratio the same? Explain.

17. **Journal** In the 1930s, most teenagers were paid about 25¢ an hour to baby-sit or mow lawns. Make a table using this rate showing the total amount charged for 5 hours of baby-sitting or for mowing 5 lawns. Then make a second table using a rate you might charge now. Choose one of your tables and write an advertisement for your own baby-sitting or lawn-mowing service, using the rates in your table.

Mixed Review

Convert to a fraction in lowest terms. *[Lesson 3-10]*

18. 0.375   **19.** 0.25   **20.** 0.42   **21.** 0.671

22. 0.15   **23.** 0.38   **24.** 0.33   **25.** 0.1234

Find the sum of the measures of the angles of each polygon. *[Lesson 5-4]*

26. Parallelogram   **27.** Pentagon   **28.** 9-sided polygon

Project Progress

Go to two or more stores in your neighborhood, and record the prices of the 6–10 items on your grocery list. Be sure you record each item's weight, capacity, or volume.

Problem Solving

Understand
Plan
Solve
Look Back

During the Renaissance, artists such as Leonardo da Vinci and Albrecht Dürer worked out ratios that describe the human figure. One unexpected result of their work was the discovery that one of those ratios had been known since ancient times. Artists and architects call it the Golden Ratio.

Human Comparisons

Materials: Ruler

1. Measure each of the following lengths on one hand as accurately as possible:

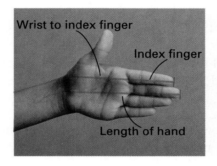

Wrist to index finger

Index finger

Length of hand

a. Distance from wrist to index finger

b. Length of the index finger

c. Length of hand

2. Calculate each ratio.

a. $\dfrac{\text{distance from wrist to finger}}{\text{length of finger}}$

b. $\dfrac{\text{length of hand}}{\text{distance from wrist to finger}}$

3. The Golden Ratio is about $\frac{21}{13}$. Since ancient times, artists have based works on this ratio, believing that its proportions are especially pleasing to the eye. For example, the length-to-width ratios of many well-known buildings and designs are equal to the Golden Ratio. Compare your ratios from Step 2 with the Golden Ratio.

4. Although other artists disagree, Albrecht Dürer claimed that there are dozens of Golden Ratio relationships in the human figure. Why might people believe that Golden Ratio proportions are especially pleasing to look at?

Number Sense Write each ratio in lowest terms.

1. 3:15   **2.** 27 to 21   **3.** $\dfrac{9}{63}$ **4.** 16:56   **5.** $\dfrac{75}{90}$

Express each rate as a unit rate.

6. Read 64 pages in 4 hours   **7.** Do 84 push-ups in 4 minutes   **8.** Earn $56 for 7 hours of work

9. Consumer Which is the better price, $2.22 for 2 baskets of blueberries or $3.54 for 3 baskets?

Operation Sense Multiply and divide to find two ratios equivalent to each ratio.

10. $\dfrac{42}{63}$ **11.** 49:70   **12.** $\dfrac{81}{108}$ **13.** 150:225   **14.** $\dfrac{320}{740}$

15. Science Many small insects flap their wings very quickly. Make a table for each insect to find five rates equivalent to each rate.

    a. Fly: 200 flaps per second   **b.** Mosquito: 600 flaps per second

16. Health The table shows how quickly a swimmer expends calories. Estimate the number of calories you expend if you swim for one hour.

Calories Expended	250	500	750	1000	1250
Time (min)	25	50	75	100	125

17. **Journal** Use an advertisement to find the price of an item you would like to buy. Construct a table to show how much it would cost to purchase different quantities of the item. Find another ad for the same item and construct another table using a different price for the item.

Test Prep

On a multiple choice test where you need to decide if two ratios are equivalent, use mental math to multiply or divide the numbers in the ratios.

18. Choose the ratio equivalent to $\dfrac{13}{4}$.

    Ⓐ $\dfrac{50}{16}$ Ⓑ $\dfrac{26}{7}$ Ⓒ $\dfrac{39}{12}$ Ⓓ $\dfrac{65}{15}$

REVIEW 6A

a Whale of a Tail

*D*o you think you could count the whales in the ocean without counting the same one twice? Marine biologists such as Gretchen Steiger of Cascadia Research are faced with this problem.

Luckily, whales do have identifying "fingerprints." Each whale has different markings on its flukes (tail fins). Gretchen photographs these flukes so she can identify individual whales. Since 1986, Cascadia Research has identified more than 600 individual humpback whales. By comparing pictures of whale flukes, Gretchen can see if a whale has been photographed before or if it is a new addition to the collection of photos.

Even with this method, it is not possible to count every single whale in an area. Biologists use a "photo-rephoto" method to estimate the whale population. After you have learned about proportional quantities, you will discover how this method works.

1 Suppose it took 10 years to count 600 whales. Express this as a unit rate.

2 Why do you think it would be difficult to count every whale in an area of the ocean? Try to give at least three reasons.

3 Name some other types of animals that might be hard to count and explain why.

6-5

Creating Proportions

You'll Learn ...

■ to use equivalent ratios to write proportions

... How It's Used

Magazine designers use proportions to scale photographs so that they fill the right amount of space.

Vocabulary

proportion

▶ **Lesson Link** You've created equivalent ratios, such as $\frac{2}{3}$ and $\frac{4}{6}$, by multiplying or dividing both parts of a ratio by the same number. Now you'll investigate equations involving equivalent ratios. ◀

Explore | Proportions

Materials: Graph paper

Antarctic Blues

The blue whale is the largest animal on earth. A blue whale can weigh 160 tons! An area of the ocean near Antarctica contains an average of 2 blue whales in every 9 square miles. Use this rate to answer the following questions.

1. On graph paper, draw a rectangle with an area of 18 square units. Let each square represent 1 square mile. How many blue whales would you expect to be in an area of the ocean this size? Explain.

2. Draw a rectangle that you would expect to contain 10 blue whales. What is its area? Explain.

3. The rate $\frac{2 \text{ whales}}{9 \text{ square miles}}$ is one way to represent the concentration of blue whales. Using your results from Steps 1 and 2, write two other rates that represent this concentration.

4. Create three more rates equivalent to $\frac{2 \text{ whales}}{9 \text{ square miles}}$. Explain what each means by describing the number of whales in each area.

5. A marine biologist surveyed an area of 140 square miles. Estimate the number of blue whales she counted.

Learn | Creating Proportions

A **proportion** is a statement that shows two ratios are equal, or *proportional*. Proportions can be written in numbers or in words.

$$\frac{1}{2} = \frac{3}{6}$$ "One is to two as three is to six."

Example

Complete the table to create three ratios equivalent to $\frac{3}{4}$. Then write three proportions using $\frac{3}{4}$.

3	6	9	12
4			

Use multiplication to complete the table.

The proportions are $\frac{3}{4} = \frac{6}{8}$, $\frac{3}{4} = \frac{9}{12}$, and $\frac{3}{4} = \frac{12}{16}$.

	3•2	3•3	3•4
3	6	9	12
4	8	12	16
	4•2	4•3	4•4

Try It

a. Complete the table to create three ratios equivalent to $\frac{2}{5}$. Then write three proportions using $\frac{2}{5}$.

2	4	6	8
5			

b. In the Sea of Cortez, marine biologists counted 3 gray whales for every 8 killer whales. Make a table of values and write two proportions related to the survey.

HINT

You can create the multiples with some calculators. Try:
3 $+$ 3 $=$. Keep pressing the $=$ and see what happens. Some calculators have a K key. If so, press 3 $+$ 3 K, then keep pressing $=$.

You can use the table in the Example to write other proportions.

$$\frac{6}{8} = \frac{9}{12} \qquad\qquad \frac{6}{8} = \frac{12}{16} \qquad\qquad \frac{9}{12} = \frac{12}{16}$$

A proportion can be written in several correct ways. Four ways to write a proportion from the data in the table are shown.

Television Sets	3	6
Homes	2	4

$$\frac{3 \text{ television sets}}{2 \text{ homes}} = \frac{6 \text{ television sets}}{4 \text{ homes}} \qquad \frac{2 \text{ homes}}{3 \text{ television sets}} = \frac{4 \text{ homes}}{6 \text{ television sets}}$$

$$\frac{2 \text{ homes}}{4 \text{ homes}} = \frac{3 \text{ television sets}}{6 \text{ television sets}} \qquad \frac{4 \text{ homes}}{2 \text{ homes}} = \frac{6 \text{ television sets}}{3 \text{ television sets}}$$

However, be careful that the numerators and the denominators match up properly! The equation $\frac{3 \text{ television sets}}{2 \text{ homes}} = \frac{4 \text{ homes}}{6 \text{ television sets}}$ is *not* a proportion.

▶ Social Studies Link

The Sea of Cortez is another name for the Gulf of California. It is on the west coast of Mexico, between the mainland and the Baja California peninsula. Many species of marine life are found there.

Check Your Understanding

1. How can you write two proportions using the ratio $\frac{5}{8}$?

2. Give an example of a proportion you find in your daily life.

3. In your own words, explain the difference between a ratio and a proportion.

Practice and Apply

1. | **Getting Started** | Follow these steps to complete the table with equivalent ratios. Then use the table to write three proportions.

2			
7			

   a. Make a table with four columns and two rows. In the left-hand column, write 2 in the top row and 7 in the bottom row.

   b. Multiply both the numerator and the denominator by 2. Put the results in the second column. Complete the third and fourth columns by multiplying the first entries by 3 and by 4.

   c. All of the ratios in the table are equivalent. Choose pairs of these ratios to create the three proportions.

Complete each table. Then write four proportions involving ratios in the table.

2.

6	12	18	24
7			

3.

5	10	20	50
9			

For each ratio, make a table and create three equal ratios. Then use your ratios to write three proportions.

4. $\dfrac{9}{20}$　　　**5.** $\dfrac{7}{8}$　　　**6.** $\dfrac{3}{11}$　　　**7.** $\dfrac{13}{15}$　　　**8.** $\dfrac{20}{7}$

9. $\dfrac{10}{14}$　　　**10.** $\dfrac{12}{13}$　　　**11.** $\dfrac{2}{100}$　　　**12.** $\dfrac{11}{5}$　　　**13.** $\dfrac{17}{19}$

14. Problem Solving A coleslaw recipe that serves 4 calls for $\frac{1}{3}$ cup of mayonnaise, $1\frac{1}{2}$ tablespoons of vinegar, and 3 cups of sliced cabbage. Change these amounts so the recipe serves 2, 3, and 4 times as many people.

Use each proportion to write two other proportions.

15. $\dfrac{1 \text{ yard}}{3 \text{ feet}} = \dfrac{7 \text{ yards}}{21 \text{ feet}}$　　　　**16.** $\dfrac{3}{4} = \dfrac{15}{20}$

17. $\dfrac{2 \text{ teachers}}{7 \text{ teachers}} = \dfrac{16 \text{ students}}{56 \text{ students}}$　　**18.** $\dfrac{60 \text{ calories}}{1 \text{ apple}} = \dfrac{180 \text{ calories}}{3 \text{ apples}}$

19. **Test Prep** Which proportion is made up of ratios equivalent to $\frac{2}{3}$?

Ⓐ $\frac{4}{9} = \frac{8}{18}$ Ⓑ $\frac{6}{9} = \frac{9}{12}$ Ⓒ $\frac{10}{15} = \frac{12}{18}$ Ⓓ $\frac{20}{30} = \frac{21}{32}$

20. **Science** A fully grown fin whale weighs about 80 tons. A bowhead whale weighs about 50 tons. At these weights, 5 fin whales weigh about as much as 8 bowhead whales. Use this ratio to create three equivalent ratios, then use the ratios to write three proportions.

Bowhead whale

Problem Solving and Reasoning

Critical Thinking Write a proportion suggested by each figure.

21.

22.

Critical Thinking Find values of the variables so that the three ratios are equivalent.

23. $\frac{2}{9}, \frac{x}{45}$, and $\frac{14}{y}$ **24.** $\frac{7}{12}, \frac{a}{60}$, and $\frac{63}{b}$ **25.** $\frac{12}{25}, \frac{48}{g}$, and $\frac{h}{300}$ **26.** $\frac{75}{120}, \frac{25}{s}$, and $\frac{t}{24}$

27. The ratio of humpback whales to blue whales seen on a series of whale-watching trips averaged 8 to 3. Can you tell how many whales of each type were seen on a particular trip? Explain.

Mixed Review

For each equation, make a table to show the value of *y* when *x* = 2, 3, 4, 5, and 6. *[Lesson 2-3]*

28. $y = x - 2$ **29.** $y = 4x$ **30.** $y = x + 17$ **31.** $y = 8x + 3$

32. $y = 4x - 5$ **33.** $y = 5x + 6$ **34.** $y = 10x - 5$ **35.** $y = 3x - 4$

Find the perimeter and area of each rectangle. *[Lesson 5-5]*

36. Length 8 cm, width 5 cm   **37.** Length 20 ft, width 14 ft

38. Base 14 in., height 23 in.   **39.** Base 9 m, height 8 m

40. Base $\frac{1}{4}$ mm, height $\frac{2}{7}$ mm   **41.** Length 2.4 mi, width 3.5 mi

Testing for Proportionality

You'll Learn ...

■ to recognize proportional relationships

... How It's Used

Officers investigating traffic accidents understand that a vehicle's stopping distance is proportional to the square of the speed at which it was traveling.

▶ **Lesson Link** You've learned to create a proportion. Now you will see how to tell whether a relationship is proportional. ◀

Explore | Proportionality

Materials: Graphing utility

Whales to Scale

While migrating, a group of killer whales might move 54 feet in 3 seconds (12 mi/hr).

Gray whale

1. Create a table of five rates that are equivalent to the killer whale's rate.

2. Use a graphing utility to make a scatter-plot of your data. Each of your rates will represent a point. Describe the scatterplot.

3. The table lists typical speeds for three other whale species. Add these points to your scatterplot. What do you notice? Explain how you can use a scatterplot to decide whether the ratios in a data set are proportional.

Species	Rate
Gray	36 ft/4 sec
Fin	36 ft/3 sec
Right	29 ft/4 sec

Learn | Testing for Proportionality

There are many ways to check whether two ratios are proportional. One is to rewrite the ratios in lowest terms and see if they are equivalent.

Example 1

Decide if the ratios $\frac{4}{12}$ and $\frac{8}{24}$ are proportional.

$\frac{4}{12} = \frac{4 \div 4}{12 \div 4} = \frac{1}{3}$ Rewrite in lowest terms by dividing by the greatest common factor.

$\frac{8}{24} = \frac{8 \div 8}{24 \div 8} = \frac{1}{3}$ Rewrite in lowest terms by dividing by the greatest common factor.

Since both ratios are equal to $\frac{1}{3}$, they are proportional.

Example 2

Two migrating gray whales were traveling at the same speed but started at different times. When the first whale had traveled 7 miles, the second whale had traveled 2 miles. When the first whale had traveled 15 miles, the second whale had traveled 10 miles. Is this a proportional relationship?

Substitute numbers in the ratio $\frac{\text{1st whale}}{\text{2nd whale}}$.
The ratios are $\frac{7}{2}$ and $\frac{15}{10}$.

Notice that $\frac{7}{2}$ is already in lowest terms.

$\frac{15}{10} = \frac{15 \div 5}{10 \div 5} = \frac{3}{2}$ Rewrite in lowest terms by dividing by the greatest common factor.

$\frac{3}{2}$ is not equal to $\frac{7}{2}$.

The relationship is not proportional.

Another way to check whether two ratios are proportional is to check whether the numerators or denominators are related by multiplication.

$$\overset{\cdot\,2}{\frac{4}{12} \overset{?}{=} \frac{8}{24}} \underset{\cdot\,2}{}$$

Both parts of the second fraction are **2** times the first.

$$\frac{4}{12} \overset{?}{=} \frac{8}{24} \cdot 3$$

Each denominator is **3** times the numerator.

Example 3

Decide if the ratios $\frac{6}{9}$ and $\frac{24}{36}$ are proportional.

Since $6 \cdot 4 = 24$ and $9 \cdot 4 = 36$, the ratios are equivalent.

$$\overset{\cdot\,4}{\frac{6}{9} \overset{?}{=} \frac{24}{36}} \underset{\cdot\,4}{}$$

$\frac{6}{9}$ and $\frac{24}{36}$ are proportional.

Try It

a. Decide if the ratios $\frac{3}{15}$ and $\frac{10}{50}$ are proportional by rewriting them in lowest terms.

b. Is the rate 32 apples in 6 boxes proportional to the rate 20 apples in 4 boxes?

c. Decide if the ratios $\frac{7}{10}$ and $\frac{21}{30}$ are proportional by seeing if they are related by multiplication.

You can also use a scatterplot to test for proportionality. When you graph equivalent ratios, a straight line through all the points will also pass through the point (0, 0).

Gasoline (gal)	2	4	5
Distance (mi)	40	80	100

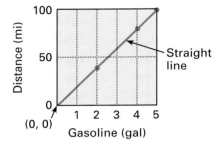

Example 4

A marine biologist plans to photograph whales. She will pay $50 to rent special photography equipment and $25 per hour for a boat. Make a table to find her total cost for 2, 4, 6, and 8 hours. Then make a scatterplot to see if the relationship between time and cost is proportional.

Time (hr)	2	4	6	8
Cost ($)	100	150	200	250

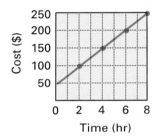

A line through the points on the scatterplot does not pass through the point (0, 0).

The relationship is not proportional.

Try It

Make a scatterplot to see if each relationship is proportional.

a.

Length of Call (min)	2	3	5	7
Cost (¢)	24	36	60	84

b.

Age	9	10	12	13
Allowance ($)	1	2	4	5

Check | Your Understanding

1. Write two ratios that are not proportional. How do you know they do not form a proportion?

2. How can you use division to decide whether two ratios are proportional?

6-6 Exercises and Applications

Practice and Apply

1. **Getting Started** Follow these steps to decide if $\frac{6}{8}$ and $\frac{9}{12}$ are proportional.

   a. Rewrite $\frac{6}{8}$ in lowest terms by dividing the numerator and denominator by the same number.

   b. Rewrite $\frac{9}{12}$ in lowest terms by dividing the numerator and denominator by the same number.

   c. Compare the ratios in lowest terms to decide if $\frac{6}{8}$ and $\frac{9}{12}$ are proportional.

Decide if the ratios are proportional.

2. $\frac{1}{2} \overset{?}{=} \frac{3}{6}$

3. $\frac{3}{9} \overset{?}{=} \frac{5}{15}$

4. $\frac{5}{8} \overset{?}{=} \frac{2}{3}$

5. $\frac{3}{1} \overset{?}{=} \frac{12}{4}$

6. $\frac{54}{2} \overset{?}{=} \frac{108}{3}$

7. $\frac{3}{4} \overset{?}{=} \frac{27}{36}$

8. $\frac{12}{18} \overset{?}{=} \frac{48}{72}$

9. $\frac{42}{7} \overset{?}{=} \frac{12}{2}$

10. $\frac{7}{9} \overset{?}{=} \frac{25}{27}$

11. $\frac{9}{18} \overset{?}{=} \frac{9}{27}$

12. $\frac{14}{17} \overset{?}{=} \frac{56}{68}$

13. $\frac{4.8}{48} \overset{?}{=} \frac{3.02}{302}$

14. $\frac{12}{13} \overset{?}{=} \frac{60}{78}$

15. $\frac{3}{5} \overset{?}{=} \frac{12}{20}$

16. $\frac{6}{18} \overset{?}{=} \frac{27}{81}$

Make a scatterplot to see if each relationship is proportional.

17.

Mike's Age	4	6	8	12
Ted's Age	6	8	10	14

18.

Dog's Weight (lb)	10	20	45	90
Amount of Food (cans)	0.5	1.5	2.5	4.5

19. **Science** Researchers tracking a pod (group) of killer whales found that the whales swam 30 miles in 4 hours on Monday, 45 miles in 6 hours on Tuesday, and 60 miles in 8 hours on Wednesday. Make a scatterplot to find out if these rates are proportional.

20. **Science** An elephant's heart rate was measured at 26 beats in 1 minute and 102 beats in 4 minutes. Are the rates proportional?

Pod of killer whales

21. | Test Prep | Choose the ratio that is proportional to $\frac{5}{9}$.

Ⓐ $\frac{1}{3}$ Ⓑ $\frac{2}{6}$ Ⓒ $\frac{7}{12}$ Ⓓ $\frac{15}{27}$

22. Use the data in the table to decide whether the ratios of brain to body weights are equal for humans and dolphins.

23. **Chance** There are 3 green marbles in a bag of 12 marbles. A larger bag has a total of 25 total marbles, including 6 green marbles. Are the chances of choosing a green marble from each bag the same? Explain.

	Body Weight (lb)	Brain Weight (lb)
Human	150	3.1
Dolphin	300	3.5

Problem Solving and Reasoning

24. **Communicate** The directions on a can of frozen orange juice say to mix 3 cans of cold water with each can of concentrate. The directions on a can of frozen orange punch say to mix $4\frac{1}{3}$ cans of cold water with each can of concentrate. Marsha correctly used 13 cans of water for 3 cans of concentrate. Did she make orange juice or punch? How do you know?

25. **Critical Thinking** Create as many proportions as you can using the numbers 2, 3, 4, 6, and 8. Show why each is a proportion.

26. **Communicate** A dolphin researcher collected the data on bottle-nosed dolphins shown in the table. Are the dolphins' weights roughly proportional to their lengths? Explain.

Length (m)	1.626	2.159	2.337	2.400	2.565
Weight (kg)	45.5	97.7	117.3	140.0	153.6

Bottle-nosed dolphin

Mixed Review

Name the inverse action of each. *[Lesson 2-4]*

27. Add 45   **28.** Multiply by 20   **29.** Divide by 10   **30.** Subtract 15

31. Add 24, then divide by 7   **32.** Multiply by 5, then add 14

Find each square root. *[Lesson 5-6]*

33. $\sqrt{81}$ **34.** $\sqrt{225}$ **35.** $\sqrt{3600}$ **36.** $\sqrt{729}$

37. $\sqrt{100}$ **38.** $\sqrt{49}$ **39.** $\sqrt{289}$ **40.** $\sqrt{6400}$

T E C H N O L O G Y

Searching the World Wide Web • Using Search Engines

Problem: What is the difference between using the words "or" and "and" when searching for information on the World Wide Web?

You can use one of the many *search engines* available on the Internet to investigate the solution to this problem. (A search engine is a program that searches Web pages for the information you've asked for.)

1 Get onto the Internet and select a search engine. Type "blue AND whale" into the search text box, then click on Search. Notice the number of documents found that match your request.

2 Now, search for "blue OR whale." Compare the number of matches for this request to the results for "blue AND whale."

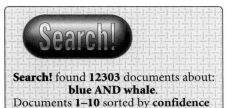

Search! found **12303** documents about:
blue AND whale.
Documents **1–10** sorted by **confidence**

84% **Blue Whale**　　Sort by Site

Search! found **52685** documents about:
blue OR whale.
Documents **1–10** sorted by **confidence**

84% **Blue Whale**　　Sort by Site

Solution: Using "and" locates documents that contain both "blue" and "whale"; using "or" locates documents that contain either word. (Note: There are differences between search engines; for instance, some use a plus sign to mean "and.")

TRY IT

a. If you wanted information about "great white sharks," would you use "and" or "or"? Try your idea.

b. If you were choosing between two topics for a science project, would you search for "whales and dolphins" or "whales or dolphins"? Explain your answer.

ON YOUR OWN

▶ What are some advantages and disadvantages of researching a topic using the World Wide Web instead of using an encyclopedia (in book form)?

Solving Proportions Using Unit Rates

You'll Learn ...

■ to use unit rates to solve a proportion

... How It's Used

Hardware store clerks use proportions when they mix paints. They need to calculate exactly the right amount of each color.

▶ **Lesson Link** You've learned how to write proportions and how to decide whether a relationship is proportional. Now you'll see how to use unit rates to find a missing part of a proportion. ◀

Explore Solving Proportions

How Do You Rate?

Materials: Watch with a second hand

Your *pulse rate* is the number of times your heart beats in 1 minute. A typical pulse rate for a person at rest is 72 beats per minute.

1. To find your pulse rate, place your index and middle fingers on your carotid artery (at the side of your neck) and count the number of beats in 10 seconds. Work out your pulse rate. Explain your calculation.

2. How many beats in 10 seconds would give a pulse rate of 72 beats per minute? Of 120 beats per minute? Explain.

3. Suppose you count 10 beats in 6 seconds. What is your pulse rate?

4. Does the method you're using give an estimate of the actual pulse rate, or does it give the exact rate? Explain why.

Learn Solving Proportions Using Unit Rates

Solving a proportion means finding a missing part of the proportion. You can use unit rates to solve a proportion. First find the unit rate. Then multiply to solve the proportion.

For instance, if you know that you can read 30 pages per hour, you can quickly predict how many pages you could read in other amounts of time.

In **2** hours I can read 30 • **2** = 60 pages.

In **5** hours I can read 30 • **5** = 150 pages.

Examples

▶ **Science Link**

The electric battery was invented by the Italian Alessandro Volta in 1800.

1 Size D batteries cost $2.19 for 3 batteries. At this rate, how much will 5 batteries cost?

> Estimate: Using compatible numbers, 1 battery costs about $2.10 ÷ 3, or $0.70. Five batteries cost about 5 • $0.70, or $3.50.

$$\frac{2.19 \text{ dollars}}{3 \text{ batteries}} = \frac{2.19 \div 3}{3 \div 3}$$ Divide by the denominator to find the unit rate.

$$= \frac{0.73 \text{ dollars}}{1 \text{ battery}}$$ The unit rate is $0.73 per battery.

$$0.73 \cdot 5 = 3.65$$ Multiply the unit rate by 5.

The cost of 5 batteries is $3.65.

2 A bottle-nosed dolphin can travel about 2.25 miles in 5 minutes. At this rate, how long does it take the dolphin to travel 8 miles?

$$\frac{5 \text{ minutes}}{2.25 \text{ miles}} = \frac{5 \div 2.25}{2.25 \div 2.25}$$ Divide by the denominator to find the unit rate.

$$\approx \frac{2.22 \text{ minutes}}{1 \text{ mile}}$$ The unit rate is about 2.22 minutes per mile.

$$2.22 \cdot 8 \approx 17.8$$ Multiply the unit rate by 8 to find the time for 8 miles.

The dolphin takes about 17.8 minutes to travel 8 miles.

▶ **Language Link**

Unit means one of anything. The French word for "one" is *un.* In Spanish, *uno* means "one." When a word starts with *uni,* think ONE!

Try It

Five CDs cost $42. At that rate, how much will 7 CDs cost?

Check | Your Understanding

1. What do car salespeople mean by their "sales per day" rate? By their "days per sale" rate?

2. Why are the words "at this rate" included in the Examples? What would happen if they weren't included?

Practice and Apply

Getting Started Find each unit rate.

1. 24 pages in 6 minutes

2. 500 miles in 12 hours

3. $1.44 per dozen

4. $1.89 for 3

5. Oranges are on sale at 6 for $0.99.
    a. Find the cost of 2 oranges.
    b. Find the cost of 4 oranges.

6. Jake earned $51.20 in 8 hours.
    a. Find his hourly rate.
    b. Find his earnings in 7 hours.

7. Sports Driving a Marmon Wasp race car, Ray Harroun completed the first 500-mile Indianapolis 500 auto race in 1911 in 6.7 hours.

    a. Find Harroun's rate in miles per hour. Round to the nearest tenth.

    b. At this rate, how far did Harroun drive in 2 hours?

    c. Find Harroun's rate in hours per mile.

    d. How long did it take Harroun to drive 400 miles?

Ray Harroun

8. Estimation Your body weight is a measure of the force of gravity. Jupiter's gravitational pull is 2.64 times that of Earth. Imagine that a scale on Jupiter shows that a whale weighs 8712 pounds. Estimate the whale's weight on Earth.

9. Literature Phileas Fogg was the hero of Jules Verne's adventure novel *Around the World in Eighty Days*. The distance around the earth is about 25,000 miles.

    a. Assuming Fogg traveled at a steady rate, how long did it take him to travel the 4000 miles from London to India?

    b. How far did Fogg travel during the final week of his trip?

10. **Test Prep** Lea earned $25.50 in 5 hours. How much did she earn per hour?

    Ⓐ $102.50   Ⓑ $5.10   Ⓒ $5.50   Ⓓ None of these

11. Sports Olympic volleyball player Bev Oden averaged 3.42 "kills" (spikes that end a rally) per game. Predict her number of kills in a 5-game match.

PRACTICE 6-7

Problem Solving and Reasoning

12. Communicate In 1991, Mike Powell of the United States set a world long-jump record of 29 ft 4.5 in. Powell is 6 ft 4 in. tall. A 5-foot-tall kangaroo can jump more than 40 feet. If Powell could jump the same distance in proportion to his height as the kangaroo can, how far could he jump? Explain how you found your answer.

13. Journal A 20-year-old man is 6 ft tall. Does that mean that a 40-year-old man is 12 ft tall? Explain why or why not.

14. Critical Thinking Gloria paid $14.99 for a new CD with 10 songs. Another CD by the same artist has 12 songs and sells for $17.99.

   a. Is the price for the second CD fair? Explain.

   b. Besides the number of songs, what other factors might help Gloria decide whether to buy the second CD?

Mixed Review

Write an algebraic expression for each phrase. *[Lesson 2-5]*

15. 5 less than a number (u)

16. 7 more than a number (x)

17. A number (g) increased by 12

18. The product of a number (z) and 10

Find the length of the unknown side. *[Lesson 5-7]*

19.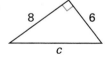

20.

21.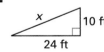

22.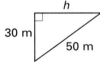

Project Progress

Decide which of the grocery stores you surveyed has the lowest overall prices. Prepare a report for your class to show your results and to explain how you decided on the lowest-priced store.

Problem Solving

Understand
Plan
Solve
Look Back

Cross Multiplication

▶ **Lesson Link** You've used unit rates to solve proportions and to help decide if two ratios form a proportion. Now you'll use a method that can do both. ◀

You'll Learn ...

■ to use cross multiplication to solve a proportion

■ to use cross multiplication to check whether two ratios form a proportion

... How It's Used

When photographers set up photos, they use proportions to determine a good exposure.

Vocabulary

cross product

Explore | Cross Multiplication

Reinventing the Whale

An aquarium has models of humpback whales hanging from the ceiling of the ticket area and the gift shop.

1. One whale in the aquarium is 45 feet long. Its flippers are 15 feet long.

Write this as a ratio:

$$\frac{\text{actual flipper length}}{\text{actual body size}} = \frac{?\ \text{ft}}{?\ \text{ft}}$$

2. The whale model in the ticket area is 21 ft long and its flippers are 7 ft long. The model in the gift shop is 12 ft long and its flippers are 4 ft long. Use this information to write two more ratios like the one you wrote in Step 1.

3. Are all three of your ratios equivalent? How do you know? Use your ratios to write two different proportions.

4. For each proportion, use its four numbers to write as many different pairs of numbers as you can. Find the product of each pair.

5. What do you notice about the pairs that give equal products? Write a sentence describing any patterns you found.

Learn | Cross Multiplication

In a proportion, the product of one numerator and the other denominator is a **cross product**. Notice that the cross products in the proportion $\frac{3}{4} = \frac{6}{8}$ are equal.

$$3 \cdot 8 = 24$$
$$4 \cdot 6 = 24$$

PROPERTY OF CROSS PRODUCTS

If two ratios form a proportion, the cross products are equal. If two ratios have equal cross products, they form a proportion.

Example 1

Check cross products to decide if the ratios $\frac{9}{21}$ and $\frac{7}{16}$ form a proportion.

$\frac{9}{21} \stackrel{?}{=} \frac{7}{16}$ Write the ratios as if they are a proportion.

$\frac{9}{21} = \frac{7}{16}$ Identify the cross products.

$9 \cdot 16 \stackrel{?}{=} 21 \cdot 7$ Write the cross products.

$144 \neq 147$ Multiply. Compare the cross products.

Since the cross products are not equal, the ratios do not form a proportion.

Test Prep

When a test asks you to compare two fractions, you can use cross products. When you find the cross products, "move" the denominators, not the numerators. If the cross products are not equal, the greater product will be on the same side as the greater fraction.

You can use cross products to find an unknown number in a proportion.

Example 2

Crustaceans called krill are some whales' only food. A 150-ton blue whale can eat 8 tons of krill a day. How many tons might a 130-ton whale eat?

Let n stand for the number of tons of krill a 130-ton whale might eat in a day.

wt. of 150-ton whale → $\quad \frac{150}{8} = \frac{130}{n} \quad$ ← wt. of 130-ton whale   Write the ratios
tons of krill →   ← tons of krill   as a proportion.

$150 \cdot n = 8 \cdot 130$ Write the cross products.

$150n = 1040$ Multiply.

$\frac{150n}{150} = \frac{1040}{150}$ To undo multiplying by 150, divide both sides by 150.

$n \approx 6.9$ Divide.

A 130-ton blue whale might eat 6.9 tons of krill in a day.

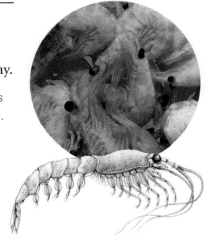

Try It

Decide whether each pair of ratios forms a proportion.

a. $\frac{4}{5} \stackrel{?}{=} \frac{11}{13}$ **b.** $\frac{5}{8} \stackrel{?}{=} \frac{15}{24}$

Solve each proportion.   **c.** $\frac{4}{7} = \frac{x}{84}$ **d.** $\frac{8}{3} = \frac{192}{k}$ **e.** $\frac{51}{35} = \frac{8.5}{n}$

WHAT DO YOU THINK?

Kimberly and Andy are on a swim team. Their training swim is 200 meters and usually takes them 3 minutes. How long, at this rate, would it take them to complete an 800-meter swim?

Kimberly thinks ...

$$\frac{200 \text{ meter}}{3 \text{ minutes}} = \frac{800 \text{ meters}}{n \text{ minutes}}$$ Write the ratios as a proportion.

$200 \cdot n = 3 \cdot 800$ Write the cross products.

$200n = 2400$ Multiply.

$$\frac{200n}{200} = \frac{2400}{200}$$ To undo multiplying by 200, divide both sides by 200.

$n = 12$ Divide.

An 800-meter swim will take 12 minutes.

Andy thinks ...

Since 800 is 4 • 200, an 800-meter swim is 4 times the length of our 200-meter swim. It should take us 4 times as long as our 3 minute training swim.

4 • 3 minutes = 12 minutes

An 800-meter swim will take 12 minutes.

What do  you think?

1. Would Andy's method have worked for a distance of 700 meters? Would Kimberly's? Explain.

2. How could you solve this problem using unit rates?

Check   Your Understanding

1. When are cross products a good way to solve a proportion? When are other methods better?

2. If you know only two of the four numbers in a proportion, can you find the other two? Why or why not?

Practice and Apply

1. **Getting Started** Follow the steps to solve the proportion $\frac{5}{x} = \frac{4}{3}$.

 a. Complete the cross products: $5 \cdot \underline{\hspace{1cm}} = 4 \cdot x$

 b. Multiply: $\underline{\hspace{1cm}} = 4x$

 c. To undo multiplying by 4, divide both sides by 4.

 d. Write and check the solution.

Find the cross products for each proportion.

2. $\frac{4}{14} = \frac{2}{7}$ 3. $\frac{2}{3} = \frac{6}{9}$ 4. $\frac{5}{8} = \frac{25}{40}$ 5. $\frac{32}{40} = \frac{8}{10}$ 6. $\frac{18}{30} = \frac{9}{15}$

Decide whether each pair of ratios forms a proportion.

7. $\frac{6}{8} \stackrel{?}{=} \frac{10}{15}$ 8. $\frac{5}{15} \stackrel{?}{=} \frac{3}{9}$ 9. $\frac{9}{15} \stackrel{?}{=} \frac{15}{25}$ 10. $\frac{6}{10} \stackrel{?}{=} \frac{25}{42}$

11. $\frac{7}{9} \stackrel{?}{=} \frac{20}{27}$ 12. $\frac{8}{22} \stackrel{?}{=} \frac{28}{77}$ 13. $\frac{15}{12} \stackrel{?}{=} \frac{4.5}{3.6}$ 14. $\frac{1.9}{2.4} \stackrel{?}{=} \frac{5.7}{7.2}$

Solve each proportion.

15. $\frac{x}{6} = \frac{1}{3}$ 16. $\frac{1}{6} = \frac{k}{12}$ 17. $\frac{3}{x} = \frac{11}{20}$ 18. $\frac{5}{2} = \frac{6}{x}$

19. $\frac{9}{1} = \frac{t}{4}$ 20. $\frac{y}{10} = \frac{3}{5}$ 21. $\frac{4}{9} = \frac{10}{x}$ 22. $\frac{5}{2} = \frac{2}{x}$

23. **Test Prep** What is the value of x in the proportion $\frac{5}{8} = \frac{10}{x}$?

 Ⓐ 8   Ⓑ 15   Ⓒ 16   Ⓓ None of these

24. **Science** An adult blue whale can be about 100 ft long and weigh about 150 tons. An adult beluga whale can be about 15 ft long and weigh about 1.5 tons. Do the ratios of the whales' lengths to weights form a proportion?

25. **History** In 1890, the United States had an area of about 3.0 million square miles and a population of about 62.9 million. In 1990, the area was about 3.5 million square miles and the population was about 248.7 million. Do the ratios of the areas to the populations form a proportion? Explain.

Beluga whale

26. Estimation According to 1993 figures from the A. C. Nielsen Company, nearly 60 million of the 95 million U.S. households own two or more television sets. Use the data shown to estimate the number of households in Texas with two or more sets.

27. Science A 380-cubic-centimeter sample of titanium has a mass of 1710 g. Find the weight of a titanium sample that has a volume of 532 cubic centimeters.

= 1 million households

Problem Solving and Reasoning

28. Choose a Strategy The ratio of teachers to students at Sam Houston Middle School is 1 to 36. If there are 720 students, how many more teachers are needed to make the teacher-to-student ratio 1 to 30? Explain.

29. Critical Thinking A chemist analyzed samples of three substances. If two samples do not contain the same proportions of carbon and hydrogen, they cannot be the same substance. Could any of these samples be the same substance? Explain.

	Sample A	Sample B	Sample C
Carbon (g)	4	6	10
Hydrogen (g)	18	25	45

Problem Solving
STRATEGIES
• Look for a Pattern
• Make an Organized List
• Make a Table
• Guess and Check
• Work Backward
• Use Logical Reasoning
• Draw a Diagram
• Solve a Simpler Problem

30. Communicate Some linguists believe that the works of 19th-century writer Thomas Jefferson Snodgrass were actually written by Mark Twain. The table shows a count of 1- and 2-syllable words in similar passages by the two writers. Does the data support the theory that Twain was Snodgrass? Explain.

	Total No. of Words	1-Syllable Words	2-Syllable Words
Twain	916	525	231
Snodgrass	655	362	179

Mixed Review

Solve each equation. *[Lesson 2-6]*

31. $x - 9 = 24$ **32.** $f + 25 = 67$ **33.** $34 = y - 18$ **34.** $659 = p + 345$

Find the missing measurements of the following triangles. *[Lesson 5-8]*

35. Base = 8, height = 6, area = ?   **36.** Base = ?, height = 24 in., area = 96 in^2

At the beginning of this section, you read about the *photo-rephoto* method that researchers use to estimate the number of whales in a particular region. You can model this technique using chips as "whales" and a bowl as an "ocean."

A Whale of a Tail

Materials: Large number of plastic chips, Bowl, Marking pen

Put the whales (chips) into the ocean (bowl). Do not count the whales.

1. **Photo** Grab a small handful of chips. Mark each of these chips with a felt-tipped pen. Count and record the number of marked chips. This number is the *first number of whales photographed.* Return the chips to the bowl and mix thoroughly.

2. **Rephoto** Grab another small handful of chips. Count and record the number of chips grabbed (the *second number of whales photographed*) and the number of marked chips in the second handful (the *number of whales rephotographed*).

3. Solve the proportion:

$$\frac{\text{number of whales rephotographed}}{\text{second number of whales photographed}} = \frac{\text{first number of whales photographed}}{x}$$

The value of *x* you obtain will be an estimate of the number of whales in your ocean.

4. Return the chips to the bowl and mix thoroughly. Repeat Steps 2 and 3 four more times. Each time, you'll obtain an estimate of the total number of whales.

5. Find the mean of your five estimates. Then count the number of chips in the bowl and compare the total with the mean you calculated.

6. Explain why it is important to mix the chips thoroughly each time you return them to the bowl. What can biologists do to make sure that the whales they photograph and rephotograph are thoroughly "mixed"?

1. Complete the table with equivalent ratios. Then write four proportions using ratios in the table.

3	6	9			
5					

Make a table and create three equal ratios. Use the ratios to write three proportions.

2. $\dfrac{3}{7}$　　　　**3.** $\dfrac{9}{8}$　　　　**4.** $\dfrac{6}{11}$　　　　**5.** $\dfrac{5}{2}$　　　　**6.** $\dfrac{9}{20}$

Decide whether each pair of ratios forms a proportion.

7. $\dfrac{9}{14} \stackrel{?}{=} \dfrac{25}{39}$　　**8.** $\dfrac{10}{35} \stackrel{?}{=} \dfrac{8}{28}$　　**9.** $\dfrac{6}{9} \stackrel{?}{=} \dfrac{12}{18}$　　**10.** $\dfrac{7}{8} \stackrel{?}{=} \dfrac{49}{56}$　　**11.** $\dfrac{18}{36} \stackrel{?}{=} \dfrac{9}{18}$

Solve each proportion.

12. $\dfrac{3}{5} = \dfrac{12}{x}$　　**13.** $\dfrac{5}{4} = \dfrac{y}{10}$　　**14.** $\dfrac{n}{27} = \dfrac{8}{18}$　　**15.** $\dfrac{18}{36} = \dfrac{10}{a}$　　**16.** $\dfrac{4}{9} = \dfrac{20}{q}$

17. Consumer Report covers sell for 8 for $5.20. Find the unit price. Then tell how many covers you can buy for $78.00.

18. Science In 1996, Keiko, the killer whale used in the filming of *Free Willy*, was moved from Mexico to Oregon. It cost $9,000,000 to airlift the 7,000 pound whale to his new home. How much did it cost per pound to move Keiko?

19. Journal A researcher tagged 200 bass and released them into a lake. A month later, he netted 16 bass and found that 5 of them were tagged. Estimate the bass population of the lake. Describe the process you used.

Test Prep

To solve a proportion on a multiple choice test, substitute each answer and check the cross products. The answer giving equal cross products is correct.

20. Solve for *x*.　$\dfrac{4}{5} = \dfrac{6}{x}$

Ⓐ 7　　　　　Ⓑ 7.5　　　　　Ⓒ 9　　　　　Ⓓ 9.5

The Tangent Ratio

The *tangent ratio* of an acute angle in a right triangle is equal to the ratio $\frac{\text{length of opposite side}}{\text{length of adjacent side}}$.

In the figure, the tangent of $\angle A$, abbreviated tan $\angle A$,
$= \frac{5}{4} = 1.25$.

The hypotenuse is *never* part of the tangent ratio.

If you know an angle's measure, you can use a scientific calculator to find its tangent. To find the tangent of 40°, enter 40 [TAN]. The result is about 0.84.

Tangent ratios can be used to make an *indirect* measurement—to find a length that cannot be measured directly.

From a point 37 feet from the bottom of a telephone pole, the angle to the top of the pole is 32°. Find h, the height of the pole.

The length of the side opposite the 32° angle is h and the length of the adjacent side is 37 feet. So:

$$\tan 32° = \frac{h}{37} \qquad \underline{\text{Set up the tangent ratio.}}$$

$$37 \times \tan 32° = h \qquad \underline{\text{Use inverse operations.}}$$

You can use a calculator to find h.

37 [×] 32 [TAN] [=] 23.12016602...

The telephone pole is about 23.1 feet tall.

Try It

Solve for h in each figure. Round answers to the nearest tenth.

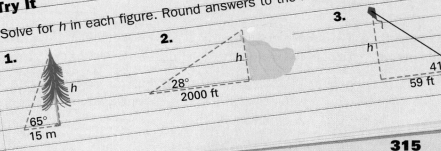

1. 65° 15 m

2. 28° 2000 ft

3. 41° 59 ft

Graphic Organizer

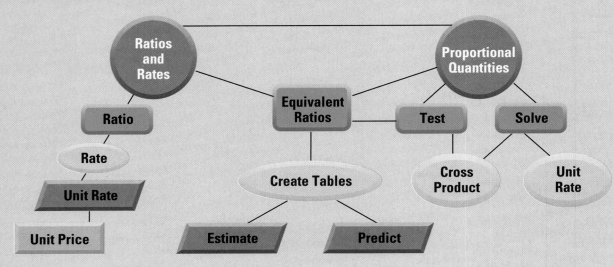

Section 6A   Ratios and Rates

Summary

- A **ratio** compares two quantities. There are three ways to write a ratio; for example, the ratios 2 to 3, $\frac{2}{3}$, and 2:3 all have the same meaning.

- A ratio is called a **rate** when the units of measure of the quantities are different. A rate shows how quantities with different units are related.

- A **unit rate** is a rate in which the measure of the second quantity is 1 unit. A **unit price** is a unit rate that gives the cost of one item.

- To find **equivalent ratios** or **equivalent rates**, multiply or divide the numerator and denominator of a given ratio or rate by the same number. You can use this method to create a table of equivalent ratios or rates.

- You can use tables to estimate and predict ratios and rates.

Review

1. Write the ratio 8 forks to 6 spoons in three ways. Write in lowest terms if possible.

2. Estimate the ratio of the height to the base of the triangle.

3. Find the unit rate: 130 miles in 2 hours. Remember to include units in your rate.

4. Express the rate as a unit rate: 102 houses along a 6-mile road.

5. Find the better buy for bread: $3.20 for 2 loaves or $5.10 for 3 loaves.

6. Hugo's car travels 108 miles on 4 gallons of gas. How far will it travel on 7 gallons of gas?

7. Multiply and divide to find two ratios equivalent to the ratio $\frac{16}{20}$.

8. Use a table to find two rates equivalent to 15 points in 4 games.

9. Using multiplication, complete the table to find 5 ratios equivalent to $\frac{3}{4}$.

3	6	9	12	15	18
4					

10. Using division, complete the table to find 5 ratios equivalent to $\frac{120}{80}$.

120	60	30	24	12	6
80					

Section 6B Proportional Quantities

Summary

- A **proportion** is an equation or statement that shows two ratios are equal.

- To test two ratios to see if they are proportional, you can reduce each ratio to lowest terms and see if they are equivalent.

- You can use unit rates to solve a proportion. First find the unit rate. Then multiply to solve the proportion.

- A **cross product** of two ratios is the product of the numerator of one ratio and the denominator of the other ratio.

- If two ratios form a proportion, the cross products are equal. If two ratios have equal cross products, they form a proportion. You can use cross products to find an unknown number in a proportion.

Review

11. Steve baked one loaf of bread using 3 cups of flour and 5 teaspoons of yeast, and another loaf using 4 cups of flour and 7 teaspoons of yeast. Are these ratios proportional?

12. Complete the ratio table. Then write four proportions involving the ratios in the table.

4	8	12	16
7			

13. Make a table and create three ratios equal to $\frac{5}{13}$. Use your ratios to write three proportions.

14. Decide if the ratios are proportional and give a reason: $\frac{9}{14} \stackrel{?}{=} \frac{13}{21}$.

15. Find the unit rate: $7.65 for 9 muffins.

16. Solve the proportion: $\frac{12}{26} = \frac{n}{65}$.

17. Decide whether the ratios form a proportion: $\frac{98}{112} \stackrel{?}{=} \frac{63}{72}$.

18. Anna earned $123.75 in 15 hours. Find her hourly rate.

1. Using multiplication, complete the table by finding 5 ratios equivalent to $\frac{5}{9}$.

5	10	15	20	25	30
9					

2. Estimate the ratio of the height to the width of the building.

3. Write the ratio 10 cats to 25 dogs in three ways. Write in lowest terms if possible.

4. Express the rate as a unit rate: 385 raisins in 7 pounds of cereal.

5. Use unit rates to find the better buy for dog food: 98 cents for 14 oz or 64 cents for 8 oz.

6. Morris was paid $34.00 for 5 hours of work. If he is paid an hourly wage, how much will he be paid for 12 hours of work?

7. Find the rate: 5 tons in 18 days. Remember to include units in your rate.

8. Use a table to find two rates equivalent to 20 feet in 34 seconds.

9. Multiply and divide to find two ratios equivalent to the ratio $\frac{12}{21}$.

10. Make a table and create three ratios equal to $\frac{3}{8}$. Use your ratios to write three proportions.

11. Using division, complete the table by finding 5 ratios equivalent to $\frac{72}{126}$.

72	36	24	12	8	4
126					

12. Complete the ratio table. Then write four proportions involving the ratios in the table.

6	12	18	24
11			

13. Hulleah ran 100 m in 15 sec, 200 m in 30 sec, and 400 m in 70 sec. Use a scatterplot to decide whether these rates are proportional.

14. Mr. Sanderson's class has 20 boys and 16 girls. Ms. Trevino's class has 15 boys and 12 girls. Are these ratios proportional?

15. Decide whether the ratios form a proportion: $\frac{75}{120} \stackrel{?}{=} \frac{96}{144}$.

16. Decide if the ratios are proportional and give a reason: $\frac{40}{56} \stackrel{?}{=} \frac{45}{63}$.

17. Solve the proportion: $\frac{16}{x} = \frac{12}{8}$.

Performance Task

Draw rectangles of dimensions 3 by 5, 6 by 10, and 9 by 15. For each pair of rectangles, find the ratio of the short sides, the ratio of the long sides, and the ratio of the areas. What do you notice?

Multiple Choice

Choose the best answer.

1. Solve $5z + 8 = 43$. [Lesson 2-7]

   Ⓐ $z = 6$ Ⓑ $z = 7$

   Ⓒ $z = 8$ Ⓓ $z = 9$

2. Express the number 3,800,000 in scientific notation. [Lesson 3-5]

   Ⓐ 38×10^5 Ⓑ 3.8×10^5

   Ⓒ 3.8×10^6 Ⓓ 3.8×10^7

3. Find the quotient $6\frac{2}{3} \div 2\frac{1}{7}$. [Lesson 4-5]

   Ⓐ $2\frac{6}{7}$ Ⓑ $3\frac{1}{9}$ Ⓒ $7\frac{1}{3}$ Ⓓ $14\frac{2}{7}$

4. Which of the following is not correct? [Lesson 5-1]

   Ⓐ A 95° angle is obtuse.

   Ⓑ A 90° angle is a right angle.

   Ⓒ An 84° angle is acute.

   Ⓓ A 91° angle is acute.

5. What is the sum of the angles in a quadrilateral? [Lesson 5-3]

   Ⓐ 180°

   Ⓑ 360°

   Ⓒ 540°

   Ⓓ It depends on the quadrilateral.

6. Which rectangle has a perimeter of 18? [Lesson 5-5]

   Ⓐ 4 by 5   Ⓑ 7 by 11

   Ⓒ 2 by 9   Ⓓ 4 by 18

7. Between which consecutive whole numbers does $\sqrt{183}$ lie? [Lesson 5-6]

   Ⓐ 12 and 13   Ⓑ 13 and 14

   Ⓒ 14 and 15   Ⓓ 15 and 16

8. Which trapezoid has the smallest area? [Lesson 5-9]

   Ⓐ Bases 7 and 8, height 19

   Ⓑ Bases 12 and 18, height 6

   Ⓒ Bases 3 and 7, height 16

   Ⓓ Bases 4 and 12, height 9

9. Which of the following does *not* represent a ratio of 12 to 8? [Lesson 6-1]

   Ⓐ 12:8   Ⓑ 3 to 2

   Ⓒ $\frac{8}{12}$ Ⓓ $\frac{12}{8}$

10. Express as a unit rate: 64 gallons in 16 hours. [Lesson 6-2]

   Ⓐ $\frac{4 \text{ gallons}}{1 \text{ hour}}$ Ⓑ $\frac{64 \text{ gallons}}{16 \text{ hours}}$

   Ⓒ $\frac{4 \text{ hours}}{1 \text{ gallon}}$ Ⓓ $\frac{8 \text{ gallons}}{1 \text{ hour}}$

11. Which rate is equivalent to 24 feet in 64 seconds? [Lesson 6-6]

   Ⓐ $\frac{6 \text{ ft}}{16 \text{ sec}}$ Ⓑ $\frac{12 \text{ ft}}{15 \text{ sec}}$

   Ⓒ $\frac{30 \text{ ft}}{84 \text{ sec}}$ Ⓓ $\frac{40 \text{ ft}}{108 \text{ sec}}$

12. Frederic bought 3 pounds of onions for $0.63. How many pounds of onions could he buy for $2.94? [Lesson 6-7]

   Ⓐ 12 pounds   Ⓑ 14 pounds

   Ⓒ 15 pounds   Ⓓ 16 pounds

13. Solve the proportion: $\frac{8}{3} = \frac{12}{p}$. [Lesson 6-8]

   Ⓐ $p = 4$ Ⓑ $p = 4.5$

   Ⓒ $p = 5.5$ Ⓓ $p = 6.5$

Cultural Link
www.mathsurf.com/7/ch7/people

Entertainment Link
www.mathsurf.com/7/ch7/ent

People of the World

To estimate what your shoe size is in Europe, measure your foot in centimeters and multiply by $\frac{3}{2}$.

Entertainment

A sand castle is a scale model of a "real" castle. The tallest sand castle ever built stood over 23 feet tall! The World Championship Sand Sculpture Competition is held each September in Harrison Hot Springs, British Columbia, Canada.

Arts & Literature

In 1726, Jonathan Swift wrote a book called *Gulliver's Travels.* The hero, Gulliver, travels to two imaginary lands: Lilliput, where people are 6 inches tall, and Brobdingnag, where toddlers are over 40 feet tall.

Science

The diameter of the sun is 109 times greater than the diameter of the earth. If you made a model of the earth the size of a golf ball, your model of the sun would have a diameter of more than 15 feet!

Social Studies

When Columbus set sail from Spain in 1492, he was trying to find a shorter route to India. He underestimated the size of the earth because he used a map with the wrong scale, and he was unaware of the North and South American continents.

KEY MATH IDEAS

The scale of a map or model relates its size to the size of the area or object it represents. You can use scales to solve problems involving maps.

By converting units, you can express the same rate in different ways.

Similar figures have the same shape but not necessarily the same size.

The ratio of the side lengths of two similar figures is the scale factor.

CHAPTER PROJECT

Problem Solving

Understand
Plan
Solve
Look Back

In this project, you will design and make a scale model of your dream house. Begin by thinking about other scale models you have seen, such as model trains and dollhouses. Then make a simple sketch of your dream house.

321

Problem Solving Focus

Identifying Missing Information

As you make a problem-solving plan, you need to be sure you have all the information you need. Sometimes you will encounter a problem that is missing important information.

Identify any additional information needed to solve each problem. If a problem is not missing any information, give its solution.

1. 7-foot 7-inch, 303-pound Gheorghe Muresan is one of the tallest players in the National Basketball Association. Estimate the ratio of Muresan's height to that of the NBA's shortest player, 132-pound Muggsy Bogues.

2. In the 1995–96 season, David Robinson of the San Antonio Spurs had 1000 rebounds in 82 games. How many rebounds per game is this?

3. Grant Hill of the Detroit Pistons averaged 20.2 points per game in 1995–96. How many points did he score that season?

4. In 1995–96, the NBA's best long-range shooter was Tim Legler of the Washington Bullets. He made 52.2% of his attempts from 3-point range. How many 3-point shots did Legler attempt?

Page 26.

Captains Lewis & Clark holding a Council with the Indians

Never Mind— I'll Draw It Myself!

Imagine finding your way to an unfamiliar place across town without a map. Now imagine that you're going across a continent instead of across town; you can't take a plane, car, or bus; and you're not sure you'll make it back alive. Sound like fun?

In 1804, Meriwether Lewis and William Clark set out from St. Louis on exactly this kind of trip. With the help of native people, they traveled from St. Louis to the Pacific Ocean and back—without a map! As they traveled, guided by a Shoshone woman, Sacajawea, Lewis and Clark recorded information so *they* could make a map of the region. They talked to Native Americans, observed the sun and stars, noted important landmarks, and estimated distances. The map they produced was extremely accurate.

Accurate mapmaking requires careful mathematics. You will learn about many of the skills mapmakers use. Then, like Lewis and Clark, you'll make a map of previously unmapped territory!

1 The Lewis and Clark expedition traveled about 8000 miles in 2 years, 4 months. How many miles per month is this?

2 Two towns separated by 20 mi are 1 in. apart on a map. How far apart should the mapmaker draw two towns that are separated by 60 mi? Explain your reasoning.

Measurement: Estimating Actual and Scale Distances

You'll Learn ...

■ to read and understand scales

■ to estimate distances from maps using scales

... How It's Used

Travel planners need to be able to read distances from maps to organize trips.

Vocabulary

scale

▶ **Lesson Link** You've used ratios to compare quantities. Now you'll see how ratios are used to compare actual distances with distances shown on maps. ◀

Explore | Maps

Materials: Paper, Yardstick or meter stick

A Map Is a Snap!

1. Choose an area around your school you would like to map.

2. Before beginning a detailed map, make a rough sketch of the area you chose. Estimate or measure important distances and record the locations of significant landmarks.

3. Draw your map. Make it as accurate as you can.

4. How did you decide how large to make objects on your map and how far apart to draw them?

5. Most people cannot draw a perfect map. Does any part of your map look distorted? If so, how can you tell?

6. Did you use ratios or proportions to draw your map? Explain.

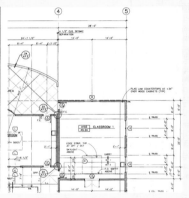

Architect's plan for school

Learn | Estimating Actual and Scale Distances

The ratio used to reduce real roads, cities, and countries so they fit on a map is the **scale**. The scale is the ratio of the distance between two points on the map to the actual distance between the points.

Suppose a 10 mi long road has a length of 1 in. on a map. Here are three ways to write the map's scale:

$\dfrac{1 \text{ in.}}{10 \text{ mi}}$ 1 in.:10 mi   1 in. = 10 mi

Examples

1 Lewis and Clark traveled from St. Louis to the Pacific coast. These points are actually about 1800 miles apart. Estimate the scale of the map.

On the map, St. Louis is about 2 in. from the Pacific coast. The scale is about

$$\frac{2 \text{ in.}}{1800 \text{ mi}}, \text{ or } \frac{1 \text{ in.}}{900 \text{ mi}}.$$

2 Main Street is $6\frac{1}{8}$ miles long. Estimate the length of Main Street on a town map with a scale of 1 in. = 4 mi.

A 4-mile road is 1 in. long on the map. So 2 mi is $\frac{1}{2}$ in. long and 6 mi (3 times as far) is $1\frac{1}{2}$ in. long on the map. Main Street's length of $6\frac{1}{8}$ mi is about $1\frac{1}{2}$ in. on the map.

Try It

Estimate the map length of a 15 mi road on a map with a scale of $\frac{1 \text{ in.}}{8 \text{ mi}}$.

► **Literature Link**

Almost every town in the United States has a Main Street. Sinclair Lewis (1885–1951) wrote a novel called *Main Street* that presented a grim picture of small-town life.

Example 3

A map uses a scale of 2 cm:5 km. Estimate the actual length of a road whose map length is 5.5 cm.

Every 2 cm represents 5 km, so 6 cm would represent 15 km. A length of 5.5 cm represents a little less than 15 km.

A good estimate for the length of the road is about 14 km.

Try It

A map uses the scale 2 cm = 75 km. If the Suez Canal is 3.9 cm long on the map, estimate the actual length of the Suez Canal.

DID YOU KNOW?

The metric system of measurement was developed in France after the French Revolution. One meter was defined as one ten-millionth of the distance from the North Pole to the Equator.

Check Your Understanding

1. Why is it important to know the scale of a map?

2. You begin a map with a scale of 1 in.:500 ft, then find that it will be too large to fit your paper. How would you change the scale? Explain.

3. Would two maps of Utah have the same shape even if the scales were different? Explain.

7-1 Exercises and Applications

Practice and Apply

1. **Getting Started** Follow these steps to estimate the distance between two cities shown $5\frac{1}{8}$ inches apart on a map with a scale of 1 in. = 15 mi.

   a. Determine the number of miles represented by 5 inches.

   b. Estimate the number of miles represented by $\frac{1}{8}$ inch.

   c. Add the numbers you found to estimate the total actual distance.

Number Sense Write each scale in two other ways.

2. 2 in.:75 mi   3. 1 in. = 225 mi   4. $\dfrac{1 \text{ cm}}{30 \text{ km}}$ 5. 6 cm:100 km   6. $\dfrac{5 \text{ in.}}{5 \text{ mi}}$

Use the following measurements to estimate the scale of each map.

7. A 60 mi road is 5 in. long.   8. A 110 km wide park is 22 cm wide.

9. A 75 mi trail is $10\frac{1}{2}$ in. long.   10. A 4866 km wide continent is 3 cm wide.

Estimation Estimate each map distance.

11. A bullet train travels 192 kilometers between the Japanese cities of Hiroshima and Kokuru. About how long will the train line appear on a map with the scale $\frac{1 \text{ cm}}{100 \text{ km}}$?

12. New York City is 205 miles from Washington, DC. About how far apart will these cities appear on a map with the scale of 1 in.:50 mi?

13. A map uses the scale 1 cm = 319 km. If South America is 27.7 cm long on the map, estimate the actual length of South America.

Use the map and a ruler to estimate each straight-line distance in miles.

14. Boise City to Forgan

15. Hardesty to Kenton

16. Tyrone to Guymon

17. Geography The students at Clissold Elementary School in Chicago, Illinois, painted a map of the world on their playground. The United States, which is about 3000 miles wide, measures 25 feet across on the playground map. Estimate the scale of their map.

18. | Test Prep | Two towns are 146 miles apart. About how far apart will they appear on a map with the scale 1 in. = 45 mi?

(A) 2 in. (B) 3 in. (C) 45 in. (D) 135 in.

Problem Solving and Reasoning

19. Critical Thinking Yellowstone Lake, in Wyoming, is the largest high-altitude lake in North America, measuring 20 mi long and 14 mi wide. About how long and wide would Yellowstone Lake appear on a map with the scale 1 in. = 3 mi?

20. Communicate Fantasy novels such as J. R. R. Tolkien's *The Hobbit* often contain maps of imaginary lands. Draw your own map of an imaginary world. Include as much detail as you like. When you are finished, write a scale next to your map. Explain how you calculated your scale.

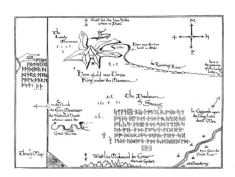

21. Critical Thinking A group of artists produced a miniature model of New York City in which every detail of the city is modeled at a much smaller scale. A 1200 ft tall building measures just 1 ft tall in the model. Express the scale used in the model in in. per ft.

Mixed Review

Estimate each sum or difference. *[Lesson 4-1]*

22. $\frac{1}{5} + \frac{3}{8}$ **23.** $\frac{2}{3} - \frac{1}{7}$ **24.** $\frac{1}{6} - \frac{1}{9}$ **25.** $\frac{5}{12} + \frac{3}{7}$ **26.** $\frac{1}{7} + \frac{4}{5}$

27. $\frac{2}{9} - \frac{1}{13}$ **28.** $\frac{4}{5} - \frac{1}{6}$ **29.** $\frac{5}{11} + \frac{1}{8}$ **30.** $\frac{7}{15} + \frac{2}{3}$ **31.** $\frac{11}{12} + \frac{1}{20}$

Find the area of each trapezoid or parallelogram. *[Lesson 5-9]*

32.
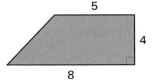

33.
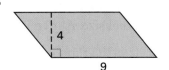

34.
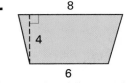

7-2

Calculating with Scales

You'll Learn ...

■ to use scales and scale drawings to calculate actual distances

... How It's Used

Mapmakers use scales as they determine the size a map will be.

Vocabulary

scale drawing

▶ **Lesson Link** You've learned how scales are used to relate map distances to actual distances. The concept of scale can also be applied to various kinds of drawings, diagrams, and even three-dimensional models. ◀

Explore Scale Drawings

Growing Roses

Materials: Graph paper

A *compass rose* is the design on a map that shows which direction is north.

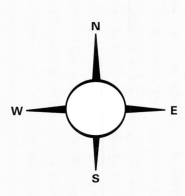

1. Trace the drawing of the compass rose onto your graph paper near the top of the page.

2. Using the grid marks on your paper as a guide, draw another compass rose whose length is twice that of the original. What is the scale of this drawing?

3. Draw a third compass rose whose length is twice that of the one you drew in Step 2. What is the scale of this drawing compared to the original compass rose? How can you tell?

4. Use the original compass rose to draw a fourth one, with a scale of 3 to 1. How did you decide how long and how wide to make your drawing?

5. Suppose that a drawing of the original compass rose has a length of 9 in. What scale do you think was used?

Learn Calculating with Scales

A **scale drawing** is often used to illustrate something that is too large or too small to show actual size. A map is one kind of scale drawing.

A drawing's scale is the ratio of a length in the drawing to the actual length it represents. When the units are the same, they can be omitted from the scale. For example, a scale of 1 in.:5 in. can be stated as 1:5 or $\frac{1}{5}$.

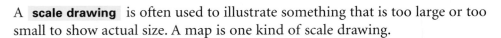

Example 1

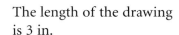

Jaime drew a picture of his car using a scale of 1 in.:4 ft. Measure his drawing and find the actual length of the car.

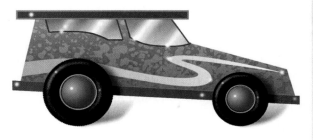

The length of the drawing is 3 in.

Since the scale means every inch on the drawing represents 4 ft, the length of the car is 3 times 4 ft, or 12 ft.

The actual length of the car is 12 ft.

Try It

Find the actual height of Jaime's car.

When you make a drawing or model that is smaller than the real thing, it is a *reduction*. A scale represents a reduction when the first number is *less* than the second number. When the first number in the scale is greater, the scale represents an *enlargement*.

Reduction   Original   Enlargement
Scale: 1:2   Scale: 2:1

Example 2

A bolt is 1.2 cm long. Find the length of an enlarged technical drawing of this bolt at a scale of 15:2.

The actual length is 1.2 cm. Let x be the length of the drawing.

$$\frac{\text{scale length}}{\text{actual length}} = \frac{x \text{ cm}}{1.2 \text{ cm}} = \frac{15}{2}$$

$2x = 1.2 \cdot 15$ Write the cross products.

$2x = 18$ Multiply.

$\dfrac{2x}{2} = \dfrac{18}{2}$ To undo multiplying by 2, divide by 2.

$x = 9$ Divide.

The new drawing has a length of 9 cm.

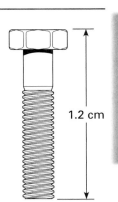

1.2 cm

WHAT DO YOU THINK?

Jacob and Jyotsna have found that Albuquerque and Santa Fe are 0.75 in. apart on a map with a scale of 1 in.:80 mi. What is the actual distance between Albuquerque and Santa Fe?

Jacob thinks ...

I'll let x represent the actual distance in miles. I can set up a proportion and use cross products to solve for x.

$$\frac{\text{map length}}{\text{actual length}} = \frac{0.75 \text{ in.}}{x \text{ mi}} = \frac{1 \text{ in.}}{80 \text{ mi}}$$

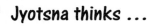

$x = 0.75 \cdot 80 = 60$. The distance is 60 mi.

Jyotsna thinks ...

I know 0.75 means the same thing as $\frac{3}{4}$. Since 1 inch represents 80 miles, $\frac{3}{4}$ of an inch must represent $\frac{3}{4}$ of 80 miles, or $\frac{3}{4} \cdot 80$.

$$\frac{3}{4} \cdot \frac{80}{1} = \frac{240}{4} = 60.$$ The distance is 60 miles.

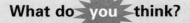

What do you think?

1. How did Jacob and Jyotsna know what units to use for their answers?

2. Can you use a different proportion to solve this problem? Explain.

Check | Your Understanding

1. How can a proportion be used to find the actual size of an object?

2. What happens to the size of a scale drawing when the scale is changed from 1 in.:4 ft to 1 in.:10 ft? Explain how you know.

3. What is the impact on a scale drawing when the scale is changed from $\frac{1 \text{ cm}}{20 \text{ m}}$ to $\frac{1 \text{ cm}}{5 \text{ m}}$? Explain.

Practice and Apply

1. **Getting Started** Follow these steps to calculate the actual length of a house if the model uses the scale 1 cm = 3 m.

   a. Measure the length of the scale model.

   b. Let x be the actual length in meters. Use your measurement and the scale of the model to set up the following proportion:

   $$\frac{\text{scale length (cm)}}{x \text{ m}} = \frac{1 \text{ cm}}{3 \text{ m}}$$

   c. Cross multiply. Write the actual length of the house.

Number Sense Measure the scale drawing and find the width of the bedroom for each scale.

2. 1 in. = 7 ft

3. 1 in. = $8\frac{1}{2}$ ft

4. 1 in. = $9\frac{3}{4}$ ft

5. 1 in. = 12.25 ft

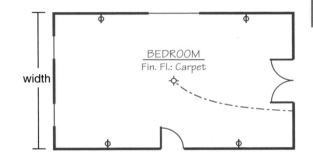

A model airplane is 6 cm long. Use each scale to find the length of the actual airplane.

6. Scale: 1 cm = 2 m

7. Scale: 1 cm = $3\frac{1}{3}$ m

8. Scale: 2 cm = 9 m

9. **Geography** Dallas is $7\frac{1}{2}$ in. from Houston on a map of Texas with a scale of $\frac{3 \text{ in.}}{100 \text{ mi}}$. What is the actual distance from Dallas to Houston?

10. When the leaders of Fort Wayne, Indiana, decided to build a huge playground called Kids Crossing, they asked students for ideas. Many students made scale drawings showing the equipment and rides they wanted. If a student made a drawing of a slide with a scale of 1 in. = 8 ft, how long would the slide actually be if it was drawn $2\frac{1}{2}$ in. long?

Solve for *x* in each proportion.

11. $\dfrac{5 \text{ in.}}{x} = \dfrac{3 \text{ in.}}{12 \text{ ft}}$

12. $\dfrac{7 \text{ cm}}{x} = \dfrac{10 \text{ cm}}{84 \text{ km}}$

13. $\dfrac{1.4 \text{ in.}}{25 \text{ mi}} = \dfrac{7 \text{ in.}}{x}$

14. $\dfrac{8 \text{ cm}}{300 \text{ km}} = \dfrac{3.2 \text{ cm}}{x}$

15. Geography Enrique has found that Lagos, Nigeria, is 12 cm from Casablanca, Morocco, on an African map with a scale of 3 cm:715 km. Find the actual distance from Lagos to Casablanca. Explain how you found your answer.

16. **Test Prep** A scale model of a truck uses the scale 1 in. = 8 ft. The model is 2.75 in. long. How long is the actual truck?

   Ⓐ 18 ft   Ⓑ 20 ft   Ⓒ 22 ft   Ⓓ 24 ft

Problem Solving and Reasoning

17. Critical Thinking Stan Herd is an artist who plants flowers and grains on large fields to create "crop art." This photo shows a work called *Saginaw Grant*.

Herd often makes a scale drawing before planting seeds and flowers. If a sketch measures 6.4 in. × 10.2 in. at a scale of 1 in. = 25 ft, what will be the dimensions of his "crop art"?

18. Critical Thinking Make a scale drawing of an object and write three different scales next to the drawing. Calculate the actual size of the object you drew based on each of the three scales.

19. Journal A *Tyrannosaurus rex* was about 40 ft long from head to tail. Suppose you wanted to make a toy *Tyrannosaurus* for a five-year-old. What scale would you use? Explain how you chose your scale. Tell why the toy shouldn't be too large or too small.

Mixed Review

Find the sum or difference. Write your answers in lowest terms. *[Lesson 4-2]*

20. $\frac{2}{21} + \frac{3}{7}$ **21.** $\frac{5}{6} - \frac{4}{5}$ **22.** $\frac{2}{3} - \frac{1}{9}$ **23.** $\frac{11}{12} + \frac{1}{15}$ **24.** $\frac{1}{3} + \frac{2}{3}$

Find the area of each figure. *[Lesson 5-10]*

25.

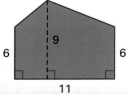

26.

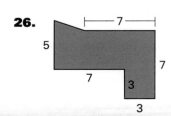

27.

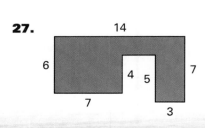

Problem Solving Using Maps

▶ **Lesson Link**   You have learned how scales relate map distances to actual distances. Maps can be used to solve many practical problems, including choosing the best route and determining arrival times. ◀

You'll Learn ...

■ to use scales to read maps and make decisions

... How It's Used

Schedulers for railroads and airlines need to be able to solve problems using maps to design efficient schedules.

Explore   Problem Solving Using Maps

Drive and Deliver!

Materials: Ruler

You are the delivery person for Furniture Paradise, location F on the map. You must make the following deliveries today, and you need to plan your route so you can deliver the furniture efficiently.

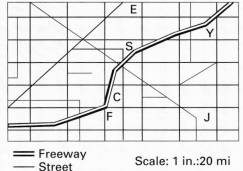

Freeway
Street

Scale: 1 in.:20 mi

Name	Location	To Be Delivered
Mr. Chavez	C	Dining table and chairs
Mrs. Smith	S	Couch
Mr. Yamamoto	Y	Entertainment center
Ms. Jones	J	Bookcases
Mr. Edwards	E	Desk, filing cabinet

1. What information can you get from the map that will help you plan your route?

2. What other information would you want before planning your route?

3. Using the map to help you, plan an efficient delivery route. Give a short written explanation of how you decided on this route.

4. Mr. Edwards calls and asks what time you expect to get to his office. If you plan to start your route at 9:00 A.M., what should you tell him? Explain your answer.

5. How can you estimate the time it will take to get somewhere? How can a map help you make such an estimate?

A map can be an important problem-solving tool. You can use the formula time $= \frac{\text{distance}}{\text{rate}}$ and your knowledge of scale to solve problems.

Example 1

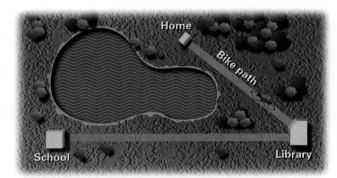

Dave leaves school at 3:15 P.M. and rides his bicycle to the library at 15 km/hr. The scale of the map is 1 cm:2 km. At about what time will he arrive?

The map distance to the library is 6.5 cm, so the real distance is 13 km. At 15 km/hr, the ride takes a little less than an hour. Dave will get to the library a little before 4:15 P.M.

Try It

Dave leaves the library at 4:55 P.M. and rides home at a rate of about 12 km/hr. At about what time do you expect him to get home?

Example 2

Antoinette is on a hike with her nature club. The hikers need to arrive at their campsite before 6:00 P.M. They can take a steep 11 km trail or a flatter 17 km trail. The hikers average 3 km/hr on the steep trail and 4 km/hr on the flatter one. Which trail is faster, and when should they leave?

The time needed to hike the flat trail is $\frac{\text{distance}}{\text{rate}} = \frac{17}{4} = 4\frac{1}{4}$ hr. (The time is in hours because the rate is in kilometers per *hour*.)

The steep trail is 11 km long, so the time to hike it is $\frac{\text{distance}}{\text{rate}} = \frac{11}{3} = 3\frac{2}{3}$ hr.

The steeper trail is faster. The hikers must leave $3\frac{2}{3}$ hr before 6:00. Since $\frac{2}{3}$ hr is 40 minutes, they must leave at 2:20 P.M.

Check | **Your Understanding**

1. How do maps make planning easier?

2. How can you estimate the scale for a map if it is not given?

Practice and Apply

1. **Getting Started** Follow these steps to find what time Shuichi will arrive home if he leaves the library at 3:30 P.M. and walks at 4 km/hr.

   a. On a map with a scale of 1 cm = 2 km, the library is 3 cm from Shuichi's home. Calculate the actual distance from the library to Shuichi's home.

   b. Use $\dfrac{\text{distance}}{\text{rate}}$ = time to calculate how long Shuichi's walk takes.

   c. Use the answer to **b** and the departure time of 3:30 P.M. to determine when Shuichi arrives home.

Ferdinand left home at 3:00 P.M. and traveled 150 mi. Find his arrival time for each of the following speeds.

2. 25 mi/hr   3. 30 mi/hr   4. 40 mi/hr   5. 55 mi/hr   6. 15 mi/hr

7. Lisa's family plans to go to a movie theater downtown at 8:00 P.M. They can drive 40 mi/hr on King Expressway.

   a. What is the expressway distance from their home to the theater?

   b. How long will it take them to get from home to the theater?

   c. When do they need to leave to get to the movie by 8:00 P.M.?

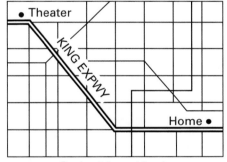

Scale: 1 in. = 12 mi

8. **Problem Solving** Carly is planning a trip from Appleton to Shore City. She can drive at an average speed of 50 mi/hr or take a train that averages 40 mi/hr. The driving distance between the cities is 180 mi. The train takes a more direct route, so the rail distance is 140 mi.

   a. Which method of travel is faster? Explain how you decided.

   b. If Carly chooses the faster method and leaves Appleton at 2:00 P.M., when will she arrive in Shore City?

9. **History** Pony Express riders delivered mail between St. Joseph, Missouri, and Sacramento, California, a distance of 1966 miles. A day's ride could cover 75 miles or more.

   a. If a rider began at 7:30 A.M. and rode at an average speed of 15 mi/hr for 75 mi, when would his ride end?

   b. If a rider began at 2:30 P.M. and rode 80 mi at 15 mi/hr, when would his ride end?

10. **Test Prep** Maria-Teresa left the library at 5:30 P.M. and began biking at the rate of 20 km/hr. By what time had she biked 35 kilometers?

Ⓐ 6:04 P.M.   Ⓑ 6:05 P.M.   Ⓒ 6:25 P.M.   Ⓓ 7:15 P.M.

Problem Solving and Reasoning

11. Critical Thinking Sela is a truck driver traveling from Dallas, Texas, to Buffalo, New York. The road distance on her map is $5\frac{1}{2}$ in. and the map's scale is 1 in.:250 mi. Her truck gets 11 mi/gal.

a. What is the actual distance Sela will drive?

b. How much gasoline will Sela use on her trip?

c. What will fuel cost for the trip if the price is $1.30 per gallon?

12. Choose a Strategy Students at Northampton East High School in North Carolina designed an electric car. At top speed, the car can travel for 6 hr. Then its batteries must be recharged for 6 hr. If this car travels 1440 miles, when would the car arrive if it left on Tuesday at noon? (Assume the driver travels at a speed of 65 mi/hr.)

Problem Solving
STRATEGIES
• Look for a Pattern
• Make an Organized List
• Make a Table
• Guess and Check
• Work Backward
• Use Logical Reasoning
• Draw a Diagram
• Solve a Simpler Problem

13. Communicate Using an atlas, plan a "fantasy trip" from your home to a place in the United States you would like to visit. Calculate how long the trip would take at an average speed of 30 mi/hr. Finally, write a trip *itinerary* (plan), telling what time you would leave and when you would reach your destination.

Mixed Review

Find each sum or difference. *[Lesson 4-3]*

14. $6\frac{2}{3} + 2\frac{1}{2}$ **15.** $8\frac{3}{5} - 5\frac{4}{5}$ **16.** $1\frac{1}{4} + 2\frac{4}{7}$ **17.** $3\frac{5}{8} - 2\frac{3}{7}$ **18.** $12\frac{4}{11} + \frac{1}{3}$

19. $5\frac{4}{9} + 10\frac{6}{7}$ **20.** $3\frac{1}{9} - 1\frac{7}{8}$ **21.** $13\frac{3}{7} + 4\frac{2}{3}$ **22.** $10\frac{11}{12} - 3\frac{1}{3}$

Write each ratio in three ways. *[Lesson 6-1]*

23. 3 pounds for 1 dollar

24. 11 people for 2 tables

Creating Scale Drawings and Scale Models

7-4

▶ **Lesson Link**   You've used scales to interpret maps and other scale drawings. Now you'll choose appropriate scales for scale drawings and scale models. ◀

You'll Learn …

■ to select a reasonable scale for a drawing, map, or model

… How It's Used

Craftspeople who construct models of ships, automobiles, or other objects need to determine a scale to create an authentic reproduction of the desired size.

Explore   Creating Scale Drawings

In Search of a Flat Earth

Materials: Earth globe, Ruler, Tape measure

Mapmakers have used many different methods to project the globe of the earth onto a flat surface. One of these methods is the Mercator projection, used to make the map shown at right.

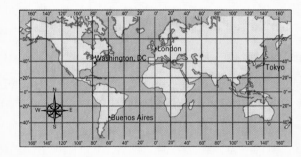

1. Do you think the Mercator map is distorted? How can you tell?

2. Washington, DC, is 5218 mi away from Buenos Aires, Argentina. Use this fact to calculate the scales of the map and the globe.

3. The distance from London, England, to Tokyo, Japan, is 5940 mi. Calculate the scales again, using London and Tokyo.

4. How are your results related to your answer to Step 1? Did any of your results surprise you? Explain.

Learn   Creating Scale Drawings and Scale Models

Fitting the round Earth onto a flat map has challenged people for centuries. In fact, it is impossible to do this without some distortion.

Fortunately, when mapping small regions or making scale drawings or models, distortion is not a significant problem, and the fit problem is solved simply by choosing a good scale. The scale must be small enough to fit the available space. It should be large enough to show important details.

Example 1

Gerald is making a scale drawing of a locomotive on an $8\frac{1}{2}$ in. × 11 in. sheet of paper turned sideways. The actual locomotive is 12 ft tall and 22 ft long. What scale should he use if he wants the drawing to be as large as possible?

The length of the drawing must be 11 in. or less. If Gerald makes the drawing 11 in. long, the scale is

$$\frac{\text{scale length}}{\text{actual length}} = \frac{11 \text{ in.}}{22 \text{ ft}} = \frac{1 \text{ in.}}{2 \text{ ft}}$$

Check that the other dimension also fits the paper. At 1 in.:2 ft, the drawing's height will be 6 in., which easily fits the paper's $8\frac{1}{2}$ in. height.

Gerald can use a scale of 1 in.:2 ft.

Try It

Marbella wants to sketch a dog that is 33 in. tall and 44 in. long on a 3 in. by 5 in. index card. What scale should she use if she wants to make the largest possible sketch?

Example 2

Heidi is designing a 60 cm × 100 cm poster showing a rectangular 7.5 cm × 16.5 cm calculator. What is the largest scale she can use?

Both dimensions of the calculator must fit. Find the largest scale possible for each dimension and choose the *lesser of the two.*

$$\text{Largest scale for width to fit} = \frac{\text{poster width}}{\text{actual width}} = \frac{60 \text{ cm}}{7.5 \text{ cm}} = 8{:}1$$

$$\text{Largest scale for height to fit} = \frac{\text{poster height}}{\text{actual height}} = \frac{100 \text{ cm}}{16.5 \text{ cm}} \approx 6{:}1$$

The largest possible scale is 6:1.

Check | Your Understanding

1. When you make a scale drawing, what factors help you decide on a good scale to use?

2. Why are scale drawings useful?

3. In Example 2, why was 6:1 chosen for the largest possible scale instead of 8:1?

Practice and Apply

1. **Getting Started** Follow these steps to find the largest scale that can be used to enlarge the picture at right to make a 21 in. × 36 in. poster.

   a. Measure the height of the picture in inches.

   b. Use the formula scale $= \dfrac{\text{scale length}}{\text{actual length}}$ to find the scale that gives you a height of 36 in.

   c. Measure the width of the picture. Find the scale that gives you a width of 21 in.

   d. Choose the smaller of your scale calculations in **b** and **c**.

A giraffe can be as much as 18 ft tall. Find the maximum scale you can use for a model giraffe if it must fit in a:

2. Room with a 9 ft ceiling   3. 6 ft tall crate

4. 2 ft tall toy box   5. 5 in. tall zoo diorama

6. Determine an appropriate scale to make a scale drawing of this figure that fills an $8\frac{1}{2}$ in. × 11 in. sheet of paper. Then make the scale drawing.

7. **Fine Arts** When developed, most film used by photographers makes negatives that measure about 24 mm high and 35 mm wide. These negatives are used to make prints that measure about 102 mm × 153 mm. What is the approximate scale of the prints?

8. **Geography** Oregon is approximately 400 miles from east to west and 300 miles from north to south. What is the largest scale that can be used to fit a map of Oregon on a sheet of $8\frac{1}{2}$ in. × 11 in. paper, if:

   a. The 11 in. side runs north-south

   b. The $8\frac{1}{2}$ in. side runs north-south

9. **Estimation** Estimate the scale of the Oregon map.

10. **Test Prep** Which of these scales is the largest that could be used to make a scale drawing of a 26 in. × 35 in. photo on a 3 in. × 5 in. card?

    Ⓐ 1:6   Ⓑ 1:8

    Ⓒ 1:9   Ⓓ 1:12

Problem Solving and Reasoning

11. Critical Thinking The Oscar Mayer Wienermobile has been a traveling advertisement for the past 60 years. The 27 ft long Wienermobile looks like a large hot dog sitting on a bun. A hot dog measures about 5 in. in length. What is the scale of the Wienermobile compared to a real hot dog?

12. Communicate A map has a scale that is given as 1:982,000. Explain how would you find how many miles are represented by 1 foot on this map.

13. Critical Thinking In a scale model of the solar system, a penny (0.019 m in diameter) is used to represent the sun, which is 139,200 km in diameter.

   a. Determine the scale being used for this model.

   b. On average, Earth is 149,600,000 km from the sun. How far from the penny should Earth be in the model?

   c. On average, Pluto is 5,950,000,000 km from the sun. How far from the penny should Pluto be in the model?

   d. The moon is about 400,000 km from Earth. How far away from Earth should it be in the model?

Mixed Review

Solve each equation. Check your answer. *[Lesson 2-7]*

14. $m \cdot 6 = 72$ **15.** $\frac{q}{5} = 12$ **16.** $6s = 42$ **17.** $15 = 3 \cdot n$ **18.** $11p = 121$

19. $t \cdot 2 = 42$ **20.** $5x = 5$ **21.** $47r = 94$ **22.** $3 = \frac{u}{7}$ **23.** $8 = \frac{w}{5}$

Express each rate as a unit rate. *[Lesson 6-2]*

24. 40 pages read in 2 days   **25.** 15 sections in 5 days   **26.** 132 desks in 4 classrooms

27. 334 miles for 10 gallons   **28.** 20 meters in 4 seconds   **29.** 48 cans in 2 cases

---

Project Progress

Decide which rooms you want in your dream house. Then decide how big you want each room to be. (Measuring rooms in your own home can help you do this.) Determine an appropriate scale for your project.

Problem Solving

Understand
Plan
Solve
Look Back

Section 7A Connect

At the beginning of Section 7A, you saw that Lewis and Clark were able to create a map of an unfamiliar territory. Now you will create a map of a very familiar territory—your classroom. You can use what you've learned about maps and scales to make a very accurate map.

Never Mind—I'll Draw It Myself!

Materials: Tape measure, Ruler

Your younger sister wants to know what your math classroom is like. When she becomes confused by your explanations, you decide to make a scale drawing so you can *show* her how it's arranged.

1. Without taking any measurements, make a rough sketch of your classroom. Show details such as doors, windows, chalkboards, and your teacher's desk.

2. What other information will you need to make an accurate scale drawing?

3. How can you be sure the drawing will fit on a single sheet of paper? Make some measurements and decide what scale to use.

4. Make any other measurements you need, then make a final drawing. Be as accurate as you can.

5. Are you pleased with your drawing? If not, tell what you would do differently the next time.

6. If you needed to make a scale drawing of your school, how would you obtain the measurements you needed? How would you decide on a scale?

REVIEW 7A

Number Sense Give two other ways to write each scale.

1. 4 in.:200 mi

2. 17 in. = 510 mi

3. $\dfrac{10 \text{ cm}}{4 \text{ km}}$

4. Measure the miniature reproduction of a painting. Find its actual dimensions given the following scales.

   a. 1 in. = 8.5 in.   **b.** 1 in. = 14.25 in.   **c.** 1 in. = $3\frac{1}{2}$ ft

Use the following measurements to find the scale of each map.

5. A 400 km state border is 2 cm long.

6. A 260 mi bike trail is 3 in. long.

7. History The Pyramid of the Sun, in Mexico, is about 200 ft tall. If a model of the pyramid uses a scale of 1.5 in.:5 ft, how tall is the model?

8. Literature In Jonathan Swift's *Gulliver's Travels*, Gulliver travels to Brobdingnag, the land of the giants. Gulliver says that a Brobdingnagian "took about ten yards at every stride." Assume that Gulliver's stride is about 2 ft long. Estimate the scale if:

   a. Gulliver is viewed as a reduced scale model of the giant

   b. The giant is viewed as an enlarged scale model of Gulliver

9. **Journal** In an atlas, a map of Korea is $13\frac{1}{2}$ in. × 24 in. Sheila needs to fit a copy of this map onto a 9 in. × 11 in. report cover. What is the largest scale she can use? Explain how you found your answer.

Piet Mondrian, *Large composition*, 1919

Test Prep

On a multiple choice test, check that your answers make sense. Even if you cannot solve a problem, you may be able to use common sense to eliminate answers.

10. Berlin, Germany, is 811 km from Stockholm, Sweden. About how far apart will these cities appear on a map with the scale 3 cm = 200 km?

   Ⓐ 12 cm   Ⓑ 27 cm   Ⓒ 270 cm   Ⓓ 12 km

Water, Water, Everywhere

Oceans cover most of the earth's surface. So why should you conserve water? First of all, ocean water is too salty to drink; we can only drink water from lakes, wells, or reservoirs. And even in a rainy climate, wasting water hurts the environment. It takes energy and chemicals to treat waste water, pump clean water to your home, and heat water for your showers.

The book 50 Simple Things You Can Do to Save the Earth, *by The EarthWorks Group, contains many water conservation tips. According to this book (which is printed on recycled paper), your family can save up to 20,000 gallons of water per year by doing simple things such as not running the faucet while you brush your teeth or wash the dishes.*

When you work with a number of gallons per year or pounds of paper per tree, you are using rates. You'll explore many different rates that have to do with conservation and the environment.

1 How much water do you use in an 8-minute shower if the water runs at a rate of 5 gallons per minute?

2 If your family saves 20,000 gallons of water per year, will they save more or less than 20,000 gallons per day? Explain how you know.

Choosing Appropriate Rates and Units

You'll Learn ...

■ to select an appropriate rate for a particular situation

■ to write reciprocal rates that have the same meaning

... How It's Used

Chefs may need to convert recipes given in small units (such as cups and ounces) to larger ones (such as quarts and pounds) when they cook for a large number of people.

▶ **Lesson Link** You know what rates are and how to use rates to solve problems. Now you will choose appropriate rates for different situations. ◀

Explore | **Using Rates**

Shake Across America!

Materials: Tape measure, Stopwatch

An environmental group is organizing a "Handshake Across America." They plan to have people line up from New York to Los Angeles and pass a handshake from east to west.

1. Have several members of your class form a line. Count how many students are in the line and measure its length.

2. Start a handshake at one end of the line. Use a stopwatch to find out how long the handshake takes to reach the end of the line.

3. Use your results from Step 1 to estimate the number of students per foot. Explain why this number is a rate.

4. The road distance from Los Angeles to New York is 2825 miles, or almost 15,000,000 ft. About how many people need to be in the line?

5. Use your results from Step 2 to estimate the speed of the handshake. How did you choose your units for this rate?

6. Estimate when the handshake would have to start so it ends on midnight in Los Angeles. Explain how you found your answer. What rates did you use to help solve this problem?

Learn | **Choosing Appropriate Rates and Units**

It's important to choose appropriate units when you use a rate. If the speedometer in your family's car read 40,000 inches per minute, it would be hard to tell whether you're speeding or blocking traffic. But if it reads 30 miles per hour, you have a better idea of how fast you're traveling.

Example 1

What are appropriate units for measuring a snail's speed?

Rates that describe speeds, such as miles per hour, have a distance unit per time unit. Snails are slow, so it is best to use a shorter unit of distance.

Appropriate units for a snail's speed might be feet per hour or inches per minute.

Try It

What are appropriate units for measuring:

a. The speed of a jet airplane?

b. The rate at which you do homework?

▶ **Science Link**

Snails are mollusks. The "horns" on a snail's head are actually its eyes. They can be extended to look around and can be retracted when the snail retreats into its shell.

Rates can be expressed in different ways that have the same meaning. The most useful way to express a rate depends on the problem you are solving.

Example 2

At a recycling center, you are paid 2.5 cents per can. Does this rate mean the same thing as 40 cans per dollar? Give a situation where each rate is useful.

If you recycle 40 cans at 2.5 cents each, you are paid $40 \times 2.5 = 100$ cents, or one dollar. The rates have the same meaning.

If you want to know *how much money* you will get for 120 cans, it's easier to use the 2.5 cents per can rate:

$120 \times 2.5 = 300$ cents ($3.00)

If you want to know *how many cans* you need to earn $10, you'd use 40 cans per dollar:

$10 \times 40 = 400$ cans

▶ **History Link**

Aluminum was once one of the most expensive metals on earth. In the 1820s, a pound of aluminum sold for more than $500!

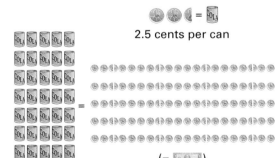

2.5 cents per can

40 cans per dollar

Try It

Ollie the collie eats 3 cups of dog food per day. Does this rate have the same meaning as Ollie eating at a rate of $\frac{1}{3}$ of a day per cup?

The rates in Example 2, $\frac{2.5 \text{ cents}}{1 \text{ can}}$ and $\frac{40 \text{ cans}}{1 \text{ dollar}}$, have the same meaning, but they are not equal. Although they may not look like it, they are *reciprocals*!

$$\frac{2.5 \text{ cents}}{1 \text{ can}} \quad \xrightarrow{\text{reciprocal}} \quad \frac{1 \text{ can}}{2.5 \text{ cents}}$$ Exchange numerator and denominator.

$$= \frac{1 \text{ can} \times 40}{2.5 \text{ cents} \times 40} = \frac{40 \text{ cans}}{100 \text{ cents}} = \frac{40 \text{ cans}}{1 \text{ dollar}}$$ Write an equivalent unit rate.

Example 3

A low-flow faucet aerator can save 2 gallons of water per minute. Give a reciprocal rate that has the same meaning. Then give a reciprocal *unit* rate.

Find a reciprocal rate by exchanging the numerator and the denominator. $\frac{2 \text{ gal}}{1 \text{ min}}$ means the same thing as $\frac{1 \text{ min}}{2 \text{ gal}}$.

To convert $\frac{1 \text{ min}}{2 \text{ gal}}$ to a unit rate, divide the numerator and denominator by 2.

$$\frac{1 \text{ min}}{2 \text{ gal}} = \frac{1 \text{ min} \div 2}{2 \text{ gal} \div 2} = \frac{\frac{1}{2} \text{ min}}{1 \text{ gal}} = \frac{0.5 \text{ min}}{\text{gal}}$$

The reciprocal unit rate is $\frac{1}{2}$ minute per gallon or 0.5 minutes per gallon.

Try It

Jorge recycles 25 pounds of newspapers, cans, and bottles per week. Give a reciprocal rate that has the same meaning. Then give the reciprocal *unit* rate.

Check | Your Understanding

1. How are the rates 6 pounds per day and 6 days per pound different? When would each be useful?

2. Describe a situation where you would want to know the number of hours per mile instead of miles per hour.

3. Name some rates that would help you plan improvements to a recycling program.

Practice and Apply

1. **Getting Started** Find the reciprocal unit rate for 20 miles per gallon.

  a. Write 20 miles per gallon as a fraction.

  b. Find a reciprocal rate by exchanging the numerator and the denominator.

  c. The rate you found in **b** is a reciprocal, but it is not a unit rate. To convert it to a unit rate, divide its numerator and denominator by the number in the denominator.

Number Sense Suggest appropriate units for each rate. You may use the same units more than once.

2. The speed of a bicycle rider

3. The rate at which a car uses gasoline

4. The rate at which your heart beats

5. The rate of pay for a baby-sitter

6. The rate at which a family recycles aluminum cans

Give a unit rate that describes each situation.

7. 75 quarts of soup for 150 students

8. 4 pounds of bananas for $1.00

9. 100 meters in 10 seconds

10. 400 raisins in 20 cookies

Do the rates in each pair have the same meaning? Write *Yes* or *No*.

11. $\dfrac{2 \text{ ft}}{\text{sec}}, \dfrac{0.5 \text{ sec}}{\text{ft}}$

12. $\dfrac{25 \text{ mi}}{\text{gal}}, \dfrac{25 \text{ gal}}{\text{mi}}$

13. $\dfrac{25 ¢}{\text{lb}}, \dfrac{4 \text{ lb}}{\text{dollar}}$

14. $\dfrac{7 \text{ days}}{\text{week}}, \dfrac{\frac{1}{7} \text{ week}}{\text{day}}$

For each rate, give a reciprocal unit rate that has the same meaning.

15. $\dfrac{5 \text{ lb}}{\$1}$

16. $\dfrac{15 \text{ mi}}{\text{hr}}$

17. $\dfrac{2 \text{ weeks}}{\text{ton}}$

18. $\dfrac{25 \text{ gal}}{\text{day}}$

19. **Science** According to *50 Simple Things Kids Can Do to Save the Earth*, about 20 *species* (types) of plants and animals become extinct every week. (Not all scientists agree with this estimate.) Does this rate have the same meaning as $\dfrac{0.2 \text{ days}}{\text{species}}$?

African Elephant Population 1979–1992

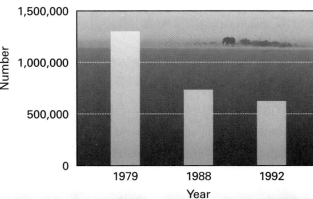

The African elephant is a threatened species

20. **Test Prep** Which of the following units are most appropriate for the rate of newspaper recycling in Illinois?

Ⓐ Miles per hour   Ⓑ Tons per week

Ⓒ Ounces per month   Ⓓ Years per pound

Problem Solving and Reasoning

21. **Journal** Suppose you want to examine your family's energy and water use. You plan to find out how efficiently your family uses these resources, and what changes you might make to increase efficiency. Name rates that will be helpful in carrying out your plan.

22. **Choose a Strategy** One of the earliest auto races was the *Chicago Times-Herald* race of 1895, covering 55 miles from Chicago, Illinois, to Evanston, Illinois. The winner, J. Frank Duryea, averaged $7\frac{1}{2}$ miles per hour. Write a reciprocal unit rate for that average speed that has the same meaning.

23. **Communicate** Two buses leave your school to take students on field trips. One bus travels for 20 minutes, covering 15 miles. The other travels 45 miles in one hour. Did both buses travel at the same rate? Explain your answer.

> **Problem Solving**
> ## STRATEGIES
> - Look for a Pattern
> - Make an Organized List
> - Make a Table
> - Guess and Check
> - Work Backward
> - Use Logical Reasoning
> - Draw a Diagram
> - Solve a Simpler Problem

Mixed Review

Solve each equation. Check your answer. *[Lesson 2-7]*

24. $m \cdot 8 = 56$ **25.** $\frac{q}{3} = 25$ **26.** $9s = 144$ **27.** $18 = 6 \cdot n$ **28.** $7p = 84$

Express each rate as a unit rate. *[Lesson 6-2]*

29. 15 millimeters in 5 seconds   **30.** 160 pages read in 8 days

31. 231 desks in 7 classrooms   **32.** $27.99 for 3 T-shirts

33. 2,000 mL in 2 L   **34.** 60 decades in 6 centuries

Project Progress

Using the measurements and decisions you made earlier, set up and solve proportions to determine the scaled-down sizes of the rooms and features to be included in a scale model of your dream house. Make a drawing of your model.

> **Problem Solving**
>
> Understand
> Plan
> Solve
> Look Back

Converting Units

▶ **Lesson Link**   You've chosen appropriate units for rates. Now you'll convert measurements from one unit to another. ◀

Explore Converting Units

How Old Are You?

Are you closer to one million seconds old or one billion seconds old?

1. What is your age in years? In days? In hours?

2. Find your age in seconds.

3. How many years equal one million seconds? One billion seconds?

4. Is your age closer to a million seconds or a billion seconds? Explain.

You'll Learn ...

■ to convert measurements from one unit to another

... How It's Used

Travelers going from one country to another need to convert their money into the local currency. Knowing the conversion rate helps them manage their money.

Vocabulary

conversion factor

Learn Converting Units

You know that 2 days = 48 hours because there are 24 hours in a day.

$$2 \text{ days} \times \frac{24 \text{ hr}}{1 \text{ day}} = 48 \text{ hours} \qquad 48 \text{ hr} \times \frac{1 \text{ day}}{24 \text{ hr}} = 2 \text{ days}$$

The fractions shown above, $\frac{24 \text{ hr}}{1 \text{ day}}$ and $\frac{1 \text{ day}}{24 \text{ hr}}$, are called **conversion factors** because they can be used to convert measurements from one unit to another.

A conversion factor equals 1 because its numerator equals its denominator (1 day is the same thing as 24 hours). So multiplying a quantity by a conversion factor changes only its units, not its value.

To convert days to hours:

$$2 \text{ days} \times \frac{24 \text{ hr}}{1 \text{ day}} = 48 \text{ hours}$$

To convert hours to days:

$$48 \text{ hr} \times \frac{1 \text{ day}}{24 \text{ hr}} = 2 \text{ days}$$

When choosing a conversion factor, be sure the unit you want to convert is in the *denominator* of the conversion factor.

Examples

1 The reticulated python is the world's longest snake. Many of these pythons are more than 20 feet long. Convert 20 feet to inches.

There are 12 inches in 1 foot, so there are two possible conversion factors:

$$\frac{12 \text{ in.}}{1 \text{ ft}} \qquad \frac{1 \text{ ft}}{12 \text{ in.}}$$

Choose the factor that has the unit you want to convert in the denominator. You want to convert *feet*, so choose the first factor.

$$\frac{20 \textbf{ ft} \times 12 \text{ in.}}{1 \textbf{ ft}} = (20 \times 12) \text{ inches} = 240 \text{ inches}$$

20 feet is equal to 240 inches.

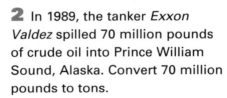

2 In 1989, the tanker *Exxon Valdez* spilled 70 million pounds of crude oil into Prince William Sound, Alaska. Convert 70 million pounds to tons.

There are 2000 pounds in 1 ton. You want to convert *pounds,* so use the conversion factor $\frac{1 \text{ ton}}{2000 \text{ lb}}$.

$$70{,}000{,}000 \textbf{ lb} \times \frac{1 \text{ ton}}{2{,}000 \textbf{ lb}} = \frac{70{,}000{,}000}{2{,}000} \text{ tons} = 35{,}000 \text{ tons}$$

The tanker spilled 35,000 tons of oil.

Try It

a. The Student Senate met for 180 minutes. Convert this time to hours.

b. In baseball, the distance between bases is 90 feet. Convert this distance to yards.

Check Your Understanding

1. How do you decide whether to use the conversion factor $\frac{16 \text{ oz}}{1 \text{ lb}}$ or $\frac{1 \text{ lb}}{16 \text{ oz}}$?

2. When you choose a conversion factor, why should the unit you want to convert from be in the denominator of the conversion factor?

Problem Solving TIP

Check to make sure your answer makes sense.

Remember

Converting to different units may give you a rate with a very large number. You may want to use scientific notation when you write this number.

[Page 126]

Practice and Apply

1. |**Getting Started**| Convert 3,000 meters to kilometers.

a. There are 1,000 meters in a kilometer. Write two fractions involving meters and kilometers that can be used as conversion factors.

b. Choose the conversion factor that has the unit you want to convert from in the denominator.

c. To convert 3,000 meters to kilometers, multiply 3,000 meters by the conversion factor you chose in **b**.

Number Sense Write two conversion factors involving each pair of units. (Use the information on page 346 if you do not remember how some of these units compare.)

2. Inches, feet

3. Days, years

4. Centimeters, meters

5. Pounds, ounces

6. Gallons, quarts

7. Grams, kilograms

Operation Sense Convert each quantity to the given units. (Use the information on page 346 if you do not remember how some of these units compare.)

8. 2 weeks to days

9. 20 feet to inches

10. 275 centimeters to meters

11. 672 ounces to pounds

12. 12 minutes to hours

13. 8 quarts to gallons

14. 500 meters to kilometers

15. 150 inches to feet

16. 7 pounds to ounces

17. 10 gallons to quarts

18. History The *cubit* was the basic unit of length used to build the pyramids of ancient Egypt. One cubit was the distance from the tip of the middle finger to the elbow. Use your arm and hand to measure the length of one cubit in inches. Write two conversion factors for your measurements.

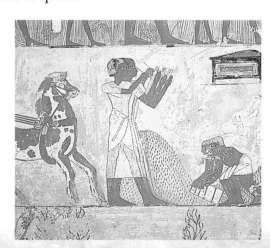

19. Literature *Twenty Thousand Leagues Under the Sea* is a famous novel by Jules Verne. A league is about 3.45 miles. Convert 20,000 leagues to feet.

The information in Exercises 20 and 21 comes from *50 Simple Things You Can Do to Save the Earth.*

20. Conservation The average office worker in the United States throws away 180 pounds of recyclable paper every year. How many ounces is this?

21. **Test Prep** The energy saved from recycling one glass bottle would light a 100-watt bulb for 4 hours. How many minutes is this?

    Ⓐ $\frac{1}{15}$ minute   Ⓑ $1\frac{2}{3}$ minutes   Ⓒ 240 minutes   Ⓓ 6,000 minutes

Problem Solving and Reasoning

22. Number Sense There are 12 inches in a foot and 3 feet in a yard.

    a. What relationship involving inches and yards could you use to convert inches to yards in one step?

    b. Use a conversion factor to make each conversion in one step: 60 inches to yards; 15 yards to inches.

    c. There are 220 yards in a furlong. What conversion factor could you use to convert furlongs to feet?

    d. In the Kentucky Derby, horses race a distance of 10 furlongs. Convert this distance to feet.

23. **Journal** Mark said that since a week is longer than a day, the number of weeks until vacation must be more than the number of days. Do you agree? Explain.

24. Critical Thinking There are 2 pints in a quart. How many pints are there in a gallon?

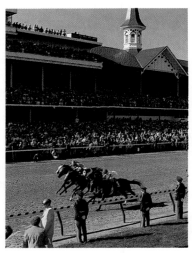

The Kentucky Derby

Mixed Review

Write each number in scientific notation. *[Lesson 3-5]*

25. 40,045.2   **26.** 538,334,892   **27.** 43.567   **28.** 3,876,576.33

29. 577   **30.** 800   **31.** 403.770   **32.** 300.8903

Complete the tables. *[Lesson 6-4]*

33. Using multiplication, complete the table to find 5 ratios equivalent to $\frac{4}{5}$.

4	8	12	16	20	24
5					

34. Using division, complete the table to find 5 ratios equivalent to $\frac{60}{90}$.

60	30	12	6	4	2
90					

Problem Solving: Converting Rates

▶ **Lesson Link** You've seen how to use a conversion factor to convert from one unit to another. Now you will use conversion factors to convert from one rate to another. ◀

You'll Learn …

■ to solve problems involving conversion of rates

… How It's Used

Physicists use rate conversions to express speeds, forces, and masses in different units.

Explore | Converting Rates

Drastic Plastic

According to *50 Simple Things You Can Do to Save the Earth,* an average person in the United States uses about 190 pounds of plastic every year.

U.S. Plastic Recycling, 1993 (Millions of tons)
Recovered–0.7
Unrecovered–18.6

1. Give two reciprocal conversion factors that involve pounds and ounces.

2. Use the appropriate conversion factor to find the number of ounces of plastic used by each person in a year.

3. In the last lesson, you saw how to convert feet to inches and pounds to tons. How are those conversions different from the conversion in Step 2? Why are conversions such as the one in Step 2 useful?

4. How could you convert your answer in Step 2 to give the number of ounces of plastic the average person in the United States uses each day? What is this number?

5. Based on the information in the circle graph, about how much of this plastic is recycled? (Hint: Use the graph and your answer to Step 4 to set up a proportion.)

Learn | Problem Solving: Converting Rates

Every rate contains two units.   50 miles per hour   18 **holidays** per **year**

You can use conversion factors to convert from one rate to another. If you need to change a unit in the *numerator* of the rate, choose a conversion factor with that unit in the *denominator,* and vice-versa.

$$\frac{miles}{hour} \cdot \frac{feet}{mile} = \frac{feet}{hour}$$

$$\frac{miles}{hour} \cdot \frac{hours}{day} = \frac{miles}{day}$$

Example 1

It takes more than 5,000,000 trees to print one week's worth of newspapers for the United States. How many trees per day is this?

There are 7 days in a week. To convert

$$\frac{\text{trees}}{\text{week}} \text{ to } \frac{\text{trees}}{\text{day}}$$

use the conversion factor that has weeks in the numerator.

$$\frac{5,000,000 \text{ trees}}{1 \text{ week}} \cdot \frac{1 \text{ week}}{7 \text{ days}} = \frac{5,000,000 \text{ trees}}{7 \text{ days}} \approx 714,286 \text{ trees per day}$$

Printing the newspapers uses about 714,286 trees per day.

Try It

a. Convert 714,286 trees per day to trees per hour.

b. Convert 12 meters per second to millimeters per second.

c. Convert 12,000 millimeters per second to millimeters per minute.

If you need to change *both* units in a rate, you can make the change one step at a time.

Example 2

A standard showerhead uses about 6 gallons of water per minute. How many ounces per second is this? (A gallon contains 128 fluid ounces.)

First, convert from gallons per minute to gallons per second.

$$\frac{6 \text{ gal}}{1 \text{ min}} \cdot \frac{1 \text{ min}}{60 \text{ sec}} = \frac{6 \text{ gal}}{60 \text{ sec}}$$

Then convert from gallons per second to ounces per second.

$$\frac{6 \text{ gal}}{60 \text{ sec}} \cdot \frac{128 \text{ oz}}{1 \text{ gal}} = \frac{768 \text{ oz}}{60 \text{ sec}} = 12.8 \text{ ounces per second}$$

A standard showerhead uses 12.8 fluid ounces of water per second.

Try It

a. Convert 65 kilometers per hour to meters per minute.

b. Convert $2.40 per pound to cents per ounce.

Check | Your Understanding

1. Why do you get an equivalent rate when you multiply a rate by a conversion factor?

2. Explain how you would convert miles per hour to feet per second. Would the new number be larger or smaller?

7-7 Exercises and Applications

Practice and Apply

1. **Getting Started** Follow the steps below to convert 16 gallons per day to quarts per day.
   a. Use 1 gal = 4 quarts to give two conversion factors of the form $\frac{? \text{ gal}}{? \text{ qt}}$ and $\frac{? \text{ qt}}{? \text{ gal}}$.
   b. Since $\frac{16 \text{ gal}}{1 \text{ day}}$ has gallons in the numerator, choose the conversion factor from **a** that has gallons in the denominator.
   c. Multiply $\frac{16 \text{ gal}}{1 \text{ day}}$ by the correct conversion factor. The result is the rate in quarts per day.

Operation Sense Convert each rate to an equivalent rate.

2. 40 kilometers per hour to kilometers per minute

3. 128 inches per second to feet per second

4. 0.45 kilograms per pound to grams per pound

5. 36 fluid ounces per day to cups per day

6. 28 feet per second to miles per hour

The information in Exercises 7–10 comes from *50 Simple Things You Can Do to Save the Earth*.

7. Every year 50 million flea collars are thrown away. How many flea collars are thrown away per day?

8. The average person in the United States uses about 640 pounds of paper each year. How much is this in ounces per year?

9. Homeowners in the United States use more than 25 million pounds of pesticides on their lawns every year. Convert this rate to ounces per hour.

10. People in the United States throw away 2.5 million plastic bottles per hour. How many bottles per year do we throw away?

11. **Test Prep** The United States is the leading garbage-producing nation on earth, with an average of 864 kg of waste produced by each person per year. On average, how much waste is produced by each person in the United States in a month?

Ⓐ 72 kg   Ⓑ 8,640 kg   Ⓒ 10,380 kg   Ⓓ 315,360 kg

Science Some of the world's fastest animals are endangered species. Use conversion factors to complete the table.

	Name of Animal	Maximum Speed (mi/hr)	Maximum Speed (ft/sec)
12.	Cheetah	70	
13.	Peregrine falcon		318
14.	Mountain zebra	40	

Problem Solving and Reasoning

15. **Journal** An ad for Spudz Potato Chips claims, "In 1995, Spudz lovers bought 329,000,000 pounds of Spudz Potato Chips. That's over 901,000 pounds a day, 625 pounds a minute, and 10 pounds a second!" Assuming the number 329,000,000 is correct, check the truth of this claim. Are the numbers exact or estimates?

16. Critical Thinking Do you use more water for a shower or for a bath? Suppose you always use 250 L of water for a bath and your shower uses 15 L of water per minute.

a. How many minutes would a 150 L shower take?

b. What is the greatest whole number of minutes you can shower and still use less water than you would use taking a bath?

Mixed Review

Use >, < , or = to compare each pair of numbers. *[Lesson 3-9]*

17. $\frac{13}{52}$ ☐ $\frac{5}{16}$ **18.** $\frac{8}{9}$ ☐ $\frac{43}{50}$ **19.** $\frac{23}{92}$ ☐ $\frac{1}{4}$ **20.** $\frac{32}{512}$ ☐ $\frac{2}{17}$

For each ratio, make a table and create three equal ratios. Then use your ratios to write three proportions. *[Lesson 6-5]*

21. $\frac{5}{3}$ **22.** $\frac{1}{2}$ **23.** $\frac{11}{44}$ **24.** $\frac{4}{7}$ **25.** $\frac{27}{36}$

Section 7B Connect

You've investigated different rates and units. Now you will use what you have learned about rates to see if a claim about the amount of water a family can save is true.

Water, Water Everywhere

According to *50 Simple Things You Can Do to Save the Earth*, a family can save 20,000 gallons of water per year by taking a few simple conservation measures. Here are four suggestions the book makes:

- Just wet and rinse your toothbrush when you brush.
- When you wash dishes, fill the basin instead of running the tap.
- Use a bucket and a hose with a shut-off nozzle when you wash the car.
- When shaving, fill the sink with water instead of keeping the water running.

The table shows savings for a family of four (with one adult who shaves).

Activity	Savings Rate (gal/min)	Time (min)	How Often
Brushing teeth	4	1	8 times a day (4 people)
Washing dishes	4	6	Once a day
Washing car	3	30	Once a week
Shaving	4	2	Once a day (one person)

1. How much car washing water can be saved per week? Per day?

2. How much tooth brushing water can be saved each day? How much dish washing water? How much shaving water?

3. Use the above answers to find the total daily water savings. Then decide whether a family could actually save 20,000 gallons of water a year. Explain how you found your answer.

Number Sense Suggest appropriate units for each rate.

1. The rate at which a book is read

2. The speed of a train

3. Logic Suppose there are 32 pizzas for 80 students. Write two unit rates that describe this situation. Which one of your rates is more useful?

Do the rates in each pair have the same meaning? Write *Yes* or *No*.

4. $\dfrac{2 \text{ miles}}{\text{day}}, \dfrac{0.5 \text{ days}}{\text{mile}}$

5. $\dfrac{\$0.40}{\text{lb}}, \dfrac{3 \text{ lb}}{\$1}$

6. $\dfrac{10 \text{ mi}}{\text{hr}}, \dfrac{0.25 \text{ hr}}{\text{mi}}$

7. $\dfrac{4 \text{ ft}}{\text{sec}}, \dfrac{0.25 \text{ sec}}{\text{ft}}$

Convert each quantity to the given units.

8. 4,000 pounds to tons

9. 84 hours to days

10. 43 meters to centimeters

Operation Sense Convert each rate to an equivalent rate.

11. 25 miles per hour to miles per day

12. $7.60 per hour to cents per hour

13. 2 gallons per minute to gallons per day

14. 3.5 centimeters per second to meters per minute

15. According to *50 Simple Things You Can Do to Save the Earth*, a mature tree consumes up to 13 pounds of carbon dioxide per year. Convert this rate to ounces per year.

16.  Suppose you hear a claim that people in the United States eat 100 acres of pizza per day. Convert this rate into reasonable units so you can evaluate this claim. Explain how you chose your units. One acre contains 43,560 square feet, and the population of the United States is about 260 million.

Test Prep

When finding an equivalent rate on a multiple choice test, you can eliminate choices that do not involve similar units. For example, when converting miles per hour, the answer must involve distance per time.

17. Which rate is equivalent to 3 pounds per hour?

    Ⓐ 1200 oz/km   Ⓑ 0.8 oz/min   Ⓒ 4.4 ft/sec   Ⓓ 11.25 oz/mile

LARGER THAN LIFE

Have you ever wondered how monster and science fiction movies such as *King Kong* and *Star Wars* were created? The creatures in these movies appear to be taller than a house, and it's hard to find a 24 foot tall actor who is willing to wear an ape suit!

In these movies, directors used scale models of the "monsters." The original version of *King Kong* was filmed using a model only 18 inches tall! Today, computers are replacing scale models. When you see a spaceship in an old *Star Trek* episode, you can be sure you're looking at a model. But recent films like *Jurassic Park* have been made using computers.

The scale models used in moviemaking are mathematically similar to the "real" objects they replace. By learning about the properties of similar figures, you can understand how these models compare to the things they represent.

1 In the movie *Honey, I Shrunk the Kids,* humans become smaller than insects. How do you think the models of insects used in this movie were different from the models of Godzilla and King Kong?

2 King Kong was supposed to be 24 feet tall. What scale was used to make the 18 in. scale model?

359

Creating and Exploring Similar Figures

You'll Learn ...

■ to identify similar figures

■ to write similarity statements

... How It's Used

Photographers produce similar figures when they enlarge or reduce their pictures.

Vocabulary

similar figures

corresponding sides

corresponding angles

● scale factor

▶ **Lesson Link**   You've seen that a scale drawing has the same shape as the original but a different size. Now you'll look at geometric figures that also have the same shape but not necessarily the same size. ◀

Explore   Similar Shapes

Oh, Give Me a Home ...

Materials: Protractor, Metric ruler, cm graph paper

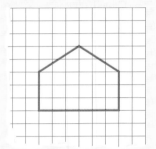

1. On your paper, draw a small "house" with five sides. Measure the length of each segment.

2. Add 3 cm to each length, then draw another house with the new dimensions. (Make sure both diagonal sides are the right length.)

3. Draw a third house, adding another 4 cm to each segment in the second house. Do your houses have the same shape?

4. Measure the angles in your houses. What do you notice?

5. Now draw a fourth house by doubling each length in the original house. Does this house have the same shape as the original house?

6. Measure the angles in your fourth house. What do you notice now?

Learn   Creating and Exploring Similar Figures

The scale model used to make *King Kong* looked like the "real" Kong but was a different size.

If one geometric figure is a scale model of another, the figures are **similar figures**. Similar figures have the same shape, but not necessarily the same size.

Matching sides and angles of similar figures are called **corresponding sides** and **corresponding angles**. The measures of these sides and angles are related in a special way.

DEFINITION OF SIMILARITY

Figures are similar if their corresponding angles are congruent and the lengths of their corresponding sides have equal ratios.

The ratio of corresponding side lengths is the **scale factor** of the figures. It has the same meaning as the map and model scales you worked with earlier. The scale factor from $\triangle MNP$ to $\triangle QRS$ is $\frac{3}{2}$, since $\frac{9}{6} = \frac{6}{4} = \frac{12}{8} = \frac{3}{2}$.

Example 1

A movie uses a model skyscraper that is similar to a real one. Find the scale factor from the actual skyscraper to the model.

In similar figures, the ratio of any pair of corresponding side lengths can be used to find the scale factor. You can use the buildings' heights *or* widths to find the scale factor.

Using heights:

$$\frac{\text{model height}}{\text{actual height}} = \frac{4}{480} = \frac{1}{120}$$

Using widths:

$$\frac{\text{model width}}{\text{actual width}} = \frac{1}{120}$$

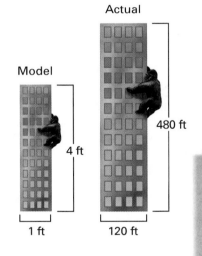

The scale factor from the actual skyscraper to the model is $\frac{1}{120}$.

The statement $\triangle ABC \sim \triangle EFD$ says that $\triangle ABC$ is similar to $\triangle EFD$. The order of the letters shows the corresponding parts. When you write a similarity statement, be sure to list the parts in the right order.

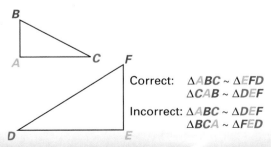

Correct: $\triangle ABC \sim \triangle EFD$
$\triangle CAB \sim \triangle DEF$

Incorrect: $\triangle ABC \sim \triangle DEF$
$\triangle BCA \sim \triangle FED$

Example 2

$\triangle PQR \sim \triangle TUS$. Find the measures of $\angle S$, $\angle T$, and $\angle U$.

Since $\triangle PQR \sim \triangle TUS$, you know:

$\angle T$ corresponds to $\angle P$, so $m\angle T = m\angle P = 72°$.

$\angle U$ corresponds to $\angle Q$, so $m\angle U = m\angle Q = 42°$.

$\angle S$ corresponds to $\angle R$, so $m\angle S = m\angle R = 66°$.

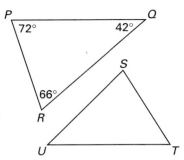

To see if two figures are similar, check that their corresponding angles are congruent *and* their corresponding side lengths have equal ratios.

Example 3

Tell whether the trapezoids are similar. If they are, write a similarity statement using ∼.

Check that corresponding angles are congruent.

$\angle A \cong \angle E$; $\angle B \cong \angle H$; $\angle C \cong \angle G$; and $\angle D \cong \angle F$.

Check that corresponding side lengths have equal ratios.

$$\frac{25}{10} = \frac{5}{2} \qquad \frac{30}{12} = \frac{5}{2} \qquad \frac{20}{8} = \frac{5}{2} \qquad \frac{15}{6} = \frac{5}{2}$$

The trapezoids are similar: $ABCD \sim EHGF$.

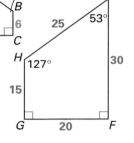

Try It

Tell if the triangles are similar. If they are, give the scale factor from $\triangle UVW$ to the other triangle and write a statement using the symbol ∼.

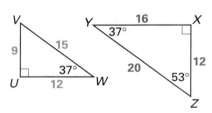

Check Your Understanding

1. Why must similar figures have congruent corresponding angles?

2. Are all squares similar? Are all rectangles similar?

3. How does the everyday use of the word *similar* differ from the mathematical use of the word?

7-8 Exercises and Applications

Practice and Apply

1. **Getting Started** Follow the steps to check that the two triangles are similar and to find the scale factor from △*ABC* to the other triangle.

   a. Decide how the figures correspond. Which angle corresponds to ∠*A*? To ∠*B*? To ∠*C*?

   b. Check that each angle has the same measure as its corresponding angle.

   c. Which side corresponds to $\overline{AB}$? Find the ratio of that side's length to the length of $\overline{AB}$. Repeat for $\overline{BC}$ and $\overline{AC}$.

   d. Check that all three ratios are equal. What is the scale factor from △*ABC* to the other triangle?

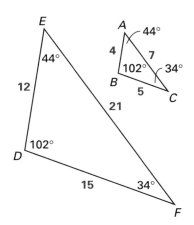

PRACTICE 7-8

Geometry Tell if the figures are similar. If they are, write a similarity statement using ~ and give the scale factor. If they're not, explain why not.

2.

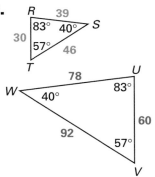

3.

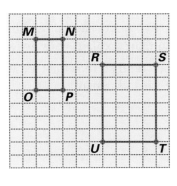

4.

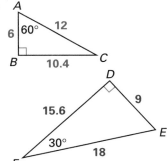

5. Draw two rectangles that are similar and two that are not similar.

6. Tammy drew the two monsters shown. Are they mathematically similar? Explain why or why not.

7. Suppose △*UVW* ~ △*ZYX*. If *m*∠*X* = 96°, *m*∠*Y* = 46°, and *m*∠*Z* = 38°, find the measures of ∠*U*, ∠*V*, and ∠*W*.

8. Suppose △*ABC* ~ △*DEF*. The length of $\overline{AB}$ is 8, the length of $\overline{BC}$ is 10, the length of $\overline{CA}$ is 12, and the length of $\overline{DE}$ is 12. Find the lengths of $\overline{EF}$ and $\overline{FD}$.

9. In the movie *Ghostbusters,* the massive Stay-Puft Marshmallow Man terrorized New York City. A child's toy version of the Marshmallow Man is 10 inches tall. Assume that the Marshmallow Man was supposed to be 800 feet tall. Find the scale factor from the toy to the "real" monster.

10. Fine Arts Motion pictures can be projected onto a screen, played on a videotape machine, broadcast over television, and even shown in clips on a computer. Which of these rectangular screens is similar to a computer screen that measures 10 in. by 14 in.?

   a. A miniature TV screen 2 in. by 3 in.

   b. A TV monitor 17.5 in. by 24.5 in.

   c. A movie screen 20 ft by 28 ft

11. **Test Prep** Which similarity statement is *not* correct?

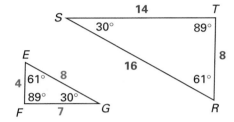

   Ⓐ $\triangle EFG \sim \triangle RTS$ Ⓑ $\triangle GEF \sim \triangle STR$

   Ⓒ $\triangle GFE \sim \triangle STR$ Ⓓ $\triangle FGE \sim \triangle TSR$

Problem Solving and Reasoning

12. Critical Thinking Do you think two quadrilaterals can have four pairs of congruent angles but not be similar? Explain your answer.

13. Communicate Where would you stand so that the tree appears taller than the lighthouse? Draw a picture and explain.

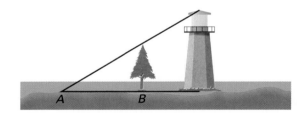

14. Critical Thinking Similar figures that have the same size are *congruent figures.* What is the scale factor for two congruent figures? Explain.

Mixed Review

Find each product. Write your answers in lowest terms. *[Lesson 4-4]*

15. $\dfrac{1}{3} \cdot \dfrac{2}{5}$ **16.** $\dfrac{2}{7} \cdot \dfrac{35}{36}$ **17.** $\dfrac{9}{10} \cdot \dfrac{90}{81}$ **18.** $\dfrac{7}{8} \cdot \dfrac{72}{105}$ **19.** $\dfrac{3}{7} \cdot \dfrac{21}{9}$

Decide if each pair of ratios is proportional. *[Lesson 6-6]*

20. $\dfrac{2}{3} \stackrel{?}{=} \dfrac{12}{18}$ **21.** $\dfrac{7}{8} \stackrel{?}{=} \dfrac{49}{56}$ **22.** $\dfrac{5}{6} \stackrel{?}{=} \dfrac{25}{36}$ **23.** $\dfrac{5}{7} \stackrel{?}{=} \dfrac{20}{28}$

TECHNOLOGY

Using Dynamic Geometry Software • Exploring Dilations

Problem: How can you construct a polygon similar to a given polygon using a scale factor of 2.5?

You can use dynamic geometry software to construct the polygon. A *dilation* is an enlargement or reduction of a geometric figure. A dilation results in a figure similar to the original figure.

1 Use your software to make a triangle. Then choose "numerical edit" from the label menu and type 2.5 somewhere outside the triangle.

2 Create a dilation of the triangle. Make point *A* the center of the dilation and use a scale factor of 2.5.

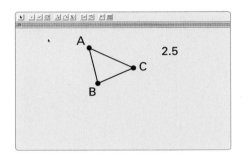

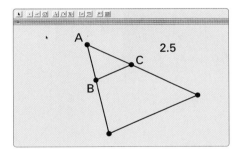

Solution: The result of the dilation is a triangle that is similar to △*ABC* using a scale factor of 2.5.

TRY IT

a. Use geometry software to draw a triangle. Then use a dilation to construct a similar triangle using a scale factor of 3. Sketch the result.

b. Use geometry software to draw a rectangle. Then use a dilation to construct a similar rectangle using a scale factor of $\frac{1}{2}$. Sketch the result.

ON YOUR OWN

▶ What do you think would happen if you dilated a figure using a scale factor of 7, then reduced the dilation using a scale factor of $\frac{1}{7}$? Use geometry software to test your idea.

▶ Why do you think you need to type a number before the computer can do the dilation?

Finding Measures of Similar Figures

▶ **Lesson Link**
You've seen that similar figures have the same shape, but not necessarily the same size. Now you'll use proportions to find side lengths in similar figures. ◀

You'll Learn ...

■ to find missing side lengths in similar figures

■ to use shadows to find the heights of tall objects

... How It's Used

The methods geographers use to find the height of a mountain are based on similar triangles.

Explore   Measures of Similar Figures

Maybe It Just LOOKS Similar!

Materials: Protractor, Ruler

1. Find all pairs of similar triangles in the set of six triangles. For each pair, write a similarity statement, using ~, and find a scale factor.

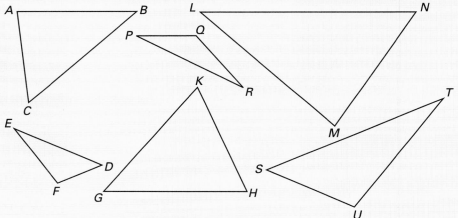

2. For each pair of similar triangles, write a paragraph explaining why you're sure they are similar.

3. Suppose $\triangle XYZ \sim \triangle ABC$ and the scale factor from $\triangle XYZ$ to $\triangle ABC$ is 3. Find the angle measures and side lengths in $\triangle XYZ$.

Learn   Finding Measures of Similar Figures

You can use proportions to solve problems about side lengths of similar figures.

By applying this idea, you may be able to find a real-world length or distance that you would not be able to measure with a ruler or tape measure. This technique is called *indirect measurement*.

Examples

▶ **Art Link**

Dollhouses are mathematically similar to real houses. The Museum of the City of New York contains a dollhouse with miniature pictures painted by famous artists such as Marcel Duchamp and Gaston Lachaise.

1 If △ABC ~ △DEF, find x, the length of $\overline{EF}$.

The triangles are similar, so corresponding side lengths are proportional.

$\dfrac{12}{15} = \dfrac{x}{10}$ Write a proportion.

$120 = 15x$ Find the cross products.

$\dfrac{120}{15} = \dfrac{15x}{15}$ To undo multiplication by 15, divide both sides by 15.

$8 = x$ Divide.

The length of $\overline{EF}$ is 8 units.

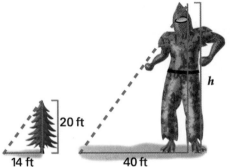

2 Director I. M. Skerry is making a new movie, *Shadows of Terror*. In one scene, the shadow of a 20-foot-tall tree is 14 feet long. At the same time, the monster's shadow is 40 feet long. How tall is the monster?

Because the sun's rays come in at the same angle, the triangles formed by the objects and their shadows are similar.

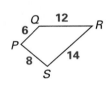
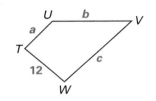

$\dfrac{h}{20} = \dfrac{40}{14}$ Write a proportion.

$14h = 800$ Find the cross products.

$\dfrac{14h}{14} = \dfrac{800}{14}$ To undo multiplication by 14, divide both sides by 14.

$h \approx 57.14$ Divide.

The monster is about 57.14 feet (nearly 57 feet 2 inches) tall.

Problem Solving TIP

When you solve for the height of an object, be sure your answer makes sense. If you get an answer like "The monster is 0.2 feet tall," go back and check your work!

Try It

PQRS ~ *TUVW*. Find *a*, *b*, and *c*.

WHAT DO YOU THINK?

The largest flying dinosaur, *Quetzalcoatlus,* had a wingspan of about 40 feet. A technician for a new dinosaur movie needs to create a scale model of a *Quetzalcoatlus* using a scale factor of $\frac{1}{25}$. What should the model's wingspan be?

Wendy thinks ...

The scale model is $\frac{1}{25}$ of the size of a *Quetzalcoatlus*, so I'll multiply $40 \cdot \frac{1}{25} = 1.6$ feet. The model has a wingspan of 1.6 feet.

Luis thinks ...

Let x be the wingspan of the model. I'll set up a proportion:

$$\frac{\text{model wingspan}}{\text{actual wingspan}} = \frac{1}{25} \quad \text{or} \quad \frac{x}{40} = \frac{1}{25}$$

$$25x = 40$$

$$x = \frac{40}{25} = \frac{8}{5} = 1.6$$

The model has a wingspan of 1.6 feet.

What do you think?

1. Why does Wendy's method work? Why does Luis's?

2. Suppose that the height of a *Quetzalcoatlus* was 18 feet. What is the height of the model?

Check | Your Understanding

1. How is the scale of a map related to the scale factor between two similar figures?

2. Describe a method for finding the height of the top of a tower on a sunny day.

Practice and Apply

1. | Getting Started | If *ABCD* ~ *EFGH*, follow the steps to find *x*, the length of $\overline{EF}$.

a. Which side in *ABCD* corresponds to $\overline{EF}$?

b. Give the ratio of *x* to the length of the corresponding side in *ABCD*.

c. Which side of *EFGH* has a known length?

d. Which side of *ABCD* corresponds to the side you named in **c**? Give the ratio of these corresponding sides.

e. The ratios in **b** and **d** are equal. Write and solve a proportion to find *x*.

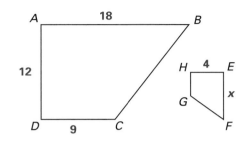

Find *x* in each pair of similar figures.

2. △*ABC* ~ △*DEF*

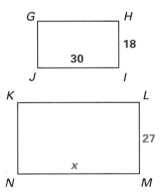

3. *GHIJ* ~ *KLMN*

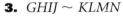

4.

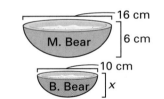

5. Problem Solving In *Terror of the Bird Thing*, the Bird Thing casts a shadow that is 60 m long. Diane is 150 cm tall. If Diane's shadow is 180 cm long, how tall is the Bird Thing?

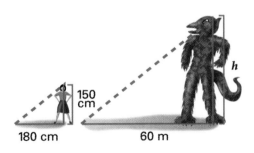

Find the missing side lengths in each pair of similar figures.

6. △*RST* ~ △*UVW*

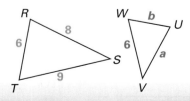

7. *EFGH* ~ *JKLM*

8. △*NPQ* ~ △*RST*

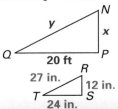

9. **Test Prep** What proportion could you use to solve for *x*?

Ⓐ $\frac{42}{x} = \frac{88}{40}$ Ⓑ $\frac{x}{42} = \frac{88}{40}$ Ⓒ $\frac{40}{42} = \frac{x}{88}$ Ⓓ $\frac{40}{x} = \frac{42}{88}$

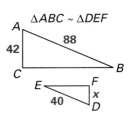

$\triangle ABC \sim \triangle DEF$

10. Ashok has enlarged an 8 in. × 10 in. photograph to make a poster. If his poster's length is 25 in., what is its width?

Problem Solving and Reasoning

11. **Journal** A photo processing lab offers to enlarge 3.5 in. × 5 in. photos to 5 in. × 7 in. Are these rectangles similar? If not, how can the photo lab make the enlargements? Explain.

12. **Choose a Strategy** You need to find the distance across the Ralimis River. If $\triangle ABC \sim \triangle DEC$, what is the distance across the river from *E* to *D*? Explain how you solved this problem.

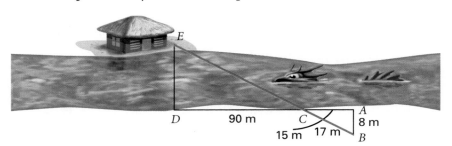

Problem Solving
STRATEGIES

- Look for a Pattern
- Make an Organized List
- Make a Table
- Guess and Check
- Work Backward
- Use Logical Reasoning
- Draw a Diagram
- Solve a Simpler Problem

13. **Critical Thinking** Maribel says that any two equilateral triangles are similar. Is she right? If she is, explain why. If she is not, sketch two equilateral triangles that are not similar.

Mixed Review

Find each product. *[Lesson 4-5]*

14. $2\frac{3}{4} \cdot 1\frac{2}{3}$ **15.** $5\frac{7}{8} \cdot 3\frac{4}{3}$ **16.** $2\frac{5}{9} \cdot 7\frac{1}{10}$ **17.** $3\frac{4}{5} \cdot 6\frac{1}{2}$ **18.** $10\frac{5}{8} \cdot 3\frac{5}{12}$

Find each unit rate. *[Lesson 6-7]*

19. 200 words in 5 minutes **20.** 14 days in 7 months **21.** $16.99 for 10 gallons

Project Progress

If possible, build the scale model of your dream house using construction paper, scissors, and tape. If this is not possible, find how much paper you would need to build your house by calculating the areas of the walls, ceiling, and roof.

Problem Solving

Understand
Plan
Solve
Look Back

Perimeters and Areas of Similar Figures

▶ **Lesson Link** You've learned how to find side lengths of similar figures. Now you'll explore perimeters and areas of similar figures. ◀

You'll Learn ...

■ to use the scale factor to find perimeters and areas of similar figures

... How It's Used

People who frame artwork need to know how the size of a painting affects its area and perimeter.

Explore | Perimeters and Areas

If It's a Lot, It Can't Be Little

Materials: Graph paper

Celluloid Creatures Studios has asked you to investigate the costs of buying and fencing different-sized lots. Lot space costs $100 per square foot. Fencing costs $12 per foot.

1. Let one grid square represent 10 ft by 10 ft. Sketch a 50 ft × 200 ft lot. Find the lot space cost, the fencing cost, and the total cost of the lot.

2. Sketch a 100 ft × 200 ft lot and a 100 ft × 400 ft foot lot. For each, find the lot space cost, the fencing cost, and the total cost.

3. Compare the lot space, fencing, and total costs of the three lots. What do you notice? Which of the larger lots would you say is "twice as big" as the original?

4. What geometric measurement is associated with the fencing of the lot? What measurement is associated with the size of the lot?

Learn | Perimeters and Areas of Similar Figures

The ratio of the perimeters of two similar figures is equal to the ratio of the side lengths—the scale factor. The ratio of their areas is equal to the *square* of the scale factor.

Examples

1 A designer is making two similar versions of a movie poster. If the scale factor from the smaller poster to the larger is 3, predict the ratio of their areas. Check your prediction by calculating the areas.

Prediction: Since the scale factor is 3, the ratio of the areas should be $3^2 = 9$.

Calculation: The area of the smaller poster is $4 \cdot 3 = 12$ square units. The area of the larger is $12 \cdot 9 = 108$ square units. The ratio of the areas is $\frac{108}{12} = 9$.

2 The perimeter of the larger of these similar figures is 38 cm and its area is 50 cm². The scale factor from the larger to the smaller is $\frac{3}{5}$. Find the perimeter and area of the smaller figure.

Multiply by the scale factor to find the perimeter of the smaller figure.

Perimeter $= 38 \cdot \frac{3}{5} = 22.8$ cm.

Multiply by the *square* of the scale factor to find the area of the smaller figure.
Area $= 50 \cdot \left(\frac{3}{5}\right)^2 = 50 \cdot \frac{9}{25} = 18$ cm².

Try It

The perimeter of the smaller of these similar figures is 64 units and its area is 44 square units. The scale factor from the smaller figure to the larger is $\frac{3}{2}$. Find the perimeter and area of the larger figure.

Check Your Understanding

1. Explain why doubling the side length of a square quadruples its area.

2. If one similar rectangle has twice the area of another, does it have twice the length and width? Explain.

Practice and Apply

1. **Getting Started** Two rectangles are similar. The scale factor from the smaller to the larger is 3. The smaller rectangle has perimeter 14 and area 28. Follow the steps to find the perimeter and area of the larger rectangle.

   a. The ratio of the perimeters is equal to the scale factor. Multiply the small rectangle's perimeter by the scale factor to find the large rectangle's perimeter.

   b. Square the scale factor. This is the ratio of the areas.

   c. Multiply the small rectangle's area by the ratio in **b** to find the large rectangle's area.

Geometry Predict the ratio of the areas of each pair of similar figures. Check your predictions by calculating the areas.

2. Scale factor 2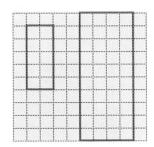

3. Scale factor 4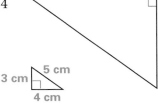

   3 cm 5 cm
   4 cm

4. An artist is drawing a larger version of the monster in this poster. The scale factor from this figure to the enlargement is $\frac{7}{3}$. If this figure has an area of 108 cm², what will the area of the larger one be? Explain.

Suppose two figures are similar. For each scale factor from the smaller to the larger, find the unknown perimeter and area.

5. Scale factor = 3, perimeter of smaller = 10 cm, area of smaller = 6 cm². Find the perimeter and area of the larger figure.

6. Scale factor = 5, perimeter of larger = 120 in., area of larger = 172 in². Find the perimeter and area of the smaller figure.

7. Scale factor = $\frac{3}{2}$, perimeter of smaller = 14 ft, area of smaller = 26 ft². Find the perimeter and area of the larger figure.

Perimeter and area ratios of similar figures are given. Find each scale factor.

8. Perimeter ratio = 100

9. Area ratio = 25

10. Area ratio = 81

11. Perimeter ratio = 0.62

12. History The ancient temple Angkor Wat was built by the Khmer people of Cambodia. The temple's enclosure is a rectangle 1000 meters long and 850 meters wide. If a museum model of the temple is built using a scale factor of $\frac{1}{8}$, what will the area of the model be?

13. **Test Prep** The ratio of the areas of two similar rectangles is $\frac{36}{25}$. What is the ratio of their perimeters?

Ⓐ $\frac{5}{6}$ Ⓑ $\frac{6}{5}$ Ⓒ $\frac{25}{36}$ Ⓓ $\frac{36}{25}$

Problem Solving and Reasoning

14. Communicate Jacob tells Renata that one of his school photographs is twice as big as another one. Renata asks Jacob what he means by "twice as big." Explain why Renata might be confused. What do you think people usually mean when they say one thing is "twice as big" as another?

15. Critical Thinking On a movie set, a 2-meter tall Godzilla casts a shadow whose area is 3 m². If the "real" Godzilla is 50 meters tall, what is the area of his shadow?

16. Critical Thinking You find that it takes 0.16 gallons of paint to paint a rectangular wall whose length is 6 ft and whose height is 8 ft. How much paint will you need to paint a wall whose length is 12 ft and whose height is 16 ft? Explain how you found your answer.

Mixed Review

Find each quotient. Write your answers in lowest terms. *[Lesson 4-6]*

17. $\frac{3}{4} \div 1\frac{2}{3}$ **18.** $5\frac{1}{2} \div 2\frac{3}{4}$ **19.** $1\frac{1}{9} \div \frac{1}{3}$ **20.** $\frac{1}{2} \div \frac{5}{12}$ **21.** $32 \div \frac{1}{2}$

Solve each proportion. *[Lesson 6-8]*

22. $\frac{x}{14} = \frac{4}{7}$ **23.** $\frac{p}{12} = \frac{3}{4}$ **24.** $\frac{5}{11} = \frac{m}{22}$ **25.** $\frac{12}{n} = \frac{6}{5}$ **26.** $\frac{b}{3} = \frac{2}{4}$

Section 7C Connect

You have seen that an enlargement or reduction of a figure is similar to the original. Now you will use two different methods to enlarge a drawing.

Larger than Life

Materials: Graph paper (with larger squares than those in drawing)

The drawing shows a simplified drawing of Rodan, who co-starred with Godzilla in several 1960s movies. You will use two methods—the *grid* method and the *projection* method—to enlarge this drawing.

1. In the grid method, you enlarge one piece of the picture at a time. Use an 8 × 8 area on your graph paper to make a larger copy of Rodan. Each square in your drawing should look like the corresponding square in the original.

2. To use the projection method:

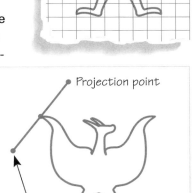

Projection point

Wing tip of enlarged drawing

a. Trace the original drawing onto an $8\frac{1}{2}$ in. × 11 in. sheet of paper. The top of your tracing should be about $2\frac{1}{2}$ in. from the top of the paper.

b. Mark dots on your tracing. These dots will be your guide for the enlargement. Mark key points, like the tips of the wings.

c. Draw a dot near the top of your paper. This is the *projection point*. Draw a line from this point through each dot on your drawing. Mark a new dot twice as far from the projection point as the original dot.

d. Using the new dots as a guide, sketch a larger drawing. What is the scale factor from the enlargement to the original?

3. How can each of these methods be used to make a drawing triple the size of the original? One-fourth the size of the original?

Geometry Tell if the figures are similar. If they are, write a similarity statement using ~ and give the scale factor. If they're not, explain why not.

1.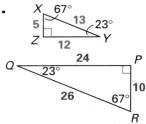

2.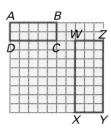

3.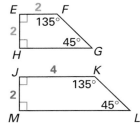

4. The mother and baby elephant shown are approximately similar. Assume the mother is 2.8 m tall and 4.2 m long. If the baby is 1.8 m long, how tall is it?

5. Two rectangles are similar, and the scale factor from the smaller to the larger is 2. The perimeter of the smaller rectangle is 20 ft and its area is 24 ft². Find the perimeter and area of the larger rectangle.

6. **Journal** In the original *King Kong*, Kong was supposed to be 24 feet tall. If the 18-inch-tall model of Kong cast a 10-inch-long shadow during one scene, how long would the shadow of the "real" Kong have been? Explain how you solved this problem.

7. **Operation Sense** Convert 740 miles per hour to miles per minute.

Test Prep

When you're asked to find a side length in a pair of similar figures on a multiple choice test, setting up a proportion can help you work more quickly.

8. Pat uses a photocopy machine to enlarge a drawing that is 6 cm wide and 8 cm long. If the enlargement has a width of 10.5 cm, what is its length? Choose the proportion that will help you find the correct answer.

   Ⓐ $\dfrac{6}{x} = \dfrac{10.5}{8}$ Ⓑ $\dfrac{6}{10.5} = \dfrac{8}{x}$ Ⓒ $\dfrac{6}{x} = \dfrac{8}{10.5}$ Ⓓ $\dfrac{x}{6} = \dfrac{8}{10.5}$

Fractal Geometry

Fractal geometry is one of the newest areas of mathematical exploration. Developed in the 1970s and 1980s, fractal geometry is the study of geometric figures with predictable patterns that repeat as the scale changes.

Fractal patterns show *self-similarity*. When you "zoom in" on a small part of a self-similar figure, the enlarged region looks similar to the original figure. In nature, clouds, coastlines, and cauliflower show self-similarity.

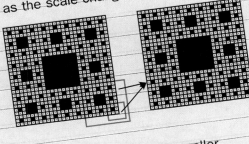

Fractal patterns can be created by repeating a rule on a smaller and smaller scale. The rule for the pattern below is "find the midpoints of each side of the square and connect them to make a new square."

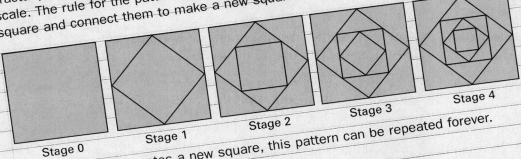

Stage 0   Stage 1   Stage 2   Stage 3   Stage 4

Since each stage creates a new square, this pattern can be repeated forever.

Try It

Stages 0–2 of a famous fractal pattern are shown. The figure created by repeating the rule an infinite number of times is called a *Sierpinski Gasket*.

1. Sketch Stage 3 of this pattern.

2. In your own words, explain the rule for this pattern.

3. List the number of shaded and unshaded triangles for each stage. Describe any patterns you see in these numbers.

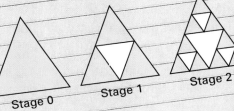

Stage 0   Stage 1   Stage 2

377

Chapter 7 Summary and Review

Graphic Organizer

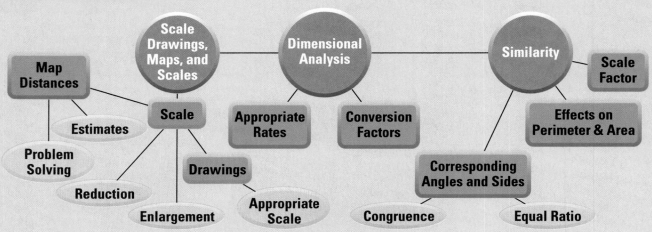

Section 7A   Scale Drawings, Maps, and Scales

Summary

- The **scale** of a map is the ratio of the distance between two points on the map to the actual distance between the points.

- A **scale drawing** is often used to illustrate something that is too large or too small to show actual size. A map is one kind of scale drawing.

- A drawing's scale is the ratio of a length in the drawing to the actual length it represents. When the units are the same, they can be omitted.

- A map can be an important problem-solving tool. You can solve problems by using the formula $\text{time} = \dfrac{\text{distance}}{\text{rate}}$ and your knowledge of scale.

Review

1. Write the scale $\dfrac{1 \text{ in.}}{25 \text{ mi}}$ in two other ways.

2. Solve the proportion $\dfrac{14 \text{ in.}}{x} = \dfrac{21 \text{ in.}}{12 \text{ yd}}$ for x.

3. A model train is 35 in. long. Find the length of the actual train if the scale is 7 in.:90 ft.

4. Find the scale of a map if a 63 km wide canyon is 14 cm wide on the map.

5. Devesh left school at 3:45 P.M. and rode his bike home at a rate of 10 mi/hr. If his home is 7 mi away from school, when did he arrive?

6. A model of a 26 ft tall dinosaur has to fit into a museum with 9 ft ceilings. Suggest an appropriate scale for the model.

Section 7B Dimensional Analysis

Summary

- For any rate, you can find the reciprocal unit rate by exchanging the numerator and denominator, then converting to a unit rate.

- **Conversion factors** are fractions that can be used to convert units. If you need to convert a unit in the *numerator* of a rate, multiply by a conversion factor that has that unit in the *denominator,* and vice versa.

Review

7. Suggest appropriate units for a rate that describes the growth rate of a plant.

8. Give a reciprocal unit rate that has the same meaning as 5 feet per second.

9. Convert 360 miles per hour to miles per minute.

10. Dr. Acevedo earns $55 per hour. Convert this rate to cents per second.

Section 7C Similarity

Summary

- **Similar** figures have the same shape but not necessarily the same size.

- Matching sides and angles of similar figures are **corresponding sides** and **corresponding angles.** Figures are similar if the corresponding angles are congruent and corresponding side lengths have equal ratios.

- The statement $\triangle ABC \sim \triangle DEF$ means that $\triangle ABC$ is similar to $\triangle DEF$. The order of the letters shows the corresponding parts.

- You can use proportions to find side lengths in similar figures.

- The ratio of the perimeters of two similar figures is equal to the scale factor. The ratio of their areas is equal to the *square* of the scale factor.

Review

11. Tell whether the figures on the grid are similar. If they are, write a similarity statement using ~ and give the scale factor. If they're not, explain why not.

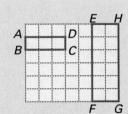

12. Two triangles are similar, with scale factor 4. The smaller triangle has perimeter 7 in. and area 5 in². Find the perimeter and area of the larger triangle.

13. Two similar octagons have an area ratio of 81. Find the perimeter ratio and the scale factor from the smaller to the larger.

1. St. Louis is 240 miles from Memphis. About how far apart will these cities appear on a map with the scale 1 in.:40 mi?

2. A model of a building is 64 cm tall, with the scale 8 cm:11 m. Find the height of the actual building.

3. Find the scale of a map if a 10 mile road is shown as 25 inches long.

4. Suggest appropriate units for a rate that tells how fast a dog can run.

5. A bicycle measures 42 in. by 54 in. What is the largest scale that can be used to make a scale drawing of the bicycle to fit in a 3 in. by 5 in. note card?

6. Carolyn plans to bicycle to her cousin's home, 26 miles away. She needs to arrive at 3:45 P.M. If she rides at an average rate of 14 miles per hour, when should she leave?

7. Write two conversion factors involving seconds and minutes.

8. Convert $45 per hour to dollars per minute.

9. Tell whether the figures $ABCD$ and $EFGH$ are similar. If they are, write a similarity statement using ~ and give the scale factor. If they're not, explain why not.

10. Two similar figures have a perimeter ratio of 13. Find the scale factor and the area ratio.

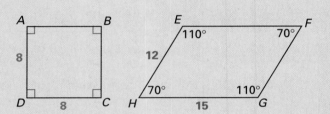

11. $\triangle HIJ \sim \triangle MLK$. Find the missing side lengths.

12. Two rectangles are similar, with scale factor 5. The larger rectangle has perimeter 30 and area 50. Find the perimeter and area of the smaller one.

13. Light travels at the rate of 300,000,000 meters per second. Convert this to kilometers per hour.

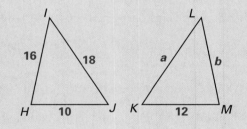

14. $\triangle JKL \sim \triangle FED$. If $m\angle J = 64°$, $m\angle K = 82°$, and $m\angle L = 34°$, find $m\angle D$, $m\angle E$, and $m\angle F$.

15. When Julianne's shadow is 4 feet long, Greuso's shadow is 22 feet long. If Julianne is 5 feet tall, how tall is Greuso?

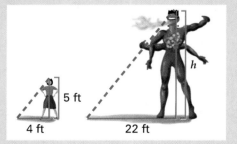

Performance Task

Use the following information to write as many conversion factors as you can: A bushel is 4 pecks. A peck is 8 quarts. A quart is 2 pints.

Performance Assessment

Choose one problem.

SPACE SCHOOL

Space station Vega 9 has been in orbit for 15 years. Its first generation of children are entering their teens. You are an architect designing a math classroom for Vega 9. Make a scale drawing of your classroom of the future. Show the scale, and label the drawing to explain the items in your classroom and how they work.

You Be the Guide!

Your school has a summer exchange program with a Japanese school. You are excited because one of the students is coming to stay with you. Use maps to plan a 10 day vacation in which you will show your guest around your city and state. Allow time for travel and sightseeing. Write a letter to the student describing your travel plans. Include a map to show her where you will be going.

I'VE BEEN WORKING ON THE RAILROAD

The Transcontinental Railroad was completed in 1869. Many Chinese and Irish laborers died during its construction. Union Pacific crews, working west from Nebraska, laid about 349 miles of track during the three years from 1866 to 1869. Central Pacific crews laid about 18 miles per month during this time. Write a newspaper article about the construction of the railroad. Include a double bar graph comparing each year's total distance for the two crews. Be sure to tell how much track each crew had laid by the time the railroad was finished.

Shadow of Castle Doom

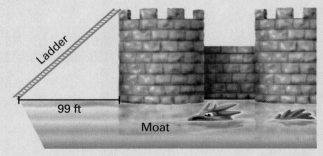

Lady Fenestra, who is 5 ft 6 in. ($5\frac{1}{2}$ ft) tall, must rescue the handsome Don Wannabe from Castle Doom. She plans to place a ladder over the moat to the top of the tower. The moat is 99 feet wide. Lady Fenestra finds that her shadow is 8 ft long when the shadow of the castle tower just covers the moat. How tall is the tower? How long a ladder will Lady Fenestra need? Explain how you found each answer.

Percents

Science Link
www.mathsurf.com/7/ch8/science

Arts & Literature Link
www.mathsurf.com/7/ch8/arts

Science

The relative humidity is a measure of the amount of water the air can hold at a particular temperature. The warmer it is, the more water the air can hold. A relative humidity of 85% at 90°F is wetter than a relative humidity of 85% at 40°F.

Arts & Literature

The Guggenheim Museum in New York City has a spiraling gallery that increases in height at a 3% grade.

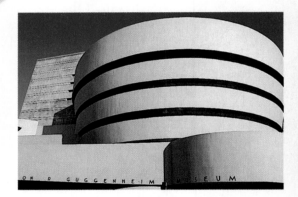

Social Studies

China produced 2,915,000 of the 10,333,000 metric tons of pears grown in one year. This is about 28% of the world's pear production.

Entertainment

Lisa Leslie, a center on the United States 1996 Olympic women's basketball team, shot 86% from the field in the gold medal game against Brazil. She made 12 of the 14 shots she took.

KEY MATH IDEAS

A **percent** is a ratio that describes a part of 100.

You can use the fact that *percent* means "out of 100" to help you rewrite a percent as a fraction or decimal.

Problems about money often involve percents. You can set up proportions or use other kinds of equations to solve a problem with percents.

You can use percents to describe an increase or decrease in a number.

People of the World

50% of the people in the world are under the age of 25.

CHAPTER PROJECT

Problem Solving

Understand
Plan
Solve
Look Back

In this project, you will plan a picnic for young children in a hospital. You must make sure that your meal is nutritious and appealing. To begin the project, make a list of some of the foods you might want to serve.

Interpreting Mathematical Phrases

When making a problem-solving plan, you need to translate words into mathematical symbols. For example, the phrase "half as much as" can mean "$\times \frac{1}{2}$," and "four times as many" can mean "$\times 4$."

Problem Solving Focus

For each problem below, write the answer and the arithmetic you used to find the answer. (For example, if you added 5 to 7 to get 12, write "5 + 7 = 12.")

1 Jaime is baking a sheet cake for a surprise party. The recipe serves eight and uses two cups of flour. Jaime has invited three times as many people as the recipe calls for. How much flour will he need?

2 Doreen is bringing Salsa Verde Cruda to the party. Her recipe for this uncooked green sauce makes one and one-half cups of salsa. Doreen decides to make four times this amount. If the recipe calls for two serrano chilies, how many more chilies than this should she buy?

3 Reggie decides to make papadum, a spicy crispbread popular in India. He usually uses $\frac{1}{2}$ teaspoon of cumin seed to make 10 pieces of papadum. If he wants to make 5 times this many pieces, how much cumin should he use?

4 Huynh, who doesn't like to cook, volunteered to bring drinks. She estimates that $\frac{2}{3}$ of the 24 people who are coming to the party will want milk with their cake. How many people should she buy milk for?

To the Batcave!

It's just before dusk. You're standing near the Congress Avenue Bridge in Austin, Texas. Suddenly you hear a whirring sound. What looks like a cloud of smoke pours out from underneath the bridge.

But it's not smoke, it's *bats*—1.5 *million* bats, the largest urban bat colony in North America. Austin's bats make up a small part of the 100 million free-tailed bats that migrate north from Mexico each spring to raise their young.

Many countries have legends about bats that attack people. Actually, most bats are harmless and many are extremely beneficial to humans. One little brown bat may eat 600 mosquitoes in one hour—an average of one insect every six seconds!

Mathematical information can help people separate fact from fiction. As you learn more about bats you'll begin your study of *percents,* which are an important way to communicate mathematical information.

1 Write 1.5 million in scientific notation.

2 Give an example showing how mathematics can help people tell fact from fiction.

3 How could you use mathematics to compare Austin's free-tailed bat population to Austin's human population?

8-1

Understanding Percents

You'll Learn ...

■ to compare quantities by using percents

... How It's Used

Marketing specialists use percents to measure the opinions of potential customers.

Vocabulary

percent

▶ **Lesson Link** You've studied several methods for comparing quantities, including rates, ratios, and scales. Now you'll compare quantities by measuring them in relation to 100. ◀

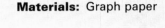

Explore Comparing Numbers Using Grids

Free Tails and Long Ears

Materials: Graph paper

1. The weight of an average Mexican free-tailed bat is about 0.8 times the usual weight of a little brown bat. Draw a 10-by-10 grid to represent the weight of a little brown bat. Shade squares to represent the weight of a free-tailed bat.

Red bat

2. Repeat Step 1 using a 10-by-4 grid to represent the little brown bat. Then repeat Step 1 using a 6-by-5 grid. Which of the three grids was easiest to use? Why?

3. The length of an average long-eared bat is about $\frac{3}{10}$ the length of a typical red bat. Draw a 10-by-10 grid to represent the length of a red bat. Shade squares to represent the length of a long-eared bat.

4. Repeat Step 3 using a grid size of your choice.

5. Compare your Step 3 and Step 4 grids with those of other students. What is the advantage of using a 10-by-10 grid?

Learn Understanding Percents

There are 60 shaded squares on this 10-by-10 grid. So $\frac{60}{100}$ of the squares are shaded. You can say that 60 **percent** (written 60%) of the grid squares are shaded. A percent is a ratio that describes a part of 100. 60% means "60 *per hundred.*" So 100% represents a whole.

Example 1

Use percents to compare the sizes of the tennis court and the picnic area.

The tennis court occupies 18 out of 100 squares. That's 18% of the park. The picnic area occupies 8 out of 100 squares. That's 8% of the park.

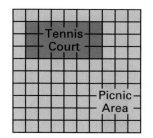

To compare ratios with different denominators, you can write each ratio with a denominator of 100. Then compare the percents.

▶ **History Link**

Percents used to be written as fractions, with the numerators over 100. Gradually, the bar of the fraction and the 100 blended together to become the percent sign we use today.

Example 2

Little brown bats spend about $\frac{11}{20}$ of their hibernation period in light sleep and about $\frac{2}{5}$ in a state of complete inactivity called "deep torpor." Use percents to compare the amount of time spent in each type of hibernation.

$$\frac{11}{20} = \frac{11 \times 5}{20 \times 5} = \frac{55}{100} = 55\%$$

Rewrite both fractions with denominators of 100.

$$\frac{2}{5} = \frac{2 \times 20}{5 \times 20} = \frac{40}{100} = 40\%$$

During hibernation, little brown bats are in light sleep about 55% of the time and in deep torpor about 40% of the time. They spend more of their time in light sleep.

▶ **Science Link**

Bats are the only mammals that can truly fly. The "flying" squirrel really only glides from tree to tree, using membranes attached to its legs.

Try It

Use percents to compare.

a. $\frac{1}{2}$ and $\frac{3}{5}$ **b.** $\frac{7}{10}$ and $\frac{3}{4}$ **c.** $\frac{13}{20}$ and $\frac{16}{25}$

Check Your Understanding

1. If all the squares on a grid are shaded, what percent of them are shaded?

2. What percent of the votes in an election would guarantee a win? Explain.

Practice and Apply

1. **Getting Started** Follow these steps to write $\frac{7}{25}$ as a percent.

a. *Percent* means "out of 100," so you need to write a fraction equal to $\frac{7}{25}$ with a denominator of 100. What number do you need to multiply 25 by to get 100?

b. Use your answer to **a** to rewrite $\frac{7}{25}$ with a denominator of 100.

c. Write the numerator of your fraction in **b** with a percent sign.

Express each fraction as a percent.

2. $\frac{47}{100}$ **3.** $\frac{75}{100}$ **4.** $\frac{25.5}{100}$ **5.** $\frac{48.3}{100}$ **6.** $\frac{8}{10}$

7. $\frac{15}{20}$ **8.** $\frac{4}{25}$ **9.** $\frac{13.5}{100}$ **10.** $\frac{2}{5}$ **11.** $\frac{3.2}{4}$

Number Sense Use percents to compare.

12. $\frac{6}{20}$ and $\frac{3}{10}$ **13.** $\frac{11}{25}$ and $\frac{1}{2}$ **14.** $\frac{1}{4}$ and $\frac{6}{25}$ **15.** $\frac{3}{4}$ and $\frac{4}{5}$ **16.** $\frac{7}{10}$ and $\frac{18}{25}$

Use percents to compare the shaded areas on each grid.

17.

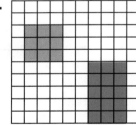

18.

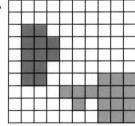

19.

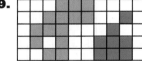

20. **Fine Arts** M. C. Escher was a Dutch artist who made many prints using interlocking figures called *tessellations*. About what percent of the Escher print shown is made up of black bats?

Measurement There are 100 cm in a meter. Express each length as a percent of a meter.

21. 1 cm   **22.** 50 cm   **23.** 63 cm

24. 37.5 cm   **25.** 100 cm   **26.** 20.1 cm

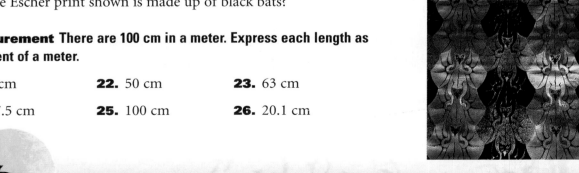

PRACTICE 8-1

Consumer Express each amount of money as a percent of a dollar.

27. A penny   **28.** Two nickels   **29.** Four quarters   **30.** Three dimes and a nickel

31. ▮Test Prep▮ Which percent is equal to $\frac{15}{25}$?

Ⓐ 4%   Ⓑ 15%   Ⓒ 25%   Ⓓ 60%

Problem Solving and Reasoning

32. Critical Thinking About 70% of all species of bats eat insects. About what percent of bat species do *not* eat insects? Explain how you found your answer.

33. ▮Journal▮ In 1972, the 26th Amendment to the Constitution lowered the voting age from 21 to 18. In 1968, 3 out of 5 eligible voters voted. This ratio is called the *voter turnout*. In 1972, voter turnout changed to 11 out of 20 eligible voters.

a. Use percents to compare the voter turnouts for these elections.

b. Explain why allowing 18- to 20-year-olds to vote might have affected the voter turnout in this way. Then give another possible explanation for the change in voter turnout.

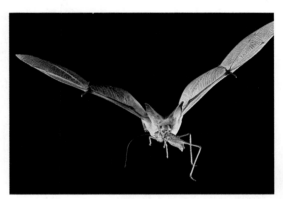

Pallid bat

34. Critical Thinking Although some bats living in the United States migrate during the cold months of the year, other bats spend the winter hibernating in caves. Most bats in the United States hibernate from early October until the end of April. What percent of the year is this?

Mixed Review

Write each decimal as a fraction in lowest terms. *[Lesson 3-10]*

35. 0.352   **36.** 0.15   **37.** 0.5505   **38.** 0.125   **39.** 0.6125

Write each fraction as a decimal. *[Lesson 3-10]*

40. $\frac{3}{7}$ **41.** $\frac{3}{8}$ **42.** $\frac{7}{10}$ **43.** $\frac{23}{50}$ **44.** $\frac{6}{17}$ **45.** $\frac{32}{96}$

Use the measurements to find the scale of each map. *[Lesson 7-1]*

46. A 40 mi road is 8 cm long.   **47.** A 50 m pool is 2.5 cm long.

48. A 2.7 mi lake is 1.5 in. long.   **49.** A 100 ft building is 5 in. wide.

Linking Fractions, Decimals, and Percents

▶ **Lesson Link** You've seen that percents are ratios. Now you'll look at relationships among percents, fractions, and decimals. ◄

Explore | Fractions, Decimals, and Percents

Making Sense of Percents

1. Copy the table. Use the patterns in the first two columns to complete the table.

Fraction	$\frac{91}{100}$	$\frac{23}{100}$	$\frac{67}{100}$			$\frac{11}{50}$		
Decimal	0.91	0.23		0.39			0.12	
Percent	91%	23%			87%			80%

2. Explain how you can write a two-digit decimal such as 0.91 as a percent.

3. Explain how you can write a percent as a fraction.

Learn | Linking Fractions, Decimals, and Percents

You can use the fact that *percent* means "out of 100" to rewrite a percent as a fraction.

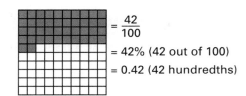

$= \frac{42}{100}$

= 42% (42 out of 100)

= 0.42 (42 hundredths)

Example 1

About 30% of the tree species in the world's tropical regions are pollinated by bats. Rewrite 30% as a fraction.

$30\% = \frac{30}{100}$ Write the percent as a fraction using 100 as the denominator.

$= \frac{3}{10}$ Rewrite the fraction in lowest terms.

Notice that 0.42 and 42% both mean "42 hundredths." Since the *second* place to the right of the decimal point is the hundredths place, you can rewrite decimals and percents by moving the decimal point *two* places.

$$42.\% = 0.42.$$
$$42\% = 0.42$$
$$0.42 = .42.\%$$
$$0.42 = 42\%$$

Examples

2 Write 0.63 as a percent.

To write a decimal as a percent, move the decimal point two places to the *right*.

$$0.63 = 63\%$$

3 In 1996, about 7.2% of the people living in the United States were between the ages of 10 and 14. Write 7.2% as a decimal.

To write a percent as a decimal, move the decimal point two places to the *left*. Annex zeros as needed.

$$7.2\% = 0.07.2$$

$$7.2\% = 0.072$$

Remember

If you know percent names for key fractions, you can use mental math to find the percent names for many others.

$\frac{1}{100} = 1\%$ $\frac{1}{10} = 10\%$

$\frac{1}{5} = 20\%$ $\frac{1}{4} = 25\%$

$\frac{1}{3} = 33\frac{1}{3}\%$ $\frac{1}{2} = 50\%$

[Previous Course]

You've used division to rewrite fractions in decimal form. By taking one more step, you can also rewrite a fraction as a percent.

Example 4

Little brown bats flap their wings about $\frac{3}{4}$ as fast as pipistrelle bats do. Write the fraction as a decimal and as a percent.

$\frac{3}{4} = 3 \div 4 = 0.75$ Use division to rewrite the fraction as a decimal.

$= 75\%$ Write the decimal as a percent.

Little brown bat

Try It

a. Write 54% as a fraction.

b. Write 0.91 as a percent.

c. Write $\frac{3}{5}$ as a percent.

d. Write 0.135 as a percent.

Check | Your Understanding

1. What are two ways to write 0.47 as a percent? Explain each method.

2. Describe two ways you could rewrite $\frac{23}{50}$ as a percent. Explain each method.

Practice and Apply

1. **Getting Started** Follow these steps to write $\frac{3}{16}$ as a percent.

   a. Write $\frac{3}{16}$ as a decimal by dividing 3 by 16.

   b. Rewrite your answer to **a** as a percent by moving the decimal point two places to the right.

Write each percent as a decimal.

2. 60%   **3.** 75%   **4.** 30%   **5.** 5%   **6.** 1%

7. 100%   **8.** 8.9%   **9.** 14.3%   **10.** 25.5%   **11.** $47\frac{1}{2}\%$

Write each percent as a fraction in lowest terms.

12. 50%   **13.** 20%   **14.** 30%   **15.** 85%   **16.** 98%

17. 55%   **18.** 65%   **19.** 28%   **20.** 12.5 %   **21.** 37.5%

Write each decimal as a percent.

22. 0.86   **23.** 0.08   **24.** 0.1   **25.** 0.875   **26.** 1.0

Write each fraction as a percent. Where necessary, use a repeating decimal to help express your percent.

27. $\frac{1}{2}$ **28.** $\frac{3}{4}$ **29.** $\frac{4}{9}$ **30.** $\frac{1}{4}$ **31.** $\frac{4}{5}$

32. $\frac{3}{8}$ **33.** $\frac{9}{20}$ **34.** $\frac{8.5}{25}$ **35.** $\frac{6.2}{40}$ **36.** $\frac{7}{9}$

37. **Estimation** The 1920 U.S. Census found the United States population to be about 106.02 million. Indiana had a population of about 2.93 million. Estimate the percent of the United States population that lived in Indiana.

38. **Science** Each fall, volunteers pick up trash from beaches around the United States. The table shows each kind of trash they find and the percent of total trash it represents. Express each percent as a fraction and as a decimal.

1920
106.02 million

INDIANA
2.93
million

Kind of Trash	Plastic	Glass	Metal	Paper	Other
Percent of Total	59%	12%	11%	11%	7%

39. **Test Prep** What percent is exactly equal to $\frac{1}{3}$?

Ⓐ 30%   Ⓑ 33%   Ⓒ $33\frac{1}{3}$%   Ⓓ 34%

Problem Solving and Reasoning

40. Critical Thinking Many bats hibernate during the winter. A wide-awake bat may breathe 200 times per minute; a hibernating bat may breathe 23 times per minute. The bat's normal heart rate of 400 beats per minute often slows to about 25 beats per minute during hibernation. Express the breathing rate and heart rate of a hibernating bat as fractions, decimals, and percents of the corresponding rates for an active bat.

Tent bat

41. Communicate In a 1 oz. serving of a brand of "reduced fat" potato chips, 54 of the 130 calories come from fat. The Department of Agriculture recommends that no more than 30% of the calories we take in come from fat. Does this brand of chips meet this recommendation? Explain. If this brand does not meet the recommendation, explain how it can be labeled "reduced fat."

42. Critical Thinking Seventeen of the 42 species of bats found in the United States are on the endangered species list. What percent of the species of bats found in the United States are endangered? Round your answer to the nearest percent.

Mixed Review

Estimate each sum or difference. *[Lesson 4-1]*

43. $\frac{4}{9} + \frac{3}{7}$ **44.** $\frac{4}{5} - \frac{1}{3}$ **45.** $\frac{7}{8} - \frac{1}{9}$ **46.** $\frac{1}{14} + \frac{1}{5}$ **47.** $\frac{3}{7} + \frac{1}{8}$

48. $\frac{3}{20} - \frac{9}{100}$ **49.** $\frac{5}{8} - \frac{1}{6}$ **50.** $\frac{2}{3} + \frac{3}{11}$ **51.** $\frac{4}{15} + \frac{1}{9}$ **52.** $\frac{7}{9} + \frac{6}{17}$

Solve for *x* in each proportion. *[Lesson 7-2]*

53. $\frac{3 \text{ in.}}{12 \text{ mi}} = \frac{x}{100 \text{ mi}}$ **54.** $\frac{4.2 \text{ cm}}{17 \text{ km}} = \frac{8 \text{ cm}}{x}$ **55.** $\frac{x}{40 \text{ mi}} = \frac{5 \text{ in.}}{250 \text{ mi}}$

56. $\frac{x}{7 \text{ ft}} = \frac{8 \text{ in.}}{14 \text{ ft}}$ **57.** $\frac{22 \text{ mm}}{x} = \frac{11 \text{ mm}}{125 \text{ m}}$ **58.** $\frac{42 \text{ cm}}{1 \text{ km}} = \frac{28 \text{ cm}}{x}$

59. $\frac{x}{14 \text{ cm}} = \frac{7.5 \text{ mm}}{2 \text{ cm}}$ **60.** $\frac{1 \text{ ft}}{25 \text{ mi}} = \frac{12 \text{ ft}}{x}$ **61.** $\frac{0.1 \text{ mm}}{5 \text{ km}} = \frac{2.2 \text{ mm}}{x}$

Percents Greater than 100 or Less than 1

You'll Learn ...

■ to use percents that are less than 1%

■ to use percents that are greater than 100%

... How It's Used

Home buyers pay close attention to changes of fractions of a percent in interest rates. The higher the interest rate is, the more money they'll pay on their mortgage each month.

▶ **Lesson Link** │ The percents you've used so far range from 1% to 100%. Now you'll use percents that are less than 1% and greater than 100%. ◀

Explore │ Large and Small Percents

Materials: Graph paper

Made in the Shade

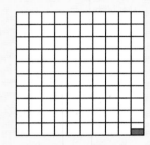

1. Draw a 10-by-10 grid. What percent of the grid does one square represent?

2. Shade half a square. How many half-squares can fit on a grid? What fraction compares one half-square with the total number of half-squares?

3. What percent of a 10-by-10 grid does a half-square represent?

4. Using two grids, shade 120 squares. What percent of one 10-by-10 grid do the squares represent?

5. If you shade *less than one square* on a 10-by-10 grid, what can you say about the percent you have shaded? If you shade *more than one complete grid*, what can you say about the percent?

Learn │ Percents Greater than 100 or Less than 1

Suppose that, during the first hour of feeding, a little brown bat ate 400 insects.

During the second hour, it ate 600 insects, 150% of the number eaten during the first.

During the third hour, it ate 1 insect, $\frac{1}{4}$% of the number eaten during the first.

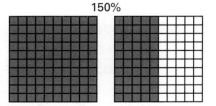

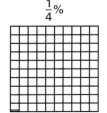

1 square = 4 insects

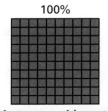

You can express a percent that is less than 1% or greater than 100% as a decimal and as a fraction.

Examples

1 Write 0.3% as a decimal and as a fraction.

To rewrite a percent as a decimal, move the decimal point two places to the left. Annex zeros as needed.

$$0.3\% = 0.00.3$$

$$0.3\% = 0.003$$

To rewrite as a fraction:

$0.3\% = \dfrac{0.3}{100}$ Rewrite with a denominator of 100.

$= \dfrac{0.3 \times 10}{100 \times 10}$ Rewrite the numerator as a whole number.

$= \dfrac{3}{1000}$ Simplify.

2 Write 140% as a decimal and as a fraction.

To rewrite a percent as a decimal, move the decimal point two places to the left.

$$140\% = 1.40 = 1.4$$

To rewrite as a fraction:

$140\% = \dfrac{140}{100}$ Rewrite with a denominator of 100.

$= \dfrac{140 \div 20}{100 \div 20}$ To rewrite in lowest terms, divide by the GCF of 140 and 100.

$= \dfrac{7}{5}$, or $1\dfrac{2}{5}$ Simplify.

You may be able to use mental math to rewrite decimals or fractions as percents.

Example 3

A large flying fox bat eats about 2.5 times its weight in fruit each night. Write 2.5 as a percent.

Think: 100% = the flying fox's weight.

So $2.5 = 2.5 \times 100\% = 250\%$.

Flying fox bat

Try It

Write as a fraction and as a decimal.   **a.** 0.4%   **b.** 125%

Remember

You can find the greatest common factor of two numbers by listing all the factors of each and finding the greatest factor that is in both lists. **[Page 139]**

WHAT DO YOU THINK?

Not many species of bats live on islands. There are about 1000 species of bats, but only one of them is native to Hawaii. Lorena and Brett need to know what percent of the species of bats are native to Hawaii.

Lorena thinks ...

I'll write the ratio as a fraction. One out of 1000 = $\frac{1}{1000}$. If I divide the numerator and denominator by 10, the fraction will be out of 100:

$$\frac{1 \div 10}{1000 \div 10} = \frac{0.1}{100}$$

So 0.1% of the species of bats are native to Hawaii.

Brett thinks ...

I'll use my calculator to put the ratio into decimal form: $1 \div 1000 = 0.001$. To rewrite this number as a percent, I move the decimal point two places to the right.

So 0.1% of the species of bats are native to Hawaii.

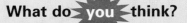

What do you think?

1. Why did Lorena divide the numerator and denominator of her fraction by 10?

2. How else could Brett have known that $1 \div 1000$ equals 0.001?

3. How else could you solve this problem?

Check | Your Understanding

1. A soccer coach said, "To win this game, you've got to give 110%." What did the coach mean?

2. Compare the numerator and denominator of a fraction that is greater than 100%.

3. How can you decide whether a decimal is less than 1%? More than 100%? Give an example for each case.

Practice and Apply

1. **Getting Started** Follow these steps to write 0.8% as a fraction.

   a. Rewrite 0.8% as a fraction with a denominator of 100.

   b. Rewrite the fraction as an equivalent fraction with a whole number numerator.

   c. If necessary, simplify the fraction.

Number Sense Classify each fraction or decimal as: (A) less than 1%, (B) greater than 100%, or (C) between 1% and 100%.

2. $\frac{240}{100}$ **3.** $\frac{1}{200}$ **4.** $\frac{1}{4}$ **5.** $\frac{3}{2}$ **6.** $\frac{4}{1000}$

7. 0.75 **8.** 1.05 **9.** 0.0001 **10.** 0.015 **11.** 3.0001

Number Sense Use >, <, or = to compare the numbers in each pair.

12. 3 ☐ 300% **13.** 9% ☐ 0.009 **14.** $\frac{1}{5}$ ☐ 20% **15.** 0.5% ☐ 0.05 **16.** 1.5 ☐ 95%

Write each fraction as a percent.

17. $\frac{0.3}{1000}$ **18.** $\frac{105}{100}$ **19.** $\frac{350}{100}$ **20.** $\frac{\frac{1}{3}}{100}$ **21.** $\frac{13}{10}$

22. $\frac{90}{10}$ **23.** $\frac{70}{25}$ **24.** $\frac{13}{20}$ **25.** $\frac{1}{125}$ **26.** $\frac{5}{4}$

Write each decimal as a percent.

27. 0.007 **28.** 5.0 **29.** 0.00125 **30.** 3.015 **31.** 0.0604

Write each percent as a decimal.

32. 0.1% **33.** 125% **34.** 1000% **35.** $\frac{1}{5}$% **36.** $\frac{3}{4}$%

37. $6\frac{1}{2}$% **38.** 205% **39.** $\frac{3}{8}$% **40.** 0.43% **41.** 0.0067%

42. **Science** Of the approximately 1000 species of bats, only 3 are vampire bats—bats that feed on the blood of living animals. About what percent of bat species are vampire bats?

43. **Problem Solving** In 1993, there were 1,316,291 dogs registered with the American Kennel Club in the top 50 breeds. Of those, 3,519 were Schipperkes. What percent of the dogs were Schipperkes?

Common vampire bat

44. Geography The world's total land area is about 57.9 million square miles. Luxembourg has an area of 999 square miles. What percent of the world's total land area does Luxembourg occupy?

45. **Test Prep** The decimal 0.0125 is equal to what fraction and what percent?

Ⓐ $\frac{1}{8}$; 1.25%   Ⓑ $\frac{1}{80}$; 1.25%

Ⓒ $\frac{1}{125}$; 125%   Ⓓ $\frac{1}{12.5}$; 12.5%

Problem Solving and Reasoning

46. Choose a Strategy A small percent of bats carries rabies—generally about $\frac{1}{2}$%. In how large a group of bats would you expect to find exactly one bat carrying rabies? Explain how you found your answer.

47. **Journal** Write a step-by-step explanation of how you can write a percent as a decimal and as a fraction. Explain why each method works.

48. Critical Thinking Eagle Creek Cave in Arizona once housed what was probably the largest bat colony ever to exist in the United States. About 30 million Mexican free-tailed bats lived in this cave in 1963. Because of vandalism and other disturbances, only 30,000 bats remain. What percent of the 1963 population lives in Eagle Creek Cave today?

Problem Solving
STRATEGIES

• Look for a Pattern
• Make an Organized List
• Make a Table
• Guess and Check
• Work Backward
• Use Logical Reasoning
• Draw a Diagram
• Solve a Simpler Problem

Mexican free-tailed bat

Mixed Review

Find each sum or difference. Rewrite in lowest terms. *[Lesson 4-2]*

49. $\frac{2}{3} + \frac{1}{4}$ **50.** $\frac{3}{5} - \frac{1}{7}$ **51.** $\frac{1}{4} + \frac{4}{9}$ **52.** $\frac{5}{8} - \frac{3}{11}$ **53.** $\frac{4}{7} + \frac{1}{3}$

54. $\frac{3}{5} + \frac{1}{7}$ **55.** $\frac{2}{13} - \frac{1}{39}$ **56.** $\frac{12}{13} + \frac{1}{5}$ **57.** $\frac{2}{5} - \frac{1}{30}$ **58.** $\frac{23}{24} + \frac{1}{2}$

Elena leaves her house at 2:30 P.M. to visit Mio. Mio lives 2.5 miles away. Find the time Elena will arrive using each method of transportation. *[Lesson 7-3]*

59. Walking at 3 mi/hr   **60.** Jogging at 6.5 mi/hr   **61.** Bicycling at 10 mi/hr

Finding a Percent of a Number Mentally

▶ **Lesson Link** You've learned the meaning of percent. Now you'll use mental math to find an exact percent of a number and to estimate a percent.◀

Explore   Finding Percents

Waiter, There's a Bat in My Soup!

When you eat at a restaurant, you usually *tip* the waiter. Tips are figured as a percent of the total bill. The better the service, the bigger the tip.

Tipping Guide

Service	Tip
Excellent	20%
Average	15%
Below Average	10%
Poor	5%

1. What fraction in lowest terms is equal to 10%?

2. Use this fraction and mental math to calculate the tip you would leave for below-average service if your bill were $40. Explain how you calculated the tip.

3. How can you mentally calculate a tip for excellent service? For poor service? What tip would you leave on a bill of $60 for these types of service?

4. What tip would you leave for average service on a bill of $30? Explain.

5. Diners often round their bill to a convenient number before calculating the tip. For a bill of $46.97, estimate the tip you would leave for each type of service.

You'll Learn ...

■ to use estimation and mental math to find a percent of a number

... How It's Used

Salespeople need to find percents quickly to determine discounts.

Learn   Finding a Percent of a Number Mentally

You can use percents such as 50%, 10%, and 1% to find other percents mentally.

50% of a number is $\frac{1}{2}$ of the number, which means $\frac{1}{2}$ *times* the number.

10% of a number is $\frac{1}{10}$ of the number.   1% of a number is $\frac{1}{100}$ of the number.

10% of 270 = 27.0 or 27   **1% of 270 = 2.70 or 2.7**

Decimal point moves one to the left.   Decimal point moves two to the left.

Examples

1 Use mental math to find 60% of 480.

Think: 60% equals 50% + 10%.

50% (half) of 480 is 240. 10% (one-tenth) of 480 is 48.

So 60% of 480 is 240 + 48 = 288.

2 The normal heart rate of a little brown bat is **400 beats per minute.** During hibernation, the heart rate falls to about **5% of normal.** Use mental math to find the hibernation heart rate.

Think: 10% of 400 is 40. So 5% of 400 must be half of 40, or 20.

The hibernation heart rate is about 20 beats per minute.

Little brown bats

3 Using mental math, estimate 68% of 612.

Think: 68% is close to 70%. 612 is close to 600.

Think: 70% of a number is 7 times 10% of the number.

10% of 600 is 60.

So 68% of 612 is about 7 times 60 or 420.

4 A restaurant bill was $42. Find the tip for average service.

The usual tip for average service is 15%.

Think: 15% is 10% plus 5%. 5% is half of 10%.

10% of $42.00 is $4.20. 5% is half of that, or $2.10.

So 15% of $42.00 is $4.20 + $2.10 = $6.30.

Try It

Use mental math to find each percent.

a. 50% of 6   **b.** 20% of 80   **c.** 5% of 300   **d.** 90% of 500

Check Your Understanding

1. Explain how you can calculate 15% of a number mentally.

2. Is 35% of 55 the same as 55% of 35? Explain.

Practice and Apply

1. **Getting Started** Follow these steps to find 15% of 34,000 mentally.
   a. Find 10% of 34,000 by moving the decimal point one place to the left.
   b. Take half of your answer to **a**.
   c. Add your answers from **a** and **b**.

Find 50%, 10%, and 1% of each number.

2. 27,000   3. 5800   4. 120   5. 244   6. 73

Number Sense Use mental math to find each percent of 8,200.

7. 15%   8. 5%   9. 70%   10. 25%   11. 40%   12. 90%

Use mental math to find each percent.

13. 25% of 500   14. 10% of $40   15. 80% of $70   16. 30% of 600   17. 5% of 2100

18. 15% of $8.00   19. 60% of 400   20. 90% of 240   21. 5% of 700   22. 15% of $22.00

Estimation Estimate each percent.

23. 10% of 39   24. 48% of 58   25. 15% of 79.7   26. 91% of 198   27. 22% of 9896

28. **Science** Only 3% of what were originally 8,000,000 Mexican free-tailed bats are now living in Carlsbad Caverns in New Mexico. How many Mexican free-tailed bats are now living in Carlsbad Caverns? (*Hint:* First find 1% of the original number of bats.)

29. **Test Prep** Choose the expression that would best help you estimate 47% of 237.
    Ⓐ 40% of 237
    Ⓑ 40% of 240
    Ⓒ 50% of 240
    Ⓓ 50% of 250

Mexican free-tailed bats, Carlsbad Caverns

Problem Solving and Reasoning

30. **Critical Thinking** In 1993, the world's population was approximately 5.5 billion people. About 15% spoke Mandarin Chinese as their primary language, about 6% spoke Hindi, and about 2% spoke German. Use mental math to find the number of native speakers of each language.

31. **Communicate** A female Mexican free-tailed bat living in Texas usually produces one baby, called a *pup*, per year. A large colony of these bats can have 4,000,000 pups.

a. One year, 50% of the pups were eaten by predators or died during the migration to Mexico. How many pups died? How many survived?

b. 25% of the remaining pups died during the winter or on the return migration in the spring. How many of these pups died? How many returned to Texas?

c. What percent of the original 4,000,000 pups returned to Texas? Explain how you solved this problem.

Bat pups in leaf

32. **Critical Thinking** People in the United States eat about 1.6 billion (1,600,000,000) gallons of ice cream each year. About 30% of this ice cream is vanilla, about 10% is chocolate, and about 5% is chocolate chip.

a. Use mental math to find the number of gallons sold for each flavor.

b. There are about 260 million people in the United States. On the average, how many gallons of vanilla ice cream does each one eat in a year?

Mixed Review

Evaluate each expression. *[Lesson 5-6]*

33. 16^2 **34.** 12^2 **35.** 23^2 **36.** 100^2 **37.** 1^2

38. $\sqrt{49}$ **39.** $\sqrt{484}$ **40.** $\sqrt{\frac{1}{4}}$ **41.** $\sqrt{361}$ **42.** $\sqrt{324}$

43. The island of Puerto Rico measures about 100 miles from east to west and 32 miles from north to south. What is the largest scale that can be used to fit a map of Puerto Rico on an $8\frac{1}{2}$ in. by 14 in. sheet of paper if the 14 in. side runs east-west? *[Lesson 7-4]*

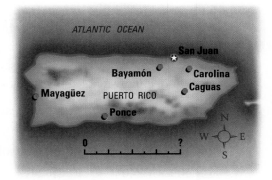

Project Progress

Make a table of the items on your picnic list. Have a column that lists the total cost for each item, and add up the costs. Make a bar graph that shows the percent of the total cost that each item represents.

Problem Solving

Understand
Plan
Solve
Look Back

In this section, you've learned how to find a percent of a number mentally. You've also linked percents, fractions, and decimals. Now you'll use these skills to learn more about the Mexican free-tailed bat.

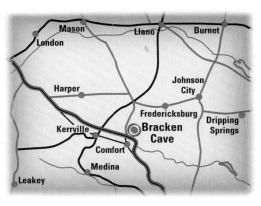

To the Batcave!

Materials: Inch ruler

1. The photo shows a swarm of Mexican free-tailed bats leaving Bracken Cave to feed near Comfort, Texas. Estimate the percent of the photo covered by bats.

2. If this photo were completely filled with bats, it might show about 1000 bats. Estimate the number of bats in the photo.

3. Bracken Cave has the largest concentration of bats in the world. Twenty million adult female bats live in the cave. About what percent of the bats in the cave are shown in the photo?

4. Bats arrive at the cave in early spring after migrating 1500 miles from Mexico. On their nightly feeding flights, they fly up to 3% of this migration distance from the cave. Using the map, find the town farthest from the cave that a bat could reach in one night.

Scale: 1 in. = 40 mi

403

Number Sense Write each fraction or decimal as a percent.

1. 0.17   **2.** $\frac{14}{50}$ **3.** $\frac{6}{20}$ **4.** $\frac{23}{25}$ **5.** $\frac{17.9}{25}$

6. $\frac{7}{100}$ **7.** $\frac{3}{5}$ **8.** $\frac{35}{25}$ **9.** $\frac{456}{1000}$ **10.** $\frac{5}{1000}$

11. 0.89   **12.** 0.04   **13.** 0.498   **14.** 0.0001   **15.** 3.07

16. Science "Maternity" caves may contain thousands of baby bats. Scientists know about 21 out of every 25 mother bats can identify their baby bats, or pups, from among thousands of similar bats. About what percent of mother bats identify their pups? About what percent do not?

Number Sense Write each percent as a decimal.

17. 30%   **18.** 6%   **19.** 423%   **20.** 1050%   **21.** 0.1%

Write each percent as a fraction in lowest terms.

22. 25%   **23.** 70%   **24.** 92%   **25.** 306%   **26.** 0.5%

Use mental math to find each percent.

27. 10% of 850   **28.** 50% of 2468   **29.** 15% of $36   **30.** 80% of 140   **31.** 5% of 6100

32. Estimation Many species of bats have "nose leaves." These may aid in locating prey by sensing sound waves reflected from the prey to the bats' noses. Other species have plain noses. If there are 355 species of plain-nosed bats and a total of 986 species, estimate the percent of plain-nosed bat species.

33. In your own words, explain how you can use mental math to find a percent of a number.

Honduran white bat

Test Prep

When you're asked to find a percent on a multiple choice test, using mental math can help you work more quickly.

34. What is 1% of $700?

    Ⓐ $7.00   Ⓑ $70,000   Ⓒ $0.07   Ⓓ $0.70

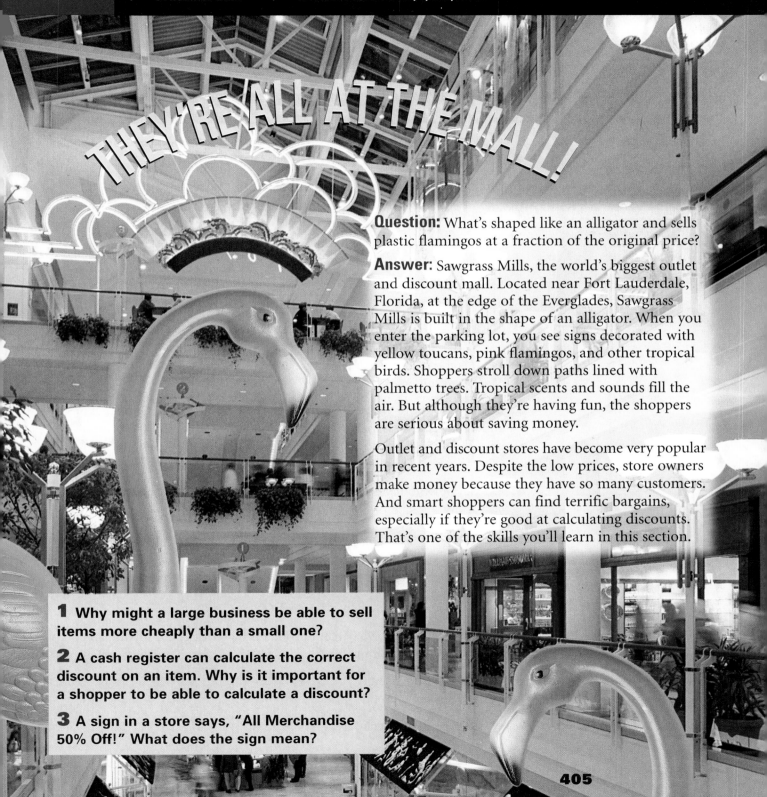

THEY'RE ALL AT THE MALL!

Question: What's shaped like an alligator and sells plastic flamingos at a fraction of the original price?

Answer: Sawgrass Mills, the world's biggest outlet and discount mall. Located near Fort Lauderdale, Florida, at the edge of the Everglades, Sawgrass Mills is built in the shape of an alligator. When you enter the parking lot, you see signs decorated with yellow toucans, pink flamingos, and other tropical birds. Shoppers stroll down paths lined with palmetto trees. Tropical scents and sounds fill the air. But although they're having fun, the shoppers are serious about saving money.

Outlet and discount stores have become very popular in recent years. Despite the low prices, store owners make money because they have so many customers. And smart shoppers can find terrific bargains, especially if they're good at calculating discounts. That's one of the skills you'll learn in this section.

1 Why might a large business be able to sell items more cheaply than a small one?

2 A cash register can calculate the correct discount on an item. Why is it important for a shopper to be able to calculate a discount?

3 A sign in a store says, "All Merchandise 50% Off!" What does the sign mean?

405

Using Equations to Solve Percent Problems

You'll Learn ...

■ to use equations to solve problems involving percents

... How It's Used

People working at oil refineries make gasolines by mixing percents of different chemical compounds.

▶ **Lesson Link** You've used models, fractions, and decimals to solve percent problems. Now you'll use equations to solve problems involving percents. ◀

Explore | Percent Equations

Think Snow!

Materials: Graph paper

It hasn't snowed for weeks, and the S'No Joke Mall is having a sale!

1. Mogulrider snowboards now sell for $40, which is 80% of the regular price. Explain how the grids show the regular price and the sale price of a Mogulrider.

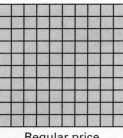
Regular price

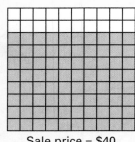
Sale price = $40

2. What is the value of each square? What is the regular price of Mogulriders? How do you know?

3. Crisis! Two more weeks of warm weather! The prices of Slippenslider snowboards are *slashed!* The new price of $48 is 60% of the original price. Use grids to show the regular price and the sale price of a Slippenslider. Then find the regular price of the board.

4. Explain how you can use grids to find the original price of an item if you know the sale price and the percent off.

Learn | Using Equations to Solve Percent Problems

Sometimes it's easiest to solve percent problems by writing and solving an equation. Here are two helpful hints for translating percent problems into equations.

• Remember that *of* usually means *times*.

• Rewrite percents as decimals.

What number is 25% of 200?

x = 0.25 · 200

x = 50

Example 1

What percent of 48 is 15?

Let p = the percent.   Choose a variable.

p percent of 48 is 15.   Reword the statement.

$\quad p \cdot 48 = 15$ Translate to an equation.

$\quad \dfrac{p \cdot 48}{48} = \dfrac{15}{48}$ Use inverse operations.

$p = 0.3125 = 31.25\%$ Divide. Write the decimal as a percent.

15 is 31.25% of 48.

Remember

When you convert a decimal to a percent, move the decimal point two places to the right.
[Page 391]

A percent *discount* describes how much you save off the original price. The percent of the original price you pay is 100% minus the percent discount.

Example 2

A Fats Domino CD is on sale at Disk Cellar at a 35% discount. The sale price is $8.06. Find the regular price.

The new price is 100% − 35% = 65% of the original price.

Let r = the regular price.

$8.06 is 65% of the regular price.

$\quad 8.06 = 0.65 \cdot r$

$\quad \dfrac{8.06}{0.65} = \dfrac{0.65r}{0.65}$

$\quad 12.40 = r$

The regular price is $12.40.

Try It

a. What percent of 120 is 36?   **b.** 12% of what number is 9?

▶ **Music Link**

Fats Domino was one of the most important rock-and-roll musicians of the 1950s. His records, which included "Blueberry Hill" and "Ain't That a Shame," sold over 65 million copies. Domino was named to the Rock and Roll Hall of Fame in 1986.

Check Your Understanding

1. Do the questions "What is 20% of 40?", "20 is what percent of 40?", and "20 is 40% of what number?" mean the same thing? Explain.

2. Write a percent problem you would solve using mental math. Write another you would use an equation to solve. Explain your thinking.

Practice and Apply

1. **Getting Started** Follow these steps to find the regular price of an item that sells for $25.20, which is 60% of the regular price.

   a. Choose a variable for the regular price.

   b. Reword the problem using the following format: _____ is _____ percent of the regular price.

   c. Translate the problem to an equation.

   d. Use the inverse operation.

   e. Solve for the variable. State the regular price of the item.

Solve each problem. If necessary, round answers to the nearest tenth.

2. What percent of 78 is 39?

3. What percent of 70 is 22?

4. 55% of 985 is what number?

5. 9% of 600 is what number?

6. 30% of what number is 45?

7. 11% of what number is 36?

8. What percent of 72 is 67?

9. 95% of 40 is what number?

10. 240% of 58 is what number?

11. 89% of what number is 178?

12. What percent of 780 is 3.9?

13. 0.1% of what number is 12?

14. **Logic** In the following sentence, fill in the blanks with numbers so that the answer is greater than 100 percent.

    What percent of _____ is _____?

15. **Consumer** Superplex Cinemas give students a 25% discount off the regular ticket price of $7.00.

    a. What percent of the regular price is the student price?

    b. What is the student ticket price?

16. **Social Studies** A student at West Milford High School, in New Jersey, was concerned because food in the school cafeteria was served on plastic foam trays rather than recyclable paper trays. She polled students to see if they would pay 5¢ extra for paper trays. Of those students, 85% responded that they would be willing to pay the extra nickel. If 480 students were polled, how many were willing to pay extra for paper trays?

17. Consumer Two candle stores are having a sale. Advertisements for Cut-Rate Candles say, "At Least 10% Off All Candles!" Flyers for Wick World say, "Up to 75% Off All Candles!" Which store is having the better sale? Explain.

18. Test Prep Which formula can be used to find 0.3% of 1829?

     Ⓐ 3×1829 Ⓑ 0.3×1829

     Ⓒ 0.03×1829 Ⓓ 0.003×1829

CANDLE SALE

Problem Solving and Reasoning

19. **Journal** The table gives data about U.S. physicians in 1994.

Physicians in the United States, 1994		
Sex	**Total**	**Under 35 Years Old**
Male	551,151	90,528
Female	133,263	43,204

  a. What percent of U.S. physicians in 1994 were women?

  b. What percent of U.S. physicians under 35 years old were women?

  c. Compare your answers to **a** and **b**. Make a prediction about the percent of female physicians in the future. Explain your reasoning.

20. Choose a Strategy Find all the whole-number percents of 182 that would equal a number less than 18. Explain how you found your answer.

21. Critical Thinking If 25% of a number is 45, is the number greater than or less than 45? If 150% of a number is 45, is the number greater than or less than 45? Explain how you can tell.

Problem Solving

STRATEGIES

- Look for a Pattern
- Make an Organized List
- Make a Table
- Guess and Check
- Work Backward
- Use Logical Reasoning
- Draw a Diagram
- Solve a Simpler Problem

Mixed Review

Determine if each triangle is a right triangle. *[Lesson 5-7]*

22.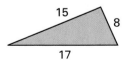
15   8   17

23.
26   10   24

24.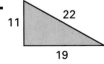
22   11   19

Number Sense Suggest appropriate units for each rate. *[Lesson 7-5]*

25. Your breathing rate   **26.** The price of potatoes   **27.** The speed of ketchup coming out of a bottle

Solving Percent Problems with Proportions

You'll Learn ...

■ to use proportions to solve percent problems

... How It's Used

Printers combined different percents of four basic colors to produce all the colors you see in this book.

▶ **Lesson Link** You've solved percent problems by solving equations. Now you'll use proportions to solve problems involving percents. ◄

Explore | Solving Percent Problems

Materials: Inch ruler, Graph paper

Attention, Shoppers!

The brochure lists the types of stores at Lakeside Mall.

1. What is the total number of stores at the mall?

2. Use an equation to find the percent of each type of store.

3. Draw a 10 unit by 10 unit square on graph paper. Your drawing will contain 100 squares.

4. Divide the large square into 5 regions that represent the percent of different types of stores. Label each region. Explain how you divided the square.

5. Write a fraction comparing the *number* of clothing stores to the total number of stores. Then rewrite the *percent* of stores that are clothing stores as a fraction. Are these fractions equal?

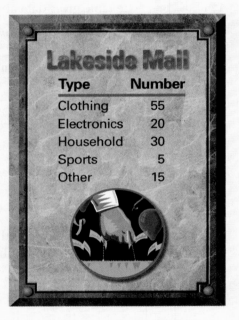

Lakeside Mall

Type	Number
Clothing	55
Electronics	20
Household	30
Sports	5
Other	15

Learn | Solving Percent Problems with Proportions

You know how to solve percent problems by using equations. However, it's sometimes easier to set up and solve these equations as proportions.

You can rewrite a percent as a fraction whose denominator is 100. This is one fraction in the proportion. The other comes from information in the problem.

Examples

1 What number is 47% of 280? Solve using a proportion.

Estimate: 47% is close to 50%, which is $\frac{1}{2}$. Half of 280 is 140. 47% of 280 should be a little less than 140.

Let n = the number.　　Choose a variable.

$\frac{47}{100} = \frac{n}{280}$　　Write a proportion.

$13{,}160 = 100n$　　Find the cross products.

$\frac{13{,}160}{100} = \frac{100n}{100}$　　Use inverse operations.

$131.6 = n$　　Divide.

131.6 is 47% of 280.

HINT

Many calculators have percent keys. To find 47% of 280 on a calculator, press 280 ⨯ 47 % = .

2 Sam chose a jacket from a "45% Off" rack. The original price was $35.00. When the clerk rang up the sale, the price, before tax, was $23.80. What percent discount did Sam get? Is this the correct discount?

The correct discount is 45%, so the sale price should be 100% − 45% = 55% of the original price.

Let p = the percent of the original price.　　Choose a variable.

$\frac{\text{sale price}}{\text{original price}} = \frac{p}{100}$　　Write a proportion.

$\frac{23.80}{35.00} = \frac{p}{100}$　　Substitute.

$2380 = 35p$　　Find the cross products.

$\frac{2380}{35} = \frac{35p}{35}$　　Use inverse operations.

$68 = p$　　Divide.

The sale price was 68% of the original price. Sam actually got a discount of 100% − 68% = 32%, which is less than the correct discount of 45%.

Test Prep

Be sure not to spend too much time on any one problem. When you're really stuck, go on to the next problem. You can return to the difficult problems later, after you solve the ones you feel confident about.

Try It

Solve using a proportion.

a. What number is 78% of 221?

b. If there are 16 girls in a class of 30, what percent of the students are girls?

Example 3

The largest shopping center in the United States is the Mall of America in Bloomington, Minnesota. The largest shopping center in the world is the West Edmonton Mall in Alberta, Canada.

The Mall of America has 350 stores. This is 43.75% of the number in the West Edmonton Mall. How many stores are there in the West Edmonton Mall?

West Edmonton Mall

Let e = number of stores in the West Edmonton Mall.   Choose a variable.

$$\frac{\text{Mall of America stores}}{\text{West Edmonton stores}} = \frac{43.75}{100}$$ Write a proportion.

$$\frac{350}{e} = \frac{43.75}{100}$$ Substitute.

$$35{,}000 = 43.75e$$ Find the cross products.

$$\frac{35{,}000}{43.75} = \frac{43.75e}{43.75}$$ Use inverse operations.

$$800 = e$$ Divide.

There are 800 stores in the West Edmonton Mall.

Try It

Solve using a proportion.

a. 41 is 25% of what number?

b. In 1988, there were about 735,000 African elephants. This was about 56% of the number of African elephants in 1979. How many African elephants were there in 1979?

Check Your Understanding

1. When you use a proportion to solve a percent problem, one of the four numbers is always the same. Which is it, and why is it always the same?

2. Juanita was using a proportion to find a percent of a number. She noticed that her proportion involved an improper fraction. If Juanita set up the proportion correctly, what does this tell you?

8-6 Exercises and Applications

Practice and Apply

1. **Getting Started** 52 is 38% of what number? Follow these steps to solve using a proportion.

    a. Choose a variable.

    b. Write a proportion involving 38% rewritten as a fraction.

    c. Multiply to find the cross products.

    d. Use the inverse operation.

    e. Solve for the variable. Round your answer to the nearest tenth.

Operation Sense Write a proportion and solve each problem. If necessary, round answers to the nearest tenth.

2. What number is 70% of 45?

3. What number is 23% of 75?

4. 45 is what percent of 90?

5. 7 is what percent of 77?

6. 15 is 25% of what number?

7. 43 is 18% of what number?

8. What number is 75% of 125?

9. 60 is what percent of 25?

10. 39 is 150% of what number?

11. 25 is what percent of 752?

12. 19 is 95% of what number?

13. What number is 0.5% of 490?

14. In part because of the popularity of outlet malls, about 300 of the 1800 traditional retail malls across the United States may close in the next few years. Find the percent of retail malls that may close.

15. **Science** The bee hummingbird is the smallest bird. It can weigh as little as 2 grams. The largest bird, the ostrich, can weigh as much as 150 kilograms. What percent of the weight of a bee hummingbird is the weight of an ostrich?

16. **Problem Solving** The U.S. Postal Service handles 170,000,000,000 pieces of mail each year. This is 40% of the world's total. How many pieces of mail are sent each year?

17. **Patterns** The fraction $\frac{1}{3}$ is equal to $33\frac{1}{3}$%. Name three other fractions that equal $33\frac{1}{3}$%.

18. **Problem Solving** A factory-outlet shoe store sells items at discounts ranging from 20% to 70%. If a pair of shoes that usually costs $45 is sold at a 25% discount, how much can you save by purchasing the shoes from this store?

19. **Statistics** The weight of a nickel is 80% of the weight of a quarter.

   a. If a nickel weighs 5 grams, how much does a quarter weigh?

   b. A dime weighs 50% as much as a nickel does. What is the weight of a dime?

20. **Test Prep** 25 is approximately what percent of 23?

   (A) 0.92%   (B) 1.1%   (C) 92%   (D) 109%

Problem Solving and Reasoning

21. **Critical Thinking** Tourists from Korea spend an average of $360 shopping when they travel abroad. Travelers from South Africa spend less—an average of $300 per person. Travelers from the United States average only about $190. Using percents, compare tourist spending for pairs of these countries. Report on all possible combinations.

22. **Journal** Describe two different ways to solve: "What number is 10% of 520?" Then explain which method seems to be the more efficient way to solve the problem.

Mixed Review

Find the missing measurements for the following triangles. *[Lesson 5-8]*

23. $b = ?, h = 14$ cm, $A = 70$ cm^2

24. $b = 4$ in., $h = 15$ in., $A = ?$

25. $b = 11$ m, $h = ?, A = 66$ m^2

26. $b = ?, h = 1$ ft, $A = 0.5$ ft^2

Convert each rate to an equivalent rate. *[Lesson 7-6]*

27. 2 feet per second to feet per minute

28. 30 kilometers per hour to meters per hour

29. 2.54 centimeters per inch to centimeters per foot

30. 60 dollars per hour to dollars per minute

Project Progress

Consult a nutrition book to find out how many calories and grams of fat a typical teenager should consume each day. Then find the calories and grams of fat your picnic meal would contain. If your meal has less than 20% or more than 35% of either amount, change your meal to bring it within those limits.

Problem Solving
Understand
Plan
Solve
Look Back

Problem Solving: Percent Increase and Decrease

► **Lesson Link**   You've used several different strategies to solve percent problems. Now you'll use percents to describe amounts of increase or decrease. ◄

You'll Learn ...

■ to solve problems involving percent increase and percent decrease

Explore   Percent Increase and Decrease

Pencil Ups and Downs

You're the manager of Just Pencils. You've decided to raise the price of Dazzlers and lower the price of Yellow Classics. Both sell for 20¢.

1. Decide on a new price for Dazzlers. Then copy the table and complete the first row. Express the values in the last three columns as percents.

Old Price	New Price	Price Change	New Price / Old Price	Price Change / Old Price	Price Change / New Price
20¢					
20¢					

2. Complete the second row of the table for Yellow Classics, *lowering* the price exactly as much as you raised the price of Dazzlers.

3. Repeat Steps 1 and 2, using a different price change.

4. Describe any patterns you see in your tables. Which percent stays the same whether you raise or lower the price?

... How It's Used

Retailers need to know how much they can discount the price of an item on sale without losing money.

Vocabulary

percent increase

percent decrease

percent change

Learn   Problem Solving: Percent Increase and Decrease

When a number changes, you can use a **percent increase** or **percent decrease** to describe the size of the change. A percent increase or decrease is always based on the original amount.

Solving the proportion $\dfrac{\text{percent change}}{100} = \dfrac{\text{amount of change}}{\text{original amount}}$ is one way to find the **percent change** .

25% decrease   25% increase

$30 ← − $10 ← $40 backpack → + $10 → $50
(original price)

Example 1

After the holiday season, the average number of customers per day at the Game Galaxy store decreased from 612 to 450. Find the percent decrease.

Solve for p to find the percent decrease.

amount of change = $612 - 450 = 162$

$$\frac{p}{100} = \frac{162}{612} \qquad \begin{matrix} \leftarrow \text{ amount of change} \\ \leftarrow \text{ original amount} \end{matrix}$$

$$612p = 16{,}200$$

$$\frac{612p}{612} = \frac{16{,}200}{612}$$

$$p \approx 26.5$$

There was a 26.5% decrease in the number of customers after the holidays.

When you know the *percent* change, you can use an equation to solve for the *amount* of change.

Example 2

Problem Solving TIP

Another way to find the number of "bad air" days is to subtract 57% from 100%, then find 43% of 47.

Los Angeles air violated federal carbon monoxide standards on 47 days in 1990. By 1993, this number was 57% lower, largely due to pollution control devices on cars. What was the number of "bad air" days in 1993?

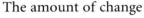

First find the amount of change (c).

The amount of change is 57% of the 1990 total.   Reword the question.

$c = 0.57 \cdot 47$ Translate to an equation.

$c = 26.79 \approx 27$ Multiply. Round to a whole number of days.

This is the amount of change, not the 1993 total. To find the new amount, subtract the amount of change from the original number.

$47 - 27 = 20$

There were 20 "bad air" days in Los Angeles in 1993.

► History Link

The first U.S. postage stamps were issued on July 1, 1847. The 5¢ stamp showed Benjamin Franklin; the 10¢, George Washington.

Try It

a. During the holiday season, daily sales at Game Galaxy grew from $125,000 to $200,000. Find the percent increase.

b. The price of a first-class postage stamp was 10¢ in 1974. By 1991, the price had risen 190%. Find the 1991 price of a first-class stamp.

Last year, the Factory Outlet had 450 employees. This year, the number grew by 12%. Find the current number of employees.

Will thinks ...

First I'll find out how many more employees there are. I want to know what number is 12% of 450.

My equation is $x = 0.12 \cdot 450$. Since $0.12 \cdot 450 = 54$, there are 54 more employees now than there were last year.

There were 450 employees last year. The new number of employees is $450 + 54 = 504$.

Nedra thinks ...

The number of employees grew by 12%. So the current number is $100\% + 12\% = 112\%$ of the original number. Since $1.12 \cdot 450$ is 504, there are 504 employees now.

What do  you think?

1. Why did Nedra add 100% to 12%?

2. When Will wrote his equation, why did he write 0.12 instead of 12%?

3. Another student used the expression $450 + (0.12 \cdot 450)$ to get the answer. Does this method work? If it does, explain why.

Check | Your Understanding

1. Suppose the number of shoppers at a mall decreased by 100% from one year to the next. What would this mean? What might have happened?

2. Is it possible for an amount of increase to be greater than the original amount? If so, what do you know about the percent increase?

Practice and Apply

1. **Getting Started** The number of cars in a mall parking lot grew from 140 at 10:00 to 259 at 11:00. Find the percent increase.

    a. Find the amount of change by subtracting the smaller value from the larger value.

    b. Write a proportion using $\dfrac{\text{percent change}}{100} = \dfrac{\text{amount of change}}{\text{original amount}}$.

    c. Find the cross products.

    d. Use the inverse operation to solve for the percent change.

Find each percent increase or decrease. If necessary, round answers to the nearest tenth.

2. 15 is increased to 20.

3. 96 is decreased to 72.

4. 13.5 is increased to 27.

5. 125 is decreased to 2.

6. 360 is increased to 361.

7. 84 is decreased to 28.

Find each amount of increase or decrease. If necessary, round answers to the nearest tenth.

8. 55 is increased by 20%.

9. 75 is decreased by 40%.

10. 58 is increased by 72%.

11. 28 is increased by 150%.

12. 506 is decreased by 57%.

13. 37.6 is decreased by 25%.

Find the new amount after each increase or decrease. If necessary, round answers to the nearest tenth.

14. $48 is increased by 35%.

15. 446 is decreased by 91%.

16. 84.5 is increased by 110%.

17. **Consumer** Hotels often have lower prices for seasons when people are less likely to take vacations. The Welcome Inn charges $52.00 a night during the summer, but $40.00 a night during the fall. What is the percent decrease?

Consumer Sales tax is an amount of increase. Find the amount of sales tax and the total price (including sales tax) for each of the following. If necessary, round answers to the nearest cent.

18. $8.99, 6% sales tax

19. $53.49, 8.25% sales tax

20. $108.05, 5% sales tax

21. $79.98, 6.5% sales tax

22. **Science** The world's tiger population was probably about 125,000 in 1900. The number of tigers has declined about 95% since then. About how many tigers are there now?

Geometry For each pair of similar figures, find the percent increase or decrease in area from Figure A to Figure B.

23. A.

B.

24. A.

100 ft
30 ft

B.

90 ft
27 ft

25. A.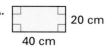

20 cm
40 cm

B.

72 cm
36 cm

26. Problem Solving A softball diamond is a 60 ft by 60 ft square. The sides of a baseball diamond are 50% longer than this. What is the percent increase in the area from the softball diamond to the baseball diamond?

27. **Test Prep** The price of a computer game is $39.99. If the sales tax is 6%, its total cost is:

(A) $39.99 × 0.06   (B) $39.99 + 0.06   (C) $39.99 × 1.06   (D) $39.99 + 1.06

Problem Solving and Reasoning

28. Choose a Strategy In 1916, 18,353,022 people voted in the U.S. presidential election. In 1919, the Nineteenth Amendment gave women the right to vote. The 1920 election had 26,768,613 voters. What was the percent increase in the number of voters? Round to the nearest percent.

29. Problem Solving Many people collect coins. The highest price ever paid for a coin is $1,500,000, for a 1907 U.S. Double Eagle $20 gold coin. What is the percent increase in the value of this coin since 1907?

30. **Journal** An item originally cost $10. It was discounted 50%, then discounted 25% off the *reduced* price. What is the sale price of the item? How much would the sale price be if the *original* price had been reduced 75%? Why isn't a 50% discount followed by a 25% discount the same thing as a 75% discount?

Problem Solving
STRATEGIES

• Look for a Pattern
• Make an Organized List
• Make a Table
• Guess and Check
• Work Backward
• Use Logical Reasoning
• Draw a Diagram
• Solve a Simpler Problem

Mixed Review

Find the area of each figure. *[Lesson 5-9]*

31.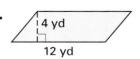

4 yd
12 yd

32.

5 in.
4 in.
7 in.

33.

8 in.
3 in.
6 in.

Convert each rate into the equivalent rate. *[Lesson 7-7]*

34. 2.5 milliliters per minute to milliliters per day

35. 42 feet per second to miles per hour

TECHNOLOGY

Using a Spreadsheet • Compound Interest

Problem: How much would an investment of $100 earning 4% interest each year be worth after 3 years?

You can use a spreadsheet to help answer this question.

1 Enter the amount of the original investment and the year numbers into the spreadsheet as shown.

	A	B
1	Year	Amount
2	0	100
3	1	
4	2	
5	3	

2 If your investment earns 4% interest per year, it increases by 4% of the beginning amount each year. In cell B3, enter the formula = B2*.04 + B2. This calculates the interest for Year 1 and adds it to the original amount.

	A	B
1	Year	Amount
2	0	100
3	1	104
4	2	
5	3	

3 Copy your formula from cell B3 and paste it into cells B4 and B5.

	A	B
1	Year	Amount
2	0	100
3	1	104
4	2	108.16
5	3	112.49

Solution: The investment will be worth $112.49 after 3 years.

This investment earns *compound* interest because each year you also earn interest on the previous interest, not just on the original amount.

TRY IT

a. How much would an investment of $100 earning 4% interest each year be worth in 10 years?

b. How much would an investment of $500 earning 8% interest each year be worth after 6 years?

ON YOUR OWN

▶ In **2**, why was B2 multiplied by .04 and not by 4?

▶ If you earn *simple* interest, interest is paid only on the original amount. How much would the $100 investment in the problem be worth if it earned 4% simple interest for three years? Compare your answer to the result of **3**.

In this section, you've applied percents to many different shopping situations. Now you'll apply what you've learned to a problem that faces every store owner in a mall: What's a fair rent to pay?

They're All at the Mall!

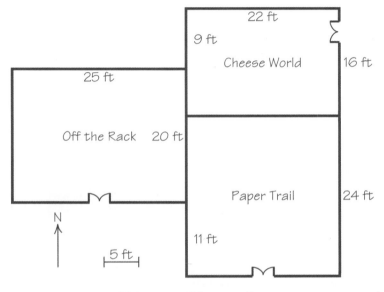

25 ft

Off the Rack   20 ft

N

5 ft

22 ft

9 ft

Cheese World   16 ft

Paper Trail   24 ft

11 ft

1. At the Northeast Ridgemont Megamall, store owners are charged $1.60 per square foot each month in rent. Calculate the area of each store and its rent charge.

2. Off the Rack has expanded its business and needs more floor space. The store owner was able to negotiate an agreement with Cheese World and Paper Trail to move its wall 5 feet to the east. Draw a dashed line to represent the placement of the new wall.

3. Find the percent increase or decrease in the area of each store.

4. By what amount should Off the Rack's rent increase? How much should the rents of Cheese World and Paper Trail decrease? Explain your reasoning.

421

Solve each problem. If necessary, round answers to the nearest tenth.

1. What percent of 108 is 24?

2. 45% of 820 is what number?

3. 17% of 620 is what number?

4. 30% of what number is 33?

5. What percent of 44 is 55?

6. 0.2% of 1100 is what number?

7. 125% of what number is 84?

8. What percent of 408 is 3?

9. **Consumer** Backstage Pass ticket agency sells concert tickets for their face value plus an 8% service fee. If the face value of a ticket is $22.00, what is the total charge, including the service fee?

10. A best-selling book that usually sells for $25.00 at Booksellers, Ltd., is on sale at a 30% discount. The same book usually sells for $20.00 at Book Warehouse, which is having a 15% off sale. Where would you buy the book? Explain how you decided.

11. **History** According to *The Good Old Days—They Were Terrible!,* by Otto Bettmann, an 1893 survey of 18 public schools in Brooklyn, New York, found that many teachers had 90 or more students. In 1993, the average number of students per teacher in New York was 15.2. What is the percent decrease from 90 to 15.2?

Use mental math to find each percent. *[Lesson 8-4]*

12. 25% of 240

13. 10% of $50

14. 60% of 120

15. 15% of $32

16. 5% of 7200

17. Use three different methods to find 80% of 50. Give a short written explanation telling why each method works.

Test Prep

When solving a percent change problem on a multiple choice test, remember to compare the change to the original number.

18. There are 820 math books in a school bookstore. After the first hour of school, 697 books are left. What is the percent decrease in the number of books?

    Ⓐ 1.5%   Ⓑ 1.76%   Ⓒ 15%   Ⓓ 17.6%

Multiple Markups and/or Discounts

On Saturday, Cho's Clothing begins a weekend sale. A $100 jacket goes on sale for a 10% discount. On Sunday, the store runs an ad that says, "Take an Additional 10% Off All Sale Prices!" What is the price of the jacket now?

It seems as if the total discount should be 10% + 10% = 20%. That would mean that the Sunday price is 80% of the original $100, or $80. But is it?

Day	Starting Price	Percent Discount	Amount of Discount	New Price
Saturday	$100	10%	$100 • 0.10 = $10	$90
Sunday	$90	10%	$90 • 0.10 = $9	$81

The Sunday price is actually $81, not $80. A close look at the table explains why. The second 10% discount is based on a price of $90, not the original $100.

When calculating the result of several discounts, several *markups* (increases), or a combination of the two, you cannot just add or subtract percents to find the overall effect. Instead, calculate the discounts or markups one at a time.

A store sells packs of basketball cards for $5.00. During the NBA Finals, the price goes up 12%. After the Finals, that price is discounted 30%. What is the final price?

Time	Starting Price	Percent Markup/Discount	Amount of Markup/Discount	New Price
During Finals	$5.00	12%	$5.00 • 0.12 = $0.60	$5.60
After Finals	$5.60	30%	$5.60 • 0.30 = $1.68	$3.92

The final price of a pack of cards is $3.92.

Try It

1. Find the sale price of an item that cost $78 originally, was marked up 50%, and was then discounted 10%.

2. Hector tried to sell his bicycle for $50. After a week, he reduced the price 20%. Then he reduced that price 35%. What was the final price?

Graphic Organizer

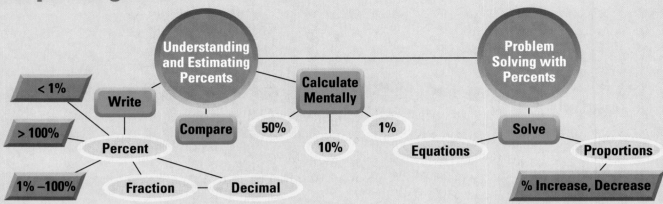

Section 8A   Understanding and Estimating Percents

Summary

- A **percent** is a ratio that compares a number with 100.

- Percents can be written as fractions or as decimals.

- To rewrite a percent as a fraction, write the percent over 100 and rewrite in lowest terms.

- To rewrite a percent as a decimal, move the decimal point two places to the left. To rewrite a decimal as a percent, move the decimal point two places to the right.

- To rewrite a fraction as a percent, first use division to rewrite it as a decimal, then move the decimal point two places to the right.

- A percent can be greater than 100% or less than 1%.

- You can find 50% of a number mentally by taking half of it; 10% of the number by moving the decimal point one place to the left; and 1% by moving the decimal point two places to the left.

Review

1. Write $\frac{27}{100}$ as a percent.

2. Use percents to compare $\frac{1}{4}$ and $\frac{1}{5}$.

3. Rewrite 22% as a fraction.

4. Rewrite 86% as a decimal.

5. Rewrite 0.73 as a percent and a fraction.

6. Rewrite 45% as a fraction and as a decimal.

7. Rewrite 0.8% as a fraction and as a decimal.

8. Rewrite 125% as a fraction and as a decimal.

9. Find 10% and 1% of 2400 mentally.

10. Find 60% of 460 mentally.

11. Find 5% of 280 mentally.

12. Find 15% of $44 mentally.

Section 8B Problem Solving with Percents

Summary

■ You can solve a percent problem by writing and solving an equation or by using a proportion.

■ To solve a percent problem using proportions, write the percent as a ratio with a denominator of 100 and use it to form one side of the proportion. Use the data in the problem to write the other ratio. Then use cross products to help solve the problem.

■ Increases and decreases in value can be measured as percents. To calculate a percent increase or decrease, use this proportion:

$$\frac{\text{percent change}}{100} = \frac{\text{amount of change}}{\text{original amount}}.$$

Review

13. 40% of 50 is what number?

14. What percent of 65 is 30?

15. 18% of what number is 12?

16. 160% of 115 is what number?

17. A bike is on sale for $170. This is 80% of the regular price. Find the regular price.

18. A $20 T-shirt is on sale at a 25% discount. What is the sale price of the shirt?

19. At a shopping mall, 45% of 220 stores sell clothing. How many clothing stores are there?

20. During a flu epidemic, 146 students out of the 680 who attend Lincoln Middle School were absent. What percent were absent?

21. DeJuan bought a $15.00 CD on sale for $12.60. What percent is this of the regular price? What percent discount did he get?

22. During the first week of school, Ms. Yamada's math class increased from 26 to 32 students. What was the percent increase?

23. A fashion buyer for Great Gear, Inc. bought 250 dresses for $45 each. Great Gear sold the dresses for $59 each. What was the percent increase?

24. There were 124 students at a baseball game. By the time the score was 15 to 1, only 32 students were left. Find the percent decrease in the number of students.

1. Of the 42 species of bats in the United States, 33 live in Texas. What percent of U.S. bat species live in Texas?

2. Use percents to compare $\frac{17}{20}$ and $\frac{4}{5}$.

3. Write 0.95 as a percent and as a fraction.

4. List from smallest to greatest: $\frac{3}{8}$, 32%, and 0.36.

5. Suppose 0.5% of the bats in a cave have rabies. What fraction of the bats is this?

6. The sales tax in Green County is 6%. Your total bill for an item would be what percent of its original price?

7. Only 5 of 850 concert tickets were not sold. Was the percent of unsold tickets greater or less than 1%?

8. At birth, a Mexican free-tailed bat weighs $\frac{1}{3}$ as much as its mother. At that time, the mother's weight is what percent of the baby's weight?

9. If a dinner bill were $43.80, how much would a 15% tip be?

10. Jorge has exactly $20. If the sales tax is 7%, can he buy a shirt that is priced at $19.95? Explain.

11. Use mental math to find 20% of 530.

12. Is 48% of 65 the same as 65% of 48? Explain.

13. Rick scored 76% on a history quiz. His score was 25% higher on the next quiz. What did he score on the second quiz?

14. What percent of 640 is 280?

15. Which is greater: 6% of 24 or 85% of 1.5?

16. A skateboard that normally sells for $84.99 is on sale for $70.00. By what percent has it been marked down?

17. After Toni received a salary increase of 4%, her salary was $35,360. What was her salary before the raise?

18. By what percent does the area of an 8 ft by 6 ft rectangle change if its length and width are both increased by 50%?

Performance Task

The label on a cereal box lists the nutritional content of the product. Give each of the figures in two other ways.

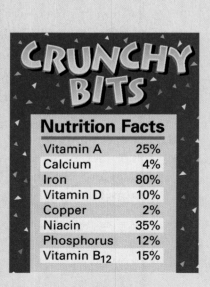

CRUNCHY BITS

Nutrition Facts

Vitamin A	25%
Calcium	4%
Iron	80%
Vitamin D	10%
Copper	2%
Niacin	35%
Phosphorus	12%
Vitamin B$_{12}$	15%

Multiple Choice

Choose the best answer.

1. Find the mode for the set of data: 38, 33, 37, 36, 36, 12, 16, 32. *[Lesson 1-4]*

Ⓐ 25　　Ⓑ 26　　Ⓒ 36　　Ⓓ 38

2. Solve: $5.2x = 18.2$ *[Lesson 3-4]*

Ⓐ $x = 3$　　　　　Ⓑ $x = 3.5$

Ⓒ $x = 23.4$　　　Ⓓ $x = 94.64$

3. Find the prime factorization for 1680. *[Lesson 3-6]*

Ⓐ $4^2 \cdot 3 \cdot 5 \cdot 7$　　Ⓑ $2^4 \cdot 7 \cdot 15$

Ⓒ $2^4 \cdot 3 \cdot 5 \cdot 7$　　Ⓓ $5 \cdot 6 \cdot 7 \cdot 8$

4. Find the product of $1\frac{1}{2} \times 1\frac{2}{3} \times 2\frac{1}{5}$. *[Lesson 4-5]*

Ⓐ $2\frac{4}{7}$　　Ⓑ $3\frac{2}{7}$　　Ⓒ $4\frac{2}{12}$　　Ⓓ $5\frac{1}{2}$

5. Fill in the blank: The *complement* of an acute angle is always a(n) _____ angle. *[Lesson 5-1]*

Ⓐ Acute　　　　Ⓑ Obtuse

Ⓒ Right　　　　Ⓓ Straight

6. Which of these sets of lengths could form the sides of a right triangle? *[Lesson 5-7]*

Ⓐ 8 m, 13 m, 18 m

Ⓑ 15 m, 20 m, 25 m

Ⓒ 7 m, 12 m, 17 m

Ⓓ 9 m, 16 m, 21 m

7. Which of these ratios is *not* equivalent to 24:45? *[Lesson 5-7]*

Ⓐ 8:15　　Ⓑ 12:23　　Ⓒ 16:30　　Ⓓ 48:90

8. Solve: $\frac{p}{18} = \frac{25}{48}$ *[Lesson 6-8]*

Ⓐ $p = 5$　　　　　Ⓑ $p = 23$

Ⓒ $p = 9.375$　　Ⓓ $p = 34.56$

9. Which of these rates is faster than 35 miles per hour? *[Lesson 7-6]*

Ⓐ 1 mile in 3 minutes

Ⓑ 1250 feet in 30 seconds

Ⓒ 10 miles in 15 minutes

Ⓓ 48 feet per second

10. Which set of conversion factors changes meters per hour into centimeters per minute? *[Lesson 7-7]*

Ⓐ $\dfrac{\text{meters}}{\text{hour}} \cdot \dfrac{\text{centimeters}}{\text{meter}} \cdot \dfrac{\text{minutes}}{\text{hour}}$

Ⓑ $\dfrac{\text{meters}}{\text{hour}} \cdot \dfrac{\text{centimeters}}{\text{meter}} \cdot \dfrac{\text{hours}}{\text{minute}}$

Ⓒ $\dfrac{\text{meters}}{\text{hour}} \cdot \dfrac{\text{hours}}{\text{centimeter}} \cdot \dfrac{\text{meters}}{\text{minute}}$

Ⓓ $\dfrac{\text{meters}}{\text{hour}} \cdot \dfrac{\text{hours}}{\text{minute}} \cdot \dfrac{\text{meters}}{\text{centimeter}}$

11. Which fraction is equivalent to 36%? *[Lesson 8-2]*

Ⓐ $\frac{1}{36}$　　Ⓑ $\frac{3}{6}$　　Ⓒ $\frac{9}{25}$　　Ⓓ $\frac{100}{36}$

12. Maria's stamp collection has increased in value by 125% since 1992, when it was worth $440. What is it worth now? *[Lesson 8-3]*

Ⓐ $2432　　　　Ⓑ $990

Ⓒ $665　　　　　Ⓓ $115

13. The sales tax is 7%. How much tax did Ranjit pay for a sweatshirt that cost $25? *[Lesson 8-5]*

Ⓐ $1750　　　　Ⓑ $17.50

Ⓒ $1.75　　　　Ⓓ $0.175

People of the World

In 1993, the annual growth rate in the Russian economy was −12%. The growth rate in the economy of Chile was +6%.

Science

The largest fuel tank on the outside of the rocket that launches the space shuttle is filled with liquid oxygen. Oxygen becomes a liquid at −183°C (−297°F).

Entertainment

Gail Graham −9
Hiromi Kobayashi −8
Beth Daniel −7
Karen Lunn −7
Nancy Lopez −6

In golf, *par* is the score a good player would normally get on a particular hole. Scores above par are shown with positive numbers, those below par are shown with negative numbers. The more negative a golf score is, the better it is.

Social Studies

The Challenger Deep, in the Pacific Ocean, is the deepest point in the world's oceans. The elevation of the Challenger Deep is −35,839 ft.

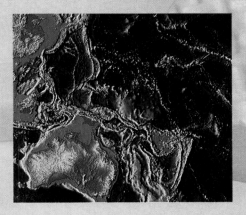

Arts & Literature

Architects use grids to lay out floor plans for new buildings.

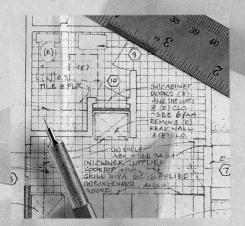

KEY MATH IDEAS

An integer is a whole number, positive or negative. Negative integers are written with a − sign.

The absolute value of an integer tells its distance from 0.

Ordered pairs can be represented by points on a coordinate plane.

When you add or subtract integers, you must take their signs into account. You can use number lines or algebra tiles to model integer addition and subtraction.

The product or quotient of two integers with the same sign is positive. The product or quotient of two integers with different signs is negative.

CHAPTER PROJECT

Problem Solving

Understand
Plan
Solve
Look Back

In this project, you'll create a personal time line showing dates that are important to you. Begin the project by drawing a number line. Put the date you were born above the center of the line and write a zero below it.

429

Problem Solving Focus

Problem Solving

Understand
Plan
Solve
Look Back

Solving the Problem

There is often more than one way to solve a problem. When you solve a problem, you may find that one plan works more easily than another. An important part of good problem solving is choosing a strategy that is easy to work with.

The following problem has already been solved using three different methods.

Squares can be used to make staircase patterns, as shown. Find the number of squares in a six-step staircase pattern.

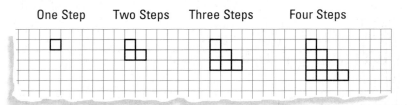

One Step   Two Steps   Three Steps   Four Steps

Draw a diagram

By counting squares, you see that there are 21 steps in a six-step staircase.

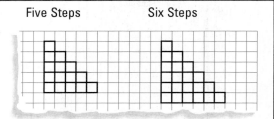

Five Steps   Six Steps

Look for a pattern

Making a table can show a pattern in the results.

Number of Steps	1	2	3	4
Number of Squares	1	3	6	10
Increase	–	2	3	4

When you add a step, the number of squares always increases by the number of steps in the new staircase. So there are 10 + **5** = 15 steps in a **five**-step staircase, and there are 15 + **6** = 21 steps in a **six**-step staircase.

Use logical reasoning

Each row of the staircase has the same number of squares as its row number.

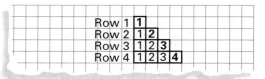

So a six-step staircase has 1 + 2 + 3 + 4 + 5 + 6 = 21 steps.

Solve the following problem. You may use one of the above methods or a method of your own.

1 How many small triangles does it take to build a triangle five rows high?

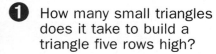

One Row   Two Rows

Journey to Inner Space

EXAMPLE:
Breccia

GRAIN:
Sharp and Angular

EXAMPLE:
Sandstone

GRAIN:
Coarse

EXAMPLE:
Gneiss

GRAIN:
Banded

EXAMPLE:
Slate

GRAIN:
Elongated

EXAMPLE:
Granite

GRAIN:
Nonbanded

EXAMPLE:
Obsidian

"I was awakened from a heavy sleep by an awful shock. The raft appeared to have struck upon a sunken rock. 'Eh, what is it?' cried my uncle, starting up. 'It is a colossal monster!' I cried, clasping my hands."

In Jules Verne's 1864 novel, *A Journey to the Center of the Earth*, a group of people travel to the earth's center. Along the way, they discover monsters, giant mushrooms, and a vast underground sea.

In reality, humans have explored very little of the earth's "inner space." The deepest *boreholes*, narrow holes drilled to collect materials, have reached depths of up to 50,000 feet. So far, they've revealed not a single monster or giant mushroom!

The top of a 20,000 ft mountain is a very different place from the bottom of a 20,000 ft borehole. As you explore integers, you'll write and compare numbers that describe opposite directions.

1 Estimate the depth of the deepest borehole in miles. Compare this to the earth's radius of about 4000 miles.

2 The height of the earth's tallest mountain is about 30,000 ft. What is the difference between this height and the depth of the deepest borehole?

Using Integers to Represent Quantities

► **Lesson Link** Most of the numbers you've studied so far have been greater than zero. Now you'll explore numbers that are less than zero. ◄

You'll Learn ...

■ to use integers to represent real-world quantities

■ to find the opposite of an integer

■ to find the absolute value of an integer

... How It's Used

Sailors need to know ocean and harbor depths to prevent their ships from running aground.

Vocabulary

negative numbers

origin

opposite numbers

integers

absolute value

Explore   Numbers Less than Zero

Hills and Valleys

In Plaquemines Parish, Louisiana, a borehole was drilled to 22,570 ft below sea level. Sea level is the average height of the earth's oceans.

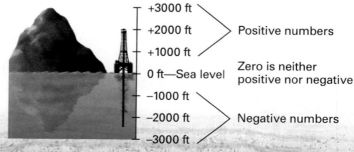

Mt. Everest, Nepal, 29,028 ft — 30,000 ft

Mt. McKinley, AK, 20,320 ft — 20,000 ft

Mt. Whitney, CA, 14,494 ft

— 10,000 ft

Guadalupe Peak, TX, 8,749 ft

0 ft—Sea level

Dead Sea, 1,312 ft

— 10,000 ft

Deepest point, Gulf of Mexico, 14,370 ft

— 20,000 ft

Plaquemines Borehole, 22,570 ft

— 30,000 ft

Deepest point, Pacific Ocean, 35,839 ft   35,000 ft

1. Which landmarks are below sea level? Above sea level?

2. Which is closer to sea level, the deepest point in the Gulf of Mexico or Mt. Whitney? How much closer?

3. Which is farther from sea level, Mt. McKinley or the Plaquemines borehole? How much farther?

4. Describe a way to show the difference between numbers of feet above sea level and below sea level.

Learn   Using Integers to Represent Quantities

A vertical number line can be used to compare heights and depths.

+3000 ft

+2000 ft ⟩ Positive numbers

+1000 ft

0 ft—Sea level   Zero is neither positive nor negative

−1000 ft

−2000 ft ⟩ Negative numbers

−3000 ft

Positive numbers, such as +1000, are greater than zero. They are usually written without a positive (+) sign. **Negative numbers**, such as −2000, are less than zero. The zero point on a number line is the **origin**.

Example 1

The greatest recorded altitude for a bird in flight, a Ruppell's vulture, is 37,000 feet above sea level. A leatherback turtle once dove 3,973 feet below sea level. Use signs to write each number.

You can use positive numbers to represent heights and negative numbers to represent depths.

Ruppell's vulture

Height of vulture: +37,000   Depth of turtle: −3,973

A number line can be drawn horizontally. The farther to the right a number is, the greater it is; the farther to the left it is, the less it is.

Opposite numbers are the same distance from zero. −2 and 2 are opposites because they are both 2 units from zero.

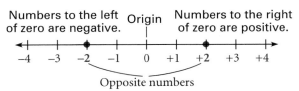

Numbers to the left of zero are negative.   Origin   Numbers to the right of zero are positive.

Opposite numbers

Whole numbers and their opposites are **integers**. Zero is a whole number, so it is an integer.

Example 2

On seven runs, a football running back gained 6, 2, −4, 0, −2, −1, and 4 yards. Which numbers are positive? Negative? Which pairs of numbers are opposites?

2, 4, and 6 are to the right of zero, so they are positive.

−4, −2, and −1 are to the left of zero, so they are negative.

−4 and 4 are opposites. −2 and 2 are opposites.

Try It

Which of the numbers −3, 5, 0, −1, 4, −5, and 3 are positive? Negative? Which pairs of numbers are opposites?

Problem Solving TIP

When you're deciding how to represent a number as an integer, remember that numbers *below* or *less than* the zero point are negative.

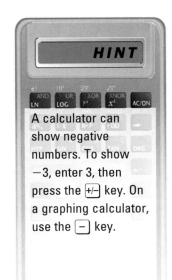

HINT

A calculator can show negative numbers. To show −3, enter 3, then press the [+/−] key. On a graphing calculator, use the [−] key.

If you fly from Chicago to Cleveland, you travel 340 miles. If you fly from Chicago to Des Moines, you go the same distance, but in the opposite direction. Do you travel −340 miles?

No! Des Moines and Cleveland are *both* 340 miles from Chicago. No matter what direction you travel, distance is a positive number.

Like distances on a map, distances on a number line are always positive.

The **absolute value** of a number is its distance from zero. Bars are used to show absolute value.

$$|2| = 2 \qquad |-17| = 17$$

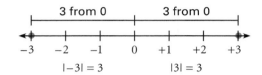

$|-3| = 3 \qquad |3| = 3$

The absolute value of a negative number is its (positive) opposite. The absolute value of a positive number or 0 is the number itself.

Example 3

The world's deepest mine is in South Africa. The bottom of this mine shaft is at −12,600 feet. How far is this from sea level?

The absolute value of a number is its distance from zero.

$$|-12,600| = 12,600$$

The bottom of the mine is 12,600 feet from sea level.

Try It

Find each absolute value. **a.** $|-17|$ **b.** $|5.25|$ **c.** $|-3298|$ **d.** $|0|$

Check Your Understanding

1. Describe some real-life situations where you might use negative numbers.

2. What is the opposite of zero? Of a positive number? Of a negative number?

Practice and Apply

1. **Getting Started** **a.** Graph each of the numbers −1, 3, 0, 1, −5, 4, and −3 on a horizontal number line.

   b. Which numbers are positive?

   c. Which numbers are negative?

   d. Which pairs of numbers are opposites?

Tell whether each number is an integer. Write *Yes* or *No*.

2. −3   **3.** 4.1   **4.** $-\frac{1}{2}$ **5.** 0   **6.** −3.14

Number Sense Use signs to write each number.

7. A borehole 31,441 feet deep   **8.** Earned $10

9. Lost 6 yards   **10.** 5280 feet above sea level

11. 2 units to the left of the origin on a horizontal number line

12. 9 units above the origin on a vertical number line

Write the opposite of each integer.

13. 3   **14.** −23   **15.** −222   **16.** 250   **17.** 5640

Find each absolute value.

18. |23| **19.** |−23| **20.** |−66| **21.** |66| **22.** |−1089|

23. |−4771| **24.** |650| **25.** |2435| **26.** |−1000| **27.** |−90,121|

28. **Science** North American geologists and geophysicists have drilled boreholes to see if temperatures at different depths are related to global warming. The table shows the depths of some of the boreholes they have drilled. Write an integer to represent each depth.

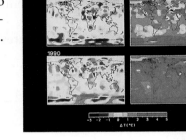

Location	Western Canada	Western Utah	Northeast United States	Alberta, Canada
Borehole Depth (m)	1000	160	710	220

PRACTICE 9-1

29. Geography The hottest recorded temperature on Earth was 136°F, at Al' Aziziyah, Libya. The coldest was −129°F, at Vostok, Antarctica. Find the absolute value of each temperature and tell which is closer to zero.

30. <u>Test Prep</u> Find the set of numbers that contains the opposites of 37, −7, and −54.

    Ⓐ −37, −7, −54   Ⓑ −37, 7, 54   Ⓒ 37, −7, 54   Ⓓ 37, 7, −54

Problem Solving and Reasoning

31. Critical Thinking The volcano Mauna Kea, on the island of Hawaii, is the world's tallest mountain from base to peak. Mauna Kea's base is 19,680 feet below the ocean's surface. Its peak is 13,796 feet above sea level. Write integers representing the height of Mauna Kea above sea level and its depth below sea level.

Mauna Kea

32. Critical Thinking The earth is covered with a rocky *crust*, which can be 25 miles thick. Underneath this is an 1800-mile-thick *mantle* of heavier rock. Below the mantle is a liquid *outer core*, about 1400 miles thick. The center of the earth is a solid *inner core*.

Use integers to describe the minimum and maximum depths of each region. (You will be able to give only the minimum depth of the inner core.)

33. |Journal| Write about a situation each measurement might represent.

    a. −30 seconds   **b.** −$20   **c.** −39°F   **d.** −12 yards

Mixed Review

Write each ratio in three ways. If possible, write in lowest terms. *[Lesson 6-1]*

34. 4 days out of 7 days

35. 2 socks for every uniform

36. 1 teacher for every 30 students

37. 12 servings for 10 people

Find x in each pair of similar figures. *[Lesson 7-9]*

38.

39.

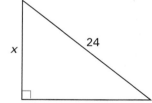

Comparing and Ordering Integers

▶ **Lesson Link** In the last lesson, you used integers to represent real-world quantities. Now you'll compare and order integers. ◄

You'll Learn …

■ to compare and order integers

… How It's Used

Quality control workers compare positive and negative numbers to tell whether a product is within desired limits.

Explore | Comparing and Ordering Integers

Forecast: Windy and Colder

Have you ever noticed that a cold day feels *colder* when the wind blows? For example, a 50 mi/hr wind makes a 35°F temperature feel like 0°F.

The *wind chill temperature* tells us how cold it feels. The chart shows actual and wind chill temperatures on a day in February, 1996.

City	Cody, WY	St. Paul, MN	Helena, MT	Idaho Falls, ID	Key West, FL
Temperature	−12°F	5°F	−16°F	0°F	73°F
Wind Chill Temperature	−25°F	−10°F	−30°F	−12°F	73°F

1. Which city had the higher actual temperature, Cody or St. Paul? How do you know?

2. Sketch a vertical thermometer and mark the ten temperatures on it.

3. Which temperature was the coldest? The warmest?

4. Which city had a *higher* wind chill temperature that day, Helena or Idaho Falls? Which temperature was farther from 0°? Explain.

Learn | Comparing and Ordering Integers

The average January temperature in Chicago is −3°C. The average July temperature is 24°C. As any Chicagoan can tell you, a positive number is always greater than a negative number.

If two integers have different signs, it's easy to decide which is greater. However, it's more difficult to compare two negative integers.

You can use a number line to compare integers.

On a horizontal number line, the farther *to the right* a number is, the greater it is.

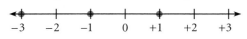

−1 is to the right of −3, so −1 > −3.

−1 is to the left of +1, so −1 < +1.

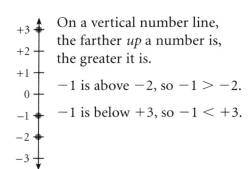

On a vertical number line, the farther *up* a number is, the greater it is.

−1 is above −2, so −1 > −2.

−1 is below +3, so −1 < +3.

On a number line, the farther to the left or farther down a number is, the *less* it is. So a negative number close to zero such as −2 is *greater* than −25,000.

Examples

1 Write an inequality to tell which is greater, −7 or −2.

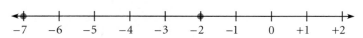

−2 is to the right of −7, so −2 > −7.

2 Order the depths of these mines from deepest to least deep: Kolar, India, −8,604 ft; Western Deep, South Africa, −12,600 ft; Nova Lima, Brazil, −8,052; Boksburg, South Africa, −11,248 ft.

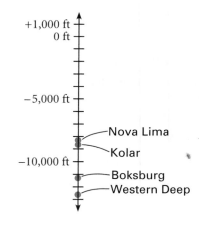

The number line shows these depths.

From deepest to least deep, the depths are −12,600 ft, −11,248 ft, −8,604 ft, and −8,052 ft.

Try It

a. Which is warmer, −67°F or 45°F?

b. Write an inequality to tell which number is greater, −22 or −1.

c. Order the depths of these Rocky Mountain caves from deepest to least deep: Papoose, −252 m; Sunray, −245 m; Silvertip, −313 m; Big Brush, −262 m.

DID YOU KNOW?

Marble Bar, Australia, had 160 consecutive days where the temperature exceeded 100°F. Langdon, North Dakota, had 92 days in a row where the temperature dropped below freezing (0°C).

Jacob and Winona were asked to compare January temperatures for four cities by ordering them from lowest to highest.

City	Albany, NY	Bismarck, ND	Duluth, MN	Fairbanks, AK
Average January Low Temperature	16°F	−2°F	0°F	−20°F

Jacob thinks ...

I'll show the temperatures on a number line.

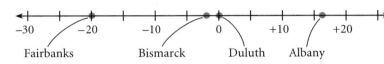

Fairbanks   Bismarck   Duluth   Albany

I can read the order of the temperatures from left to right. From lowest to highest, the temperatures are −20°, −2°, 0°, and 16°.

Winona thinks ...

I'll use the signs of the numbers to help put them in order.

The only positive temperature is 16°. So, this is the highest temperature and it comes last in the list.

Zero is greater than any negative number, so 0° comes next.

−2° is closer to zero than −20°, so −20° is less than −2°.

The temperatures are −20°, −2°, 0°, and 16°.

What do you think?

1. How could Jacob and Winona use their methods to compare −2 and 2?

2. How can Winona use her method to decide which is greater, 8 or 4?

Check | Your Understanding

1. Explain why −5,000 is greater than −1,000,000.

2. What is the greatest negative integer?

Practice and Apply

1. **Getting Started** Follow these steps to determine which number is greater, -6 or -8.

   a. Draw a number line. Locate -6 and -8.

   b. Determine which number is farther to the right. This is the greater number.

Number Sense Using the number line, write an inequality to tell which number is greater.

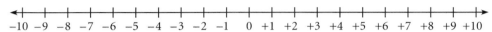

2. $-3, -8$ 3. $-7, -5$ 4. $0, 6$ 5. $-8, 5$ 6. $6, -4$

7. $-9, -7$ 8. $0, -10$ 9. $-3, -2$ 10. $1, -1$ 11. $-4, 3$

Use >, <, or = to compare each pair of numbers.

12. $-4 \;\square\; 5$ 13. $-4 \;\square\; 0$ 14. $-34 \;\square\; -25$ 15. $-679 \;\square\; -769$

16. $-901 \;\square\; -910$ 17. $|5| \;\square\; |-5|$ 18. $|-56| \;\square\; |-61|$ 19. $-100 \;\square\; -104$

Order each set of numbers from greatest to least.

20. $-2°, 12°, 54°, 0°, -18°, -5°$

21. $\$12, -\$7, \$11, \$0, -\$2, -\$5, \$8$

22. $32°, -24°, -10°, 0°, 212°$

23. $-3551, -3155, -3515, -3151, -3555$

24. **Science** The map shows the depth below sea level of several boreholes.

    a. Represent each depth as an integer.

    b. Order the integers in **a** from least to greatest.

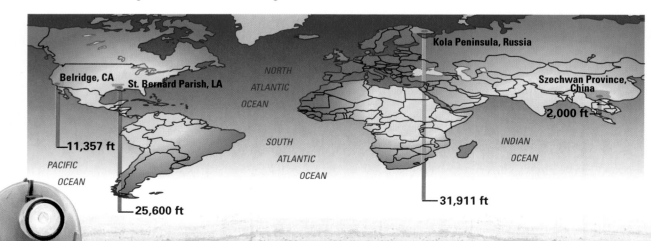

25. Logic Fill in the blanks with *sometimes*, *always*, or *never*.

   a. A positive integer is _____ greater than a negative integer.

   b. The absolute value of a positive integer is _____ greater than the absolute value of a negative integer.

   c. If two integers are positive, the one closer to zero is _____ greater.

   d. Zero is _____ greater than any negative integer.

26. Problem Solving The table shows minimum estimated surface temperatures for several planets. Order the temperatures from greatest to least.

Planet	Mercury	Venus	Earth	Mars	Jupiter	Pluto
Temperature	−300°F	890°F	−130°F	−190°F	−240°F	−390°F

27. **Test Prep** Determine which statement is true.

   Ⓐ −13 > −4   Ⓑ −18 < −12   Ⓒ −2 > 0   Ⓓ −14 < −16

Problem Solving and Reasoning

28. Choose a Strategy The table shows elevations of the *lowest* points in five states. Write each as an integer, then order from least to greatest.

State	Alabama	California	Colorado	Louisiana	Wyoming
Lowest Point	Sea level	282 ft below sea level	3350 ft	8 ft below sea level	3099 ft

29. Communicate Changes in stock prices are listed using positive and negative numbers. For instance, "$-1\frac{1}{2}$" means that a share lost $1.50 in value. Explain what each price change means.

   a. $-2\frac{3}{4}$ **b.** $-3\frac{1}{4}$ **c.** $+1\frac{1}{4}$ **d.** -4

> ### Problem Solving
> ## STRATEGIES
> • Look for a Pattern
> • Make an Organized List
> • Make a Table
> • Guess and Check
> • Work Backward
> • Use Logical Reasoning
> • Draw a Diagram
> • Solve a Simpler Problem

Mixed Review

Express each rate as a unit rate. *[Lesson 6-2]*

30. 360 miles on 12 gallons

31. 30 pages in 60 minutes

32. 24 sets of markers for 3 classrooms

33. 10 hours of homework in 5 days

Find the perimeter and area of each figure. *[Lesson 7-10]*

34. Scale factor 1.5

35. Scale factor 3

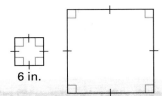

6 in.

The Coordinate Plane

You'll Learn ...

■ to graph points on a coordinate plane

... How It's Used

Archaeologists use grids to record the locations of the artifacts they find at a dig site.

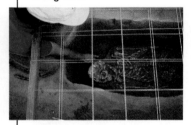

Vocabulary

coordinate system

x-y coordinate plane

x-axis

y-axis

origin

quadrants

ordered pair

x-coordinate

y-coordinate

▶ **Lesson Link** You've made scatterplots by plotting points with positive coordinates. Now you'll plot points with negative coordinates. ◀

Explore The Coordinate Plane

X Marks the Spot

Materials: Tracing paper, Ruler

An oil company plans to drill a borehole near Odessa, Texas. It needs to give a precise description of its location.

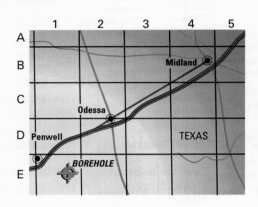

1. Use the letters and numbers on the map to describe Midland's location.

2. Now describe the location of the borehole.

　a. Draw intersecting vertical and horizontal number lines on your tracing paper. Let the intersection point be the origin of both lines.

　b. Place the tracing paper so the origin is over Midland. Be sure your vertical number line points north.

　c. Use the integers on your lines to describe the location of the borehole. Explain how you found your answer.

3. Move your tracing paper so the origin is over Odessa. What is the location of the borehole now?

Learn The Coordinate Plane

Maps often use a grid of numbers and letters to help locate landmarks. The Parliament Building in Victoria, British Columbia, is located at R38 on the map.

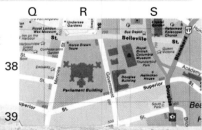

You can locate points with a similar **coordinate system** of intersecting horizontal and vertical number lines.

The **x-y coordinate plane** is based on two number lines. The horizontal line is the **x-axis** and the vertical line is the **y-axis**. They intersect at the **origin** of the coordinate plane.

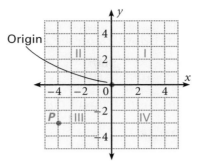

The axes divide the plane into four **quadrants**, numbered I, II, III, and IV. Point P is in quadrant III.

The axes are not in any quadrant.

Any point can be described by an **ordered pair**, such as $(-3, 5)$. The first number is the **x-coordinate**. It tells how far to the left or right of the origin the point is, as measured along the x-axis. The **y-coordinate** tells how far up or down the point is, as measured along the y-axis. The origin itself is at $(0, 0)$.

Examples

Plot each point on a coordinate plane.

1 $(4, -3)$

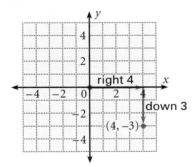

Start at the origin. Move 4 units to the right on the x-axis. Then move 3 units down (parallel to the y-axis). Plot the point.

2 $(-400, 0)$

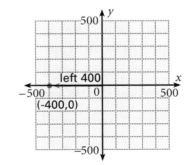

Start at the origin. Move 400 units to the left on the x-axis. Plot the point. (Since the y-coordinate is 0, do not move up or down.)

Try It

Plot each point on the same coordinate plane.

a. $(-3, 4)$ **b.** $(4, -3)$ **c.** $(2, 0)$ **d.** $(0, -5)$

e–h. Name the quadrant or axis that contains each point in **a–d**.

Example 3

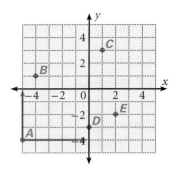

Find the coordinates of point *A*.

A is below −5 on the *x*-axis, so its *x*-coordinate is −5. *A* is to the left of −4 on the *y*-axis, so its *y*-coordinate is −4.

The coordinates of point *A* are (−5, −4).

Try It

Using the grid for Example 3, find the coordinates of points *B*, *C*, *D*, and *E*.

You can tell which quadrant a point is in from the signs of its *x*- and *y*-coordinates. For example, quadrant I contains all points that are to the right of and above the origin. So any point whose coordinates are both positive must be in quadrant I.

Example 4

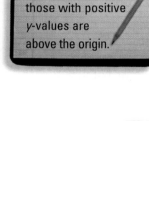

Study TIP

Remember that quadrants with positive *x*-values are to the right of the origin, and those with positive *y*-values are above the origin.

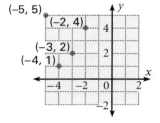

What are the signs of the *x*- and *y*-coordinates of points in quadrant II?

Four points in quadrant II are plotted. Notice these patterns in the signs:

• The *x*-coordinate of each point is negative.
• The *y*-coordinate of each point is positive.

In quadrant II, the *x*-coordinate of any point is negative and the *y*-coordinate is positive.

Try It

What are the signs of the *x*- and *y*-coordinates of points in quadrant III?

Check | Your Understanding

1. What is the *x*-coordinate of a point on the *y*-axis? What is the *y*-coordinate of a point on the *x*-axis?

2. On a number line, the coordinate of the origin is 0. Why does the origin on a coordinate plane have coordinates (0, 0)?

3. Is the point (−4, 5) the same as the point (5, −4)? Explain.

Practice and Apply

1. **Getting Started** Follow these steps to plot the point $(-3, -5)$.

   a. Draw and label a horizontal x-axis and a vertical y-axis.

   b. Since the x-coordinate is negative, move 3 units *to the left* on the x-axis.

   c. Since the y-coordinate is negative, move 5 spaces *down,* parallel to the y-axis.

   d. Plot the point.

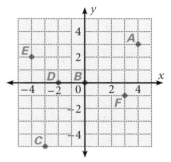

Find the coordinates of each point.

2. A **3.** B **4.** C **5.** D **6.** E **7.** F

8. Patterns What are the signs of the x- and y-coordinates of points in quadrant IV?

Plot each point on the same coordinate plane.

9. $(4, 4)$ **10.** $(-2, 0)$ **11.** $(3, -1)$ **12.** $(-1, -5)$ **13.** $(0, -3)$

Plot each point on the same coordinate plane.

14. $(16, -6)$ **15.** $(20, 14)$ **16.** $(-5, 10)$ **17.** $(-11, 9)$ **18.** $(-14, -12)$

19. **Industry** The depth of a geologic formation is not always the same. Two hundred feet from point A, the formation shown is 100 feet deep. It is 200 feet deep at a distance of 500 feet from A.

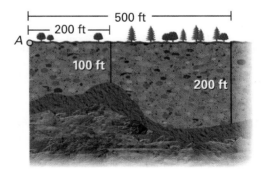

   a. Use two ordered pairs to describe this data. Let the x-coordinate of each point be the distance from A and the y-coordinate be the depth of the formation.

   b. Plot these ordered pairs on a coordinate plane. Choose a scale that fits the data.

20. **Geometry** Draw a trapezoid on a coordinate plane so that each of its vertices is in a different quadrant. Label the coordinates of each point.

Logic Name the quadrant that contains each point.

21. $(7, -3)$ **22.** $(-4, -9)$ **23.** $(6, 3)$ **24.** $(-5, 8)$ **25.** $(-2, -2)$

26. $(17, 26)$ **27.** $(40, -60)$ **28.** $(-324, 119)$ **29.** $(404, 15)$ **30.** $(-628, -705)$

31. **Test Prep** In which quadrant would you find $(-6, -3)$?

Ⓐ I   Ⓑ II   Ⓒ III   Ⓓ IV

Problem Solving and Reasoning

32. Critical Thinking Follow these steps to *translate* a geometric figure. A translation moves a figure but does not change its size or shape.

a. Plot the ordered pairs $(4, 1)$, $(3, 2)$, and $(2, 1)$. Connect the points.

b. Make three new ordered pairs by subtracting 2 from the *x*-coordinates and adding 3 to the *y*-coordinates of the original points. Plot these points and connect them.

c. Describe the new figure. How does it compare to the original?

33. Critical Thinking The *latitude-longitude* system describes locations on the earth's surface. Latitude measures degrees north or south of the equator. Longitude measures degrees east or west of a line called the *prime meridian*. For instance, Dakar is at 15° north, 17° west.

Use the map to give the approximate latitude and longitude of Cairo and Zanzibar.

34. **Journal** On a coordinate plane, plot all the points whose *x*-coordinates and *y*-coordinates are equal. Connect the points. Describe the result.

Mixed Review

Multiply and divide to find two ratios equivalent to each ratio. *[Lesson 6-3]*

35. $\dfrac{8}{22}$ **36.** $\dfrac{6}{14}$ **37.** $\dfrac{20}{42}$ **38.** $\dfrac{18}{20}$ **39.** $\dfrac{42}{100}$

Express each fraction as a percent. *[Lesson 8-1]*

40. $\dfrac{9}{12}$ **41.** $\dfrac{67}{100}$ **42.** $\dfrac{4}{25}$ **43.** $\dfrac{17}{50}$ **44.** $\dfrac{4}{5}$

Project Progress

Put tick marks on your time line to the left and right of the origin. Use these marks to represent years before and after your birth. List events and dates you'd like to include on your time line. Ask your parents or look in books to find out about events that happened before you were born.

Problem Solving

Understand

Plan

Solve

Look Back

You've used integers to describe and compare real-world quantities. Now you'll learn about a relationship between depth and temperature as you examine measurements that were taken when a giant drill bored deep into the earth.

Journey to Inner Space

Materials: Graph paper

As they descended to the center of the earth, Jules Verne's fictional characters found the temperature unexpectedly comfortable. Ten thousand feet below sea level, the temperature was about 63°F. Now you'll see what temperatures are *really* like in the earth's interior. The following data comes from measurements taken during the drilling of a borehole in South Africa.

Depth (ft)	Temp. (°F)	Depth (ft)	Temp. (°F)	Depth (ft)	Temp. (°F)
−2094	75.4	−597	68.6	−3644	82.9
−4747	88.2	−8937	110.3	−6860	100.1
−9904	114.0	−5806	92.6	−7912	105.6

1. Write each pair of data values as an ordered pair, with depth as the *x*-coordinate and temperature as the *y*-coordinate.

2. Order the points according to temperature, from coldest to hottest.

3. Order the points according to depth, from deepest to least deep.

4. Are the sets of points you made in Steps 2 and 3 in the same order?

5. Plot the points on a coordinate graph. What patterns do you notice?

6. Use your graph to predict the temperature at each depth. Explain how you made your predictions.

   a. −5000 ft   **b.** −20,000 ft   **c.** Sea level

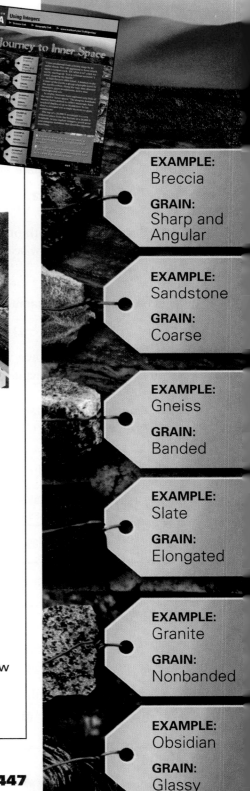

EXAMPLE:
Breccia

GRAIN:
Sharp and Angular

EXAMPLE:
Sandstone

GRAIN:
Coarse

EXAMPLE:
Gneiss

GRAIN:
Banded

EXAMPLE:
Slate

GRAIN:
Elongated

EXAMPLE:
Granite

GRAIN:
Nonbanded

EXAMPLE:
Obsidian

GRAIN:
Glassy

Section 9A Review

Number Sense Write the opposite of each integer.

1. -4 **2.** 50 **3.** 0 **4.** -726 **5.** 201

Find each absolute value.

6. $|-6|$ **7.** $|6|$ **8.** $|-1800|$ **9.** $|613|$ **10.** $|-24{,}789|$

Use $>$, $<$, or $=$ to compare each pair of numbers.

11. $-3 \,\square\, -8$ **12.** $-12 \,\square\, 12$ **13.** $-702 \,\square\, -720$ **14.** $0 \,\square\, |-10|$

15. Science The depth of the bottom of the earth's crust varies from 5 to 25 miles below sea level. Write integers to represent these two numbers.

Plot each point on the same coordinate plane.

16. $(1, 5)$ **17.** $(-2, -4)$ **18.** $(5, -3)$ **19.** $(3, 0)$ **20.** $(-4, 2)$

21. In your own words, explain the difference between the *absolute value* of a number and the *opposite* of a number.

22. Geography The table shows the lowest point of every continent except Antarctica. Order the elevations from lowest to highest.

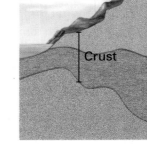

Crust

Continent	Africa	North America	South America	Asia	Australia	Europe
Location	Lake Assal	Death Valley	Vakles Peninsula	Dead Sea	Lake Eyre	Caspian Sea
Lowest Elevation (ft)	−509 ft	−282 ft	−131 ft	−1312 ft	−52 ft	−92 ft

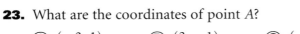
Test Prep

When you're asked to find the coordinates of a point on a multiple choice test, be sure to pay attention to the scales on the axes.

23. What are the coordinates of point *A*?

Ⓐ $(-3, 1)$ Ⓑ $(3, -1)$ Ⓒ $(-300, 10)$ Ⓓ $(-300, -100)$

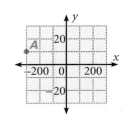

Operations with Integers

For Your Amusement

The floor drops open beneath you. You crawl to a height of 150 feet, pause, then plunge 128 feet, reaching speeds of more than 60 miles per hour. You and your stomach spin through a 104-foot vertical loop, two 45-degree loops, a 60-foot loop *underground*, and a corkscrew. Just three minutes after you started, you stumble out of the car. Congratulations—you've survived Montu™, one of the world's tallest and longest inverted steel roller coasters!

Montu opened in 1996 at Busch Gardens®, in Tampa, Florida. At full capacity, Montu thrills about 1700 riders every hour.

Roller coaster designers use mathematics to model the motions and forces of the rides they create. Then they analyze the ride on a computer. By the time Montu was built, its designers were confident that it would be safe as well as breathtaking. Now you'll use integers to investigate amusement park rides and games.

1 A car on Montu goes up 150 ft, then down 128 ft. How could you use integers to represent these values? What is the height of the car after its 128 ft drop? Explain your reasoning.

2 If you dropped 128 ft three times in a row, how many feet would you drop in all? Explain.

Adding Integers

▶ **Lesson Link**
In the last section, you learned basic properties of integers. Now you'll see how to add integers. ◀

You'll Learn ...

■ to add integers

... How It's Used

Weather forecasters use integers to describe changes in temperatures and barometric pressures.

Wind, rain aiming at the Nor

Vocabulary

additive inverse

zero pair

Explore | Adding Integers

Materials: Algebra tiles

It All Adds Up!

Adding Integers

+2 + (−3)

- To model 2 + (−3), model positive integers with yellow tiles and negative integers with red tiles.

- +1 + (−1) = 0, so you can remove any yellow-red pair without changing the value of the pile.

- Use the remaining tile(s) to find the sum.

$$\boxed{\quad \blacksquare\,} = 0$$

$$\boxed{\quad \blacksquare\,} = 0$$

1. Use algebra tiles to find each sum.

　a. 2 + 1　　**b.** −1 + (−2)　　**c.** 3 + (−1)

　d. −1 + 2　　**e.** 1 + (−2)　　**f.** −4 + 2

+2 + (−3) = −1

2. When you add two positive integers, is the sum positive, negative, or impossible to predict? Can you predict the sign of the sum when you add two negative integers? A positive and a negative integer? Explain.

3. How is adding integers different from adding whole numbers?

Learn | Adding Integers

You can use a number line or algebra tiles to add integers.

Number Line

To add a *positive* number, move to the right.

To add a *negative* number, move to the left.

−1 + 3

$$\xleftarrow{\quad} \underset{-3\ \ -2\ \ -1\ \ \ 0\ \ +1\ \ +2\ \ +3}{+\!\!+\!\!+\!\!+\!\!+\!\!+\!\!+} \xrightarrow{\quad}$$

+3 + (−5)

Algebra Tiles

Use yellow tiles to represent positive integers and red tiles to represent negative integers.

Remove yellow-red pairs. The number of tiles left is the sum.

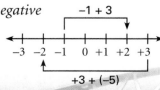

Example 1

Use a number line and algebra tiles to add: $-2 + (-4)$

Number Line

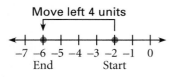

$-2 + (-4) = -6$

Algebra Tiles

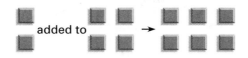

The sum is 6 red tiles.

$$-2 + (-4) = -6$$

Try It

Use algebra tiles or a number line to find each sum.

a. $-2 + (-1)$ **b.** $3 + 2$ **c.** $-5 + (-3)$ **d.** $1 + 5$

In Example 1, two numbers with the *same* sign were added.

When you add numbers with *unlike* signs, you use **additive inverses** . The additive inverse of a number is its opposite. For instance, the additive inverse of -5 is 5.

To see how additive inverses work, think of buying 3 tickets at an amusement park, then using them to go on a 3-ticket ride. How many tickets do you have left?

THE INVERSE PROPERTY OF ADDITION

In words: The sum of an integer and its additive inverse is 0.

In symbols: $3 + (-3) = 0$ $a + (-a) = 0$

$1 + (-1) = 0$, so the tiles [ ] [ ] form a **zero pair** .

Remember

Inverse operations undo each other. Addition and subtraction are inverse operations.
[Page 75]

Example 2

Use algebra tiles to add: $-5 + 3$

Use five red tiles to represent -5 and three yellow tiles to represent $+3$.

Remove the three zero pairs. (Notice that -3 and 3 are additive inverses.) There are two red tiles left.

$-5 + 3 = -2$

Example 3

Players win a token for each basket they make playing Hoop Shoot. Clark spent 6 tokens to play and made 9 baskets. Use a number line to find how many more tokens he had when he finished than when he began.

Use negative numbers to represent tokens spent. Use positive numbers to represent tokens won.

tokens spent + tokens won = total

$$-6 \quad + \quad 9 \quad = \quad 3$$

Clark left the game with 3 tokens more than when he began.

Move right 9 units

-6 Start   0   3 End

Try It

Use algebra tiles or a number line to find each sum.

a. $-1 + 4$ **b.** $3 + (-4)$ **c.** $-2 + 1$ **d.** $2 + (-2)$

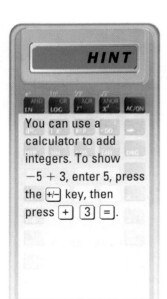

HINT

You can use a calculator to add integers. To show $-5 + 3$, enter 5, press the ⊞⊟ key, then press ⊞ ③ ⊜.

As Example 1 shows, adding integers with the same sign is similar to whole-number addition. Examples 2 and 3, where addends have opposite signs, look more like whole-number subtraction. These results are summarized below.

INTEGER ADDITION RULES

Adding Integers with the Same Sign
- *Add* the absolute values of the numbers.
- Use the sign of the numbers.

Adding Integers with Different Signs
- *Subtract* the absolute values of the numbers.
- Use the sign of the number with the larger absolute value.

Examples

Find each sum.

4 $-7 + (-14)$

$$7 + 14 = 21$$ Add the absolute values.

$$-7 + (-14) = -21$$ Use the sign of the numbers.

5 $23 + (-12)$

$$23 - 12 = 11$$ Subtract the absolute values.

$$23 + (-12) = 11$$ Use the sign of the number with the larger absolute value.

1. How do you find the sum of two integers with different signs?

2. How is the Zero Property of Addition related to the idea of zero pairs?

9-4 Exercises and Applications

Practice and Apply

1. **Getting Started** Follow these steps to find $2 + (-5)$ using algebra tiles.
   a. Sketch two positive tiles. Color them yellow (or leave them empty).
   b. Sketch five negative tiles. Color them red (or shade them in).
   c. Remove zero pairs.
   d. Count the remaining tiles. Write the sum.

Write the addition problem and the sum for each model.

2.   3.  4.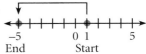

Find the additive inverse of each integer.

5. -6 6. 8 7. -15 8. 1 9. 0

Use algebra tiles or a number line to find each sum.

10. $2 + 4$ 11. $-7 + (-3)$ 12. $6 + (-2)$ 13. $-4 + 9$ 14. $6 + (-6)$

15. $9 + (-5)$ 16. $-5 + 8$ 17. $-4 + (-6)$ 18. $7 + (-8)$ 19. $-4 + 4$

Operation Sense Find each sum.

20. $-16 + 37$ 21. $23 + (-12)$ 22. $-25 + (-15)$

23. $-81 + 35$ 24. $64 + (-23)$ 25. $97 + (-75)$

26. $42 + 14$ 27. $-55 + (-55)$ 28. $123 + (-60)$

29. Binh spent 15 game tokens in an amusement park arcade. She won 11 tokens while she was playing the games. If she has no tokens left when she leaves the arcade, how many did she buy while she was playing the games? Explain your answer.

PRACTICE 9-4

Patterns Write the next integer in each pattern.

30. $-18, -14, -10,$ _____   **31.** $8, 2, -4,$ _____   **32.** $-8, -1, 6,$ _____

33. | Test Prep | A football team gains 7 yards on one play, then loses 15 yards on the next. What is the team's total gain?

   Ⓐ 8 yards   Ⓑ -8 yards   Ⓒ 22 yards   Ⓓ -22 yards

34. Science Although mercury is a metal, it is a liquid at room temperature. Mercury melts at about $-39°C$. If the temperature of a block of mercury starts at $-54°C$ and increases by $22°C$, does the mercury melt? Explain your answer.

Problem Solving and Reasoning

35. Critical Thinking The first Ferris wheel operated at Chicago's World's Columbian Exposition in 1893. The top of the Ferris wheel was 264 feet above the ground.

   a. Bertram's car was at the top of the Ferris wheel. Then it descended 127 feet. Write a sum you could use to find the height of Bertram's car after this descent.

   b. How far off the ground was Bertram?

36. Write an addition equation using one positive integer and one negative integer so that:

   a. The sum is positive   **b.** The sum is negative

   c. The sum is zero   **d.** The sum is -14

Mixed Review

Use multiplication or division to complete each table. *[Lesson 6-4]*

37. Find five ratios equivalent to $\frac{3}{7}$.

3	6	9	12	15	18
7					

38. Find five ratios equivalent to $\frac{60}{96}$.

60	30	20	15	10	5
96					

Write each percent as a fraction in lowest terms. *[Lesson 8-2]*

39. 50%   **40.** 80%   **41.** 5%   **42.** 36%   **43.** 45%

44. 98%   **45.** 11.2%   **46.** 47%   **47.** 52%   **48.** 0.5%

Subtracting Integers

▶ **Lesson Link** In the last lesson, you added integers. Now you'll explore integer subtraction. ◀

You'll Learn ...

■ to subtract integers

... How It's Used

Business owners need to add and subtract integers to see whether their business is making or losing money.

Explore | **Subtracting Integers**

What Difference Does It Make?

Materials: Algebra tiles

Subtracting Integers

2 – 3

- To model 2 − 3, use algebra tiles to model the first number in the difference.

- The second number in the difference tells you how many tiles to "take away." If you do not have enough to take away, add yellow-red pairs until you have the right number.

  Now there are 3 positive tiles to take away.

- Take away the number of tiles equal to the second number in the difference. Use the remaining tile(s) to write the difference.

  Take away 3 tiles.

1. Use algebra tiles to find each difference.

2 – 3 = –1

  a. 5 − 3   **b.** −7 − (−2)   **c.** −6 − (−4)

  d. 2 − 3   **e.** 2 − (−3)   **f.** −3 − (−5)

2. Why can you add yellow-red pairs to the original number of tiles?

3. When you subtract a negative integer from a number, how does the result compare to the original number? Explain why this happens.

Learn | **Subtracting Integers**

You can model subtraction with algebra tiles. To subtract a number, take away that number of tiles. To subtract 5 − 3:

Start with 5 positive tiles.

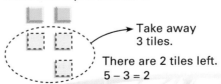

Take away 3 tiles.

There are 2 tiles left.
5 – 3 = 2

When you use algebra tiles to subtract integers, you may not have enough tiles to take away. You can add zero pairs to provide the tiles you need.

Example 1

Use algebra tiles to subtract: $-2 - 3$

Start with two negative tiles.

You don't have three positive tiles to take away. To introduce the three positive tiles you need, add three zero pairs. (Since you're adding zero, the value of the pile does not change.)

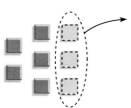

Now subtract by taking away three positive tiles. There are five negative tiles left.

$$-2 - 3 = -5$$

Try It

Use algebra tiles to find each difference.

a. $4 - 3$ **b.** $2 - 5$ **c.** $-3 - 3$ **d.** $-2 - (-6)$

> **► History Link**
>
> The Italian mathematician Leonardo Fibonacci published *Liber Abaci* (The Book of Numbers) in A.D. 1202. In it, he explained that "5 diminished by 8" would result in "a debt of 3." This is one of the earliest known references to a negative number.

You can use a number line to subtract integers. When you subtract a positive number, the difference is *less* than the original number, so you move to the *left*. To subtract a negative number, move to the *right*.

Example 2

Use a number line to subtract: $-6 - (-4)$

Start at -6. To subtract *negative* 4, move four units to the *right*.

$$-6 - (-4) = -2$$

Move right 4 units

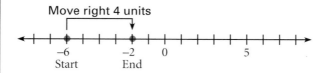

Try It

Use a number line to find each difference.

a. $5 - 3$ **b.** $-2 - 3$ **c.** $-1 - (-4)$ **d.** $0 - (-2)$

You can use a number line to show a very important relationship between integer addition and subtraction.

Compare the subtraction problem $-4 - (-3)$ to the addition problem $-4 + 3$.

To subtract negative 3, move *right*.   To add positive 3, move *right*.

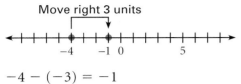

$$-4 - (-3) = -1 \qquad\qquad\qquad -4 + 3 = -1$$

In both cases, you start at the same point, move in the same direction, and get the same answer. This idea is summarized in the following property:

Subtracting a number is the same as adding its opposite.

Example 3

During the biggest drop of the Mean Streak roller coaster at Cedar Point®, in Sandusky, Ohio, your altitude changes by -155 feet. The longest drop of the Texas Giant™, at Six Flags® Over Texas, has a -137 ft change. How much farther do you drop on the Mean Streak?

$$-155 - (-137) = -155 + 137 \qquad \text{Rewrite as addition.}$$

$$= |-155| - |137| \qquad \text{The integers have different signs. Subtract their absolute values.}$$

$$= 155 - 137$$

$$= 18, \text{but write } -18 \qquad \text{Take the sign of the number with the larger absolute value.}$$

You drop 18 feet farther on the Mean Streak.

DID YOU KNOW?

The Mean Streak can reach speeds of 65 miles per hour.

Try It

The Drop Zone™ Stunt Tower at Paramount's Great America® has a free-fall altitude change of -129 ft. It replaces the Edge™, which had a -60 ft change. How much farther do you free-fall in the Drop Zone?

Check Your Understanding

1. How is subtraction related to addition?

2. Michelle subtracted a negative integer from another integer. Was her answer greater than or less than the original integer? Explain your answer.

PRACTICE 9-5

Practice and Apply

1. **Getting Started** Follow these steps to find the difference $1 - (-4)$ by using algebra tiles.

   a. Draw a positive algebra tile to represent 1.

   b. You don't have 4 negative tiles to take away, so sketch 4 zero pairs.

   c. Subtract by taking away 4 negative tiles.

   d. Count the remaining tiles. Write the difference.

Use algebra tiles to find each difference.

2. $3 - (-3)$ **3.** $-5 - 4$ **4.** $-2 - 7$

Use a number line to find each difference.

5. $5 - (-5)$ **6.** $-3 - (-4)$ **7.** $8 - (-4)$

Operation Sense Find each difference.

8. $-12 - 33$ **9.** $42 - (-14)$ **10.** $-39 - (-45)$ **11.** $-60 - (-120)$ **12.** $85 - (-30)$

13. $-18 - 3$ **14.** $22 - (-17)$ **15.** $52 - 82$ **16.** $-75 - (-75)$ **17.** $-147 - (-56)$

18. $-67 - 136$ **19.** $271 - (-312)$ **20.** $-430 - (-650)$ **21.** $43 + (-15) - (-102)$

Patterns Write the next integer in each pattern.

22. $5, 0, -5,$ _____   **23.** $13, 4, -5,$ _____   **24.** $16, 2, -12,$ _____

Find the unknown number in each difference.

25. $-23 - x = -35$ **26.** $7 - y = -5$

27. $-7 - w = 0$ **28.** $11 - z = 26$

29. **Geography** The table shows the highest and lowest temperatures ever recorded in several states. Find the temperature range for each state. Which state has the widest range? The narrowest range?

Extreme Temperatures					
State	Alaska	California	Hawaii	North Dakota	West Virginia
High Temperature	100°F	134°F	100°F	121°F	112°F
Low Temperature	−80°F	−45°F	14°F	−60°F	−37°F

Death Valley, California

30. **Test Prep** A professional golfer scores 5 under par (-5), 3 under par, 6 under par, and 4 under par for the four days of a tournament. What is her total score?

Ⓐ $+18$　　　Ⓑ $+8$　　　Ⓒ -18　　　Ⓓ -8

Problem Solving and Reasoning

31. **Choose a Strategy** Evaluate the following expressions if $x = -10$ and $y = 20$. Write an equation for each expression.

a. $x - y$　　　**b.** $y - x$　　　**c.** $x - x$　　　**d.** $y - y$

32. **Critical Thinking** The climb from the start to the top of the first hill on the I Scream, You Scream roller coaster is 115 ft.

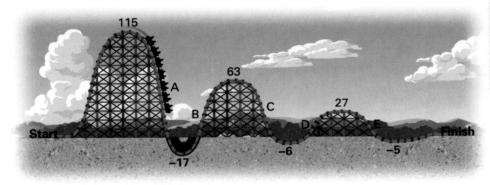

a. What is the change in altitude for drop A, where the coaster plunges into an underground tunnel (from 115 ft to -17 ft)?

b. Find the changes for each of the other climbs and drops (B–E).

c. How did you find the change for climb E?

Mixed Review

Use factor trees to find the prime factorization of the following numbers. If possible, express multiple factors as exponents. *[Lesson 3-6]*

33. 1024　　**34.** 132　　**35.** 66　　**36.** 375　　**37.** 144

38. 210　　**39.** 2730　　**40.** 192　　**41.** 96　　**42.** 2310

Write each decimal as a percent. *[Lesson 8-3]*

43. 0.52　　**44.** 0.17　　**45.** 0.9　　**46.** 0.07　　**47.** 2.43

48. 1　　**49.** 9.87654　　**50.** 0.00003　　**51.** 10.2　　**52.** 0.1053

Problem Solving

STRATEGIES

• Look for a Pattern
• Make an Organized List
• Make a Table
• Guess and Check
• Work Backward
• Use Logical Reasoning
• Draw a Diagram
• Solve a Simpler Problem

TECHNOLOGY

Using a Spreadsheet • Duplicating Formulas

Problem: Magdalena's family owns a cafe. The sales totals for the first five months of the year are shown. What are the average sales per day each month?

You can use your spreadsheet's ability to duplicate formulas to answer this question.

Jan.	$7050
Feb.	$5784
Mar.	$8992
Apr.	$7231
May	$9067

① Enter the data and the number of days in each month into the spreadsheet.

Then, to find January sales per day, divide the value in cell B2 by the number of days in cell B3. This formula is =B2/B3. Enter it into cell B4, and press return.

	A	B	C	D	E	F
1	Month	January	February	March	April	May
2	Sales	7050	5784	8992	7231	9067
3	Days in month	31	28	31	30	31
4	Sales per day	227.42				

② To find sales per day for the other months, you could enter =C2/C3 into cell C4, =D2/D3 into cell D4, and so on. But, except for the letters, these formulas are the same as the one used in cell B4. In this case, you can COPY the formula and PASTE it into cells C4 through F4. The spreadsheet automatically updates the cell references—if you look in cell E4, it shows the formula =E2/E3.

	B
1	January
2	7050
3	31
4	227.42

	A	B	C	D	E	F
1	Month	January	February	March	April	May
2	Sales	7050	5784	8992	7231	9067
3	Days in month	31	28	31	30	31
4	Sales per day	227.42	206.57	290.06	241.03	292.48

Solution: The sales per day are shown in the last row of the table.

TRY IT

Misha's Market is open every day. In the first 13 weeks of the year, customers bought 20, 21, 24, 19, 18, 23, 22, 26, 28, 24, 30, 34, and 48 Super Sleety drinks. Use a spreadsheet to find the average sold per day for each week.

ON YOUR OWN

▶ Why is it helpful to be able to copy and paste formulas in a spreadsheet?

▶ You can also copy and paste numbers in a spreadsheet. Suppose Magdalena's family owned a second restaurant and wanted to find out its sales per day for the first four months. What numbers from the spreadsheet shown in ① would it be useful to copy and paste?

Multiplying Integers

▶ **Lesson Link** │ You know how to add and subtract integers. Now you'll investigate multiplication of integers. ◀

You'll Learn ...

■ to multiply integers

... How It's Used

Civil engineers use integer multiplication when they calculate the forces on a bridge.

Explore │ **Multiplying Integers**

One Good Turn Deserves Another

Latasha videotaped her sister Tonya riding a Ferris wheel. During the first half of the ride, the wheel turned forward (clockwise). During the second half of the ride, the wheel turned backward. Later, the girls played the video on their VCR.

1. On the video, did the wheel appear to turn forward or backward during the first half of the ride?

2. Did the wheel appear to turn forward or backward during the second half of the ride?

3. For fun, the girls decided to run the video backward. Did the wheel appear to turn forward or backward during the first half of the ride? How did the wheel appear to turn during the second half of the ride? Explain.

4. Using your answers to Questions 1–3, copy and complete the table. Describe any patterns you notice.

Ferris Wheel Motion	Forward	Backward	Forward	Backward
VCR Motion	Forward	Forward	Backward	Backward
***Apparent* Motion of Wheel**				

When you multiply two integers, you need to know whether the product is positive or negative. There are four cases to think about:

First Number	Second Number	Example
+	+	2 · 3
+	−	2 · (−3)
−	+	−2 · 3
−	−	−2 · (−3)

The first case is easy. From arithmetic, you know *the product of two positive numbers is positive.*

You can use algebra tiles to investigate the second case.

Think: 2 · (−3) means "two groups of negative three."

There are six red tiles, so 2 · (−3) = −6.

From the Commutative Property of Multiplication, you know that the order of multiplication does not affect the product. For the third case, −3 · 2 must also equal −6. Therefore, *the product of two integers with different signs is negative,* and −2 · 3 also equals −6.

Examples

Find each product.

1 12 • 5

Both numbers are positive, so the product is positive.

12 • 5 = 60

2 −6 • 8

−6 is negative and 8 is positive, so the product is negative.

−6 • 8 = −48

3 7 • (−2)

7 is positive and −2 is negative, so the product is negative.

7 • (−2) = −14

Try It

Find each product.

a. −4 • 4

b. 10 • 2

c. 9 • (−6)

d. −11 • 3

e. 28 • (−5)

f. −19 • 0

Example 4

When the 32 passengers on a roller coaster went through a loop, an average of 65¢ in change fell out of each of their pockets. How much money did the passengers lose in all?

Use -65 to represent a loss of 65¢.

$32 \cdot (-65) = -2080$ The factors have opposite signs, so the product is negative.

The passengers lost 2080¢, or $20.80.

To decide what happens when both numbers are negative, study the pattern in the table. What predictions can you make about $-3 \cdot (-1)$ and $-3 \cdot (-2)$?

Each product is 3 more than the preceding one. Continuing the pattern, $-3 \cdot (-1) = 3$ and $-3 \cdot (-2) = 6$. This shows that *the product of two negative integers is positive.*

Here is a summary of rules for multiplying integers.

-3×4	=	-12
-3×3	=	-9
-3×2	=	-6
-3×1	=	-3
-3×0	=	0
$-3 \times (-1)$	=	?
$-3 \times (-2)$	=	?

Study TIP

You can remember that the product of two negative numbers is positive by imagining their two minus signs forming a plus sign.

INTEGER MULTIPLICATION RULES

- The product of two numbers with the same sign is positive.
- The product of two numbers with different signs is negative.

Examples

5 Multiply: $-34 \cdot (-9)$

Both numbers have the same sign, so the product is positive.

$-34 \cdot (-9) = 306$

6 Multiply: $-2 \cdot (-3) \cdot (-4)$

$-2 \cdot (-3) \cdot (-4) = 6 \cdot (-4)$ The signs are the same, so the product is positive.

$\qquad 6 \cdot (-4) = -24$ The signs are different, so the product is negative.

MENTAL MATH

When you're multiplying a series of integers, look for compatible numbers to multiply first.

Try It

Find each product.

a. $-4 \cdot (-8) \cdot 2$ **b.** $5 \cdot 3 \cdot (-2)$ **c.** $6 \cdot (-2) \cdot (-2)$

1. Explain why $3 \cdot 4 = -3 \cdot (-4)$.

2. What can you say about the signs of two numbers if their product is positive? Negative?

9-6 Exercises and Applications

Practice and Apply

Getting Started Copy and complete each pattern.

1. $4 \times 4 = 16$
$4 \times 3 = 12$
$4 \times 2 = ?$
$4 \times 1 = ?$
$4 \times 0 = 0$
$4 \times (-1) = ?$
$4 \times (-2) = ?$

2. $-5 \times 3 = -15$
$-5 \times 2 = -10$
$-5 \times 1 = ?$
$-5 \times 0 = 0$
$-5 \times (-1) = ?$
$-5 \times (-2) = ?$
$-5 \times (-3) = ?$

3. $-9 \times 3 = ?$
$-9 \times 2 = -18$
$-9 \times 1 = -9$
$-9 \times 0 = ?$
$-9 \times (-1) = ?$
$-9 \times (-2) = ?$
$-9 \times (-3) = 27$

Operation Sense Give the sign of each product.

4. $+ \times +$

5. $+ \times -$

6. $- \times +$

7. $- \times -$

Operation Sense Find each product.

8. $8 \cdot 9$

9. $-8 \cdot (-9)$

10. $-8 \cdot 9$

11. $8 \cdot (-9)$

12. $-8 \cdot 0$

13. $-5 \cdot (-9)$

14. $12 \cdot (-3)$

15. $-20 \cdot 5$

16. $-14 \cdot (-10)$

17. $27 \cdot (-5)$

18. $-81 \cdot 1$

19. $-25 \cdot (-5)$

20. $100 \cdot (-10)$

21. $-16 \cdot 7$

22. $-50 \cdot (-50)$

23. $-2 \cdot (-2) \cdot (-2)$

24. $-5 \cdot 2 \cdot (-3)$

25. $-7 \cdot 3 \cdot 4$

26. $10 \cdot (-6) \cdot (-5)$

27. $8 \cdot (-8) \cdot 8$

28. Science The underlying rock ledge of Canada's Horseshoe Falls is cut back about 2 ft each year by erosion.

    a. Write the erosion rate as a negative integer.

    b. Calculate how much the rock ledge will erode over a seven-year period.

PRACTICE 9-6

29. **Sports** A hockey player's plus-minus rating compares the number of goals scored by his or her team (plus) to the number scored by the opponents (minus) while he or she is playing. In 1996, eight players on the San Jose Sharks had an average plus-minus rating of -17. What was the total of their ratings?

30. **Estimation** Estimate the product $-5 \cdot 19 \cdot (-11)$. Explain how you made your estimate.

31. **Test Prep** Miguel withdrew $20 per week from his bank account for 4 weeks. Which expression shows the change in his account balance?

    Ⓐ $-20 + 4$ Ⓑ $-20 - 4$ Ⓒ -20×4 Ⓓ $-20 \div 4$

Problem Solving and Reasoning

32. **Communicate** In this exercise, you will look for patterns in powers of negative numbers.

    a. Evaluate $(-2)^2$, $(-2)^3$, $(-2)^4$, $(-2)^5$, and $(-2)^6$.

    b. Evaluate $(-3)^2$, $(-3)^3$, $(-3)^4$, $(-3)^5$, and $(-3)^6$.

    c. What patterns do you notice in your results? Explain why the patterns make sense.

33. **Communicate** How is multiplying integers like multiplying whole numbers? How is it different?

34. **Critical Thinking** Suppose an amusement park bought a merry-go-round for $92,000, and 42,512 people paid $2 each to ride the merry-go-round in its first year of operation. Ignoring the cost of operation, how much money did the park earn or lose on this ride in its first year?

Mixed Review

Find the GCF for each pair of numbers. *[Lesson 3-7]*

35. 45, 75   **36.** 132, 55   **37.** 68, 187   **38.** 76, 361

39. 147, 168   **40.** 51, 129   **41.** 273, 54   **42.** 36, 72

Use mental math to find each percent. *[Lesson 8-4]*

43. 15% of 400   **44.** 10% of 42   **45.** 75% of 120   **46.** 20% of 40

47. 5% of 30   **48.** 80% of 50   **49.** 15% of $36   **50.** 60% of 200

Dividing Integers

▶ **Lesson Link** You know how to add, subtract, and multiply integers. Now you'll use your knowledge of multiplication to develop division rules for integers. ◀

Explore | Dividing Integers

A Pretty Mean Drop

The table gives altitude changes for free-fall drops in five amusement park rides.

1. Plot these altitude changes on a number line.

Name of Ride	Desperado	Drop Zone™	Steel Force®	Loch Ness Monster®	Mantis
Change (ft)	−225	−137	−205	−114	−137

2. Estimate a point on the line that represents the mean of these changes. How did you choose the point? Is the mean positive or negative? (Recall that the mean of a data set is the sum of the values divided by the number of values.)

3. Without adding, tell whether the sum of the changes is positive or negative. Explain how you decided.

4. Without dividing, tell whether the sum of the changes divided by 5 is positive or negative. Explain how you know.

5. Two rides not listed above have altitude changes of −100 ft and −200 ft. Find the mean change for these rides. How did you find the mean?

Learn | Dividing Integers

Multiplication and division are inverse operations. If you know the product of two numbers, you can find two quotients.

$$3 \cdot 4 = 12$$

$$12 \div 4 = 3 \qquad\qquad 12 \div 3 = 4$$

Examples

Use the given product to find each quotient.

1 $8 \cdot 6 = 48$ **2** $-2 \cdot 4 = -8$ **3** $-3 \cdot (-2) = 6$ **4** $9 \cdot (-6) = -54$

$48 \div 8 = ?$ $-8 \div 4 = ?$ $6 \div (-3) = ?$ $-54 \div (-6) = ?$

$48 \div 8 = 6$ $-8 \div 4 = -2$ $6 \div (-3) = -2$ $-54 \div (-6) = 9$

Try It

Use the given product to find each quotient.

a. $7 \cdot 4 = 28$ **b.** $5 \cdot (-3) = -15$ **c.** $-2 \cdot 9 = -18$ **d.** $-3 \cdot (-3) = 9$

$28 \div 7 = ?$ $-15 \div (-3) = ?$ $-18 \div 9 = ?$ $9 \div (-3) = ?$

Because of the relationship between multiplication and division, the rules for dividing integers are the same as those for multiplying integers.

INTEGER DIVISION RULES

- The quotient of two numbers with the same sign is positive.
- The quotient of two numbers with different signs is negative.

Example 5

Shelley played miniature golf at an amusement park. *Par* is a typical number of strokes (shots) for a hole. Scores above par are positive, scores below par are negative.

On the first five holes, Shelley's scores were -2, -1, $+1$, -2, and -1. What was her mean score for these holes?

To find the mean, divide the total score by the number of holes.

$$\frac{-2 + (-1) + 1 + (-2) + (-1)}{5} = \frac{-5}{5} = -1$$

Shelley's mean score for the first five holes was -1 (1 under par).

Try It

Here are the results of six plays for the Elbmuf Junior High football team. Find the mean gain per play.

$-3, -5, 19, -7, -24, -4$

Problem Solving TIP

You can use additive inverses to simplify sums of integers. In Example 5, you can first add -1 and $+1$ to make 0, then add the remaining numbers.

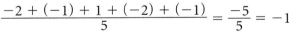

WHAT DO YOU THINK?

With their spelunking club, Andy and Jyotsna want to explore a cave passage whose elevation is −56 ft. They plan to descend at a rate of −8 ft/min. They need to know how long it will take to reach the cave.

Andy thinks ...

I'll ignore the positive and negative signs.

56 divided by 8 is 7.

The two integers −56 and −8 have the same sign, so the quotient is positive 7.

It will take us 7 minutes to reach the passage.

Jyotsna thinks ...

I'll turn this into a multiplication problem.

We'll go −56 feet at −8 feet per minute.

Since rate × time = distance, I need to know what number times −8 is −56. I know 56 is 8 times 7. A negative product must come from two numbers with different signs, so the number I'm looking for is positive 7.

It will take us 7 minutes to reach the passage.

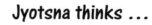

What do you think?

1. Did Andy really ignore the positive and negative signs? Explain.

2. After exploring the cave, Andy and Jyotsna took 28 minutes to return to the surface. How would each calculate the speed of their ascent?

| **Check** | **Your Understanding** |

1. The quotient of two integers is positive. What do you know about the signs of the integers?

2. The quotient of two integers is negative. What do you know about the signs of the integers?

Practice and Apply

1. **Getting Started** Altitude changes for the longest drops of some of the world's largest roller coasters are shown. Follow these steps to find the average change.

Name	Steel Phantom	Moonsault Scramble	Mean Streak	Texas Giant™
Change (ft)	−225	−207	−155	−137

   a. Add the four altitude changes.
   b. Divide the sum by 4 to find the average change.
   c. Write your answer as an integer.
   d. Does this represent a drop or a rise?

Operation Sense Give the sign of each quotient.

2. $+ \div +$
3. $+ \div -$
4. $- \div +$
5. $- \div -$

Use the given product to find each quotient.

6. $7 \cdot 4 = 28$
   $28 \div 4 = ?$

7. $-3 \cdot 17 = -51$
   $-51 \div 17 = ?$

8. $-7 \cdot (-9) = 63$
   $63 \div (-7) = ?$

9. $8 \cdot (-4) = -32$
   $-32 \div (-4) = ?$

Find each quotient.

10. $-18 \div (-9)$
11. $-18 \div 9$
12. $0 \div (-8)$
13. $16 \div (-2)$
14. $-63 \div (-7)$
15. $-81 \div (-1)$
16. $-40 \div 10$
17. $80 \div (-5)$
18. $-105 \div 5$
19. $-300 \div (-20)$
20. $400 \div 0$
21. $-1000 \div 125$
22. $-256 \div (-16)$
23. $-56 \div 7 \div (-2)$

24. **Science** A cold wave gripped much of the United States during the first week of February 1996. The lowest temperatures in four Ohio cities that week were: Cleveland, −10°F; Cincinnati, −11°F; Columbus, −3°F; Toledo, −8°F. What was the average lowest temperature for these cities?

25. **Statistics** Antonio had scores of −1, −2, −1, −2, 0, 2, −1, −2, and −2 for nine holes on a miniature golf course. What was his mean score?

PRACTICE 9-7

26. **Test Prep** If you divide one negative number by another, the quotient is:

 Ⓐ Greater than either number   Ⓑ Less than either number

 Ⓒ Equal to one of the numbers   Ⓓ Not enough information to tell

Problem Solving and Reasoning

27. Communicate What is the mean of five negative integers and their opposites? Explain how you know.

28. Critical Thinking The table gives *Amusement Business* magazine's estimated 1993–1995 attendance figures for the four best attended amusement and theme parks in the United States.

Find the average change in attendance for these parks from 1993 to 1994. Compare this to the average change from 1994 to 1995. Express your answers as integers, and explain what their signs mean.

Park Attendance, 1993–1995	1993	1994	1995
The Magic Kingdom®	12,000,000	11,200,000	12,900,000
Disneyland®	11,400,000	10,300,000	14,100,000
EPCOT®	10,000,000	9,700,000	10,700,000
Disney–MGM Studios	8,000,000	8,000,000	9,500,000

Mixed Review

Express each fraction in lowest terms. *[Lesson 3-8]*

29. $\frac{33}{75}$ **30.** $\frac{10}{20}$ **31.** $\frac{9}{45}$ **32.** $\frac{12}{48}$ **33.** $\frac{52}{65}$ **34.** $\frac{4}{4}$ **35.** $\frac{5}{25}$ **36.** $\frac{240}{375}$

Solve each problem. If necessary, round answers to the nearest tenth. *[Lesson 8-5]*

37. What percent of 56 is 28?   **38.** 20% of what number is 5?   **39.** 11% of 200 is what number?

40. 16% of 50 is what number?   **41.** What percent of 144 is 36?   **42.** 45% of 40 is what number?

Project Progress

Use your list of events to complete your time line. Illustrate your time line by cutting out or drawing pictures to show different events. Make a list showing the time that passed between several pairs of events on your time line. Include events before and after your birth, and in your future.

Problem Solving

Understand
Plan
Solve
Look Back

You've added, subtracted, multiplied, and divided integers. Now you'll show how these integer operations relate to the "real" world of roller coasters, water slides, and merry-go-rounds.

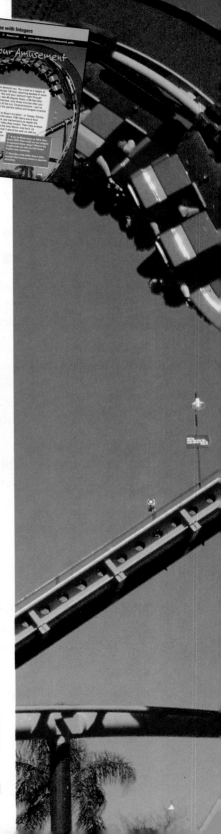

For Your Amusement

Your class has just been put in charge of an amusement park, and you're part of the public relations (PR) team. Your job is to explain the relationship between mathematics and amusement parks to other students.

1. Write four problems involving mathematics in your amusement park.

   • Each problem should involve a different operation ($+$, $-$, $\times$, $\div$).

   • One problem should involve a ride, one should involve a game, and one should involve money.

   • The fourth problem can be about a topic of your choice.

   • At least two of the problems should involve negative integers.

2. Solve each of your problems in writing. Be sure to show your solutions clearly so other students can learn from them. Explain how you know your solutions are correct.

3. Prepare a presentation of your problems and solutions that you could give to your class.

Find each sum, difference, product, or quotient.

1. $7 + (-7)$ **2.** $-9 - (-3)$ **3.** $5 \cdot (-10)$ **4.** $-24 \div 6$ **5.** $-11 + 20$

6. $-24 \div (-3)$ **7.** $-15 \cdot (-10)$ **8.** $-37 - 47$ **9.** $-59 + (-181)$ **10.** $-17 \cdot 101$

11. $108 - (-274)$ **12.** $-17 \cdot (-1001)$ **13.** $288 \div (-18)$ **14.** $0 \div (-52)$ **15.** $17 \cdot (-10,001)$

Evaluate each expression.

16. $3 + (-4) - 8$ **17.** $(-2)(-8)(-10)$ **18.** $16 \div (-2) \div (-4)$ **19.** $-5 + 6 \div (-2) + (-4) \cdot (-2)$

Plot each point on the same coordinate plane. *[Lesson 9-3]*

20. $(-3, 7)$ **21.** $(-5, -8)$ **22.** $(9, -2)$ **23.** $(-6, 0)$ **24.** $(-3, 4)$

25. Explain why subtracting an integer gives the same result as adding its opposite. You may wish to draw algebra tiles or number lines to illustrate your explanation.

26. History After Chicago's World's Columbian Exposition in 1893, the number of amusement parks in the United States grew rapidly. By 1919, there were about 1520 parks. Because of the Great Depression, which began in 1929, only 400 were left by 1935. Find the rate of change in the number of parks from 1919 to 1935. Give your answer in parks per year.

27. Science The highest temperature ever recorded was 136°F (58°C), in Libya. The lowest ever recorded was −129°F (−89°C), in Antarctica. Find the difference between these extreme temperatures in °F and in °C.

Test Prep

When you're asked to find the mean (average) of several integers on a multiple choice test, you can use mental math to estimate the sign and size of the answer. By doing this, you may be able to eliminate some answer choices.

28. What is the mean of −29, −12, 39, −48, and 20?

 Ⓐ −60 Ⓑ −6 Ⓒ −0.6 Ⓓ 6

Negative Exponents and Scientific Notation

You've seen how scientific notation is used to write large numbers. To convert a number to scientific notation, rewrite it as a number greater than or equal to 1, but less than 10, multiplied by a power of 10.

For instance, 2300 is 2.3×10^3 in scientific notation. The exponent of 10 is positive 3 because you have moved the decimal point *three* places to the left.

Scientific notation can also be used to write small numbers. Look at the pattern in the table.

Number	2,300	230	23	2.3	0.23	0.023
Scientific Notation	2.3×10^3	2.3×10^2	2.3×10^1	2.3×10^0	2.3×10^{-1}	2.3×10^{-2}

Notice that to convert 0.023 to scientific notation, the decimal point must be moved *two* places to the *right*. This tells you that the exponent of 10 is *negative* 2.

$$0.023 = 2.3 \times 10^{-2}$$

Two places to the right.

Here's how to convert 0.000794 to scientific notation.

Move the decimal point to between the 7 and the 9, so the number is 1 or more but less than 10. This moves the decimal point four places to the right, so the power of 10 is −4.

$$0.000794 = 7.94 \times 10^{-4}$$

You can write a number such as 1.175×10^{-6} without scientific notation. The exponent −6 tells you that the decimal point must be moved 6 places to the *left*. Annex 6 zeros before moving the decimal point. The sixth zero is added because we prefer to show decimal numbers with a digit in front of the decimal point.

$$0000001.175 \times 10^{-6} = 0.000001175$$

Try It

Write each number in scientific notation.

1. 0.0031   **2.** 0.24   **3.** 0.00000913   **4.** 0.00004001   **5.** 0.005515

Write each number without scientific notation.

6. 2.8×10^{-3} **7.** 8.55×10^{-1} **8.** 8.03×10^{-6} **9.** 1.284×10^{-4}

Graphic Organizer

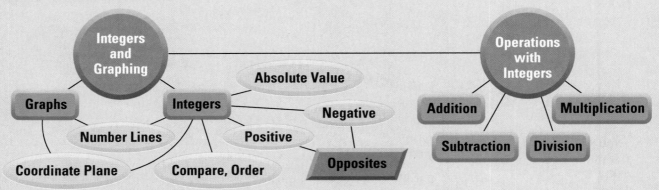

Section 9A Using Integers

Summary

- A **number line** can be horizontal or vertical. Its zero point is the **origin**.

- **Positive numbers** are greater than zero. **Negative numbers** are less than zero and are written with a − sign.

- Distances on a number line are always positive. The **absolute value** of a number is its distance from zero.

- Whole numbers (including zero) and their opposites are **integers**.

- The **x-y coordinate plane** is based on a horizontal number line (x-axis) and a vertical number line (y-axis). The axes intersect at the **origin**.

- Any point can be described by an **ordered pair,** like $(-3, 5)$. The first number (the **x-coordinate**) tells how far to the left or right of the origin the point is. The **y-coordinate** tells how far up or down the point is.

Review

1. Tell whether -1.75 is an integer.

2. Use a sign to write the number: lost $25

3. Write the opposite of 42.

4. Find the absolute value: $|-87|$

5. Use $>$, $<$, or $=$ to compare the numbers: $-18 \ \square \ -91$

6. Order the set of numbers from least to greatest: $18, -4, 0, 10, -8$

7. Draw a square so that each of its vertices is in a different quadrant. Label the coordinates of each vertex.

8. Plot each point on the same coordinate plane.
   a. $(-3, 2)$ **b.** $(0, 4)$ **c.** $(1, 3)$

Summary

■ You can use a number line to add integers. To add a positive number, move right. To add a negative number, move left.

■ Algebra tiles can be used to represent integers. The tiles ▢ ▣ form a **zero pair**. You can use algebra tiles to add or subtract integers. After all zero pairs are removed, the tiles left represent the sum or difference.

■ The **additive inverse** of an integer is its opposite. The **Inverse Property of Addition** says that the sum of an integer and its additive inverse is 0.

■ To add two integers with the same sign, add their absolute values and use the sign of the numbers. To add two integers with different signs, subtract their absolute values and use the sign of the number with the larger absolute value. To subtract an integer, add its opposite.

■ To multiply two integers, multiply their absolute values and then decide the correct sign. The product is positive if the numbers have the same sign; it is negative if they have different signs.

■ To divide two integers, divide their absolute values and then decide the correct sign. The quotient is positive if the numbers have the same sign; it is negative if they have different signs.

Review

9. Write the addition problem and the sum modeled in the picture.

10. Use algebra tiles or a number line to find the sum $3 + (-7)$.

11. Write the next integer in the pattern: $-16, -10, -4,$ _____

12. Find each sum.
   a. $-2 + 8$
   b. $-7 + (-4)$
   c. $-41 + (-24)$
   d. $-25 + (-62) + 25$

13. Find each difference.
   a. $4 - 7$
   b. $-2 - (-6)$
   c. $-73 - 28$
   d. $-85 - (-97) - 12$

14. Find each product.
   a. $-7 \cdot 12$
   b. $-10 \cdot (-4)$
   c. $21 \cdot 6 \cdot (-2)$
   d. $32 \cdot (-3) \cdot (-5)$

15. Find each quotient.
   a. $110 \div (-5)$
   b. $-32 \div (-8)$
   c. $-54 \div 9$
   d. $168 \div 4 \div 2$

16. Wanda's business lost $42,000 over a period of eight years. What was the average annual loss?

17. The lowest point in the United States is Death Valley, California, 282 ft below sea level. The highest point is Mt. McKinley, Alaska, 20,320 ft above sea level. Subtract to find the range of elevations.

1. Use a sign to write the number: 23 degrees below zero

2. Write the opposite of -54.

3. Find the absolute value: $|-327|$

4. Use $>$, $<$, or $=$ to compare the pair of numbers: $5 \boxed{} -21$

5. Order the set of numbers from least to greatest: $5, -28, -3, 0$

6. Find the coordinates of each point.

    a. A　　　**b.** B　　　**c.** C　　　**d.** D　　　**e.** E

7. Plot each point on the same coordinate plane.

    a. $(-4, 1)$　　**b.** $(-3, 0)$　　**c.** $(3, 1)$　　**d.** $(1, -2)$

8. Name the quadrant or axis that contains $(-18, -12)$.

9. Write the next integer in the pattern: $17, 8, -1, \underline{}$

10. Write the addition problem and the sum modeled in the picture.

11. Use algebra tiles or a number line to find the sum $-2 + 6$.

12. Find each sum, difference, product, or quotient.

    a. $-2 + 5$ 　　　　**b.** $17 + (-11)$ 　　**c.** $-26 + (-31)$ 　　**d.** $5 - (-4)$

    e. $-23 - 8$ 　　　**f.** $-75 - 53$ 　　　**g.** $-13 \cdot (-7)$ 　　**h.** $8 \cdot (-11)$

    i. $-5 \cdot (-6) \cdot (-7)$ 　**j.** $-50 \div 25$ 　　　**k.** $78 \div (-6)$ 　　**l.** $-93 \div (-3)$

13. Gerry's bank account has a balance of $146. What will his balance be after he deposits $100 and then withdraws $33?

14. Fill in the blank with *sometimes*, *always*, or *never*: The product of two negative integers is _____ greater than the product of a negative integer and a positive integer.

Performance Task

The figure on the left is called a *magic square* because the whole numbers in each row, column, and diagonal add up to the same number. Use integers to complete a copy of the magic square on the right. Then make up a magic square of your own that contains positive and negative integers.

6	7	2
1	5	9
8	3	4

	3	−4
	−1	
2		

Performance Assessment

Choose one problem.

Good Game!

Design your own board or card game that uses integer addition, subtraction, multiplication, and division to determine the number of points a player has. The game can involve skill, chance, or a combination of the two.

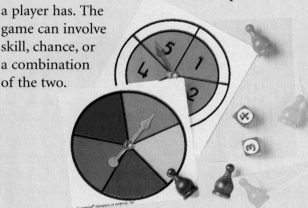

THE BIG CHILL

The table shows the lowest known temperatures for five states and the elevations of the places where they occurred, to the nearest hundred meters. Graph this data on a coordinate plane, then describe any patterns you see. Predict the elevation for a record low temperature of −33°F.

State	Elev. (m)	Temp. (°F)
California	1,700	−45°
Georgia	300	−17°
New Mexico	2,200	−50°
Texas	1,000	−23°
West Virginia	700	−37°

What Goes Up May Come Down

You can show negative values on a bar graph by drawing bars that go below the horizontal axis. Draw a bar graph that shows last week's performance of the stocks in Mr. Takagi's portfolio.

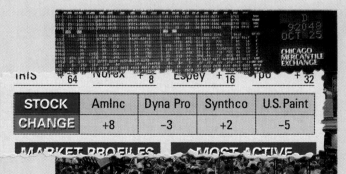

STOCK	AmInc	Dyna Pro	Synthco	U.S. Paint
CHANGE	+8	−3	+2	−5

HOME, SWEET HOME

Draw a simple pentagonal house on a coordinate plane. Place the tip of the "roof" on the y-axis, the corners of the roof in quadrants I and II, and the bottom of the house in quadrants III and IV. Draw a second house by doubling the coordinates of each vertex of your original house. Compare the shapes, perimeters, and areas of the two houses.

Science Link
www.mathsurf.com/7/ch10/science

Science

To convert Fahrenheit temperatures to Celsius, subtract 32 and multiply the result by $\frac{5}{9}$. The only temperature that is the same in both scales is $-40°$.

People of the World

In fifteenth-century Italy, the merchant's key was a rule used to determine how much a quantity of an item would cost. The merchant would find the unit cost and multiply it by the quantity that the customer wanted.

LISA LESLIE

JENNIFER AZZI

TERESA EDWARDS

SHERYL SWOOPES

DAWN STALEY

Entertainment

In fantasy sports leagues, people "pick teams" of professional athletes. Formulas are used to analyze the athletes' perform-ances and to see whose team did the best.

and Graphs

Arts & Literature Link
www.mathsurf.com/7/ch10/arts

Social Studies

Businesspeople use graphs to show trends in their company's profits.

Arts & Literature

Fractal patterns like the one shown below are generated by mathematical rules. Some fractals are made by substituting coordinates for many different points into an equation, then tracing the results for each point.

KEY MATH IDEAS

Quantities whose values can change are variables. Those whose values do not change are constants. The relationship between two variables can be shown in a table or graph.

A sequence is a pattern of numbers. By writing an algebraic rule for a sequence, you can find any of its terms.

You can solve an equation by using a graph or a table. If you find the value of the known variable on the graph or in the table, you can read the value of the unknown variable.

You can also solve an equation involving integers by using algebra tiles or algebraic symbols. When solving by these methods, you must always do the same thing to both sides of the equation.

CHAPTER PROJECT

Problem Solving

Understand
Plan
Solve
Look Back

In this project, you'll investigate the population of your city, town, or state. Begin by choosing the population you're interested in. Then do some research to find this population for several different years.

Problem Solving Focus

Checking for a Reasonable Answer

It is important to look back at your answer to a problem to make sure it's reasonable. You can use an estimate to evaluate the reasonableness of your exact answer.

Each of the problems below has an answer, but the answer is not exactly right. Tell if each answer is "close enough," "too low," or "too high," and explain why.

1 The tallest mountain in the world, Mount Everest, is 29,028 ft tall. It is located on the border of China and Nepal. The tallest mountain in the Americas is Aconcagua, which is 5,994 ft shorter than Mount Everest. How tall is Aconcagua?
Answer: 21,100 ft

2 Mount Kanchenjunga, on the border between Nepal and Sikkim, is 12 ft less than twice as tall as Pike's Peak in Colorado. If Pike's Peak is 14,110 ft tall, how tall is Mount Kanchenjunga?
Answer: 28,200 ft

3 What is the mean of the heights of Mount Everest and Alaska's 20,320 ft Mount McKinley, the tallest mountain in the United States?
Answer: 26,300 ft

4 The highest waterfall in the world is 1000-meter-tall Angel Falls in Venezuela. It is 6 meters less than twice as tall as Takkakaw Falls in British Columbia, Canada. What is the height of Takkakaw Falls?
Answer: 500 meters

5 The second- and third-highest waterfalls in the world are 914-meter-tall Tugela Falls in South Africa and Cuquenán Falls in Venezuela. The height of Cuquenán Falls is $\frac{2}{3}$ of the height of Tugela Falls. How tall is Cuquenán Falls?
Answer: 400 meters

6 Sutherland Falls, in New Zealand, is 580 meters tall. It is 486 meters taller than Lower Yellowstone Falls, in Wyoming. How tall is Lower Yellowstone Falls?
Answer: 200 meters

Howdy, Ant Bee!

A summer picnic in a city park—what could be nicer? Unfortunately, these outings can turn into a battle for the survival of the fittest. While you're brushing the ants off your fruit salad with one hand and slapping mosquitoes with the other, you're trying to dodge a swarm of bees who think your insect repellent smells like a flower!

When most people think of insects, only the annoying ones come to mind. Yet of the more than one million species of insects, probably less than 2% are pests. In fact, many of these six-legged creatures are essential to our survival. About one-third of our food is a direct result of insect pollination of plants.

Entomologists use mathematics to model insect behavior and the growth of insect populations. Now you will investigate many of the mathematical tools these scientists use.

1. There are about 4600 species of mammals. How many times more species of insects are there?

2. Suppose an adult human consumes 2100 food calories in a day. On average, how many of these calories are a direct result of insect pollination?

481

Quantities, Constants, and Variables

You'll Learn ...

■ to identify variables and constants

... How It's Used

The quantities measured by medical tests are variables that can be used to diagnose illnesses.

Vocabulary

constant

▶ **Lesson Link** You've used variables to help you solve many different types of problems. Now you'll take a closer look at variables and other numbers. ◀

Explore | **Types of Numbers**

Flying Lesson

Think about each of the numbers described below. Make a table showing the numbers that can change and those that always stay the same.

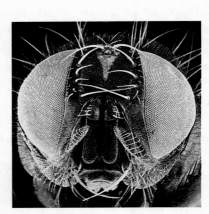

1. Number of legs on a normal housefly

2. Amount of food eaten by a housefly in one day

3. Distance a housefly flies in an hour

4. Weight of a male housefly

5. Number of wings on a normal housefly

6. Add other fly-related numbers to your table. Include at least one number that stays the same and another that can change.

7. Give the actual value of any number in Step 6 that you know about. What do you notice about all of these numbers?

Learn | **Quantities, Constants, and Variables**

A *quantity* is anything that can be measured by a number. The number of inches in a foot and the number of ladybugs on a leaf are quantities. The *value* for the first of these quantities is 12 inches; the second value might be 1 ladybug.

As you've seen, quantities whose values may change are called *variables*. Quantities whose values cannot change are called **constants**.

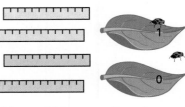

Always 12 in.
→ **constant**

Can change
→ **variable**

Examples

Tell whether each quantity is a variable or a constant.

1 The number of times a butterfly's wings beat in one minute

The number of beats in a minute can change, so this quantity is a variable.

2 The number of antennae on a butterfly

Butterflies always have two antennae, so this quantity is a constant.

Try It

Tell whether each quantity is a variable or a constant.

a. Your height

b. The number of centimeters in a meter

c. The number of locusts in a swarm

d. The number of quarters in a dollar

► **Science Link**

A swarm of locusts may contain 28 billion insects, weighing a total of 70 tons.

Although variables can take on different values, you can make an educated guess at a reasonable *range* of values for many real-world quantities.

Examples

For each quantity, define a variable and give a range of reasonable values.

3 The length of a cricket

Let c = the length of a cricket. By looking at a ruler, you can estimate that c is between 1 cm and 4 cm.

4 The number of songs on a CD

Let s = the number of songs. For most CDs, s is between 8 and 15.

Try It

For each quantity, define a variable and give a range of reasonable values.

a. The time it takes to get to school

b. The wingspan of a butterfly

Check | Your Understanding

1. Explain the difference between variable and constant quantities.

2. Why do you think we use letters instead of numbers to represent the values of variable quantities?

Practice and Apply

PRACTICE 10-1

1. **Getting Started** Fill in each blank with the appropriate word.
   a. Quantities whose values change are _____.
   b. Quantities whose values do not change are _____.

Tell whether each quantity is a variable or a constant.

2. The number of days in a year

3. The weight of a puppy

4. The number of hornets in a nest

5. The number of students absent each day

6. The number of feet in a mile

7. The speed of a car

Hornets' nest

Number Sense For each quantity, define a variable and give a reasonable range of values.

8. The length of a grasshopper

9. The weight of a newborn baby

10. The height of a two-story building

11. The time it takes to eat lunch

12. The price of a movie ticket

13. The height of a school desk

Measurement Give an appropriate unit of measurement for each quantity.

14. The weight of a mosquito

15. The length of a room

16. The amount of milk in a glass

17. The amount of time it takes to play a board game

18. **Problem Solving** You're planning your school's Valentine's Day dance. You originally expected 200 people to attend, but a flu virus hit the school. Now you think only 100 people will attend.
    a. Name two quantities related to the dance that will change.
    b. Name two quantities related to the dance that will remain the same.

19. **Geometry** The formula for the area of a triangle is $A = \frac{1}{2}bh$. What quantities in this formula can vary? What remains constant?

20. **Social Studies** In 1996, California had 52 representatives in the House of Representatives, Florida had 23, and Alaska had 1. Every state has 2 senators. Which quantity is a constant, the number of senators or the number of representatives? Which quantity is a variable?

21. **Test Prep** Marcus is a nurse. He works the same number of days each week, but a different number of hours each day. Which of the following is true?

Ⓐ Hours worked per day is constant   Ⓑ Hours worked per week is constant

Ⓒ Days worked per month is constant   Ⓓ Days worked in two weeks is constant

Problem Solving and Reasoning

22. **Critical Thinking** Certain types of animals always have the same number of legs, while others may have a varying number. Which of the quantities described are constants and which are variables?

   a. The walking stick has 6 legs, as do all insects.

   b. Sunstars, a type of starfish, can have up to 50 arms.

   c. The cardinal has 2 legs, as do all other birds.

23. **Communicate** Ginny measured a room and found that it was 4.1 meters long. Alex measured the same length but found that it was 13.5 feet long. They said that the room's length is a variable, since they got different measurements. What do you think?

24. **Journal** You've just gotten off a bus. During the bus ride, was the speed of the bus a constant or a variable? Is the *average* speed of the bus for your trip a constant or a variable? Explain your answers.

Walking stick

Mixed Review

Estimate the map distance. *[Lesson 7-1]*

25. Omaha, Nebraska, is 833 miles from Salt Lake City, Utah. About how far apart will these cities appear on a map with a scale 1 in.:70 mi?

Order each set of numbers from greatest to least. *[Lesson 9-2]*

26. $10, −$9, $7, $0, −$1, $3, −$8   27. −42°, 41°, 32°, 3°, −15°, −3°

28. −4, 3, −2, 1, 0, −5, 6   29. −4221, −4122, −4212, −4111, −4222

10-2 Relating Graphs to Stories

You'll Learn ...

■ to match a graph to a story

■ to write a story for a graph

... How It's Used

Quality control experts analyze graphs to decide when product quality is declining and a manufacturing process needs to be corrected.

Vocabulary

increasing graph

decreasing graph

constant graph

> ► **Lesson Link** You've investigated quantities that can change. Now you'll explore a way to show relationships between variables visually. ◄

Explore | Relating Graphs to Stories

Breaking Out of Hives

1. The graph shows the population of bees in a hive over time. Look at the change in the graph between points A and B. Explain what might have happened during this time period.

2. In what way did the population change between points B and C? Explain what might have happened between these times.

3. How is the increase in the number of bees between points C and D different from that between points A and B?

4. What might have happened between point D and point E?

Learn | Relating Graphs to Stories

The direction of a graph can show a relationship between the quantities on its axes.

When the graph is **increasing** from left to right, the quantities on the axes go up together.

When the graph is **decreasing**, one quantity goes down when the other goes up.

When the graph is **constant**, one quantity stays the same when the other changes.

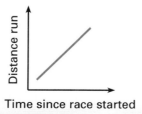

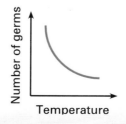

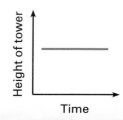

Example 1

A bee flies from the hive to the flower garden, stays a while to get some pollen, and then flies back to the hive. Which graph could show its flight?

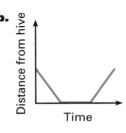

a. Distance from hive / Time

b. Distance from hive / Time

c. Distance from hive / Time

When the bee leaves, its distance from the hive *increases*. Then it stops at the garden, so the graph is *constant*. As the bee returns to the hive, the distance *decreases*. The answer is **c.**

Try It

Another bee was at the flower garden. It flew to the hive, stayed a while, and then flew back to the garden. Which of the graphs above could show its flight?

Example 2

The graph shows the number of homework exercises Leilani did one night. Tell a story that fits the graph.

Leilani did about half of the exercises. Then she stopped doing homework while she talked to her friend. Next, she did the rest of the problems, but worked more slowly than she had at first.

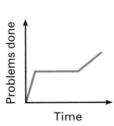

Problems done / Time

Try It

The graph shows the number of students in a classroom over time. Tell a story that fits the graph.

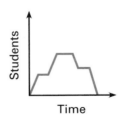

Students / Time

Check Your Understanding

1. How can you tell from a graph whether two quantities have an increasing relationship? A decreasing relationship? A constant relationship?

2. None of the graphs in this lesson had numbers on their axes. How is it possible to get useful information from these graphs?

Practice and Apply

1. **Getting Started** You're flying from Tulsa to Oklahoma City. As the time increases, tell whether each of the following quantities increases, decreases, or stays constant.

   a. The miles remaining to Oklahoma City
   b. The amount of fuel in the airplane
   c. The number of pilots on the airplane
   d. The miles from Tulsa

Number Sense Name another quantity that each given quantity might depend on.

2. The height of a termite mound

3. The area of a square

4. The amount of money a business makes

5. The height of a teenager

Termite mound

For Exercises 6 and 7, choose the graph that best shows the story.

6. You notice a few fleas on your dog. You decide they'll probably go away on their own. Instead, the problem gets much worse!

   a.
   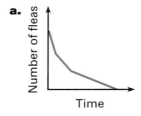

   b.
   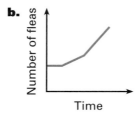

   c.
   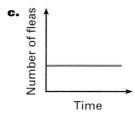

7. You bicycle to your friend's apartment and stay there for lunch. Then the two of you ride to an arcade and play some games. After you finish, you ride straight home.

   a.
   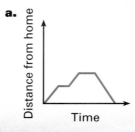

   b.
   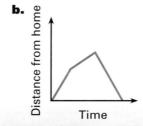

   c.
   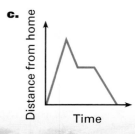

For Exercises 8–10, tell a story that fits each graph.

8.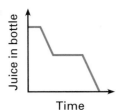

9.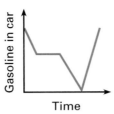

10.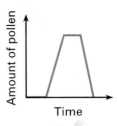

11. Problem Solving A fly soars into the air, looks for a picnic, and then dives onto your plate. Sketch a graph that shows the relationship between time and height for the fly.

12. | Test Prep | Which of these statements is true about the graph?

Ⓐ Increases from X to Y

Ⓑ Decreases from Y to Z

Ⓒ Stays constant from W to X

Ⓓ None of the above

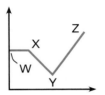

Problem Solving and Reasoning

13. Critical Thinking The graphs show performances by three runners in the same race. If the time scales are the same, which graph shows the winner's performance? Explain.

a.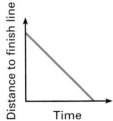

b.

c.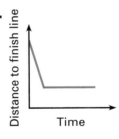

14. [Journal] Draw a graph that includes at least one section sloping upward, at least one sloping downward, and at least one flat section. Make up a story to fit the graph. Label your graph's axes so they match the story.

Mixed Review

A model boat is 4 cm long. Use each scale to find the length of the actual boat. *[Lesson 7-2]*

15. Scale: 1 cm = 2 m

16. Scale: 1 cm = $4\frac{1}{4}$ m

17. Scale: 2 cm = 7 m

Plot each point on the same coordinate plane. *[Lesson 9-3]*

18. $(-4, 3)$

19. $(2, 0)$

20. $(5, -1)$

21. $(-4, -2)$

22. $(0, -1)$

Tables and Expressions

▶ **Lesson Link** You've seen how graphs can show relationships between quantities. Now you'll see how those relationships can be shown in a table. ◀

You'll Learn ...

■ to write rules for sequences

■ to identify arithmetic and geometric sequences

... How It's Used

Biologists use sequences to analyze population growth.

Vocabulary

sequence

term

arithmetic sequence

geometric sequence

Explore | Tables

Patterns, Patterns Everywhere

Materials: Centimeter cubes or graph paper

1. Use cubes to build the figures shown, or sketch them on graph paper.

2. Continue the pattern. How many cubes would it take to make the fourth figure? The fifth? Organize your findings in a table.

1st   2nd   3rd

3. Describe any patterns you see in your table.

Figure Number (n)	1	2	3	4	5	6
Number of Cubes	2	4	6			

4. Predict the number of cubes in the 100th figure. Explain how you made your prediction.

5. If we use the variable n to represent the number of a figure, how could we use n to describe the number of cubes? Explain.

Learn | Tables and Expressions

As you've seen, you can use tables to write equivalent fractions. The fractions in this table can be used to create several proportions.

The numerators and denominators in the table both show consistent patterns. Lists of numbers like these are called **sequences**. The numbers 4, 8, 12, 16, ... form a sequence. Each number in the sequence is a **term**.

$1 \cdot 2 \quad 1 \cdot 3 \quad 1 \cdot 4$

Numerator	1	2	3	4
Denominator	4	8	12	16

$4 \cdot 2 \quad 4 \cdot 3 \quad 4 \cdot 4$

Sequences often follow patterns that can be described by an expression. Looking at the numerical position (number) of a term can help you find the pattern.

Examples

1 Write an expression describing the rule for the numbers in the sequence 6, 7, 8, 9, 10, 11, …. Then give the 100th number in the sequence.

Make a table pairing a term number to each number in the sequence.

Term Number (*n*)	1	2	3	4	5	6	…	*n*
	↓ + 5	↓ + 5	↓ + 5	↓ + 5	↓ + 5	↓ + 5		↓ + 5
Number in Sequence	6	7	8	9	10	11	…	?

In words, the rule is "*add five to the term number.*" This translates to $n + 5$.

The 100th number in the sequence is $100 + 5 = 105$.

2 Silk is a fabric made from silkworm cocoons. Write a rule showing the relationship between the number of silk kimonos and the number of cocoons. Then tell how many cocoons it would take to make 12 kimonos.

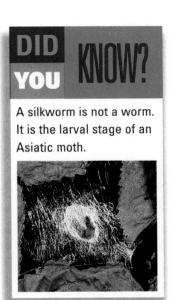

Number of Kimonos (*k*)	1	2	3	4	5	…	*k*
Number of Cocoons	1700	3400	5100	6800	8500	…	?

In words, the rule is "*multiply the number of kimonos by 1700.*" This translates to the expression $1700k$.

So, to make 12 kimonos, it would take $1700 \cdot 12 = 20{,}400$ silkworm cocoons!

3 Write a rule showing the relationship between the figure number and the number of squares.

Make a table to show the relationship.

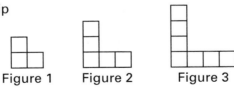

Figure 1   Figure 2   Figure 3

In words, the rule is "*add one to twice the figure number.*" (This is because two more squares are added to the corner square each time.) This translates to the expression $2n + 1$.

Figure Number (*n*)	1	2	3	…	*n*
Number of Squares	3	5	7	…	?

Try It

Write an expression describing the rule for the numbers in the sequence 3, 6, 9, 12, ….

If you are given an expression describing the rule for a sequence, you can make a table of numbers in the sequence.

Example 4

The rule for a sequence is 2^n. Make a table showing the first 4 terms.

Make a table and fill in the term numbers. Use the rule to complete the table.

Term Number (n)	1	2	3	4
Number in Sequence, 2^n	$2^1 = 2$	$2^2 = 4$	$2^3 = 8$	$2^4 = 16$

Try It

The rule for a sequence is $10x$. Make a table showing the first 6 terms.

In Example 1, the terms in the second row of the table form the sequence 6, 7, 8, 9, 10, 11, …. In this sequence, each term is 1 more than the previous term. Sequences where the difference between consecutive terms is always the same are **arithmetic sequences**.

In Example 4, each term in the sequence 2, 4, 8, 16, … was 2 times as large as the previous one. Sequences like these are **geometric sequences**.

Arithmetic Sequence	**Geometric Sequence**

2   5   8   11   14   17
 \ /\ /\ /\ /\ /
 +3 +3 +3 +3 +3

1   3   9   27   81
 \ /\ /\ /\ /
 •3 •3 •3 •3

Each term is 3 **more than** the previous term.

Each term is 3 **times as much as** the previous term.

Example 5

Tell whether the sequence is arithmetic, geometric, or neither. Then give the next two terms.

18, 23, 28, 33, 38, …

Each term is 5 more than the previous one, so the sequence is arithmetic. The next two terms are $38 + 5 = 43$ and $43 + 5 = 48$.

Check | Your Understanding

1. When writing a rule for a sequence, why is it helpful to list the term numbers?

2. Why might it be useful to describe a rule for a sequence with an expression?

Practice and Apply

1. |Getting Started| Follow the steps to describe the rule for the numbers in the sequence 7, 14, 21, 28, 35, ...

a. Make a table with two rows. In the first row, list term numbers 1, 2, 3, 4, 5, and n.

b. Fill in the first five numbers in the second row with the numbers in the sequence. Leave the cell under n blank.

c. Compare each number in the sequence to its term number. When you recognize a pattern, write an expression using n to describe the rule. Test your rule to be sure it works.

Logic Give the next term in each sequence or the next picture in each pattern.

2. 2, 4, 6, 8, ...

3. $-4, -3, -2, -1, ...$

4. $\frac{1}{2}, \frac{1}{3}, \frac{1}{4}, \frac{1}{5}, ...$

5. 5, 5, 5, 5, ...

6. 25, 20, 15, 10, ...

7. 1, 2, 4, 8, ...

8.  ...

9.  ...

10.  ...

Write an expression describing the rule for each sequence. Then give the 100th term for the sequence.

11. 11, 12, 13, 14, ...

12. 4, 8, 12, 16, ...

13. $\frac{1}{2}, 1, \frac{3}{2}, 2, ...$

14. 9, 18, 27, 36, ...

15. 0.1, 0.2, 0.3, 0.4, ...

16. $-5, -4, -3, -2, ...$

17. 1, 4, 9, 16, ...

18. 3, 5, 7, 9, ...

19. Science A queen termite can lay 8000 eggs a day for years, making it the insect with the greatest reproduction rate.

Days	1	2	3	4	5	6	7
Total Eggs	8,000	16,000	24,000	32,000	40,000	48,000	56,000

a. Write a rule showing the relationship between the number of days and the number of eggs.

b. How many eggs can the queen termite lay in one year? Explain how you found your answer.

Make a table showing the first four terms of the sequence for each rule.

20. $6n$

21. $n + 8$

22. $-7x$

23. $2c + 5$

24. 3^n

25. A pattern of squares is shown.

a. Sketch the fourth and fifth figure in this pattern.

b. Make a table comparing the figure number to the number of squares. Write an expression for the number of squares in the *n*th figure.

c. How many squares would there be in the 100th figure?

26. [**Test Prep**] The cicada was once a terrible pest in the United States. It would appear in large numbers, devour trees, then disappear for 17 years. If a swarm was seen in 1980, in which of these sequences of years is the cicada likely to appear?

   Ⓐ 1917, 2017, 2117   Ⓑ 1997, 2014, 2031

   Ⓒ 1980, 1981, 1982   Ⓓ 2000, 2017, 2034

Tell whether each sequence is arithmetic, geometric, or neither. Then give the next two terms.

27. 1, 3, 5, 7, …   **28.** 2, 4, 8, 16, …   **29.** 11, 22, 33, 44, …

30. 11, 111, 1,111, 11,111, …   **31.** 10, 100, 1,000, 10,000, …

32. −3, 9, −27, 81, …   **33.** $\frac{1}{2}, \frac{2}{3}, \frac{3}{4}, \frac{4}{5}, \dots$

Problem Solving and Reasoning

34. Choose a Strategy The fifth term of an arithmetic sequence is 96. The difference between consecutive terms is 4. Find the first four terms.

35. Critical Thinking Suppose a female fruit fly (generation 1) lays 100 eggs in her lifetime. If half of those eggs contain female flies, each of which survives to lay 100 eggs, how many flies will there be in the fifth generation? Explain your answer.

> **Problem Solving**
> ## STRATEGIES
> - Look for a Pattern
> - Make an Organized List
> - Make a Table
> - Guess and Check
> - Work Backward
> - Use Logical Reasoning
> - Draw a Diagram
> - Solve a Simpler Problem

Mixed Review

Wilson left home at 3:00 P.M. and traveled 60 miles. Find his arrival time for each of the following speeds. *[Lesson 7-3]*

36. 15 mi/hr   **37.** 10 mi/hr   **38.** 20 mi/hr   **39.** 25 mi/hr   **40.** 48 mi/hr

Operation Sense Find each sum. *[Lesson 9-4]*

41. 22 + (−14)   **42.** −27 + (−12)   **43.** −49 + 22   **44.** −51 + 45

45. −71 + 23   **46.** 88 + (−53)   **47.** −102 + (−77)

48. 256 + (−101)   **49.** (−127) + (−341)   **50.** −917 + (−497)

Understanding and Writing Equations

▶ **Lesson Link** You've written expressions to describe sequences. Now you'll see how to write equations to describe the relationship between two quantities. ◀

Explore | Showing Relationships with Tables

Faster than a Speeding Beetle?

Some of the fastest-moving insects are beetles. The table shows how fast one type of beetle can crawl.

Time (sec)	1	2	3	4	5	...	t
Distance (in.)	4	8	12	16	20	...	?

1. Describe any patterns you see in the table. Write an expression using t for the final box in the distance row.

2. Use words to describe the relation-ship between the distance traveled and the time.

3. If this beetle crawled for 60 seconds, how far would it go?

4. How long would it take this beetle to crawl 36 inches?

5. Explain how you found your answers to Steps 3 and 4. What is differ-ent about the questions asked in these steps?

Learn | Understanding and Writing Equations

When two expressions name the same quantity, we can link them with an equation. Writing an equation is an important way to show a relationship between variables.

The geometric formulas you've worked with are equations. For instance, since the perimeter of a square is four times the length of a side, we write $p = 4s$. The equal sign shows that p and $4s$ always have the same value.

$$p = 4s$$

Examples

1 Write an equation to show the relationship between x and y. Use the equation to find y when $x = 9$.

x	1	2	3	4
y	1	4	9	16

Notice that each y-value is equal to the *square* of its x-value. The equation $y = x^2$ shows this relationship.

To find y when $x = 9$, substitute 9 into the equation for x.

$y = 9^2 = 81$. When $x = 9$, $y = 81$.

2 Write an equation to describe the relationship between the number of trips a bee makes and the amount of pollen it carries to its hive. Use the equation to find the amount of pollen the bee can carry in 12 trips.

Trips	Pollen (mg)
1	25
2	50
3	75
4	100

Test Prep

When you're writing an equation to model a real-world situation, be sure the equation gives results that make sense.

Let t = the number of trips, and p = the amount of pollen. The table shows that the bee carries 25 mg of pollen in each trip. The equation is $p = 25t$.

To find the amount of pollen carried in 12 trips, substitute 12 for t.

$p = 25(12) = 300$ mg

The bee can carry 300 mg of pollen in 12 trips.

Try It

Write an equation to show the relationship between x and y. Then use the equation to find the value of y when $x = 17$.

x	1	2	3	4	5
y	0.25	0.5	0.75	1	1.25

You can use equations to make tables of values.

Example 3

Make a table of six pairs of values for the equation $y = 3x + 2$.

Choose six x-values, then substitute each into $y = 3x + 2$ to find the y-values.

x	1	2	3	4	5	6
y	5	8	11	14	17	20

Try It

A bee colony needs about 20 kg of pollen each year. In y years, it will need $20y$, so $p = 20y$. Make a table of six pairs of values for this equation.

Check Your Understanding

1. How does an equation show a relationship between quantities?

2. What does an equation tell you that a table of values does not? What information is in a table of values that isn't shown in an equation?

10-4 Exercises and Applications

Practice and Apply

1. Getting Started Follow the steps to make a table of five values for the equation $y = 3x - 4$.

a. Make a table with two rows (or columns). Begin the first with the letter x, then fill in five x-values of your choice.

b. Begin the second row (or column) with the letter y. Substitute the first x-value into the equation. Simplify to find the y-value for this x-value.

c. Repeat until you complete the table.

For each table, write an equation to show the relationship between *x* and *y*. Use the equation to find *y* when *x* = 7.

2.

x	1	2	3	4
y	3	4	5	6

3.

x	1	2	3	4
y	−5	−10	−15	−20

Complete each table. Then write an equation to show the relationship between the variables.

4.

r	D
40	80
50	100
55	110
60	
65	

5.

n	C
0	0
2	7.00
4	14.00
6	
8	

6.

s	A
1	1
2	4
3	9
4	
6	

7.

t	d
1	35
2	70
3	
4	
5	

Make a table of six pairs of values for each equation.

8. $y = 2x$

9. $y = x + 8$

10. $c = -7b$

11. $k = g - 3$

12. $y = \frac{1}{3}x$

13. $y = 3x + 1$

14. $d = -14t - 22$

15. $y = 0.22x$

16. $y = -x$

17. $h = \frac{k}{4} + 1$

18. The relationship between the number of jumps a locust makes and the distance it covers is shown. Write an equation to describe this relationship. Then use the equation to find the distance the locust would cover in 25 jumps.

Jumps	1	2	3	4	5	6
Distance (in.)	20	40	60	80	100	120

19. **Test Prep** As shown in the table, the cost of boarding a cat in a kennel depends on the number of days it stays.

Days	2	4	5	7
Cost ($)	6	12	15	21

Which equation represents the relationship between cost and number of days?

Ⓐ $C = d + 4$ Ⓑ $C = \dfrac{d}{3}$ Ⓒ $C = 3d$ Ⓓ $C = 6d$

Problem Solving and Reasoning

20. Critical Thinking An important rule for a mathematical sequence is $\dfrac{n(n + 1)}{2}$.

a. Find the first five terms of this sequence.

b. Find the sums $1 + 2$, $1 + 2 + 3$, $1 + 2 + 3 + 4$, and $1 + 2 + 3 + 4 + 5$. Compare your results to the sequence in **a**. Why is this rule important?

21. Communicate Draw a square pattern of your own invention, like the ones shown on page 490 and 491. Label each figure with a number.

a. If you can, write an equation that describes the pattern. If you can't, explain why not.

b. Find the number of squares in the 100th figure in your pattern.

Mixed Review

A bottlenose dolphin can be 12 feet long. Find the maximum scale you can use for a model dolphin if it must fit in each of the following. *[Lesson 7-4]*

22. A 6 ft long crate

23. A 3 in. long toy box

24. A 50 ft long exhibit hall

25. A 5 in. long carton

Operation Sense Find each difference. *[Lesson 9-5]*

26. $37 - 58$

27. $-10 - (-15)$

28. $-79 - 32$

29. $51 - (-51)$

30. $171 - 239$

31. $481 - (-308)$

TECHNOLOGY

Using a Graphing Utility • Choosing a Window Size and Scale

**Problem: How can you select an appropriate viewing "window"
for the graph of $y = 100x + 250$?**

You can use a graphing utility to investigate this question.

1 Enter the function
$y = 100x + 250$ as Y1.
Go to ZOOM and select
the standard window, then
press GRAPH to graph the
function.

2 The graph appears almost
vertical. To spread it out,
limit the range of x-values
and extend the range of
y-values. Go to WINDOW
and enter Xmin $= -3$,
Xmax $= 1$, Ymin $= -300$,
and Ymax $= 300$. Press
GRAPH to see the result.

3 Notice that the "tick marks"
are very spread out on
the x-axis and very close
together on the y-axis.
To change this, go to
WINDOW. Change Xscl to
0.5 and Yscl to 50. Press
GRAPH to see the result.

Solution: Values that give an appropriate viewing window are
Xmin $= -3$, Xmax $= 1$, Ymin $= -300$, Ymax $= 300$, Xscl $= 0.5$, and
Yscl $= 50$.

ON YOUR OWN

TRY IT

► What do Xmin, Xmax, Ymin, Ymax, Xscl, and Yscl mean?

► If you and a friend graphed $y = 25x - 100$ using different values for the viewing window, would the graphs
look the same? Explain.

Determine an appropriate viewing window
for each graph.

a. $y = 200x - 100$
b. $y = 0.25x + 10$ **c.** $y = x^2 + 2$

You'll Learn ...

■ to draw the graph of an equation

... How It's Used

Sound recording engineers use three-dimensional sound graphs when recording albums.

▶ **Lesson Link** You've seen how equations and graphs show how quantities are related. Now you'll see how you can draw a graph of an equation. ◀

Explore | **Showing Relationships in Graphs**

These Bees Are "Killer"!

Honey is produced in the United States mostly by European-type bees, often called honeybees. They average 24 kg of honey per hive each season.

1. The scatterplot shows the amount of honey produced by 1 hive, 2 hives, 3 hives, 4 hives, and 5 hives of European bees in one season. Copy the table below, then use the scatterplot to complete it.

European Bee Honey Production

Hives	1	2	3	4	5
Honey (kg)					

2. African ("killer") bees produce up to 90 kg of honey per hive, as shown in the scatterplot. Make and complete a table like the one above for African bee honey production.

3. If a beekeeper has 10 European honeybee hives, approximately how many kg of honey would they produce in one season? How much honey could she get from 10 African bee hives? Explain.

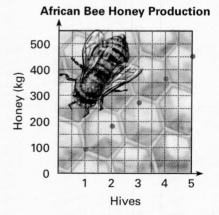

4. Assuming that African bees are safe, should the beekeeper change bees? Why or why not? Explain how the tables and scatterplots support your choice.

To make a scatterplot from data in a table, you can write the data as ordered pairs and plot the points on a coordinate plane.

Graphing an equation is similar to creating a scatterplot. You can begin by making a table of values, then plotting the ordered pairs these values represent.

$y = 3x$ ⟶

x	y
−1	−3
0	0
2	6

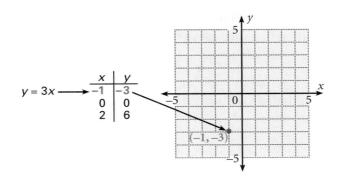

Example 1

Graph the equation $y = 3x$ on a coordinate plane.

First make a table of values. Choose several values for x. It's a good idea to include 0 and a negative value.

Next, plot the ordered pairs $(−1, −3)$, $(0, 0)$, $(1, 3)$, $(2, 6)$, and $(3, 9)$ represented by the table.

All of these points fall in a line.

Although these points are on the graph of the equation, they are not the *only* points on the graph. Although the math would not have been as easy, we could have used x-values like $2\frac{1}{2}$ and 1.0001.

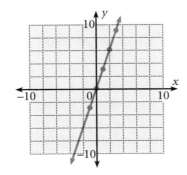

x	y
−1	−3
0	0
1	3
2	6
3	9

To show that points between and beyond the ones in the table are also on the graph, we connect the points.

Try It

Graph each equation on a coordinate plane.

a. $y = 5x$ **b.** $y = x + 4$ **c.** $y = −2x$

You can use graphs to model relationships in the real world. However, when you do this, be sure the values you choose for your table make sense in the real-world situation.

Example 2

A dragonfly can reach speeds of 50 km/hr. An equation to represent the dragonfly's speed is $d = 50t$, where d represents the distance in kilometers and t represents the time in hours. Graph this equation on a coordinate plane.

First make a table of values. For this situation, use only non-negative t-values.

Time (hr)	Distance (km)
0	0
1	50
2	100
3	150
4	200
5	250

Then graph the points in the table on a coordinate plane and connect the points.

Notice that this graph is shown only in the first quadrant, since negative numbers do not make sense in this situation.

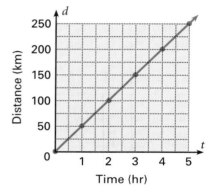

DID YOU KNOW?

Dragonfly wings move at a rate of 30–50 beats per second. The wings of a housefly, which have a different structure, move at 200 wingbeats per second.

Try It

The fastest insect in the world, a type of horsefly, flies at speeds of up to 87 mi/hr.

An equation to represent the horsefly's speed is $d = 87t$, where d represents the distance in miles and t represents the time in hours. Graph this equation on a coordinate plane.

Check Your Understanding

1. In your own words, describe a method for graphing an equation.

2. Give an example of a graph of a real-world situation that would *not* be in the first quadrant only.

Practice and Apply

1. | Getting Started | Follow the steps to graph the equation $y = 2x + 3$.

a. Make a table with two rows (or columns). Begin the first with the letter x, then fill in several x-values of your choice. Include at least one negative value and zero.

b. Begin the second row (or column) with the letter y. Then substitute the first x-value into the equation. Simplify to find the y-value for this x-value. Write this y-value next to its corresponding x-value.

c. Repeat until you complete the table.

d. Each x-y pair of values in the table represents a point. Plot these points on a coordinate plane. Then connect the points to show the graph.

In Exercises 2–5, a table of points is given for each equation. Graph each equation on a coordinate plane.

2. $y = x + 2$

x	y
−1	1
0	2
1	3
2	4
3	5

3. $y = 4x$

x	y
−2	−8
0	0
1	4
2	8
4	16

4. $y = x - 1$

x	y
−1	−2
0	−1
3	2
4	3
5	4

5. $y = -2x + 5$

x	y
−2	9
0	5
2	1
4	−3
6	−7

Graph each equation on a coordinate plane.

6. $y = 2x$ **7.** $y = x + 1$ **8.** $y = -3x$ **9.** $y = 4x - 5$ **10.** $y = x$

11. Look at the graphs for the equations in Exercises 2–10. Compare the equations whose graphs go through the origin to the equations whose graphs do not. What do you notice?

12. Science The Goliath beetle is the world's heaviest insect. One Goliath beetle can weigh 3.5 ounces. An equation to represent the weight of several Goliath beetles is $w = 3.5b$, where w represents the weight in ounces and b represents the number of beetles. Graph this equation.

Graph each equation on the same coordinate plane.

13. $y = \frac{1}{2}x$ **14.** $y = \frac{1}{2}x - 1$ **15.** $y = \frac{1}{2}x + 1$ **16.** $y = \frac{1}{2}x - 3$

17. What do you notice about the graphs in Exercises 13–16?

18. **Test Prep**   Which of these equations has a graph that contains the origin?

     Ⓐ $y = x + 2$ Ⓑ $y = 2x$ Ⓒ $y = 2x + 1$ Ⓓ $y = x - 2$

Problem Solving and Reasoning

19. **Critical Thinking** When an insect is active, its heart can beat at a rate of 140 beats per minute. When it is inactive and cold, its heart rate can slow to 1 beat per hour.

     a. Write an equation to represent each of these rates.

     b. Graph both equations on the same coordinate plane. Describe similarities and differences between these graphs. How can you tell by looking which graph represents the lesser rate?

20. **Communicate** Why does the graph of $y = 2x + 1$ contain the point $(2, 5)$? Why does it *not* contain $(2, 6)$?

21. **Critical Thinking** Graph each pair of equations on the same coordinate plane.

     a. $y = 2x$ and $y = -2x$ **b.** $y = 3x$ and $y = -3x$ **c.** $y = 10x$ and $y = -10x$

     d. Describe the differences between the graphs in each pair.

Mixed Review

Number Sense Use percents to compare. *[Lesson 8-1]*

22. $\frac{61}{100}$ and $\frac{3}{5}$ **23.** $\frac{9}{20}$ and $\frac{1}{2}$ **24.** $\frac{1}{4}$ and $\frac{4}{25}$ **25.** $\frac{1}{4}$ and $\frac{1}{5}$ **26.** $\frac{3}{10}$ and $\frac{7}{25}$

Operation Sense Find each product. *[Lesson 9-6]*

27. $7 \cdot 9$ **28.** $-3 \cdot (-5)$ **29.** $-4 \cdot 11$ **30.** $6 \cdot (-10)$ **31.** $-16 \cdot 0$

32. $42 \cdot (-10)$ **33.** $-12 \cdot (-9)$ **34.** $-5 \cdot 23$ **35.** $18 \cdot (-15)$ **36.** $-1 \cdot -1 \cdot -1$

Project Progress

Create a table of the population data you found for your city, town, or state. Then see if you can find an equation that fits the data. If there is no exact equation, see if you can find an equation that comes close. (*Hint:* It may help to number the years from 0 instead of using the actual dates.)

Problem Solving

Understand
Plan
Solve
Look Back

You've analyzed relationships between quantities by using graphs, tables, and equations. Now you'll apply those skills to add some spice to your diet.

Howdy, Ant Bee!

Materials: Graph paper

Have you ever swallowed an insect accidentally? You may have felt a little uneasy at the time, but you got the better of the deal. In fact, many insects are good for you!

The following table gives nutritional information for 1-ounce servings of different types of animals.

Nutritional Content of Edible Insects and Other Animals				
	Energy (cal)	Protein (g)	Calcium (mg)	Iron (mg)
Daily Requirements (adult)	2850	37	1000	18
Termites	172	4.0	11.3	2.1
Weevils	159	1.9	52.7	3.7
Beef (lean ground)	62	7.8	3.4	1.0
Chicken (roasted white meat)	47	9.0	3.1	0.4
Fish (broiled cod)	48	8.1	8.8	0.3

1. Make a table and a graph of the amount of iron in 1, 2, 3, 4, and 5 ounces of termites.

2. Use your graph or your table to find the approximate amount of iron in $4\frac{1}{2}$ ounces of termites. Explain how you found your answer.

3. Approximately how many ounces of termites would an adult have to eat to get the minimum daily requirement of iron?

4. How many ounces of fish would you have to eat to get as much calcium as there is in 1 ounce of weevils?

5. Approximately how many ounces of weevils would an adult have to eat to get the minimum daily requirement of calcium?

6. Compare the amounts of each type of food that you would need to eat to get an adult's minimum requirement of calories. What do you notice?

1. **History** In 1519, Ferdinand Magellan left Spain on a voyage around the world. After Magellan died in the Philippines, Juan del Cano assumed command. He waited until the ships were repaired, then returned to Spain in 1522. Which graph could show this voyage?

a.

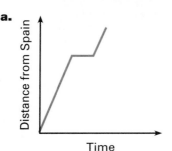

b.

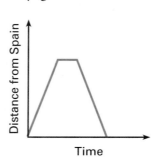

Write an expression describing the rule for each sequence. Then give the 100th term for the sequence.

2. 4, 5, 6, 7, …   **3.** 2, 4, 6, 8, …   **4.** 0.3, 0.6, 0.9, 1.2, …   **5.** −5, −10, −15, −20, …

For each table, write an equation to show the relationship between x and y. Use the equation to find y when $x = 9$.

6.

x	1	2	3	4
y	3	6	9	12

7.

x	1	2	3	4
y	−5	−4	−3	−2

Graph each equation on a coordinate plane.

8. $y = x$ **9.** $y = x - 4$ **10.** $y = -4x$ **11.** $y = 2x + 2$ **12.** $y = -x$

13. **Journal** Explain the relationship between an equation, a table of values for the equation, and the graph of the equation.

Test Prep

When asked to find the next number in a sequence on a multiple choice test, remember that the sequence may follow a rule that can't be written as an expression.

14. What is the next number in the sequence 2, 3, 5, 7, 11, …?

ⓐ 12   ⓑ 13   ⓒ 14   ⓓ 15

IT IS MY BUSINESS!

It started as a garden in South Central Los Angeles. In 1992, after riots devastated their community, 38 Crenshaw High School students cleared a patch of weeds and began to raise vegetables. They sold some for scholarship money and donated some to homeless shelters. Then they had an idea: We know vegetables, so let's make salad dressing!

Biology teacher Tammy Bird helped the students. The group experimented until they found the right recipe. They got advice from Norris Bernstein, founder of Bernstein's salad dressings. Finally they set up their own company, Food From the 'Hood. In 1994, more than 2000 grocery stores began selling their product, Straight Out 'the Garden salad dressing.

When they graduate, the students receive their profits as scholarship money. Food From the 'Hood is on target to earn $50,000 for its student owners! Now you'll see how young entrepreneurs like the owners of Food From the 'Hood use mathematics in their businesses.

1 Explain how you calculate the profit for a business if you know its income and its costs.

2 How do you think the student owners of Food From the 'Hood use mathematics in their business?

507

Solving Equations Using Tables

▶ Lesson Link You've made tables of values and drawn graphs of equations. Now you'll use tables and graphs to solve equations. ◀

Explore · Tables and Equations

Up to Her Necklace in Sales!

As a seventh-grader, Solangel Brujan of New York City borrowed $50 and began a jewelry business. In just 3 years, she made $3000. One item she stocked was a faux-pearl necklace that sold for $5.

1. Let n be the number of "pearl" necklaces purchased by one customer. Let c be the customer's total cost. Write an equation showing the relationship between these variables.

2. Make a table showing how much 1 to 12 necklaces would cost. How much would 7 necklaces cost? 24 necklaces? Explain.

3. How many necklaces would Solangel have to sell to pay back the amount she borrowed? Explain how you found the answer.

Learn · Solving Equations Using Tables

By using a table of x and y values for an equation, you can read the x-value that goes with a specific y-value.

Example 1

Make a table of values for $y = x + 2$. Use x-values of -1, 0, 1, 2, 3, and 4. Then find the value of x when y is 1, 3, and 6.

x	−1	0	1	2	3	4
y	1	2	3	4	5	6

To make the table, substitute each x-value into the equation.

When $y = 1$, $x = -1$; when $y = 3$, $x = 1$; and when $y = 6$, $x = 4$.

You can use a table of values to solve an equation. To solve $8 = x + 5$, first make a table for the *related* equation $y = x + 5$. Then find the x-value for $y = 8$.

Example 2

Use a table to solve $14 = 3x - 4$.

The related equation is $y = 3x - 4$. A table for this equation is shown.

x	-2	0	2	4	6	8
y	-10	-4	2	8	14	20

From the table, $x = 6$ when $y = 14$.

Try It

Make and use a table to solve each equation.

a. $7 = x - 3$ **b.** $42 = -7x$ **c.** $15 = 3k + 2$ **d.** $-6 = 2x + 8$

You may be able to use a table to estimate the solution to an equation.

Example 3

The MelMaps Company was started by 11-year-old Melissa Gollick of Denver. Melissa uses a computer to draw maps for real estate firms. Each map sells for $40. How many maps does she need to sell to earn $280?

Let m = the number of maps. We need to solve $280 = 40m$.

Let y = the amount earned. The table gives values for $y = 40m$.

Maps, m	2	4	6	8	10
Income, y ($)	80	160	240	320	400

$y = 280$ does not appear in the table. However, you can *estimate* that 280 is halfway between 240 and 320.

In the m-row, the value halfway between 6 and 8 is 7. Melissa must sell 7 maps.

Check Your Understanding

1. What is the related equation for $14 = 7x$? How are these equations "related"?

2. In Example 3, how could we check whether 7 maps is the correct answer?

Practice and Apply

1. **Getting Started** Follow the steps to solve $8 = x + 3$ by using a table.

a. Write the related equation for $8 = x + 3$ by replacing 8 with y.

b. Make a table of values for the related equation.

c. Look for a y-value of 8 in your table. The x-value for this y-value is the solution to the equation.

The table below represents the equation $y = -2x$. Use it to solve the related equations below the table.

x	-2	-1	0	1	2	3	4	6	8
y	4	2	0	-2	-4	-6	-8	-12	-16

2. $-6 = -2x$ **3.** $-2x = 4$ **4.** $0 = -2x$ **5.** $-2x = -8$

6. **Estimation** Use the table above to estimate the solution to $3 = -2x$. Explain how you found your answer.

Make and use a table to solve each equation.

7. $4 = x - 2$ **8.** $3x = 9$ **9.** $-16 = 5r + 4$ **10.** $200 = 10n - 50$

Estimation Make and use a table to estimate the solution to each equation.

11. $7 = 2x$ **12.** $-5b = 18$ **13.** $-17 = 3z - 2$ **14.** $3\frac{1}{2} = 2k - 7$

15. **Geometry** Recall that the circumference of a circle is equal to π times its diameter, so $C = \pi d$.

a. Make a table of values for $C = \pi d$.

b. Use your table to estimate the diameter of a circle whose circumference is 11 cm.

16. **Industry** Champ Cookies and Things is a business that began in a Washington, DC, school in 1987. Students bought the supplies, baked the cookies, and packaged and sold the cookies. Suppose the ingredients for one dozen cookies cost 35¢. Use a table to decide how many dozen cookies could be made for $7.70.

17. Literature In *The Cricket in Times Square*, by George Selden, Mario talks to his mother and father about crickets while he sells newspapers at their newsstand. (Excerpt below from *The Cricket in Times Square* (New York: Farrar, Straus and Giroux, 1960). Copyright ©1960 by George Selden Thompson.)

"So you spend less time playing with cricketers, you'll sell more papers," said Mama.

"Oh now, now," Papa soothed her. *"Mario couldn't help it if nobody buys."*

"You can tell the temperature with crickets too," said Mario. *"You count the number of chirps in a minute, divide by four, and add forty. They're very intelligent."*

Make a table to find the number of times a cricket would chirp in a minute if the temperature were 90°F.

18. **Test Prep** Which of these equations matches the table?

Ⓐ $g = -f + 3$ Ⓑ $g = 1 - 2f$

Ⓒ $g = 2f - 1$ Ⓓ $g = 2 - 3f$

f	-1	0	1	2
g	3	1	-1	-3

Problem Solving and Reasoning

19. Choose a Strategy Some tables don't come from equations, but they can still be used to make predictions. Use the table to predict the percent of women in the United States who will be working by the year 2000. Explain how you made your prediction.

Women 16 and Over in the Civilian Labor Force							
Year	1930	1940	1950	1960	1970	1980	1990
Percent	22.0	25.4	33.9	37.7	43.3	51.5	57.5

Problem Solving
STRATEGIES

- Look for a Pattern
- Make an Organized List
- Make a Table
- Guess and Check
- Work Backward
- Use Logical Reasoning
- Draw a Diagram
- Solve a Simpler Problem

20. **Journal** When you use a table to solve an equation, how do you decide which *x*-values to use? (*Hint:* Would you choose different values to solve $12 = 3x$ than to solve $27,954 = 3x$?)

Mixed Review

Write each percent as a decimal. *[Lesson 8-2]*

21. 50%   **22.** 20%   **23.** 90%   **24.** 2%   **25.** 7%

26. 120%   **27.** 5.6%   **28.** 22.2%   **29.** 84.62%   **30.** $12\frac{1}{2}$%

Find each quotient. *[Lesson 9-7]*

31. $-12 \div (-4)$ **32.** $-12 \div 4$ **33.** $0 \div (-17)$ **34.** $22 \div (-2)$ **35.** $-56 \div (-8)$

36. $-44 \div (-1)$ **37.** $-60 \div 15$ **38.** $80 \div (-12)$ **39.** $-170 \div 5$ **40.** $-300 \div 0$

Solving Equations Using Graphs

You'll Learn ...

■ to use graphs to solve equations

... How It's Used

Materials scientists "design" the metals and plastics that products are made from. They consult graphs to decide whether a material will be a solid, liquid, or gas at a particular temperature and pressure.

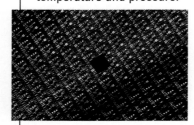

▶ **Lesson Link**   You've used tables and graphs to solve one-step equations. Now you'll use these methods to solve two-step equations. ◀

Explore   Equations and Graphs

Racking Up the Profits

Materials: Graphing utility

In 1992, Lizzie Denis and Louise Kramer of St. Paul, Minnesota, decided that cookies take too long to bake in a single-layer pan. So the two 11-year-olds invented the Double Decker Baking Rack. Their company, L&L Products, markets the rack through stores and catalogs. It sells for about $20.

Suppose a store buys $1000 worth of racks and earns $4 for each rack sold. The store's manager wants to know how many racks the store needs to sell:

• To break even ($0 profit)   • To make $4500

1. Let x represent the number of racks sold, and let y represent the amount of money made. Write an equation in the form y = _____ relating x and y. Remember to subtract the original $1000 investment.

2. Graph the equation on a graphing utility. Describe the graph.

3. To find out how many racks need to be sold to reach the break-even point ($0 profit), use TRACE to move along your graph until the y-value equals 0. What is the x-value? What does this tell you?

4. Use TRACE to find out how many racks need to be sold for the store to earn $4500.

Learn | Solving Equations Using Graphs

Just as you can with a table, you can use a graph to find the value of x that goes with a particular value of y.

Example 1

Graph $y = -2x$. Then find the values of x when y is -2 and 4.

Make a table of a few values for the equation.

x	-1	0	1	2
y	2	0	-2	-4

Plot the points on a coordinate plane and connect them.

To find the value of x when $y = -2$, go to -2 on the y-axis. Then move across to the line. When you reach the line, move up to the x-axis.

When $y = -2$, $x = 1$.

You can use the same method to find the value of x when $y = 4$. In this case, you need to move *down* from the line to reach the x-axis.

When $y = 4$, $x = -2$.

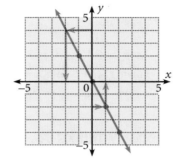

▶ **History Link**

In 1903, an African American, Maggie Lena Walker, became the first female bank president in the United States. She founded Saint Luke's Penny-Saving bank in Richmond, Virginia. During the Great Depression, Walker's bank merged with others to become the Richmond Consolidated Bank and Trust.

You can use a graph to solve an equation.

Example 2

Use a graph to solve $16 = 3x - 8$.

Graph the *related* equation $y = 3x - 8$.

x	-2	0	2	4
y	-14	-8	-2	4

Go to 16 on the y-axis. Move across to the line, then down to the x-axis. You reach the x-axis at 8.

The solution is $x = 8$.

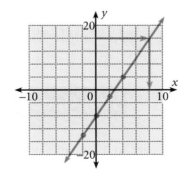

Try It

Use a graph to solve each equation.

a. $4 = x - 2$

b. $12 = -3x$

c. $-10 = 4x + 2$

Problem Solving TIP

Be sure you make the scale on the y-axis large enough to include the value you're looking for—here, the y-axis needed to include 16.

WHAT DO YOU THINK ?

Ben Narasin is the founder of Boston Prepatory Co. sportswear. He got his first taste of big business at age 12 when he paid $65 to buy and sell comics at a comic book convention. His one-day profit: $2500!

Suppose you pay $65 to sell n comic books at an average profit of $10. Your profit, p, is given by $p = 10n - 65$. How many comic books would you need to sell to earn $2500?

Will thinks ...

I'll use the equation $p = 10n - 65$ to make a table.

Number of Comics Sold, n	50	100	150	200	250	300
Profit, p ($)	435	935	1435	1935	2435	2935

At $p = 2435$, $n = 250$. 2500 is a little more than 2435, so I'll estimate $n = 260$. I'd need to sell about 260 comic books.

Kimberly thinks ...

I'll graph the equation $p = 10n - 65$ first.

Starting at $p = 2500$ on the "Profit" axis, I'll move over to the line, then down. I end at about 260 on the "Comic Books" axis.

I'd need to sell about 260 comic books.

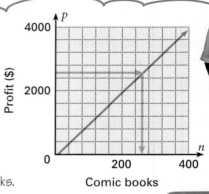

What do you think?

1. Why did Will and Kimberly both look for $p = 2500$?

2. Why does $p = 10n - 65$ give the amount of profit?

Check | Your Understanding

1. Is it easier to use a table or a graph to estimate solutions? Explain.

2. When you solve an equation by graphing, why do you need to move across to the graph from a point on the y-axis instead of moving up or down?

Practice and Apply

 Getting Started A graph of $y = x + 3$ is shown at the right. Use it to solve the related equations.

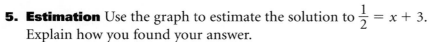

1. $2 = x + 3$ **2.** $x + 3 = -1$ **3.** $4 = x + 3$ **4.** $x + 3 = 0$

5. Estimation Use the graph to estimate the solution to $\frac{1}{2} = x + 3$. Explain how you found your answer.

6. Follow the steps to solve $10 = 3x - 2$ by graphing.

   a. Write the related equation for $10 = 3x - 2$ by replacing 10 with y.

   b. Make a table of values for the related equation.

   c. Plot the points in your table on a coordinate plane. Connect the points.

   d. Start at 10 on the y-axis of your coordinate plane. Go across until you reach the graph. Then drop vertically to the x-axis and read the solution.

Use a graph to solve each equation.

7. $5 = x + 3$ **8.** $2x = 8$ **9.** $-5 = 3p - 2$ **10.** $500 = 8n - 100$

Estimation Use a graph to estimate the solution to each equation.

11. $6 = 2x - 3$ **12.** $-7 = 4x + 2$ **13.** $35 = -3t - 11$ **14.** $22.75 = 5n - 8$

15. Problem Solving When you *lease* an automobile, you return it to the dealer after you have driven it for a certain amount of time. Suppose a car lease requires an initial payment of $1500 and payments of $300 at the end of each month. After how many months will the total cost of the lease be $4500? Use a graph to answer this question.

16. **Test Prep** Darryl is going on a business trip. His company allows him $140 per day in expenses, up to a total of $1000. Which equation can Darryl use to find the greatest number of days his expenses can last?

   Ⓐ $1000 = 140d$ Ⓑ $1000 = \dfrac{d}{140}$

   Ⓒ $d = 140 \cdot 1000$ Ⓓ $1000 = \dfrac{140}{d}$

17. Industry When she was in fifth grade, Alexia Abernathy of Cedar Rapids, Iowa, invented the Oops! Proof™ spill-proof bowl. She gets part of the money from the sales of her bowl.

Suppose a family spends $1200 developing an invention, and that they earn $2.00 for each one sold.

a. How much money does the family earn if *n* items are sold?

b. What were the family's expenses?

c. *Profit* is the difference between money earned *(income)* and expenses. Write an equation for the profit. Graph the equation.

d. How many items must be sold to have a profit of $3000? Explain how you found your answer.

Problem Solving and Reasoning

18. Critical Thinking You are a vice president at a toy company. You are going to make a presentation about a new toy that sells for $15.

a. You think people will want to know how many toys the company would need to sell to make $50,000, $125,000, and $250,000. Prepare a graph and a table to answer these questions. What are the answers?

b. In the actual presentation, when might you use the table? When might you use the graph? Explain the advantages and disadvantages of each.

19. Communicate Suppose a bank charges its customers $5.00 each month plus a $0.25 fee for each check they write during that month.

a. Write an equation for the total amount the bank would charge a customer in one month.

b. How much would a customer be charged if she wrote 10 checks in a month?

c. If a customer were charged $8.75, how many checks did he write? Explain.

Mixed Review

Write each fraction as a percent. *[Lesson 8-3]*

20. $\frac{1}{1000}$ **21.** $\frac{135}{100}$ **22.** $\frac{920}{100}$ **23.** $\frac{\frac{1}{2}}{100}$ **24.** $\frac{57}{10}$

Write the opposite of each integer. *[Lesson 9-1]*

25. 7   **26.** −5   **27.** −417   **28.** 550   **29.** −114

30. 5,040   **31.** −22,714   **32.** 101   **33.** 4×10^4 **34.** 0

Relating Equations and Inequalities

▶ **Lesson Link** You've used tables and graphs to solve equations. Now you'll use your knowledge of equations to solve inequalities. ◀

You'll Learn ...

■ to graph inequalities on a number line

■ to write the inequality represented by a graph

... How It's Used

Inequalities are used to describe how long you can talk on a telephone before the rates change.

Explore   Inequalities

Net Profits

As high school juniors, Rachel Rief and Margaret Kowalski founded FUNdamentals Summer Soccer Camp Just-For-Girls in Yakima, Washington. They charged $22 per player for a week of soccer training.

1. Make a table showing the income for training 1 to 10 players. Let *n* represent the number of players.

2. In your table, find the value(s) of *n* that will produce an income that is:

   a. Equal to $110   **b.** Less than $110   **c.** Greater than $110

3. Explain how you found these values from your table.

Vocabulary

inequality

solutions of an inequality

Learn   Relating Equations and Inequalities

An equation consists of two expressions separated by an equal sign. Two expressions separated by an inequality sign form an **inequality**. Examples of inequalities include $4 + 3 < 12$, $5 - 2 \leq 3$, and $x + 12 \geq 15$.

The **solutions of an inequality** are the values that make the inequality true. They can be graphed on a number line. A filled-in circle shows that the number below it satisfies the inequality.

$x > -2$ ("greater than")

$-5\ -4\ -3\ -2\ -1\ \ 0\ \ 1\ \ 2\ \ 3\ \ 4\ \ 5$

$x < -2$ ("less than")

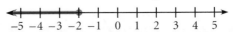

$-5\ -4\ -3\ -2\ -1\ \ 0\ \ 1\ \ 2\ \ 3\ \ 4\ \ 5$

$x \geq -2$ ("greater than or equal to")

$-5\ -4\ -3\ -2\ -1\ \ 0\ \ 1\ \ 2\ \ 3\ \ 4\ \ 5$

$x \leq -2$ ("less than or equal to")

$-5\ -4\ -3\ -2\ -1\ \ 0\ \ 1\ \ 2\ \ 3\ \ 4\ \ 5$

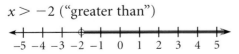

Examples

1 Graph the inequality $x \geq 3$ on a number line.

The x values *greater* than 3 are to the right of 3. Since the inequality has a greater than *or equal to* sign, the circle is filled in.

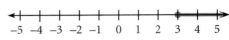

2 Write an inequality for the graph.

The inequality includes points less than 1, but does not include 1.

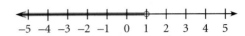

The inequality $x < 1$ fits the graph.

Try It

a. Graph the inequality $x \leq -1$.

b. Write an inequality for the graph.

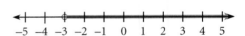

Examples

3 Write a real-world statement for the inequality $n < 150$.

The statement shows a quantity that is less than 150. So a statement like "The number of skateboards sold last week was less than 150" fits the inequality.

4 Write an inequality for the statement "Last week's profits were greater than $800." Graph the inequality.

Let p = profits.   Define a variable.

$p > 800$ Use an inequality symbol to write an inequality.

The arrow points to the right because the inequality is "greater than." The circle is open.

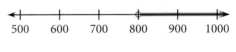

Try It

Write an inequality for the statement "The cost of advertising soccer camp was less than $450." Graph the inequality.

Check Your Understanding

1. How can you check the graph of an inequality?

2. Is the inequality $x > 4$ the same as the inequality $4 < x$? Explain.

Practice and Apply

1. **Getting Started** Follow the steps to graph the inequality $x \leq -3$.

a. Draw a number line that includes -3.

b. Make a circle at -3. Since the inequality includes the "equal to" possibility, fill in the circle.

c. Since x-values *less than* -3 make the inequality true, draw an arrow that starts at the filled-in circle and goes to the left.

Graph each inequality on a number line.

2. $x > 1$ **3.** $x \geq 0$ **4.** $k \leq 4$ **5.** $t > -3$ **6.** $x \geq 7$

7. $p \leq 40$ **8.** $r > 25$ **9.** $d \geq 100$ **10.** $n < -32$ **11.** $v \geq 2{,}000$

For each inequality, tell whether the number in bold is a solution.

12. $x > 4;$ **8**   **13.** $z > -12;$ **-13**   **14.** $x + 4 \geq 7;$ **3**   **15.** $2m \leq -5;$ **-3**   **16.** $2x + 1 < 0;$ **-1**

Write an inequality for each graph.

17.

-5 -4 -3 -2 -1 0 1 2 3 4 5

18.

-5 -4 -3 -2 -1 0 1 2 3 4 5

19.

0 10 20 30 40 50 60 70 80

20.

-10 -9 -8 -7 -6 -5 -4 -3 -2 -1 0

Write a real-world statement for each inequality.

21. $n > 150$ **22.** $t \leq 12$ **23.** $g \geq 90$ **24.** $t \leq 0.06$ **25.** $s \leq 65$

26. **Industry** Stephen Lovett started his own car-washing business at age 13. Within 5 years, it grew into a custom cleaning and car detailing business. Lovett charged up to $80 to work on a car.

a. Write an inequality to represent the amount Lovett charged to work on a car.

b. Draw a graph of the inequality you wrote in **a.**

Write and graph an inequality for each statement.

27. Every item in the store costs a dollar or less!

28. The population of China is at least 1,000,000,000 people.

29. **Number Sense** If $20 + 40 > m$, is $m > 20 + 40$? Explain your answer.

30. **Science** Most elements have a freezing point and a boiling point. Below the freezing point, the element is a solid. Above the boiling point, the element is a gas. Write and graph an inequality to show each temperature range.

   a. The freezing point of mercury is $-39°C$. For what temperatures is mercury a solid?

   b. The boiling point of silver is $2210°C$. For what temperatures is silver a gas?

31. **Test Prep** Which of these values for c makes $c + 0.25 < 19.75$ true?

   (A) 19   (B) 19.75   (C) 20   (D) 20.25

Mercury is the only metal that is a liquid at room temperature.

Problem Solving and Reasoning

32. **Communicate** Is the statement $|-5| < |3|$ true or false? Explain.

33. **Critical Thinking** Make a table of the *equation* $x + 3 = y$. Then use your table to investigate the *inequality* $x + 3 > 7$. Find at least three values of x that make this inequality true. (You may need to add a few entries to your original table.)

34. **Critical Thinking** Answer each question for the integers -5 to 5. It may help to make a table.

   a. When is $n = n^2$?   **b.** When is $n < n^2$?   **c.** When is $n > n^2$?

Mixed Review

Estimate each answer. *[Lesson 8-4]*

35. 10% of 41   36. 52% of 74   37. 15% of $13.92   38. 26% of 392

Use $>$, $<$, or $=$ to compare each pair of numbers. *[Lesson 9-2]*

39. $-3 \square 3$ 40. $-7 \square 0$ 41. $-27 \square -26$ 42. $-1 \square -905$

43. $-707 \square -770$ 44. $|17| \square |-17|$ 45. $|-27| \square |-26|$ 46. $1 \square -1,000,000$

Project Progress

Make a table and a scatterplot of the population data you've gathered. If you've written an equation to fit your data, show the graph of that equation on your scatterplot.

Problem Solving

Understand
Plan
Solve
Look Back

You've seen some of the ways businesses can use tables, graphs, and equations. Now you'll apply what you've learned to questions that could face the student owners of Food From the 'Hood.

It IS My Business!

Materials: Graph paper

Food From the 'Hood earns $1.25 on each bottle of Creamy Italian or Honey Mustard salad dressing it sells at the full retail price.

1. Write an equation relating the income to the number of bottles sold.

2. Make a table showing the income from sales of 20, 40, 60, 80, and 100 bottles. Use the table to draw a graph.

3. Estimate the number of bottles that must be sold to make $105. Explain how you made your estimate.

Food From the 'Hood has a goal of earning $50,000 in 1996–1997, which will be distributed as scholarship money to the student owners when they graduate.

4. Suppose that Food From the 'Hood has expenses of $35,000 and earns $1.25 for every bottle of salad dressing it sells. Write a two-step equation to show that its income minus its expenses gives a profit of $50,000.

5. Solve the equation you wrote in Step 4. What is your solution, and what does it mean? Explain how you solved the equation.

The table represents the equation $y = -2x + 6$. Use it to solve the related equations beneath the table.

x	−2	−1	0	1	2	3	4	5	6
y	10	8	6	4	2	0	−2	−4	−6

1. $6 = -2x + 6$

2. $-2x + 6 = -2$

3. $10 = -2x + 6$

4. $-2x + 6 = 0$

The graph of $y = 5x + 30$ is shown at the right. Use it to solve the related equations.

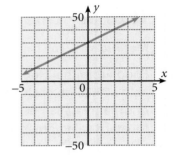

5. $30 = 5x + 30$

6. $40 = 5x + 30$

7. $5x + 30 = 10$

8. Estimation Use the graph to estimate the solution to $25 = 5x + 30$.

9. Journal Explain the difference between an equation and an inequality.

10. The cost of a plane ticket from Anchorage, Alaska, to Biloxi, Mississippi, is greater than $500. Write and graph an inequality for this statement.

11. Industry When she was 13, Amy Kumpel and her friends began making pillows and having them autographed by famous people. The pillows were sold at an auction, and the proceeds went to benefit homeless children.

a. The pillows sold for an average of about $72. Write an equation for the amount of money, m, made from selling p pillows.

b. Make a table of values for your equation in **a.** Use the table to estimate the number of pillows sold to make $4000.

Write an expression describing the rule for each sequence. Then give the 100th term for the sequence. *[Lesson 10-3]*

12. $-2, -1, 0, 1, \ldots$

13. $6, 12, 18, 24, \ldots$

14. $0.2, 0.4, 0.6, 0.8, \ldots$

15. $1, 8, 27, 64, \ldots$

Test Prep

When you're asked a question about an inequality on a multiple choice test, remember to consider negative numbers, fractions, and zero.

16. Which of these inequalities is *always* true for any number n?

Ⓐ $n^2 > n$ Ⓑ $2n > n$ Ⓒ $n + 4 > n$ Ⓓ $-n < n$

Weathering the Storm

On September 11, 1995, tropical storm Luis hit Newfoundland, Canada. Its strong winds and torrential rains washed out roads and flooded low-lying areas. The storm caused millions of dollars in damage and claimed one life. A fearsome storm, right? Yes, but ...

This was only the last fizzling gasp of what was once Hurricane Luis. As it smashed through the Caribbean, packing winds whose gusts reached 170 mi/hr, Hurricane Luis caused billions of dollars worth of damage. It destroyed hotels and hospitals on Antigua, and ripped the roofs off three-quarters of the homes in the island nation of St. Kitts-Nevis.

Obviously, warning people about the approach of a storm such as Hurricane Luis can save thousands of lives. Meteorologists use physics, mathematics, and data from satellites to develop weather forecasts. Equations such as the ones you're about to investigate play an important role in predicting our wild, wild weather.

1 Name some weather conditions that have affected your state in the past year.

2 Make a list of some information that you think is involved in predicting the weather.

3 Name some examples of mathematics used in weather reports.

Integer Addition and Subtraction Equations

▶ **Lesson Link** You've solved equations using graphs and tables. Now you'll use algebra to solve equations involving addition and subtraction of integers. ◀

Explore | Modeling Integer Equations

Tiling the Day Away

Materials: Algebra tiles

You must follow these rules when using algebra tiles to solve equations:

Zero Pairs

x

$-x$

-1 1

• Whatever you do to one side of the equation, you must do to the other.

• Any zero pairs on one side of the equation can be removed.

• The equation is solved when a positive x-tile is alone on one side.

1. Write the equation modeled by each equation box. Then use algebra tiles and the rules to solve each equation. State your final equation for each problem, and give the solution.

a.  b. 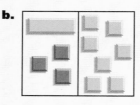 c.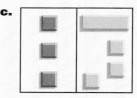

2. Make up and solve an equation that involves x and integers.

Learn | Integer Addition and Subtraction Equations

When you solve an equation, it helps to think of a balanced scale.

To preserve the balance, you must do the same thing to each side of the equation.

Examples

1 Solve: $x + (-3) = -5$

The algebra tiles illustrate the steps. Each side of the equation box represents a side of the equation.

$$x + (-3) = -5$$

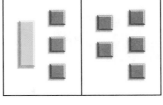

$$x + (-3) + 3 = -5 + 3 \qquad \text{To isolate } x, \text{ add}$$
positive 3 to both sides.

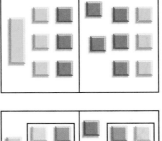

$$x = -5 + 3 \qquad -3 + 3 = 0$$

$$x = -2 \qquad \text{Add.}$$

Remember

When you add two integers with different signs, subtract their absolute values and use the sign of the number with the larger absolute value. **[Page 452]**

2 The greatest recorded one-day temperature change was 100°F, recorded at Browning, Montana. If the high temperature was 44°F, what was the low temperature?

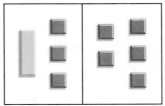

Let l = the low temperature.

$$l + 100 = 44 \qquad \text{Write an equation.}$$

$$l + 100 - 100 = 44 - 100 \qquad \text{Use inverse operations.}$$

$$l = -56 \qquad \text{Subtract.}$$

The low temperature was −56°F. Since −56 + 100 = 44, the solution checks.

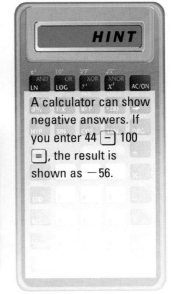

HINT

A calculator can show negative answers. If you enter 44 − 100 = , the result is shown as −56.

Try It

Solve each equation.

a. $x + 1 = -4$ **b.** $x + 5 = -2$ **c.** $x + 11 = -29$ **d.** $x + (-7) = 41$

Notice that in Example 1, the *additive inverse* was used to undo addition, and in Example 2, an *inverse operation* was used. Both strategies work.

WHAT DO YOU THINK?

Jacob and Jyotsna live in Helena, Montana. As they get ready for school, the local weather report states that the temperature is expected to rise 15°F to −7°F during the day. What is the temperature now?

Jyotsna thinks ...

I'll write an equation. If the temperature is t now, $t + 15 = -7$.

I have to get t by itself. To get rid of adding 15 to t, I'll subtract 15.

$$t + 15 - 15 = -7 - 15$$
$$t = -22$$

It must be −22° now.

Jacob thinks ...

I'll find an equation. Let's say it's t degrees out now. If it goes up 15 degrees, it'll be −7, so $t + 15 = -7$.

To undo adding positive 15, I'll add negative 15.

$$t + 15 + (-15) = -7 + (-15)$$
$$t = -22$$

I agree—it must be −22° now. Is school really open?

What do  think?

1. Why do these methods give the same result?

2. Explain how Jyotsna knows that −7 − 15 is equal to −22.

Check | Your Understanding

1. Describe how an equation looks when you've finished solving it.

2. Suppose you're solving $x + 7 = 12$. Does it matter whether you add −7 to each side or subtract 7 from each side? Explain why or why not.

Practice and Apply

1. **Getting Started** Follow the steps to solve $x + (-2) = (-11)$.

   a. To isolate x, you need to undo the addition of -2. To do this, add (positive) 2 to both sides of the equation.

   b. The left side of the equation simplifies to x. Use your rules for integer addition to simplify the right side of the equation.

   c. Check your answer by substituting it into the original equation.

Write the equation represented by each equation box. Then solve the equation.

2.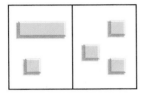

3.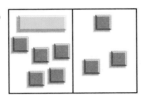

4.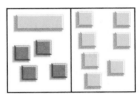

For each equation, tell whether the number in bold is a solution.

5. $m - (-4) = -5;$ **-1**   6. $x + 18 = 3;$ **-15**   7. $24 + b = -2;$ **26**   8. $c + (-4) = -1;$ **-5**

Solve each equation. Check your solutions.

9. $x + 2 = -3$ 10. $m + 1 = -9$ 11. $z - 7 = -8$ 12. $x + (-7) = -8$

13. $-10 + k = 17$ 14. $p - 45 = -32$ 15. $x - (-33) = 28$ 16. $(-4) + x = -19$

17. $22 + x = 11$ 18. $n + 111 = 95$ 19. $x - (-59) = -1$ 20. $b + (-61) = -85$

21. **Science** The fastest recorded temperature rise was 49° in 2 minutes, in Spearfish, South Dakota. If the temperature after the rise was 45°F, what was the temperature before the rise?

22. **Social Studies** The amount of profit a business (or a government) makes is equal to its income minus its expenses. As an equation: $P = I - E$. In 1994, the United States government had a deficit of about 203 billion dollars. (This means the same thing as a profit of -203 billion dollars.) If the government's expenses were about 1461 billion dollars that year, what was its income?

23. Science Atmospheric pressure is sometimes measured in *millibars*. Low pressure is associated with severe weather. The pressure at the center of Hurricane Luis dropped 73 millibars in ten days, to a low of 948 millibars. What was the original pressure?

24. **Test Prep** At sunset on the moon, the temperature is about 58°F. After night falls, the temperature can drop to -261°F. Which equation could be used to find the difference between the two temperatures?

    Ⓐ $D = 261 - 58$ Ⓑ $D = 58 - 261$

    Ⓒ $D = 58 - (-261)$ Ⓓ $D = -261 + 58$

Problem Solving and Reasoning

25. Communicate Write a problem that could be modeled by the equation $x + 5 = -55$. Then give the solution to your problem.

26. Choose a Strategy The Dow Jones Industrial Average measures the prices of important stocks on the New York Stock Exchange. Suppose the Dow Jones average ends the week at 5602.10. The average lost 8.70 points on Monday, gained 37.70 on Tuesday, lost 11.25 on Wednesday, gained 24.90 on Thursday, and gained 27.15 on Friday. What was the Dow Jones average at the start of the week?

27. Critical Thinking Suppose you're given the equation $-x + 27 = -32$.

    a. What is the difference between this equation and other addition and subtraction equations you've solved?

    b. Solve this equation. Explain how you found the solution.

> **Problem Solving**
> ## STRATEGIES
> • Look for a Pattern
> • Make an Organized List
> • Make a Table
> • Guess and Check
> • Work Backward
> • Use Logical Reasoning
> • Draw a Diagram
> • Solve a Simpler Problem

Mixed Review

Complete each table to create equal ratios. Then write four proportions involving ratios in the table. *[Lesson 6-5]*

28.

2	4	8	16
3			

29.

1	3	4	7
5			

Write a proportion and solve each problem. If necessary, round answers to the nearest tenth. *[Lesson 8-6]*

30. What percent of 24 is 11?

31. 20% of what number is 12?

32. 90% of 1210 is what number?

33. 0.1% of what number is 57?

Integer Multiplication and Division Equations

▶ **Lesson Link** │ You've solved equations that involve adding and subtracting integers. Now you'll solve equations with multiplication and division of integers. ◀

You'll Learn ...

■ to solve multiplication and division equations involving positive and negative integers

... How It's Used

Submarine crews can solve an equation involving their ascent rate to determine when they will reach the surface.

Explore │ Modeling Multiplication Equations

Materials: Algebra tiles

Divide and Conquer!

1. A set of equations is modeled by algebra tiles. Write the equation for each equation box.

a.

b.

c.

d.

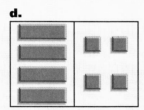

e.

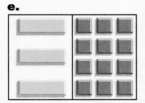

f.

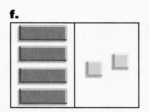

2. Use the tiles to solve each equation. Check your solutions.

3. Explain how you solved these equations. Tell why the method you used does not break any of the rules for solving equations.

Learn │ Integer Multiplication and Division Equations

You've seen that multiplication and division are inverse operations. You can use this fact to solve multiplication and division equations with negative numbers.

When you solve these equations, you'll need to remember the rules for multiplication and division of signed numbers.

When two numbers have the same sign, their product or quotient is positive; when the numbers have different signs, their product or quotient is negative.

Algebra tiles can be used to show why the steps for solving a multiplication equation work. Notice how division is shown in the equation boxes.

Examples

1 Solve: $3x = -9$

The algebra tiles illustrate the steps. Each side of the equation box represents a side of the equation.

$3x = -9$

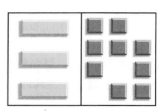

$\dfrac{3x}{3} = -\dfrac{9}{3}$ To undo multiplying by 3, divide by 3.

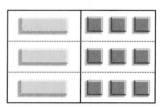

$x = -3$ Divide. The quotient of a negative and a positive number is negative.

The solution is $x = -3$.

2 In Yakutsk, Russia, the average high temperature drops 20°F per month ($-20°$) from July to January. How long does it take before the average high temperature changes (drops) by $-90°F$?

Let $m =$ the number of months.   Define a variable.

$-20m = -90$ Write an equation for the problem.

$\dfrac{-20m}{-20} = \dfrac{-90}{-20}$ Use inverse operations.

$m = \dfrac{-90}{-20} = \dfrac{9}{2} = 4\dfrac{1}{2}$ Divide. The quotient of two negative numbers is positive.

The average high temperature changes by $-90°F$ in $4\dfrac{1}{2}$ months.

Try It

Solve each equation.

a. $2x = -4$ **b.** $-18h = -80$ **c.** $-15x = 65$

It's difficult to model division equations with algebra tiles. However, these equations can be solved by using inverse operations.

Examples

3 Solve: $\dfrac{x}{-10} = 20$

$$\dfrac{x}{-10}(-10) = 20(-10) \qquad \text{Use inverse operations.}$$

$$x = -200 \qquad \text{Multiply.}$$

The solution is $x = -200$. To check, substitute into the original equation.

$$\dfrac{-200}{-10} = 20$$

$$20 = 20 \checkmark$$

4 In a flood in Kansas City, Missouri, and Kansas City, Kansas, the Kansas River rose an average of 6 inches per hour for 40 hours, when it spilled over a restraining wall and flooded the cities. How much did the waters rise over this time?

Let $r =$ the rise in the waters. Define a variable.

$$\dfrac{r}{40} = 6 \qquad \text{Write an equation for the problem.}$$

$$\dfrac{r}{40} \cdot 40 = 6 \cdot 40 \qquad \text{Use inverse operations.}$$

$$r = 240 \qquad \text{Multiply.}$$

The flood waters rose 240 inches, or 20 feet.

▶ **History Link**

The Salton Sea in California did not exist until 1905, when the Colorado River flooded a human-made canal. The water rushed into a salt flat known as the Salton Sink, creating a huge inland lake.

Try It

Solve each equation.

a. $\dfrac{y}{5} = -30$ **b.** $\dfrac{w}{-6} = -220$ **c.** $\dfrac{m}{-2} = -224$

Check | Your Understanding

1. Explain how you could use algebra tiles to solve $-3x = 6$.

2. Can you tell the sign of the answer to a multiplication equation before you solve it? If so, explain how. If not, explain why not.

PRACTICE 10-10

Practice and Apply

1. **Getting Started** Follow the steps to solve $-3x = -15$.

a. To isolate x, you need to undo multiplication by -3. To do this, divide both sides of the equation by -3.

b. The left side of the equation simplifies to x. Use your rules for integer division to simplify the right side of the equation.

c. Check your answer by substituting it into the original equation.

Write the equation represented by each equation box. Then solve the equation.

2.

3.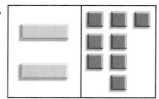

4.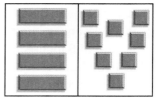

For each equation, tell whether the number in bold is a solution.

5. $-4p = -20; \mathbf{-5}$ **6.** $\dfrac{x}{4} = -16; \mathbf{-4}$ **7.** $8t = -168; \mathbf{-21}$ **8.** $\dfrac{v}{-2} = 12; \mathbf{-24}$

Solve each equation. Check your solutions.

9. $3m = 99$ **10.** $11g = -44$ **11.** $-8z = -80$ **12.** $84 = -2s$

13. $\dfrac{c}{4} = -16$ **14.** $\dfrac{g}{7} = -11$ **15.** $\dfrac{d}{-3} = -12$ **16.** $\dfrac{f}{-8} = -22$

17. $-1x = 19$ **18.** $\dfrac{n}{-25} = -101$ **19.** $-5.2x = -18.2$ **20.** $\dfrac{y}{-107} = 0$

21. **Science** The wettest inhabited place in the world is Buenaventura, Colombia. Its average annual rainfall is 6,743 mm—over 22 ft of rain! Buenaventura's rainfall is 13,486 times as great as the rainfall of the driest inhabited place, Aswan, Egypt. What is the annual rainfall in Aswan?

Aswan, Egypt

22. Geometry If the area of a parallelogram is 42 cm² and its length is 14 cm, what is its width? Explain how you solved this problem.

23. Operation Sense Write two different division equations that have a solution of −4.

24. | Test Prep | Yakutat, Alaska, has an average annual rainfall of about 135 inches. This is about 5 times the annual rainfall of Minneapolis, Minnesota. Which equation can be used to find the approximate annual rainfall for Minneapolis?

Ⓐ $r = 135 \cdot 5$ Ⓑ $r = 135 + 5$ Ⓒ $r = 135 - 5$ Ⓓ $r = \dfrac{135}{5}$

25. Consumer Using a sunscreen can help prevent skin cancer. A sunscreen with an SPF of 15 means you can stay in the sun 15 times as long without burning as you could with no sunscreen. Jules tends to burn after 30 minutes in the sun. If he is buying sunscreen for a 12-hour hike in a sunny canyon, what is the smallest SPF number he should look for?

Problem Solving and Reasoning

26. Communicate Write a problem that could be modeled by the equation $-5x = -100$. Then give the solution to your problem.

27. [Journal] Although it's difficult to use algebra tiles to model a division equation, it's not impossible! Explain a way that you could use algebra tiles to solve a division equation. Then show how your method works by sketching the solution to a division equation.

28. Critical Thinking Suppose the average low temperature for a 4-day period in Chicago, Illinois, is −8°F. After the next day, the 5-day average is −9°F. What was the low temperature for the fifth day? Explain your reasoning.

Mixed Review

29. George earned $12.00 for working 2 hours and $35.00 for working 5 hours. Are the rates proportional? *[Lesson 6-6]*

Find the new amount after each increase or decrease. If necessary, round answers to the nearest tenth. *[Lesson 8-7]*

30. $80 is increased by 55%

31. 1580 is decreased by 90%

32. 22.7 is increased by 120%

33. $108 is decreased by 34%

Problem Solving TIP

Draw a picture to help you write an algebraic equation.

Solving Two-Step Equations

▶ **Lesson Link** You've solved integer equations involving just one step. Now you'll solve two-step equations. ◀

You'll Learn ...

■ to solve two-step equations involving positive and negative integers

... How It's Used

Two-step equations can help you analyze memberships or subscriptions that have a small initial payment plus a monthly fee.

Explore | **Modeling Two-Step Equations**

Doing the Two-Step

Materials: Algebra tiles

1. Model the equation $3x + (-2) = 4$ with algebra tiles.

2. Use the rules for solving equations to solve this equation. Record each step and check your answer when you finish.

3. In solving this equation, which did you undo first, the addition of -2 to x or the multiplication of x by 3? Why did you choose to undo this operation first?

4. Try to use the tiles to solve the equation in Step 1 in a different way. If you are able to solve the equation another way, explain how you did it. If you can't solve the equation, explain why not.

Learn | **Solving Two-Step Equations**

You may recall the idea of an inverse operation machine. This machine always gives back the same number that goes in. Notice that it undoes operations in the *opposite* of their original order.

multiply by 4   subtract 3   add 3   divide by 4

$$3 \longrightarrow 12 \longrightarrow 9 \longrightarrow 12 \longrightarrow 3$$

You can use this idea to help you solve two-step equations. Because you *do* addition and subtraction last in the order of operations, you need to *undo* them first when solving equations.

Examples

1 Solve: $3 + 2x = -5$

$$3 + 2x = -5$$

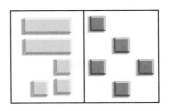

Study TIP

When solving problems involving positive and negative numbers, predict the sign your answer will have *before* you begin the problem.

$$3 + (-3) + 2x = -5 + (-3)$$ First undo adding 3.

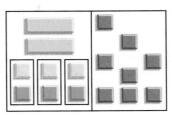

$$2x = -8$$ Add.

$$\frac{2x}{2} = \frac{-8}{2}$$ Then undo multiplication by 2.

$$x = -4$$ Divide.

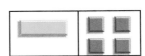

2 Solve: $\frac{x}{-3} + 7 = -2$

$$\frac{x}{-3} + 7 - 7 = -2 - 7$$ Undo addition first.

$$\frac{x}{-3} = -9$$ Subtract.

$$\frac{x}{-3}(-3) = -9(-3)$$ Use inverse operations.

$$x = 27$$ Multiply.

Try It

Solve each equation.

a. $2x + 2 = -4$ **b.** $12 - 8c = 76$ **c.** $\frac{x}{5} - 11 = -5$ **d.** $\frac{x}{-4} + 2 = 7$

Some real-world situations can be modeled by two-step equations.

Example 3

As you go up in altitude, the temperature decreases. Typically, there is a decrease of about 6.5°C for every kilometer you go up.

Suppose you begin a mountain climbing trip. During the day, the temperature increases 18°C. However, due to your altitude gain, you feel a drop of about 8°C. How many kilometers did you climb?

Let k = the number of kilometers you climbed.

The temperature change due to altitude is $-6.5k$. Adding this to 18° gives a drop of $-8°$. The equation is:

$$-6.5k + 18 = -8$$
$$-6.5k + 18 - 18 = -8 - 18$$
$$-6.5k = -26$$
$$\frac{-6.5k}{-6.5} = \frac{-26}{-6.5}$$
$$k = 4$$

You climbed 4 kilometers.

Try It

a. In Example 3, suppose you feel an *increase* of 5°C instead of a decrease of 8°C. How many kilometers did you climb?

b. In Example 3, suppose you feel a decrease of 14.5°C. How many kilometers did you climb?

| Check | Your Understanding |

1. When you solve a two-step equation, why do you undo addition or subtraction before you undo multiplication or division?

2. Suppose you're given a two-step equation to solve. Can you tell what you'll need to do to solve it just by looking at the equation? If so, explain how you can tell. If not, explain why it's not possible to tell.

► **Science Link**

10-11 Exercises and Applications

Practice and Apply

1. **Getting Started** Follow the steps to solve $-4x - 2 = -14$.

   a. First undo subtracting 2 by adding 2 to both sides of the equation.

   b. The left side of the equation simplifies to $-4x$. Use your rules for integer addition to simplify the right side of the equation.

   c. To isolate x, you need to undo multiplication by -4. To do this, divide both sides of the equation by -4.

   d. The left side of the equation simplifies to x. Use your rules for integer division to simplify the right side of the equation.

   e. Check your answer by substituting it into the original equation.

Write the equation represented by each equation box. Then solve the equation.

2.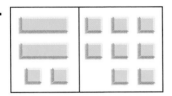

3.

4.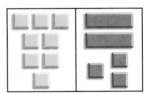

For each equation, tell whether the number in bold is a solution.

5. $4 = 2x + 10$; **−3**

6. $\dfrac{m}{3} + 3 = 3$; **2**

7. $2j + (-5) = -3$; **−4**

8. $\dfrac{y}{-2} + 4 = -8$; **6**

Solve each equation. Check your solutions.

9. $2x - 1 = 1$

10. $2m + 3 = -5$

11. $\dfrac{t}{6} - 1 = -7$

12. $3 = 5w + (-2)$

13. $8 = -5g - 7$

14. $96 = \dfrac{v}{-2} + 90$

15. $5n + 100 = 60$

16. $2e + 6 = 6$

17. $\dfrac{x}{-4} - (-8) = -12$

18. $2k - 11 = -22$

19. $\dfrac{f}{7} + 52 = -108$

20. $6p + 27 = -3$

21. **Science** The greatest one-day rainfall ever recorded was 72 inches (six *feet!*) on January 7–8, 1966, on the island of Réunion. This is 14 inches less than twice the greatest recorded one-day rainfall in United States history. Find the greatest one-day United States rainfall.

22. Geometry Write and solve an equation to find the length of this rectangle if its perimeter is 32 m.

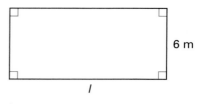

6 m

l

23. **Test Prep** The snow depth at a ski resort is 64 in. now, and snow is falling at the rate of 2 in. per hour. Which equation could be used to find the number of hours it will take for the snow depth to reach 77 in.?

Ⓐ $2h + 64 = 77$

Ⓑ $\frac{h}{2} + 64 = 77$

Ⓒ $2h - 64 = 77$

Ⓓ $\frac{h}{2} - 77 = 64$

Problem Solving and Reasoning

24. Critical Thinking Abraham Lincoln's famous speech, the Gettysburg Address, begins, "Four score and seven years ago." Lincoln was referring to the fact that the Declaration of Independence had been written 87 years earlier.

a. How many years are there in a score? Explain your answer.

b. If the Declaration of Independence was written in 1776, when did Lincoln give the Gettysburg Address?

25. Communicate Write two different two-step equations that each have a solution of -3.

26. Critical Thinking Solve the equation $\frac{2}{3}x + 7 = -19$. (Remember that your goal is to isolate x, and that you must do the same thing to both sides of the equation.) Explain how you were able to solve this equation.

Mixed Review

Convert to a decimal. Tell if the decimal terminates or repeats. *[Lesson 3-10]*

27. $\frac{2}{9}$

28. $\frac{5}{11}$

29. $\frac{7}{8}$

30. $\frac{26}{39}$

31. $\frac{7}{16}$

Corn is on sale at 5 ears for $1.25. Find each cost. *[Lesson 6-7]*

32. The cost of 1 ear of corn

33. The cost of 12 ears of corn

Project Progress

Choose a population figure that your town, city, or state seems to be moving toward.

Then make a mathematical estimate of the year the population will reach that figure.

You may choose to use graphs, tables, or equations to help make your estimate.

Problem Solving

Understand

Plan

Solve

Look Back

Problem Solving with Integer Equations

> **Lesson Link** You've solved equations with positive and negative numbers. Now you'll use those methods to solve real-world problems. ◄

You'll Learn ...

■ to solve real-world problems by using integer equations

... How It's Used

Movie producers need to solve equations involving integers to see whether or not a film will make a profit.

Explore Problem Solving with Integer Equations

Materials: Graph paper

Forecast: Flood!

Raging River is 8 ft deep at 9:00 A.M. Heavy rainfall is causing the river to rise.

1. The river will overflow its banks and flood the town if it reaches a depth of 32 ft. It is rising at a rate of 3 ft/hr. You need to know how long it will be until the river floods. Write an equation to model this problem.

2. Make a graph or a table to solve the equation you wrote in Step 1. At what time will the river flood? Check that your answer makes sense.

3. Write a short report explaining how you solved this problem.

Learn Problem Solving with Integer Equations

You can use your equation-solving abilities to answer real-world questions.

Example 1

After takeoff, a plane ascends at a rate of 750 feet per minute. How long will it take to reach a cruising altitude of 30,000 feet?

Let m = the number of minutes to reach cruising altitude.

$$750m = 30{,}000$$

$$\frac{750m}{750} = \frac{30{,}000}{750}$$

$$m = 40$$

The plane will take 40 minutes to reach an altitude of 30,000 feet.

Examples

Problem Solving TIP

If you are having trouble solving an equation with large numbers, it may help to solve a similar equation with smaller numbers first. The method you use to solve the simpler equation may help you see how to solve the more difficult one.

2 Between 1990 and 1992, the population of St. Louis, Missouri, declined by 12,952 people. If the 1992 population was 383,733, what was the 1990 population?

Let p = the 1990 population.

$$p - 12{,}952 = 383{,}733$$

$$p - 12{,}952 + 12{,}952 = 383{,}733 + 12{,}952$$

$$p = 396{,}685$$

The 1990 population of St. Louis was 396,685.

3 In Bismarck, North Dakota, the average high temperature in July is about 28°C. Between July and January, the high temperature drops an average of 6°C each month. At this rate of decrease, how long will it be before the average high temperature is 4°C?

Let m = the number of months. The temperature change in m months is $-6m$.

The starting temperature is 28°C, so the temperature after m months is $28 + (-6m)$. We need to know when this number will equal 4°C.

$$28 + (-6m) = 4$$

$$28 - 28 + (-6m) = 4 - 28$$

$$-6m = -24$$

$$\frac{-6m}{-6} = \frac{-24}{-6}$$

$$m = 4$$

The temperature will equal 4°C in 4 months.

Try It

a. Between 1980 and 1990, the per capita income in the United States increased by $9,202. If the 1990 per capita income was $18,696, what was the per capita income in 1980?

b. Luisa wants to buy a pair of basketball shoes that cost $60. She earns about $15 each week doing odd jobs. Before she can buy the shoes, she must pay her mother back $15. How long will it take before Luisa can afford the shoes?

Check Your Understanding

1. The equation in Example 2 could have been written with a negative integer instead of using subtraction. Write this form of the equation.

2. Suppose you solve a real-world problem and come up with a negative answer. Have you done something wrong? If not, in what kinds of problems might a negative answer make sense?

10-12 Exercises and Applications

Practice and Apply

Getting Started | **Write an equation for each statement. Do not solve the equation.**

1. The number of hours (h) increased by 2 equals 14.

2. The number of inches of snowfall (s) multiplied by 3 is 6.

3. Twice the temperature (t) decreased by 7 equals -27.

4. A number (x) divided by -5, then increased by 4, equals 100.

5. Problem Solving Suppose that the temperature drops 17° to -12°F. What was the starting temperature?

6. Industry The formula $D = 2A + V$ is used by the Forest Department to describe the damage potential, D, that a forest fire can cause to an area. A represents the average age of the brush, and V is the *value class,* used to describe the worth of the resources and structures in the area. If the value class of an area is 5 and the damage potential is 25, what is the average age of the brush?

7. Science Bagdad, California, went over 2 years without measurable rainfall. This is $\frac{1}{7}$ the number of years that Arica, Chile, went without rain. How long did Arica go without rain?

8. Science The pressure at sea level is 1 *atmosphere.* Undersea divers must plan on 1 additional atmosphere of pressure for every 33 ft of depth. Pressure can be found using the formula $P = \frac{d}{33} + 1$, where P is the pressure in atmospheres and d is the depth in ft. Find the number of atmospheres experienced by:

a. A diver at a depth of 33 ft.

b. The record-holding bathyscaphe *Trieste* at a depth of 35,817 ft.

9. [Test Prep] Carole took a car trip through California. After leaving the lowest point in Death Valley, she gained 1597 meters in altitude to cross Towne Pass. If the elevation of Towne Pass is 1511 m, what is the elevation of the lowest point in Death Valley?

Ⓐ −282 m   Ⓑ −86 m   Ⓒ 86 m   Ⓓ 3108 m

Problem Solving and Reasoning

10. Critical Thinking Suppose it costs 25¢ for the first minute of a long distance phone call and 15¢ for each additional minute. The cost of a phone call can then be expressed by the formula $c = 0.25 + 0.15(m − 1)$, where c is the total cost in dollars and m is the number of minutes.

  a. For $1.75, how long can you talk?

  b. What is the cost of a call that lasts 1 hour 15 minutes?

11. Communicate According to some scientists, the average temperature of the earth has increased about $\frac{1}{2}$°C over the last 100 years. This phenomenon is called *global warming*. If this trend continues, and the current average temperature is about 17°C, when will the earth's average temperature reach:

  a. 18°C ?   **b.** 20°C?   **c.** 21°C?

  d. In the last ice age, about 15,000 years ago, the average temperature was about 5°C less than it is today. Find the average rate of temperature increase over this 15,000-year period. How does it compare to the current rate of global warming?

Area Covered by Ice

CANADA

UNITED STATES

Mixed Review

Solve each proportion. *[Lesson 6-8]*

12. $\dfrac{x}{5} = \dfrac{4}{10}$ **13.** $\dfrac{1}{6} = \dfrac{k}{18}$ **14.** $\dfrac{5}{x} = \dfrac{25}{20}$ **15.** $\dfrac{1}{10} = \dfrac{6}{x}$

16. $\dfrac{8}{1} = \dfrac{t}{7}$ **17.** $\dfrac{y}{9} = \dfrac{12}{27}$ **18.** $\dfrac{4}{9} = \dfrac{6}{x}$ **19.** $\dfrac{3}{2} = \dfrac{2}{x}$

Find each absolute value. *[Lesson 9-1]*

20. $|10|$ **21.** $|-10|$ **22.** $|-108|$ **23.** $|0|$ **24.** $|-4.6|$

25. $|75|$ **26.** $|8.14|$ **27.** $|-32|$ **28.** $|-3007|$ **29.** $|101|$

30. $|5 + 9|$ **31.** $|-5 + (-9)|$ **32.** $|9 - 5|$ **33.** $|-9 + 5|$ **34.** $|-\pi|$

You've investigated many different ways to solve equations involving positive and negative integers. Now you'll apply your skills to solve some real-world problems about an important hurricane.

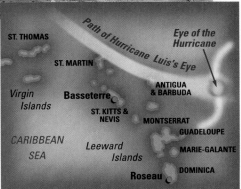

Weathering the Storm

Hurricane Luis was one of the most powerful storms of this century. It left a terrible path of destruction through the Caribbean Sea during August and September 1995.

Write and solve an equation for each of the following questions. Explain how you solved each problem.

1. From August 30 to September 2, Luis's wind speeds increased by 100 mi/hr. If Luis's wind speed was 140 mi/hr on September 2, what was its wind speed on August 30?

2. On September 3, at 11:00 P.M., the *eye* (center) of Hurricane Luis was 355 miles east of the Leeward Islands. It was moving west at a speed of 14 mi/hr. If its path and speed did not change, when did Luis's center reach the Leeward Islands?

3. On September 6, Luis's wind speed was 130 mi/hr. During the next few days, this speed declined by about 8 mi/hr per day. By what day had Luis's sustained wind speed declined to 90 mi/hr?

Write the equation represented by each equation box. Then solve the equation.

1.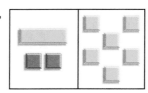

2.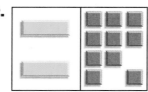

3.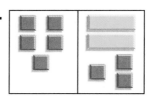

For each equation, tell whether the number in bold is a solution.

4. $x + (-7) = -22; \mathbf{-15}$ **5.** $\frac{g}{3} = -81; \mathbf{-27}$ **6.** $38 = -2p; \mathbf{-19}$ **7.** $-4g - 18 = (-22); \mathbf{1}$

Solve each equation. Check your solutions.

8. $w + 70 = 65$ **9.** $3p = -66$ **10.** $s - 85 = 50$ **11.** $\frac{x}{-6} = -30$

12. $-19 = f + (-19)$ **13.** $64 = \frac{d}{2}$ **14.** $-2h + 6 = -24$ **15.** $\frac{x}{-4} + 2 = 10$

16. Science Since land heats up and cools down faster than water, areas far from oceans tend to have a wide temperature range. Verkhoyansk, Russia, has one of the widest temperature ranges in the world. According to the *Guinness Book of World Records*, the highest temperature there was 98°F. If this was 192° greater than the lowest recorded temperature, what was the lowest temperature?

Solve each equation using a table. Then solve it using a graph.
[Lesson 10-6]

17. $4 = x - 1$ **18.** $10 = x + 4$ **19.** $2x = 8$ **20.** $56 = 8x$

Test Prep

When you're asked to identify an equation that describes a problem on a multiple choice test, use key words in the problem, like *times, less than,* or *added to,* to identify the operations that should be in the equation.

21. In the blizzard of 1888, Albany received about 48 inches of snow. This was 4 times the amount Boston received. Which equation would you use to find Boston's snowfall?

  Ⓐ $48 + 4 = s$ Ⓑ $48 - 4 = s$ Ⓒ $48 \cdot 4 = s$ Ⓓ $\frac{48}{4} = s$

Quadratic and Absolute Value Graphs

Not all graphs of equations are straight lines.

The equation $y = x^2 - 5$ is *quadratic*. Quadratic equations have squared terms, such as the x^2 in this equation.

You can graph a quadratic equation by making a table of values. Here is a table for $y = x^2 - 5$.

x	−3	−2	−1	0	1	2	3
y	4	−1	−4	−5	−4	−1	4

Plotting and connecting these points gives the graph of the quadratic equation. Notice that the equation is somewhat U-shaped. This shape is called a *parabola*.

You can also graph equations involving the absolute value of a variable.

To graph $y = |x| - 2$, begin by making a table of values.

x	−3	−2	−1	0	1	2	3
y	1	0	−1	−2	−1	0	1

Then plot and connect the points.

Notice that the graph of this absolute value equation has a V shape. This is typical of the graphs of these equations. There is a V shape because the part of the equation inside the absolute value bars cannot be less than zero.

Try It

Graph each quadratic or absolute value equation on a coordinate plane.

1. $y = x^2$ **2.** $y = x^2 + 2$ **3.** $y = |x| - 5$ **4.** $y = |x - 5|$ **5.** $y = 5 - x^2$

545

Graphic Organizer

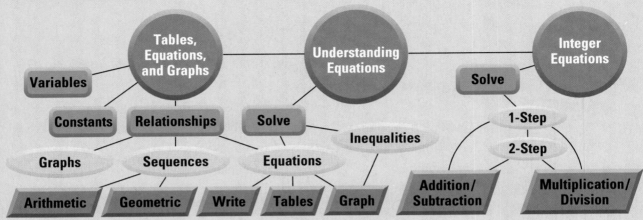

Section 10A Tables, Equations, and Graphs

Summary

- A quantity is a *variable* if its value may change and a **constant** otherwise.

- The direction of a graph (**increasing, decreasing,** or **constant**) can help show the relationship between the quantities on its axes.

- A **sequence** is a list of numbers, or **terms**. Sequences often follow a pattern that can be described using an expression.

- You can graph an equation by making a table of values, plotting the ordered pairs these values represent, and connecting the points.

Review

1. Define a variable and give a reasonable range of values for the number of petals on a flower.

2. Name a quantity that the volume of a cylinder might depend on.

3. Write a rule for the sequence 6, 12, 18, 24, …, and give the 100th term of the sequence.

4. Make a table of six pairs of values for the equation $y = 2x + 5$.

5. Tell a story that fits the graph.

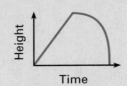

6. For the table below, write an equation to show the relationship between x and y. Use the equation to find y when $x = 9$.

x	1	2	3	4
y	4	8	12	16

7. Graph each equation on a coordinate plane.

    a. $y = x - 3$ **b.** $y = x^2 - 4$

Section 10B Understanding Equations

Summary

- You can use a table or a graph to solve an equation.

- An **inequality** uses an inequality sign to compare two expressions. The **solutions** of an inequality are the values of the variable that make the inequality true. They can be graphed on a number line.

Review

8. The table below was created from the equation $y = -2x + 3$. Use it to solve the following related equations.

   a. $-3 = -2x + 3$ **b.** $3 = -2x + 3$

x	0	1	2	3	4
y	3	1	−1	−3	−5

9. Use a graph to solve $-7 = 3x + 5$.

10. Write and graph an inequality on a number line to show that the cost was less than $7.

Section 10C Integer Equations

Summary

- Solving equations with negative integers involves the same rules as solving equations with only positive integers. The goal is to isolate the variable, and whatever you do to one side of the equation, you must do to the other.

- You can use algebra tiles to model and solve equations. Solve the equation by getting a single x-tile on one side and unit tiles on the other.

Review

11. Solve the equation $-3s + 5 = 14$. Check your solution.

12. The length of a rectangle is 15 cm. If its perimeter is 36 cm, what is its width?

13. Solve each equation. Check your solutions.

   a. $4x = -16$ **b.** $\dfrac{t}{-2} = -10$

14. Tapes are $9 each and there is a $5 shipping charge. Kadie paid $41 for some tapes. How many did she buy?

15. Write the equation modeled in the equation box. Solve the equation. Sketch your steps.

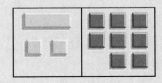

16. Solve each equation. Check your solutions.

   a. $x + 3 = 7$ **b.** $k + (-3) = -4$

17. For each equation, tell whether the number in **bold** is a solution.

   a. $-2x = 24;\ \mathbf{-12}$ **b.** $\dfrac{g}{3} = -18;\ \mathbf{-6}$

1. Tell whether the number of ounces in 500 pounds is a variable or a constant.

2. Define a variable and give a reasonable range of values for the number of hours a student spends doing homework on a weeknight.

3. You ride your bicycle to school in the morning. After school, you ride most of the way home before remembering that you need your math book. You go back to get it, and then you ride home. Sketch a graph that shows the relationship between time and your distance from home.

4. Give the next picture in the pattern.

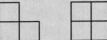 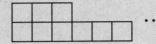 ...

5. Write a rule for the sequence $-4, -3, -2, -1, \ldots$, and give the 100th term of the sequence.

6. Complete the table and write an equation to show the relationship between the variables.

u	3	4	5	6	7
v	9	12	15		

7. Make a table of six pairs of values for the equation $y = 2x - 5$.

8. Graph each equation on a coordinate plane.

   a. $y = -2x$ b. $y = x + 2$

9. The table at the right was created from the equation $u = 5t - 7$. Use it to solve the following related equations.

t	0	1	2	3	4
u	-7	-2	3	8	13

   a. $13 = 5t - 7$ b. $-2 = 5t - 7$

10. Graph the inequality $x \geq -4$ on a number line.

11. Write an inequality for the graph.

12. Solve each equation. Check your solutions.

   a. $z - 18 = -7$ b. $\dfrac{w}{6} = -9$ c. $-7t + 12 = 33$

13. One winter day, the temperature rises 29° to reach a high of 12°F. What was the low temperature that day?

Performance Task

Write a story describing your typical day at school. Choose a fixed location at school, such as your locker or your homeroom. Then sketch a graph that shows the relationship between time and your distance from your chosen location.

Multiple Choice

Choose the best answer.

1. For the data set below, which of the following is equal to 6.5? *[Lesson 1-4]*

   3, 7, 9, 9, 8, 5, 4, 6, 7, 7, 5, 8

   Ⓐ Mean
   Ⓑ Median
   Ⓒ Mode
   Ⓓ Mean and median

2. Evaluate: $8 \cdot 4 + 3 \cdot 5$ *[Lesson 2-2]*

   Ⓐ 47   Ⓑ 105   Ⓒ 152   Ⓓ 280

3. Round 6.938471 to the nearest thousandth. *[Lesson 3-2]*

   Ⓐ 6.94
   Ⓑ 6.938
   Ⓒ 6.9385
   Ⓓ 6.939

4. Find the difference: $5\frac{5}{12} - 2\frac{11}{18}$ *[Lesson 4-3]*

   Ⓐ $2\frac{7}{18}$ Ⓑ $2\frac{29}{36}$ Ⓒ $3\frac{23}{36}$ Ⓓ $3\frac{29}{36}$

5. What is the sum of the angle measures in a hexagon? *[Lesson 5-4]*

   Ⓐ 360°   Ⓑ 540°   Ⓒ 720°   Ⓓ 900°

6. Solve the proportion: $\frac{15}{z} = \frac{27}{99}$ *[Lesson 6-8]*

   Ⓐ $z = 45$
   Ⓑ $z = 55$
   Ⓒ $z = 66$
   Ⓓ $z = 85$

7. Myra left home at 4:35 P.M. and rode her bike to the library at a rate of 12 mi/hr. If the library is 5 mi away from home, what time did she arrive? *[Lesson 7-3]*

   Ⓐ 4:40   Ⓑ 4:47   Ⓒ 5:00   Ⓓ 5:35

8. The value of Ron's coin collection has gone up 25% since last year. If it was worth $500 last year, how much is it worth now? *[Lesson 8-7]*

   Ⓐ $400
   Ⓑ $525
   Ⓒ $625
   Ⓓ $12,500

9. Which quadrant contains $(3, -2)$? *[Lesson 9-3]*

   Ⓐ I   Ⓑ II   Ⓒ III   Ⓓ IV

10. Fill in the blank: The sum of two positive numbers is ____ greater than the sum of a positive number and a negative number. *[Lesson 9-4]*

    Ⓐ Always   Ⓑ Sometimes   Ⓒ Never

11. Find the product: $-3 \cdot (-4)$ *[Lesson 9-6]*

    Ⓐ -12 Ⓑ -7 Ⓒ 7   Ⓓ 12

12. Where is the graph increasing? *[Lesson 10-2]*

    Ⓐ P to Q
    Ⓑ Q to R
    Ⓒ R to S
    Ⓓ Nowhere

    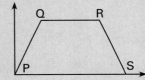

13. Which equation shows the relationship between the variables in the table shown below? *[Lesson 10-4]*

x	1	2	3	4
y	−6	−12	−18	−24

    Ⓐ $y = 6x$
    Ⓑ $y = x - 7$
    Ⓒ $y = -6x$
    Ⓓ $x = -6y$

14. Solve the equation: $k + (-18) = -11$ *[Lesson 10-9]*

    Ⓐ $k = -29$
    Ⓑ $k = -7$
    Ⓒ $k = 7$
    Ⓓ $k = 29$

15. Solve the equation: $-3x = -27$ *[Lesson 10-10]*

    Ⓐ $x = -81$
    Ⓑ $x = -9$
    Ⓒ $x = 9$
    Ⓓ $x = 81$

16. Solve the equation: $5x - 4 = 21$ *[Lesson 10-11]*

    Ⓐ $x = 4$
    Ⓑ $x = 5$
    Ⓒ $x = 6$
    Ⓓ $x = 7$

Social Studies Link
www.mathsurf.com/7/ch11/social

Arts & Literature Link
www.mathsurf.com/7/ch11/arts

Social Studies

Longitude and latitude lines are imaginary circles. The circles that make longitude lines are all the same size. The longest latitude line is the equator.

Arts & Literature

The Alhambra palace was built for the Islamic rulers of Granada, Spain. Tile patterns on the walls and floors of the Alhambra show reflections and rotations of geometric figures.

Entertainment

Old music boxes play music that is "recorded" on cylinders. Indentations or bumps in the cylinders represent notes.

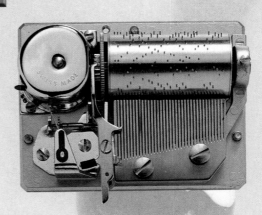

Transformations

Geography Link
www.mathsurf.com/7/ch11/people

Science

Most animals have right and left sides that are mirror images of each other.

People of the World

Many cultures build homes that do not have square corners. Mongolian nomads live in cylindrical tents called *yurts*.

KEY MATH IDEAS

A polyhedron is a three-dimensional figure whose surfaces, or faces, are polygons.

The surface area of a three-dimensional figure is the total area of all its faces. The volume of the figure is the amount of space it takes up.

A circle is a set of points that are at the same distance (the radius) from its center point. A circle's perimeter is called its circumference.

A cylinder has two circular bases. The formula for the area of a circle is important for finding the surface area and volume of a cylinder.

A figure has symmetry if a reflection or rotation of the figure is identical to the original. When you slide (translate), reflect, or rotate a geometric figure, you create a transformation.

CHAPTER PROJECT

Problem Solving

Understand
Plan
Solve
Look Back

In this project, you'll design and build a single-serving beverage container. Begin the project by thinking about the different shapes of the containers that juices and soft drinks are sold in.

551

Problem Solving Focus

Checking the Rules of the Problem

After you solve a problem, look back to make sure your answer or answers satisfy the rules described in the problem.

Identify the correct answer. Tell which rule the other two answers didn't follow.

1 A wild animal park has an African elephant, a black rhinoceros, a giraffe, and a Komodo monitor. Their weights total 17,000 lb. The rhinoceros weighs 100 lb more than the giraffe. The giraffe weighs 15 times as much as the Komodo monitor. The monitor weighs 10,500 lb less than the elephant. How much does each weigh?

Answer 1: Komodo monitor, 100 lb; giraffe, 1,500 lb; elephant, 10,600 lb; rhinoceros, 1,600 lb.

Answer 2: Komodo monitor, 200 lb; giraffe, 3,000 lb; elephant, 10,700 lb; rhinoceros, 3,100 lb.

Answer 3: Komodo monitor, 150 lb; giraffe, 2,250 lb; elephant, 10,650 lb; rhinoceros, 3,950 lb.

2 The Komodo monitor, giraffe, elephant, and rhinoceros can reach a total age of 175 years in captivity. The Komodo monitor's life span is $\frac{5}{7}$ of the giraffe's. The giraffe's life span is 50% of the elephant's. The rhino's life span is 10 years longer than the giraffe's. What is the life span of each animal?

Answer 1: Komodo monitor, 45 years; giraffe, 30 years; elephant, 60 years; rhinoceros, 40 years.

Answer 2: Komodo monitor, 35 years; giraffe, 49 years; elephant, 98 years; rhinoceros, 59 years.

Answer 3: Komodo monitor, 25 years; giraffe, 35 years; elephant, 70 years; rhinoceros, 45 years.

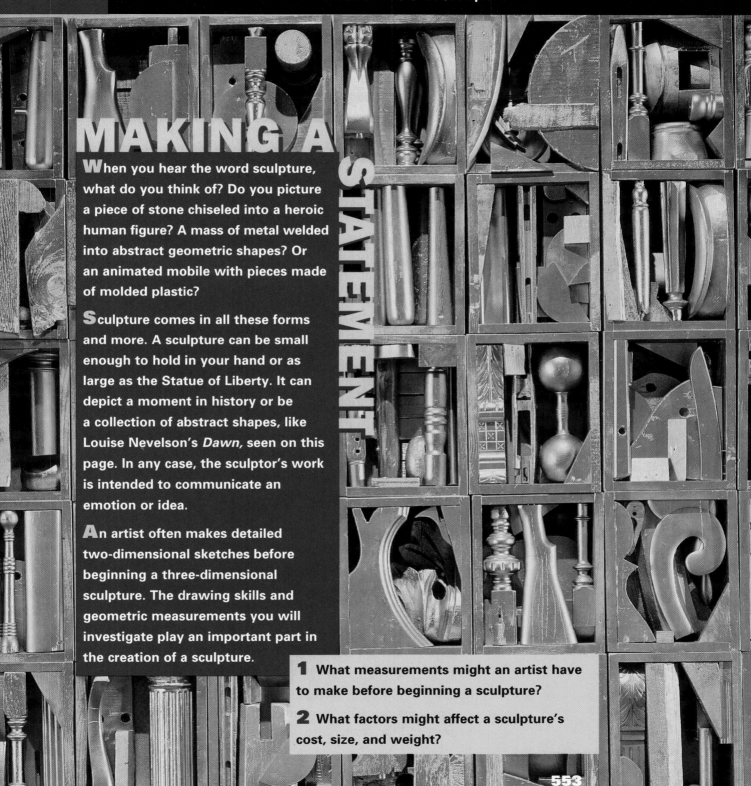

MAKING A STATEMENT

When you hear the word sculpture, what do you think of? Do you picture a piece of stone chiseled into a heroic human figure? A mass of metal welded into abstract geometric shapes? Or an animated mobile with pieces made of molded plastic?

Sculpture comes in all these forms and more. A sculpture can be small enough to hold in your hand or as large as the Statue of Liberty. It can depict a moment in history or be a collection of abstract shapes, like Louise Nevelson's *Dawn,* seen on this page. In any case, the sculptor's work is intended to communicate an emotion or idea.

An artist often makes detailed two-dimensional sketches before beginning a three-dimensional sculpture. The drawing skills and geometric measurements you will investigate play an important part in the creation of a sculpture.

1 What measurements might an artist have to make before beginning a sculpture?

2 What factors might affect a sculpture's cost, size, and weight?

11-1

Exploring Polyhedrons

You'll Learn ...

■ to name polyhedrons

■ to sketch polyhedrons

... How It's Used

Gemologists grind and polish irregularly shaped stones into polyhedrons.

Vocabulary

solid

face

polyhedron

edge

vertex

prism

base

pyramid

▶ **Lesson Link** You've worked with two-dimensional polygons. Now you'll investigate three-dimensional geometric figures. ◄

Explore Three-Dimensional Figures

A Touch of Classification

1. Several three-dimensional figures are shown. Decide on a way to sort these figures into at least three categories. Explain your classification system.

A.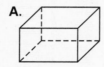

B.

C.

D.

E.

F.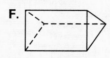

G.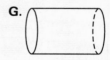

H.

2. Find and explain two other ways to classify these figures.

3. Suppose you're describing one of these figures to an artist who is making a preliminary sketch for a sculpture. What are some characteristics you would include in your description?

Learn Exploring Polyhedrons

The geometric figures you've investigated so far are two-dimensional, since they are flat. However, anything that takes up space is a three-dimensional object.

A three-dimensional object, or **solid**, whose **faces** are polygons is a **polyhedron**. The segments joining the faces are **edges**, and the corners are **vertices**.

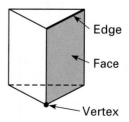

A **prism** is a polyhedron whose **bases** are congruent and parallel. A **pyramid** has a polygonal base but comes to a point.

The name of a prism or pyramid tells the shape of its base.

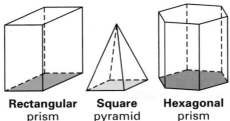

Rectangular prism   **Square** pyramid   **Hexagonal** prism

When you're drawing a three-dimensional figure, you can show depth by imagining that you're in front of and above the object. Show hidden edges as dashed lines.

▶ **Science Link**

Many minerals form crystals that are prisms. Fluorite has cubic crystals. Quartz, staurolite, and vanadinite are sometimes found as hexagonal prisms.

Examples

1 Name the polyhedrons in the sculpture.

In the sculpture, you can see cubes and other rectangular prisms.

2 Sketch a right triangular prism.

Sketch one base.   Draw an identical base below the first.   Add vertical lines joining the vertices of the bases. Make the hidden edge dashed.

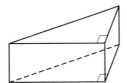

Try It

Name each polyhedron.

a.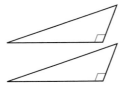

b.

c. Sketch a pentagonal prism.

Remember

A polygon is named according to the number of sides it has. A *triangle* has three sides, a *quadrilateral* has four, a *pentagon* has five, and a *hexagon* has six. **[Page 227]**

Check | Your Understanding

1. Is a cube a prism? Explain. What is another name for a cube?

2. Give real-world examples of at least three polyhedrons.

Practice and Apply

1. **Getting Started** Follow these steps to sketch a rectangular prism.
   a. Draw a parallelogram to show one rectangular base in perspective.
   b. Draw a second parallelogram directly below the first.
   c. Add vertical lines joining the vertices of the bases.
   d. Decide which edges are hidden. Make these dashed lines.

Geometry Use the sketch of the prism to answer each question.

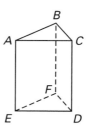

2. Name the polyhedron.

3. Name the polygons that are the faces of the prism. How many of each type of polygon are there?

4. How many edges, faces, and vertices does the polyhedron have?

Name each polyhedron.

5.

6.

7.

Sketch each polyhedron.

8. An octagonal prism
9. A triangular pyramid
10. A hexagonal prism

Fine Arts Name the polyhedrons in each sculpture.

11.

12.

13. **Test Prep** How many faces, edges, and vertices does a square pyramid have?
    Ⓐ 4 faces, 8 edges, 6 vertices
    Ⓑ 4 faces, 6 edges, 4 vertices
    Ⓒ 5 faces, 8 edges, 5 vertices
    Ⓓ 5 faces, 9 edges, 6 vertices

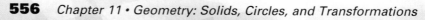

14. Science Different minerals form differently shaped crystals. Name the shape of each mineral.

a. Halite (rock salt)

b. Beryl

Problem Solving and Reasoning

15. Critical Thinking *Platonic solids,* named for the Greek philosopher Plato, are polyhedrons whose faces are all regular polygons. Three of the five Platonic solids are shown.

Tetrahedron

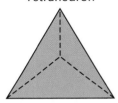

Hexahedron (cube)

Octahedron

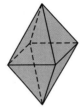

a. Find the number of faces, edges, and vertices in each Platonic solid.

b. There is an equation relating the number of faces, vertices, and edges of a polyhedron. Use your results from **a** to find the equation.

16. In your own words, describe the similarities and differences between pyramids and prisms.

17. Critical Thinking The sculpture *Untitled,* by Donald Judd, is made up of ten identical rectangular prisms. What is the total number of faces, edges, and vertices for the prisms in this sculpture?

Mixed Review

Draw each pair of angles. *[Lesson 5-1]*

18. Two complementary angles, one with measure 45°

19. Two supplementary angles, one with measure 105°

20. Two complementary angles, one with measure 80°

Plot and label each point on the same coordinate plane. Name the quadrant or axis that contains each point. *[Lesson 9-3]*

21. $(-3, 4)$ **22.** $(0, -2)$ **23.** $(-5, -3)$ **24.** $(5, 0)$ **25.** $(6, 2)$

You'll Learn ...

■ to match isometric and orthographic views

■ to draw front, side, and top views of a solid

■ to draw a figure in perspective from its front, top, and side views

... How It's Used

Draftspeople make orthographic drawings to show exact specifications for a manufactured part.

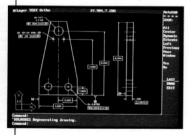

Vocabulary

isometric drawing

orthographic drawing

▶ **Lesson Link** You've named and sketched different polyhedrons. Now you'll investigate techniques for drawing any three-dimensional object. ◄

Explore Three-Dimensional Figures

Materials: Centimeter cubes

What's Your View?

You're the construction crew! Front, side, and top views of three simple buildings are shown.

1. Use cubes to construct each building. Is there more than one way to construct any or all of them?

2. Sketch the buildings you made in Step 1. Do your best to make your sketches look three-dimensional.

3. Design and build a cube building of your own. Draw front, side, and top views of your building.

4. When you're describing a building, what advantages and disadvantages do front, side, and top views have compared to drawings such as the one you made in Step 2?

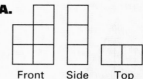
A.
Front   Side   Top

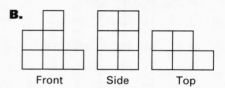
B.
Front   Side   Top

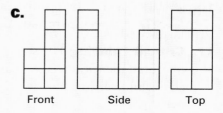
C.
Front   Side   Top

Learn Isometric and Orthographic Drawing

Artists of many cultures have tried to give the illusion of depth to their paintings. In Babylonian sculpture, the figures in front partially block our view of those in back. During the Renaissance, European artists developed a mathematical way to show perspective.

Isometric drawing is one method used to give perspective to a drawing. Using isometric dot paper makes isometric drawing easier.

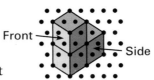
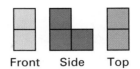

Front — Side

However, isometric drawing can distort angles. The right angles of the cube look like obtuse and acute angles.

Orthographic drawing shows angles and lengths accurately. In an orthographic view, you look directly at the object from front, side, and top views. More than one view is needed to describe the object completely.

Front   Side   Top

Example 1

Match each isometric drawing with a set of orthographic views.

Problem Solving **TIP**

1.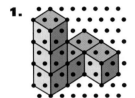

A.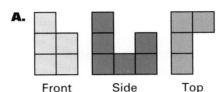

Front   Side   Top

Use the heights of the stacks of cubes to help you match isometric and orthographic drawings.

2.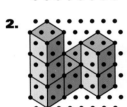

B.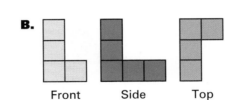

Front   Side   Top

Isometric drawing 2 has a stack of two cubes; drawing 1 does not. The front and side views of **A** show stacks of two cubes in the proper location to match drawing 2.

Drawing 1 matches with **B** and drawing 2 with **A**.

Try It

Match the isometric drawing with a set of orthographic views.

1.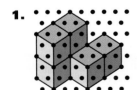

A.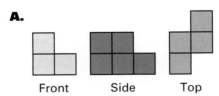

Front   Side   Top

2.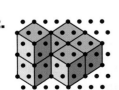

B.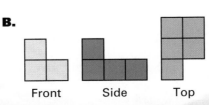

Front   Side   Top

Examples

2 Sketch front, top, and side views of the object shown.

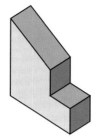

The three views are shown. Notice how the lines in the side and top views show changes in the object.

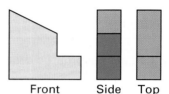

Front   Side   Top

3 Make a perspective sketch of the metal plate. (The dotted lines represent the two holes.)

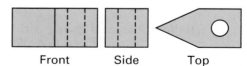

Front   Side   Top

The sketch is shown.

Try It

a. The sculpture shown is in downtown New York City. Sketch front, top, and side views of the sculpture.

b. Make a perspective sketch of the object shown.

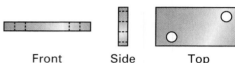

Front   Side   Top

► **History Link**

The Colossus of Rhodes was one of the seven ancient wonders of the world. The bronze statue of Apollo was 120 ft tall and stood atop a 25 ft tall marble base. About 220 B.C., just 60 years after its completion, the Colossus broke at the knees and fell during an earthquake. It was later sold as scrap metal.

Check | Your Understanding

1. Name some situations where orthographic views would be more useful than an isometric drawing. When might the isometric drawing be more helpful?

2. If you were given the front view of a set of cubes, would you be able to sketch the back view? If so, explain how; if not, explain why not.

Practice and Apply

1. **Getting Started** Follow these steps to draw front, side, and top orthographic views of the cubes.

   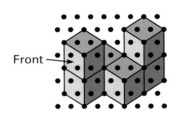

   Front →

   a. Imagine yourself in front of the cubes. Decide how many stacks of cubes you would see. Then decide how many cubes you would see in each stack. Draw the front view.

   b. Imagine that you move to the side of the "building" to your right. Repeat **a** to draw the side view.

   c. Imagine yourself directly above the cubes. Repeat **a** to draw the top view.

Find the number of cubes in each figure. Assume all cubes are visible.

2.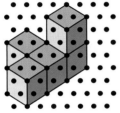

3.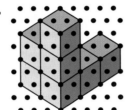

4.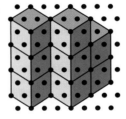

Match each isometric drawing with a set of orthographic views.

5.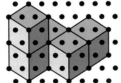

6.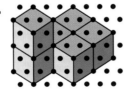

7.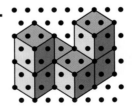

8.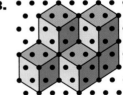

A.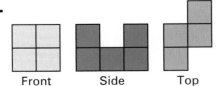

Front   Side   Top

B.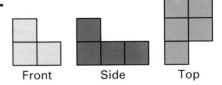

Front   Side   Top

C.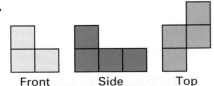

Front   Side   Top

D.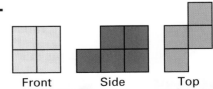

Front   Side   Top

Sketch front, top, and side views of each object.

9.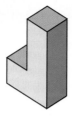

10.

11.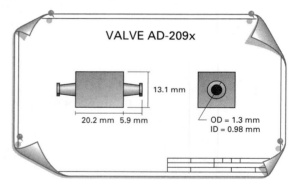

Make a perspective sketch of each object.

12.

Front   Side

Top

13.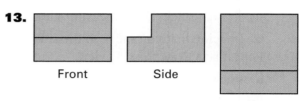

Front   Side

Top

Problem Solving and Reasoning

14. Communicate The photograph of *Black Sun*, by Isamu Noguchi, is nearly a front view of the sculpture. Sketch what you think the top and side views look like.

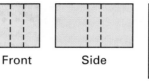

15. Communicate Technical drawings of manufactured parts are orthographic drawings. Explain why orthographic drawings are used to picture these parts.

VALVE AD-209x

13.1 mm

20.2 mm   5.9 mm

OD = 1.3 mm
ID = 0.98 mm

Mixed Review

Write the word that describes the lines or line segments. *[Lesson 5-2]*

16. A double yellow line on the street

17. The top and side edges of a door

18. The sideline and end line of a playing field

19. Joined edges of a floppy disk

Tell which quantities are variables and which are constants. *[Lesson 10-1]*

20. Number of students in a classroom

21. Number of inches in a foot

22. Amount of water you drink in a day

23. Number of leaves on a tree

Polyhedron Nets and Surface Areas

▶ **Lesson Link**   You know how to calculate areas of two-dimensional figures. Now you'll apply those skills to find surface areas of three-dimensional figures. ◀

You'll Learn ...

■ to find the surface area of a polyhedron

... How It's Used

Parade volunteers must know the surface area of a float to decide how much decorative material they need.

CITY OF SOUTH PASADENA

Vocabulary

surface area

Explore   Nets for Polyhedrons

Polyhedron Wrap

Materials: Graph paper, Scissors, Tape

A *net* is a two-dimensional pattern that folds up into a three-dimensional object.

1. Copy each net onto graph paper. Cut out each net, then fold and tape the sides together to make a polyhedron.

2. Name the polyhedron for each net. Then give the name of each of its faces. How many of each type of face are there?

3. Can you look at a net and predict the polyhedron it will make? Explain.

4. Create your own net for a polyhedron. Test it to see if it works.

Learn   Polyhedron Nets and Surface Areas

The **surface area** of a three-dimensional figure is the sum of the areas of its faces. The faces include the base(s) of the polyhedron.

The surface area of a gift box is equal to the area of the paper you'd need to wrap it, assuming no gaps or overlap.

By drawing a net for a polyhedron, you can see the shapes and dimensions of its faces. Then you can use area formulas to help you calculate surface areas.

Examples

Study TIP

On the day of a test, take a few minutes to skim the material you studied the night before. A quick review can help refresh your memory.

1 Sketch a net for the polyhedron. Then find its surface area.

The net is shown.

To find the surface area, first find the area of each face.

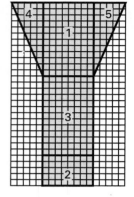

Face 1: Area = 12 cm • 8 cm = 96 cm²

Face 2: Area = 5 cm • 8 cm = 40 cm²

Face 3: Area = 13 cm • 8 cm = 104 cm²

Faces 4 and 5: Area = $2(\frac{1}{2} \cdot 12 \text{ cm} \cdot 5 \text{ cm}) = 60 \text{ cm}^2$

Surface area = 96 cm² + 40 cm² + 104 cm² + 60 cm²

= 300 cm²

2 Find the surface area of the prism.

11 in. by 14 in. rectangular face: Area = 11 in. • 14 in. = 154 in²

Two 5 in. by 11 in. rectangular faces: Area = 2(5 in. • 11 in.) = 110 in²

8 in. by 11 in. rectangular face:
Area = 8 in. • 11 in. = 88 in²

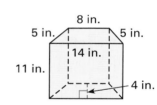

Two trapezoidal faces, bases 8 in. and 14 in., height = 4 in.:
Area = $2(\frac{1}{2} \cdot (8 \text{ in.} + 14 \text{ in.}) \cdot 4 \text{ in.}) = 88 \text{ in}^2$

Surface area = 154 in² + 110 in² + 88 in² + 88 in² = 440 in²

Try It

a. Sketch a net for this "sculpture." Then find its surface area.

b. Find the surface area of the prism.

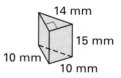

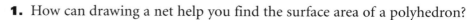

Check | Your Understanding

1. How can drawing a net help you find the surface area of a polyhedron?

2. Why is surface area measured in square units?

Practice and Apply

1. **Getting Started** Follow the steps to find the surface area of the triangular prism.

   a. Find the area of the 10 by 4 rectangular face.

   b. Find the area of the 10 by 13 rectangular face.

   c. Find the area of the 10 by 15 rectangular face.

   d. Find the total area of the two triangular bases.

   e. Add the areas in **a–d** to find the surface area.

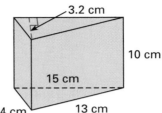

Sketch a net for each polyhedron.

2.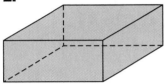

3.

4.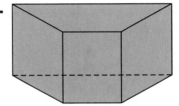

Sketch a net for each polyhedron, then find its surface area.

5.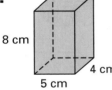

6. 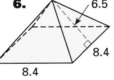 **square pyramid**

7. 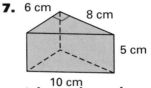 **triangular prism**

8. 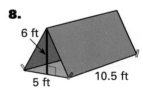 **triangular prism**

9. **Consumer** You need to paint the outside of the house shown. A gallon of paint covers between 300 and 400 square feet. How many gallons will you need to buy? (Ignore the areas of windows and doors, and do not paint the roof!)

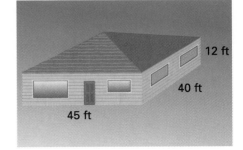

10. **Literature** In *Flat Stanley*, Stanley is, "four feet tall, about a foot wide, and half an inch thick." Assuming Stanley is a rectangular solid, what is his surface area? (Excerpt from *Flat Stanley* by Jeff Brown (New York: Harper and Row, 1964.) Copyright ©1964 by Jeff Brown.)

11. **Test Prep** Which formula gives the surface area of a cube whose sides are *s* units long?

    Ⓐ s^2 Ⓑ $3s^2$ Ⓒ $6s^2$ Ⓓ s^3

PRACTICE 11-3

12. Estimation Estimate the surface area of the polyhedron.

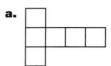
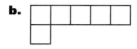

13. Identify the nets that can be folded into a cube.

a. 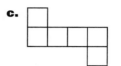 **b.** 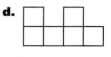 **c.** **d.**

14. Fine Arts Artist Larry Bell created this cube-shaped sculpture entitled *Memories of Mike*. Each side of the cube is $24\frac{1}{4}$ inches long.

a. What is the surface area of the sculpture?

b. Draw a net of this sculpture. Label the measure of each side.

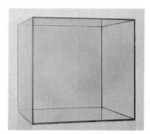

Problem Solving and Reasoning

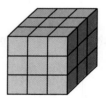

15. Critical Thinking A large cube is made of small cubes as shown. Can you remove one cube from the figure and

a. Increase its surface area? If so, how?

b. Decrease its surface area? If so, how?

c. Keep its surface area the same? If so, how?

16. Communicate Find a formula for the surface area of the outside of an *open* box whose length is *l*, width is *w*, and height is *h*. Explain why your formula works.

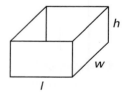

Mixed Review

Classify each polygon in as many ways as you can. *[Lesson 5-3]*

17.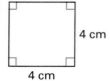

4 cm

4 cm

18.

19.

Name a quantity each value might depend on. *[Lesson 10-2]*

20. Distance traveled in a car **21.** Area of a triangle **22.** Your grade in a class

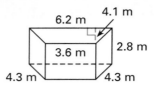

Volumes of Prisms

▶ **Lesson Link** You know how to find the surface area of a prism. Now you'll investigate another measure of a prism's size—its volume. ◀

Explore | Filling Rectangular Solids

Box 'Em Up!

Materials: Centimeter cubes, Centimeter graph paper, Scissors, Tape

You can make a box out of graph paper by cutting a square out of each corner, then folding up the sides. What's the *largest* box you can make?

1. Cut a 16 cm by 12 cm rectangle from your graph paper. Cut a 1 cm square out of each corner, then fold and tape the sides to make a box.

2. How many centimeter cubes does your box hold? Record the dimensions of the box and the number of cubes it can hold.

3. Now make a box by cutting 2 by 2 squares out of a 16 by 12 rectangle. Find out how many cubes it holds. Repeat, cutting out larger and larger squares, until you find the box that holds the most cubes.

4. What are the dimensions of the box that holds the most cubes? How many cubes does it hold? Why are you sure this is the largest box?

You'll Learn ...

■ to find the volume of a prism

... How It's Used

Packaging designers calculate volumes as they decide the best ways to create packages that are both efficient and attractive.

Vocabulary

volume

height

Learn | Volumes of Prisms

The **volume** of a three-dimensional object is the amount of space it takes up. Volume describes the number of cubes an object can hold, so it is measured in cubic units.

Volume = 24 units³

A prism has two identical bases. The distance between the bases is the **height**, h, of the prism. Thinking of the prism as a stack of bases h units tall leads to a formula for the volume of a prism.

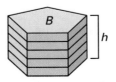

> **VOLUME OF A PRISM**
>
> The volume of a prism whose base area is B and height is h is given by $V = Bh$.

Examples

1 Find the volume of the right triangular prism.

The volume is equal to the base area times the height.

6 ft

8 ft

7 ft

$B = \dfrac{1}{2} \cdot 8 \cdot 6 = 24 \text{ ft}^2$ $\qquad\qquad$ $h = 7$ ft

$V = Bh = 24 \cdot 7 = 168 \text{ ft}^3$

2 A prism has a base area of 32 cm² and a height of 7 cm. Find its volume.

$V = Bh = 32 \cdot 7 = 224 \text{ cm}^3$

The prism has a volume of 224 cm³.

Try It

a. At Devil's Postpile National Monument, basalt, a volcanic rock, forms hexagonal columns. If one column has a base area of 2 ft² and a height of 24 ft, what is the volume of the column?

b. Find the volume of the trapezoidal prism.

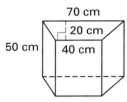

70 cm

20 cm

50 cm

40 cm

The area of the base of a rectangular prism is lw, so the formula for the volume of a rectangular prism is $V = lwh$.

Example 3

Find the volume of a rectangular prism whose height is 4 mm, length is 10 mm, and width is 8 mm.

Use $V = lwh$ for a rectangular prism.

$V = 10 \cdot 8 \cdot 4 = 320 \text{ mm}^3$

Check | Your Understanding

1. Describe the difference between surface area and volume.

2. If you measure the volume of a prism in cubic centimeters, do you get a greater volume than if you measure the volume in cubic inches? Explain.

Practice and Apply

1. **Getting Started** Follow these steps to find the volume of the prism.

   a. Find the area of the base. Since the base of this prism is a triangle, use the formula for the area of a triangle.

   b. Multiply the base area by the height.

   c. Write your answer. Be sure to use cubic units.

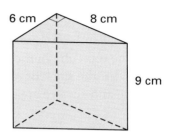

Find the volume of each prism.

2.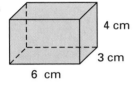
   4 cm
   3 cm
   6 cm

3.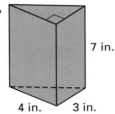
   7 in.
   4 in. 3 in.

4.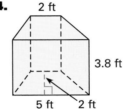
   2 ft
   3.8 ft
   5 ft 2 ft

5.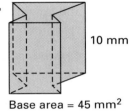
   10 mm
   Base area = 45 mm²

6. **Fine Arts** The sculpture *Untitled*, by Donald Judd, is made up of ten rectangular prisms. The length of each prism is 40 in., the width is 31 in., and the height is 9 in. What is the volume of one of these prisms?

7. Sarah's family is thinking of installing a swimming pool in their backyard, and they want to know how much it will increase their water use. The pool would be a rectangular prism with dimensions 10 m by 8 m by 2 m. What is the maximum volume of water it could hold?

8. **Consumer** The two boxes of sugar are the same price. Which one is the better buy? Explain your answer.

A.
20 cm
5 cm
12 cm

B.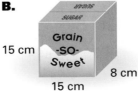
15 cm
8 cm
15 cm

9. **Test Prep** An artist uses 2280 cm³ of modeling clay to make a prism. If the area of the prism's base is 152 cm², what is its height?

Ⓐ 15 cm   Ⓑ 25 cm   Ⓒ 2128 cm   Ⓓ 346,560 cm

10. Assume that the edges of the cubes in the figures are 1 cm long. All cubes are visible.

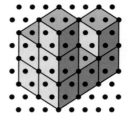 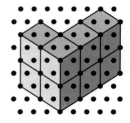

a. What is the volume of the first figure?

b. What is its surface area?

c. Suppose the top cube in the stack of three is moved to "fill in" the stack of one as shown. How do the volume and surface area change?

Problem Solving and Reasoning

11. Critical Thinking The volume of a pyramid is given by the formula $V = \frac{1}{3}Bh$. Suppose you had a rectangular pyramid with the same base and height measurements as a rectangular prism. How would their volumes compare?

12. Choose a Strategy Suppose each dimension (length, width, and height) of a rectangular solid is changed as described. How does the volume of the box change? Try several examples for each change.

a. Each dimension is doubled.   **b.** Each dimension is tripled.

c. Each dimension is quadrupled.   **d.** Each dimension is halved.

e. Describe any pattern you see in your results.

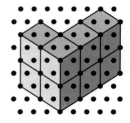

Problem Solving
STRATEGIES

- Look for a Pattern
- Make an Organized List
- Make a Table
- Guess and Check
- Work Backward
- Use Logical Reasoning
- Draw a Diagram
- Solve a Simpler Problem

Mixed Review

Find the sums of the measures of the angles of each polygon. *[Lesson 5-4]*

13. 12-sided polygon   **14.** 14-sided polygon   **15.** 17-sided polygon

Give the next term in each sequence. Write a rule for each. *[Lesson 10-3]*

16. 5, 9, 13, 17, _____   **17.** 3, 3, 3, 3, _____   **18.** −4, −2, 0, 2, _____   **19.** $\frac{1}{6}, \frac{1}{8}, \frac{1}{10}, \frac{1}{12},$ _____

Project Progress

Design a beverage container in the shape of a prism. The container must have a volume of 360 cm³. Sketch a net for your container and show its dimensions on the net.

Problem Solving

Understand
Plan
Solve
Look Back

Section 11A Connect

You've explored ways to sketch polyhedrons, and you've calculated their surface areas and volumes. Now you'll use all these skills to design and analyze a sculpture of your own.

Making a Statement

Materials: Construction paper, Ruler, Scissors, Tape

Many artists and sculptors use geometric figures in their art. Now you'll make a piece of geometric sculpture that uses polyhedrons.

1. Decide how you want your sculpture to look. (Include at least one prism in the design.) Sketch a three-dimensional picture of your sculpture. Then sketch front, side, and top views.

2. Use construction paper, scissors, and tape to construct your sculpture.

3. *Gold leaf* is solid gold that has been rolled into a thin sheet. It costs about 11¢ per square inch. How much would it cost to cover your sculpture with gold leaf?

4. An overseas museum wants to display your sculpture! The sculpture must be packed for shipping in a crate that is a rectangular prism. Find the dimensions and volume of a crate large enough to hold your sculpture. Explain how you found your answers.

Tell whether each statement is true or false. If it is false, explain why.

1. A cube is a rectangular prism.

2. Some pyramids are prisms.

3. A square pyramid has five vertices.

4. A cylinder is a polyhedron.

Sketch each polyhedron.

5. A rectangular prism

6. A right triangular pyramid

7. A pentagonal prism

8. Sketch a net for the square pyramid at right. Then find its surface area.

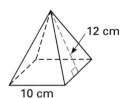

12 cm

10 cm

Find the surface area and volume of each figure.

9.

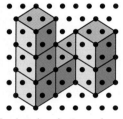

Each edge is 1 cm long.

10.

20 in.

32 in.

20 in.

11.

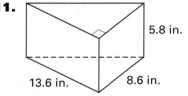

5.8 in.

13.6 in.   8.6 in.

triangular prism

12. Fine Arts This sculpture, by Hubert Dalwood, is made of aluminum, wood, and gilt. Sketch front, top, and side views of the sculpture.

13. Suppose you wanted to build a doghouse for your dog Melvin. When planning the doghouse, would you need to think about its surface area, its volume, or both? Explain your answer.

Test Prep

When asked to find a volume on a multiple choice test, you may be able to use mental math to eliminate some of the answer choices.

14. Find the volume of the rectangular prism.

Ⓒ 10.5 in³   Ⓑ 842 in³   Ⓔ 1,050 in³   Ⓕ 13,500 in³

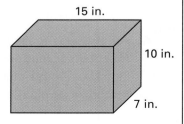

15 in.

10 in.

7 in.

TOYS 'ROUND THE WORLD

What do a Frisbee®, a marble, a soccer ball, a Hula Hoop®, and a yo-yo have in common? They're all fun to play with, of course. But they wouldn't be nearly as much fun (and some would be downright dangerous!) if it weren't for their other common trait. All of these toys are *round* in some way.

People have been making toys with circular shapes almost since they discovered that round

things roll. A 3800-year-old toy cart was found at Mohenjo Daro, in what is now Pakistan. The wooden horse on wheels shown at lower left was made by Egyptians about A.D. 200. All around the world, people have fun rolling hoops, bouncing balls, and spinning disks.

As you explore the mathematics of circles and circular objects, you'll learn more about the measurements that describe round toys.

1 Which of the toys listed in the first paragraph would be impossible to play with if they were square instead of round? Explain your answer.

2 Although a marble, a Hula Hoop, and a yo-yo are all "round," they have different shapes. Describe the differences in the shapes of these toys.

Circles and Circle Graphs

You'll Learn ...

■ to make circle graphs

... How It's Used

Newspaper editors use circle graphs to show the data in a news story.

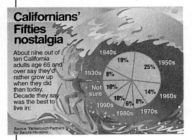

Californians' Fifties nostalgia

About nine out of ten California adults age 65 and over say they'd rather grow up when they did than today. Decade they say was the best to live in:

1940s 19%
1950s 25%
1930s 8%
Not sure 10%
1960s 14%
1990s 10%
1980s 6%
1970s 8%

Source: Yankelovich Partners for Secure Horizons

Vocabulary

circle

center

central angle

▶ **Lesson Link** You've interpreted data shown on circle graphs. Now you'll explore properties of a circle and draw your own circle graphs. ◀

Explore | Making Circle Graphs

Circular Reasoning

Which of these toys would you have liked best when you were younger?

Materials: Compass, Colored pencils or markers

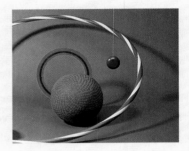

1. Survey the class to find the number of students who prefer each toy.

2. Copy the frequency table. Enter the number of votes for each toy. Then find the percent of the class that voted for each toy.

3. Draw a circle and mark its center. Using your knowledge of percents, make a circle graph showing the results from Step 2.

4. Explain how you made your circle graph.

Toy	Number	Percent

Learn | Circles and Circle Graphs

The circle graph shows where the world's computers were in 1993. It also shows important parts of a circle.

All of the points on a **circle** are the same distance from its **center**.

Each "slice" of the circle graph is a *sector* of the circle. The **central angle** that determines the size of the sector has its vertex at the center of the circle.

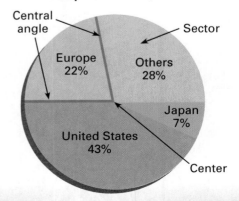

Computers in Use, 1993

Central angle

Sector

Europe 22%

Others 28%

Japan 7%

United States 43%

Center

To make a circle graph, you must find out how large the central angle of each sector should be. You can use the fact that there are 360° in a circle to find the central angles.

Example 1

In 1996, the Pittsburgh Penguins played 82 regular-season hockey matches. They won 49 matches, lost 29, and tied 4. Draw a circle graph to display this data.

Find the percent of wins, losses, and ties.

$$\text{Wins} = \frac{49}{82} \approx 0.60 = 60\% \qquad \text{Losses} = \frac{29}{82} \approx 0.35 = 35\%$$

$$\text{Ties} = \frac{4}{82} \approx 0.05 = 5\%$$

To find each central angle, multiply the percent (in decimal form) by 360°.

Wins: $0.60 \cdot 360° = 216°$ Losses: $0.35 \cdot 360° = 126°$ Ties: $0.05 \cdot 360° = 18°$

Draw a circle. Use a protractor to draw each central angle that measures less than 180°. Label each sector of the circle graph, and give the graph a title.

Notice that since the Penguins won more than 50% of their games, the central angle of the "Wins" sector measures *more* than 180°. The angle is *past* a straight line.

1996 Pittsburgh Penguins Record

Try It

Draw a circle graph to show each data set.

a. A recent survey showed that 89% of the people in the United States had heard of a Slinky®. (*Hint:* What percent had *not* heard of a Slinky?)

b. In the 1992 presidential election, about 44 million people voted for Bill Clinton, 39 million for George Bush, and 20 million for Ross Perot.

Check   Your Understanding

1. Suppose 25% of the people in a survey name pizza as their favorite food. How large would the central angle in the "pizza" sector be in a circle graph? How do you know?

2. Can a circle graph have two central angles that measure more than 180°? Explain.

Practice and Apply

1. **Getting Started** In 1990, about 29% of the people in the United States were less than 20 years old, 40% were between 20 and 44, and 31% were 45 and older. Follow these steps to make a circle graph of this data.

   a. Find the central angle for the "Below 20" sector by multiplying 29% (in decimal form) by 360°.

   b. Find the central angle for each of the other two sectors.

   c. Draw a circle and mark the center.

   d. Use a protractor to draw each central angle.

   e. Label and shade each sector, and title your circle graph.

Data Use the circle graph to answer Exercises 2 and 3.

2. **Estimation** Estimate the percent of governors in each category.

3. Identify any sectors that have central angles greater than 180°. Explain how you can tell.

United States Governors, 1996

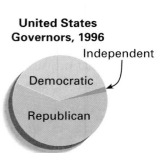

Estimation Sketch a circle graph to show each data set. (Do *not* calculate or measure the central angles.)

4. **Sports** Through the 1994 season, Steve Young was the National Football League's highest-rated quarterback of all time. About 64% of his passes were caught, 33% were incomplete, and 3% were intercepted.

5. **Science** Of the total mass of the planets in the solar system, Jupiter contains about 71%, Saturn contains 21%, and the other planets (including Earth) contain the other 8%.

6. **Test Prep** Which category in the circle graph represents about 15% of the data?

   Ⓐ A   Ⓑ B   Ⓒ C   Ⓓ D

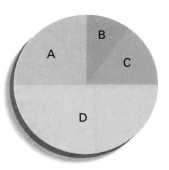

7. **Number Sense** If a circle graph shows that 72% of 1200 students in a middle school are interested in music, how many students does this represent?

Data In Exercises 8-10, draw a circle graph to show each data set.

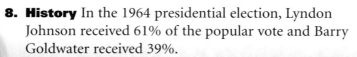

8. **History** In the 1964 presidential election, Lyndon Johnson received 61% of the popular vote and Barry Goldwater received 39%.

9.

United States Exports, 1994				
Category	Food and Agricultural	Machinery and Transport	Manufactured Goods	Other
Percent of Total Value	8%	29%	18%	45%

10. Geography

Land Areas of the Continents (Millions of Square Miles)							
Continent	Africa	Antarctica	Asia	Australia and Oceania	Europe	N. America	S. America
Area	11.7	6.0	17.2	3.3	4.0	9.4	6.9

Problem Solving and Reasoning

11. Critical Thinking In the game of Disc Golf, a flying disc is thrown at a series of far-off targets. Analyze the score data, and make a circle graph to show your results.

Hole Number	1	2	3	4	5	6	7	8	9	10	11	12	13	14	15	16	17	18
Score	3	4	4	5	4	4	4	4	4	5	4	4	4	3	3	4	3	3

12. **Journal** Determine the number of hours you spend in different activities on a typical school day. Make a circle graph of your data.

13. Communicate Your student council wants to survey the student body to decide how to spend this year's entertainment fund. They plan to allow each student to give more than one choice. Explain to the student council why they should *not* display the poll results in a circle graph.

Mixed Review

Find the area and perimeter of each rectangle. *[Lesson 5-5]*

14. $l = 10$ cm, $w = 7$ cm

15. $l = 17$ in., $w = 4$ in.

16. $l = 8.2$ ft, $w = 7.4$ ft

17. $l = 18$ cm, $w = 0.4$ cm

18. $l = \frac{3}{4}$ in., $w = \frac{1}{2}$ in.

19. $l = 145$ mi, $w = 75$ mi

Copy and complete each table of values. *[Lesson 10-4]*

20. $y = 2x + 5$

x	−2	−1	0	1	2	3
y						

21. $y = -x - 10$

x	−2	−1	0	1	2	3
y						

Pi and Circumference

You'll Learn ...

■ the meaning of π

■ to find the circumference of a circle

... How It's Used

The circumference of a car tire affects its gasoline mileage. Drivers need to keep tires properly inflated to get the most miles per gallon.

Vocabulary

diameter

radius

circumference

π (pi)

▶ **Lesson Link**   You know that all points on a circle are the same distance from the center. Now you'll investigate the ratio of that distance to the circle's perimeter. ◀

Explore | A Circle Ratio

I Get Around

Materials: Spreadsheet software, Tape measure, Round objects

1. Measure the distance around and the distance across five of the round objects provided. Set up a table like this one on a spreadsheet and record your results.

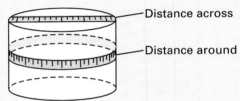
Distance across
Distance around

	A	B	C	D	E	F
1	Object	1	2	3	4	5
2	Distance Around					
3	Distance Across					

2. Find the ratio $\dfrac{\text{distance around}}{\text{distance across}}$ for each object you've measured.

3. Write a conclusion about the $\dfrac{\text{distance around}}{\text{distance across}}$ ratio of a circle.

Learn | Pi and Circumference

There are three ways you can describe the size of a Hula Hoop® or other circular object.

The **diameter** of a circle is the distance across the circle through its center. The **radius** is the distance from the center to any point on the circle. The perimeter of a circle is its **circumference**.

The diameter of a circle is twice its radius: $d = 2r$.

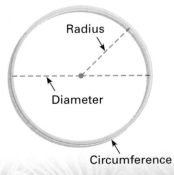
Radius
Diameter
Circumference

Example 1

If the radius of a Hula Hoop® is 88 cm, what is its diameter?

The diameter is twice the radius: $d = 2r = 2 \cdot 88 = 176$ cm.

More than four thousand years ago, Egyptians knew that the $\dfrac{\text{circumference}}{\text{diameter}}$ ratio is the same for every circle. This ratio is named by a Greek letter, **π (pi)**. It is approximately equal to 3.14, or $\frac{22}{7}$. Since $\pi = \frac{C}{d}$, $C = \pi d$.

HINT

Most calculators have a π key. You usually have to press INV or 2ND before pressing the key.

> **CIRCUMFERENCE FORMULAS**
> The circumference of a circle is given by $C = \pi d = 2\pi r$.

Examples

2 The diameter of a volleyball is $8\frac{1}{4}$ inches. Find its circumference.

Use $C = \pi d$.

$C \approx \left(\frac{22}{7}\right)\left(8\frac{1}{4}\right)$ Substitute. Since the diameter is a fraction, use $\frac{22}{7}$ for π.

$C \approx \left(\frac{22}{7}\right)\left(\frac{33}{4}\right)$ Convert $8\frac{1}{4}$ to an improper fraction.

$C \approx \frac{726}{28} = \frac{363}{14}$ Multiply and simplify.

The circumference is about $\frac{363}{14} = 25\frac{13}{14}$ inches.

3 If a yo-yo's circumference is 16 cm, what is its diameter? Round to the nearest tenth.

Use $C = \pi d$.

$16 \approx 3.14 \cdot d$ Substitute.

$\dfrac{16}{3.14} \approx \dfrac{3.14d}{3.14}$ Use inverse operations.

$5.0955\ldots \approx d$. The diameter is about 5.1 cm.

> ▶ **Language Link**
>
> The yo-yo was brought to the United States from the Philippines. The word *yo-yo* comes from the Tagalog language widely spoken in that country.

Try It

Find the diameter and circumference of a circle whose radius is 32 in.

Check | Your Understanding

1. Explain why the formula $C = 2\pi r$ works.

2. Examples 2 and 3 used ≈ signs after π was replaced with a number. Why?

Practice and Apply

1. **Getting Started** Follow these steps to find the diameter and circumference of a circle whose radius is 5 cm.

   a. The diameter of a circle is twice its radius. Use $d = 2r$ to find the diameter. Remember to include units with your answer.

   b. The circumference of a circle is 2π times its radius. Use $C = 2\pi r$ to find the circumference. (Use $\pi \approx 3.14$.) Include units with your answer.

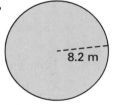
5 cm

2. **Logic** Explain another way to find the circumference in Exercise 1b.

Find the diameter and circumference of each circle given its radius. Use $\pi \approx 3.14$ and round answers to the nearest tenth.

3.
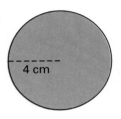
4 cm

4.
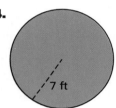
7 ft

5.
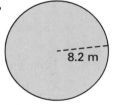
8.2 m

Find the circumference of each circle given its radius. Use $\pi \approx \frac{22}{7}$ and express your answers in lowest terms.

6.
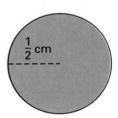
$\frac{1}{2}$ cm

7.
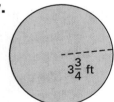
$3\frac{3}{4}$ ft

8.
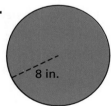
8 in.

Given the radius, diameter, or circumference of a circle, find the other two measurements. Use $\pi \approx 3.14$. If necessary, round answers to the nearest tenth.

9. $r = 8$ cm   10. $d = 22$ mi   11. $C = 6$ mm   12. $r = 17.5$ in.   13. $d = 51$ ft

14. $C = 17.8$ mm   15. $r = 100$ in.   16. $d = 4.9$ m   17. $C = 88$ ft   18. $C = \pi$ cm

19. **Test Prep** The earth's orbit around the sun is nearly circular. Our average distance from the sun is 93,000,000 miles. What is the best estimate for the circumference of the earth's orbit?

   Ⓐ 3×10^7 mi   Ⓑ 6×10^7 mi   Ⓒ 3×10^8 mi   Ⓓ 6×10^8 mi

20. History The Aztec Calendar Stone contains carvings representing the days of the Aztec month. Its circumference is about 36 feet. Find the diameter of the Calendar Stone to the nearest tenth of a foot.

21. Problem Solving The world's largest yo-yo measures 50 inches in diameter and weighs 256 pounds. It was tested using an 80-foot crane! Find the circumference of this yo-yo to the nearest inch.

Problem Solving and Reasoning

22. Critical Thinking The running track is made up of two half-circles at either end of a rectangle. Find the distance around the track.

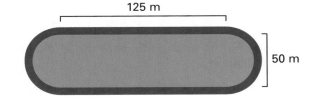

125 m

50 m

23. Communicate A friend claims that the bigger a circle is, the greater its $\dfrac{\text{circumference}}{\text{diameter}}$ ratio should be. In writing, explain to your friend why this claim is incorrect.

24. Choose a Strategy An audio CD is 12.5 cm in diameter and a CD player spins 200 times each minute. How far does a spot on the outside edge of a CD travel in 1 minute? In 30 minutes?

Problem Solving

STRATEGIES

- Look for a Pattern
- Make an Organized List
- Make a Table
- Guess and Check
- Work Backward
- Use Logical Reasoning
- Draw a Diagram
- Solve a Simpler Problem

Mixed Review

Give a unit rate or ratio that describes each situation. *[Lesson 7-5]*

25. 153 miles in 3 hours

26. 4 car washes for $10.00

27. 510 students for 30 teachers

28. 750 words on 3 pages

Graph each equation on the same coordinate grid, and tell how the lines differ from each other. *[Lesson 10-5]*

29. $y = x$

30. $y = 3x$

31. $y = 4x$

32. $y = \dfrac{2}{3}x$

TECHNOLOGY

Using Dynamic Geometry Software • Investigating Circles and Tangent Lines

Problem: How can you:

- Check that the $\dfrac{\text{circumference}}{\text{diameter}}$ ratio is constant for a circle of any size?

- Construct a line that touches a circle in only one point?

You can use dynamic geometry software to explore these problems.

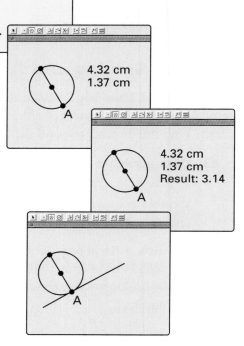

1 Use your software to make a circle. Place and label a point *A* on the circle. Draw a diameter by drawing a segment from *A,* through the center, to another point on the circle. Measure the circumference and diameter.

2 Choose "calculate" from the measurement menu. Click on the circumference, the ÷ key, the diameter, and the = key. Drag the result onto the screen. Click on the circle and drag to change the size of the circle. What do you notice about $\dfrac{C}{d}$?

3 Use the software to construct a line through *A* that is perpendicular to the diameter. The new line is a *tangent line*—a line that touches a circle at just one point. The tangent line through any point on a circle is perpendicular to the radius drawn to that point.

TRY IT

a. Draw a new circle with its radius. Measure the radius, then resize the circle until its radius is 1 cm. Predict the circumference of this circle. Then use the measurement tool to find the circumference.

b. Construct a tangent line to the circle you drew in **a.**

Solutions: The $\dfrac{\text{circumference}}{\text{diameter}}$ **ratio for a circle of any size is** π**. To construct a line that touches a circle at only one point, draw a line perpendicular to a radius at that point.**

ON YOUR OWN

▶ Explain how you could use pencil and paper to draw a tangent line to a circle.

Area of a Circle

▶ **Lesson Link** You've used a formula to find the circumference of a circle. Now you'll develop and apply a formula for the area of a circle. ◀

You'll Learn ...
■ to find the area of a circle

... How It's Used

The radius of a radio station's signal determines the area it can reach.

Explore Area of a Circle

Pie Are Squared

Materials: Graph paper, Compass, Spreadsheet software

You can count squares on graph paper to estimate the area of a circle.

1. Use your compass to draw several different-sized circles on graph paper. Make the radius of each circle a whole number.

2. Count squares to estimate the area of each circle.

3. Record the radius (r) and area (A) of each circle in two rows of a spread-sheet. In another row, calculate $\frac{A}{r^2}$ for each circle. What do you notice?

4. Use your conclusion from Step 3 to write an equation with $\frac{A}{r^2}$.

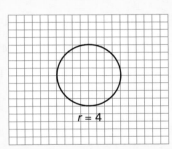

$r = 4$

Learn Area of a Circle

A dart board is divided into sectors.

If the sectors are cut apart and arranged as shown below, the new figure looks like a parallelogram.

The height of the parallelogram is the radius of the circle, and its base is half the circumference, so its area is $A = bh = \frac{1}{2}Cr$.

Since the circumference of the circle is equal to $2\pi r$,

$A = \frac{1}{2}(2\pi r)r = \pi \cdot r \cdot r = \pi r^2.$

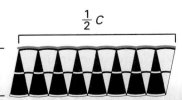

$\frac{1}{2}C$

r

> **AREA OF A CIRCLE**
>
> The area of a circle whose radius is r is given by $A = \pi r^2$.

Examples

Problem Solving TIP

In the order of operations, powers come before multiplication. Be sure to square the radius *first* when using $A = \pi r^2$.

1 The radius of a toy wagon wheel is 3.8 cm. Estimate the area of a circular surface of the wheel.

Use $A = \pi r^2$.

3.8 is close to 4, so use $r = 4$. Use 3 to approximate π to the nearest whole number.

$A \approx 3 \cdot 4^2$	Substitute.
$A \approx 3 \cdot 16$	Calculate powers before multiplying.
$A \approx 48$	Multiply.

The area of a circular surface of the wheel is about 48 cm^2.

2 Find the area of the circle. Round to the nearest tenth.

First find the radius. Since the diameter of the circle is 22 ft, the radius is 11 ft.

Then use $A = \pi r^2$.

$A \approx 3.14 \cdot 11^2$	Substitute.
$A \approx 379.94 \approx 379.9$	Multiply. Round your answer.

The area of the circle is about 379.9 ft^2.

22 ft

Try It

Find the area of each object. Round to the nearest tenth. Use $\pi \approx 3.14$.

a. A dart board whose radius is 20 in.

b. A CD whose diameter is 12.5 cm.

Check | Your Understanding

1. Explain how you can find the area of a circle if you know its diameter.

2. Name some circular objects in your classroom. Estimate the area of one of these objects. Explain how you made your estimate.

Practice and Apply

1. **Getting Started** Follow the steps to find the area of a circle with a diameter of 16 in.

    a. The area formula for a circle involves the radius of the circle. Find the radius by dividing the diameter by 2.

    b. The area of a circle is π times its radius squared. Use $A = \pi r^2$ to find the area. (Use $\pi \approx 3.14$.) Include units with your answer.

2. **a.** Estimate the area of the circle by counting grid squares. Assume each square represents 1 cm².

    b. Use $A = \pi r^2$ to find the area of the circle. Compare this area to your estimate in **a.**

Find the area of each circle given its radius. Use $\pi \approx 3.14$, and round answers to the nearest tenth.

3.

3 cm

4.

14 in.

5.

22.5 ft

Find the area of each circle given its diameter or radius. Use $\pi \approx \frac{22}{7}$, and express answers in lowest terms.

6.

$\frac{3}{4}$ in.

7.

7 ft

8.

14 mm

Given the radius or diameter of a circle, find its area. Round answers to the nearest tenth. Use $\pi \approx 3.14$.

9. $r = 2$ cm   **10.** $r = 22$ m   **11.** $r = 153$ ft   **12.** $r = 37.4$ in.

13. $d = 10$ cm   **14.** $d = 36$ in.   **15.** $d = 8.8$ m   **16.** $d = 0.8$ mm

17. **History** The people of Yap, an island group in the Pacific Ocean, once used huge stone disks as ceremonial money. These disks were as large as 12 feet in diameter. What was the area of one side of a Yapese coin?

18. Estimation Estimate the area of a circle whose radius is 5.87 in. Explain how you made your estimate.

19. Number Sense The first six digits of π are 3.14159. (You can't write down the last digit—π goes on forever!) Which approximation is closer to π, 3.14 or $\frac{22}{7}$? Explain your answer.

20. Test Prep What is the exact area of a circle whose radius is 2 cm?

Ⓐ 12.56 cm² Ⓑ 12.6 cm² Ⓒ 4π cm² Ⓓ $\frac{88}{7}$ cm²

Problem Solving and Reasoning

21. Journal Todaro's Pizzeria sells 9 in. diameter cheese pizzas for $8.00. What would a fair price be for a cheese pizza with a 13 in. diameter? Explain how you decided on this price.

22. Critical Thinking Is the combined area of two circles with the same radius the same as the area of one circle with twice the radius? Explain your reasoning.

23. Social Studies Native American children sometimes used hoops to practice their aim. A screen was put in the center of the hoop. Then the hoop was rolled along the ground between two lines of players, who hurled darts at the rapidly moving target. If a target hoop had a circumference of 60 in., what was its area?

24. Problem Solving Each time its wheels go around, a toy car moves a distance equal to their circumference. If a toy car moves forward 12.1 mm each time its wheels go around, what is the area of a circular surface of one of its wheels? Round to the nearest tenth.

Mixed Review

Convert each quantity to the given units. (See the chart on page 346 if you do not remember how some of these units compare.) *[Lesson 7-6]*

25. 2 days to hours **26.** 200 centimeters to meters **27.** 80 ounces to pounds

28. 52 inches to feet **29.** 672 cups to gallons **30.** 5.2 centimeters to millimeters

Graph y = x + 35. Use the graph to solve each equation. *[Lesson 10-7]*

31. 40 = x + 35 **32.** 65 = x + 35 **33.** 10 = x + 35 **34.** 35 = x + 35

Surface Areas of Cylinders

▶ **Lesson Link**   You know how to find surface areas of polyhedrons and areas of circles. You will use both of these skills to calculate surface areas of cylinders. ◀

Explore   Nets for Cylinders and Cones

Cans and Cones

Materials: Graph paper, Cylindrical and conical objects, Scissors, Tape

By looking at the faces of a polyhedron, you can see the shapes in its net. What do nets for cylinders and cones look like?

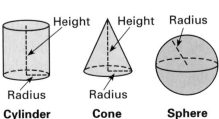

1. Choose a cylinder and make a net for it on graph paper. First trace circles for the top and bottom. Then cut a strip that will wrap around the outside.

2. Tape the pieces of the net together to make a cylinder. What shapes do you find in the net? Do you think *any* cylinder would have these shapes in its net? Explain.

3. What shapes do you think there are in the net for a cone?

4. Use your graph paper to make a net for a cone. Tape the pieces of your net together to be sure it makes a cone. What shapes do you find?

You'll Learn ...

■ to find the surface area of a cylinder

... How It's Used

Farmers store grain in cylindrical silos. The surface area of the cylinder represents the amount of material needed to make the silo.

Vocabulary

cylinder

cone

sphere

Learn   Surface Areas of Cylinders

All of a polyhedron's faces are flat. Other three-dimensional objects have circular faces and curved sides.

A **cylinder** has two parallel circular bases with the same radius. A **cone** has one circular base.

A **sphere** is the three-dimensional version of a circle. All the points on a sphere are the same distance from its center.

The net for a cylinder has two circles and a rectangle. You can use the surface area formulas for those figures to find the surface area of a cylinder.

Because the "tube" wraps around the base, its length is equal to the base's circumference. This is important to remember when you're finding the area of the rectangular "tube."

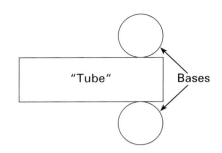

Example 1

Find the surface area of a cylinder whose height is 10 cm and radius is 8 cm. Round to the nearest tenth.

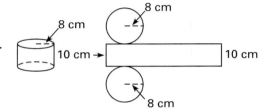

- Use $A = \pi r^2$ to find the areas of the circles.

  For one circle:

  $A = \pi r^2 \approx 3.14 \cdot 8^2 \approx 201.0$ cm^2

  The combined area of *both* circles is about $201.0 \cdot 2 = 402.0$ cm^2.

- Use $A = lw$ to find the area of the rectangle. First find the length.

  $l = C = 2\pi r \approx 2 \cdot 3.14 \cdot 8 = 50.2$ cm   The length equals the circumference of a base.

  $A = lw = 50.2 \cdot 10 = 502.0$ cm^2

- To find the surface area, add the area of the circles to the area of the rectangle.

  Surface area $= 402.0 + 502.0 = 904.0$ cm^2

  The surface area is about 904.0 cm^2.

Try It

a. A rainstick uses pebbles to mimic the sound of a rainstorm. If a toy rainstick has a height of 12 in. and a diameter of 2 in., find its surface area. Round to the nearest tenth.

b. Find the surface area of a cylinder whose radius and height are both 5.4 in. Round to the nearest tenth.

Luis and Paula are painting a toy drum whose radius is 6 in. and height is 5 in. What is its surface area?

Luis thinks ...

I'll add the areas of the circular bases to the area of the tube of the drum.

The area of each circular base is $\pi r^2 \approx 3.14 \cdot 6 \cdot 6 = 113.04$ in^2. There are two bases, so their total area is about $2 \cdot 113.04 = 226.08$ in^2.

Now I need to find the circumference of a base. This is $2\pi r$, or about $2 \cdot 3.14 \cdot 6 = 37.68$ in.

The height of the drum is 5 in., so the tube's area is $5 \cdot 37.68 = 188.4$ in^2.

The surface area of the drum is about 226.08 in^2 + 188.4 in^2 = 414.48 in^2.

Paula thinks ...

I'll find a formula.

The area of each circular base is πr^2, so the area of two bases is $2\pi r^2$.

The area of the tube is its width times its height. The width is the circumference of a base, so $w = 2\pi r$. The area of the tube is $2\pi rh$.

The surface area formula is $SA = 2\pi r^2 + 2\pi rh$. I can substitute $r = 6$ and $h = 5$.

$$SA \approx 2 \cdot 3.14 \cdot 6^2 + 2 \cdot 3.14 \cdot 6 \cdot 5 = 226.08 + 188.4$$
$$= 414.48 \text{ in}^2$$

The surface area of the drum is about 414.48 in^2.

What do you think?

1. How is Luis's method similar to Paula's? How is it different?

2. Would Paula's formula apply to any cylinder? Explain why or why not.

1. How is a cylinder like a prism? How is it different?

2. Explain why a cylinder's net contains a rectangle.

11-8 Exercises and Applications

Practice and Apply

1. **Getting Started** Follow the steps to find the surface area of the cylinder shown. Use $\pi \approx 3.14$.

   a. Use $A = \pi r^2$ to find the area of one of the circles.

   b. Since there are two ends, multiply your answer to **a** by 2.

   c. The "tube" is a rolled-up rectangle. Its length is the circumference of one of the circles. Use $C = 2\pi r$ to find the length.

   d. Multiply your answer to **c** by the height to find the area of the "tube."

   e. To find the surface area, add your answers to **b** and **d**. Remember to include units.

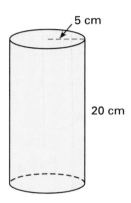

5 cm

20 cm

Make a perspective drawing of each object.

2. A cylinder

3. A cone

4. A sphere

5. **Test Prep** Which of these is a net for a cylinder?

Ⓐ 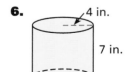   Ⓑ    Ⓒ 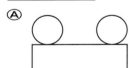   Ⓓ

Find the surface area of each cylinder. Use $\pi \approx 3.14$, and round to the nearest tenth.

6.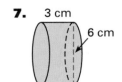
4 in.
7 in.

7. 3 cm
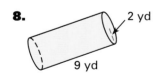
6 cm

8.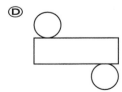
2 yd
9 yd

9. 5 m
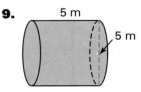
5 m

10. **Estimation** A cylindrical soup can has a radius of 1.3 in. and a height of 3.9 in. Estimate the area of its label. Explain how you made your estimate.

11. **History** The first phonographs were invented in the late 1800s by Thomas Edison and others. These phonographs used hollow wax cylinders to record and reproduce sound. If a recording cylinder was about 4 in. long and had a 2 in. diameter, what was its surface area?

12. **Problem Solving** A painter needs to paint a cylindrical railroad tank car. The car's diameter is 9 ft and its length is 22 ft. What is the area to be painted?

Problem Solving and Reasoning

13. **Critical Thinking** A Chinese toy called a *diabolo* is juggled with sticks and a rope. Suppose a diabolo is $5\frac{1}{2}$ in. tall and has a 5 in. diameter. If the diabolo is sold in a cylindrical container that fits it exactly, find the surface area of the container.

14. **Critical Thinking** A cylinder with a radius of 5 cm has a surface area of 345.4 cm². What is its height?

15. **Communicate** Some Alaskan native tribes and Native American tribes in the Pacific Northwest make totem poles. These cylindrical poles display the animals and birds, or *totems,* associated with a tribe's clans. Totem poles can be up to 80 ft tall.

Design your own totem pole. Label your drawing with diameter and radius measurements. Then find the surface area of your totem pole.

Mixed Review

Operation Sense Convert each rate to an equivalent rate. *[Lesson 7-7]*

16. 3 meters per second to meters per minute

17. 35 miles per hour to feet per hour

18. 12,800 fluid ounces per second to gallons per second

The table was created from the equation $y = 3x + 4$. Use it to solve each related equation. *[Lesson 10-6]*

x	−2	−1	0	1	2	3	4
y	−2	1	4	7	10	13	16

19. $13 = 3x + 4$ 20. $-2 = 3x + 4$ 21. $10 = 3x + 4$ 22. $1 = 3x + 4$

You'll Learn ...

■ to find the volume of a cylinder

... How It's Used

Oil refinery workers need to know the volumes of cylindrical tanks and barrels.

▶ **Lesson Link** You know how to calculate the volume of a prism. A cylinder is like a prism with circular bases. You'll investigate how finding the volume of a cylinder is similar to and different from finding the volume of a prism. ◀

Explore   **Volume of a Cylinder**

Cube It!

Materials: Centimeter cubes, Ruler, Cylindrical jar, glass, or mug

You may have entered contests where you guessed the number of jelly beans in a jar. Now you'll investigate how many centimeter cubes a cylindrical object can hold.

1. Estimate the number of cubes your cylinder can hold. How did you make your estimate?

2. Fill the cylinder with centimeter cubes. Empty the cylinder and count the cubes. How many cubes fit inside the cylinder? How close was your estimate in Step 1?

3. Do you think the number of cubes you found in Step 2 is greater than, less than, or equal to the volume of the cylinder? How did you decide?

4. Measure the diameter (d) and height (h) of your cylinder. Calculate the volume of a *prism* with height h and a square base d units on a side. Do you think this volume is greater or less than the volume of your cylinder? Why?

5. Estimate your cylinder's volume. How did you make this estimate?

Learn   **Volumes of Cylinders**

Recall that the volume of a prism is equal to its base area times its height.

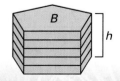

Like a prism, a cylinder has two identical bases, so its volume is also given by $V = Bh$. Since the base is a circle, $B = \pi r^2$. These results are summarized below.

> **VOLUME OF A CYLINDER**
> The volume of a cylinder is given by $V = Bh = \pi r^2 h$.

Although you can't completely fill a cylinder with cubes, the volume of a cylinder, like any other volume, is measured in cubic units.

Examples

1 A kaleidoscope has a height of 20.5 cm and a diameter of 4.2 cm. Estimate its volume.

The volume is equal to the base area times the height.

The base area is πr^2. π is close to 3. The radius is half of the 4.2 cm diameter or about 2 cm.

$B \approx 3 \cdot 2^2 = 12$ cm^2

The height is about 20 cm.

$V = Bh \approx 12 \cdot 20 = 240$ cm^3

The kaleidoscope's volume is about 240 cm^3.

2 Find the volume of the cylinder.

For the circular base, $B = \pi r^2$.

$B = \pi r^2 \approx 3.14 \cdot 10 \cdot 10 = 314$ in^2

$V = Bh \approx 314 \cdot 6 = 1884$ in^3

The volume of the cylinder is about 1884 in^3.

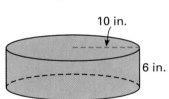

10 in.

6 in.

Test Prep

Remember that you find the volumes of both prisms and cylinders by multiplying the base area by the height.

Try It

a. The height of the tennis ball can shown is about 24 cm and its radius is about 3.8 cm. Estimate its volume.

b. Find the volume of the cylinder. Round to the nearest tenth.

9 in.

7 in.

Volume is the amount of space an object takes up. When we measure the amount of liquid a container can hold, we use different units. These units are called units of *capacity*.

Customary System	Metric System
Volume units include: yd³, ft³, in³	Volume units include: m³, cm³, mm³
Capacity units include: teaspoon (tsp), cup (c), pint (pt), quart (qt), gallon (gal)	Capacity units include: kiloliter (kL), liter (L), milliliter (mL)

Converting from volume to capacity units is not easy in the customary system. For instance, 1 cubic foot is equivalent to 7.481 gallons.

In the metric system, there is a direct connection, so conversions are simpler.

1 liter = 1000 cubic centimeters

1 milliliter = 1 cubic centimeter

Example 3

An iced tea can has a diameter of 6.3 cm and height of 12.3 cm. Find its capacity to the nearest milliliter.

First find the volume.

The radius is $6.3 \div 2 = 3.15$ cm.

$V = Bh = \pi r^2 h \approx 3.14 \cdot 3.15^2 \cdot 12.3$

$V \approx 383.227$ cm³

Since 1 mL = 1 cm³, the can's capacity is about 383 mL.

Try It

A cylindrical drinking glass is 15 cm tall and has a diameter of 7 cm. Find its capacity to the nearest milliliter.

Check | Your Understanding

1. Name some products that are packaged in cylinders. Which is usually greater, the height of the package or the radius? Why do you think this might be?

2. How is the formula for the volume of a cylinder similar to the formula for the volume of a prism? How are they different?

Practice and Apply

1. **Getting Started** Follow the steps to find the volume of the cylinder shown to the nearest tenth. Use $\pi \approx 3.14$.

   a. A cylinder has a circular base. Use $A = \pi r^2$ to find the area of one of the circles.

   b. The volume of a cylinder is equal to its base area times its height. Multiply your answer to **a** by the height of the cylinder.

   c. Round your answer to the nearest tenth. Remember to include units.

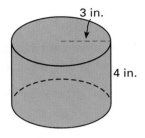

3 in.

4 in.

2. **Problem Solving** A yo-yo is nearly cylindrical, with a base area of about 3 in² and a height of 2 in. Find the volume of a cylinder with this base area and height.

3. **Estimation** Estimate the volume of a cylinder whose height is 24.8 cm and radius is 2.2 cm. Explain how you made your estimate.

Find the volume of each cylinder. Use $\pi \approx 3.14$, and round answers to the nearest tenth.

4.
   3 ft
   5 ft

5.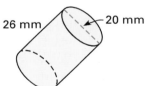
   26 mm 20 mm

6.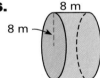
   8 m
   8 m

7.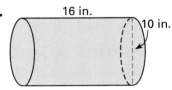
   16 in.
   10 in.

8.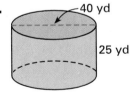
   40 yd
   25 yd

9.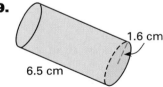
   1.6 cm
   6.5 cm

10. **Problem Solving** A typical soft drink can has a height of about 4.8 in. and a diameter of about 2.5 in. A case that holds 12 cans is a rectangular prism about 5 in. tall, 11 in. long, and 7.6 in. wide.

    a. What is the total volume of the 12 cans?

    b. What is the volume of the case?

    c. What percent of the space in the case is taken up by the cans?

11. Industry In 1956, inventors attempting to develop a wallpaper cleaner created Play-Doh® modeling clay. If a cylindrical can of Play-Doh has a diameter of $2\frac{1}{2}$ in. and a height of $3\frac{1}{8}$ in., what is its volume?

12. **Test Prep**   What is the volume of a 680 mL container?

Ⓐ 0.68 L   Ⓑ 680 cm   Ⓒ 680 mm³   Ⓓ 680 cm³

Given the height and radius, find the capacity of each cylindrical can to the nearest tenth of a milliliter. Use $\pi \approx 3.14$.

13. $h = 10$ cm, $r = 6$ cm   **14.** $h = 14$ cm, $r = 5$ cm   **15.** $h = 19.4$ cm, $r = 3.8$ cm

Problem Solving and Reasoning

16. Critical Thinking The volume formula for a cone is $\frac{1}{3}Bh$. Suppose a movie theater sells cylindrical popcorn containers that have a volume of 140 in³ and are 7 in. tall.

a. If the theater sold cone-shaped popcorn containers with the same volume and radius as the cylindrical ones, what would their height be?

b. If the cone-shaped containers had the same volume and height as the cylindrical containers, what would their radius be?

17. Communicate Many foods, like canned fruits and vegetables, come in cylindrical containers. Others, like most cereals and cake mixes, come in boxes (rectangular prisms). In general, what types of foods are sold in cans? What types of foods are usually sold in boxes? Give some possible reasons for this match between food type and container shape.

Mixed Review

18. Are these cards similar to a rectangular 3 in. by 5 in. card? *[Lesson 7-8]*

a. A 6 in. by 10 in. card   **b.** A 5 in. by 7 in. card   **c.** A 20 in. by 12 in. card

For each inequality, tell whether the number in bold is a solution. *[Lesson 10-8]*

19. $x + 7 > 14$; **6**   **20.** $m - 8 < 18$; **23**   **21.** $3k + 7 \leq 10$; **1**   **22.** $9 \geq n$; **10**

Project Progress

Design a cylindrical beverage container with a volume of 360 cm³. Sketch a net for this container, and show its dimensions on the net.

Problem Solving

Understand
Plan
Solve
Look Back

You've used the properties of a circle to make circle graphs and to calculate circumferences, areas, surface areas, and volumes. Now you'll use your knowledge of circles to analyze a popular toy.

Toys 'Round the World

Slinky® toys have been walking down the stairs of homes in the United States since 1945. Use your knowledge of circles and cylinders to analyze the dimensions of two Slinkies.

1. Although a Slinky is not a cylinder, it has a cylindrical shape. Find the surface areas of the cylinders suggested by these Slinkies.

2. Find the volumes of the cylinders.

3. Compare the ratio of the two surface areas to the ratio of the volumes. Which ratio is larger?

4. If you straightened out these Slinkies, how long would they be? (*Hint:* Count or estimate the number of loops. How can you find the circumference of one loop?)

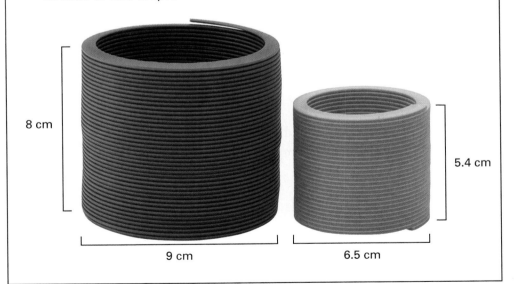

8 cm

5.4 cm

9 cm

6.5 cm

1. **Data** In 1994, an average two-income family in the United States spent its money as shown in the table. Draw a circle graph to show this data.

Category	Taxes	Housing and Household	Medical Care	Food	Other
Percent	40%	16%	10%	10%	24%

Find the circumference and area of each circle given its diameter or radius. Use π ≈ 3.14, and round answers to the nearest tenth.

2.
2 mm

3.
18 cm

4.
5.4 in.

5. **History** In the 1800s, children sometimes used steel wheel rims as hoop toys. If the circumference of a wagon wheel was 10 ft, find the radius of the hoop.

Find the surface area and volume of each cylinder. Use π ≈ 3.14, and round answers to the nearest tenth.

6.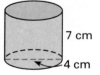
7 cm
4 cm

7.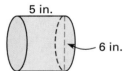
5 in.
6 in.

8. Find the surface area and volume of a rectangular solid whose height is 6 cm, length is 8 cm, and width is 5 cm. *[Lessons 11-3 and 11-4]*

Test Prep

When you're given the circumference of a circle and are asked to find its radius on a multiple choice test, it may be faster to check which one of the answers works instead of solving the equation for the radius.

9. The circumference of a circle is 18.8 cm. Find its radius to the nearest cm.

   Ⓐ 3 cm   Ⓑ 4 cm   Ⓒ 5 cm   Ⓓ 6 cm

When Worlds Kaleide

Question: What's less than a foot long and filled with millions of intricate works of art? *Hint:* If you don't like the art, you can change it with a twist of your wrist.

Answer: A kaleidoscope!

In 1816, a Scottish scientist, Sir David Brewster, discovered that if he placed a chamber full of colored glass objects at the end of a cylinder with mirrors inside it, the reflections created beautiful geometric patterns. The kaleidoscope was born!

Over the years, kaleidoscopes have been made with different mirror arrangements that create a wide variety of pattern types. The objects used to make those patterns include seashells, stones, beads, fake pearls floating in oil, and the world itself.

When you look through a kaleidoscope, the sections of the pattern you see are copies of each other in different positions. Now you'll begin to investigate the slides, flips, and twists that describe these patterns.

1. Look at the circled kaleidoscope pattern. Describe two ways you could fold this pattern so the two halves are mirror images of each other.

2. Look at the top half and bottom half of the circled kaleidoscope image. What do you notice? What about the left side and right side?

3. Describe any slides, flips, or twists you see in the circled kaleidoscope pattern.

Translations

► **Lesson Link** You've plotted points in all four quadrants of a coordinate plane. Now you'll use those skills to investigate slides of geometric figures. ◄

You'll Learn ...

■ to draw translations on a coordinate plane

■ to write rules for translations

... How It's Used

Computer animators use translations to move figures across a scene.

Vocabulary

transformation

translation

Explore | Slides on a Coordinate Plane

Which Way Did He Go?

Materials: Graph paper, Scissors

1. On graph paper, trace and cut out a copy of one of the right triangles shown on the coordinate plane. Then copy the axes and triangles onto another sheet of graph paper.

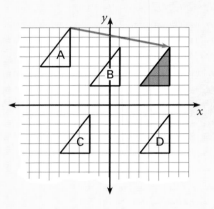

2. Draw an arrow to show the path of a slide from the top vertex of triangle *A* to the top vertex of the shaded triangle. Then draw arrows for triangles B, C, and D.

3. Position the cutout triangle on top of triangle A. Slide it along the arrow until it exactly matches the shaded triangle. Think of a way to describe this slide to someone whose graph paper does not show the shaded triangle.

4. Repeat Step 3 to describe slides from triangles B, C, and D to the shaded triangle.

5. Have a classmate test your directions from Steps 3 and 4.

Learn | Translations

When you change the position or size of a figure, you have performed a **transformation** . A **translation** is a transformation that slides a figure without changing its size or orientation.

Example 1

Which lettered figure is a translation of the shaded figure?

Although all the figures are moved to new positions, A has also been twisted, B has been flipped, and D has been reduced.

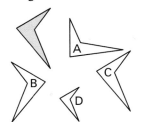

C is a translation of the shaded figure.

Try It

Identify the lettered figures in the kaleido-scope pattern that are translations of the shaded quadrilateral.

▶ **Social Studies Link**

Clothing designs in many cultures show repeating patterns that involve translations. African, Greek, and Native American embroidery often use translation-based designs.

When a figure is translated on a coordinate plane, you can use coordinates to describe the translation.

In the translation shown, every point is moved right 5 units and up 4 units. For instance, $(4, 0)$ slides to $(9, 4)$. The translation of point A is labeled A' ("A prime").

Since every point moves 5 units to the right, every x-coordinate increases by 5. Since every point moves 4 units up, every y-coordinate increases by 4.

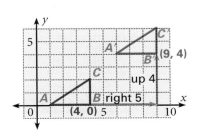

Remember

The **x-coordinate** of a point tells how far to the left or right of the origin the point is along the x-axis. The **y-coordinate** tells how far up or down the point is along the y-axis. **[Page 443]**

To describe the translation "right 5, up 4," we can write the rule $(x, y) \rightarrow (x + 5, y + 4)$.

Examples

2 Write a rule for the translation "left 6, down 3."

Left and down are negative directions. *Subtract* from both coordinates.

The rule is $(x, y) \rightarrow (x - 6, y - 3)$.

3 A line segment has endpoints at $(0, 0)$ and $(-3, -2)$. Give the endpoints of its translated segment using the rule $(x, y) \rightarrow (x + 1, y - 3)$.

$(0, 0) \rightarrow (0 + 1, 0 - 3) = (1, -3)$
$(-3, -2) \rightarrow (-3 + 1, -2 - 3) = (-2, -5)$

Try It

A triangle has vertices at $(0, 0)$, $(0, 4)$, and $(2, 3)$. Give the vertices of its translation using the rule $(x, y) \rightarrow (x - 5, y + 1)$.

Shawon and Lorena are using a translation to create a pattern on a coordinate plane. What is the translation of a parallelogram with vertices at (0, 0), (3, 0), (1, 2), and (4, 2) if they use the rule $(x, y) \rightarrow (x - 2, y + 3)$?

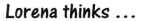

Lorena thinks ...

I'll use the meaning of the rule.

Subtracting 2 from x moves the parallelogram 2 units left. Adding 3 to y moves it 3 units up. So I'll slide the parallelogram "left 2, up 3."

Shawon thinks ...

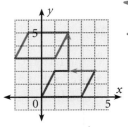

I'll use the rule to find the vertices of the translation, then draw the parallelogram.

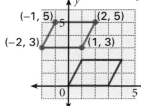

$$(0, 0) \rightarrow (0 - 2, 0 + 3) = (-2, 3)$$

$$(3, 0) \rightarrow (3 - 2, 0 + 3) = (1, 3)$$

$$(1, 2) \rightarrow (1 - 2, 2 + 3) = (-1, 5)$$

$$(4, 2) \rightarrow (4 - 2, 2 + 3) = (2, 5)$$

What do you think?

1. Why do these two methods give the same result?

2. Whose method would be easier to use if the rule involved very large numbers? Explain your reasoning.

Check | Your Understanding

1. Describe a translation from your desk to the classroom door in terms of steps forward or back and right or left.

2. How can you tell whether or not two sets of coordinates represent a translation?

Practice and Apply

1. **Getting Started** Sketch the translation of △*MNP* using the rule $(x, y) \rightarrow (x + 2, y - 1)$.

   a. Find the coordinates of point *M′* by adding 2 to *M*'s *x*-coordinate and subtracting 1 from its *y*-coordinate. Plot *M′*.

   b. Repeat **a** to plot points *N′* and *P′*.

   c. Draw the translated triangle △*M′N′P′* by connecting its vertices.

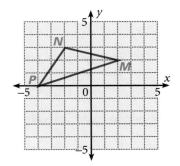

For each group of figures, identify all lettered polygons that are translations of the shaded polygon.

2.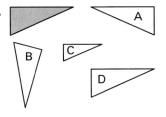

3.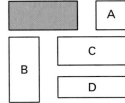

4.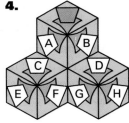

5. **Science** Some kaleidoscopes use four perpendicular mirrors. These kaleidoscopes produce images like the one shown. Use transformations to describe this image.

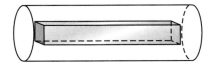

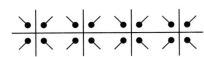

Write a rule for each translation.

6. Right 1, up 2   7. Left 5, up 7   8. Left 6, down 5   9. Down 3

Point *A* is at (2, −3). Use each rule to find the coordinates of *A′*.

10. $(x, y) \rightarrow (x + 3, y - 1)$ 11. $(x, y) \rightarrow (x - 2, y + 3)$

12. $(x, y) \rightarrow (x, y - 4)$ 13. $(x, y) \rightarrow (x - 5, y + 7)$

14. **Test Prep** If you translate (4, −2) three units to the right and five units down, what are the coordinates of the translated point?

    Ⓐ (7, −7)   Ⓑ (1, −7)   Ⓒ (7, 3)   Ⓓ (1, 3)

Using each rule, draw a translation of figure *ABCD* on a coordinate plane. Give the coordinates of the vertices of the translation.

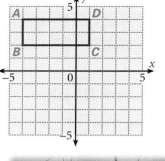

15. Right 3 units

16. $(x, y) \rightarrow (x + 1, y - 3)$

17. $(x, y) \rightarrow (x - 1, y - 1)$

18. Geography The map shows counties in southern Iowa. Describe any translations that you see.

Problem Solving and Reasoning

19. Communicate A transformation of $\triangle ABC$ moves $A(2, -3)$ to $D(0, -2)$, $B(1, 4)$ to $E(-1, 5)$, and $C(-2, 1)$ to $F(-4, 2)$. Is $\triangle DEF$ a translation of $\triangle ABC$? If so, what is the rule for the translation? If not, why not?

20. Critical Thinking When creating animations, computer programmers use translations to describe the ways images will move across a screen. Suppose that the figure moves as shown by the arrow. Write a rule for the translation of this figure.

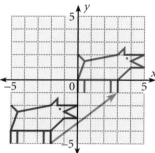

Mixed Review

Find the missing side lengths in each pair of similar figures. *[Lesson 7-9]*

21.

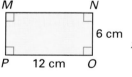 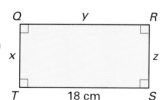

22.

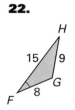 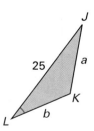

Solve each equation. Check your solutions. *[Lesson 10-11]*

23. $5a - 4 = 11$

24. $6v + 2 = 44$

25. $\frac{c}{10} + 11 = 13$

26. $3x - 75 = 75$

27. $\frac{m}{2} - 5 = -3$

28. $-4b + 2 = 10$

29. $2f - 5 = 14$

30. $7c - 11 = -4$

31. $\frac{c}{3} + 7 = 0$

32. $-2x - 5 = -13$

33. $8k + 6 = -10$

34. $700t + 2800 = 4200$

Reflections and Line Symmetry

▶ **Lesson Link** │ You've transformed figures by sliding them. Now you'll investigate transformations made by flipping figures. ◀

You'll Learn ...

■ to identify lines of symmetry

■ to reflect figures on a coordinate plane

... How It's Used

Judges at dog shows look for symmetry when choosing champion dogs.

Explore │ Reflections

Mirror, Mirror, on the Graph

Materials: Graph paper, Markers

1. Set up *x*- and *y*-axes on your graph paper. Use a marking pen to sketch a simple cartoon character or irregular design in the second quadrant of your coordinate system.

2. Fold your paper along the *y*-axis so the original figure is on the outside. Turn your paper over and trace your figure onto the other half of the paper.

3. Unfold your paper. Compare your original figure to the tracing. Are the figures identical? If not, what differences do you see?

4. Choose a point on your original figure. How far is the point from the *y*-axis? How far is the matching point on your tracing from the *y*-axis?

Vocabulary

symmetry

line symmetry

line of symmetry

reflection

Learn │ Reflections and Line Symmetry

A balance, or **symmetry** , is often found in nature and in art.

When one half of an object is a mirror image of the other, the object has **line symmetry** , and the imaginary "mirror" is the **line of symmetry** .

Since kaleidoscopes use several mirrors, the patterns they produce have many lines of symmetry.

Examples

Decide whether each figure has line symmetry. If it does, copy the figure, then draw and number the lines of symmetry.

1 Regular pentagon

A regular pentagon has 5 lines of symmetry.

2 Square

A square has 4 lines of symmetry.

3 Scalene triangle

A scalene triangle has no lines of symmetry.

Try It

Decide whether each figure has line symmetry. If it does, copy the figure, then draw and number the lines of symmetry.

a. Isosceles triangle

b. Rectangle

c. Regular hexagon

Whether it has line symmetry or not, any figure can be reflected in a mirror. The reflections in kaleidoscope images can be produced by irregular objects.

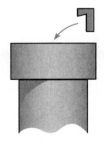

The transformation created by flipping a figure is a **reflection** .

When you reflect a figure across a line, every point on the original figure is the same distance from the line as the matching point on its reflection.

You can use this idea to help you draw reflections on a coordinate plane.

Example 4

The vertices of △FGH are F(−4, 1), G(−2, 5), and H(4, 3). Draw the reflection of △FGH across the x-axis. Give the coordinates of the reflection's vertices.

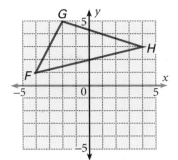

Draw the reflection by reflecting the vertices, then connecting the points.

To reflect a point, find the distance to the line of reflection. Go the same distance on the other side of the line and mark the reflection point.

For instance, since point F is one unit *above* the x-axis, its reflection F' is one unit *below* the axis.

The coordinates of the vertices of the reflection are F'(−4, −1), G'(−2, −5), and H'(4, −3).

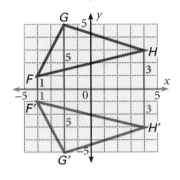

Try It

The vertices of △ABC are A(3, 2), B(−3, 4), and C(0, 5). Draw a reflection of △ABC across the x-axis, and give the coordinates of its vertices.

The coordinates of points in Example 4 demonstrate an important pattern. When a point is reflected across the x-axis:

- its x-coordinate stays the same
- its y-coordinate is multiplied by −1

There is a similar rule for reflections across the y-axis. When a point is reflected across the y-axis:

- its x-coordinate is multiplied by −1
- its y-coordinate stays the same

Study TIP

If a point is on the line of reflection, it is its own reflection. Think of touching your fingertip to a mirror. Where is your fingertip's reflection?

Check Your Understanding

1. How are the ideas of line symmetry and reflection related? What are some differences between them?

2. Explain how to sketch the reflection of a polygon across a line.

3. If a figure is reflected across a line, does the reflection have line symmetry? Explain your answer.

Practice and Apply

1. **Getting Started** Follow these steps to draw the reflection of $\triangle DEF$ across the y-axis.

   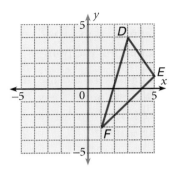

   a. Since the reflection is across the y-axis, find the coordinates of point D' by multiplying the x-coordinate of D by -1 and keeping the y-coordinate the same. Plot point D'.

   b. Repeat **a** to plot points E' and F'.

   c. Draw the reflected triangle $\triangle D'E'F'$ by connecting its vertices.

Geometry Decide whether each figure has line symmetry. If it does, copy the figure, then draw and number the lines of symmetry.

2. Equilateral triangle

   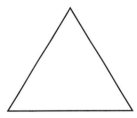

3. Rhombus

   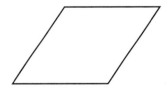

4. Regular octagon

   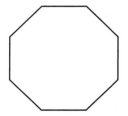

Decide whether each pattern or object has line symmetry. If it does, make a simplified copy of the figure, then draw and number the lines of symmetry.

5. Kaleidoscope pattern

6. **Science** Diatom (microscopic plant)

   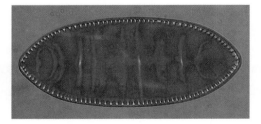

7. **Test Prep** If you reflect the point $(3, -5)$ over the y-axis, what are the coordinates of the reflection?

   Ⓐ $(3, 5)$ Ⓑ $(-3, -5)$ Ⓒ $(3, -5)$ Ⓓ $(-3, 5)$

8. Draw the reflection of △*JKL* across the *x*-axis. Give the coordinates of the reflection's vertices.

9. Draw the reflection of △*JKL* across the *y*-axis. Give the coordinates of the reflection's vertices.

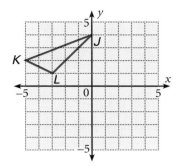

Draw each figure and its reflection on a coordinate plane.

10. △*RST* with *R*(1, 3), *S*(5, 4), and *T*(4, 1), reflected across the *y*-axis.

11. *VWXY* with *V*(1, 2), *W*(2, 4), *X*(5, 5), and *Y*(6, 1), reflected across the *x*-axis.

12. **Geography** Tell how many lines of symmetry there are in each state flag.

a.
Arizona

b.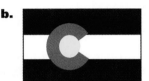
Colorado

c.
New Mexico

d.
Texas

Problem Solving and Reasoning

13. **Communicate** Sketch regular polygons with different numbers of sides, and see how many lines of symmetry each has. What do you notice? Explain the pattern you see.

Look for a pattern.

14. **Critical Thinking** Draw a quadrilateral with exactly two lines of symmetry. What type did you draw? Are other types possible? Explain.

15. **Journal** Explain why reflecting a point across the *x*-axis multiplies its *y*-coordinate by −1 but does not change its *x*-coordinate.

Mixed Review

Suppose two figures are similar. For each scale factor of the smaller to the larger, find the unknown perimeter and area. *[Lesson 7-10]*

16. Scale factor = $\frac{1}{4}$, perimeter of smaller = 15 cm, area of smaller = 9 cm². Find the perimeter and area of the larger figure.

17. Scale factor = $\frac{1}{3}$, perimeter of larger = 90 in., area of larger = 450 in². Find the perimeter and area of the smaller figure.

Solve each equation. Check your solutions. *[Lesson 10-9]*

18. $-6 + x = 26$

19. $m + 42 = -3$

20. $t - 12 = 144$

21. $y + 100 = 100$

22. $-72 + a = 100$

23. $d + (-4) = 38$

24. $22 - r = 38$

25. $17 - z = -35$

11-12 Rotations and Rotational Symmetry

You'll Learn ...

■ to identify figures with rotational symmetry

■ to determine how far a figure has been rotated

■ to rotate figures on a coordinate plane

... How It's Used

Woodworkers use rotating lathes to create symmetric designs.

Vocabulary

rotation

rotational symmetry

point symmetry

▶ **Lesson Link** You've explored translations and reflections. Now you'll see a transformation that turns a figure. ◀

Explore The Symmetry of Turns

A Big Turnaround

Materials: Graph paper, Push pin, Ruler, Scissors, Cardboard

1. Set up *x*- and *y*-axes on a sheet of graph paper. Then cut a 4 by 4 square and a 2 by 4 rectangle out of another sheet.

2. Place the cardboard behind your coordinate plane. Use the push pin to attach the center of your square to the origin of the graph. Label the upper right vertex *A* on the graph paper *and* on the square. Trace around the square.

3. Turn the square clockwise until it matches its starting position. Notice where *A* is. Continue turning the square. How many perfect overlaps are there before the square returns to its starting position?

4. Repeat Steps 2 and 3 for the rectangle.

5. Trace and cut out the regular hexagon shown, then repeat Steps 2 and 3 for this figure.

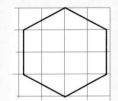

Learn Rotations and Rotational Symmetry

A **rotation** is a transformation that pivots a figure around a point. A full turn is a 360° rotation. So a $\frac{1}{4}$ turn is a 90° rotation, a $\frac{1}{2}$ turn is a 180° rotation, and a $\frac{3}{4}$ turn is a 270° rotation.

Original position

90° clockwise rotation

180° clockwise rotation

270° clockwise rotation

360° rotation = original position

A figure has **rotational symmetry** if a rotation of less than 360° rotates the figure onto itself. If a figure has 180° (half-turn) rotational symmetry, it has **point symmetry**.

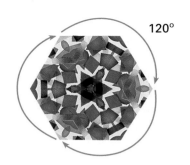

120°

▶ **Science Link**

Different arrangements of mirrors in a kaleidoscope produce different types of images. Three-mirror kaleidoscopes produce patterns with 120° and 240° rotational symmetry.

Examples

1 Decide whether this parallelogram has rotational symmetry. If it does, name all clockwise fractional turns that rotate the figure onto itself.

Imagine the figure rotating around its center. The original figure is shown in blue.

$\frac{1}{4}$ turn $\frac{1}{2}$ turn **overlaps** $\frac{3}{4}$ turn

The parallelogram has half-turn rotational symmetry (point symmetry).

2 Give the smallest fractional turn that this figure has been rotated clockwise. Then express your answer in degrees.

Imagine the figure rotating around its center.

$\frac{1}{4}$ turn $\frac{1}{2}$ turn $\frac{3}{4}$ turn

The figure has been rotated $\frac{3}{4}$ of a turn, or 270°.

Try It

Decide whether this trapezoid has rotational symmetry. If it does, name all clockwise fractional turns that rotate the figure onto itself.

DID YOU KNOW?

When someone says an object has "symmetry," they usually mean it has *line* symmetry.

You can use coordinates to help describe rotations.

Example 3

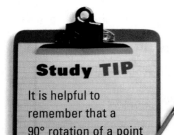

Give the coordinates of rotations of △*RST* after clockwise rotations of 90° ($\frac{1}{4}$ turn), 180° ($\frac{1}{2}$ turn), 270° ($\frac{3}{4}$ turn), and 360° (full turn) around the origin.

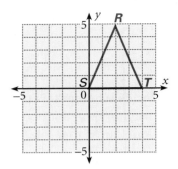

90°: Since *S* is the center of the rotation, its "rotations" do not move. So *S'* is at (0, 0). *T'* is on the *y*-axis. It is still 4 units from the origin, so *T'* is at (0, −4). *R'* is at (5, −2).

180°: *S"* is at (0, 0). *T"* is on the negative side of the *x*-axis, 4 units from *S*, at (−4, 0). *R"* is at (−2, −5).

270°: *S'''* is at (0, 0). *T'''* is on the positive side of the *y*-axis, so its coordinates are (0, 4). *R'''* is at (−5, 2).

360°: The triangle is back in its original position, with vertex coordinates (0, 0), (4, 0), and (2, 5).

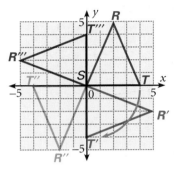

Notice that the *shape* of a figure does not change as it is rotated.

When you rotate an object, the only point that does not move is the center of the rotation. You can use this fact to identify the center of a rotation.

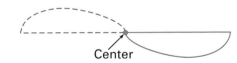

Center

Check Your Understanding

1. What happens when you rotate a figure 360°?

2. Identify some objects in your classroom that have rotational symmetry.

3. If a figure has point symmetry, does it have rotational symmetry? If it has rotational symmetry, does it have point symmetry? Explain your answer.

4. Is it possible for a figure to have line symmetry but not rotational symmetry? If it is, sketch such a figure; if not, explain why it is not possible.

Practice and Apply

1. **Getting Started** Follow the steps to decide whether the figure has rotational symmetry.

   a. Copy the original figure.

   b. Slowly rotate your copy. As you turn the figure, check to see whether it matches the original. Be especially sure to check after each $\frac{1}{4}$ turn.

   c. If the copy matches the original at any time before you have made a full turn, it has rotational symmetry.

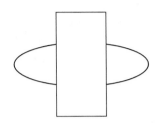

Decide whether each figure has rotational symmetry. If it does, name all clockwise fractional turns that rotate the figure onto itself.

2. Square

3. Parallelogram

4. Isosceles triangle

5. Computer-generated kaleidoscope pattern

6. **Fine Arts** Ellsworth Kelly's *Blue, Green, Yellow, Orange, Red*

7. List all the images in Exercises 2–6 that have point symmetry.

8. On a coordinate plane, draw rectangle *WXYZ* with *W*(0, 0), *X*(2, 0), *Y*(2, 3), and *Z*(0, 3). Give the coordinates of rotations of *WXYZ* after clockwise rotations around the origin of:

   a. 90° $\left(\frac{1}{4} \text{ turn}\right)$ **b.** 180° $\left(\frac{1}{2} \text{ turn}\right)$ **c.** 270° $\left(\frac{3}{4} \text{ turn}\right)$ **d.** 360° (full turn)

9. **Test Prep** How many degrees does $\frac{3}{4}$ of a rotation represent?

   Ⓐ 90°   Ⓑ 180°   Ⓒ 270°   Ⓓ 360°

PRACTICE 11-12

Give the smallest fractional turn that each figure has been rotated clockwise. Then express your answer in degrees.

10. Social Studies Swiss flag

11.

12. Science Water (H_2O) molecule

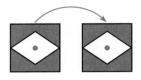

13. Give the coordinates of rotations of $\triangle DEF$ after clockwise rotations around the origin of:

a. $90°$ $\left(\frac{1}{4} \text{ turn}\right)$ **b.** $180°$ $\left(\frac{1}{2} \text{ turn}\right)$ **c.** $270°$ $\left(\frac{3}{4} \text{ turn}\right)$

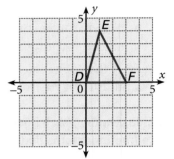

Problem Solving and Reasoning

14. Critical Thinking How can you tell if a figure has been rotated $180°$ or reflected over a line?

15. Communicate Decide whether each of these regular polygons has rotational symmetry. If it does, name all clockwise fractional turns that rotate the figure onto itself.

a. Equilateral triangle   **b.** Square   **c.** Regular pentagon   **d.** Regular hexagon

e. What pattern of rotational symmetry is there for regular polygons?

Mixed Review

Write a proportion and solve each problem. If necessary, round answers to the nearest tenth. *[Lesson 8-6]*

16. What is 30% of 220?   **17.** 25 is what percent of 125?   **18.** 12 is 5% of what number?

Solve each equation. Check your solutions. *[Lesson 10-10]*

19. $5x = 105$ **20.** $\frac{y}{12} = 3$ **21.** $4m = 52$ **22.** $\frac{g}{-3} = 5$

23. $7v = 56$ **24.** $\frac{h}{11} = 11$ **25.** $-12x = 12$ **26.** $15n = 30$

Project Progress

Decide which of your containers you prefer. Then design a label for your container, using transformations and symmetry. Finally, copy the net for the container you chose, decorate it with the label design, and make the container.

Problem Solving

Understand
Plan
Solve
Look Back

You've used reflections, rotations, and translations to transform objects. Now you'll use transformations to create a kaleidoscopic tessellation.

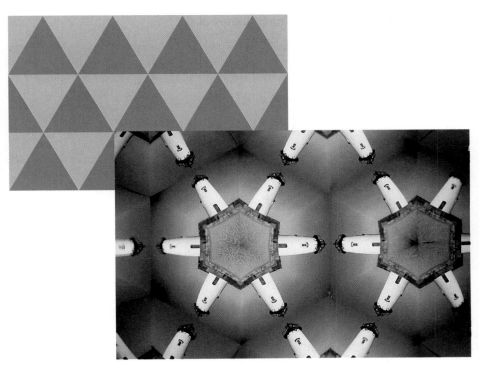

When Worlds Kaleide

A *tessellation* is a pattern of congruent shapes that covers a flat surface without gaps or overlaps.

1. Look at the kaleidoscope pattern that tessellates. Identify the basic (largest) geometric figure in the kaleidoscope tessellation.

2. Examine the pattern within one of the basic figures (*cells*) you identi- fied in Step 1. Describe some of the symmetries—line or rotational— you see.

3. Design one cell of a simple kaleidoscope pattern that uses at least one transformation. Then repeat the pattern to make a tessellation.

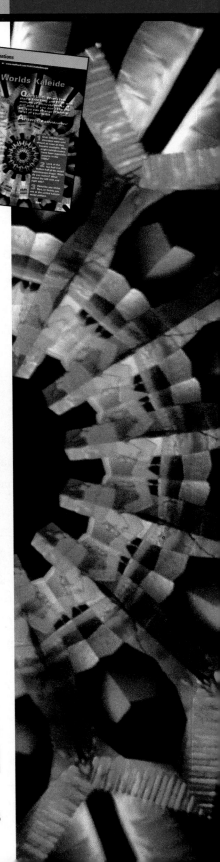

1. Copy the coordinate plane and draw the reflection of △*ABC* across the *x*-axis. Give the coordinates of the reflection's vertices.

2. Give the coordinates of rotations of △*ABC* after clockwise rotations around the origin of:

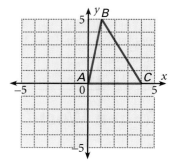

a. 90° $\left(\frac{1}{4} \text{ turn}\right)$

b. 180° $\left(\frac{1}{2} \text{ turn}\right)$

c. 270° $\left(\frac{3}{4} \text{ turn}\right)$

d. 360° (full turn)

Point *D* is at (−4, −1). Use each translation rule to find the coordinates of *D'*.

3. $(x, y) \rightarrow (x + 5, y + 3)$

4. $(x, y) \rightarrow (x - 3, y - 4)$

5. Explain how the kaleidoscope image shows reflections and rotations.

6. Language Arts The Cyrillic alphabet is used in Russia and other Eastern European countries. Ten of its thirty-two letters are shown.

Б Д Е Ж И К П Ф П Щ

a. Which letters have a horizontal line of symmetry?

b. Which letters have a vertical line of symmetry?

c. Which letters have rotational symmetry?

Test Prep

When you are asked to identify a figure with point symmetry on a multiple choice test, remember that point symmetry means half-turn rotational symmetry.

7. Which of these figures has point symmetry?

Ⓐ

Ⓑ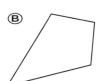

Ⓒ

Ⓓ

Inscribed and Circumscribed Polygons

When a polygon is *inscribed* in a circle, all its vertices lie on the circle.

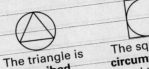

The triangle is **inscribed** inside the circle.

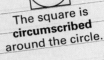

The square is **circumscribed** around the circle.

When a polygon is *circumscribed* around a circle, the circle just touches all its sides.

You can use a compass and straightedge to construct inscribed regular polygons.

To inscribe a regular hexagon or an equilateral triangle inside a circle:

- Draw a circle. Mark a point *P* on the circle.

- Do not change the setting of your compass. Move the tip of your compass to *P*. Swing an arc that intersects another point on the circle.

- Move the compass tip to the place where your first arc intersected the circle. Make another arc that intersects the circle. Repeat this step until you come back to point *P*.

- To inscribe a hexagon, draw segments that connect the points of intersection. To inscribe an equilateral triangle, connect every other intersection point.

To inscribe a square inside a circle:

- Draw a circle. Mark its center and draw a diameter of the circle.

- Construct the perpendicular bisector of one diameter of the circle. (If you need a reminder of how to do this, see page 221.) Extend the bisector until it is a second diameter of the circle.

- Draw a square whose vertices are the endpoints of the diameters.

Try It

1. Use a compass to draw a circle. Inscribe a square inside the circle.
2. Use a compass to draw a circle. Inscribe an equilateral triangle and a regular hexagon inside the circle.

Graphic Organizer

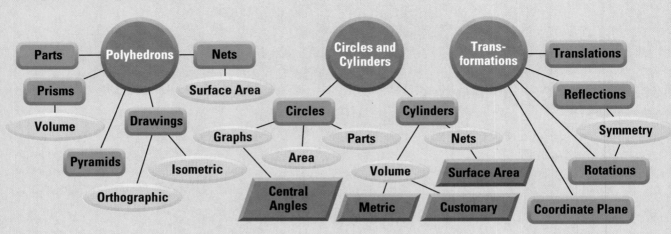

Section 11A   Polyhedrons

Summary

- A **polyhedron** is a 3-dimensional object, or **solid,** whose **faces** are polygons. A **prism** is a polyhedron whose **bases** are congruent and parallel. A **pyramid** has a polygonal base and one more vertex above or below the base.

- **Isometric drawing** shows perspective. **Orthographic drawing** shows angles and lengths accurately in front, top, and side views.

- The **surface area** of a polyhedron is the sum of the areas of its faces. You can use a net to help calculate surface area.

- The **volume** of a 3-dimensional object is the amount of space it takes up. Prism volumes are given by the formulas $V = Bh$ and $V = lwh$.

Review

1. Find the number of cubes in the figure at the right. Assume all cubes are visible.

2. Sketch a square pyramid. How many edges, faces, and vertices does it have?

3. The bases of the prism are right triangles.
    a. Sketch a net for this prism.
    b. Find its surface area and volume.

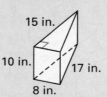

15 in.

10 in.   17 in.

8 in.

Section 11B   Circles and Cylinders

Summary

- A **circle** is the set of all points in a plane that are the same distance (the **radius**) from the center. The **diameter** is twice the radius.

- The **circumference** is the distance around a circle: $C = \pi d$ or $C = 2\pi r$. The area of a circle is given by $A = \pi r^2$. **Pi** (π) is the ratio of the circumference of a circle to its diameter.

- A **cylinder** has two circular bases and a **cone** has one circular base.

Review

4. The data shows Hal's time at work. Make a circle graph. Label each sector.

Typing	Filing	Telephone	Meetings
35%	25%	30%	10%

5. Find the circumference and area of a circle whose radius is 21.98 m. Use 3.14 for π. Round to the nearest tenth.

6. Find the surface area and the volume of the cylinder. Use 3.14 for π.

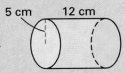

5 cm   12 cm

Section 11C   Transformations

Summary

- A **translation** slides every point on a figure.

- A **line of symmetry** divides a figure into two mirror-image halves. The **reflection** of a figure is its mirror image across a line.

- A **rotation** turns a figure. A figure has **rotational symmetry** if you can rotate it a fraction of 360° and it matches the original figure exactly.

Review

7. Copy the figure. Draw all lines of symmetry. Then tell whether or not it has rotational symmetry.

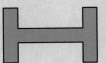

8. Point A is at $(-4, -1)$. Use the translation rule $(x, y) \to (x - 3, y + 2)$ to find the coordinates of A'.

9. $ABCD$ has coordinates $A(0, 0)$, $B(4, 0)$, $C(6, 3)$, and $D(2, 5)$.

  a. Draw the figure on a coordinate plane.

  b. Draw the reflection of $ABCD$ across the x-axis. Give the coordinates of the reflection's vertices.

  c. Give the coordinates of a rotation of $ABCD$ for a 90° clockwise rotation around the origin.

1. Sketch a pentagonal prism. How many edges, faces, and vertices does it have?

2. Make a perspective sketch of the object shown at the right.

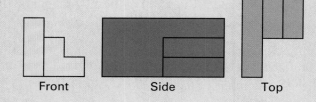

Front   Side   Top

3. Last week, Auto Imports sold 3 yellow cars, 7 blue cars, 5 white cars, 4 red cars, and 6 green cars. Make a circle graph to show this data.

4. A rectangular prism is shown.

   a. Sketch a net for the prism.

   b. Find the surface area and volume of the prism.

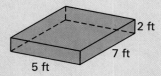

5. A circle has a diameter of 8 cm. Find its radius, area, and circumference. Use 3.14 for π. Round to the nearest tenth.

6. Marc jogged one circuit around a large circular lawn with area 15,000 m². How far did Marc jog?

7. A child's cylindrical block is 4 in. long and has a diameter of 2 in. Find its surface area and volume. Use 3.14 for π. Round to the nearest tenth.

Use the figure at the right for Exercises 8–10.

8. Draw the reflection of ABCD across the x-axis. Give the coordinates of the reflection's vertices.

9. Give the coordinates of a rotation of ABCD for a 180° clockwise rotation around the origin.

10. Sketch the image formed by translating ABCD using the translation rule $(x, y) \rightarrow (x + 4, y - 5)$.

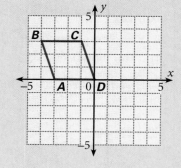

11. For the digits **1, 2, 3, 6,** and **8:**

   a. Which have no lines of symmetry?

   b. Which have just one line of symmetry?

   c. Which have two lines of symmetry?

   d. Which have rotational symmetry?

Performance Task

Wheelchair ramps are often triangular prisms. Design a wheelchair ramp with a horizontal length of 40 ft. The angle between the ground and the ramp must measure 4°. Use a net to make a scale model of your ramp, and calculate its surface area and volume.

Performance Assessment

Choose one problem.

BLOCK SCHEDULE

Design a set of four building blocks using the shapes you have learned about in this chapter. Draw top, front, and side views of each block. Make a net for each one, then build your set of blocks. Calculate or estimate the volume and surface area of each of your blocks.

Rolling Along

Each number on a number cube has a $\frac{1}{6}$ probability of coming up on any roll. Sometimes game designers want to use a solid where all of the probabilities are *not* $\frac{1}{6}$.

Five special polyhedrons are called *Platonic solids*. All of the faces of these polyhedrons are regular polygons. Research the names and shapes of the five Platonic solids. Build a model of each one and number its faces. Which solid would you roll if you wanted each number to come up $\frac{1}{4}$ of the time? $\frac{1}{6}$? $\frac{1}{8}$? $\frac{1}{12}$? $\frac{1}{20}$?

Circles, Circles, Circles

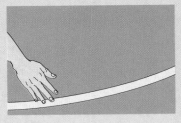

Use a compass to draw circles that have the same center and the following radii: $\frac{1}{2}$ in., 1 in., $1\frac{1}{2}$ in., 2 in., $2\frac{1}{2}$ in., 3 in., $3\frac{1}{2}$ in., and 4 in. How does the circumference of each circle compare to that of the one inside it? Now imagine that $\frac{1}{2}$ in. masking tape is used to make a circle with a radius of 1 mile. There are really *two* circles, one corresponding to the inside border of the tape and one corresponding to the outside border of the tape. How do the circumferences of these two circles compare?

Making Money

For this experiment, you will need two small rectangular mirrors, a coin, and a protractor.

Place the coin on a tabletop. Set the two mirrors together so that you can see the coin's reflection. How many coins do you see?

Experiment with the angle between the mirrors. Use a protractor to measure the angles that give different numbers of reflections. Make a table that shows the relationship between the angle and the number of coins you see.

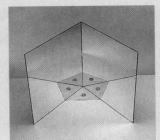

Is there a way to "make" an infinite amount of money with your mirrors? If so, explain how.

Science Link
www.mathsurf.com/7/ch12/science

Social Studies

Before the Civil War, the Underground Railroad helped thousands of slaves reach free states and Canada. Harriet Tubman was the most famous "conductor" on the Railroad. For each of the 300 or more people she guided, the probability of reaching freedom was 100%.

Science

According to NASA, the odds of the earth colliding with an asteroid or comet over 1 km in diameter in the next century is less than 1 out of 1000.

Arts & Literature

According to *What the Odds Are,* by Les Krantz, once you submit a book to a publisher, the odds of having it published are between 1:50 and 1:100.

A Tail Of Two Cities
by Chuck Dickens

REJECT

Chapter 1

It was the best of times, it was pretty lame, it was the age of wisdom, it was the age of really dumb stuff,

People of the World

The probability that a randomly chosen person lives in India is about 16%.

Entertainment

According to *Numbers,* by Andrea Sutcliffe, the odds that you will go to jail during a game of Monopoly® are 1 to 1.74.

KEY MATH IDEAS

You can find the number of different outcomes for a series of events by using a tree diagram, or by multiplying the number of possibilities for each item.

A permutation is a possible way to put a set of items in order. A combination is an arrangement of items where the order does not matter.

The odds of an event are the ratio of the number of ways it could happen to the number of ways it could not happen. The (theoretical) probability of an event is the ratio of the number of ways it could happen to the total number of possible outcomes.

Two events are independent if the outcome of one does not change the probabilities of the outcome for the second; otherwise, the events are dependent

CHAPTER PROJECT

Problem Solving

Understand
Plan
Solve
Look Back

In this project, you'll design an experiment to simulate the typical performance of a favorite player, such as the free-throw percentage of a basketball player or the batting average of a baseball or softball player. Begin the project by choosing a sports star whose skills you'll simulate.

623

Checking for a Reasonable Answer

Even if you use a calculator to help you solve a problem, you should look back to check whether your answer is reasonable. You can use estimation and common sense to help you.

Problem Solving Focus

Each of the problems below has an answer, but the answer is not exactly right. Tell if each answer is "close enough," "too low," or "too high," and explain why.

1 A 1996 television viewing survey showed that 15,440,000 viewers watched suspense and mystery programming. Approximately 4% of this audience was made up of teens between the ages of 12 and 17. About how many teens watched suspense and mystery programming?
Answer: 61,760,000

2 The survey found that 2,720,000 more viewers watched situation comedies than suspense and mystery programs. About 30% of situation comedy viewers were men aged 18 or older. About how many men 18 or older watched situation comedies?
Answer: 5,400,000

3 A 1995 survey found that female teenagers spent less time watching television than any other age group, averaging 160 minutes per day. Male teens' viewing time was about 129% of that amount. About how many minutes per day did male teens watch television?
Answer: 320 minutes

4 Women aged 55 or older spent the most time watching television. Their average daily viewing time was 199% of the viewing time of female teenagers. About how many minutes per day did women 55 or older watch television?
Answer: 320 minutes

Someday My Prints Will Come

"It is a capital mistake to theorize before you have all the evidence [said Sherlock Holmes]. It biases the judgment."
—Arthur Conan Doyle
A Study in Scarlet

Ever since Arthur Conan Doyle introduced the world to Sherlock Holmes, people have enjoyed reading detective stories. It's fun to try to solve the mystery along with (or faster than!) a super-sleuth like Agatha Christie's Miss Marple.

In real life, a fingerprint is one of a detective's most important clues. Every person has unique fingerprints, so a match between a suspect and a fingerprint at a crime scene is powerful evidence.

Fingerprint experts use a classification system based on 3 basic patterns. Along with the computerized Automated Fingerprint Identification System, this classification system helps compare a fingerprint to the millions on file. The mathematics of arranging and counting you are about to investigate is an important part of this system.

1 Look at one of your fingertips closely. Describe any patterns you see in your fingerprint.

2 Compare the fingerprints on your two little fingers. What do you notice?

3 Why do you think fingerprint experts needed to devise a system for classifying fingerprints?

625

Counting Methods

You'll Learn ...

■ to use tree diagrams and the Counting Principle to find all the outcomes for a set of choices

... How It's Used

Biologists use tree diagrams to analyze what might happen in different generations of animals.

Vocabulary

tree diagram

outcome

Counting Principle

▶ **Lesson Link** You've had experience making organized lists. Now you'll see how organized lists can help you count efficiently. ◀

Explore | Classifying Characteristics

I Spy a Crook

You are a detective interviewing witnesses at a burglary scene. Your goal is to get an accurate description of the suspect.

1. Make a list of all the characteristics you can think of that you will ask the witnesses about.

2. For each characteristic, what are the possible responses? (For instance, possible responses for observed hair color might include blonde, brown, red, and black.)

3. How many of your characteristics would you expect a witness to be able to remember? Explain your answer.

4. Give some different possibilities for the description of your suspect.

Learn | Counting Methods

Suppose a witness sees a burglar running from a robbery and can describe the color and length of the suspect's hair. You can make an organized list to count the number of possible descriptions.

Hair Color	Hair Length		Hair Color	Hair Length	
Black	Short		Brown	Short	
Black	Medium		Brown	Medium	
Black	Long		Brown	Long	
Blonde	Short		Red	Short	
Blonde	Medium		Red	Medium	
Blonde	Long		Red	Long	

You can see that, if there are 4 hair colors and 3 lengths, there are 12 different combinations of hair length and color.

There are other organized ways to count the information shown in this table. One is to use a **tree diagram** . The structure of the tree shows all the possibilities, or **outcomes** , in a given situation.

Example 1

Use a tree diagram to show all of the different outcomes for 4 hair colors (black, blonde, brown, and red) and 3 hair lengths (short, medium, and long).

From the starting point, draw a "branch" for each of the 4 hair colors.

For each color, draw 3 "twigs," one for each possible length.

Counting the twigs shows that there are 12 different outcomes for hair length and color.

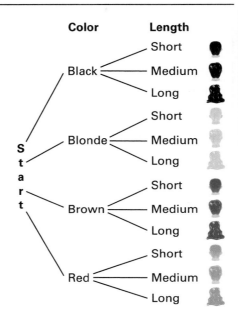

Try It

Hector's Juice-O-Rama sells 2 types of juice, orange and apple. You can order a small, medium, or large glass of either type. Use a tree diagram to show how many different juice orders are possible.

In Example 1, the tree diagram had 4 branches and each branch had 3 twigs. Notice that the number of possible combinations, 12, is equal to 4 • 3.

4 branches times 3 twigs equals 12 combinations.

$4 \times 3 = 12$

This idea is summarized in the **Counting Principle** .

COUNTING PRINCIPLE

To find the number of different outcomes for making choices in a sequence, multiply together the number of possibilities for each item.

Examples

2 A school has 3 mathematics teachers, 4 English teachers, and 2 Spanish teachers. Using the Counting Principle, find how many different sets of teachers a student could have for these 3 subjects.

Multiply the number of choices for each type of teacher.

$3 \cdot 4 \cdot 2 = 24$

There are 24 possible sets of teachers.

3 A detective is planning a disguise. He can choose from 2 wigs (red or blonde), 2 fake noses (bulbous or pointy), and 2 pairs of glasses (green or mirrored). How many different disguises can he create, and what are they?

Using the Counting Principle, there are $2 \cdot 2 \cdot 2 = 8$ disguises. However, we need to make an organized list, such as a tree diagram, to describe the disguises.

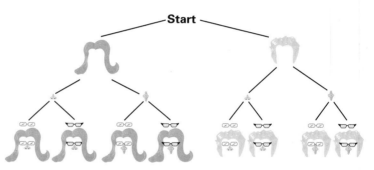

Counting the tips of the twigs confirms that there are 8 possible disguises. The tips of the twigs show the different disguises.

Try It

A softball coach has 5 pitchers, 2 catchers, and 2 shortstops on her team. Using the Counting Principle, find out how many different sets of players she can use for these positions.

Check | Your Understanding

1. In the tree diagram in Example 1, would you get a different number of outcomes if the branches were hair lengths and the twigs were colors? Explain.

2. Describe a situation where the Counting Principle is more useful than a tree diagram. Describe a situation where a tree diagram is more useful.

Practice and Apply

1. **Getting Started** Follow the steps to find out how many different sundaes you can make choosing one flavor of ice cream, one sauce, and one topping from the list.

   a. Multiply the number of ice cream flavors by the number of sauce flavors.

   b. Multiply your answer to **a** by the number of toppings. The product is the number of different sundaes you can make.

   c. What is the name of the principle you used to solve this problem?

Ice Cream Flavors	Sauce Flavors	Toppings
Vanilla Chocolate Strawberry Peach	Chocolate Caramel Butterscotch	Nuts Whipped Cream Sprinkles

Operation Sense Use the Counting Principle to find the number of outcomes in each situation.

2. Parakeets: 2 types, 5 colors. How many choices?

3. Clothing: 3 shirts, 4 pairs of pants, 2 pairs of shoes. How many outfits?

4. Bicycles: 5 colors, 3 sizes, 3 styles. How many choices?

5. Lunch: 2 drinks, 4 different sandwiches, 3 kinds of fruit. How many choices?

6. **Logic** You are taking a true-false test. The test has 3 questions, and there are 2 choices (T and F) for each.

   a. Make a tree diagram to show the possible outcomes for answers for this test. How many outcomes are there? What are the outcomes?

   b. Suppose the correct answers are FFT. How many of the outcomes in **a** give all 3 right answers? 2 right answers? 1 right answer?

7. **Social Studies** On a 1996 ballot in San Jose, California, there were 8 candidates for President, 5 for U.S. Representative, and 3 for State Senator. How many different ways could a voter select one candidate for each office?

8. The Out To Lunch restaurant chain offers customers their choice of one kind of soup and one sandwich. On Monday, the soups are chicken noodle and tomato, and the sandwiches are roast beef, turkey, and veggie. How many different lunches can be selected, and what are they?

PRACTICE 12-1

9. Police artists draw *composite sketches* of suspects. The FaceKit imaging system allows detectives to create composite sketches on a computer. Among other features, FaceKit has 96 different head shapes, 248 noses, 176 mouths, and 224 chins. How many combinations of these features can FaceKit make?

10. **Test Prep** There are 4 roads from City A to City B, 2 from B to C, and only 1 highway from C to D. How many different routes are there from A to B to C to D?

    Ⓐ 7   Ⓑ 8   Ⓒ 9   Ⓓ 10

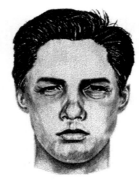

Image created by FaceKit
Pacer Infotec, Inc.

Problem Solving and Reasoning

11. **Critical Thinking** Ms. Potatohead® comes with: a straw hat, a yellow visor, a red baseball cap, a flowered bonnet; eyes with glasses, eyes without glasses; open lips with teeth, closed lips, open lips with tongue sticking out; green, purple, and pink shoes; and two different noses. How many different versions of Ms. Potatohead could you create if you use one choice for each feature?

12. **Critical Thinking** Suppose you have x choices for your first period class, y choices for your second period class, and z choices for your third period class.

  a. How many possible ways are there to select these classes?

  b. Give possible values of x, y, and z if there are 42 ways to select the classes.

13. **Journal** Write an interactive story where the reader is allowed to make 2 decisions. (For instance, at one point you could ask, "Should Ana go into the dragon's cave? If you answer yes, go on to the next paragraph. If no, go to paragraph 5.") There should be at least 6 possible versions of the story.

PROBLEM SOLVING 12-1

Mixed Review

Sketch each polyhedron. *[Lesson 11-1]*

14. Square pyramid   **15.** Triangular prism   **16.** Hexagonal prism

Make a perspective sketch of each object. *[Lesson 11-2]*

17.

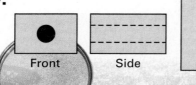

Front   Side

Top

18.

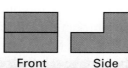

Front   Side   Top

Arrangements

▶ Lesson Link You've found the number of outcomes for a series of events. Now you will investigate situations where the *order* of the events is important. ◀

Explore Arrangements

This Isn't a Chorus Line!

Materials: Index cards or slips of paper

Police Chief Iva Gottam is planning a police *lineup,* where witnesses to a crime try to pick the criminal out of a group of people. How many different ways can she line up 3 people from left to right?

1. Write the names of the 3 people in the lineup on cards and arrange them in all the possible orders. (You'll need several cards for each person.) Record your results and count the arrangements.

Gil Tee   Ann Ocent   Al E. Bye

2. Take the cards and arrange them in a tree diagram to show all the possibilities. Again, record your results and count the arrangements.

3. After you placed the first person in a lineup, how many choices did you have for the second? After the first two were placed, how many choices did you have for the third?

4. How is this situation different from the combinations you've investigated so far?

You'll Learn ...

■ to count the number of ways items can be arranged

■ to use factorial products to count arrangements

... How It's Used

You use permutations when arranging a selection of photographs in a frame.

Vocabulary

permutation

Learn Arrangements

When you arrange a set of books on a shelf, each one you place leaves one less possibility for the next. When the order of the items in an arrangement is important, each possible ordering is called a **permutation** .

The fact that you have one less choice at each stage of the decision is very important when finding the number of permutations.

Example 1

► **Language Link**

The word *permutation* comes from the Latin *permutare,* "to change thoroughly."

Today, Azucena, Bert, and Chao-Yee are going to give their reports in math class. In how many orders can these students give their reports?

There are 3 possibilities for the first report.

Once the first student gives his or her report, there are 2 choices (shown by the branches) for the second.

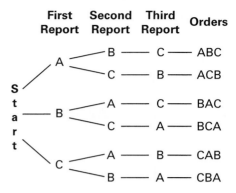

First Report	Second Report	Third Report	Orders
A	B	C	ABC
A	C	B	ACB
B	A	C	BAC
B	C	A	BCA
C	A	B	CAB
C	B	A	CBA

Finally, there is only 1 person left for the third report, as shown by having 1 twig for each branch.

There are 6 possible orders for the student reports.

Notice that there are 3 "trunks," each trunk has 2 "branches," and each branch has 1 "twig," resulting in the $3 \cdot 2 \cdot 1 = 6$ permutations.

The Counting Principle can help determine the number of possible permutations in a given situation.

Example 2

There are 4 people in Darryl's family. In how many different ways can they line up for a family portrait?

There are 4 possible choices for the person on the left. There are 3 choices for the second spot, 2 for the third, and the remaining person must stand on the right.

By the Counting Principle, there are $4 \cdot 3 \cdot 2 \cdot 1 = 24$ ways Darryl's family can line up for the portrait.

Try It

The Fotomatic Camera Store, Gemie's Jewelry, Handy Hardware, Igloo Yogurt, and Joe's Junque Shoppe were burglarized in Napoleonville last night. In how many different orders could the burglaries have taken place?

Did you notice a pattern in the multiplications in Examples 1 and 2? The factors decreased by 1 each time, since every step reduced the number of choices by 1.

Another way to write 4 · 3 · 2 · 1 is 4!. This is read "four factorial" (not "four!!"). The exclamation point is the sign for factorial.

Factorial products, and portions of factorial products, are important in calculating numbers of permutations.

Examples

Give each factorial product.

3 5!

5! = 5 · 4 · 3 · 2 · 1 = 120

4 8!

8! = 8 · 7 · 6 · 5 · 4 · 3 · 2 · 1
　　= 40,320

5 Cycleville uses a 3-digit number for each of its bicycle license plates. Zeros are not used, and no digit appears more than once in a license. Chief Pedals wants to know how many different licenses he can issue.

There are **9** possibilities (1–9) for the first digit. Suppose you choose a 7 for the first digit.

Then there are only **8** possibilities left for the second: 1, 2, 3, 4, 5, 6, 8, and 9.

If you choose a 4 for the second digit, there are **7** possibilities left for the third: 1, 2, 3, 5, 6, 8, and 9.

Once you choose the third digit, the license is finished.

There are **9** · **8** · **7** = 504 different license numbers.

Try It

Give each factorial product.

a. 4!

b. 10!

c. Chief Pedals (from Example 5) decides that 504 license numbers are not enough for Cycleville. If he uses 4-digit numbers instead, how many different license plate numbers will there be?

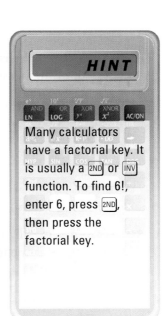

Check Your Understanding

1. Write the values of 2! through 6! and see how quickly the size of a factorial product grows. Why do you think these products grow so quickly?

2. Explain why, when you order a set of items, the number of possibilities decreases by 1 at each step in the ordering process.

Practice and Apply

1. **Getting Started** On a Saturday, you plan to go shopping, eat lunch, call a friend, and see a movie. Follow the steps to determine how many different orders there are for these activities.

   a. Decide how many choices there are for the first activity.

   b. After you do the first activity, how many choices do you have for the second?

   c. How many choices are left for the third activity?

   d. How many choices are left for the fourth?

   e. Multiply your answers to **a, b, c,** and **d** to find the number of different orders for these activities.

Operation Sense Give each factorial product.

2. 3!   3. 7!   4. 11!   5. 9!

6. **Problem Solving** A detective plans to dust a crime scene for fingerprints, make casts of footprints, collect hair samples, and collect fiber samples. In how many different orders can he do these tasks?

7. **Sports** In the 1996 Olympics, the gold, silver, and bronze medalists in the women's marathon were Yuko Arimori, Japan; Fatuma Roba, Ethiopia; and Valentina Yegorova, Russia — but not in that order. List all of the possible orders of finish for these athletes.

8. **Science** Many animal groups have *pecking orders*. An animal dominates those below it in the pecking order. Use factorial notation to give the number of possible pecking orders for:

   a. A flock of 15 chickens   **b.** A pack of 22 wolves

9. List all possible orderings of the letters A, B, C, and D (without repeating letters). Do any of these orderings form words?

10. **Consumer** Polly must make up a 4-digit secret code for her ATM card. If she can choose any of the digits 1–6, but is not allowed to repeat digits, how many possibilities are there for her code?

11. **Test Prep** How many different 4-digit license plates can be made from the digits 0–9 if no digits are repeated?

    Ⓐ 10   Ⓑ 3,024   Ⓒ 5,040   Ⓓ 362,880

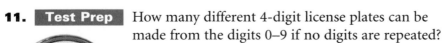

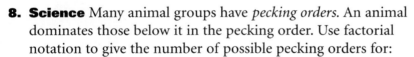

12. Kadim and Mary have been asked to design a school flag. They have decided to make a flag with three horizontal stripes, similar to the flag of Sierra Leone at right. They can choose from green, white, red, and yellow stripes. How many different possibilities are there for the design if the three stripes must have different colors? (Assume a green-white-red flag is different from a red-white-green flag.)

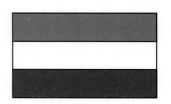

Problem Solving and Reasoning

13. Communicate Complete the table below for the equation $y = x!$. Then graph your results. What do you notice about the growth of factorial products?

x	2	3	4	5	6	7	8	9	10
$y = x!$									

14. Choose a Strategy There are 4 boys and 4 girls in a square-dancing class.

   a. How many possible orders are there for the 4 boys?

   b. How many possible orders are there for the 4 girls?

   c. How many different pairs of 1 boy and 1 girl can be made?

   d. How many possible orders are there for 4 pairs of boys and girls in the class? Explain how you found your answer.

Problem Solving

STRATEGIES

- Look for a Pattern
- Make an Organized List
- Make a Table
- Guess and Check
- Work Backward
- Use Logical Reasoning
- Draw a Diagram
- Solve a Simpler Problem

Mixed Review

Sketch a net for each polyhedron. Then find its surface area. *[Lesson 11-3]*

15.

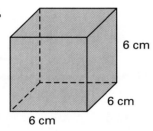

6 cm
6 cm
6 cm

16.

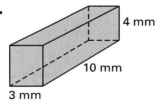

4 mm
10 mm
3 mm

17. Square pyramid

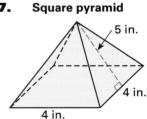

5 in.
4 in.
4 in.

Find the volume of each prism. *[Lesson 11-4]*

18.

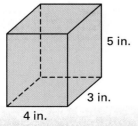

5 in.
3 in.
4 in.

19.

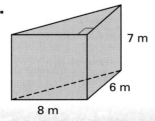

7 m
6 m
8 m

20.

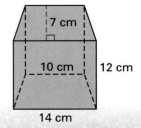

7 cm
10 cm
12 cm
14 cm

12-3 Choosing a Group

▶ **Lesson Link** You've found the number of permutations, where the order of a set of items is important. Now you'll explore methods to count the number of ways to choose things where the order does not matter. ◀

You'll Learn ...

■ how to calculate the number of ways to choose some items out of a larger group when the order is unimportant

... How It's Used

Coaches use combinations when they're selecting a starting lineup.

Vocabulary

combination

Explore   Choosing a Group

Materials: Index cards or slips of paper

Pick a Pair of Perpetrators

Eyewitnesses say that 2 burglars stole the Secret Sauce recipe at the Burger Bungalow. The detectives have narrowed down the list of suspects to Ally Eagle, Ray Kinn, Lars Sonny, and Kat Berglar. Help the detectives discover how many possible pairs of these suspects there are.

1. Write the names or initials of the suspects on index cards.

2. Find all the possible pairs that can be made with these suspects.

3. When you think you've found all the possible pairs, check your answer by making a list or drawing a picture.

4. How many pairs of burglars can you make from the list of 4 suspects? Explain how you know that you've found all the possibilities.

Ally Eagle   Ray Kinn

Lars Sonny   Kat Berglar

Learn   Choosing a Group

When you solved problems involving permutations, you were concerned with the order the items were in.

 ≠

Now you will count the number of ways a few items can be selected from a larger group. In these problems, the order does *not* matter.

A selection of items where the order does not matter is a **combination**.

Examples

1 At a crime scene, a detective collected 3 clothing fiber samples labeled A, B, and C. The crime lab has time to analyze 2 samples before the case goes to trial. How many different pairs of the samples could be analyzed? What are the pairs?

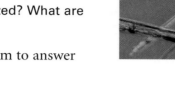

▶ **Literature Link**

Sherlock Holmes, the famous detective created by Arthur Conan Doyle, popularized the science of criminology.

You can use a tree diagram to answer this question.

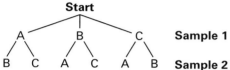

There are 6 pairs listed at the bottom of the tree diagram. However, the pairs in red are duplicates of those in black.

There are 3 different pairs of samples that could be analyzed. They are AB, AC, and BC.

2 There are 4 candidates, Winnie, Xavier, Yolanda, and Zeke, running for 3 positions on the student council. How many different ways are there to choose 3 of the 4?

Test Prep

When you check your answer to a combination problem, make sure you've eliminated all the possibilities that are duplicates of each other.

You can make an organized list of the possibilities to answer this question.

First find all the choices that include Winnie. Be sure to list all the possibilities for the other 2 candidates.

W XY   W XZ   W YZ

Then find all the choices that don't include Winnie. Since there are only 3 other candidates, there's only 1 possibility.

XYZ

There are 4 different ways to choose 3 candidates.

Try It

a. Suppose you can choose 2 out of these 3 electives: Drawing, Metal Shop, or Journalism. How many different options do you have?

b. In Example 2, suppose there is a fifth candidate to choose from, Victor. How many different combinations are there for 3 of the 5 candidates?

WHAT DO YOU THINK?

Taro and Lorena are going to a pizza parlor because of a special offer. They can choose 2 out of the 4 following toppings for no charge: green peppers, mushrooms, onions, and pepperoni. How many combinations can be made using 2 of the 4 toppings?

Taro thinks ...

I can make an organized list of the possibilities.

First I'll list all the possibilities that include green peppers.

Then I'll list all the combinations that have mushrooms, but *don't* have green peppers.

Finally, I'll list the remaining combination.

There are 6 different combinations of the 4 toppings.

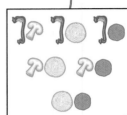

Lorena thinks ...

I'll make a tree diagram.

After crossing out duplicate pairs, I see that there are 6 different combinations of the 4 toppings.

Start

GM GO GP   MG MO MP   OG OM OP   PG PM PO

What do you think?

1. Why does Lorena's tree diagram give each combination more than once?

2. When Taro made the second row of his list, why did he make sure *not* to list combinations with green peppers?

Check | Your Understanding

1. How are combinations different from permutations?

2. How can writing an organized list help you find all of the possible combinations for a given situation? What do you need to remember to do?

Practice and Apply

1. **Getting Started** Alex, Bess, and Chandra are running for two seats on the student council. Follow the steps to find all possible combinations of two of these candidates.

   a. List all pairs of candidates that include Alex. Remember that the order does not matter.

   b. List all pairs of candidates that *do not* include Alex. Again, remember that the order does not matter.

   c. The results of **a** and **b** give a complete list of the possible combinations. How many combinations are there?

Decide whether or not order matters in each situation. Write *Yes* or *No*.

2. Choosing 4 CDs out of a list of 100 in a record club offer

3. Choosing digits for an alarm code

4. Seating students in a classroom

You are at a pizza parlor that offers four toppings: anchovies, olives, pineapple, and sausage. How many different combinations of these items can you make if you choose:

5. Two toppings?

6. Three toppings?

7. Four toppings?

8. Secret agents 001, 002, 003, 004, and 005 are available to be sent on a case. Their boss, Agent 000, decides to send only two of them. How many different pairs of these agents are there?

9. **Problem Solving** A florist uses 6 different types of flowers to make bouquets: asters, begonias, carnations, daisies, roses, and zinnias. In how many different ways can he select 3 of these types of flowers?

10. Five stores in town were recently burglarized: Alice's Aquariums, Boris's Bagels, Carlos's Candy, Dorinda's Dolls, and Ellis's Electronics. Detective Wilson knows the same person committed 3 of the crimes. How many different combinations of 3 of these stores are there?

Problem Solving TIP

Use a letter to represent each store. Then make an organized list of the possibilities, starting with all of the possibilities that include A (Alice's Aquariums).

11. **Test Prep** How many different ways can a student choose 2 books from a reading list of 5 books?

   Ⓐ 5   Ⓑ 10   Ⓒ 20   Ⓓ 50

PRACTICE 12-3

Problem Solving and Reasoning

12. Critical Thinking There is another way to answer the question in the What Do You Think scenario on page 638. You can find all of the ways to choose 2 out of 4 toppings by drawing all of the segments that can connect them. Using this method, show how you can use a pentagon to solve Exercise 11.

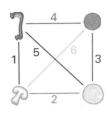

13. Communicate Mr. Marble won an all expenses paid trip for being Outstanding Detective of the Year. He can choose to visit any 3 of the following countries: Argentina, Brazil, Chile, Ecuador, Peru, and Uruguay.

a. How many different trips can Mr. Marble take if the order of the countries is not considered?

b. How many different trips can he take if the order is considered?

c. Which number is greater, the one you found in **a** or the one you found in **b**? Explain why this makes sense.

14. Critical Thinking Suppose you can choose 1, 2, 3, *or* 4 of the following fruits for a fruit shake: banana, blueberry, pineapple, and strawberry. How many different shakes are possible?

Mixed Review

15. In 1994, about 41% of the cars made in the United States were made by General Motors, 25% by Ford, 8% by Chrysler, and 26% by other companies. Draw a circle graph to show this data. *[Lesson 11-5]*

Find the circumference of each circle given its radius or diameter. Use $\pi \approx 3.14$, and round answers to the nearest tenth. *[Lesson 11-6]*

16.

2 cm

17.

8 in.

18.

15 ft

19.

5.5 mm

Project Progress

Think about all of the things that could possibly happen when your sports star performs the skill you are interested in, like shooting a free throw or going to bat. Then list all of the possible outcomes of performing this skill twice.

Problem Solving

Understand

Plan

Solve

Look Back

PROBLEM SOLVING 12-3

Section 12A Connect

You've seen how you can use tree diagrams, organized lists, and the Counting Principle to help count the possibilities in different situations. Now you'll use some of those skills to analyze your own fingerprints.

Someday My Prints Will Come

Materials: Tape, Index cards, Magnifying glasses, Calculators

There are 3 basic types of fingerprint patterns: *whorls, loops,* and *arches.*

1. You may have a different fingerprint pattern (whorl, loop, or arch) on each finger. How many different combinations of these patterns can occur on your right hand? (*Hint:* Does the order make a difference?)

Whorl

2. Suppose you have a different fingerprint pattern on the ring and pinky fingers of your left hand. How many possible pairs of patterns are there for those two fingers?

3. Take a #2 pencil and rub it so that you cover about 1 square inch of paper with the graphite. Rub the index finger of your nonwriting hand over the graphite. Then take a piece of tape and wrap it around your fingertip. Remove the tape carefully and place it on a card.

Loop

4. Compare your fingerprint to the patterns. How would you characterize your fingerprint?

Arch

Section 12A Review

Operation Sense Use the Counting Principle to find the number of outcomes in each situation.

1. Drinks: 3 flavors, 4 sizes. How many choices?

2. Entertainment: 6 movies, 2 ways to get there, 12 rows. How many choices?

3. Problem Solving A burglar cut his hand during a car break-in, and tests will reveal whether the blood he left behind is type A, B, AB, or O. Also, by analyzing scratches from the break-in, detectives will be able to tell whether he is right- or left-handed. Make a tree diagram to show all the possibilities for blood type and handedness. How many possibilities are there?

Distribution of Blood Types

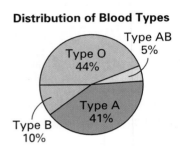

Operation Sense Give each factorial product.

4. 4!   **5.** 8!   **6.** 10!   **7.** 6!

8. Science The genetic coding in our bodies is called DNA. The "rungs" in the spiral ladder of a strand of DNA are made of 2 out of 4 *bases:* adenine, cytosine, guanine, and thymine.

a. How many ways can you select 2 out of these 4 bases?

b. Adenine and thymine are always paired. How many pairs of bases are actually possible, and what are they?

Computer model of DNA strand

9. How many different three-number license plates can be made from the digits 0–9 if:

a. Digits can be repeated?   **b.** Digits can't be repeated?

10. *Journal* Explain why factorial products and partial factorial products are important for calculating numbers of permutations.

Test Prep

When you're solving a counting problem on a multiple choice test, be sure to think about whether or not the order makes a difference.

11. How many different combinations of 3 letters can be made from the letters A, B, C, and D?

   Ⓐ 4   Ⓑ 12   Ⓒ 16   Ⓓ 24

Chance and Probability

Do NOT Pass Go!

What's your favorite board game? Do you prefer a game of pure skill, like chess or Go? Or would you rather play a game like Monopoly®, where all of your skill and cunning can be destroyed by an unlucky roll of the dice?

People have played games where luck is involved for hundreds of years. Cubes with dots have been found in Egyptian tombs, and 2500-year-old dice have been unearthed in Chinese excavations. In ancient India, instead of rolling a cube when playing a game, people tossed six cowrie shells.

Whether you play Chutes and Ladders®, Scrabble®, or a modern version of an ancient game like Pachisi (from India) or Hyena Chase (from North Africa), winning or losing depends, at least in part, on chance. As you investigate chance and probability, you'll get a better understanding of the mathematics of games.

1 In Monopoly®, you roll number cubes to find out how far to move. Does Monopoly® depend on luck?

2 What number or numbers would you use to describe the chance that a tossed coin lands heads? How did you decide on the number(s)?

3 A cowrie shell has a flat side and a rounded side. How do you think six cowrie shells might have been used when playing a game?

Odds and Fairness

You'll Learn ...

■ to find the odds that an event happens

... How It's Used

Bird breeders need to know the odds of certain traits appearing in their chicks.

Vocabulary

experiment

event

odds

fair games

▶ **Lesson Link**   In the last section, you found methods of counting all the ways that something can happen. Now you'll see how knowing all the possible outcomes can help you find the odds of an event. ◀

Explore | Fairness

Materials: Number cubes

Multiplication Toss

You and a partner are about to play a game of chance called Multiplication Toss. Here are the rules of the game.

• Decide which player will be "even" and which will be "odd."

• Take turns rolling the cubes. For each roll, find the product of the numbers rolled. If the product is odd, the odd player gets a point; if it's even, the even player gets a point.

• Repeat until each player has rolled 10 times. The player with the most points wins.

1. Play Multiplication Toss several times. Switch from "even" to "odd" each time.

2. If you could choose to be the "even" player or the "odd" player, which would you prefer? Why?

3. Would you ever expect the "odd" player to win this game? Explain.

4. Is Multiplication Toss a fair game? Explain why or why not.

Learn | Odds and Fairness

When you hear the word *experiment*, you probably think of a science lab. In probability, an **experiment** can be anything that involves chance—like the toss of a coin or the roll of a number cube.

The result of an experiment is an *outcome*. For a coin toss, the possible outcomes are heads and tails.

Examples

Name the possible outcomes of each experiment.

1 Rolling a number cube.

The possible outcomes are the numbers 1, 2, 3, 4, 5, and 6.

2 Drawing one marble from a bag with red, white, and blue marbles.

The possible outcomes are drawing a red marble, drawing a white marble, and drawing a blue marble.

An **event** is any outcome (or set of outcomes) we're interested in. We can use **odds** to describe the chance that an event will happen.

ODDS OF AN EVENT
The odds of an event are:
number of ways the event can happen : number of ways it cannot happen

Examples

Give the odds of each event.

3 Rolling a 2 on a number cube.

There is only one way for the event to happen—you roll a 2. The other **five** rolls (1, 3, 4, 5, and 6) are ways it does *not* happen.

The odds of rolling a 2 on a roll of a number cube are 1:5.

4 Drawing a blue marble from a bag with 2 blue, 5 red, and 4 white marbles.

There are two ways for the event to happen—the 2 blue marbles. The other 9 marbles are ways it does not happen.

The odds of drawing a blue marble are 2:9.

Try It

Give the odds of each event.

a. Getting heads on the toss of a coin.

b. Getting a 2 or a 5 on a roll of a number cube.

> ► **History Link**
>
> There have been 44 vice presidents of the United States before Al Gore. So far, the odds that a vice president will eventually become president are 14:30.

In some games, both players start with equal forces. In others, like the South Asian game of Cows and Leopards, one player starts at a disadvantage.

A game where all players have the same odds of winning is a **fair game**.

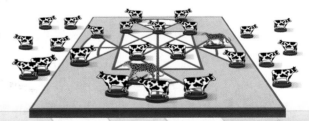

GO BACK 7 SPACES

LOSE A TURN

Examples

For each game described, give each player's odds of winning. Then tell whether the game is fair.

5 Alice, Bess, Cedric, and Deepak take turns spinning the spinner shown. Each player gets a point if the letter the spinner lands on matches the initial of his or her name.

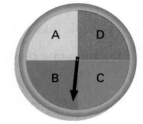

On any spin, each player has 1:3 odds of getting a point. The game is fair.

6 Clarissa, Melissa, and Narissa are playing a number cube game. Clarissa gets a point every time a 1 is rolled, Melissa gets a point for any even number, and Narissa gets a point for a 3 or a 5.

The table shows the odds for each player. The game is not fair.

Player	Winning Roll(s)	Non-winning Roll(s)	Odds
Clarissa	1	2, 3, 4, 5, 6	1:5
Melissa	2, 4, 6	1, 3, 5	3:3
Narissa	3, 5	1, 2, 4, 6	2:4

Try It

For each game described, give each player's odds of winning. Then tell whether the game is fair.

a. Alex and Bronwyn play a number cube game. Alex gets a point for each odd number rolled, Bronwyn gets a point for each even number.

b. Two players spin the spinner shown. Player A gets a point if the spinner lands in a shaded area; player B gets a point if it lands in an unshaded area.

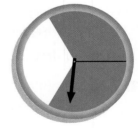

c. Evan rolls a number cube. He gets a point if the number he rolls is even, Primo gets a point if it is prime, and Trace gets a point if the number is divisible by 3.

Check | Your Understanding

1. If the two numbers given in an odds ratio are equal, how would you describe the chances of an event?

2. Is an event more likely if its odds are 9:2 or 2:9? Explain.

Practice and Apply

1. **Getting Started** Follow the steps to find the odds of rolling a 5 or a 6 on a number cube.

   a. Decide how many ways the event you are looking for can happen.

   b. Decide how many ways the event can *not* happen.

   c. Write the ratio of the number in **a** to the number in **b**. This ratio represents the odds of rolling a 5 or a 6.

Name possible outcomes for each experiment.

2. Tossing a coin

3. Spinning the spinner at the right

4. Putting a coin into a vending machine and pressing a button

Give the odds of each event.

5. Getting tails on the toss of a coin

6. Getting a number greater than or equal to 2 on a roll of a number cube

7. Drawing a green marble from a bag with 2 green and 3 red marbles

8. Drawing a vowel out of a bag containing 3 tiles lettered A, B, and C

9. **Social Studies** In the 1992 presidential election, about 104 million of the 170 million people of voting age in the United States went to the polls. What were the odds of a voting-age person going to the polls in 1992?

The game of Rummikub® contains 13 red tiles, 13 blue tiles, 13 black tiles, 13 orange tiles, and 2 jokers. The red, blue, black, and orange tiles are numbered 1–13. If you choose one Rummikub tile, what are the odds that it is:

10. Blue?

11. A joker?

12. Numbered 4?

13. Blue or orange?

14. Not a joker?

15. A multiple of 3?

GO BACK 7 SPACES

LOSE A TURN

Logic For each game described, give each player's odds of winning. Then tell whether the game is fair.

16. Toss a coin. Player A gets a point for heads; player B, for tails.

17. Roll a number cube. Player A gets a point for a 1, player B gets a point for 2, 3, 4, or 5, and player C gets a point for 6.

18. **Test Prep** What are the odds of rolling a 3 or a 4 on a number cube?

    Ⓐ 1:3   Ⓑ 2:4   Ⓒ 3:4   Ⓓ 4:2

Problem Solving and Reasoning

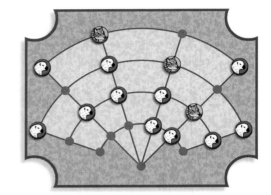

19. **Journal** Lambs and Tigers is a game played in India. One player has 3 pieces called tigers, and the other has 15 lambs. Tigers remove lambs by jumping them, and lambs remove tigers by trapping them. Is this likely to be a fair game? Why or why not?

20. **Communicate** Choose a page from a book or newspaper. Look at the first 50 letters that appear on the page.

   a. How many of the letters are vowels? How many are consonants?

   b. Based on your results, what are the odds that a letter chosen at random is a vowel? A consonant?

   c. Do you think your results would be similar for any language? Explain.

21. **Critical Thinking** This spinner is used in a game where one team is yellow and one is green. If the spinner lands on yellow, the yellow team gets 6 points. If it lands on green, the green team gets 2 points. The first team to reach 6000 points wins. Is this a fair game? Justify your answer.

Mixed Review

Find the area of each circle given its radius or diameter. Use $\pi \approx 3.14$, and round answers to the nearest tenth. *[Lesson 11-7]*

22.

11 mm

23.

15 in.

24.

5.2 cm

25.

1 m

26. Find the surface area of a cylinder whose height is 12 cm and radius is 8 cm. Use $\pi \approx 3.14$, and round your answer to the nearest tenth. *[Lesson 11-8]*

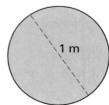

Probability

▶ **Lesson Link**   You've used odds to describe the likelihood of an event. Now you'll use *probability* to describe how likely an event is to happen. ◀

Explore   Measuring Likelihood

A Likely Story?

1. Sketch a "likelihood line" like the one shown.

Impossible   Certain

2. Use your intuition to estimate the likelihood of each event below. Place each event on the likelihood line.

  a. Getting a head on a coin toss

  b. Getting a 3 on a roll of a number cube

  c. Getting either a head or a tail on a coin toss

  d. Drawing a red marble out of a bag full of green and white marbles

  e. That tomorrow will be a sunny day

  f. Getting an odd number on a roll of a number cube

  g. That you will see a train this week

  h. That you will travel to the moon during your lifetime

3. Explain how you placed these events on the line. Did you place any of the events at the halfway point? If so, which one(s), and why?

You'll Learn ...

■ to find the probability of an event

... How It's Used

Geologists use probabilities to describe the likelihood that an earthquake will occur on a fault within a certain number of years.

Vocabulary

probability

Learn   Probability

When you play a game that involves chance, you think about how likely different events are. Should you risk rolling the dice once more if a total of 12 will put you in jail? What's the chance that the spinner will land on "Lose a Turn"?

You can use probability to assign numbers to these chances.

GO BACK 7 SPACES

LOSE A TURN

The **probability** of an event compares the number of ways it can occur to the number of possible outcomes. Expressed as a fraction:

$$\text{Probability(event)} = \frac{\text{number of ways the event can happen}}{\text{number of possible outcomes}}$$

A probability can also be expressed as a percent, a decimal, or a ratio.

Examples

Give the probability of each event as a fraction, a percent, and a decimal.

1 Rolling an even number on a number cube.

This event can happen three ways: by rolling a 2, 4, or 6. There are six outcomes (the numbers 1–6).

$P(\text{even number})$ is $\frac{3}{6} = \frac{1}{2} = 50\% = 0.5$.

2 Spinning "Lose a Turn" on the spinner at the right.

One of the four equal-sized sectors represents "Lose a Turn."

$P(\text{Lose a Turn})$ is $\frac{1}{4} = 25\% = 0.25$.

3 *Not* spinning "Lose a Turn" on the spinner.

Three of the four sectors do *not* represent "Lose a Turn."

The probability of not spinning "Lose a Turn" is $\frac{3}{4} = 75\% = 0.75$.

Try It

Give the probability of each event as a fraction, a percent, and a decimal.

a. Spinning "Bankrupt" on the spinner at right

b. Rolling a prime number on a number cube

c. Pulling a pink jelly bean out of a bag with 3 pink ones, 1 yellow one, 2 purple ones, and 4 green ones

In Examples 2 and 3, notice that the probabilities that an event *does* happen and that it does *not* happen added up to 1 (100%). Since an event either happens or it doesn't, this is always true.

You can use the odds of an event to find its probability and vice versa.

Examples

4 If the odds of an event are 3:10, what is its probability?

The first number in the odds tells us that the event can happen in 3 ways. The second number tells us that it can *not* happen in 10 ways. So there are $3 + 10 = 13$ possible outcomes.

The probability of the event is $\frac{3}{13}$.

5 In the game of Scrabble®, players draw lettered tiles out of a bag. Of the 100 tiles, 42 are vowels. What is the probability that the first letter drawn is a vowel? What are the odds?

Since 42 of the 100 tiles are vowels, P(vowel) is $\frac{42}{100}$. Since $100 - 42 = 58$, 58 of the tiles are *not* vowels, and the odds of drawing a vowel are 42:58.

Try It

a. If the odds of an event are 7:1, what is its probability?

b. In Scrabble, there is only one Z tile. What is the probability that the first tile drawn is the Z? What are the odds?

If there is no way an event can happen, its probability is 0. If an event is certain to happen, its probability is 1.

Probabilities

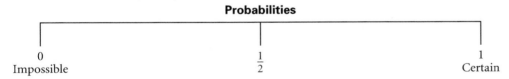

| 0 | $\frac{1}{2}$ | 1 |
| Impossible | | Certain |

Example 6

Give the probability that a roll of a typical number cube comes up π.

Since π does not appear on a typical number cube, $P(\pi) = 0$.

Check Your Understanding

1. Why is the sum of the probability that an event happens and the probability that it does *not* happen always equal to 100%?

2. Explain how you can find the odds of an event if you know its probability. Why does your method work?

GO BACK 7 SPACES

LOSE A TURN

Practice and Apply

1. **Getting Started** Follow the steps to find the probability of drawing a red marble out of a bag containing 3 red, 5 blue, and 4 yellow marbles.

   a. Find the total number of marbles.

   b. Write a fraction with the number of red marbles in the numerator and the total number of marbles in the denominator.

   c. Rewrite the fraction in lowest terms.

Give the probability of each event as a fraction, a percent, and a decimal.

2. Rolling a 1, 3, 4, or 5 on a number cube

3. Spinning "Spin Again" on the spinner at right

4. Drawing a purple marble from a bag containing:

   a. 2 yellow, 4 purple, and 1 red marble

   b. 5 purple marbles

   c. 2 pink marbles

5. **Data** The circle graph shows commuting habits of 26- to 44-year-olds. What is the probability that a randomly selected person in this age group:

   a. Drives alone to work

   b. Does *not* drive alone

   c. Uses either public transit or carpools

Commuting boom

About 60 million baby boomers (26 to 44 years old) commute to work, averaging 22 minutes of travel. Percent who:

Use other means 1.2%
Use public transit 5.2%
Drive alone 75.1%
Carpool 13.2%
Walk/work at home 5.3%

Copy and complete the table.

	Probability of Event	Probability That Event Does Not Happen	Odds of Event
6.	$\frac{1}{4}$		
7.	$\frac{1}{8}$		
8.			4:6
9.		$\frac{1}{2}$	

PRACTICE 12-5

10. In Yahtzee®, players have 3 turns to roll any or all of 5 number cubes. The highest-scoring result is a Yahtzee, where all 5 dice have the same number. Suppose 4 of the cubes show a 4, and you roll the fifth cube again. What is the probability that you get a Yahtzee on this roll?

Give the probability that corresponds to each of the odds.

11. 1:1   **12.** 3:2   **13.** 1:7   **14.** 11:9   **15.** 55:44

Assume you are drawing the first tile in a Scrabble® game. Use the table to find each probability. Express each as a percent.

16. $P(E)$ **17.** $P(Q)$

18. $P(\text{blank})$ **19.** $P(\text{consonant})$

20. **Test Prep** Which of these odds means the same thing as a probability of 25%?

   Ⓐ 1:5   Ⓑ 1:4   Ⓒ 1:3   Ⓓ 1:2

Tile	Number	Tile	Number	Tile	Number
A	9	J	1	S	4
B	2	K	1	T	6
C	2	L	4	U	4
D	4	M	2	V	2
E	12	N	6	W	2
F	2	O	8	X	1
G	3	P	2	Y	2
H	2	Q	1	Z	1
I	9	R	6	Blank	2

Problem Solving and Reasoning

21. **Critical Thinking** Name an event that has a probability of 1 and another that has a probability of 0.

22. **Communicate** Tell whether you would express each probability as a fraction, a decimal, or a percent. Explain each answer.

  a. The probability that you will catch the flu this winter

  b. The probability that you will roll a 1 or a 3 on a number cube

  c. The probability that it will rain tomorrow

Mixed Review

Find the volume of each cylinder. Use $\pi \approx 3.14$ and round answers to the nearest tenth. *[Lesson 11-9]*

23.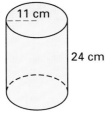
11 cm, 24 cm

24.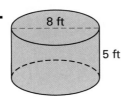
8 ft, 5 ft

25.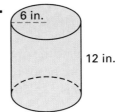
6 in., 12 in.

26.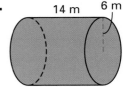
14 m, 6 m

Write a rule for each translation. *[Lesson 11-10]*

27. Right 4, down 6   **28.** Right 2, up 7   **29.** Left 0.2, up 7   **30.** Up 6

Experimental Probability

You'll Learn ...

- to use experimental probability to estimate probabilities

- to find probabilities involving geometric figures

... How It's Used

A batting average is the experimental probability that the batter will get a hit.

Vocabulary

theoretical probability

experimental probability

geometric probability

▶ **Lesson Link** You've computed the probabilities of many different events. Now you'll use probability experiments to estimate the probability of an event. ◀

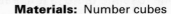

Explore **Experimental Probability**

Rolling Right Along

Materials: Number cubes

1. Write down the possible outcomes for a roll of a number cube. What is the probability of rolling a 6? Of rolling any even number? Express your probabilities as percents.

2. Roll a number cube 12 times. Record your results. What percent of the rolls came up 6? What percent came up even? Are these percents equal to the probabilities you found in Step 1?

3. Roll the number cube 12 more times. Compute the percent of sixes and of even rolls for all 24 rolls. Compare these percents to the probabilities of a 6 and of an even number. What do you notice? What changes do you see from your Step 2 results?

4. Combine the results for your 24 rolls with those of another student. How do the combined results compare to the probabilities?

5. What do you think would give percents closer to the true probabilities, rolling a number cube 6 times or rolling a number cube 600 times? Explain.

Learn **Experimental Probability**

To calculate the probability that a tossed coin lands heads, you don't need to toss a coin. Since heads represents one out of the two sides, the **theoretical probability** of heads is $\frac{1}{2} = 50\%$.

However, while mathematician John Kerrich was a prisoner of war during World War II, he tossed a coin 10,000 times and got 5,067 heads. His **experimental probability** of heads was $\frac{\text{number of heads}}{\text{number of tosses}} = \frac{5{,}067}{10{,}000} = 50.67\%$.

It's easy to find the probability of tossing heads or tails. But other theoretical probabilities are difficult—or even impossible—to calculate. In these cases, we may be able to estimate the probability by doing an experiment.

Example 1

Of Kerrich's first 10 coin tosses, 6 were tails. What is the experimental probability of tails for these tosses? Express the answer as a decimal.

The experimental probability is $\dfrac{\text{number of tails}}{\text{total number of tosses}} = \dfrac{6}{10} = 0.6$.

Since there are 6 numbers on a number cube, the Counting Principle tells us that there are $6 \cdot 6 = 36$ possible outcomes for a roll of two cubes, as shown.

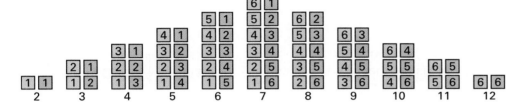

Example 2

In Monopoly®, one way to get out of jail is to roll a "double" with two number cubes. Suppose you roll a pair of number cubes 24 times and get doubles 6 times. What is the experimental probability of getting doubles? Compare this to the theoretical probability of getting doubles.

Experimental probability $= \dfrac{\text{number of doubles}}{\text{number of rolls}} = \dfrac{6}{24} = \dfrac{1}{4}$

From the chart: Theoretical probability $= \dfrac{\text{ways a double can happen}}{\text{number of outcomes}} = \dfrac{6}{36} = \dfrac{1}{6}$

The experimental probability of $\dfrac{1}{4}$ is larger than the theoretical probability of $\dfrac{1}{6}$.

Try It

a. If you drop a piece of bread with jelly on one side 100 times, and it lands "jelly side down" 58 times, what is the experimental probability of "jelly side down"? Express your answer as a decimal.

b. Suppose you roll a pair of number cubes 72 times and get a sum of 7 eight of those times. What is the experimental probability of a sum of 7? Use the figure above to compare this to the theoretical probability of this sum.

► **Science Link**

According to some geologists, there is a 50% probability of a strong earthquake (Richter scale magnitude of 6 or more) on the New Madrid fault in Missouri before the year 2000.

When a probability involves a geometric figure, you can find the theoretical probability by comparing areas, perimeters, or other measurements. A probability calculated in this way is called a **geometric probability**.

Examples

3 What is the geometric probability that a coin tossed randomly onto this "chessboard" lands mostly on a red square?

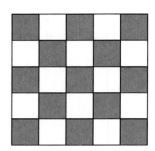

$$P(\text{red}) = \frac{\text{number of red squares}}{\text{total number of squares}} = \frac{13}{25}$$

4 In the carnival game shown, you win a prize if you toss a marker onto the shaded area of the square table. While Saskia watches, 15 out of 80 tosses win a prize.

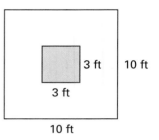

a. If the markers land randomly on the table, what is the theoretical probability of winning a prize? Express your answer as a percent.

The area of the shaded region is $3^2 = 9$ ft^2, and the area of the table is $10^2 = 100$ ft^2.

The theoretical probability of winning is $\dfrac{\text{area of winning region}}{\text{total area}} = \dfrac{9}{100} = 9\%$.

b. What is the experimental probability of winning a prize?

The experimental probability of winning is $\dfrac{\text{games won}}{\text{total games}} = \dfrac{15}{80} = 18.75\%$.

Try It

If a dart lands randomly on this "dart board," what is the theoretical probability that it lands in the triangular region?

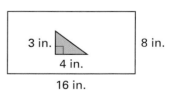

Check | Your Understanding

1. Is the experimental probability of an event always the same? Explain.

2. What would you think if the experimental probability for a coin toss turned out to be very different from its theoretical probability?

3. In Example 4, why do you think the experimental probability of winning the game might have been higher than the theoretical probability?

Practice and Apply

1. **Getting Started** A dart lands randomly on the dart board shown. Follow the steps to find the geometric probability that the dart lands in the shaded area.

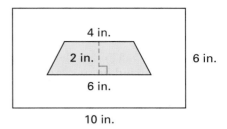
4 in.
2 in.
6 in.
6 in.
10 in.

a. Find the area of the shaded region. Use the area formula for a trapezoid.

b. Find the area of the dart board. Use the area formula for a rectangle.

c. Write a fraction with the area of the shaded region in the numerator and the area of the entire dart board in the denominator. Rewrite the fraction in lowest terms.

The tally sheet shows the results for several rolls of two number cubes. Use the sheet to find the experimental probability of each event.

Roll	Frequency
2	2
3	5
4	9
5	8
6	10
7	15
8	7
9	8
10	5
11	2
12	1

2. Rolling a 3

3. Rolling a 4

4. Rolling a 6

5. Rolling a 7

6. Rolling an 8

7. Rolling a 12

8–13. Use the figure on page 655 to find the *theoretical* probability of each event in Exercises 2–7. Compare the probabilities.

14. **Test Prep** You roll a pair of number cubes 36 times and roll a sum of 8 five times. How does the experimental probability of rolling a sum of 8 compare to the theoretical probability?

Ⓐ Less than

Ⓑ Equal to

Ⓒ Greater than

Ⓓ Not enough information

15. **History** Over the years, many cultures have used cowrie shells as a kind of dice. African cultures have used them in games of chance, and they were the dice in early versions of the Indian game of Pachisi. If a cowrie shell lands "mouth up" in 48 of 80 tosses, what is the experimental probability of "mouth up" for a cowrie shell? Express your answer as a percent.

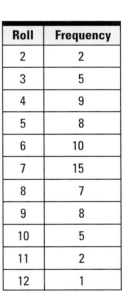
PRACTICE 12-6

GO BACK 7 SPACES

LOSE A TURN

16. A fly lands on the checkered picnic blanket shown. What is the theoretical probability that it lands on a green square?

17. An experimental probability is an estimate of the true probability of an event. Would you be more confident of an experimental probability that came from 10 trials or 1000 trials? Explain.

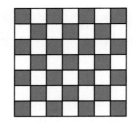

In a coin toss game, you earn points for landing on the shaded figures. Assume coins land randomly in the large square. What is the probability that a coin:

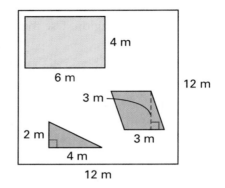

18. Lands on the shaded rectangle?

19. Lands on the non-rectangular parallelogram?

20. Lands on the right triangle?

Problem Solving and Reasoning

21. Choose a Strategy Fire fighting is an occupation with a high probability of injury. For every fire fighter who is injured, 3.6 are not.

   a. Do these numbers represent an experimental or a theoretical probability?

   b. Create a data set that would give this probability of injury. Explain how you created the data set.

22. [Journal] Find the theoretical probability of an event. Then design an experiment, and calculate an experimental probability for the event. Compare your findings.

Problem Solving

STRATEGIES

• Look for a Pattern
• Make an Organized List
• Make a Table
• Guess and Check
• Work Backward
• Use Logical Reasoning
• Draw a Diagram
• Solve a Simpler Problem

Mixed Review

Decide whether each figure has line symmetry. If it does, copy the figure and draw and number the lines of symmetry. *[Lesson 11-11]*

23. Isosceles right triangle

24. Regular pentagon

25. Isosceles trapezoid

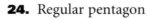

26. Suppose a jacket comes in 3 colors, 2 styles, and 5 sizes. Use the Counting Principle to find the number of different jackets. *[Lesson 12-1]*

Independent and Dependent Events

▶ **Lesson Link**   You've found probabilities for many different types of events. Now you'll use these skills to help you find the probability that *two* particular things will happen. ◀

Explore   Independent and Dependent Events

Materials: Number cubes

Eight Is for Elephant

An ancient African dice game matches numbers with animals. Suppose that a sum of 8 on a roll of two cubes stands for "elephant."

Use experimental probability to investigate each question. Roll the number cube 20 times for each experiment.

1. What is the probability that you roll "elephant" on a roll of the cubes?

2. Suppose you roll the cubes one at a time. If you roll a 1 on the first cube, what is the probability of "elephant"? Explain how you know.

3. If you roll a 4 on the first cube, what is the probability of "elephant"? Explain.

4. If your answers for Steps 1–3 were the same, explain why this makes sense. If not, explain why you think the probabilities are different.

You'll Learn ...

■ to decide whether two events are dependent or independent

■ to find probabilities of dependent and independent events

... How It's Used

Genetic researchers use dependent probabilities when they identify genes causing diseases such as cystic fibrosis.

Vocabulary

independent events

dependent events

compound event

sample space

Learn   Independent and Dependent Events

If a coin lands heads several times in a row, many people think that the probability of heads on the next toss will be less than 50%. But even though it has a head, a coin doesn't have a memory! The probability of the next toss landing heads is still $\frac{1}{2}$.

When the outcome of one event does not change the probability of another, the events are **independent** . Two coin tosses are independent, since the result of the first toss doesn't affect the second.

Now, how did I land the last time?

GO BACK 7 SPACES

LOSE A TURN

Suppose there are 11 jellybeans in a bag, and 2 are purple. If you take a jellybean out of the bag and don't put it back, you change the probability of getting a purple jellybean on the next draw.

The two draws of a jellybean are **dependent events** —the probability of the second depends on the results of the first.

P (purple) = $\frac{2}{11}$ Take one out P (purple) = $\frac{1}{10}$

Examples

Tell whether the events are dependent or independent.

1 Rolling an even number on the first roll of a number cube, then rolling an odd number on the second.

The first roll does not affect the second. The events are independent.

2 Being sick on Monday, then being sick on Tuesday.

If you are sick one day, you are more likely than usual to be sick the next. The events are dependent.

Study TIP

When deciding whether two events are dependent, decide whether knowing the results of the first would help predict the results of the second.

A **compound event** is made up of two or more individual events. To find the **sample space**, or set of all possible outcomes, for a compound event, make an organized list of all the possibilities for each event.

Examples

3 A marble bag holds 1 red marble and 3 green marbles. Give the sample space for drawing two marbles if you replace the first.

The possibilities for the first draw are red and green. The possibilities for the second are also red and green.

The sample space is (red, red), (red, green), (green, red), and (green, green).

4 To win a game, you must roll a 5 on a number cube, then spin "Return to Base" on the spinner. Use the Counting Principle to determine the probability you will win the game.

There are 6 possible rolls of the cube, and 4 equal sectors on the spinner. According to the Counting Principle, there are $6 \cdot 4 = 24$ possible outcomes. Only 1 of those 24 is the winning combination.

The probability that you will win is $\frac{1}{24}$.

In Example 4, notice that $P(5) = \frac{1}{6}$ and $P(\text{Return to Base}) = \frac{1}{4}$. The product $\frac{1}{6} \times \frac{1}{4}$ equals $\frac{1}{24}$, which is the probability that these independent events *both* happen.

PROBABILITY OF TWO INDEPENDENT EVENTS

The probability that two independent events A and B both happen is given by:

$P(A, B) = P(A) \times P(B)$.

Examples

5 For a coin toss and a roll of a number cube, find $P(\text{heads}, 4)$.

The events are independent. $P(\text{heads}) = \frac{1}{2}$, and $P(4) = \frac{1}{6}$.

Therefore, $P(\text{heads}, 4) = \frac{1}{2} \times \frac{1}{6} = \frac{1}{12}$.

6 Cheryl is drawing the first 2 tiles in a Scrabble® game. What is the probability that both are A's? (Note: 9 of the 100 tiles are A's.)

The first draw changes the number of tiles left, and may change the number of A's, so the events are dependent.

The probability of an A on the first draw is $\frac{9}{100}$. The probability of getting an A on the second draw *after* getting an A on the first is $\frac{8}{99}$, since there are 8 A's and 99 tiles left after the first A is drawn.

$P(A, \text{then } A) = \frac{9}{100} \times \frac{8}{99} = \frac{72}{9900} = \frac{2}{275}$.

> ▶ **Social Studies Link**
>
> Once a person in the United States has been in prison, the probability that he or she will return to jail at some time is greater than 60%.

Try It

a. Find the sample space for the marble bag in Example 3 if you do *not* replace the first marble.

b. For a coin toss and a spin of the spinner, find $P(\text{tails, red})$.

c. A drawer contains 8 black socks and 8 blue socks. If you draw 2 socks out of the drawer in the dark, what is the probability that both are blue?

Check | Your Understanding

1. Explain the difference between dependent and independent events.

2. Give two ways to find the probability of two independent events.

Practice and Apply

1. **Getting Started** Five red cubes and five green cubes are in a bag. Follow the steps to find *P*(green, green)—the probability that you pull two green cubes out of the bag in a row.

    a. What is the probability that the first cube taken from the bag is green?

    b. After a green cube is taken out of the bag, how many green cubes are left? How many cubes are left all together?

    c. What is the probability that the second cube taken from the bag is green?

    d. Find the product of your answers from **a** and **c.** Write your answer in lowest terms.

Tell whether the events are dependent or independent.

2. One tossed coin landing heads and the next landing tails

3. Rolling two sixes in a row on a number cube

4. Being the tallest person in your class one year, then being the tallest again the next year

Exercises 5–7 refer to rolling a number cube, then spinning the spinner shown. Find each probability.

5. *P*(rolling a 2, spinning an A)

6. *P*(rolling an even number, spinning a vowel)

7. *P*(rolling a number less than 3, spinning a consonant)

8. **Social Studies** During Hanukkah, children play with a *dreidel*. The dreidel has four sides, with the Hebrew letters that correspond to the letters N, G, S, and H. The children spin the dreidel like a top, and the letter that comes up determines the result for each turn.

    a. Are the spins of a dreidel dependent or independent events?

    b. What is the probability of spinning 2 Hs in a row?

9. **Science** Suppose the weather report says there is a 25% chance of rain for the next two days.

    a. If the events are independent, what is the probability that it rains *both* days?

    b. Do you think these events are actually independent? Explain why or why not.

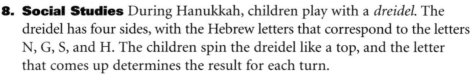

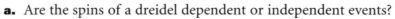

POINT
BONUS

Give the sample space for each compound event.

10. A toss of a coin and a roll of a number cube.

11. Two draws of a marble from a bag with 3 red marbles, 2 blue marbles, and 1 yellow marble. The first marble is not replaced before the second draw.

12. Problem Solving A teacher has students change desks every month. To do this, he has students draw desk numbers from a hat. You and your best friend draw the first two numbers. If there are 20 desks, what is the probability that you will choose desk 1 and she will choose desk 2?

Problem Solving TIP

Cutting out slips of paper and acting out the draws may help you understand the problem better.

13. **Test Prep** A spinner is divided into five equal sections, numbered 1 through 5. What is the probability of spinning two 5s in a row?

Ⓐ $\frac{1}{5}$ Ⓑ $\frac{1}{10}$ Ⓒ $\frac{1}{15}$ Ⓓ $\frac{1}{25}$

Problem Solving and Reasoning

14. **Journal** Suppose you toss a coin several times.

a. What is the theoretical probability that the first two tosses land heads? Toss coins to find an experimental probability for this event. Conduct at least 20 experiments. How do your experimental results compare to the theoretical probability?

b. What is the theoretical probability that the first three tosses land heads? The first four?

c. What is the theoretical probability of *n* heads in a row? Explain your thinking.

15. **Critical Thinking** The circle graphs show results of a survey by the American Games Association. If the preferences for game type and group size are independent, what is the probability that a person prefers solitaire card games? Large group word games?

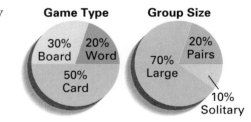

Game Type
30% Board 20% Word 50% Card

Group Size
70% Large 20% Pairs 10% Solitary

Mixed Review

16. This summer, you plan to visit Austin, Houston, and San Antonio, Texas. In how many different orders can you visit those cities? *[Lesson 12-2]*

You are joining a book club. You get free books for joining the club. How many choices do you have in each situation? *[Lesson 12-3]*

17. If you can choose 2 out of 4 books

18. If you can choose 3 out of 4 books

GO BACK 7 SPACES

LOSE A TURN

TECHNOLOGY

Using a Graphing Calculator • Simulations with Random Numbers

Problem: Washington, DC, has about 124 days with precipitation each year. How can you estimate the probability that there will be precipitation in a given week?

You can use a graphing or scientific calculator to answer this question.

1 Find the probability of precipitation on a particular day and express the answer as a decimal. The probability is $\frac{124}{365} \approx 0.34$.

2 Press the MATH button on your graphing calculator, then choose PRB and Rand.

3 When you press ENTER twice, you get a random number between 0 and 1. If this number is less than 0.34, it represents a day with precipitation. (The number on the screen does not, since it is greater than 0.34.)

4 Pressing ENTER six more times gives you a whole "week." Determine whether there was precipitation during the week, and record this result. (In the week modeled here there was precipitation on days 4 and 6.)

5 Generate several more weeks. Record whether or not it rained in each one.

Solution: To estimate the probability of precipitation in a given week, divide the number of weeks with rain in your simulation by the total number of weeks.

TRY IT

a. Belem, Brazil, has about 251 days of rain each year. Use random numbers to estimate the probability that it doesn't rain for 3 consecutive days in Belem.

b. Suppose the probability that a baseball player gets a hit is 0.310. Use random numbers to estimate the probability that he gets two hits in a row.

ON YOUR OWN

▶ Suppose you wanted to use random numbers to simulate spins of a spinner with numbers from 0 to 9. How could you do this?

Section 12B Connect

You've investigated odds, fair games, and several ways to find probabilities. Now you'll combine those skills to design a game of your own.

Do NOT Pass Go!

Materials: Compass, Protractor, Cardboard, Pushpin, Paper clip, Number cubes

In this investigation, you'll make a game of your own. If you choose to use a spinner in your game, here's how you can make one.

- Use a compass to draw a circle.

- Decide how many sectors you want your spinner to have. Use your protractor to measure the central angles, then draw the sectors.

- Put the paper with your circle on top of the cardboard, and place the paper clip over the center of the circle. Then push the pushpin into the center of the circle so the clip can be used as a spinner.

1. Use what you've learned about probability to design a game of chance. Your game must use at least two different ways to generate outcomes (for instance, a coin and a number cube). Once you've come up with a game you like, play a few rounds to see if any changes are needed.

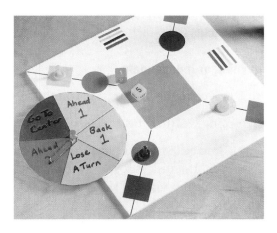

2. Is your game a fair game? Explain why or why not.

3. Does your game involve dependent events? If it does, tell what they are.

4. Identify at least two events that could happen in your game. Find the probability of each of these events. Explain how you found each probability.

Section 12B Review

Name the possible outcomes for each experiment.

1. Spinning a spinner whose sectors are numbered 1 through 10.

2. Rolling two number cubes and finding the sum of the two numbers.

Give the odds of each event.

3. Rolling a number less than or equal to 4 on a number cube.

4. Spinning red on the spinner at the right.

5. **Journal** In a game, player A gets a point if a tossed coin lands heads and the roll of a number cube is even. Player B gets a point if the tossed coin lands tails and the roll is odd. Otherwise, neither player gets a point. Is this game fair? Explain why or why not.

A bag contains 5 red, 3 blue, and 2 yellow marbles. Give the probability of each event as a fraction, a percent, and a decimal. (Round answers if necessary.)

6. P(red) **7.** P(blue) **8.** P(orange) **9.** P(*not* yellow)

10. If you draw two marbles out of the bag, what is P(blue, blue)? Assume you don't put the first marble back.

Tell whether the events are dependent or independent.

11. Getting heads on the first toss of a coin, then getting tails on the second.

12. Sunny weather one day, then rainy weather the next.

13. **Social Studies** A Hawaiian game called Lu-Lu uses disks of volcanic stone that are marked on one side. If a disk is tossed twice, what is the probability that both tosses land on the marked side?

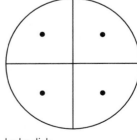

Lu-Lu disk

Test Prep

When you're asked to find the odds of an event on a multiple choice test, remember that the second number in the ratio represents the number of ways it can *not* happen, not the total number of possible outcomes.

14. What are the odds of rolling a sum of 12 on two number cubes?

ⓐ 1:36 ⓑ 1:35 ⓒ 2:12 ⓓ 12:2

Venn Diagrams and If-Then Statements

A Venn diagram shows relationships between sets of items, or *elements*.

If regions in a Venn diagram do not overlap, they have no common elements.

Overlapping regions contain elements that are in both sets. The overlapping region in this Venn diagram contains bats, since bats are mammals that fly.

If one region contains another, all elements in the smaller region also belong in the larger. The diagram shows that *if* a figure is a triangle, *then* it is also a polygon.

If-then statements like the one above are an important part of the language of logic. The "if" part of an if-then statement is its *hypothesis*, and the "then" part is its *conclusion*. For the statement to be true, the conclusion must be true whenever the hypothesis is true.

True or false? If a figure is a square, then it is a rectangle. The statement is true. Suppose a figure is a square. The conclusion *must* be true, since all squares have four sides and four right angles. In the Venn diagram, the oval that shows the hypothesis "fits" the conclusion.

True or false? If an animal is a bird, then it can fly. This statement is false. Some types of birds cannot fly. In the Venn diagram, the oval representing the hypothesis goes outside the oval that shows the conclusion.

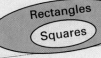

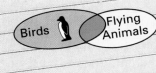

Try It

Draw a Venn diagram to show the relationships between:

1. Triangles and squares
2. Lions, bears, and animals

Explain whether each if-then statement is true or false. Draw a Venn diagram.

3. If an angle measures 30°, then it is acute.
4. If a vehicle has four wheels, then it is a car.

Graphic Organizer

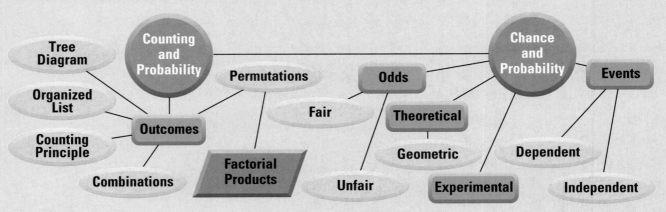

Section 12A Counting

Summary

- You can count the possible **outcomes** for a series of choices by making an organized list, making a **tree diagram,** or using the **Counting Principle.**

- A **permutation** is the number of possible arrangements of a collection of items. You can use the Counting Principle or **factorials** to count permutations.

- A **combination** is a selection of items where the order does not matter.

Review

1. For lunch, Jo's Restaurant offers 3 soups, 4 main courses, and 5 desserts. Use the Counting Principle to find the number of different lunches consisting of soup, main course, and dessert.

2. A used-music store has separate bins for CDs and cassettes in each category: jazz, popular, classical, and other. Make a tree diagram to show how many bins the store needs.

3. Fifth State Bank offers 3 different checking accounts and 5 different savings accounts. How many ways are there to open both a checking account and a savings account?

4. A club is electing a president, vice president, secretary, and treasurer. Only Jed, Karl, Lori, and Marti are eligible to hold office. In how many ways can the officers be chosen?

5. List all the possible orderings of the letters T, U, and V, without repeating letters.

6. Reggie has 7 books he intends to read. How many different ways can he choose 2 of the books to take on a vacation?

Summary

- In probability, an **experiment** is anything that involves chance. The possible results of an experiment are outcomes. An **event** is any outcome (or set of outcomes) we are interested in.

- The **odds** of an event are the ratio of the number of ways the event can happen to the number of ways it can fail to happen.

- In a **fair** game, all players have the same odds of winning.

- The **probability,** or **theoretical probability,** of an event is given by
$$\text{Probability(event)} = \frac{\text{number of ways the event can happen}}{\text{number of possible outcomes}}.$$ An impossible event has probability 0. An event that is certain to happen has probability 1.

- The **experimental probability** of an event is the number of times the event occurred divided by the number of times the experiment was carried out.

- When the occurrence of one event does not change the probability of another, the events are **independent**. Otherwise, they are **dependent**.

Review

7. A bag contains 5 red marbles and 3 blue marbles. A marble is chosen at random. Find the odds that the marble is red.

8. A spinner has 7 equal sections, numbered 1 to 7. Melanie wins if an odd number is spun, and Nathan wins if an even number is spun. Give each player's odds of winning. Then determine whether the game is fair.

9. A number cube is rolled. Find the probability of rolling a number:

   a. Less than 5   **b.** *Not* less than 5

10. Use the table on page 653 to find the probability of choosing a U, V, or W when drawing the first tile in a Scrabble® game. Express your answer as a percent.

11. Paula flipped a coin 25 times and got heads 14 times. Find the experimental probability of tails.

12. A fly lands on the dart board. What is the probability that it lands in the shaded region?

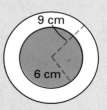

13. A number cube is rolled twice. What is the probability of getting a 5 on the first roll, then an even number on the second?

14. Sandy draws 2 marbles from a bag with 5 green and 6 black marbles. What is the probability that both are green?

1. Crafty Computer Company offers a choice of 4 processors, 3 hard drives, and 3 installed software packages. Use the Counting Principle to find the number of different computers.

2. A cafeteria's lunch special includes a choice of soup or salad; hamburger, chicken, or vegetable casserole; and fruit juice or soda. Make a tree diagram to show the number of ways to order a lunch special. How many outcomes are there?

3. Calculate 6!.

4. Pearl, Quan, Raul, Sally, and Tim need to line up in single file to buy movie tickets. In how many different orders can they line up?

5. Vanilla Heaven offers only one flavor of ice cream, but customers can choose any 3 of 4 available toppings. How many different combinations of 3 toppings are there?

6. A bag contains 3 yellow marbles, 4 purple marbles, and 7 clear marbles. Give the possible outcomes for drawing 1 marble.

7. In a game, a number cube is rolled. Xien wins if a 1 or a 3 is rolled; Yoshi wins if a 2 or a 6 is rolled; and Zelda wins if a 4 or a 5 is rolled. Give each player's odds of winning. Then tell if the game is fair.

8. Sam drew a Scrabble® tile from a bag 100 times, replacing his selection each time. If his draws included 10 A's, 3 B's, and 2 C's, what was the experimental probability of drawing an A, B, or C?

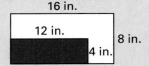

9. A coin lands randomly on the board shown. Find the probability that it lands in the shaded region.

10. Hans drew a marble from the bag described in Exercise 6. He then drew another one without replacing the first. Are his results for the two draws *independent* or *dependent* events?

11. Art tossed a coin and a number cube at the same time. Find P(heads, 6).

Performance Task

Roll a pair of number cubes 36 times and record the sums. Find the experimental probability of rolling a 2, of rolling a 3, and so on. Compare your results to the theoretical probabilities. Then roll the cubes another 36 times and combine your results for all 72 rolls. Which results are closer to the theoretical probabilities, those for 36 rolls or those for 72 rolls?

Multiple Choice

Choose the best answer.

1. Which number is divisible by 2, 3, and 5? *[Lesson 3-6]*

ⓐ 270 ⓑ 276 © 280 ⓓ 285

2. Find the product: $3\frac{3}{8} \cdot 2\frac{2}{3}$ *[Lesson 4-5]*

ⓐ $1\frac{17}{64}$ ⓑ $6\frac{1}{4}$ © $8\frac{17}{24}$ ⓓ 9

3. The hypotenuse of a right triangle is 12 ft long and one leg is 7 ft long. Which of the following is the approximate length of the other leg? *[Lesson 5-7]*

ⓐ 5.0 ft ⓑ 8.3 ft © 9.7 ft ⓓ 13.9 ft

4. Use unit rates to determine which is the best buy for avocados. *[Lesson 6-2]*

ⓐ $3.45 for 3 ⓑ $3.60 for 4

© $4.30 for 5 ⓓ $6.00 for 6

5. 32 is 8% of which number? *[Lesson 8-5]*

ⓐ 2.56 ⓑ 4 © 256 ⓓ 400

6. Which point is in quadrant II? *[Lesson 9-3]*

ⓐ $(-3, 4)$ ⓑ $(-5, -7)$

© $(2, 2)$ ⓓ $(4, -1)$

7. The graph of which equation does *not* include the origin? *[Lesson 10-5]*

ⓐ $y = -x$ ⓑ $y = 2x$

© $y = 3x - 3$ ⓓ $y = x^2$

8. How many faces does a rectangular pyramid have? *[Lesson 11-1]*

ⓐ 4 ⓑ 5 © 6 ⓓ 8

9. A building is a rectangular prism whose base measures 65 ft by 80 ft. Its volume is 624,000 ft^3. How tall is it? *[Lesson 11-4]*

ⓐ 96 ft ⓑ 120 ft © 520 ft ⓓ 7800 ft

10. Which net *cannot* be folded into a cube? *[Lesson 11-3]*

ⓐ 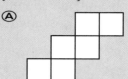 ⓑ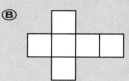

© 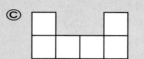 ⓓ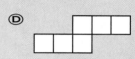

11. Find the surface area of a cylinder with radius 8 m and height 5 m. Use 3.14 for π. *[Lesson 11-8]*

ⓐ 251.2 m^2 ⓑ 408.2 m^2

© 452.16 m^2 ⓓ 653.12 m^2

12. Soap is available in 3 scents. Each is available in 4 sizes. How many different choices are there? *[Lesson 12-1]*

ⓐ 3 ⓑ 4 © 7 ⓓ 12

13. Stella is joining a music club. If the available selections include 5 albums she wants, how many ways can she choose 3 selections? *[Lesson 12-3]*

ⓐ 6 ⓑ 10 © 60 ⓓ 120

14. A bag contains 8 blue marbles and 5 black ones. Find the probability of drawing a black marble. *[Lesson 12-5]*

ⓐ $\frac{8}{5}$ ⓑ $\frac{5}{8}$ © $\frac{5}{13}$ ⓓ $\frac{8}{13}$

15. Which of the following describes the results of 2 consecutive rolls of a number cube? *[Lesson 12-7]*

ⓐ Independent events ⓑ Unfair game

© Dependent events ⓓ Fair game

Chapter Review

Chapter 1 Review

1. Use estimation to identify the month with the largest difference between cost and revenue.

2. The lengths of seven discus throws, in meters, were 52, 34, 39, 50, 59, 64, 43. Make a bar graph of the data.

3. Find the mean, median, and mode(s) of the data values: 9, 19, 15, 4, 23, 14, 20, 15, 7

4. Make a stem-and-leaf diagram of the data: 57, 76, 75, 61, 53, 68, 75, 59, 64, 67

5. Make a bar graph with a broken vertical axis to display this data for the four most popular films of the 1980s. Explain why your graph could be misleading.

6. Find the median and mode(s) of the data values displayed in the stem-and-leaf diagram. Are there any outliers?

Stem	Leaf
8	4 5 5 6 9 9
9	0 0 0 1 4 5 7 7 9 9
10	1 1 2 3 3 3 5 6
11	8

7. Make a line plot to show the finishing times of swimmers in a race.

8. The table gives the total number of points scored in the Super Bowl for each year. Make a line graph to display the data.

9. Make a scatterplot of the data for the players on a tennis team. Draw a trend line and use it to predict the expected number of winners for a player with 15 unforced errors.

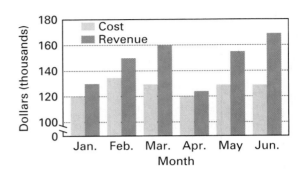

Box Office Receipts—1980s Films	
Movie	**Receipts ($ million)**
E.T.—The Extra-Terrestrial	228
Return of the Jedi	168
Batman	151
The Empire Strikes Back	142

Seconds	40	45	50	55	60	65	70
Finishers	3	4	5	4	3	6	1

Total Points Scored in Super Bowl					
Year	1991	1992	1993	1994	1995
Points	39	61	69	43	75

Winners	24	12	17	20	10
Unforced Errors	19	8	14	14	5

1. A long distance call costs $1.50 plus $0.80 for each minute. Let $C = 0.8m + 1.5$, where C is the cost and m is the number of minutes. How much would a 12-minute call cost?

Evaluate each expression.

2. $7 + 3 \times 5$ **3.** $48 - 36 \div (11 - 2)$

4. Tell which operation you would do first to evaluate $\dfrac{3 \times (9 - 5)}{6}$.

5. Find a formula relating the variables.

x	1	2	3	4	5	6	7
y	5	6	7	8	9	10	11

6. Which property is suggested by the formulas $A = lw$ and $A = wl$?

7. Use the formula $r = \dfrac{d}{t}$ to make a table of values showing the speed (r) needed to travel a distance (d) of 120 miles in 2, 3, 4, 5, and 6 hours (t).

8. Name the inverse action of walking 3 miles west.

Tell if the number in bold is a solution to the equation.

9. $x - 24 = 9$; **15**   **10.** $j \cdot 14 = 56$; **4**

Solve each equation. Check your answer.

11. $a - 31 = 47$ **12.** $53 = c + 17$ **13.** $18m = 396$

14. $\dfrac{n}{7} = 6$ **15.** $15k + 32 = 77$ **16.** $7 = \dfrac{n}{3} - 5$

17. A number is multiplied by 2, then 13 is added to the result. What operations are needed to return the original number?

18. Write an equation for this statement: The number of students decreased by 4 is 31.

19. Write an algebraic expression for the product of 8 and a number (n).

20. Lauren bought 6 chewing bones for each of her dogs. She bought 24 bones all together. Write and solve an equation to find the number of dogs (d) she has.

Write a phrase for each algebraic expression.

21. $a + 4$ **22.** $8n - 1$ **23.** $\dfrac{h}{3} - 2$ **24.** $\dfrac{5}{x + 9}$

1. Give the value of each 6 in 4168.9206.

2. Use $<$, $>$, or $=$ to compare: 2.89 ☐ 2.091

3. Round 4.9275 to the nearest thousandth.

Estimate.

4. $294.91 \cdot 5.81$

5. $141.83 + 308.11$

6. Find the sum: $129.56 + 85.403$

7. Find the quotient: $\dfrac{766.38}{31.8}$

Solve each equation.

8. $x + 64.1 = 331.09$

9. $129.98 = 9.7y$

10. $\dfrac{n}{5.2} = 9.1$

11. $x - 10.5 = 22.9$

12. $1.01x = 102.01$

13. $\dfrac{w}{35.74} = 13.45$

14. Write 4.597×10^6 in standard form.

15. Write 385,000 in scientific notation.

16. Use a factor tree to find the prime factorization of 300.

17. Find the GCF of 120 and 144.

18. Find the LCM of 16 and 20.

19. Give two fractions that are equivalent to $\dfrac{24}{39}$.

Rewrite each fraction in lowest terms.

20. $\dfrac{56}{77}$

21. $\dfrac{40}{64}$

22. $\dfrac{75}{225}$

23. $\dfrac{18}{99}$

24. $\dfrac{13}{52}$

25. $\dfrac{72}{160}$

Compare using $<$, $>$, or $=$.

26. $\dfrac{8}{11}$ ☐ $\dfrac{16}{21}$

27. $\dfrac{15}{24}$ ☐ $\dfrac{35}{56}$

28. $\dfrac{18}{45}$ ☐ $\dfrac{24}{60}$

Convert each decimal to a fraction in lowest terms.

29. 0.124

30. 0.85

31. 0.25

32. 0.625

33. 0.32

34. 0.05

35. Convert $\dfrac{14}{18}$ to a decimal. Tell if the decimal terminates or repeats.

Chapter 4 Review

Estimate each sum or difference.

1. $\frac{4}{5} + \frac{1}{10}$ **2.** $\frac{7}{15} - \frac{1}{4}$

3. Use compatible numbers to estimate the quotient $48\frac{1}{3} \div 5\frac{5}{8}$.

4. About how many $4\frac{3}{4}$-inch pieces can be cut from a string measuring $32\frac{7}{8}$ inches? Estimate to find your answer.

Find each sum or difference. Write answers in lowest terms.

5. $\frac{4}{15} + \frac{8}{15}$ **6.** $\frac{7}{8} - \frac{2}{3}$ **7.** $\frac{2}{5} + \frac{1}{4}$

8. $\frac{5}{6} - \frac{1}{3}$ **9.** $\frac{7}{18} + \frac{11}{24}$ **10.** $\frac{10}{50} - \frac{1}{10}$

11. Solve the equation: $x - \frac{1}{4} = \frac{2}{5}$

12. Write $4\frac{5}{6}$ as an improper fraction.

Find each sum or difference.

13. $6\frac{7}{9} - 4\frac{8}{9}$ **14.** $14\frac{3}{5} + 9\frac{2}{3}$ **15.** $9\frac{1}{6} - 8\frac{1}{3}$

16. $22\frac{3}{7} + 19\frac{8}{21}$ **17.** $9\frac{9}{99} - 8\frac{8}{88}$ **18.** $1\frac{17}{18} + 3\frac{2}{3}$

19. Find the area of a picture frame with dimensions $\frac{11}{12}$ ft by $\frac{3}{4}$ ft.

20. One package is $2\frac{1}{3}$ times as heavy as another. If the lighter package weighs 9 lb, how much does the heavier package weigh?

Find each product or quotient. Write answers in lowest terms.

21. $\frac{4}{5} \cdot \frac{7}{12}$ **22.** $6\frac{2}{5} \cdot 4\frac{7}{8}$ **23.** $\frac{5}{7} \div \frac{25}{4}$

24. $4\frac{5}{8} \div 1\frac{7}{12}$ **25.** $1\frac{2}{5} \cdot 3\frac{3}{4}$ **26.** $\frac{1}{4} \div \frac{16}{64}$

27. The area of one plot of land is $1\frac{1}{4}$ acres. How many plots with this area are contained in 20 acres of land?

28. A jar holds $\frac{7}{8}$ of a gallon. How many jars of this size are needed to hold 28 gallons?

1. Draw a ray $\overrightarrow{AB}$ and a line $\overleftrightarrow{CD}$ intersecting to form $\angle BEC$.

2. What is the sum of the measures of the angles of an octagon?

3. If $\angle ABC$ measures 63°:

   a. What is the measure of an angle complementary to $\angle ABC$?

   b. What is the measure of an angle supplementary to $\angle ABC$?

4. Lines $\overleftrightarrow{AB}$ and $\overleftrightarrow{CD}$ are parallel. List the angles congruent to $\angle CFE$, and explain why they are congruent.

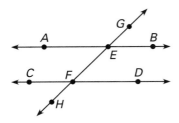

5. Find the area and perimeter of the base of a rectangular building 36 ft wide and 52 ft long.

6. Fill in the blanks: All sides of a square are _____. All sides of an equilateral triangle are _____. The sides of any other regular polygon are _____.

7. Find a perfect square between 60 and 70.

8. Find $\sqrt{42}$ to three decimal places.

9. Find the length of the shorter leg of a right triangle whose hypotenuse is 13 m long and whose longer leg is 12 m long.

10. Find the area of a triangle whose height is 6.4 in. and whose base is 5 in.

11. Find the area of the trapezoid.

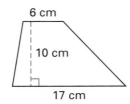

12. Find the area of the stage.

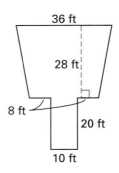

1. Estimate the ratio of the width to the length of the rectangle shown.

2. Find the rate: 144 feet in 6 seconds. Remember to include units in your rate.

3. Express the rate as a unit rate: $46.00 for 8 hours of work

4. Use unit rates to find the better gas mileage: 162 miles on 6 gallons of gas or 203 miles on 7 gallons

5. Corner Market sells 3 pounds of apples for $6.45. At this rate, how much will 5 pounds of apples cost?

6. Multiply and divide to find two ratios equivalent to $\frac{14}{24}$.

7. Use a table to find two rates equivalent to 45 jumping jacks in 2 minutes.

8. Using multiplication, complete the table to find five ratios equivalent to $\frac{2}{5}$.

2	4	6	8	10	12
5					

9. Using division, complete the table to find five ratios equivalent to $\frac{288}{216}$.

288	144	48	16	8	4
216					

10. Complete the ratio table. Then write four proportions involving the ratios.

5	10	15	20
6			

11. Sam baked one apple pie using 4 apples and 3 tablespoons of sugar, and a larger pie using 6 apples and 5 tablespoons of sugar. Are these ratios proportional?

12. Decide whether these ratios form a proportion: $\frac{84}{124} \stackrel{?}{=} \frac{42}{60}$

13. Decide if these ratios are proportional and give a reason: $\frac{5}{8} \stackrel{?}{=} \frac{17}{24}$

14. Find the unit rate: 54 pages in 9 minutes

15. Kamilah's mother drove 138 miles on 6 gallons of gas. Find the gas mileage for her car.

16. Solve the proportion: $\frac{16}{20} = \frac{n}{35}$

1. Write 5 cm:20 m in two other ways.

2. Find the scale of a map if a 42 km wide lake is 9 cm wide on the map.

3. A scale model of a truck is 3.5 in. long. Find the length of the actual truck if the scale is 1 in.:6 ft.

4. Solve the proportion: $\dfrac{8 \text{ in.}}{6 \text{ mi}} = \dfrac{28 \text{ in.}}{x}$

5. Paul needs to be at school at 8:30 A.M. If the school is 6 miles away from his home and the bus travels at 30 mi/hr, when does the bus need to leave his home?

6. Anne begins running at 4:15 P.M. and runs at a rate of 8 km/hr. If she runs 6 km, what time does she finish?

7. A model of an 82 ft long train has to fit in a display case that is 10 in. long. Suggest an appropriate scale for the model.

8. A photograph is 4 in. by 6 in. What is the largest scale that can be used to make an enlargement to fit in a 60 in. by 85 in. frame?

9. Suggest appropriate units for the rate at which your hair grows.

10. Give a reciprocal unit rate that has the same meaning as 4 gal for $1.

11. Convert 84 inches per second to feet per second.

12. Ting bicycles at a speed of 20 miles per hour. Convert this rate to feet per second.

13. Tell whether the triangles at right are similar. If they are, write a similarity statement using $\sim$ and give the scale factor. If they are not, explain why not.

14. Two trapezoids are similar, with scale factor 3:1. The smaller trapezoid has perimeter 15 cm and area 20 cm^2. Find the perimeter and area of the larger trapezoid.

15. Two similar pentagons have an area ratio of 36:1. Find the ratio of their perimeters and the scale factor.

16. Rectangle $ABCD$ has an area of 44 cm^2 and a perimeter of 30 cm. Rectangle $EFGH$ is similar to $ABCD$. If the area of $EFGH$ is 11 cm^2, what is its perimeter?

1. Rewrite $\frac{19}{25}$ as a percent. **2.** Rewrite 56% as a fraction. **3.** Rewrite 31% as a decimal.

Rewrite each decimal as a fraction and a percent.

4. 0.24 **5.** 1.5 **6.** 0.002 **7.** 0.75

Rewrite each percent as a fraction and a decimal.

8. 0.2% **9.** 96% **10.** 120% **11.** 36%

Find each of the following mentally.

12. 10% of 340 **13.** 50% of 410 **14.** 1% of $50

15. 80% of 35 is what number? **16.** What percent of 72 is 40?

17. 12% of what number is 60? **18.** 220% of 145 is what number?

19. A compact disc player is on sale for $119. This is 85% of the regular price. Find the regular price.

20. In one town, 20% of the 165 restaurants sell pizza. How many restaurants sell pizza?

21. Of the 700 students at Central School, 112 went on a field trip. What percent of the students went on the field trip?

22. A $15 book is on sale at a 30% discount. What is the sale price of the book?

23. Nate bought a $42 sweater on sale for $36.96. What percent is this of the regular price? What percent discount did he get?

24. Over a holiday weekend, the number of cats at a kennel increased from 35 to 48. What was the percent increase?

25. After Janine received a salary increase of 6%, her salary was $44,520. What was her salary before the raise?

26. Maria was given 120 raffle tickets to sell. She sold 29 of them in one week. What percent decrease in the tickets was this?

27. The number of birds on a nature reserve increased from 2980 to 3610. What was the percent increase?

28. There were 650 students at an all-day concert. By the time the last band played, 480 students were left. Find the percent decrease in the number of students.

Chapter 9 Review

1. Tell whether -4.5 is an integer.

2. Use a sign to write this number: 2000 feet below sea level

3. Write the opposite of -19.

4. Find the absolute value: $\left|-53\right|$

5. Use $>$, $<$, or $=$ to compare: $-47\ \square\ -35$

6. Order this set of numbers from least to greatest: $24, -6, 7, -13, -2$

7. Fill in the blank with *sometimes, always,* or *never:* An integer is _____ equal to its absolute value.

8. Plot each point on the same coordinate plane.

    a. $(2, 4)$ **b.** $(1, -2)$ **c.** $(-3, 0)$

9. Name the quadrant or axis that contains the point $(-4, -7)$.

10. Draw a parallelogram so that each of its vertices is in a different quadrant. Label the coordinates of each point.

11. Write the addition problem and the sum modeled in the picture.

12. Write the next integer in the pattern: $-14, -5, 4,$ _____ .

Find each sum or difference.

13. $24 + (-11)$ **14.** $-9 + (-7)$ **15.** $-63 + 91$ **16.** $37 + (-38)$

17. $8 - 15$ **18.** $-4 - (-7)$ **19.** $-29 - 45$ **20.** $-18 - (-57) - 39$

21. The highest average temperature in the world is 95°F, in Dalol Danakil Depression, Ethiopia. The lowest average temperature is -72°F, in Plateau Station, Antarctica. Subtract to find the range of average temperatures.

Find each product or quotient.

22. $-8 \cdot (-5)$ **23.** $-12 \cdot 3$ **24.** $15 \cdot (-4) \cdot 3$ **25.** $-7 \cdot (-9) \cdot (-8)$

26. $84 \div (-12)$ **27.** $-54 \div (-6)$ **28.** $-90 \div 3 \div (-5)$ **29.** $-39 \div 3$

30. The profits from Rocia's business for the first five months of 1996 were \$3500, $-\$2200$, $-\$2900$, \$800, and $-\$1700$. What was the average monthly profit?

1. Tell a story that fits the graph at right.

2. Define a variable and give a reasonable range of values for the height of a car.

3. Name a quantity that the volume of a cone might depend on.

4. Write a rule for the sequence 5, 10, 15, 20, …, and give the 100th term of the sequence.

5. For the table below, write an equation to show the relationship between x and y. Use the equation to find y when $x = 7$.

x	1	2	3	4
y	3	4	5	6

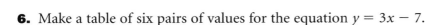

6. Make a table of six pairs of values for the equation $y = 3x - 7$.

Graph each equation on a coordinate plane.

7. $y = x + 2$

8. $y = x^2 + 1$

9. The table below was created from the equation $y = -4x + 2$. Use it to solve each related equation.

x	0	1	2	3	4
y	2	-2	-6	-10	-14

   a. $-2 = -4x + 2$ **b.** $-14 = -4x + 2$

10. Use a graph to solve $-11 = 2x - 5$.

11. Write the equation modeled in the equation box. Solve the equation. Sketch your steps.

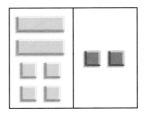

12. Write and graph an inequality to show that at least 150 students attended a play.

Solve each equation. Check your solution.

13. $p - 14 = -6$ **14.** $a + 11 = 36$ **15.** $\dfrac{d}{-6} = -72$

16. $-9r = 63$ **17.** $3x + 4 = 1$ **18.** $\dfrac{c}{3} - 2 = 5$

19. A cab ride costs $3 plus $2 per mile. Alonzo paid $17 for a cab ride. How many miles did he travel?

1. Sketch a triangular prism. How many edges, faces, and vertices does it have?

2. Find the number of cubes in the figure at right. Assume all cubes are visible.

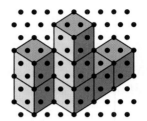

3. A rectangular prism is shown below.

   a. Sketch a net for this prism.

   b. Find its surface area.   **c.** Find its volume.

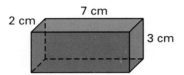

4. The data shows the season summary for Phil's baseball team. Make a circle graph. Label each sector.

Wins	Losses	Ties
40%	50%	10%

5. Find the circumference and area of a circle whose diameter is 12.54 cm. Use 3.14 for π. Round to the nearest hundredth.

6. Find the surface area and the volume of the cylinder shown. Use 3.14 for π. Round to the nearest tenth.

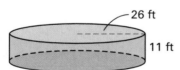

7. Copy the figure. Draw all lines of symmetry. Then tell whether or not it has rotational symmetry.

8. Point A is at $(3, -1)$. Use the translation rule $(x, y) \rightarrow (x - 4, y - 1)$ to find the coordinates of A'.

9. The coordinates of a triangle are $A(0, 0)$, $B(-4, 4)$, and $C(-1, 2)$.

   a. Draw the figure on the coordinate plane.

   b. Draw the reflection of ABC across the y-axis. Give the coordinates of the reflection's vertices.

   c. Give the coordinates of a rotation of ABC for a 90° clockwise rotation around the origin.

1. Mama's Pizza Parlor offers 3 types of crust, 2 choices of cheese, and 6 choices of toppings. Use the Counting Principle to find the number of different pizzas consisting of one type of crust, cheese, and topping.

2. A bookstore has separate sections for hardcover and paperback books in each of these categories: fiction, mystery, nonfiction, science fiction, and poetry. Make a tree diagram to show the possible outcomes. How many sections does the bookstore need?

3. A contest awards four prizes. Sandra, Miguel, Tasha, and Jimmy are the four finalists. In how many ways can first, second, third, and fourth place be assigned?

4. List all of the possible orderings of the numbers 1, 2, and 3, without repeating digits.

5. Elena has 10 CDs she wants to take on a trip, but she can't fit all of them into her luggage. How many different ways can she choose 4 of the CDs to take?

6. A bag contains 4 red, 6 blue, and 3 yellow marbles. A marble is chosen at random. Find the odds that the marble is:

   a. Blue   **b.** Yellow

7. A spinner has 6 equal sections, labeled A, B, C, D, E, and F. Pramit wins if a vowel is spun and Molly wins if a consonant is spun. Give each player's odds of winning. Then determine whether the game is fair.

8. A number cube is rolled. Find the probability of each event.

   a. Rolling a number greater than 4   **b.** Rolling a number that is *not* greater than 4

9. Find the probability of rolling a sum of 9 when rolling two number cubes. Express your answer as a percent.

10. Mike flipped a coin 20 times and got heads 7 times. Find each of the following:

    a. Theoretical probability of getting heads   **b.** Experimental probability of getting heads

11. A dart hits the dart board shown. What is the probability that it lands in the shaded region?

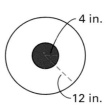

12. A number cube is rolled twice. What is the probability of getting a number less than 3 on the first roll, then a 6 on the second?

13. Roberto draws two coins from his pocket, which contains 4 quarters and 5 nickels. What is the probability that both coins are quarters?

Geometric Formulas

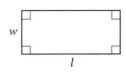

Rectangle

Area: $A = lw$

Perimeter: $p = 2l + 2w$

Square

Area: $A = s^2$

Perimeter: $p = 4s$

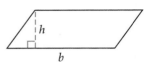

Parallelogram

Area: $A = bh$

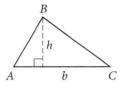

Triangle

Area: $A = \frac{1}{2}bh$

$m\angle A + m\angle B + m\angle C = 180°$

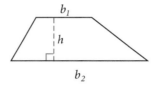

Trapezoid

Area: $A = \frac{1}{2}h(b_1 + b_2)$

Polygon

Sum of angle measures for

n-sided polygon: $S = (n - 2)180°$

Perimeter: sum of measures of

all sides

Circle

Area: $A = \pi r^2$

Circumference: $C = \pi d = 2\pi r$

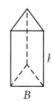

Prism

Volume: $V = Bh$

Surface Area: $SA = ph + 2B$

Cylinder

Volume: $V = \pi r^2 h$

Surface Area: $SA = 2\pi rh + 2\pi r^2$

Measurement Conversion Factors

Metric Measures of Length
1000 meters (m) = 1 kilometer (km)
100 centimeters (cm) = 1 m
10 decimeters (dm) = 1 m
1000 millimeters (mm) = 1 m
10 cm = 1 decimeter (dm)
10 mm = 1 cm

Area
100 square millimeters = 1 square centimeter
(mm^2) (cm^2)
$10,000\ cm^2 = 1$ square meter (m^2)
$10,000\ m^2 = 1$ hectare (ha)

Volume
1000 cubic millimeters = 1 cubic centimeter
(mm^3) (cm^3)
$1000\ cm^3 = 1$ cubic decimeter (dm^3)
$1,000,000\ cm^3 = 1$ cubic meter (m^3)

Capacity
1000 milliliters (mL) = 1 liter (L)
1000 L = 1 kiloliter (kL)

Mass
1000 kilograms (kg) = 1 metric ton (t)
1000 grams (g) = 1 kg
1000 milligrams (mg) = 1 g

Temperatures in Degrees Celsius (°C)
0°C = freezing point of water
37°C = normal body temperature
100°C = boiling point of water

Time
60 seconds (sec) = 1 minute (min)
60 min = 1 hour (hr)
24 hr = 1 day

Customary Measures of Length
12 inches (in.) = 1 foot (ft)
3 ft = 1 yard (yd)
36 in. = 1 yd
5280 ft = 1 mile (mi)
1760 yd = 1 mi
6076 ft = 1 nautical mile

Area
144 square inches = 1 square foot
(in^2) (ft^2)
$9\ ft^2 = 1$ square yard (yd^2)
43,560 sq $ft^2 = 1$ acre (A)

Volume
1728 cubic inches = 1 cubic foot
(cu in.) (cu ft)
27 cu ft = 1 cubic yard (cu yard)

Capacity
8 fluid ounces (fl oz) = 1 cup (c)
2 c = 1 pint (pt)
2 pt = 1 quart (qt)
4 qt = 1 gallon (gal)

Weight
16 ounces (oz) = 1 pound (lb)
2000 lb = 1 ton (T)

Temperatures in Degrees Fahrenheit (°F)
32°F = freezing point of water
98.6°F = normal body temperature
212°F = boiling point of water

TABLES

Symbols

$+$	plus or positive	$\llcorner$	right angle
$-$	minus or negative	$\perp$	is perpendicular to
$\cdot$	times	$\|\|$	is parallel to
$\times$	times	AB	length of $\overline{AB}$; distance between A and B
$\div$	divided by		
$\pm$	positive or negative	$\triangle ABC$	triangle with vertices A, B, and C
$=$	is equal to	$\angle ABC$	angle with sides $\overrightarrow{BA}$ and $\overrightarrow{BC}$
$\neq$	is not equal to	$\angle B$	angle with vertex B
$<$	is less than	$m\angle ABC$	measure of angle ABC
$>$	is greater than	$'$	prime
$\leq$	is less than or equal to	a^n	the nth power of a
$\geq$	is greater than or equal to	$\|x\|$	absolute value of x
$\approx$	is approximately equal to	$\sqrt{x}$	principal square root of x
$\%$	percent	π	pi (approximately 3.1416)
$a{:}b$	the ratio of a to b, or $\frac{a}{b}$	(a, b)	ordered pair with x-coordinate a and y-coordinate b
$\cong$	is congruent to		
$\sim$	is similar to	$P(A)$	the probability of event A
$\circ$	degree(s)	$n!$	n factorial
$\overleftrightarrow{AB}$	line containing points A and B		
$\overline{AB}$	line segment with endpoints A and B		
$\overrightarrow{AB}$	ray with endpoint A and containing B		

Squares and Square Roots

N	N²	√N		N	N²	√N
1	1	1		51	2,601	7.141
2	4	1.414		52	2,704	7.211
3	9	1.732		53	2,809	7.280
4	16	2		54	2,916	7.348
5	25	2.236		55	3,025	7.416
6	36	2.449		56	3,136	7.483
7	49	2.646		57	3,249	7.550
8	64	2.828		58	3,364	7.616
9	81	3		59	3,481	7.681
10	100	3.162		60	3,600	7.746
11	121	3.317		61	3,721	7.810
12	144	3.464		62	3,844	7.874
13	169	3.606		63	3,969	7.937
14	196	3.742		64	4,096	8
15	225	3.873		65	4,225	8.062
16	256	4		66	4,356	8.124
17	289	4.123		67	4,489	8.185
18	324	4.243		68	4,624	8.246
19	361	4.359		69	4,761	8.307
20	400	4.472		70	4,900	8.367
21	441	4.583		71	5,041	8.426
22	484	4.690		72	5,184	8.485
23	529	4.796		73	5,329	8.544
24	576	4.899		74	5,476	8.602
25	625	5		75	5,625	8.660
26	676	5.099		76	5,776	8.718
27	729	5.196		77	5,929	8.775
28	784	5.292		78	6,084	8.832
29	841	5.385		79	6,241	8.888
30	900	5.477		80	6,400	8.944
31	961	5.568		81	6,561	9
32	1,024	5.657		82	6,724	9.055
33	1,089	5.745		83	6,889	9.110
34	1,156	5.831		84	7,056	9.165
35	1,225	5.916		85	7,225	9.220
36	1,296	6		86	7,396	9.274
37	1,369	6.083		87	7,569	9.327
38	1,444	6.164		88	7,744	9.381
39	1,521	6.245		89	7,921	9.434
40	1,600	6.325		90	8,100	9.487
41	1,681	6.403		91	8,281	9.539
42	1,764	6.481		92	8,464	9.592
43	1,849	6.557		93	8,649	9.644
44	1,936	6.633		94	8,836	9.695
45	2,025	6.708		95	9,025	9.747
46	2,116	6.782		96	9,216	9.798
47	2,209	6.856		97	9,409	9.849
48	2,304	6.928		98	9,604	9.899
49	2,401	7		99	9,801	9.950
50	2,500	7.071		100	10,000	10

TABLES

Glossary

absolute value   A number's distance from zero, shown by | |. Example: |−7| = 7 [p. 434]

acute angle   An angle that measures less than 90°. [p. 213]

acute triangle   A triangle with three acute angles. [p. 223]

addend   A number added to one or more others.

additive inverse   A number's opposite. Example: The additive inverse of 2 is −2. [p. 451]

algebraic expression   An expression containing a variable. Example: 2(x − 9) [p. 78]

alternate interior angles   A pair of angles formed by two lines and a transversal. In the figure below, ∠1 and ∠3 are a pair of alternate interior angles, and ∠2 and ∠4 are a pair of alternate interior angles. [p. 218]

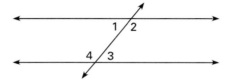

angle   Two rays with a common endpoint. [p. 213]

angle bisector   A ray bisecting an angle. [p. 214]

area   The number of square units needed to cover a figure. [p. 233]

arithmetic sequence   A sequence where the difference between consecutive terms is always the same. Example: 3, 6, 9, … [p. 492]

Associative Property of Addition   The fact that grouping does not affect the sum of three or more numbers. a + (b + c) = (a + b) + c [p. 62]

Associative Property of Multiplication   The fact that grouping does not affect the product of three or more numbers. a(bc) = (ab)c [p. 62]

average   See *mean*.

axes   See *x-axis* and *y-axis*.

bar graph   A graph that uses bars to display data. [p. 7]

base (in numeration)   A number multiplied by itself the number of times shown by an exponent. Example: $5^2 = 5 \cdot 5$, where 5 is the base and 2 is the exponent. [p. 125]

base (of a polygon)   Any side of the polygon, or the length of that side. [pp. 233, 249]

base (of a solid)   See examples below. [pp. 555, 587]

binary number system   A base-two place value system. [p. 159]

bisect   To divide an angle or segment into two congruent angles or segments. [pp. 214, 218]

box-and-whisker plot   A graph showing how a collection of data is distributed. [p. 26]

capacity   The volume of a figure, given in terms of liquid measure. [p. 594]

center   The point at the exact middle of a circle or sphere. [pp. 574, 587]

central angle   An angle whose vertex is at the center of a circle. [p. 574]

circle   A plane figure whose points are all the same distance from its center. [p. 574]

circle graph   A circular graph that uses wedges to represent portions of the data set. [p. 7]

circumference   The perimeter of a circle. [p. 578]

circumscribed figure   A figure containing another. A polygon is circumscribed around a circle if the circle touches each of its sides. [p. 617]

combination   A selection of items where the order does not matter. [p. 636]

common denominator   A denominator that is the same in two or more fractions. [p. 150]

common factor   If a number is a factor of two or more numbers, it is a common factor of that set of numbers. [p. 139]

common multiple   A number that is a multiple of each of two given numbers. Example: 24 is a common multiple of 4 and 3. [p. 141]

Commutative Property of Addition   The fact that ordering does not affect the sum of two or more numbers. a + b = b + a [p. 62]

Commutative Property of Multiplication   The fact that ordering does not affect the product of two or more numbers. ab = ba [p. 62]

complementary angles   Two angles whose measures add up to 90°. [p. 214]

composite number   A whole number greater than 1 that has more than two factors. [p. 136]

cone   A solid with one circular base. [p. 587]

congruent angles   Two angles that have equal measures. [p. 214]

congruent segments   Two segments that have equal lengths. [p. 218]

constant   A quantity whose value cannot change. [p. 482]

constant graph   A graph in which the height of the line does not change. [p. 486]

conversion factor   A fraction, equal to 1, whose numerator and denominator represent the same quantity but use different units. [p. 349]

coordinates   A pair of numbers used to locate a point on a coordinate plane. [p. 443]

coordinate system (coordinate plane)   A system of intersecting horizontal and vertical number lines, used to locate points. [p. 443]

corresponding angles   Angles formed by two lines and a transversal. $\angle 1$ and $\angle 5$, $\angle 2$ and $\angle 6$, $\angle 4$ and $\angle 8$, and $\angle 3$ and $\angle 7$ are corresponding angles. [p. 218]

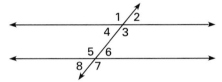

corresponding angles (in similar figures)   Matching angles on similar figures. [p. 361]

corresponding sides   Matching sides on similar figures. [p. 361]

counterexample   An example that shows a statement is false. [p. 265]

Counting Principle   To find the number of outcomes for selecting several items, multiply the number of possibilities for each item. [p. 627]

cross product   In a proportion, the product of a numerator on one side with the denominator on the other. [p. 308]

cube (geometric figure)   A 6-sided prism whose faces are congruent squares.

cube (in numeration)   A number raised to the third power.

customary system of measurement   The measurement system often used in the United States: inches, feet, miles, ounces, pounds, tons, cups, quarts, gallons, etc.

cylinder   A solid with two parallel circular bases with the same radius. [p. 587]

decagon   A polygon with 10 sides.

decimal system   A base-10 place value system.

decreasing graph   A graph in which the height of the line decreases from left to right. [p. 486]

deductive reasoning   Using logic to show that a statement is true. [p. 265]

degree (°)   A unit of measure for angles. [p. 213]

denominator   The bottom number in a fraction. [p. 144]

dependent events   Events for which the outcome of one affects the probability of the other. [p. 660]

diameter   The distance across a circle through its center. [p. 578]

difference   The answer to a subtraction problem.

Distributive Property   The fact that $a(b + c) = ab + ac$. [p. 62]

dividend   The number to be divided in a division problem. In $8 \div 4 = 2$, 8 is the dividend, 4 is the *divisor*, and 2 is the *quotient*.

divisible   A number is divisible by a second number if it can be divided by that number with no remainder. [p. 134]

divisor   See *dividend*.

double-bar graph   A single graph comparing bar graphs for two related data sets. [p. 12]

double-line graph   A single graph comparing line graphs for two related data sets. [p. 32]

edge   A segment joining two faces of a polyhedron. [p. 554]

equally-likely outcomes   Outcomes that have the same probability.

equation   A mathematical statement that two expressions are equal. Example: $x - 10 = 6$ [p. 82]

equilateral triangle   A triangle whose sides are all the same length. [p. 222]

equivalent fractions   Two fractions representing the same number, such as $\frac{1}{2}$ and $\frac{8}{16}$. [p. 144]

equivalent rates   Rates corresponding to equivalent fractions. [p. 282]

equivalent ratios   Ratios corresponding to equivalent fractions. [p. 282]

estimate   An approximation for the result of a calculation.

event   An outcome or set of outcomes of an experiment or situation. Example: Rolling a 3 or higher is one possible event produced by a dice roll. [p. 645]

689

experiment   In probability, any activity involving chance (such as a dice roll). [p. 644]

experimental probability   A probability based on the statistical results of an experiment. [p. 654]

exponent   A number telling how many times the base is being used as a factor. Example: $8^3 = 8 \cdot 8 \cdot 8$, where 3 is the exponent and 8 is the base. [p. 125]

expression   A mathematical phrase made up of variables and/or numbers and operations. Example: $3x - 11$ [p. 60]

face   A flat surface on a solid. [p. 554]

factor   A whole number that divides another whole number evenly. Example: 8 is a factor of 48. [p. 134]

factorial   The factorial of a number is the product of all whole numbers from 1 to that number. The symbol for factorial is an "!" [p. 633]

factor tree   A diagram showing how a whole number breaks down into its prime factors. [p. 136]

fair games   Games where all players have the same odds of winning. [p. 645]

formula   A rule showing relationships among quantities. Example: $A = bh$ [p. 56]

fractal   A pattern with self-similarity. If you zoom in on a small part of a fractal, the enlarged region looks similar to the original figure. [p. 377]

fraction   A number in the form $\frac{a}{b}$. [p. 144]

function   A rule that matches two sets of numbers. [p. 97]

geometric probability   A probability based on comparing measurements of geometric figures. [p. 656]

geometric sequence   A sequence where the ratio between consecutive terms is always the same. Example: 3, 6, 12, … [p. 492]

greatest common factor (GCF)   The largest factor two numbers have in common. Example: 6 is the GCF of 24 and 18. [p. 139]

height   On a triangle or quadrilateral, the distance from the base to the opposite vertex or side. On a prism or cylinder, the distance between the bases. [pp. 233, 249, 567, 587]

heptagon   A seven-sided polygon.

hexadecimal number system   A base-16 place value system. [p. 159]

hexagon   A six-sided polygon. [p. 227]

histogram   A type of bar graph where the categories are equal ranges of numbers. [p. 47]

hypotenuse   The side opposite the right angle in a right triangle. [p. 244]

if-then statement   A logical statement that uses *if* and *then* to show a relationship between two conditions. Example: *If* a triangle is scalene, *then* none of its sides are congruent. [p. 667]

improper fraction   A fraction greater than 1. [p. 178]

increasing graph   A graph in which the height of the line increases from left to right. [p. 486]

independent events   Events for which the outcome of one does not affect the probability of the other. [p. 660]

inductive reasoning   Using a pattern to draw a conclusion. [p. 265]

inequality   A statement that two expressions are not equal. Examples: $3x < 11$, $x + 2 \le 6$ [p. 517]

inscribed figure   A figure that just fits inside another. A polygon is inscribed in a circle if all of its vertices lie on the circle. [p. 617]

integer   A whole number, its opposite, or zero. The integers are the numbers … −3, −2, −1, 0, 1, 2, 3, …. [p. 433]

interval   The space between marked values on a bar graph's scale. [p. 11]

inverse operations   Operations that "undo" each other, such as addition and subtraction. [p. 75]

isometric drawing   A perspective drawing. [p. 559]

isosceles triangle   A triangle with at least two congruent sides. [p. 222]

least common denominator (LCD)   The least common multiple (LCM) of two or more denominators. [p. 174]

least common multiple (LCM)   The smallest common multiple of two numbers. Example: 56 is the LCM of 8 and 14. [p. 141]

leg   A side of a right triangle other than the hypotenuse. [p. 244]

line   A straight set of points that extends without end in both directions. [p. 212]

line graph   A graph that uses a line to show how data changes over time. [p. 30]

line of symmetry   The imaginary "mirror" in line symmetry. [p. 605]

line plot   A plot, using stacked ×'s, showing the distribution of values in a data set. [p. 17]

line segment   Two points, called the *endpoints* of the segment, and all points between them. [p. 218]

line symmetry   A figure has line symmetry if one half is the mirror image of the other half. [p. 605]

lowest terms   A fraction with a numerator and denominator whose only common factor is 1. [p. 145]

mean   The sum of the values in a data set divided by the number of values. Also known as the *average.* [p. 22]

measurement error   The uncertainty in a measurement. The greatest possible error in a measurement is half the smallest unit used. [p. 203]

median   The middle value in a data set when the values are arranged in order. [p. 22]

metric system of measurement   The most commonly used measurement system throughout the world: centimeters, meters, kilometers, grams, kilograms, milliliters, liters, etc.

midpoint   The point that divides a segment into two congruent smaller segments. [p. 218]

mixed number   A number made up of a nonzero whole number and a fraction. [p. 169]

mode   The value(s) that occur most often in a data set. [p. 22]

multiple   The product of a given number and another whole number. Example: Since 3 • 7 = 21, 21 is a multiple of both 3 and 7. [p. 141]

negative numbers   Numbers that are less than zero. [p. 433]

negative relationship   Two data sets have a negative relationship when the data values in one set increase as the values in the other decrease. [p. 37]

no relationship   Two data sets have no relationship when there is no positive or negative relationship. [p. 37]

numerator   The top number in a fraction. [p. 144]

obtuse angle   An angle that measures more than 90° and less than 180°. [p. 213]

obtuse triangle   A triangle with one obtuse angle. [p. 223]

octagon   An eight-sided polygon. [p. 227]

odds   The ratio of the number of ways an event can happen to the number of ways it cannot. [p. 645]

opposite numbers   Numbers that are the same distance from zero but on opposite sides, such as 5 and –5. [p. 433]

ordered pair   A pair of numbers, such as (12, –8), used to locate points on a coordinate plane. [p. 443]

order of operations   A rule telling in what order a series of operations should be done. The order of operations is (1) compute within grouping symbols; (2) compute powers; (3) multiply and divide from left to right; (4) add and subtract from left to right. [p. 61]

origin   The zero point on a number line, or the point (0, 0) where the axes of a coordinate system intersect. [pp. 433, 443]

orthographic drawing   A drawing of an object using front, side, and top views. [p. 559]

outcome (in probability)   One way an experiment or situation could turn out. [p. 627]

outlier   A value widely separated from the others in a data set. [p. 17]

parallel lines   Lines in a plane that never meet. [p. 217]

parallelogram   A quadrilateral with parallel and congruent opposite sides. [p. 223]

pentagon   A five-sided polygon. [p. 227]

percent   A ratio comparing a number to 100. Example: 29% = $\frac{29}{100}$ [p. 386]

percent change   The amount of a change, divided by the original amount, times 100. [p. 415]

percent decrease   A percent change describing a decrease in a quantity. [p. 415]

percent increase   A percent change describing an increase in a quantity. [p. 415]

perfect square   The square of a whole number. [p. 240]

perimeter   The distance around the outside of a figure. [p. 233]

permutation   One of the ways to order a set of items. [p. 631]

perpendicular   Lines, rays, or line segments that intersect at right angles. [p. 219]

perpendicular bisector   A line, ray, or segment that intersects a segment at its midpoint and is perpendicular to it. [p. 219]

pi (π)   The ratio of a circle's circumference to its diameter: $\pi \approx 3.14159265....$ [p. 579]

place value   The value given to the place a digit occupies.

plane   A flat surface that extends forever. [p. 217]

point symmetry   A figure has point symmetry if it looks unchanged after a 180° rotation. [p. 611]

polygon   A geometric figure with at least three sides. [p. 227]

polyhedron   A solid whose faces are polygons. [p. 554]

positive numbers   Numbers greater than zero. [p. 433]

positive relationship   Two data sets have a positive relationship when their data values increase or decrease together. [p. 37]

power   A number produced by raising a base to an exponent. Example: $16 = 2^4$, so 16 is the 4th power of 2. [p. 125]

prime factorization   Writing a number as a product of prime numbers. Example: $60 = 2^2 \cdot 3 \cdot 5$ [p. 136]

prime number   A whole number greater than 1 whose only factors are 1 and itself. The primes start with 2, 3, 5, 7, 11, ... [p. 136]

prism   A polyhedron whose bases are congruent and parallel. [p. 555]

probability   The number of ways an event can occur divided by the total number of possible outcomes. [p. 650]

product   The answer to a multiplication problem.

proportion   A statement showing two ratios are equal. [p. 294]

protractor   A tool for measuring angles. [p. 213]

pyramid   A polyhedron with one polygonal base. [p. 555]

Pythagorean Theorem   In a right triangle where c is the length of the hypotenuse and a and b are the lengths of the legs, $a^2 + b^2 = c^2$. [p. 245]

quadrants   The four regions determined by the axes of a coordinate plane. [p. 443]

quadratic equation   An equation with squared terms. Example: $x^2 + 3 = 12$ [p. 545]

quadrilateral   A four-sided polygon. [p. 223]

quotient   See *dividend*.

radical sign $\sqrt{}$, used to represent a square root. [p. 241]

radius   The distance from the center of a circle to a point on the circle. [p. 578]

range (in statistics)   The difference between the least and greatest numbers in a data set. [p. 22]

rate   A ratio showing how quantities with different units are related. Example: $\frac{72 \text{ dollars}}{8 \text{ hours}}$ [p. 278]

ratio   A comparison of two quantities, often written as a fraction. [p. 274]

ray   Part of a line that has one endpoint and extends forever. [p. 212]

reciprocals   Two numbers whose product is 1. Example: $\frac{5}{7}$ and $\frac{7}{5}$ are reciprocals. [p. 198]

rectangle   A quadrilateral with four right angles. [p. 223]

reflection   A transformation that flips a figure over a line. [p. 606]

regular polygon   A polygon with all sides and angles congruent. [p. 228]

repeating decimal   A decimal number that repeats a pattern of digits. Example: $2.313131... = 2.\overline{31}$ [p. 154]

rhombus   A parallelogram with all sides congruent. [p. 223]

right angle   An angle that measures 90°. [p. 213]

right triangle   A triangle with one right angle. [p. 223]

rotation   A transformation that turns a figure around a point. [p. 610]

rotational symmetry   A figure has rotational symmetry if it looks unchanged after a rotation of less than 360°. [p. 611]

rounding   Estimating a number to a given place value. Example: 2153 rounded to the nearest hundred is 2200. [p. 110]

scale (graphical)   The evenly spaced marks on a bar graph's vertical axis, used to measure the heights of the bars. [p. 11]

scale (in scale drawings and maps)   The ratio of the distance between two points on the map or drawing to the actual distance. [p. 324]

scale drawing   A drawing that uses a scale to make an enlarged or reduced picture of an object. [p. 328]

scale factor   The ratio used to enlarge or reduce similar figures. [p. 361]

scalene triangle   A triangle whose sides have different lengths. [p. 222]

scatterplot   A graph showing paired data values as points. [p. 35]

scientific notation   A number written as a decimal greater than or equal to 1 and less than 10, times a power of 10. Example: $937 = 9.37 \times 10^2$ [p. 126]

sector   A wedge-shaped part of a circle. [p. 7]

segment   See *line segment*.

segment bisector   A line, ray, or segment through the midpoint of a segment. [p. 218]

sequence   A list of numbers, such as −1, 4, 9, 14, ... [p. 490]

similar figures   Figures with the same shape but not necessarily the same size. [p. 360]

simulation (in probability)   A model of a probability experiment. [p. 664]

solid   A three-dimensional object. [p. 554]

solutions of an equation or inequality   Values of a variable that make an equation or inequality true. [pp. 82, 517]

solve To find the solutions of an equation or inequality. [p. 82]

sphere A solid whose points are all the same distance from the center. [p. 587]

square (geometric figure) A quadrilateral with four congruent sides and four right angles. [p. 223]

square (in numeration) A number raised to the second power. [p. 240]

square root The length of the side of a square with an area equal to a given number. [p. 240]

standard form The usual way of writing numbers (in contrast to scientific notation). [p. 126]

stem-and-leaf diagram A table showing the distribution of values in a data set by splitting each value into a stem and a leaf. [p. 17]

straight angle An angle that measures 180°. [p. 213]

substitute To replace a variable with a known value. [p. 57]

sum The answer to an addition problem.

supplementary angles Two angles whose measures add up to 180°. [p. 214]

surface area For a solid, the sum of the areas of its surfaces. [p. 563]

symmetry See *line symmetry, point symmetry,* and *rotational symmetry.*

tangent line A line that touches a circle at only one point. [p. 582]

tangent ratio In a right triangle, the tangent of an angle is the ratio of the length of the side opposite the angle to the length of the side adjacent to it. [p. 315]

term One number in a sequence. [p. 490]

terminating decimal A decimal number that ends. Example: 2.31 [p. 154]

tessellation A set of repeating figures that fills a flat surface with no gaps or overlaps. [p. 615]

theoretical probability The ratio of the number of ways an event can happen to the total number of possible outcomes. [p. 654]

transformation A change in the size or position of a figure. [p. 600]

translation A transformation that slides a figure. [p. 600]

transversal A line intersecting two or more lines. [p. 217]

trapezoid A quadrilateral with exactly two parallel sides. [p. 223]

tree diagram A branching diagram showing all possible outcomes for a given situation. [p. 627]

trend A clear direction in a line graph suggesting how the data will behave in the future. [p. 31]

trend line A line drawn through a set of data points to show a trend in the data values. [p. 41]

triangle A three-sided polygon.

unit price A unit rate giving the cost of one item. [p. 279]

unit rate A rate in which the second quantity is one unit. Example: $\frac{55 \text{ miles}}{1 \text{ hour}}$ [p. 278]

variable A quantity whose values may vary. [p. 56]

Venn diagram A diagram that uses regions to show relationships. [p. 667]

vertex On an angle, the endpoint of the rays forming the angle. On a polygon, a corner where two sides meet. On a polyhedron, a corner where edges meet. [pp. 213, 227, 554]

vertical angles Angles on opposite sides of the intersection of two lines. $\angle 1$ and $\angle 2$ are a pair of vertical angles. [p. 218]

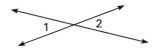

volume The amount of space taken up by a solid. [p. 567]

whole number A number in the set {0, 1, 2, 3, ...}.

x-axis The horizontal line in an x-y coordinate system. [p. 443]

x-coordinate The first number in an ordered pair. [p. 443]

x-y coordinate plane A coordinate system for locating points based on two number lines, the x- and y-axes. [p. 443]

y-axis The vertical line in an x-y coordinate system. [p. 443]

y-coordinate The second number in an ordered pair. [p. 443]

zero pair A number and its opposite. Example: 23 and (–23) [p. 451]

Selected Answers

Chapter 1

1-1 Try It (Examples 1–2)

Public service and trade

Try It (Examples 3–4)

A bar graph

1-1 Exercises & Applications

1. a. Ruiz; Hekla **b.** Colima and Etna **c.** Height in feet **3. a.** Bar graph **b.** Circle graph **c.** Circle graph **5.** C **7.** Gardening **13.** 16,002 **15.** 133 **17.** 938 **19.** 108

1-2 Try It

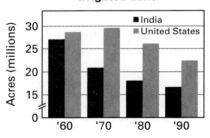

Irrigated Land

1-2 Exercises & Applications

1. a. 250,000,000 **b.** 50,000,000 **3.** B **5.** Possible answer: Scale 1000–5000, Interval 1000. **7.** Possible answer: Scale 120–360, Interval 40. **13.** four hundred twenty-eight **15.** forty-three thousand one hundred eighty-five **17.** three million seven hundred thirty-four thousand seven hundred ninety **19.** 16 **21.** 186

1-3 Try It

a.

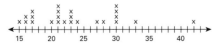

b.

Stem	Leaf
4	2
3	0, 0, 0, 0, 3
2	0, 1, 1, 1, 1, 2, 3, 3, 3, 4, 7, 8
1	5, 6, 6, 7, 7, 7

1-3 Exercises & Applications

1. a. 29 **b.** 36

c.

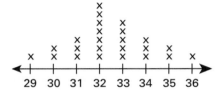

29 30 31 32 33 34 35 36

d. 1

e.

x
x   x
x   x
x   x   x
x   x x x x x
x x x x x x x x x

29 30 31 32 33 34 35 36

f. No **3.** 47; 0 **5.** D

7.

x
x   x   x   x
x x   x   x   x   x

11 12 13 14 15 16 17

9.

Stem	Leaf
3	8
2	0 3 3 5 5 8
1	2 4 6 7 9
0	5 8

11. a.

Stem	Leaf
6	1 1 4 5 8
5	0 1 2 4 4 6 7 7 7 7 8
4	6 8 9 9

13. 410 **15.** 3560 **17.** 8060 **19.** 354,450 **21.** 20,861 **23.** 101,000 **25.** 24,000 **27.** 4000 **29.** 0 **31.** 10,000

1-4 Try It

a. Mean 38.4, median 41, range 45.
b. Mean 46, median 40.5, range 67.

1-4 Exercises & Applications

1. a. 5, 6, 17, 19, 23, 26, 34; Median is 19. **b.** 27, 38, 39, 45, 47, 48, 49, 52; Median is 46. **3. a.** Mean ≈ 59.7 in., median 59.5 in., range 7 in., mode 59 in. **5.** Mean ≈ 320.1; Median 321.5; Modes 320 and 327; Range 202. **7. a.** ≈ 6,000,000 people **9.** Mean 11.87, median 10, mode 6. **11.** C **17.** 9 R2 **19.** 97 R3 **21.** 6999; 7286; 8003 **23.** 28; 82; 288; 2228; 8282; 8822; 8882

Section 1A Review

1. 25% **3.** Yes
5.

Stem	Leaf
3	1 2 2 2 2 3 4 4 6 6 7 8 9
2	3 3 3 6 6 7 7 8 8 9 9 9
1	9

7. China

1-5 Try It

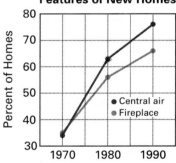

Features of New Homes

1-5 Exercises & Applications

1. An increasing trend—more nations compete each time.

3.

Josie's Bowling Score

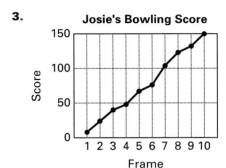

9. C **13.** 13,951 **15.** 101,555
17. 771,936 **19.** Possible answer:
Scale 100–700, Interval 50.
21. Possible answer: Scale 0–150,
Interval 10. **23.** Possible answer:
Scale 0–50, Interval 5.

1-6 Try It (Example 1)

Famous U.S. Bridges

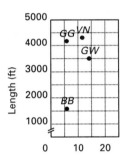

1-6 Try It (Examples 2–3)

a. Negative **b.** Positive

1-6 Exercises & Applications

3. Gorilla: 50; Rhinoceros: 72
5.

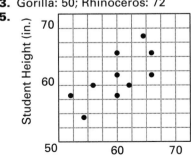

7. Negative **9.** D **15.** 38 R6
17. 118 R24 **19.** 17,269,827

21.

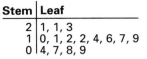

Stem	Leaf
2	1, 1, 3
1	0, 1, 2, 2, 4, 6, 7, 9
0	4, 7, 8, 9

1-7 Try It

a.

Books Read and TV Watching

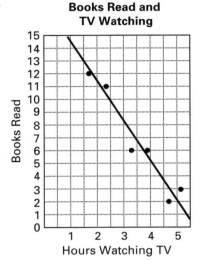

b. About 1

1-7 Exercises & Applications

3.

CD Price and Number of Songs

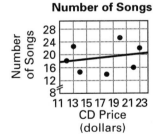

5. a.

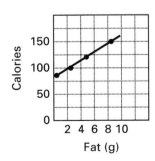

11. 3530 **13.** 54,566
15. 1,521,688 **17.** Mean 34.67,
median 36.5, mode 38. **19.** Mean
101, median 98, no mode.

Section 1B Review

1. a.

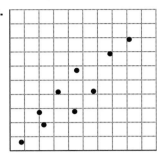

b.

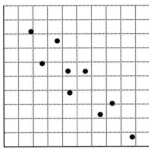

c.

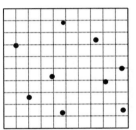

5.

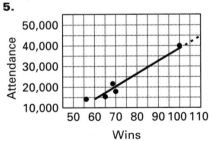

Chapter 1 Summary & Review

1.

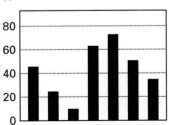

2. Mean 20.3, median 21, mode 23, range 44

3.

Stem	Leaf
4	1 2 5
3	2 3 4 7
2	2 3 8

4. A circle graph   **5.** Asia and Africa

6.

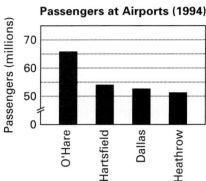

Passengers at Airports (1994)

7.

8. c

9.

Ranking for Conchita Martinez

10.

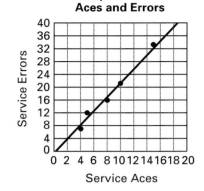

Volleyball Service Aces and Errors

Chapter 2

2-1 Try It

a. 14   **b.** $160

2-1 Exercises & Applications

1. a. *p*, *l* and *w*   **b.** 20 cm   **3.** 230 m²   **5.** 240 ft²   **7.** ≈ 0.435 km/hr   **9.** 0.6 km/hr   **11.** 9 miles   **13.** B   **17.** 24,000   **19.** 7,500   **21.** 296,000   **23.** 74,600   **25.** 146,000   **27.** 3,820,000

2-2 Try It (Examples 1–2)

a. 7   **b.** 2   **c.** 14   **d.** 26

2-2 Try It (Example 3)

a. 2430   **b.** 2456   **c.** 2460

2-2 Exercises & Applications

1. Multiplication   **3.** Division   **5.** Yes; Parentheses   **7.** Yes; Division bar   **9.** 13   **11.** 89   **13.** 66   **15.** B   **17.** $18 + 12 \div (3 + 1) = 21$ **19.** $7 \times (2 + 3 \times 6) = 140$ **21.** Associative Property of Multiplication   **23.** Commutative Property of Multiplication   **25.** Commutative Property of Multiplication   **27. a.** $65.10 **b.** $65.10   **31.** 80   **33.** 190   **35.** 170   **37.** 220

2-3 Try It (Example 1)

s (in.)	2	3	5	8	10	12
A (in²)	4	9	25	64	100	144

2-3 Try It (Example 2)

a. $y = 8x$ **b.** $n = m - 4$

2-3 Exercises & Applications

1. a. 72   **b.** 96

c.

Days	3	4	5	6	7	8
Hours	72	96	120	144	168	192

3.

C	0°	20°	40°	60°	80°	100°
K	273°	293°	313°	333°	353°	373°

5. $y = 5x$ **7.** $n = 6m$ **9.** $v = 0.1w$

11.

A	4	8	12	16
C	1	2	3	4

15. 50   **17.** 170   **19.** 270   **21.** 4600

Section 2A Review

1. 10   **3.** 7   **5.** 16   **7.** $9 \times (9 - 9) \div 9 = 0$ **9.** $(9 \times 9) - (9 \div 9) = 80$ **11.** 120   **13.** $y = 3x$ **16.** B

2-4 Try It

a. 12   **b.** Subtract 3, then multiply by 2

2-4 Exercises & Applications

1. Drive 5 mi west   **3.** Run down 3 flights of stairs   **5.** Subtract $4.50   **7.** 25, 30, 240, 30, 25   **9.** 44, 49, 392, 49, 44   **11.** Multiply by 4, subtract 7   **13.** Set his watch ahead 3 hours   **15.** 2   **19.** 240   **21.** 1500   **23.** 52,000   **25.** 3,000,000   **27.** 1000   **29.** 125   **31.** 10,000   **33.** 100,000   **35.** 32,768

2-5 Try It (Examples 1–2)

a. $h \div 2$ **b.** $25 + d$ **c.** $d(v - 5)$

2-5 Try It (Examples 3–4)

a. Twelve decreased by a number (*g*)   **b.** The sum of the products of 3 and a number (*a*) and 4 and a number (*b*)   **c.** The product of 11 and the difference between 5 and a number (*r*).

2-5 Exercises & Applications

1. Subtraction **3.** Addition **5.** $2k$
7. $u - 4$ **9.** $2c + 8$ **11.** $4(n - 6)$
13. $3(x + 15)$ **15.** 6 decreased by a number (x) **17.** The sum of twice a number (r) and 3 **19.** Half a number (f) **21.** The product of 3 and the sum of a number (d) and 3 **23.** 4 more than the quotient of 3 and the sum of a number (c) and 2
25. a. $267n$ **b.** $267n - 25$
27. $5 + 2y$ **29. a.** $2x + 6$
b. $2(x + 3)$ **33.** 16 **35.** 4 **37.** 20
39. 40 **41.** $P = 102$ ft; $A = 620$ ft^2
43. $P = 204$ m; $A = 2480$ m^2

2-6 Try It

a. $x = 181$ **b.** $b + 67 = 122$;
$b = 55$; $55

2-6 Exercises & Applications

1. Add 80 to both sides: $d - 80 + 80 = 70 + 80$ **3.** Subtract 16 from both sides: $f + 16 - 16 = 32 - 16$
5. Yes **7.** No **9.** $d = 9$ **11.** $f = 9$
13. $x = 88$ **15.** $p = 0$ **17.** $h = 68$
19. $f = 1000$ **21.** $g = 12$ **23.** $c = 149$ **25.** D **27.** $p - 25 = 180$
29. $n = 59 - 17$; $n = 42$ **31.** $n + 127 = 250$; $n = 123$ **33.** $t \approx 1400$
35. $s \approx 6000$ **37.** 13 was added to both sides. **39.** $h = 1300 - 115$, $h = 1185$ **41.** Add 17 **43.** Divide by 20 **45.** 7 **47.** 3 **49.** 16
51. 18

2-7 Try It

a. $x = 245$ **b.** $s = 222$ **c.** 120 kilowatts

2-7 Exercises & Applications

1. Divide both sides by 15: $15d \div 15 = 1200 \div 15$ **3.** Multiply both sides by 16: $\frac{f}{16} \times 16 = 32 \times 16$
5. No **7.** No **9.** $m = 2$
11. $p = 1$ **13.** $d = 15$ **15.** $y = 1$
17. $r = 21$ **19.** $h = 3484$ **21.** A
23. Rectangle with 4 cm base has a height of 3 cm and rectangle with 6 cm base has a height of 2 cm.
25. About 3,775,000 mi^2
27. $k \approx 30$ **29.** $t \approx 20,000$ **31.** C
35. $n = 1235 \div 36$; $n \approx 34.31$; Hua must buy 35 rolls of film.
37. About $\frac{1}{4}$ mi **41.** $2c - 3$
43. $r - 10$

2-8 Try It

a. $x = 51$ **b.** $5t + 48 = 73$. He worked 5 hours.

2-8 Exercises & Applications

1. Addition **3.** Subtraction
5. $n = 1$ **7.** $u = 1$ **9.** $m = 7.5$
11. $s = 1$ **13.** $u = 4$ **15.** $s = 5$
17. $x = 7$ **19.** $s = 16$ **21.** $8 = 4 + 2x$; 2 oz **23. a.** 176 chirps per minute **b.** 16 chirps per minute
25. No **27.** 4 days **29.** First 6 was subtracted from both sides, then both sides were multiplied by 4. **31.** $x = 26$ **33.** $x = 76$
35. $x = 63$ **37.** $x = 857$
39. $e = d + 4$ **41.** $y = 9x$

Section 2B Review

1. She unfastens her seatbelt, opens the door, stands up, gets out of the car, closes the door.
3. $32 + y$ **5.** 28 decreased by a number (f) **7.** The product of 6 and the difference of g and 8 **9.** 1
11. 21 **15.** $k = 8$ **17.** $z = 38$
19. $x = 2$ **21.** $k = 49$ **23.** $m = 4$

Chapter 2 Summary & Review

1. 20 ft^2 **2.** It will cost $20 to travel 6 miles. **3.** 23 **4.** 10 **5.** Addition
6. The distributive property
7. $y = 4x$
8.

Time (t) in hr	0	1	2	3	4	5
Distance (d) in mi	0	40	80	120	160	200

9. Flying 260 miles south.
10. Yes, $35 \div 5 = 7$ **11.** $d + 7 = 23$; $d = 16$ **12.** Multiplication by 11
13. No, $18 + 6 \neq 26$. **14.** $x = 13$
15. $a = 17$ **16.** $n = 96$ **17.** $x = 135$ **18.** $x = 120$ **19.** Division by 3, and subtraction of 18.
20. a. $k + 21$ **b.** $10u$ **21.** $x = 7$
22. a. The product of 5 and a number (z). **b.** The product of 12 and 4 less than a number (j). **c.** The quotient of 5 more than a number (d) and 14.

Cumulative Review
Chapters 1–2

1. B **2.** B **3.** C **4.** A **5.** B
6. D **7.** C **8.** A **9.** C **10.** A

Chapter 3

3-1 Try It

a. > **b.** =

3-1 Exercises & Applications

1. Thirty-six and five-tenths
3. Four thousand, seven hundred ninety-two and six hundred thirty-nine thousandths **5.** $\frac{6}{100}$ **7.** $\frac{6}{10}$
9. 6 thousands, 6 hundreds, $\frac{6}{10}$, $\frac{6}{100}$
11. < **13.** < **15.** <
17. Greatest: 1993; Least: 1991
19. a. Country Yogurt **25.** 23, 29, 34, 43, 45, 46, 65, 78, 89; Median is 45 **27.** 2, 3, 3, 3, 4, 5, 5, 6, 6, 6, 7, 8, 8, 9; Median is 5.5 **29.** 7 less than a number (x) **31.** The product of 8 and 4 less than a number (n)
33. The quotient of 3 more than a number (d) and 4 **35.** 5 reduced by a number (n)

3-2 Try It (Example 1)

7.9; 7.87; 7.865

3-2 Try It (Examples 2–4)

a. $\approx 68 - 32 = 36$ **b.** $\approx 10 \times 60 = 600$ **c.** $\approx 450 \div 90 \approx 5$

3-2 Exercises & Applications

1. 3.1 **3.** 17.5 **5.** 15 **7.** 10
9. 15, 1; 15 **11.** 2, 9; 18 **13.** ≈ 800
15. ≈ 9 **17.** ≈ 290 **19.** ≈ 240
21. ≈ 9600 **23.** ≈ 7 **25.** ≈ 2.5
27. ≈ 550 **29. a.** 23.38 **b.** 23.4
c. 23.383 **31. a.** 19.01 **b.** 19.0
c. 19.010 **33. a.** 0.05 **b.** 0.0
c. 0.046 **35. a.** 43.43 **b.** 43.4
c. 43.434 **37.** $\approx $240 **39.** B
41. Mars: 0.2 years; Jupiter: 1.3 years; Saturn: 2.7 years; Neptune: 9.3 years **47.** $x = 22$ **49.** $m = 197$
51. $y = 3$ **53.** $n = 55$

3-3 Try It

a. $x = 13.1$ **b.** $x = 21.35$

3-3 Exercises & Applications

1. a. $42.4 > 42.268$ **d.** 0.132
3. ≈ 170 **5.** ≈ 0.4 **7.** ≈ 0.6
9. ≈ 0.01 **11.** ≈ 0.04 **13.** ≈ 0.26
15. $x = 84.304$ **17.** $x = 16.395$
19. $x = 0.015667$ **21.** A
23. 2.3125 points **25.** Fuel used = 33.39 kg; Fuel remaining = 22.31 kg
31. $v = 12$ **33.** $c = 140$ **35.** $w = 60$ **37.** $d = 72$

3-4 Try It (Example 1)

a. $x = 1.6173$ **b.** $x = 152.165$

3-4 Try It (Examples 2–3)

a. 34.5 **b.** 0.66

3-4 Try It (Example 4)

a. $x \approx 9.47$ **b.** $n \approx 197.95$

3-4 Exercises & Applications

1. a. $\frac{x}{9} \approx 4$; $x \approx 36$ **b.** 38.22
c. 38.22 and 36 are close, so the answer is reasonable. **3.** ≈ 36
5. ≈ 12.5 **7.** 2 **9.** 20 **11.** 0.5
13. ≈ 0.4 **15.** ≈ 0.004 **17.** ≈ 20
19. ≈ 24 **21.** ≈ 0.05 **23.** $u = 0.46552$ **25.** $x \approx 2.8147$ **27.** $a = 0.9968$ **29.** $k = 0.5068$ **31.** B
33. $10.68 **35.** $w \approx 3.0698$
37. 364 **39.** 1 **41.** $g = 7$ **43.** $x = 14$ **45.** $w = 826$ **47.** $c = 306$

3-5 Try It

a. 3.17×10^{10} **b.** 9.6005×10^3
c. 410,000 **d.** 2,894,000,000,000

3-5 Exercises & Applications

1. a. 1.6120000 **b.** 7
c. 1.612×10^7 **3.** 9 **5.** 10,000
7. 9.37×10^9 **9.** 1.75×10^2
11. 1.01×10^9 **13.** 3.654×10^7
15. 9.9×10^{17} **17.** 2.43×10^8
19. C **21.** 600,000,000
23. 1,200,000,000,000 **25.** 498,000
27. 5,690,000 **29.** $18,157.69
31. 2.2744×10^9 **33.** $5,446
37. Subtract 5 **39.** Sit down
41. 12.0 **43.** 6.5 **45.** 109
47. 88

Section 3A Review

1. a. $>$ **b.** $<$ **c.** $=$ **3.** ≈ 69
5. ≈ 82 **7.** 2 **9.** 0.2 **11.** $x \approx 9$; $x = 8.96$ **13.** $x \approx 5.3$; $x \approx 4.90$
15. a. 1.21×10^4 **b.** 5.206×10^6
c. 4.86×10^9 **19.** About $6 **21.** C

3-6 Try It (Example 2)

a. 2, 3, 4, and 6 **b.** 5 **c.** 2, 4, and 8
d. 2, 3, 6, and 9

3-6 Try It (Example 3)

a. $2^2 \times 31$ **b.** $3^2 \times 7$ **c.** $2^2 \times 7 \times 11$ **d.** $2 \times 3 \times 17$

3-6 Exercises & Applications

1. No **3.** Yes **5.** Yes **7.** Yes
9. 3 **11.** 3, 5, and 9 **13.** 2, 4, 5, 8, and 10 **15.** 2, 3, 6, and 9
17. Composite **19.** Composite
21. Composite **23.** Composite
25. 2×3^2 **27.** 5×37 **29.** $2^3 \times 3^2 \times 5$ **31.** $3^2 \times 5^3$ **33.** C **35.** 1, 2, 3, 6, 7, 9, 14, 18, 21, 27, 42, 54, 63, 126, and 189 seconds
43. 1,758,289,144
45.

Stem	Leaf
4	13
3	18
2	3 6 9
1	5 7

47.

Stem	Leaf
11	7
10	3 5
9	4 5 9
8	6 7

49. $>$ **51.** $<$ **53.** $>$ **55.** $>$

3-7 Try It (Example 2)

a. 18 **b.** 24 **c.** 13 **d.** 2

3-7 Try It (Examples 3–4)

a. 15 **b.** 48 **c.** 60 **d.** 63

3-7 Exercises & Applications

1. a. 1, 2, 3, 6, 7, 14, 21, 42 **b.** 1, 3, 7, 9, 21, 63 **c.** 1, 3, 7, 21 **d.** 21
3. 12 **5.** 17 **7.** 54 **9.** 81 **11.** 45
13. 60 **15.** 56 **17.** 120 **19.** The 300th customer **21.** 85 bars

31. ≈ 160 **33.** ≈ 0.28
35. ≈ 4 **37.** ≈ 100

3-8 Try It (Example 1)

Possible answers: **a.** $\frac{2}{3}, \frac{12}{18}$
b. $\frac{5}{6}, \frac{50}{60}$ **c.** $\frac{5}{6}, \frac{30}{36}$ **d.** $\frac{5}{7}, \frac{30}{42}$

3-8 Try It (Example 2)

a. No **b.** No **c.** Yes **d.** Yes

3-8 Exercises & Applications

1. a. 1, 2, 4, 8, 16 **b.** 1, 2, 3, 4, 6, 8, 12, 24 **c.** GCF = 8 **d.** $\frac{2}{3}$ **3.** $\frac{5}{9}, \frac{30}{54}$
5. $\frac{8}{11}, \frac{32}{44}$ **7.** $\frac{2}{3}$ **9.** $\frac{7}{9}$ **11.** $\frac{4}{5}$ **13.** $\frac{2}{3}$
15. $\frac{3}{4}$ **17.** $\frac{3}{4}$ **19.** $\frac{2}{3}$ **21.** $\frac{1}{7}$ **23.** $\frac{13}{27}$
25. $\frac{18}{25}$ **27.** $\frac{5}{22}$ **29.** $\frac{24}{53}$ **31.** C
33. About $\frac{11}{20}$ **35.** $x = 21$ **37.** $x = 75$ **41.** $t = 9$ **43.** $x = 2$ **45.** $n = 204$ **47.** $y = 408$ **49.** 31 **51.** 470
53. 87 **55.** 56

3-9 Try It

a. $>$ **b.** $>$ **c.** $<$

3-9 Exercises & Applications

1. a. $\frac{48}{56}$ **b.** $\frac{49}{56}$ **c.** $\frac{7}{8} > \frac{6}{7}$ **3.** $=$
5. $<$ **7.** $>$ **9.** $>$ **11.** $=$ **13.** $=$
15. $=$ **17.** $=$ **27.** 4.756×10^5
29. 9.3×10^7 **31.** 8.3×10^2
33. 5.0×10 **35.** 46,000
37. 620,000,000 **39.** 347,000
41. 749,000,000,000,000 **43.** $\frac{25}{51}$

3-10 Try It (Example 1)

a. $\frac{3}{10}$ **b.** $\frac{3}{4}$ **c.** $\frac{46}{125}$

3-10 Try It (Examples 2–3)

a. 0.85; terminating **b.** $0.\overline{6}$; repeating **c.** 0.28125; terminating

3-10 Exercises & Applications

1. a. $\frac{25}{1000}$ **b.** $\frac{1}{40}$ **3.** $\frac{3}{25}$ **5.** $\frac{1}{25}$
7. $\frac{27}{250}$ **9.** $\frac{203}{250}$ **11.** $0.\overline{571428}$, repeating **13.** $0.\overline{6}$, repeating **15.** 0.8, terminating **17.** 0.52, terminating

19. C **21.** $\frac{5}{6}$ **23.** $\frac{2}{11}$ **27.** 63.25
29. 56.625
31.

Gallons	1	2	3	4	5
Miles	36	72	108	144	180

Section 3B Review

1. < **3.** > **5.** > **7.** > **9.** $w = 8.5$
11. $c = 26.72$ **13.** 2×3^3 **15.** $5^2 \times 7$ **17.** $2^4 \times 3^2$ **19.** GCF: 9; LCM: 810 **21.** GCF: 27; LCM: 810
23. $\frac{1}{32}$; one thirty-second
25. $0.\overline{428571}$ **27.** $0.\overline{6}$

Chapter 3 Summary & Review

1. $400, \frac{4}{1000}$ **2.** $8.041 > 8.04$
3. 18.64 **4.** ≈ 840 **5.** ≈ 6
6. 343.615 **7.** $y = 43.783$
8. 29.555 **9.** $e = 58.824$ **10.** $p = 45.3$ **11.** 723,400 **12.** 1.739×10^6
13. 2, 3, 5, 6, and 10 **14.** $2^2 \times 3 \times 23$ **15.** 5 **16.** 60 **17.** Possible
answer: $\frac{5}{6}, \frac{30}{36}$ **18.** $\frac{1}{4}$ **19.** $\frac{5}{11}$
20. $\frac{24}{31} > \frac{23}{31}$ **21.** $\frac{9}{16} > \frac{5}{9}$ **22.** $\frac{6}{25}$
23. $\frac{66}{125}$ **24.** $0.\overline{81}$; the decimal
repeats

Chapter 4

4-1 Try It (Example 1)

a. $\approx \frac{1}{2}$ **b.** ≈ 1 **c.** ≈ 2

4-1 Try It (Example 2)

a. ≈ 9 **b.** ≈ 4 **c.** ≈ 21

4-1 Try It (Examples 3–4)

a. ≈ 5 **b.** ≈ 5 **c.** ≈ 176

4-1 Exercises & Applications

1. $\frac{1}{2}$ **3.** 0 **5.** 0 **7.** $\approx \frac{1}{2}$ **9.** ≈ 0
11. ≈ 1 **13.** $\approx \frac{1}{2}$ **15.** ≈ 1
17. ≈ 12 **19.** ≈ 1 **21.** ≈ 14
23. ≈ 4 **25.** ≈ 4 **27.** ≈ 8
29. ≈ 7 **31.** ≈ 9 **33.** 30–35 times
35. ≈ 5 pieces **39.** South;
Mountain **41.** > **43.** > **45.** <

4-2 Try It

a. $d = \frac{7}{12}$ **b.** $w = \frac{14}{15}$ **c.** $h = \frac{1}{3}$

4-2 Exercises & Applications

1. As written **3.** Rewritten **5.** As
written **7.** 12 **9.** 24 **11.** 20
13. $\frac{4}{5}$ **15.** $\frac{7}{8}$ **17.** $\frac{5}{12}$ **19.** $\frac{13}{18}$ **21.** $\frac{1}{2}$
23. $y = \frac{2}{9}$ **25.** $n = \frac{9}{28}$ **27.** $\frac{7}{8}$
29. A **31.** Stock A **33.** $p = 7$
35. $u = 7\frac{1}{11}$ **37.** $a = 996$ **39.** $x = 2976$ **41.** ≈ 49 **43.** ≈ 1260
45. ≈ 111 **47.** ≈ 1500 **49.** ≈ 55
51. ≈ 470 **53.** ≈ 130 **55.** ≈ 5000

4-3 Try It

a. $8\frac{1}{8}$ **b.** $1\frac{2}{3}$ **c.** $3\frac{9}{10}$

4-3 Exercises & Applications

1. $3\frac{3}{3}$ **3.** $3\frac{7}{9}$ **5.** $4\frac{7}{8}$ **7.** $\frac{25}{8}$ **9.** $\frac{31}{4}$
11. $\frac{55}{8}$ **13.** $4\frac{1}{4}$ **15.** $2\frac{2}{7}$ **17.** $6\frac{4}{5}$
19. $2\frac{7}{8}$ **21.** $n = 3\frac{5}{12}$ **23.** $y = 6\frac{13}{20}$
25. a. $1\frac{4}{5}$ in. **b.** $1\frac{3}{4}$ in. **27.** $5\frac{1}{5}$ AU
29. a. $\frac{1}{8}$ **b.** $\frac{1}{16}$ **33.** $d = 50$ mi
35. $d = 375$ km **37.** $d = 220$ mi
39. $x = 68.86$ **41.** $x = 45.56$
43. $p = 0.049$

Section 4A Review

1. ≈ 1 **3.** $\approx 1\frac{1}{2}$ **5.** ≈ 0 **7.** ≈ 8
9. ≈ 21 **11.** $\frac{19}{24}$ **13.** $\frac{43}{45}$ **15.** $8\frac{1}{5}$
17. $4\frac{4}{5}$ **19.** $6\frac{5}{8}$ **21.** $z = 3\frac{7}{20}$
23. $x = 9\frac{7}{8}$ **25.** 2 ft $5\frac{1}{4}$ in. **27.** D

4-4 Try It (Examples 1–2)

a. $\frac{15}{56}$ **b.** $\frac{2}{3}$ **c.** $\frac{1}{4}$ **d.** $\frac{1}{6}$ **e.** $\frac{1}{10}$

4-4 Try It (Examples 3–4)

a. $\frac{8}{9}$ **b.** $\frac{1}{3}$ **c.** $\frac{27}{125}$ **d.** $\frac{1}{2}$ **e.** $\frac{1}{4}$

4-4 Exercises & Applications

1. $\frac{1}{3}$ **3.** $\frac{8}{45}$ **5.** $\frac{3}{20}$ **7.** $\frac{2}{5}$ **9.** $\frac{1}{3}$
11. $\frac{3}{10}$ **13.** $\frac{1}{7}$ **15.** $\frac{1}{6}$ **17.** $\frac{1}{4}$ **19.** $\frac{5}{14}$
21. $\frac{4}{25}$ **23.** $\frac{3}{14}$ **25.** $\frac{1}{5}$ **27.** B
29. $\approx 13,000$ **31.** $1\frac{1}{3}$ **37.** $p = 1.15$
39. $u = 3.8$ **41.** $x = 2.65$
43. $y = 9.26$

4-5 Try It

a. 18 **b.** 6 **c.** $4\frac{1}{2}$ **d.** $16\frac{1}{2}$ **e.** $17\frac{1}{3}$

4-5 Exercises & Applications

1. $\frac{27}{8}$ **3.** $\frac{71}{8}$ **5.** $\frac{13}{6}$ **7.** 14
9. 16 **11.** 16 **13.** 56 **15.** 9
17. $6\frac{2}{3}$ **19.** $73\frac{1}{8}$ **21.** $3\frac{23}{27}$ **23.** $43\frac{1}{2}$
25. $9\frac{2}{7}$ **29.** 26 **31.** $6\frac{3}{8}$ grams
39. 1.8×10^1 **41.** 4.21×10^7
43. 1.27×10^8 **45.** 1.933×10^4
47. 2.7×10^2 **49.** 9.3×10^7

4-6 Try It

a. 35 **b.** $\frac{3}{4}$ **c.** $1\frac{1}{3}$

4-6 Exercises & Applications

1. 2 **3.** $\frac{10}{3}$ **5.** 4 **7.** $\frac{7}{2}, \frac{2}{7}$ **9.** $\frac{19}{4}, \frac{4}{19}$
11. $\frac{3}{8} \times 4 = 1\frac{1}{2}$ **13.** $\frac{3}{5} \times 3 = 1\frac{4}{5}$
15. $\frac{5}{8} \times \frac{2}{7} = \frac{5}{28}$ **17.** $\frac{12}{5} \times \frac{6}{5} = 2\frac{22}{25}$
19. $\frac{5}{7}$ **21.** $2\frac{1}{2}$ **23.** $1\frac{25}{44}$ **25.** $4\frac{13}{20}$
27. C **29.** $13\frac{1}{3}$ or 14 hats
31. Possible answer: A whole number is the sum of that many ones. A proper fraction is less than one, so there must be more of them contained in the whole number.
33. a. $x = 1\frac{5}{9}$ **b.** $x = 8\frac{8}{25}$ **37.** 2, 3, 6 **39.** 2, 5, 10

Section 4B Review

1. $\frac{5}{21}$ **3.** $3\frac{7}{8}$ **5.** $\frac{1}{8}$ **7.** $1\frac{7}{10}$ **9.** $\frac{7}{12}$
11. $1\frac{2}{25}$ **13.** $5\frac{4}{9}$ **15.** 2 **17.** $\frac{1}{8}$
19. $\frac{8}{25}$ **21.** $\frac{203}{325}$ **23.** $\frac{65}{96}$ **25.** ≈ 42 ft
27. A

Chapter 4 Summary & Review

1. $\approx 1\frac{1}{2}$ **2.** ≈ 0 **3.** ≈ 5
4. ≈ 29 **5.** $1\frac{17}{30}$ **6.** $\frac{13}{18}$ **7.** $\frac{19}{60}$
8. $\frac{31}{8}$ **9.** $9\frac{3}{8}$ **10.** $5\frac{13}{15}$ **11.** $\frac{6}{11}$
12. $1\frac{3}{7}$ **13.** $\frac{5}{16}$ ft^2 **14.** 36 yr
15. 18 **16.** $61\frac{39}{40}$ **17.** $\frac{9}{16}$
18. $1\frac{13}{55}$ **19.** $41\frac{2}{3}$ or 42 disks
20. 8

Cumulative Review
Chapters 1–4

1. C **2.** C **3.** B **4.** C **5.** B **6.** C
7. B **8.** C **9.** C **10.** B **11.** A
12. D **13.** C **14.** C

Chapter 5

5-1 Try It

Complement: 47°; Supplement: 137°

5-1 Exercises & Applications

3. $\angle XYZ$; 140° **5.** $\angle LMN$; 100°
7. None; 45° **9.** 56°; 146° **11.** 145°
13. 13° **15.** Obtuse **17.** Acute
19. A **23.** < **25.** > **27.** >
29. > **31.** GCF = 5; LCM = 2805
33. GCF = 12; LCM = 672
35. GCF = 33; LCM = 2178
37. GCF = 4; LCM = 504

5-2 Try It (Example 1)

a. Corresponding **b.** Vertical
c. Alternate Interior **d.** 59° **e.** 121°
f. 121° **g.** 59°

5-2 Try It (Example 2)

a. The midpoint of the shorter
"stick" is at the point where it is
intersected by the longer one.
b. The longer stick is the perpendicular bisector of the shorter; The
longer stick intersects the shorter at
its midpoint and forms a right angle.

5-2 Exercises & Applications

1. Parallel **3.** Perpendicular
5. Parallel **7.** Perpendicular
9. Perpendicular **11.** $\overleftrightarrow{EF}$ and $\overleftrightarrow{GH}$
13. Possible answer: $\angle 1$ and $\angle 2$
19. A **25.** ≈ 85 **27.** ≈ 15
29. ≈ 35 **31.** ≈ 1000 **33.** $\frac{1}{3}$
35. $\frac{6}{13}$ **37.** $\frac{24}{35}$ **39.** $\frac{9}{16}$

5-3 Try It

a. 90°

5-3 Exercises & Applications

1. a. Known: 87°, 76°, 98°; Unknown:
m **b.** 87 + 76 + 98 + m = 360
c. 261 − 261 + m = 360 − 261

d. 99 **3.** Right scalene **5.** Right
isosceles **7.** Quadrilateral, parallelogram **9.** Quadrilateral, rectangle,
parallelogram **11.** Quadrilateral,
rhombus, parallelogram **13.** t =
38° **15.** x = 177° **21.** y = 31.95
23. x = 12.78 **25.** k = 106.575
27. > **29.** < **31.** < **33.** <

5-4 Try It

a. 1080° **b.** 1800°

5-4 Exercises & Applications

1. Regular hexagon **3.** Nonregular
quadrilateral **5.** Sides are not congruent. **7.** Sides and angles not
congruent. **11.** 900° **13.** 3240°
17. C **19.** 13 **21.** 108° **23.** 135°
27. m = 3.6 **29.** y = 1.46 **31.** x =
9.84 **33.** b = 12.8 **35.** 0.4375;
Terminates **37.** 0.428571; Repeats
39. 0.13125; Terminates **41.** 0.875;
Terminates

5-5 Try It

a. 268 ft **b.** 4200 ft²

5-5 Exercises & Applications

1. a. 48 ft **b.** A = 14 ft × 10 ft
c. 140 ft² **3.** P: 80 m; A: 364 m²
5. P: 346 yd; A: 6360 yd² **7.** P:
9,232 ft; A: 5,270,220 ft² **9.** P: 42 ft;
A: 108 ft² **11.** 2760 m² **17.** 10%
19. ≈ 12 **21.** ≈ 16 **23.** ≈ 12
25. ≈ 34 **27.** ≈ 35

Section 5A Review

1. 143° **3.** 13° **5.** Nonregular
hexagon **7.** 1260° **9.** 2520°
11. P: 800 ft; A: 33,600 ft²

5-6 Try It (Example 1)

a. 9 **b.** 11 **c.** 15 **d.** 100 **e.** 8

5-6 Try It (Examples 2–3)

a. 9.22 **b.** 6.40 **c.** 8.54
d. 9.49 **e.** 17.32

5-6 Exercises & Applications

1. 16 **3.** 625 **5.** 81 **7.** 0.0121
9. $\frac{9}{64}$ **11.** Yes **13.** Yes **15.** No
17. 10 **19.** 9 **21.** 15 **23.** 100
25. 25 **27.** 23.32 **29.** 27.04

31. 9.90 **33.** 7.55 **35.** 3.46 **37.** 1
39. ≈ 115 ft **41.** B **43.** 36 and 64
47. $\frac{1}{6}$ **49.** $\frac{43}{75}$ **51.** $1\frac{1}{80}$ **53.** $\frac{87}{91}$
55. $\frac{11}{60}$ **57.** $\frac{189}{1100}$

5-7 Try It

a. c = 25 ft **b.** b ≈ 10.39 ft

5-7 Exercises & Applications

1. Hypotenuse r; legs p and q
3. Hypotenuse s; legs t and u
5. $j^2 + h^2 = k^2$ **7.** $w^2 + v^2 = u^2$
9. Yes **11.** No **13.** a = 9 in.
15. y = 35 cm **17.** ≈ 127.3 ft
19. C **25.** $20\frac{7}{48}$ **27.** $22\frac{18}{35}$
29. $3\frac{51}{70}$ **31.** $36\frac{1}{21}$

5-8 Try It

a. 42 in² **b.** 152 in² **c.** 60 ft²

5-8 Exercises & Applications

1. a. 9 **b.** 4 **c.** 36 **d.** 18 sq. units
3. $62\frac{1}{2}$ ft² **5.** $6\frac{2}{3}$ in² **7.** 22 ft²
9. 810 m² **11.** 18 ft **13.** 90 in.
15. 18 yd **17.** 26 in. **19.** 7 in²
25. 3 **27.** 5 **29.** 2, 4 **31.** None
33. $\frac{7}{12}$ **35.** $\frac{7}{15}$ **37.** $\frac{2}{9}$ **39.** $\frac{56}{225}$
41. $\frac{55}{96}$ **43.** 1

5-9 Try It (Example 1)

a. $\frac{15}{4}$ in² **b.** 253 m² **c.** 2.88 km²

5-9 Try It (Example 3)

a. 19.5 in² **b.** 13.25 cm²
c. 8.4375 in²

5-9 Exercises & Applications

1. Height n; base m **3.** Height x;
base y **5.** $A = \frac{1}{2}h(b_1 + b_2)$
7. $A = bh$ **9.** 175.2 cm² **11.** $\frac{2}{9}$ in²
13. 96 cm² **15.** $\frac{9}{16}$ in² **17.** 64 cm²
19. A **25.** GCF = 2; LCM = 2376
27. GCF = 42; LCM = 840
29. GCF = 30; LCM = 13,260
31. GCF = 30; LCM = 3780

33. $18\frac{6}{7}$ **35.** $55\frac{1}{4}$ **37.** $16\frac{11}{18}$
39. $14\frac{7}{12}$

5-10 Try It

700 ft²

5-10 Exercises & Applications

1. c. Area = 39 m² **3.** 328 ft²
5. 615 in² **7.** 690 yd² **9.** 191.5 in²
11. 6144 m² **13.** 864 in² **15.** $\frac{5}{7}$
17. $\frac{2}{9}$ **19.** $\frac{21}{32}$ **21.** $\frac{13}{25}$ **23.** $\frac{27}{56}$
25. 4 **27.** $\frac{55}{108}$ **29.** $\frac{5}{12}$

Section 5B Review

1. Perimeter = 74 m; Area = 300 m²
3. Perimeter = $15\frac{1}{4}$ in.; Area =
$14\frac{7}{32}$ in² **5.** 11 **7.** $\frac{81}{100}$ **9.** 30 in.
11. 2 yd **13.** 17.1 cm² **15.** 0.9 mi²
19. A

Chapter 5 Summary & Review

1.

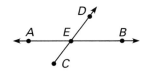

2. 1440° **3. a.** 132° **b.** 42°
4. ∠EFD, an alternate interior angle
5. Area: 24 ft²; Perimeter: 20 ft
6. Right; acute; obtuse **7.** 49
8. 4.123 **9.** 10 ft **10.** 28 cm²
11. 5.425 cm² **12.** 260 ft²

Chapter 6

6-1 Try It

1:2

6-1 Exercises & Applications

1. a. 12 **b.** 36 **c.** $\frac{12}{36}$; $\frac{1}{3}$ **3.** $\frac{7}{8}$; 7:8;
7 to 8 **5.** $\frac{4}{3}$; 4:3; 4 to 3 **7.** 44; 44:1;
44 to 1 **9.** $\frac{37}{1}$ **11.** $\frac{22}{70}$ **13.** $\frac{29}{99}$
15. 1:7 **17.** B **21.** 40 sec
23. Obtuse; 133°

6-2 Try It

a. $\frac{1}{4}$ inch per hour **b.** $8.42 for 5
videotapes

6-2 Exercises & Applications

1. a. $\frac{480}{8}$ **b.** $\frac{60}{1}$ **c.** 60 miles per
hour **3.** $\frac{65 \text{ miles}}{2 \text{ gallons}} = \frac{32.5 \text{ miles}}{1 \text{ gallon}}$
5. $4.00 per notebook **7.** 3 cookies
per student **9.** $5.50 per hour of
work **11.** $2.07 for 3 baskets
13. $3.36 for 24 slices **15.** No
17. Yes **19.** No **21.** $\frac{12}{1000} = \frac{3}{250}$
23. 108,000 mi/hr **25.** A **29.** 144
31. 13 **33.** 9 **35.** 8
37. $\overleftrightarrow{AD}$ and $\overleftrightarrow{AC}$

6-3 Try It

a. Possible answer: $\frac{3}{7}$ and $\frac{12}{28}$
b. 2 cups

6-3 Exercises & Applications

1–11. Possible answers given.
1. a. 2 **b.** $\frac{16}{40}$ **c.** 4 **d.** $\frac{4}{10}$ **3.** $\frac{20}{28}$; $\frac{5}{7}$
5. $\frac{44}{48}$; $\frac{11}{12}$ **7.** $\frac{54}{90}$; $\frac{3}{5}$ **9.** $\frac{80}{150}$; $\frac{8}{15}$
11. $\frac{200}{350}$; $\frac{4}{7}$ **13.** 1000 pesetas
15. 60 sec **17.** 720; $\frac{720 \text{ frames}}{30 \text{ seconds}}$
21. < **23.** < **25.** > **27.** <
29. Right isosceles

6-4 Try It

$\frac{4}{10}$; $\frac{6}{15}$; $\frac{8}{20}$; $\frac{10}{25}$; $\frac{12}{30}$

6-4 Exercises & Applications

1. a–d.

4	8	12	16	20	24
7	14	21	28	35	42

3. $\frac{24}{36}$; $\frac{16}{24}$; $\frac{12}{18}$; $\frac{8}{12}$; $\frac{6}{9}$ **5.** $\frac{16}{32}$; $\frac{4}{8}$; $\frac{1}{2}$; $\frac{64}{128}$
7. 11 video games **15.** B **19.** $\frac{1}{4}$
21. $\frac{671}{1000}$ **23.** $\frac{19}{50}$ **25.** $\frac{617}{5000}$ **27.** 540°

Section 6A Review

1. 1:5 **3.** $\frac{1}{7}$ **5.** $\frac{5}{6}$ **7.** 21 push-ups
per minute **9.** $2.22 for 2 baskets

6-5 Try It

a. Missing table entries are 10, 15,
20; $\frac{2}{5} = \frac{4}{10}$, $\frac{2}{5} = \frac{6}{15}$, $\frac{2}{5} = \frac{8}{20}$
b. $\frac{3 \text{ gray whales}}{8 \text{ killer whales}} = \frac{6 \text{ gray whales}}{16 \text{ killer whales}}$,
$\frac{3 \text{ gray whales}}{8 \text{ killer whales}} = \frac{9 \text{ gray whales}}{24 \text{ killer whales}}$

6-5 Exercises & Applications

1. a–b.

2	4	6	8
7	14	21	28

c. $\frac{2}{7} = \frac{4}{14}$; $\frac{2}{7} = \frac{6}{21}$; $\frac{2}{7} = \frac{8}{28}$

3.

5	10	20	50
9	18	36	90

$\frac{5}{9} = \frac{10}{18}$; $\frac{5}{9} = \frac{20}{36}$; $\frac{5}{9} = \frac{50}{90}$; $\frac{10}{18} = \frac{20}{36}$

5.

7	14	21	28
8	16	24	32

$\frac{7}{8} = \frac{14}{16}$; $\frac{7}{8} = \frac{21}{24}$; $\frac{7}{8} = \frac{28}{32}$

7.

13	26	39	52
15	30	45	60

$\frac{13}{15} = \frac{26}{30}$; $\frac{13}{15} = \frac{39}{45}$; $\frac{13}{15} = \frac{52}{60}$

9.

10	20	30	40
14	28	42	56

$\frac{10}{14} = \frac{20}{28}$; $\frac{10}{14} = \frac{30}{42}$; $\frac{10}{14} = \frac{40}{56}$

11.

2	4	6	8
100	200	300	400

$\frac{2}{100} = \frac{4}{200}$; $\frac{2}{100} = \frac{6}{300}$; $\frac{2}{100} = \frac{8}{400}$

13.

17	34	51	68
19	38	57	76

$\frac{17}{19} = \frac{34}{38}$; $\frac{17}{19} = \frac{51}{57}$; $\frac{17}{19} = \frac{68}{76}$ **19.** C
23. x = 10; y = 63 **25.** g = 100;
h = 144 **37.** P = 68 ft; A = 280 ft²
39. P = 34 m; A = 72 m²

6-6 Try It (Example 3)

a. Yes, both are equal to $\frac{1}{5}$. **b.** No
c. Yes: 7 · 3 = 21 and 10 · 3 = 30

6-6 Try It (Example 4)

a. Proportional

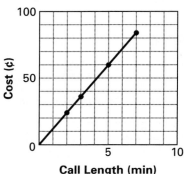

Cost (¢) vs. Call Length (min)

b. Not proportional

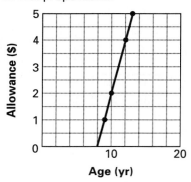

Allowance ($) vs. Age (yr)

6-6 Exercises & Applications

1. a. $\frac{3}{4}$ **b.** $\frac{3}{4}$ **c.** They are equal and proportional. **3.** Yes **5.** Yes **7.** Yes **9.** Yes **11.** No **13.** No **15.** Yes **19.** Yes **21.** D **23.** No **27.** Subtract 45 **29.** Multiply by 10 **31.** Multiply by 7, then subtract 24 **33.** 9 **35.** 60 **37.** 10 **39.** 17

6-7 Try It

$58.80

6-7 Exercises & Applications

1. 4 pages per minute **3.** $0.12 for one **5. a.** $0.33 **b.** $0.66 **7. a.** 74.6 miles per hour **b.** 149.2 miles **c.** 0.0134 hours per mile **d.** 5.36 hours **9. a.** 12.8 days **b.** 2187.5 miles **11.** 17 **15.** $u - 5$ **17.** $g + 12$ **19.** 10 **21.** 26 ft

6-8 Try It

a. No **b.** Yes **c.** $x = 48$ **d.** $k = 72$ **e.** $n = 5.83$

6-8 Exercises & Applications

1. a. 3 **b.** 15 **d.** $x = 3.75$ **3.** 18 **5.** 320 **7.** No **9.** Yes **11.** No **13.** Yes **15.** $x = 2$ **17.** $x = 5.\overline{45}$ **19.** $t = 36$ **21.** $x = 22.5$ **23.** C **25.** No **27.** 2394 g **31.** $x = 33$ **33.** $y = 52$ **35.** 24 units^2

Section 6B Review

7. No **9.** Yes **11.** Yes **13.** 12.5 **15.** 20 **17.** $0.65; 120

Chapter 6 Summary & Review

1. 4 to 3; 4:3; $\frac{4}{3}$ **2.** $\frac{3}{5}$ **3.** 65 miles per hour **4.** 17 houses per mile **5.** $3.20 for 2 loaves **6.** 189 miles **7.** Possible answer: $\frac{32}{40}, \frac{8}{10}$ **8.** Possible answer: $\frac{30 \text{ points}}{8 \text{ games}}, \frac{45 \text{ points}}{12 \text{ games}}$ **9.** $\frac{6}{8}, \frac{9}{12}, \frac{12}{16}, \frac{15}{20}, \frac{18}{24}$ **10.** $\frac{60}{40}, \frac{30}{20}, \frac{24}{16}, \frac{12}{8}, \frac{6}{4}$ **11.** No

12.

4	8	12	16
7	14	21	28

$\frac{4}{7} = \frac{8}{14}; \frac{4}{7} = \frac{12}{21}; \frac{4}{7} = \frac{16}{28}; \frac{8}{14} = \frac{12}{21}$

13.

5	10	15	20
13	26	39	52

$\frac{5}{13} = \frac{10}{26}; \frac{5}{13} = \frac{15}{39}; \frac{5}{13} = \frac{20}{52}$ **14.** No; Their cross products are not equal. **15.** $0.85 per muffin **16.** $n = 30$ **17.** Yes **18.** $8.25 per hour

Cumulative Review
Chapters 1–6

1. B **2.** C **3.** B **4.** D **5.** B **6.** A **7.** B **8.** D **9.** C **10.** A **11.** A **12.** B **13.** B

Chapter 7

7-1 Try It (Examples 1–2)

A little less than 2 inches: $\approx$ 1.9 inches

7-1 Try It (Example 3)

$\approx$ 150 km

7-1 Exercises & Applications

1. a. 75 miles **b.** $\approx$ 1.9 miles **c.** $\approx$ 76.9 miles **3.** 1 in.:225 mi, $\frac{1 \text{ in.}}{225 \text{ mi}}$ **5.** 6 cm = 100 km, $\frac{6 \text{ cm}}{100 \text{ km}}$ **7.** 1 in.:10–12 mi **9.** 1 in.:7–8 mi **11.** $\approx$ 2 cm **13.** $\approx$ 9000 km **15.** $\approx$ 100 mi **17.** 25 ft:3000 mi $\approx$ 1 ft:100 mi **19.** $\approx$ 7 in. long, $\approx$ 5 in. wide **21.** 1 in.:100 ft **23.** $\approx \frac{1}{2}$ **25.** $\approx$ 1 **27.** $\approx$ 0 **29.** $\approx \frac{1}{2}$ **31.** $\approx$ 1 **33.** 36 sq. units

7-2 Try It

5 feet

7-2 Exercises & Applications

1. a. 3 cm **b.** $\frac{3 \text{ cm}}{x \text{ m}} = \frac{1 \text{ cm}}{3 \text{ m}}$ **c.** 9 m **3.** 12.75 ft **5.** 18.375 ft **7.** 20 m **9.** 250 mi **11.** $x = 20$ ft **13.** $x = 125$ mi **15.** 2860 km **17.** 160 ft $\times$ 255 ft **21.** $\frac{1}{30}$ **23.** $\frac{59}{60}$ **25.** 82.5 sq. units **27.** 71 sq. units

7-3 Try It

About 5:35 P.M.

7-3 Exercises & Applications

1. a. 6 km **b.** $1\frac{1}{2}$ hours **c.** 5:00 P.M. **3.** 8:00 P.M. **5.** $\approx$ 5:45 P.M. **7. a.** $\approx$ 30 mi **b.** $\approx$ 45 min **c.** $\approx$ 7:15 P.M. **9. a.** 12:30 P.M. **b.** 7:50 P.M. **11. a.** 1,375 mi **b.** 125 gallons **c.** $162.50 **15.** $2\frac{4}{5}$ **17.** $1\frac{11}{56}$ **19.** $16\frac{19}{63}$ **21.** $18\frac{2}{21}$ **23.** 3 pounds:1 dollar; $\frac{3 \text{ pounds}}{1 \text{ dollar}}$; 3 pounds = 1 dollar

7-4 Try It

1:11

7-4 Exercises & Applications

1. a. 2.5 in. **b.** 14.4:1 **c.** 2 in.; 10.5:1 **d.** Scale is 10.5:1 **3.** 1 ft:3 ft **5.** 1 in.:3.6 ft **7.** $\approx$ 4.25:1 **9.** 1 in.:200 mi **11.** 27 ft:5 in. = 1 ft:0.185 in. **13. a.** $\approx$ 1:7,326,300,000 **b.** $\approx$ 20.4 m **c.** $\approx$ 812.1 m **d.** $\approx$ 0.06 m = 6 cm **15.** $q = 60$ **17.** $n = 5$ **19.** $t = 21$ **21.** $r = 2$ **23.** $w = 40$ **25.** 3 sections per day

27. 33.4 miles per gallon **29.** 24 cans per case

Section 7A Review

1. $\frac{4 \text{ in.}}{200 \text{ mi}}$, 4 in. = 200 mi
3. 10 cm:4 km, 10 cm = 4 km
5. 2 cm:400 km **7.** 60 in.

7-5 Try It (Example 1)

a. Miles per hour **b.** Problems per hour

7-5 Try It (Example 2)

Yes

7-5 Try It (Example 3)

$\frac{1 \text{ wk}}{25 \text{ lbs}}$, $\frac{0.04 \text{ wk}}{1 \text{ lb}}$

7-5 Exercises & Applications

1. a. $\frac{20 \text{ miles}}{1 \text{ gallon}}$ **b.** $\frac{1 \text{ gallon}}{20 \text{ miles}}$
c. $\frac{0.05 \text{ gallons}}{\text{mile}}$ **3–5.** Possible answers given: **3.** Gallons per mile **5.** Dollars per hour **7.** $\frac{1}{2}$ quart of soup per student **9.** 10 meters per second **11.** Yes **13.** Yes
15. $\frac{\$0.20}{1 \text{ lb}}$ **17.** $\frac{0.5 \text{ ton}}{\text{week}}$ **19.** No
23. Yes **25.** $q = 75$ **27.** $n = 3$
29. 3 mm per second **31.** 33 desks per classroom **33.** 1000 mL per L

7-6 Try It

a. 3 hrs **b.** 30 yds

7-6 Exercises & Applications

1. a. $\frac{1000 \text{ m}}{1 \text{ km}}$ and $\frac{1 \text{ km}}{1000 \text{ m}}$ **b.** $\frac{1 \text{ km}}{1000 \text{ m}}$
c. 3 km **3.** $\frac{365 \text{ days}}{1 \text{ year}}$, $\frac{1 \text{ year}}{365 \text{ days}}$
5. $\frac{1 \text{ pound}}{16 \text{ ounces}}$, $\frac{16 \text{ ounces}}{1 \text{ pound}}$ **7.** $\frac{1000 \text{ grams}}{1 \text{ kilogram}}$, $\frac{1 \text{ kilogram}}{1000 \text{ grams}}$ **9.** 240 inches
11. 42 pounds **13.** 2 gallons
15. 12.5 feet **17.** 40 quarts
21. C **25.** 4.00452×10^4
27. 4.3567×10^1 **29.** 5.77×10^2
31. 4.03770×10^2

7-7 Try It (Example 1)

a. ≈ 29,762 trees per hour
b. 12,000 millimeters per second
c. 720,000 millimeters per minute

7-7 Try It (Example 2)

a. ≈ 1083.3 meters per minute
b. 15 cents per ounce

7-7 Exercises & Applications

1. a. $\frac{1 \text{ gal.}}{4 \text{ qt}}$, $\frac{4 \text{ qt}}{1 \text{ gal}}$ **b.** $\frac{4 \text{ qt}}{1 \text{ gal}}$ **c.** $\frac{64 \text{ qt}}{1 \text{ day}}$
3. $10\frac{2}{3}$ feet per second **5.** $4\frac{1}{2}$ cups per day **7.** ≈ 137,000 flea collars per day **9.** ≈ 46,000 ounces per hour **11.** A **13.** ≈ 216.8 miles per hour **17.** $\frac{13}{52} < \frac{5}{16}$ **19.** $\frac{23}{92} = \frac{1}{4}$
21. $\frac{5}{3} = \frac{10}{6}$, $\frac{10}{6} = \frac{15}{9}$, $\frac{15}{9} = \frac{20}{12}$
23. $\frac{11}{44} = \frac{22}{88}$, $\frac{22}{88} = \frac{33}{132}$, $\frac{33}{132} = \frac{44}{176}$
25. $\frac{27}{36} = \frac{9}{12}$, $\frac{9}{12} = \frac{3}{4}$, $\frac{3}{4} = \frac{54}{72}$

Section 7B Review

1. Possible answer: Pages per hour
3. $\frac{2.5 \text{ pizzas}}{1 \text{ student}}$, $\frac{0.4 \text{ pizza}}{1 \text{ student}}$ **5.** No **7.** Yes
9. 3.5 days **11.** 600 miles per day
13. 2880 gallons per day **15.** 208 ounces per year **17.** B

7-8 Try It

Yes; Scale factor is $\frac{4}{3}$; $\triangle UVW \sim \triangle XZY$

7-8 Exercises & Applications

1. a. $\angle E$, $\angle D$, $\angle F$
b. Corresponding angles are congruent. **c.** $\overline{ED}$, $\frac{1}{3}$; $\overline{DF}$, $\frac{1}{3}$; $\overline{EF}$, $\frac{1}{3}$
d. The ratios are equal; scale factor is $\frac{1}{3}$. **3.** Not similar **7.** $m\angle U = 38°$; $m\angle V = 46°$; $m\angle W = 96°$
9. 960 **11.** B
13.

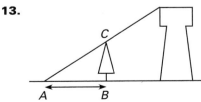

Anywhere on line segment $\overline{AB}$.

15. $\frac{2}{15}$ **17.** 1 **19.** 1 **21.** Yes
23. Yes

7-9 Try It

$a = 9$, $b = 18$, $c = 21$

7-9 Exercises & Applications

1. a. $\overline{AB}$ **b.** $\frac{x}{18}$ **c.** $\overline{HE}$ **d.** $\overline{DA}$; $\frac{1}{3}$
e. $\frac{x}{18} = \frac{1}{3}$; $x = 6$ **3.** $x = 45$ **5.** 50 m
7. $t = 3$, $s = 5$, $u = 3$ **9.** A
13. Yes **15.** $25\frac{11}{24}$ **17.** $24\frac{7}{10}$
19. 40 words per minute
21. $1.699 per gallon

7-10 Try It

Perimeter = 96 units; Area = 99 square units

7-10 Exercises & Applications

1. a. 42 **b.** 9 **c.** 252 sq. units
3. 16 **5.** Perimeter = 30 cm; Area = 54 cm^2 **7.** Perimeter = 21 ft; Area = 58.5 ft^2 **9.** 5 **11.** 0.62
13. B **15.** 1875 m^2 **17.** $\frac{9}{20}$
19. $3\frac{1}{3}$ **21.** 64 **23.** $p = 9$
25. $n = 10$

Section 7C Review

1. Yes; $\triangle XYZ \sim \triangle RQP$; 2 **3.** No
5. Perimeter = 40 ft; Area = 96 ft^2
7. $12\frac{1}{3}$ miles per minute

Chapter 7 Summary & Review

1. 1 in.:25 mi; 1 in. = 25 mi **2.** $x = 8$ yd **3.** 450 ft **4.** 14 cm = 63 km or 1 cm = 4.5 km **5.** 4:27 p.m.
6. About 1:3 **7.** Answers may vary. **8.** $\frac{0.2 \text{ sec}}{\text{foot}}$ **9.** 6 miles per minute **10.** ≈ 1.5 cents per second
11. Similar **12.** Perimeter = 28 in.; Area = 80 in^2 **13.** Perimeter ratio = 9; Scale factor = 9

Chapter 8

8-1 Try It

a. $\frac{1}{2} = 50\%$; $\frac{3}{5} = 60\%$; $\frac{1}{2} < \frac{3}{5}$ **b.** $\frac{7}{10} = 70\%$; $\frac{3}{4} = 75\%$; $\frac{7}{10} < \frac{3}{4}$ **c.** $\frac{13}{20} = 65\%$; $\frac{16}{25} = 64\%$; $\frac{13}{20} > \frac{16}{25}$

8-1 Exercises & Applications

1. a. 4 **b.** $\frac{28}{100}$ **c.** 28% **3.** 75%
5. 48.3% **7.** 75% **9.** 13.5%
11. 80% **13.** $\frac{11}{25} = 44\%$, $\frac{1}{2} = 50\%$;
$\frac{11}{25} < \frac{1}{2}$ **15.** $\frac{3}{4} = 75\%$, $\frac{4}{5} = 80\%$;
$\frac{3}{4} < \frac{4}{5}$ **17.** 9% < 15% **19.** 16% <
28% **21.** 1% **23.** 63% **25.** 100%
27. 1% of a dollar **29.** 100% of a
dollar **31.** D **35.** $\frac{44}{125}$ **37.** $\frac{1101}{2000}$
39. $\frac{49}{80}$ **41.** 0.375 **43.** 0.46 **45.** $0.\overline{3}$
47. 1 cm:20 m **49.** 1 in.:20 ft

8-2 Try It

a. $\frac{27}{50}$ **b.** 91% **c.** 60% **d.** 13.5%

8-2 Exercises & Applications

1. a. 0.1875 **b.** 18.75% **3.** 0.75
5. 0.05 **7.** 1.0 **9.** 0.143 **11.** 0.475
13. $\frac{1}{5}$ **15.** $\frac{17}{20}$ **17.** $\frac{11}{20}$ **19.** $\frac{7}{25}$
21. $\frac{3}{8}$ **23.** 8% **25.** 87.5%
27. 50% **29.** $44.\overline{4}\%$ **31.** 80%
33. 45% **35.** 15.5% **37.** ≈ 3%
39. C **41.** No; 54 of the 130 calories ≈ 41.5%. **43.** ≈ 1 **45.** ≈ 1
47. ≈ $\frac{1}{2}$ **49.** ≈ $\frac{1}{2}$ **51.** ≈ $\frac{1}{2}$
53. x = 25 in. **55.** x = 0.8 in.
57. x = 250 m **59.** x = 52.5 mm
61. x = 110 km

8-3 Try It

a. $\frac{1}{250}$, 0.004 **b.** $1\frac{1}{4}$, 1.25

8-3 Exercises & Applications

1. a. $\frac{0.8}{100}$ **b.** $\frac{8}{1000}$ **c.** $\frac{1}{125}$ **3.** A
5. B **7.** C **9.** A **11.** B **13.** >
15. < **17.** 0.03% **19.** 350%
21. 130% **23.** 280% **25.** 0.8%
27. 0.7% **29.** 0.125% **31.** 6.04%
33. 1.25 **35.** 0.002 **37.** 0.065
39. 0.00375 **41.** 0.000067
43. ≈ 0.27% **45.** B **49.** $\frac{11}{12}$
51. $\frac{25}{36}$ **53.** $\frac{19}{21}$ **55.** $\frac{5}{39}$ **57.** $\frac{11}{30}$
59. 3:20 P.M. **61.** 2:45 P.M.

8-4 Try It

a. 3 **b.** 16 **c.** 15 **d.** 450

8-4 Exercises & Applications

1. a. 3,400 **b.** 1,700 **c.** 5,100
3. 2,900; 580; 58 **5.** 122; 24.4; 2.44
7. 1,230 **9.** 5,740 **11.** 3,280
13. 125 **15.** $56 **17.** 105
19. 240 **21.** 35 **23.** ≈ 4
25. ≈ 12 **27.** ≈ 2000 **29.** C
31. a. 2,000,000 died; 2,000,000
survived **b.** 500,000 died; 1,500,000
returned to Texas. **c.** 37.5 **33.** 256
35. 529 **37.** 1 **39.** 22 **41.** 19
43. 14 in.:100 mi ≈ 1 in.:7.1 mi

Section 8A Review

1. 17% **3.** 30% **5.** 71.6% **7.** 60%
9. 45.6% **11.** 89% **13.** 49.8%
15. 307% **17.** 0.3 **19.** 4.23
21. 0.001 **23.** $\frac{7}{10}$ **25.** $3\frac{3}{50}$ **27.** 85
29. $5.40 **31.** 305

8-5 Try It

a. 30% **b.** 75

8-5 Exercises & Applications

1. a. Let regular price be r.
b. $25.20 is 60% of the regular price.
c. 25.20 = 0.6 • r **d.** $\frac{25.20}{0.6} = \frac{0.6}{0.6} • r$
e. r = 42. The regular price is
$42.00. **3.** 31.4% **5.** 54 **7.** 327.3
9. 38 **11.** 200 **13.** 12,000
15. a. 75% **b.** $5.25 **17.** It is not
possible to tell. **21.** Greater than
45; Less than 45 **23.** Yes Possible
answers for Exercises 25 and 27:
25. Breaths per minute **27.** Cubic
centimeters per minute

8-6 Try It (Examples 1–2)

a. 172.38 **b.** $53.\overline{3}\%$

8-6 Try It (Example 3)

a. 164 **b.** 1,312,500 African
elephants

8-6 Exercises & Applications

1. a. x **b.** $\frac{38}{100} = \frac{52}{x}$ **c.** 38x = 5200
d. $\frac{38x}{38} = \frac{5200}{38}$ **e.** 136.8 **3.** 17.3

5. 9.1% **7.** 238.9 **9.** 240%
11. 3.3% **13.** 2.5 **15.** 7,500,000%
17. Possible answer: $\frac{4}{12}$, $\frac{8}{24}$, $\frac{16}{48}$
19. a. 6.25 grams **b.** 2.5 grams
23. b = 10 cm **25.** h = 12 m
27. 120 feet per minute **29.** 30.48
centimeters per foot

8-7 Try It

a. 60% **b.** 29¢

8-7 Exercises & Applications

1. a. 119 **b.** $\frac{c}{100} = \frac{119}{140}$ **c.** 140c =
11,900 **d.** 85% **3.** 25% **5.** 98.4%
7. 66.7% **9.** 30 **11.** 42 **13.** 9.4
15. 40.1 **17.** ≈ 23.1% **19.** Tax:
$4.41; Price: $57.90 **21.** Tax: $5.20;
Price: $85.18 **23.** 56.25%
25. 224% **27.** C **29.** 7,499,900%
31. 48 yd^2 **33.** 21 in^2 **35.** $28.\overline{63}$
miles per hour

Section 8B Review

1. 22.2% **3.** 105.4 **5.** 125%
7. 67.2 **9.** $23.76 **11.** $83\frac{1}{9}\%$
13. $5 **15.** $4.80

Chapter 8 Summary & Review

1. 27% **2.** $\frac{1}{4} = 25\%$; $\frac{1}{5} = 20\%$; $\frac{1}{4} > \frac{1}{5}$
3. $\frac{11}{50}$ **4.** 0.86 **5.** 73%, $\frac{73}{100}$ **6.** $\frac{9}{20}$,
0.45 **7.** $\frac{1}{125}$, 0.008 **8.** $\frac{5}{4}$, 1.25
9. 240, 24 **10.** 276 **11.** 14
12. $6.60 **13.** 20 **14.** ≈ 46.2%
15. $66\frac{2}{3}$ **16.** 184 **17.** $212.50
18. $15.00 **19.** 99 **20.** ≈ 21.5%
21. 84%; 16% **22.** ≈ 23.1%
23. $31\frac{1}{9}\%$ **24.** ≈ 74.2%

Cumulative Review
Chapters 1–8

1. C **2.** B **3.** C **4.** D **5.** A **6.** B
7. B **8.** C **9.** C **10.** B **11.** C
12. B **13.** C

Chapter 9

9-1 Try It (Examples 1–2)

3, 4, 5; −1, −3, −5; −3 and 3, −5 and 5

9-1 Try It (Example 3)

a. 17 **b.** 5.25 **c.** 3298 **d.** 0

9-1 Exercises & Applications

1. a.

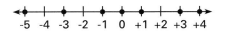

b. 1, 3, 4 **c.** −1, −3, −5 **d.** −1 and 1, −3 and 3 **3.** No **5.** Yes
7. −31,441 **9.** −6 **11.** −2
13. −3 **15.** 222 **17.** −5640
19. 23 **21.** 66 **23.** 4771
25. 2435 **27.** 90,121 **29.** 136°;
129°; −129° **31.** 13,796; −19,680
35. $\frac{2}{1}$, 2:1, 2 to 1 **37.** $\frac{12}{10}$, 12:10, 12
to 10 **39.** $x = 15$

9-2 Try It

a. 45°F **b.** −1 > −22
c. −313, −262, −252, −245

9-2 Exercises & Applications

1. a.

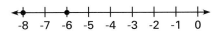

b. −6 **3.** −5 > −7 **5.** 5 > −8
7. −7 > −9 **9.** −2 > −3 **11.** 3 >
−4 **13.** < **15.** > **17.** = **19.** >
21. $12, $11, $8, $0, −$2, −$5, −$7
23. −3151, −3155, −3515, −3551,
−3555 **25. a.** Always
b. Sometimes **c.** Never **d.** Always
27. B **29. a.** Lost $2.75 **b.** Lost
$3.25 **c.** Gained $1.25 **d.** Lost
$4.00 **31.** A half a page per minute
33. 2 hours per day **35.** Perimeter
of first: 24; Area of first: 36;
Perimeter of second: 72; Area of
second: 324

9-3 Try It (Examples 1–2)

a–d.

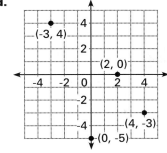

e. II **f.** IV **g.** x-axis **h.** y-axis

9-3 Try It (Example 3)

$B(-4, 1)$, $C(1, 3)$, $D(0, -3)$, $E(2, -2)$

9-3 Try It (Example 4)

They are negative.

9-3 Exercises & Applications

1. a–d.

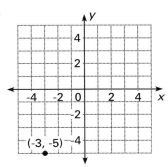

3. (0, 0) **5.** (−2, 0) **7.** (3, −1)
19. a. (200, −100); (500, −200)
b.

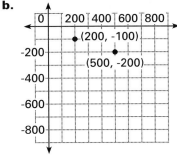

21. IV **23.** I **25.** III **27.** IV **29.** I
31. C **33.** Cairo: 30° north, 31°
east; Zanzibar: 6° south, 39° east
Possible answers for 35–39: **35.** $\frac{4}{11}$,
$\frac{16}{44}$ **37.** $\frac{10}{21}$, $\frac{40}{84}$ **39.** $\frac{21}{50}$, $\frac{84}{200}$ **41.** 67%
43. 34%

Section 9A Review

1. 4 **3.** 0 **5.** −201 **7.** 6 **9.** 613
11. > **13.** > **15.** −5, −25 **23.** C

9-4 Try It (Example 1)

a. −3 **b.** 5 **c.** −8 **d.** 6

9-4 Try It (Examples 2–3)

a. 3 **b.** −1 **c.** −1 **d.** 0

9-4 Exercises & Applications

1. a–b.

c.

d. −3 **3.** 4 + (−6) = −2 **5.** 6
7. 15 **9.** 0 **11.** −10 **13.** 5 **15.** 4
17. −10 **19.** 0 **21.** 11 **23.** −46
25. 22 **27.** −110 **29.** 4 tokens
31. −10 **33.** B **35. a.** 264 + (−127)
b. 137 ft **37.** $\frac{6}{14}$, $\frac{9}{21}$, $\frac{12}{28}$, $\frac{15}{35}$, $\frac{18}{42}$ **39.** $\frac{1}{2}$
41. $\frac{1}{20}$ **43.** $\frac{9}{20}$ **45.** $\frac{14}{125}$ **47.** $\frac{13}{25}$

9-5 Try It (Example 1)

a. 1 **b.** −3 **c.** −6 **d.** 4

9-5 Try It (Example 2)

a. 2 **b.** −5 **c.** 3 **d.** 2

9-5 Try It (Example 3)

69 feet

9-5 Exercises & Applications

1. a–b.

c.

d. 5 **3.** −9 **5.** 10 **7.** 12 **9.** 56
11. 60 **13.** −21 **15.** −30 **17.** −91
19. 583 **21.** 130 **23.** −14 **25.** 12
27. −7 **29.** Alaska: 180; California:
179; Hawaii: 86; North Dakota: 181;
West Virginia: 149; Widest: North
Dakota; Narrowest: Hawaii
31. a. −10 − 20 = −30

b. $20 - (-10) = 30$ **c.** $-10 - (-10) = 0$ **d.** $20 - 20 = 0$ **33.** 2^{10}
35. $2 \times 3 \times 11$ **37.** $2^4 \times 3^2$
39. $2 \times 3 \times 5 \times 7 \times 13$ **41.** $2^5 \times 3$
43. 52% **45.** 90% **47.** 243%
49. 987.654% **51.** 1020%

9-6 Try It (Examples 1–3)

a. -16 **b.** 20 **c.** -54 **d.** -33
e. -140 **f.** 0

9-6 Try It (Examples 4–6)

a. 64 **b.** -30 **c.** 24

9-6 Exercises & Applications

1. $8, 4, -4, -8$ **3.** $-27, 0, 9, 18$
5. $-$ **7.** $+$ **9.** 72 **11.** -72
13. 45 **15.** -100 **17.** -135
19. 125 **21.** -112 **23.** -8
25. -84 **27.** -512 **29.** -136
31. C **33.** You can multiply integers as you would whole numbers, but you have to look at the signs to figure out what sign the product is.
35. 15 **37.** 17 **39.** 21 **41.** 3
43. 60 **45.** 90 **47.** 1.5 **49.** \$5.40

9-7 Try It (Examples 1–4)

a. 4 **b.** 5 **c.** -2 **d.** -3

9-7 Try It (Example 5)

-4

9-7 Exercises & Applications

1. a. -724 **b.** -181 **c.** -181
d. a drop **3.** $-$ **5.** $+$ **7.** -3 **9.** 8
11. -2 **13.** -8 **15.** 81 **17.** -16
19. 15 **21.** -8 **23.** 4 **25.** -1
27. 0 **29.** $\frac{11}{25}$ **31.** $\frac{1}{5}$ **33.** $\frac{4}{5}$ **35.** $\frac{1}{5}$
37. 50% **39.** 22 **41.** 25%

Section 9B Review

1. 0 **3.** -50 **5.** 9 **7.** 150
9. -240 **11.** 382 **13.** -16
15. $-170,017$ **17.** -160 **19.** 0
27. 265°F; 147°C

Chapter 9 Summary & Review

1. No **2.** $-\$25$ **3.** -42 **4.** 87
5. $>$ **6.** $-8, -4, 0, 10, 18$

7. Possible answer:

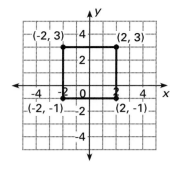

8.

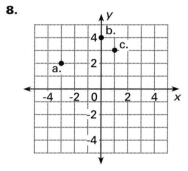

9. $5 + (-9) = -4$
10. Possible answer:

Sum is -4.
11. 2 **12. a.** 6 **b.** -11 **c.** -65
d. -62 **13. a.** -3 **b.** 4 **c.** -101
d. 0 **14. a.** -84 **b.** 40 **c.** -252
d. 480 **15. a.** -22 **b.** 4 **c.** -6
d. 21 **16.** $-\$5250$ **17.** 20,602 ft

Chapter 10

10-1 Try It (Examples 1–2)

a. Variable **b.** Constant
c. Variable **d.** Constant

10-1 Try It (Examples 3–4)

Possible answers: **a.** Let $T =$ the time it takes to get to school; Between 5 and 60 minutes **b.** Let $W =$ wingspan of a butterfly; Between 1 cm and 10 cm

10-1 Exercises & Applications

1. a. Variables **b.** Constants
3. Variable **5.** Variable

7. Variable Possible answers for Exercises 9–17: **9.** Let $W =$ weight of newborn; Between 5 and 12 lb
11. Let $T =$ time it takes to eat lunch; Between 5 and 45 min
13. Let $H =$ height of desk; Between 2 and 4 ft **15.** Feet or meters
17. Minutes or hours **19.** The measurements of the area, the base, and the height can change; The $\frac{1}{2}$ is constant. **21.** D **23.** The length is constant. **25.** About 12 in.
27. $41°, 32°, 3°, -3°, -15°, -42°$
29. $-4111, -4122, -4212, -4221, -4222$

10-2 Try It (Example 1)

b

10-2 Try It (Example 2)

There were no students at the start of the day, a few students arrived and stayed for the first class, more students came and stayed for a second class, some students left before a third class, then everyone left the room.

10-2 Exercises & Applications

1. a. Decreases **b.** Decreases
c. Stays constant **d.** Increases
Possible answers for Exercises 3 and 5: **3.** The length of a side **5.** The age of the teenager **7.** a
9. Possible answer: You start with a full tank. You stop driving for a while, then drive for a bit longer. Then you fill the tank. **13.** b
15. 8 m **17.** 14 m

10-3 Try It (Examples 1–3)

$3n$

10-3 Try It (Example 4)

x	1	2	3	4	5	6
$10x$	10	20	30	40	50	60

10-3 Exercises & Applications

1.

Term #	1	2	3	4	5	n
# in Seq.	7	14	21	28	35	$7n$

3. 0 **5.** 5 **7.** 16 **11.** $n + 10$; 110
13. $\frac{n}{2}$; 50 **15.** $\frac{n}{10}$; 10 **17.** n^2; 10,000
19. a. 8000n **b.** 2,920,000
25. b. 3n **c.** 300 **27.** Arithmetic;
9, 11 **29.** Arithmetic; 55, 66
31. Geometric; 100,000; 1,000,000
33. Neither; $\frac{5}{6}$, $\frac{6}{7}$ **35.** 625,000,000
37. 9:00 P.M. **39.** 5:24 P.M. **41.** 8
43. -27 **45.** -48 **47.** -179
49. -468

10-4 Try It (Examples 1–2)

$y = \frac{x}{4}$; $y = 4.25$

10-4 Try It (Example 3)

Possible answers:

y	1	2	3	4	5	6
p	20 kg	40 kg	60 kg	80 kg	100 kg	120 kg

10-4 Exercises & Applications

1. Possible answer:

x	1	2	3	4	5
y	-1	2	5	8	11

3. $y = -5x$; $y = -35$ **5.** $C = 21.00$,
$C = 28.00$; $C = 3.5n$ **7.** $d = 105$,
$d = 140$, $d = 175$; $d = 35t$ **19.** C
23. 1 in.:4 ft **25.** 1 in.:2.4 ft **27.** 5
29. 102 **31.** 789

10-5 Try It (Example 1)

a.

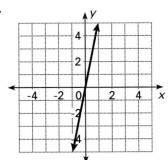

b.

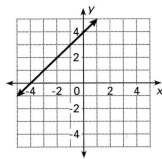

c.

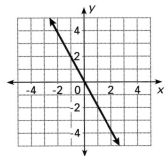

10-5 Try It (Example 2)

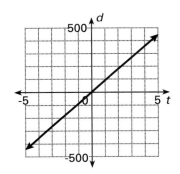

10-5 Exercises & Applications

1.

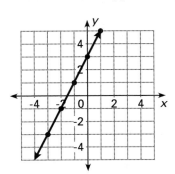

3.

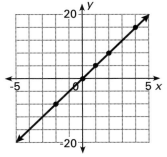

11. The graphs that go through the origin don't have a number subtracted or added at the end of the equation.
13, 15.

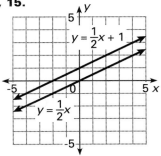

17. They are parallel lines.
19. a. Let r = rate and m = minutes;
$r = 140m$ and $r = \frac{m}{60}$. **b.** The line with the steeper slope represents the greater rate. **21. d.** The lines are images of each other reflected over the y-axis. **23.** $\frac{9}{20} = 45\%$; $\frac{1}{2} = 50\%$; $\frac{9}{20} < \frac{1}{2}$ **25.** $\frac{1}{4} = 25\%$; $\frac{1}{5} = 20\%$; $\frac{1}{4} > \frac{1}{5}$ **27.** 63 **29.** -44 **31.** 0
33. 108 **35.** -270

Section 10A Review

1. b **3.** 2n; 200 **5.** $-5n$; -500
7. $y = x - 6$; 3
9.

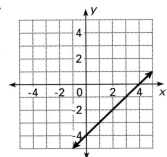

11.

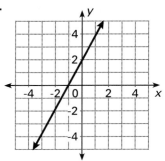

10-6 Try It

a. $x = 10$ **b.** $x = -6$ **c.** $k = 4\frac{1}{3}$
d. $x = -7$

10-6 Exercises & Applications

1. a. $y = x + 3$ **c.** $x = 5$ **3.** $x = -2$
5. $x = 4$ **7.** $x = 6$ **9.** $r = -4$
11. $x = 3\frac{1}{2}$ **13.** $z = -5$ **15. b.** $d \approx$
$3\frac{1}{2}$cm **17.** 200 times **19.** Possible
answer: About 63.4% **21.** 0.5
23. 0.9 **25.** 0.07 **27.** 0.056
29. 0.8462 **31.** 3 **33.** 0 **35.** 7
37. -4 **39.** -34

10-7 Try It

a. $x = 6$ **b.** $x = -4$ **c.** $x = -3$

10-7 Exercises & Applications

1. $x = -1$ **3.** $x = 1$ **5.** $x = -2\frac{1}{2}$
7. $x = 2$ **9.** $p = -1$ **11.** $x = 4\frac{1}{3}$
13. $t \approx -15\frac{1}{3}$ **15.** 10 months
17. a. $2n$ **b.** $1200 **c.** $y = 2n -$
1200 **d.** 2100 items **19. a.** $A =$
$5 + 0.25c$ **b.** $7.50 **c.** 15 checks
21. 135% **23.** 0.5% **25.** -7
27. 417 **29.** 114 **31.** 22,714
33. -4×10^4

10-8 Try It (Examples 1–2)

a.

b. $x > -3$

10-8 Try It (Examples 3–4)

$A < 450$

10-8 Exercises & Applications

1. a–c.

3.

5.

13. No **15.** Yes **17.** $x \geq -2$
19. $x > 40$ **21.** The number of tickets sold was greater than 150.
23. The plane needed at least 90
gallons of fuel. **25.** There were no
more than 65 sofas in the shipment.
27. $C \leq 1$ **29.** No **31.** A
33. Tables may vary; Any values of
x greater than 4 solve the inequality.
35. ≈ 4 **37.** $\approx \$2.10$ **39.** $<$
41. $<$ **43.** $>$ **45.** $>$

Section 10B Review

1. $x = 0$ **3.** $x = -2$ **5.** $x = 0$
7. $x = -4$ **11. a.** $m = 72p$
b. Need to sell about 55 pillows to
make $4000. **13.** $6n$; 600 **15.** n^3;
1,000,000

10-9 Try It

a. $x = -5$ **b.** $x = -7$ **c.** $x = -40$
d. $x = 48$

10-9 Exercises & Applications

1. a. $x + (-2) + 2 = (-11) + 2$
b. $x = -9$ **c.** $(-9) + (-2) = (-11)$;
$-11 = -11$ **3.** $x + (-5) = -3$; $x = 2$
5. No **7.** No **9.** $x = -5$ **11.** $z =$
-1 **13.** $k = 27$ **15.** $x = -5$
17. $x = -11$ **19.** $x = -60$
21. $-4°F$ **23.** 1021 millibars
25. $x = -60$ **27. a.** The variable is
preceded by a minus sign.
b. $x = 59$ **29.** 15, 20, 35; Possible
answers: $\frac{1}{5} = \frac{3}{15}, \frac{3}{15} = \frac{4}{20}, \frac{4}{20} = \frac{7}{35},$
$\frac{3}{15} = \frac{7}{35}$ **31.** $\frac{1}{5} = \frac{12}{x}$; $x = 60$
33. $\frac{1}{1000} = \frac{57}{m}$; $m = 57,000$

10-10 Try It (Examples 1–2)

a. $x = -2$ **b.** $h = 4.\overline{4}$ **c.** $x = -4.\overline{3}$

10-10 Try It (Examples 3–4)

a. $y = -150$ **b.** $w = 1320$
c. $m = 448$

10-10 Exercises & Applications

1. a. $\frac{-3x}{-3} = \frac{-15}{-3}$ **b.** $x = 5$
c. $-3(5) = -15, -15 = -15$
3. $2x = -8$; $x = -4$ **5.** No **7.** Yes
9. $m = 33$ **11.** $z = 10$ **13.** $c = -64$
15. $d = 36$ **17.** $x = -19$ **19.** $x =$
3.5 **21.** 0.5 mm **23.** Possible
answers: $\frac{12}{m} = -3$ and $\frac{n}{-2} = 2$
25. 24 **29.** No **31.** 158
33. $71.30

10-11 Try It (Examples 1–2)

a. $x = -3$ **b.** $c = -8$ **c.** $x = 30$
d. $x = -20$

10-11 Try It (Example 3)

a. 2 km **b.** 5 km

10-11 Exercises & Applications

1. a. $-4x - 2 + 2 = -14 + 2$
b. -12 **c.** $\frac{-4x}{-4} = \frac{-12}{-4}$ **d.** $x = 3$
e. $-4(3) - 2 = -14, -12 - 2 = -14,$
$-14 = -14$ **3.** $3x + 2 = -1$;
$x = -1$ **5.** Yes **7.** No **9.** $x = 1$
11. $t = -36$ **13.** $g = -3$ **15.** $n =$
-8 **17.** $x = 80$ **19.** $f = -1120$
21. 43 inches **23.** A **25.** Possible
answers: $3m + 11 = 2$ and $3 - 2n =$
9 **27.** $0.\overline{2}$; Repeats **29.** 0.875;
Terminates **31.** 0.4375; Terminates
33. $3.00

10-12 Try It

a. $9494 **b.** 5 weeks

10-12 Exercises & Applications

1. $h + 2 = 14$ **3.** $2t - 7 = -27$
5. 5°F **7.** 14 years **9.** B **11. a.** In
200 years **b.** In 600 years **c.** In
800 years **d.** 0.0003°C per year;
This is $\frac{1}{15}$ of the current rate.
13. $k = 3$ **15.** $x = 60$ **17.** $y = 4$
19. $x = 1.\overline{3}$ **21.** 10 **23.** 0 **25.** 75
27. 32 **29.** 101 **31.** 14 **33.** 4

Section 10C Review

1. $x - 2 = 6$; $x = 8$ **3.** $-5 = 2x - 3$; $x = -1$ **5.** No **7.** Yes **9.** $p = -22$ **11.** $x = 180$ **13.** $d = 128$ **15.** $x = -32$ **17.** $x = 5$ **19.** $x = 4$ **21.** D

Chapter 10 Summary & Review

1. Possible answer: p = number of petals on a flower; $5 - 50$ petals **2.** Possible answers: diameter, circumference, height **3.** $6n$; 600 **4.** Possible table values for (x, y): (1, 7), (2, 9), (3, 11), (4, 13), (5, 15), (6, 17) **5.** Possible answer: Over a 3-month period a plant grew to 3 feet and then with lack of water over the next 3 months withered down to the ground. **6.** $y = 4x$; 36
7. a.

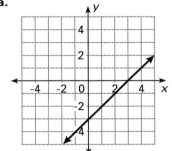

b.

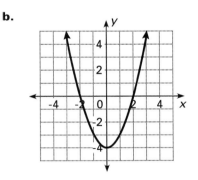

8. a. $x = 3$ **b.** $x = 0$ **9.** $x = -4$
10. $y < 7$

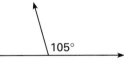

11. -3 **12.** 3 cm **13. a.** $x = -4$
b. $t = 20$ **14.** 4 tapes **15.** $x + 2 = -8$; $x = -10$ **16. a.** $x = 4$ **b.** $k = -1$ **17. a.** Yes **b.** No

Cumulative Review
Chapters 1–10

1. A **2.** A **3.** B **4.** B **5.** C **6.** B
7. C **8.** C **9.** D **10.** B **11.** D
12. A **13.** C **14.** C **15.** C **16.** B

Chapter 11

11-1 Try It

a. Triangular prism **b.** Pentagonal pyramid
c.

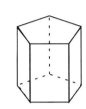

11-1 Exercises & Applications

1. Possible answer:

3. 2 triangles, 3 rectangles
5. Pentagonal prism **7.** Right triangular prism **11.** Rectangular pyramid **13.** C **15. a.** Tetrahedron: 4 faces, 6 edges, 4 vertices; Hexahedron: 6 faces, 12 edges, 8 vertices; Octahedron: 8 faces, 12 edges, 6 vertices **b.** Number of faces + Number of vertices − Number of edges = 2 **17.** 60 faces, 120 edges, 80 vertices
19.

21. II **23.** III **25.** I

11-2 Try It (Example 1)

1. A **2.** B

11-2 Try It (Examples 2–3)

a.

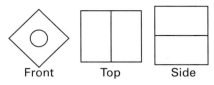

Front Top Side

b.

11-2 Exercises & Applications

1. a–c.

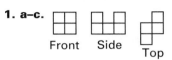

Front Side Top

3. 7 **5.** C **7.** A **17.** Perpendicular
19. Perpendicular **21.** Constant
23. Variable

11-3 Try It

a.

112 ft^2 **b.** 610 mm^2

11-3 Exercises & Applications

1. a. 40 cm^2 **b.** 130 cm^2 **c.** 150 cm^2
d. 48 cm^2 **e.** 368 cm^2 **5.** 184 cm^2
7. 168 cm^2 **9.** $\approx$ 7 gal **11.** C **13.** a and c **15. a.** Yes; Any piece other than a corner **b.** No **c.** Yes; Any corner piece **17.** Quadrilateral, parallelogram, rectangle, rhombus, square **19.** Obtuse, scalene triangle **21.** Measure of base or height

11-4 Try It

a. 48 ft^3 **b.** 55,000 cm^3

11-4 Exercises & Applications

1. a. 24 cm^2 **b.** $24 \cdot 9 = 216$
c. 216 cm^3 **3.** 42 in^3 **5.** 450 mm^3
7. 160 m^3 **9.** A **11.** The volume of the prism would be 3 times the volume of the pyramid. **13.** 1800°
15. 2700° **17.** 3; Always 3 **19.** $\frac{1}{14}$; $\frac{1}{2n + 4}$

Section 11A Review

1. True **3.** True **9.** Area: 30 cm²; Volume: 7 cm³ **11.** Area: ≈ 339 in²; Volume: 339.184 in³

11-5 Try It

a.

No 11%

Yes 89%

People who've heard of Slinky

b.

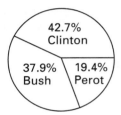

42.7% Clinton

37.9% Bush   19.4% Perot

11-5 Exercises & Applications

1. a. 104.4° **b.** 40% is 144°; 31% is 111.6°
c–e.

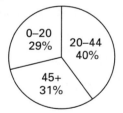

0–20 29%   20–44 40%

45+ 31%

Ages of People in the US, 1990

3. Republican; The sector is greater than 50% of the circle. **7.** 864
15. $A = 68$ in²; $P = 42$ in. **17.** $A = 7.2$ cm²; $P = 36.8$ cm **19.** $A = 10,875$ mi²; $P = 440$ mi **21.** $y = -8, -9, -10, -11, -12, -13$

11-6 Try It

$d = 64$ in.; $C \approx 201$ in.

11-6 Exercises & Applications

1. a. 10 cm **b.** 31.4 cm **3.** $d = 8$ cm; $C = 25.1$ cm **5.** $d = 16.4$ m;

$C = 51.5$ m **7.** $\approx 23\frac{4}{7}$ ft **9.** $d = 16$ cm; $C \approx 50.2$ cm **11.** $d \approx 1.9$ mm; $r \approx 1.0$ mm **13.** $r = 25.5$ ft; $C \approx 160.1$ ft **15.** $d = 200$ in.; $C \approx 628.0$ in. **17.** $d \approx 28.0$ ft; $r \approx 14.0$ ft **19.** D **21.** 157 in. **23.** The $\frac{\text{circumference}}{\text{diameter}}$ ratio for all circles is π. It doesn't matter how big or small the circle is. **25.** 51 mi/hr **27.** 17 students for 1 teacher

11-7 Try It

a. 1256 in² **b.** 122.7 cm²

11-7 Exercises & Applications

1. a. 8 in. **b.** $A \approx 200.96$ in²
3. 28.3 cm² **5.** 1589.6 ft²
7. $38\frac{1}{2}$ ft² **9.** 12.6 cm²
11. 73,504.3 ft² **13.** 78.5 cm² **15.** 60.8 m² **17.** ≈ 113.04 ft²
19. $\frac{22}{7} = 3.1428571...$ is closer.
23. ≈ 286 in² **25.** 48 hr **27.** 5 lb
29. 42 gallons **31.** $x = 5$
33. $x = -25$

11-8 Try It

a. 81.6 in² **b.** 366.2 in²

11-8 Exercises & Applications

1. a. ≈ 78.5 cm² **b.** 157 cm²
c. 31.4 cm **d.** 628 cm²
e. 785 cm² **5.** D **7.** 113.0 cm²
9. 117.8 m² **11.** ≈ 25.1 in²
13. ≈ 125.6 in² **17.** 184,800 ft/hr
19. $x = 3$ **21.** $x = 2$

11-9 Try It (Examples 1–2)

a. ≈ 1152 cm³ **b.** 1384.7 in³

11-9 Try It (Example 3)

577 mL

11-9 Exercises & Applications

1. a. ≈ 28.26 in² **b.** 113.04 in³ **c.** 113.0 in³ **3.** 300 cm³ **5.** 8164 mm³
7. 1256 in³ **9.** 52.2 cm³
11. About 15.3 in³ **13.** 1130.4 mL
15. 879.6 mL **17.** Liquid foods, or foods packed in liquid, tend to come in cans; dry foods tend to come in boxes. Liquids need to be packed in metal (or plastic), not cardboard, and metal boxes are difficult to

make (and dangerous to have on tall shelves). **19.** No **21.** Yes

Section 11B Review

3. $C = 56.5$ cm; $A = 254.3$ cm²
5. About 1.6 ft **7.** $V = 141.3$ in³; $SA = 150.7$ in² **9.** A

11-10 Try It (Example 1)

C and D

11-10 Try It (Examples 2–3)

$(-5, 1), (-5, 5), (-3, 4)$

11-10 Exercises & Applications

1. a-c.

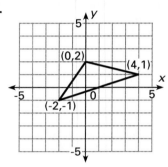

(0,2)   (4,1)

(-2,-1)

3. C **5.** The image shows horizontal translations of a basic pattern.
7. $(x, y) \rightarrow (x - 5, y + 7)$
9. $(x, y) \rightarrow (x, y - 3)$ **11.** (0, 0)
13. $(-3, 4)$ **15.** $(-1, 4), (4, 4)$, $(-1, 2)$, and $(4, 2)$ **17.** $(-5, 3)$, $(0, 3), (-5, 1)$, and $(0, 1)$ **19.** Yes; $(x, y) \rightarrow (x - 2, y + 1)$ **21.** x and z are 9 cm, y is 18 cm **23.** $a = 3$
25. $c = 20$ **27.** $m = 4$ **29.** $f = 9.5$
31. $c = -21$ **33.** $k = -2$

11-11 Try It (Examples 1–3)

a.

1

b.

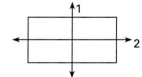

1

2

c.

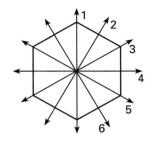

11-11 Try It (Example 4)

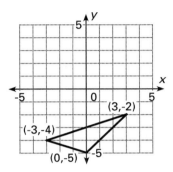

$A'(3, -2)$, $B'(-3, -4)$, $C'(0, -5)$

11-11 Exercises & Applications

1. a–c.

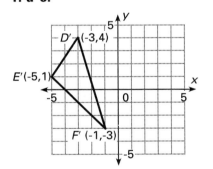

3. Yes **5.** Yes **7.** B **9.** (0, 4), (3, 1), and (5, 2) **13.** Regular polygons have the same number of lines of symmetry as they have sides. **17.** Perimeter: 30 in.; Area: 50 in^2 **19.** $m = -45$ **21.** $y = 0$ **23.** $d = 42$ **25.** $z = 52$

11-12 Try It

No

11-12 Exercises & Applications

1. Yes, it has 180° rotational symmetry. **3.** $\frac{1}{2}$ **5.** $\frac{1}{4}, \frac{1}{2}, \frac{3}{4}$ **7.** 2, 3, 5 **9.** C **11.** 180° **13. a.** $D'(0, 0)$, $E'(4, -1)$, $F'(0, -3)$ **b.** $D'(0, 0)$, $E'(-1, -4)$, $F'(-3, 0)$ **c.** $D'(0, 0)$, $E'(-4, 1)$, $F'(0, 3)$ **15. a.** $\frac{1}{3}, \frac{2}{3}$ **b.** $\frac{1}{4}$, $\frac{1}{2}, \frac{3}{4}$ **c.** $\frac{1}{5}, \frac{2}{5}, \frac{3}{5}, \frac{4}{5}$ **d.** $\frac{1}{6}, \frac{1}{3}, \frac{1}{2}, \frac{2}{3}, \frac{5}{6}$ **e.** A regular polygon with n sides has rotational symmetry for every multiple of the quotient of $\frac{360°}{n}$. **17.** $\frac{x}{100} = \frac{25}{125}$; $x = 20$ **19.** $x = 21$ **21.** $m = 13$ **23.** $v = 8$ **25.** $x = -1$

Section 11C Review

1. (0, 0), (4, 0), and (1, -5) **3.** (1, 2) **7.** D

Chapter 11 Summary & Review

1. 6

2.

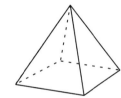

8 edges, 5 faces, 5 vertices
3. a. Answers will vary. **b.** SA = 520 in^2, V = 600 in^3

4.

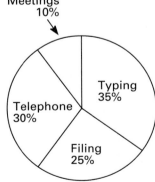

5. Circumference, 138.0 m; Area, 1517.0 m^2 **6.** Surface area, 533.8 cm^2; Volume, 942 cm^3

7.

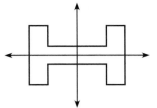

Yes **8.** $A'(-7, 1)$ **9. b.** $A'(0, 0)$, $B'(4, 0)$, $C'(6, -3)$, and $D'(2, -5)$ **c.** $A'(0, 0)$, $B'(0, -4)$, $C'(3, -6)$, and $D'(5, -2)$

SELECTED ANSWERS

Chapter 12

12-1 Try It (Example 1)

There are 6 different outcomes for juice orders.

12-1 Try It (Examples 2–3)

20

12-1 Exercises & Applications

1. a. 12 **b.** 36 **c.** Counting Principle **3.** 24 **5.** 24 **7.** 120 **9.** 144 **11.** 144

12-2 Try It (Examples 1–2)

120

12-2 Try It (Examples 3–5)

a. 24 **b.** 3,628,800 **c.** 3024

12-2 Exercises & Applications

1. a. 4 **b.** 3 **c.** 2 **d.** 1 **e.** 24 **3.** 5040 **5.** 362,880 **7.** ARY, AYR, RAY, RYA, YAR, YRA (A = Arimora, R = Roba, Y = Yegorova) **9.** ABCD, ABDC, ACBD, ACDB, ADBC, ADCB, BACD, BADC, BCAD, BCDA, BDAC, BDCA, CABD, CADB, CBAD, CBDA, CDAB, CDBA, DABC, DACB, DBAC, DBCA, DCAB, DCBA; None of the orderings form words. **11.** C **13.** The factorial product $x!$ increases very quickly as x increases. **15.** Surface area = 216 cm^2 **17.** Surface area = 56 in^2 **19.** 168 m^3

12-3 Try It

a. 3 **b.** 10

12-3 Exercises & Applications

1. a. Alex and Bess, Alex and Chandra   **b.** Bess and Chandra
c. 3   **3.** Yes   **5.** 6   **7.** 1   **9.** 20
11. B   **13. a.** 20   **b.** 120   **c.** The number in b is greater   **17.** 25.1 in.
19. 34.5 mm

Section 12A Review

1. 12   **3.** There are 8 possibilities.
5. 40,320   **7.** 720   **9. a.** 1000
b. 720   **11.** A

12-4 Try It (Examples 3–4)

a. 1:1   **b.** 2:4

12-4 Try It (Examples 5–6)

a. 1:1 odds for both; Fair   **b.** Odds for A = 2:1, odds for B = 1:2; Unfair
c. Odds for Evan = 3:3, odds for Primo = 3:3, odds for Trace = 2:4; Unfair

12-4 Exercises & Applications

1. a. 2   **b.** 4   **c.** 2:4   **3.** 1, 2, 3, 4, 5, 6, 7, or 8   **5.** 1:1   **7.** 2:3   **9.** 104:66
11. 2:52   **13.** 26:28   **15.** 16:38
17. Odds for A = 1:5, odds for B = 4:2, odds for C = 1:5; Unfair
21. Yes   **23.** 706.5 in^2 **25.** 0.8 m^2

12-5 Try It (Examples 1–3)

a. $\frac{1}{3} \approx 33.3\% = 0.333$ **b.** $\frac{1}{2} = 50\% = 0.5$ **c.** $\frac{3}{10} = 30\% = 0.3$

12-5 Try It (Examples 4–5)

a. $\frac{7}{8}$ **b.** $\frac{1}{100}$; 1:99

12-5 Exercises & Applications

1. a. 12   **b.** $\frac{3}{12}$ **c.** $\frac{1}{4}$ **3.** $\frac{1}{6} \approx 16.7\% = 0.167$ **5. a.** 75.1%   **b.** 24.9%
c. 18.4%   **7.** Probability does not $= \frac{7}{8}$; Odds = 1:7   **9.** Probability $= \frac{1}{2}$; Odds = 1:1   **11.** $\frac{1}{2}$ **13.** $\frac{1}{8}$
15. $\frac{55}{99} = \frac{5}{9}$ **17.** 1%   **19.** 56%

21. Possible answers: A dropped ball will fall down (probability 1); A person will jump to the moon tomorrow (probability 0).
23. 9118.6 cm^3 **25.** 1356.5 in^3
27. $(x + 4, y - 6)$
29. $(x - 0.2, y + 7)$

12-6 Try It (Examples 1–2)

a. 0.58   **b.** $\frac{8}{72} = \frac{1}{9}$; Less than the theoretical probability of $\frac{6}{36} = \frac{1}{6}$

12-6 Try It (Examples 3–4)

$\frac{6}{128} = \frac{3}{64}$

12-6 Exercises & Applications

1. a. 10 in^2 **b.** 60 in^2 **c.** $\frac{10}{60} = \frac{1}{6}$
3. $\frac{9}{72} = \frac{1}{8}$ **5.** $\frac{15}{72} = \frac{5}{24}$ **7.** $\frac{1}{72}$ **9.** $\frac{3}{36} = \frac{1}{12}$; Less than experimental
11. $\frac{6}{36} = \frac{1}{6}$; Less than experimental
13. $\frac{1}{36}$; Greater than experimental
15. $\frac{48}{80} = 60\%$ **17.** An estimate from 1000 trials would give more confidence.   **19.** $\frac{9}{144} = \frac{1}{16}$
21. a. Experimental   **b.** Possible data set: 10 injured fire fighters, 36 uninjured   **23.** Figure has one line of symmetry.   **25.** Figure has one line of symmetry.

12-7 Try It (Examples 1–2)

a. Dependent   **b.** Independent

12-7 Try It (Examples 4–5)

a. $\frac{1}{10}$ **b.** $\frac{7}{30}$

12-7 Exercises & Applications

1. a. $\frac{5}{10}$ **b.** 4 green cubes; 9 cubes
c. $\frac{4}{9}$ **d.** $\frac{2}{9}$ **3.** Independent   **5.** $\frac{1}{48}$
7. $\frac{1}{4}$ **9. a.** $\frac{1}{16} = 6.25\%$ **b.** No
13. D   **15.** 5%, 14%   **17.** 6

Section 12B Review

1. 1, 2, 3, 4, 5, 6, 7, 8, 9, 10   **3.** 4:2
7. $\frac{3}{10} = 30\% = 0.3$ **9.** $\frac{4}{5} = 80\% = 0.8$
11. Independent   **13.** $\frac{1}{4}$

Chapter 12 Summary & Review

1. 60   **2.** The store needs 8 bins.
3. 15   **4.** 24   **5.** TUV, TVU, UVT, UTV, VTU, VUT   **6.** 21   **7.** 5:3
8. Melanie's odds = 4:3, Nathan's odds = 3:4; Unfair   **9. a.** $\frac{4}{6} = \frac{2}{3}$
b. $\frac{2}{6} = \frac{1}{3}$ **10.** 8%   **11.** $\frac{11}{25}$ **12.** $\frac{4}{9}$
13. $\frac{1}{12}$ **14.** $\frac{5}{11} \cdot \frac{4}{10} = \frac{2}{11}$

Cumulative Review
Chapters 1–12

1. A   **2.** D   **3.** C   **4.** C   **5.** D   **6.** A
7. C   **8.** B   **9.** B   **10.** C   **11.** D
12. D   **13.** B   **14.** C   **15.** A

Photographs

Cover/Spine   Dugald Bremner/Tony Stone Images

Front Matter   iii GHP Studio*   iii (background) John Banagan/The Image Bank   v–xvi T (border) GHP Studio*   xviii BC GHP Studio*   xviii TC Thomas Johnson/Earthviews   xviii TL David Madison   xviii BR Adam Peiperl/The Stock Market   xix T Parker/Boon Productions and Dorey Sparre Photography*   xix B Dennis Geaney,* Ken Karp* and Parker/Boon Productions and Dorey Sparre Photography*   xxi Anne Dowie*   xxii Anne Dowie*   xxiii Anne Dowie*   xxiv Roz Chast © 1995 from The New Yorker Magazine, Inc.   xxv Richard Steinheimer   xxvi Ken Karp*   xxviii Ken Karp*   xxix William R. Sallaz/Duomo

Chapter 1   2–3 (background) Allen Lee Page/The Stock Market   2 TL Giraudon/Art Resource, NY   2 BL SEF/Art Resource, NY   2 R Reed Saxon/AP Photo   2 TR Cheryl Fenton*   3 Ken Karp*   4 Cheryl Fenton*   5 L Don Mason/The Stock Market   5 R Geoffrey Nilsen Photography*   6 Lawrence Migdale/Tony Stone Images   8 Shaw McCutcheon/Bruce Coleman Inc.   10 Nathan T. Wright/Bruce Coleman Inc.   11 L J. Messerschmidt/ Bruce Coleman Inc.   11 R ©1996, USA TODAY. Reprinted with permission. Photo by Cheryl Fenton*   12 UPI/Corbis-Bettmann   13 T Cameramann/The Image Works   13 R Rich Iwasaki/Tony Stone Images   15 Library of Congress   16 Tim Davis*   18 Chad Ehlers/Tony Stone Images   19 GHP Studio*   20 Stanley King Collection   21 R Dan Dancer/Herd/Sipa Press   21 L Ken Karp*   24 Robie Price*   27 T Don Mason/The Stock Market   27 R Geoffrey Nilsen Photography*   28 Will & Deni McIntyre/Photo Researchers   29 TL David Madison   29 TR David Madison/Bruce Coleman Inc.   29 B Jim Cummins/FPG International   30 Court Mast/FPG International   31 Culver Pictures   32 Cheryl Fenton*   33 Andrea Sperling/FPG International   34 Otto Greule/Allsport   35 Geoffrey Nilsen Photography*   36 Bill Losh/FPG International   38 Andy Lyons/Allsport   40 R David Madison   40 L Clive Mason/Allsport   41 The Image Bank   42 R Parker/Boon Productions and Dorey Sparre Photography*   42 L Dennis Geaney*   43 T David Madison   43 B Cheryl Fenton*   44 T Stephen Dunn/Allsport   45 Jim Cummins/FPG International   46 Stephen Dunn/Allsport   47 Geoffrey Nilsen Photography*   51 TL David Madison   51 BL (capitol) Richard Pasley/Stock, Boston   51 BL (tiles) Cheryl Fenton*   51 TR Cheryl Fenton*   51 BR George B. Fry III*

Chapter 2   52–53 (background) GHP Studio*   52 B Photo © Michael Holford/Collection British Museum   52 TL David Madison   52 TR Jenny Thomas*   53 B Cheryl Fenton*   53 T Joe McDonald/Animals, Animals   54 T E. R. Degginger/Animals, Animals   54 B Johnny Johnson/DRK Photo   55 Cindy Lewis   56 Will & Deni McIntyre/Tony Stone Images

58 Renee Lynn/Davis-Lynn Images   59 Ford Motor Company   60 L Phil Degginger/Bruce Coleman Inc.   60 R Cheryl Fenton*   61 GHP Studio*   62 Cindy Lewis   63 Tim Davis/Davis-Lynn Images   66 Anne Dowie*   68 Ken Karp*   69 Archive Photos   70 Maxell Corporation of America   71 Cindy Lewis   72 Tony Arruza/The Image Works   73 (inset) The Bancroft Library, University of California   73 (background) Steve Solum/Bruce Coleman Inc.   74 L Mindscape, Inc.   74 R Jenny Thomas*   77 Art Wolfe/Tony Stone Images   78 Cheryl Fenton.* Drawing from the collection of Jeff Kelly   80 Detroit Industry, North Wall (detail of fresco), 1932–1933 by Diego Rivera. Accession no. 33.10N (detail). Photograph © 1996 The Detroit Institute of Arts, Gift of Edsel B. Ford.   81 Long Term Parking, sculpture by Arman. Photo by Gianfranco Gorgoni/Sygma   82 Rene Sheret/Tony Stone Images   83 Photo © Michael Holford/Collection British Museum   84 L Charles D. Winters/Photo Researchers   84 R Eric Gravé/Photo Researchers   85 Culver Pictures   86 Dr. Jeremy Burgess/SPL/Photo Researchers   87 NMAI/Smithsonian Institution   88 Ken Karp*   89 David J. Sams/Stock, Boston   90 Cheryl Fenton*   91 Jose L. Pelaez/The Stock Market   92 Corbis-Bettmann   93 GHP Studio*   94 David Madison   95 Steve Solum/Bruce Coleman Inc.   97 Geoffrey Nilsen Photography*

Chapter 3   102–103 (background) M. L. Sinibaldi/The Stock Market   102 TL Cheryl Fenton*   102 TC Ulrike Welsch   102 TR Ulrike Welsch   102 BL Alfred Pasieka/G&J Images/The Image Bank   103 T Cheryl Fenton*   103 B Naomi Duguid/Asia Access   104 T Cheryl Fenton*   104 B Aneal F. Vohra/Unicorn Stock Photos   105 World Perspectives/Tony Stone Images   106 Topham/The Image Works   110 L Richard Hutchings/Photo Researchers   110 R USGS/NASA   113 Ken Karp*   114 Julian Baum/SPL/Photo Researchers   115L NASA/JPL Special Services   115R Cheryl Fenton*   116 James Balog/Tony Stone Images   117 T Ken Karp*   117 B Parker/Boon Productions and Dorey Sparre Photography*   118 fotos international/Archive Photos   119 Finley Holiday Film   120 John Lei*   121 NASA   123 Francois Gohier/Photo Researchers   124 Finley Holiday Film   125 John Lei*   127 Yerkes Observatory Photograph   129 Biophoto Associates/Photo Researchers   130 Cheryl Fenton*   131 World Perspectives/Tony Stone Images   132 NASA/Dan McCoy/The Stock Market   133 Ken Karp*   134 L Peter Beck/The Stock Market   134 R G. Holz/The Image Works   137 Jane Lidz   139 L GHP Studio*   139 R Mike Greenlar/The Image Works   140 Ken Karp*   141 Ken Karp   143 Cheryl Fenton*   144 L Mark Loader/Uniphoto Picture Agency   144 R Cheryl Fenton*   146 Ken Karp*   147 Courtesy of The Selmer Company   148 Wolfgang Kaehler   149 Anne Dowie*   150 Cheryl Fenton*   151 G. C. Kelley/Photo Researchers   152 Bob Daemmrich/Stock, Boston   153 L Cheryl Fenton*   153 R Anne Dowie*   154 Richard Pasley/Liaison International

155 T JPL/NASA   155 B GHP Studio*   156 Cheryl Fenton*   157 L GHP Studio*   157 R Ken Karp*   158 Cheryl Fenton*   159 Geoffrey Nilsen Photography*   163 TL Ken Karp*   163 TR Cheryl Fenton*   163 BL Renee Lynn/Davis-Lynn Images   163 BR GHP Studio*

Chapter 4   164–165 (background) Cheryl Fenton*   164 TL Cheryl Fenton*   164 TR GHP Studio*   164 B Photo © Michael Holford/Collection British Museum   165 T Anne Dowie*   165 B T. A. Wiewandt/DRK Photo   166 T GHP Studio*   166 B John Margolies/Esto   167 T Jonathan Kirn/Liaison International   167 C Jon Riley/Tony Stone Images   167 B Tim Flach/Tony Stone Images   168 Ed Bock/The Stock Market   169 Ken Karp*   170 Bryan F. Peterson/The Stock Market   171 L Joe McDonald/Animals, Animals   171 C Stephen Green-Armytage/The Stock Market   171 R Roy Morsch/The Stock Market   172 Roger Tully/Tony Stone Images   173 Pierre Boulat/Cosmos/Woodfin Camp & Associates   175 Laima Druskis/Photo Researchers   176 Adam Lubroth/Liaison International   178 Joe Quever*   179 Ed Lallo/Liaison International   180 L Dennis Geaney*   180 R Ken Karp*   181 UPI/Corbis-Bettmann   183 L Ken Karp*   183 TR Jonathan Kirn/Liaison International   183 CR Jon Riley/Tony Stone Images   183 BR Tim Flach/Tony Stone Images   184 Tim Davis/Photo Researchers   185 Ken Karp*   186 Crandall/The Image Works   187 Union Pacific Railroad   189 Ken Karp*   190 Tim Fitzharris/Masterfile   191 Joe Quever*   193 L Ken Karp*   193 R Dennis Geaney*   194 Porter Gifford/Liaison International   195 Cheryl Fenton*   197 Cheryl Fenton*   200 Bob Daemmrich/Stock, Boston   201 Ken Karp*   202 L Zefa Germany/The Stock Market   202 R Tim Davis/Tony Stone Images   203 Geoffrey Nilsen Photography*

Chapter 5   208–209 (background) Rafael Macia/Photo Researchers   208 TR GHP Studio*   208 L ©1997 photo by Kunio Hirano/ORION PRESS, Tokyo   209 T Roberto de Gugliemo/SPL/Photo Researchers   209 B Bob Burch/Bruce Coleman Inc.   210 T Cheryl Fenton*   210 B Parker/Boon Productions and Dorey Sparre Photography*   211 Jon Simon/Liaison International   212 L Marty Katz/Woodfin Camp & Associates   212 R David Barnes/Tony Stone Images   213 Cheryl Fenton*   214 Ron Sanford/Tony Stone Images   216 Ken Kay/Fundamental Photographs   217 TL Ken Karp*   217 TR Greg Stott/Masterfile   217 B Robert Fried/Stock, Boston   219 GHP Studio*   220 1994 by Rand McNally R.L. 94-S-140   221 L Bob Krist/The Stock Market   221 R P. Hammerschmidt/Okapia/Photo Researchers   222 L Lisl Dennis/The Image Bank   223 Cheryl Fenton*   224 Harvey Lloyd/The Stock Market   226 L Rafael Macia/Photo Researchers   226 C Catherine Karnow/Woodfin Camp & Associates   226 R M. Granitsas/The Image Works   227 T Michal Heron/The Stock Market   227 TL Cheryl Fenton*   227 B Tony Craddock/SPL/Photo Researchers   228 J. C. Carton/Bruce Coleman Inc.

713

714

CREDITS

CREDITS

Index

716

D

Dalwood, Hubert, 572
Dams, 9
Data, 114, 124, 131, 143, 147, 152, 156, 190,
    195, 200, 243, 247, 298, 427, 504, 520,
    575–577, 598, 652
    analysis, 26
    bar graphs, 11–15
    graphs, 6–10
    line graph, 30–34
    line plot, 16–20
    mean, 21–28
    median, 21–28
    mode, 21–28
    range, 21–28
    scatterplots, 35–39
    stem-and-leaf diagram, 16–20
    trend line, 40–46
da Vinci, Leonardo, 275, 277, 291
Davy, Humphry, 84
Decagon, 689
Decartes, René, 444
Decimal
    comparing and ordering, 106–109
    converting to fraction, 153–158
    converting to percent, 390–398
    multiplication, 126
    products and quotients, 120–124
    rounding, 110–114
    scientific notation, 125–132
    sums and differences, 115–119
Decimal system, 689
Decreasing graph, 486, 546, 689
Deductive reasoning, 265, 689
Degree, 213, 689
del Cano, Juan, 506
Denominator
    common, 150–152
    definition, 144
    glossary term, 689
    least common, 174–177
    unlike, adding and subtracting fractions
        with, 173–177
Dependent event, 623, 660–662, 665,
    668–670, 689
Diameter, 578–582, 689
Dickens, Charles, 52
Did You Know?, 8, 17, 22–23, 57, 83, 92,
    111, 116, 121–122, 135, 169, 178, 218, 234,
    245, 255, 279, 299–300, 329, 334, 354, 372,
    400, 412, 438, 452, 457, 491, 502, 509, 530,
    575, 611, 627, 651, 655
Difference, 689. *See also* Subtraction
Dilation, 365
Distributive Property, 62, 191–194, 689
Dividend, 689
Divisible, 134–135, 137–138, 161, 671, 689
Division
    decimals, 120–124
    in equations, 86–94, 529–542
    fractions, 197–200
    integers, 466–470

Divisor, 689
DNA, 642
Double-bar graph, 12–13, 15, 48, 51, 689
Double-line graph, 32–34, 49, 689
Doubling time, 16
Doyle, Arthur Conan, 625, 637
Dürer, Albrecht, 291
Duryea, J. Frank, 348

E

Earth, 110–111, 115, 120–121, 128, 131, 155,
    162–163, 190, 340, 436, 441, 447
Echolocation, 400
Edge, 554–557, 562, 620, 689
Edison, Thomas, 591
Enlargement, 329, 375, 378
Entertainment, 2, 52, 102, 165, 208, 270,
    320, 383, 428, 478, 550, 623
Equally-likely outcomes, 689
Equation
    addition and subtraction, 82–85
    decimal, 115–119, 121–124
    definition, 82
    fractions, 173–184
    glossary term, 689
    graphing, 500–504
    and inequalities, 517–520
    multiplying and dividing, 86–90
    and proportion, 317
    quadratic, 545
    scientific notation, 131–132
    solving using graphs, 512–516
    solving using inverse operations, 82–94
    solving using tables, 508–511
    solving with integers, 524–542
    two-step, 91–94, 534–538
    writing, 495–497
Equilateral triangle, 222, 689
Equivalent
    fractions, 144–148
    glossary terms, 689
    rates, 282–290
    ratios, 282–290
Eratosthenes, 136
Escher, M. C., 388
Estimation, 85, 122, 169, 276–277, 289, 306,
    312, 326, 339, 392, 401, 404, 465, 510, 515,
    522, 566, 576, 586, 590, 595
    of fractions, 168–172
    glossary term, 689
    of percents, 399–402
    of rates, 278–281
    of ratios, 274–277
    by rounding, 110–114
    of scale distances, 324–327
Event, 623, 645–647, 649–654, 656–659,
    661–662, 665–666, 668–670, 689
Experiment, 644–645, 647, 654–655, 666,
    669, 690
Experimental probability, 654–659,
    668–669, 690

Explore, 6, 11, 21, 30, 35, 40, 56, 60, 66, 74,
    78, 82, 86, 91, 106, 110, 115, 120, 125, 134,
    139, 144, 149, 153, 168, 173, 178, 186, 191,
    197, 212, 217, 222, 227, 233, 240, 244, 253,
    258, 274, 278, 282, 286, 294, 298, 304, 308,
    324, 328, 333, 337, 344, 349, 353, 360, 366,
    371, 386, 390, 394, 399, 406, 410, 415, 432,
    437, 442, 450, 455, 461, 466, 486, 490, 508,
    512, 524, 534, 539, 554, 578, 626, 631, 636,
    644, 649, 654, 659
Exponent, 125–126, 136–137, 690
Expression
    algebraic, 78–81, 307, 517, 547
    definition, 60
    glossary term, 690
    and tables, 490–494
Extend Key Ideas, 47, 97, 159, 203, 265,
    315, 377, 423, 473, 545, 617, 667

F

Face, 554, 690
Factor
    definition, 134
    glossary term, 690
    lowest or greatest common, 139–143
    prime, 134–138
Factorial, 633, 668, 690
Factor tree, 136–138, 161–162, 459, 690
Fahrenheit, Gabriel Daniel, 36
Fahrenheit conversion, 478
Fair games, 644–645, 648, 665, 669, 670, 690
Fibonacci, Leonardo, 456
Fine Arts, 81, 133, 339, 364, 388, 556, 566,
    569, 572, 613
Fingerprint classification, 625
Formula
    area of circle, 583
    area of irregular figures, 258–263
    area of parallelogram, 253–257
    area of rectangle, 58, 186–187, 191,
        233–234
    area of square, 67
    area of trapezoid, 254–257
    area of triangle, 248–252, 485
    average of two numbers, 57
    batting average, 148
    Celsius to Fahrenheit, 478
    Celsius to Kelvin temperatures, 69, 118
    circumference of circle, 510, 579
    definition, 56
    distance, speed, time relation, 58, 122,
        182, 277
    glossary term, 690
    order of operations, 60–64
    perimeter of rectangle, 64
    Pythagorean Theorem, 245
    shoe size, 94
    and spreadsheets, 65, 196
    sum of angles in polygon, 229
    and tables, 66–72
    and variables, 56–59
    volume of cylinder, 593

glossary term, 691
and right angles, 244, 266
tangent as, 582
Perpendicular bisector, 219–221, 691
Pi, 579, 582–586, 588–590, 593–595, 691
Pioneer 12, 110
Place value, 106–107, 159, 691
Plane, 217, 691
Platonic solids, 557, 621
Pluto, 128, 131, 163, 340, 441
Point symmetry, 611–613, 616, 691
Polygon
angles in, 230–231, 290
area, 233–235
classification, 227–229
definition, 227
glossary term, 691
perimeter, 233
Polyhedron
classification, 554–557
definition, 554
glossary term, 691
surface area of, 563–566
volume of, 567–570
Population, 2, 5–6, 12–15, 24, 27, 44, 50, 311, 392, 479, 540, 576
Positive numbers, 433, 474, 691
Positive relationship, 37, 45–46, 49, 691
Power, 125, 692
Prime factorization, 136–140, 142, 158, 161, 459, 692
Prime meridian, 446
Prime number, 103, 136, 161, 692
Prism
definition, 555
glossary term, 692
naming, 555
surface area, 563–566
volume, 567–570
Probability
and counting, 649–653
definition, 650
dependent event, 659–663
experimental, 654–658
geometric, 656
glossary term, 692
independent event, 659–663
odds and fairness, 644–648
simulation, 664
Problem Solving *The development of problem-solving skills is a key goal of this math program and is found throughout the book.*
adding and subtracting fractions, 177
adding and subtracting mixed numbers, 182
adding integers, 454
angles, 231
area, 591, 609
area of irregular figures, 262
arrangements, 634
circle graph, 577
circumference, 581
combinations, 642

conversion, 356
converting rates, 353–356
Counting Principle, 630
decimals, 109, 115, 120–124, 156
decimals, percents, 393
diameter, 586
distance/rate formula, 335
dividing fractions, 200
dividing integers, 470
equations, 85, 90–91, 94, 504, 528, 532, 541–542
equivalent fractions, 148
estimation, 172, 327
factorials, 635
formulas, 56–59, 66–70, 564, 568, 579, 583, 593
fractions, 152, 156
geometric shapes, 226, 557
graphs, 10, 15, 34, 489, 515–516
groups, 639–640
handbook, xix–xxix
integers, 436, 459
inverse operations, 77
maps, 333–336
mean, median, mode, 25
multiplying fractions, 190
multiplying integers, 465
multiplying mixed numbers, 195
ordering integers, 441
order of operations, 64
parallel and perpendicular lines, 221
parallelogram area, 257
percent, 389, 397–398, 401, 409, 413–414, 419
perimeter and area, 236
prime factorization, 143
probability, 648, 653, 658, 663
proportion, 296–297, 302, 307
Pythagorean Theorem, 247
quantities, 484–485
rates, 281, 285, 348
ratio, 277, 289, 312
rotational symmetry, 614
rounding, 114
scale, 336, 340, 370, 374
scale drawing, 332
scatterplot, 39, 44
scientific notation, 129
sequences, 494, 498
similar figures, 364, 369
square root, 243
strategies. *See* Problem Solving Strategies
surface area, 566
tables, 70, 511
translation, 446, 604
triangle area, 252
two-step equations, 538
unit conversion, 352
volume, 570, 595–596
Problem Solving Focus
check for a reasonable answer, 480, 624
checking the rules of the problem, 552

finding unnecessary information, 54, 166
identifying missing information, 210, 322
interpreting mathematical phrases, 272, 384
reading the problem, 4, 104
solving the problem, 430
Problem Solving Handbook, xix–xxix
Problem Solving Strategies
act out the problem, 663
choose a strategy, 25, 59, 81, 85, 90, 114, 129, 138, 148, 177, 182, 190, 195, 231, 236, 247, 252, 277, 312, 336, 348, 370, 398, 409, 419, 441, 459, 494, 511, 528, 570, 581, 635, 658
draw a diagram, xxviii, 430
guess and check, xxv
look for a pattern, xxii, 66, 430
make an organized list, xxiii, 18
make a table, xxiv
solve a simpler problem, xxix, 540
use logical reasoning, xxvii, 430
work backward, xxvi
Problem Solving Tip, 17–18, 31, 66, 74, 121, 150, 287, 350, 367, 400, 416, 433, 467, 513, 540, 559, 584, 639, 650, 663
Product, 692. *See also* Multiplication
Profit, 516, 527
Project Progress, 15, 39, 64, 77, 124, 143, 182, 200, 226, 262, 290, 307, 340, 348, 370, 402, 414, 446, 470, 504, 520, 538, 570, 596, 614, 640, 663
Proportion *The development of proportional reasoning is a key goal of this math program and is found throughout the book.*
creating, 294–297
cross multiplication, 308–312
definition, 294
glossary term, 692
testing for, 298–302
unit rate and, 304–307
Protractor, 213, 692
Pulse rate, 304
Pyramid, 555–557, 570, 692
Pyramid of the Sun, 342
Pythagoras, 133
Pythagorean Theorem, 244–247, 265, 267, 692
Pythagorean triple, 245

Q

Quadrant, 443–446, 692
Quadratic equation, 545, 692
Quadrilateral
angle measures in, 224
classification, 223–226
definition, 223
glossary term, 692
nonregular, 228
Quantity, 386, 482–483, 495, 497
Quartile, 26
Quotient, 692. *See also* Division

INDEX

INDEX

INDEX